مختصر زاد المعاد

Provisions for the Hereafter
(Abridged)

First Edition: September 2003

Supervised by:

ABDUL MALIK MUJAHID

Headquarters:
P.O. Box: 22743, Riyadh 11416, KSA
Tel: 00966-1-4033962/4043432
Fax: 00966-1-4021659
E-mail: darussalam@naseej.com.sa
Website: http://www.dar-us-salam.com
Bookshop: Tel: 00966-1-4614483
         Fax: 00966-1-4644945

Branches & Agents:

K.S.A.
• Jeddah: Tel & Fax: 00966-2-6807752
• Al-Khobar: Tel: 00966-3-8692900
         Fax: 00966-3-8691551

U.A.E.
• Tel: 00971-6-5632623 Fax: 5632624

PAKISTAN
• 50-Lower Mall, Lahore
  Tel: 0092-42-7240024 Fax: 7354072
• Rahman Market, Ghazni Street
  Urdu Bazar, Lahore
  Tel: 0092-42-7120054 Fax: 7320703

U.S.A.
• Houston: P.O. Box: 79194 Tx 77279
  Tel: 001-713-722 0419
  Fax: 001-713-722 0431
  E-mail: sales @ dar-us-salam.com
  Website: http:// www.dar-us-salam.com
• New York: 572 Atlantic Ave, Brooklyn
  New York-11217
  Tel: 001-718-625 5925

U.K.
• London: Darussalam International
  Publications Ltd., 226 High Street,
  Walthamstow, London E17 7JH U.K.
  Tel: 0044-208 520 2666

Mobile: 0044-794 730 6706
Fax: 0044-208 521 7645
• Darussalam International Publications
Limited, Regent Park Mosque,
146 Park Road, London NW8 7RG,
Tel: 0044-207 724 3363

FRANCE
• Editions & Libairie Essalam
135, Bd de Ménilmontant 75011
Paris (France)
Tél: 01 43 381956/4483 - Fax 01 43 574431
Website: http: www.Essalam.com
E-mail: essalam@essalam.com

AUSTRALIA
• Lakemba NSW: ICIS: Ground Floor
165-171, Haldon St.
Tel: (61-2) 9758 4040 Fax: 9758 4030

MALAYSIA
• E&D BOOKS SDN. BHD.
321 B 3rd Floor, Suria Klcc,
Kuala Lumpur City Center 50088
Tel: 00603-216 63433 Fax: 459 72032

SINGAPORE
• Muslim Converts Association of Singapore
Singapore-424484
Tel: 0065-440 6924, 348 8344
Fax: 440 6724

SRILANKA
• Darul Kitab 6, Nirmal Road, Colombo-4
Tel: 0094-1-589 038 Fax: 0094-74 722433

KUWAIT
• Islam Presentation Committee
Enlightenment Book Shop, P.O. Box: 1613
Safat 13017 Kuwait
Tel: 00965-244 7526 Fax: 240 0057

مختصر زاد المعاد

Provisions for the Hereafter

(Abridged)

By

Imam Ibn Qayyim Al-Jawziyyah ﷺ

Summarized by

Imam Muhammad Ibn Abdul Wahhab At-Tamimi ﷺ

DARUSSALAM
Publishers & Distributors
Riyadh, Saudi Arabia

بِسْمِ اللهِ الرَّحْمَنِ الرَّحِيمِ

Contents

In the Name of Allâh, the Most Beneficent, the Most Merciful.

All praise and thanks be to Allâh for those beautiful Names and sublime Attributes which are His. We praise him for the plenteous bounty and gifts which He has bestowed upon us; and we testify that none is worthy of worship except Allâh, Most High Alone, without equals or partners and we also testify that Muhammad is His slave and His Messenger, whom He sent with the most complete Law and the best of guidance – may the Peace and Blessings of Allâh be upon him and upon his family and Companions and those who conform to his path and follow his guidance forever and for all time.

As for what follows: Verily, one of the mightiest of the Blessings which Allâh has bestowed upon His slaves is that He sent this noble Messenger with guidance and the Religion of truth in order that it may supersede all other religions and completed through him His Favour upon us and chose for his people Islam as their Religion and he granted them succession in the earth and granted authority for them to practise their Religion and gave them in exchange safety after their fear and all of this was from the blessing brought about due to their affirming the Oneness of Allâh and obeying Him and their strict adherence to the guidance of His Prophet ﷺ, which is the best guidance.

And since it was the condition of his followers – may the Peace and Blessings of Allâh be upon him – that they followed his path, the scholars of the (Islamic) community have attached great importance to it and written down what they knew or what they deduced from his guidance – Peace and Blessings of Allâh be upon him – for those who came after them regarding acts of worship, dealings and habits. And one of the most famous works written on this subject is the book: *Zad Al-Ma'ad Fee Hadi Khairil-Ibad* which was compiled by the Scholar and researcher, the Imam, Ibn Qayyim Al-Jawziyyah – may Allâh have mercy on him and bestow on him a blessed abode – for he has compiled and deduced that which would not have been easy for another and the book has been printed many times and widely distributed and (many people) have benefitted from it.

And because he has discussed some of the topics in great detail and dwelt at great length on the differences of opinion and dealt with the evidences exhaustively, which might well be burdensome for one who is in a hurry, Allâh has granted success to the Imam of this Najdi *Da'wah*, Shaikh Muhammad Ibn 'Abdul Wahhab – may Allâh have mercy on him – in abbreviating it and he has been able to capture the essence of it and to sum it up in one small volume and to embody that which is important and that which was intended by the writing of the original work.

And Allâh has inspired the Islamic University of Imam Muhammad Ibn Sa'ûd in Riyadh to take up the endeavour of keeping alive the heritage of the Shaikh – may Allâh have mercy on him – by printing those of his works which have not previously been printed or renewing what has been lost of them in various fields of knowledge.

The task of the aforementioned work: *Zad Al-Ma'ad* was given to me and two handwritten copies of it were found which were collected by the Saudi Library in Riyadh: The first of them was under number 48/86 which was completed by Yoosuf Ibn Muhammad Ibn 'Abdil Hadi in the year 1241 A. H. and its text is legible, but it is not without mistakes and some topics – possibly as much as several pages – are missing and we considered it to be the original due to its being preserved and none of its writing having been altered.

As for the second copy, it is under number 49/86 and it was completed in the year 1237 A. H. and the writer did not give his name. It is more clearly and nicely written than the first and some correctors have added comments to it and has added and subtracted from it and appended many notes to it, most likely derived from *Zad Al-Ma'ad* and his intention in doing this was to complete the benefit of it and make the meaning clearer. There is also something missing from it, but it is less than the first.

We have undertaken a comparison of the two works and where they differ in the text or in the correction, we have referred to *Zad Al-Ma'ad* and confirmed what is in it where the situation requires, when we could not confirm that the wording was abbreviated and that the writer has changed the wording of the original. In such cases, we have confirmed what is most fitting for the sentence and where we have found something missing from both copies, we have depended upon the second copy along with the original.

As for the appendages and the additions which are in the margins of the second copy, we have removed them in most cases, especially at the end of the book where they were numerous and we have confirmed them in some places in brackets in order to provide clarity.

We did not see any benefit in pointing out every difference in the copies in the footnotes, unless there was some pressing need for it. We ask Allâh that He make this abbreviated work of benefit, as He made the original of it of benefit and that He reward its author and all of those who have striven to produce it and distribute it and that He prevent us not from His plenteous bounty, for verily, He is Near and He answers (supplications). And may peace and blessings be upon our Leader, Muhammad and upon his family.

14/10/1397 A. H.

The Corrector,

'Abdullah Ibn 'Abdur-Rahman Ibn Jibreen.

بِسْـــمِ اللَّهِ الرَّحْمَنِ الرَّحِيـــمِ

وبه الثقة والعصمة

"In the Name of Allâh, the Most Beneficent, the Most Merciful and in Him We Trust and it is He Who Protects Us."

All praise and thanks be to Allâh, the Lord of the worlds, and I testify that none has the right to be worshipped except Allâh, Alone, without partners and I testify that Muhammad is His slave and His Messenger.

As for what follows: Verily, all creation and choosing is in the Hands of Allâh, Most Glorified, Most High; He, Most High says:

﴿وَرَبُّكَ يَخْلُقُ مَا يَشَاءُ وَيَخْتَارُ مَا كَانَ لَهُمُ الْخِيَرَةُ سُبْحَنَ اللَّهِ وَتَعَـٰلَىٰ عَمَّا يُشْرِكُونَ﴾

"And your Lord creates whatsoever He wills and chooses, no choice have they (in any matter). Glorified is Allâh, and exalted above all that they associate (as partners with Him)."[1]

– and what is meant by choosing here is selecting and picking; and His Words:

﴿مَا كَانَ لَهُمُ الْخِيَرَةُ﴾

"no choice have they (in any matter)."

mean that they have no part in this choosing, so just as He is Alone in His Creating, so He is Alone in His Choosing, for He knows better regarding the circumstances of His Choice, as He, Most High says:

﴿اللَّهُ أَعْلَمُ حَيْثُ يَجْعَلُ رِسَالَتَهُ﴾

"Allâh knows best with whom to place His Message."[2]

and as He, Most High says:

---

[1] *Sûrah Al-Qasas 28:68*

[2] *Sûrah Al-An'âm 6:124*

$$﴿وَقَالُوا لَوْلَا نُزِّلَ هَذَا الْقُرْآنُ عَلَى رَجُلٍ مِنَ الْقَرْيَتَيْنِ عَظِيمٍ ۝ أَهُمْ يَقْسِمُونَ رَحْمَتَ رَبِّكَ نَحْنُ قَسَمْنَا بَيْنَهُم مَّعِيشَتَهُمْ فِي الْحَيَاةِ الدُّنْيَا وَرَفَعْنَا بَعْضَهُمْ فَوْقَ بَعْضٍ دَرَجَاتٍ﴾$$

"And they say: "Why is not this Qur'an sent down to some great man of the two towns (Makkah and Ta'if)?" Is it they who would portion out the Mercy of your Lord? It is We Who portion out between them their livelihood in this world, and We raised some of them above others in ranks."[1]

So He, Most Glorified has negated choice for them and informed us that that is for the One Who portions out for them their livelihood and He has raised some of them over others in rank. And in His Words:

$$﴿سُبْحَانَ اللَّهِ وَتَعَالَى عَمَّا يُشْرِكُونَ﴾$$

"Glorified and Exalted be He above all that they associate as partners with Him!",

He declares Himself to be above all that their *shirk*[2] necessitates, such as their suggestion or their choice. And their *shirk* does not include an affirmation of the attribute of creation for anyone besides Him, so that it would be necessary for Him to declare Himself above it. And the Verse is mentioned after His Words:

$$﴿فَأَمَّا مَن تَابَ وَآمَنَ وَعَمِلَ صَالِحًا فَعَسَى أَن يَكُونَ مِنَ الْمُفْلِحِينَ ۝﴾$$

"But as for him who repented (from polytheism and sins), believed (in the Oneness of Allâh, and in His Messenger Muhammad ﷺ), and did righteous deeds (in the life of this world), then he will be among those who are successful."[3]

And just as He created them, He chose from among them and that choice comes back to the Wisdom of Him, Most Glorified and His Knowledge as to who is worthy of it, not to the choice or suggestion of

---

[1] *Sûrah Az-Zukhruf* 43:31-32

[2] *Shirk*: Associating partners with Allâh.

[3] *Sûrah Al-Qasas* 28:67

those people. And this choice in this world is one of the mightiest signs of His Lordship and the greatest evidences of His Oneness and His perfect Attributes and of the truthfulness of His Messengers (ﷺ).

And included in this is His selection from among the angels, as the Prophet (ﷺ) said:

«اللَّهُمَّ رَبَّ جِبْرِيلَ وَمِيكَائِيلَ وَإِسْرَافِيلَ، فَاطِرَ السَّمَوَاتِ وَالأَرْضِ، عَالِمَ الْغَيْبِ وَالشَّهَادَةِ، أَنْتَ تَحْكُمُ بَيْنَ عِبَادِكَ فِيمَا كَانُوا فِيهِ يَخْتَلِفُونَ، اهْدِنِي لِمَا اخْتُلِفَ فِيهِ مِنَ الْحَقِّ بِإِذْنِكَ، إِنَّكَ تَهْدِي مَنْ تَشَاءُ إِلَى صِرَاطٍ مُسْتَقِيمٍ»

"Oh, Allâh! Lord of Jibreel, Meeka'eel and Israfeel, the Originator of the heavens and the earth, Knower of the unseen and the seen! You judge between Your slaves in the matters in which they used to differ; guide me by Your Leave to the truth in those matters in which there is differing, for verily, You guide whomsoever You will to the Straight Path."[1]

Likewise is His choice of the Prophets from among the sons of Adam ﷺ and His Choice of the Messengers from among them and His Choice of *'Ulul-'Azm* from them – and they are the five mentioned in *Sûrahs Al-Ahzâb* and *Ash-Shu'râ'*[2] and His choice of *Al-Khaleelan* from them: Abraham and Muhammad – may the Peace and Blessings of Allâh be upon both of them and upon all of the Prophets and Messengers. And included in this is His selection of the sons of Isma'eel from among the nations of the sons of Adam, then He chose from them Banu Kinanah from Khuzaimah, then He chose from the

---

[1] Narrated by Muslim in his *'Saheeh'* (770) regarding the prayer of the travellers, in the *Hadeeth* of 'A'ishah ﷺ and by Abu 'Awanah.

[2] A reference to the Words of Him, Most High:

﴿وَإِذْ أَخَذْنَا﴾

"And (remember) when We took (33:7) and:

﴿شَرَعَ لَكُم﴾

"He (Allâh) has ordained for you (42:13).

sons of Kinanah Quraish and from Quraish He chose Banu Hashim. Then from Banu Hashim, He chose the Leader of the children of Adam 🙵 – Muhammad 🙵 and He chose his people over all of the peoples of the world, as reported in *'Al-Musnad'*[1] on the authority of Mu'awiyah Ibn Haidah 🙵 in a *Marfu'*[2] form: "You complete (in Arabic: *Tûfûna*) seventy nations. You are the best of them and the most noble of them in Allâh's Sight."[3]

And it is reported in *'Musnad Al-Bazzar'*, in the *Hadeeth* of Abu Ad-Darda' 🙵: "Verily, Allâh, Most Glorified, Most High said to Jesus the son of Mary: "I will send after you a people who, when something which they like comes to them, praise Allâh and thank Him and if something they dislike afflicts them, they hope for a reward (from Allâh) and they patiently persevere without gentleness or knowledge" He (Jesus ['Isa 🙵]) said: "Oh, Lord! How can they be without gentleness or knowledge?" He said: "I give them from My Gentleness and My Knowledge."

---
[1] *Al-Musnad*: *Musnad Al-Imam Ahmad.*

[2] *Marfu'*: With a chain of narrators connecting to the Prophet (🙵).

[3] In Imam Ahmad's *'Musnad'*, 5/5, printed by Al-Maktab Al-Islami, it says: *"Waffaitum"* (not *"Tûfûna"*). As for *"Tûfûna"*, it is in another narration.

Allâh Has Accorded to Himself Goodness

And what is meant by this is that Allâh, Most Glorified has chosen from every race the best of it and accorded it to himself, for He, Most Glorified, Most High does not love anything except that which is good and He does not accept words, deeds or charity except those which are good.

And from this the signs of the slave's happiness and wretchedness are known, for nothing suits the good person except that which is good and he does not accept anything except it, nor does he feel at ease except with it, nor is his heart at rest except with it.

He speaks good words which are the only words that ascend to Allâh and he is the most averse to obscene words, lying, backbiting, tale-bearing, slander, false testimony and every kind of evil speech.

Similarly, he does not like any deeds except the best of them – and they are those upon whose goodness sound natural instincts are agreed, along with the Prophetic Laws and which are attested to by rational minds, such as his worshipping Allâh, Alone, without partners and preferring His Pleasure to his own whims and desires and draws closer to Allâh due to his striving and he behaves towards His creation in the best way he can, treating them as he would like them to treat him.

His traits of character are the best, such as gentleness, dignity, patience, compassion, loyalty, honesty, a true heart, modesty and he protects his countenance from surrender or humility towards anyone besides Allâh.

Likewise, he does not choose any but the best and purest of foods, which are those that are lawful and wholesome and nourish the body and the mind in the best way without causing any ill-effect to the body.

Nor does he select except the best of women as a wife, nor as friends and companions except those who are good. Such a person is one of those of whom Allâh said:

$$﴿ٱلَّذِينَ تَتَوَفَّىٰهُمُ ٱلۡمَلَـٰٓئِكَةُ طَيِّبِينَ يَقُولُونَ سَلَـٰمٌ عَلَيۡكُمُ ٱدۡخُلُوا۟ ٱلۡجَنَّةَ بِمَا كُنتُمۡ تَعۡمَلُونَ ٣٢﴾$$

"Those whose lives the angels take while they are in a pious state (i.e. pure from all evil, and worshipping none but Allâh Alone) saying (to them): "*Salamun 'Alaikum* (peace be on you) enter you Paradise, because of that (the good) which you used to do (in the world).""[1]

-- and to whom the guardians of Paradise say:

$$﴿سَلَـٰمٌ عَلَيۡكُمۡ طِبۡتُمۡ فَٱدۡخُلُوهَا خَـٰلِدِينَ ٧٣﴾$$

"*Salamun 'Alaikum* (peace be upon you)! You have done well, so enter here to abide therein forever."[2]

And the use of the letter (*Fa'*) in the Verse implies causality, i.e. because of your good deeds, enter it.

And Allâh, Most High says:

$$﴿ٱلۡخَبِيثَـٰتُ لِلۡخَبِيثِينَ وَٱلۡخَبِيثُونَ لِلۡخَبِيثَـٰتِۖ وَٱلطَّيِّبَـٰتُ لِلطَّيِّبِينَ وَٱلطَّيِّبُونَ لِلطَّيِّبَـٰتِۚ أُو۟لَـٰٓئِكَ مُبَرَّءُونَ مِمَّا يَقُولُونَۖ لَهُم مَّغۡفِرَةٌ وَرِزۡقٌ كَرِيمٌ ٢٦﴾$$

"Bad statements are for bad people (or bad women for bad men) and bad people for bad statements (or bad men for bad women). Good statements are for good people (or good women for good men) and good people for good statements (or good men for good women): such (good people) are innocent of (every) bad statement which they say; for them is forgiveness, and *Rizqun Karım* (generous provision, i.e. Paradise)."[3]

---

[1] *Sûrah An-Naḥl* 16:32
[2] *Sûrah Az-Zumar* 39:73
[3] *Sûrah An-Nûr* 24:26

This Verse has been explained as meaning that evil words belong to evil people and good words belong to good people. It has also been explained as meaning that good women are for good men and vice versa and (in fact,) it includes this meaning and others. And Allâh, Most Glorified has placed all manner of good in Paradise due to and all manner of evil in the Fire, so the former is an abode which was chosen for good, while the latter is an abode which was chosen for evil. And there is an abode in which good and evil are mixed and that is this abode (i.e. the life of this world). So when the Appointed Day comes, Allâh will distinguish between the evil and the good and then the matter will rest upon two abodes only.

And what is meant is that Allâh has made signs for the wretchedness and happiness by which they are known. And there might be two components in a man (i.e. good and evil), so whichever of them is preponderant, he belongs to its people; so if Allâh wishes good for His slave, He will purify him before death and he will not require cleansing by the Fire. The Wisdom of Him, Most High rejects that He should make the slave to be accompanied in his abode by his evil deeds and so He places him in the Fire in order to cleanse him of sins. And the time for which he will remain in the Fire is dependent upon the rapidity or slowness with which the sins are removed.

But since the polytheist is evil by nature, the Fire does not cleanse him, just as if a dog enters the sea (it is not cleansed), while because the Believer is free from sins, the Fire is forbidden to him, since there is nothing in him which necessitates cleansing; so Glorified be He Whose Wisdom overwhelms the minds.

Chapter

Regarding the Obligation to Know the Guidance of the Messenger ﷺ

From here it is understood the overriding necessity for the slaves to know the Messenger ﷺ and the Message which he brought, because there is no path to success except at his hands, nor to know good from evil except through him, so no matter how urgent the need or how great the necessity, the need of the slave for the Messenger ﷺ is far above it.

And what is your opinion regarding one whose guidance is concealed from you and whose message corrupts your heart in a moment? But only a living heart feels this, for a wound is not felt by a dead man.[1]

And if happiness is dependent upon his ﷺ guidance, then it is incumbent upon every person who loves salvation for himself to know his guidance and his life story (*Seerah*) and all his affairs in order to avoid the path of the ignorant.

And the people in this matter vary between those with a little knowledge, this with much knowledge and those who know nothing whatsoever; and Bounty is in Allâh's Hand, He gives it to whom He wills and Allâh is the Owner of great Bounty.

---------- ❖ ❖ ❖ ----------

---

[1] The end of a verse of poetry by Al-Mutanabbi: That begins:.Whoever dwells in disgrace, gets used to it.

Regarding His ﷺ Guidance in *Wûdu'* (Ablution)

He ﷺ used to perform ablution for every prayer most of the times, although sometimes he might pray with one ablution. Sometimes he would perform ablution with a *Mudd*[1] of water, sometimes with two thirds of a *Mudd* and sometimes more. And he was the most frugal of the people in pouring water for ablution and he warned his people against wasting it. It has been authentically reported from him that he performed ablution washing each limb once, twice and three times.

Sometimes he would wash some limbs twice and others three times, and he would rinse his mouth (*Madmadah*) and sniff water into his nose (*Istinshaq*) sometimes with one handful of water, sometimes with two and sometimes with three and he used to combine the rinsing of the mouth and the sniffing of water into his nose (i.e. he used to do both with the same handful of water); and he used to sniff the water with his right hand and expel it (*Istinthar*) using his left hand. Sometimes he would wipe over the whole of his head and sometimes he would pass his hands back and forth, but it has not been authentically reported from him that he ever wiped over only a part of his head. But if he wiped over his forelock, he would complete the wiping over his headdress. He never performed ablution without rinsing his mouth and sniffing water into his nose and it has not been recorded from him that he even once abandoned them. Likewise, he never even once abandoned the sequence of actions and continuity in ablution. And he would wash his feet if they were not in leather socks

---

[1] *Mudd*: A measure of two–third of a kilogram (approx.)

or ordinary socks and he would wipe over his ears both outside and in along with his head.

And every *Hadeeth* reported concerning the *Adhkar*[1] of ablution is a lie except saying *"Bismillah"* (In the Name of Allâh) at the beginning of it and the words:

«أَشْهَدُ أَنْ لَا إِلَهَ إِلَّا اللهُ وَحْدَهُ لَا شَرِيكَ لَهُ وَأَشْهَدُ أَنَّ مُحَمَّدًا عَبْدُهُ وَرَسُولُهُ، اللَّهُمَّ اجْعَلْنِي مِنَ التَّوَّابِينَ وَاجْعَلْنِي مِنَ الْمُتَطَهِّرِينَ»

"Ash-hadu Alla Ilaha Illallahu Wahdahu La Shareeka Lahu Wa Ash-hadu Anna Muhammadan 'Abduhu Wa Rasûluh. Allâhumaj'alnee Minat-Tawwabeen Waj'alnee Minal-Mutatahhireen"

"(I testify that none is worthy of worship except Allâh, Alone and I testify that Muhammad is His slave and His Messenger. Oh, Allâh! Make me one of those who turn [to You] in repentance and make me among those who purify them-selves).*"*

There is another *Hadeeth* in *'Sunan An-Nasa'i'*:

«سُبْحَانَكَ اللَّهُمَّ وَبِحَمْدِكَ أَشْهَدُ أَنْ لَا إِلَهَ إِلَّا أَنْتَ أَسْتَغْفِرُكَ وَأَتُوبُ إِلَيْكَ»

"Subhanakallahumma wa behamdika Ash-hadu Alla Ilaha Illa Anta Astagfiruka, wa Atubu Ilaika"

"(Glory be to You, oh, Allâh and praise and thanks. I testify that none is worthy of worship except You. I seek forgiveness from You and I turn to You in repentance).*"*

He never said at the beginning of it: "I make the intention", nor did any of the Companions ☀ ever did so; and he never repeated the washing of his limbs more than three times.

Likewise, it has not been authentically reported from him that he washed above the elbows or the ankles, nor was it his habitual practice to dry his limbs.

He used to run his fingers through his beard sometimes, but it was not his regular practice to do so. He also used to wash between his

---

[1] *Adhkar*: (sing. *Dhikr*) mentioning Allâh's Name using a certain formula.

fingers and toes, but he did not always do so. As for moving the ring, a weak *Hadeeth* has been reported in this regard.

It has been authentically reported from him that when at home and when traveling, he would wipe over his socks: The time for the resident being a day and a night and for the traveller three days and three nights. He used to wipe over the tops of his leather socks and he wiped over his ordinary socks and he wiped over his headdress and his forelock, contenting himself with that; it is possible that this was only in special circumstances dictated by need and it is also possible that it is general – and this is more likely.

He did not act at variance with the circumstances of his feet; rather, if they were encased in leather socks, he would wipe over them and if they were uncovered, he would wash them.

He would perform *Tayammum* by striking the ground upon which he intended to pray once for his hands and his face,[1] regardless of whether it was dust, soil or sand. And it has been authentically reported from him that he said:

«حَيْثُمَا أَدْرَكَتْ رَجُلًا مِنْ أُمَّتِي الصَّلَاةُ فَعِنْدَهُ مَسْجِدُهُ وَطَهُورُهُ»

"Wherever any man from amongst my people happened to be when the time for prayer overtook him, he has his mosque and his means of purifying himself."

When he traveled with his Companions ﷺ during the Tabuk campaign, they crossed those sands and their water became scarce and it was not reported from him that he carried dust with him, nor did he order it and nor did any of his Companions ﷺ do so; and if anyone thinks upon this, he must affirm that he performed *Tayammum* with sand.

It has not been authentically reported from him that he performed *Tayammum* for every prayer (i.e. that he renewed it), nor that he ordered it; indeed, he declared it to be general and affirmed that it took the place of ablution.

---

[1] Narrated by Al-Bukhari and Muslim on the authority of 'Ammar Ibn Yasir ﷺ.

Regarding His ﷺ Guidance in Prayer

When he ﷺ stood up to pray, he would say: *"Allâhu Akbar"* (Allâh is Most Great) and he would not say anything before it, nor did he pronounce the intention and none of the *Tabi'ûn*[1] or the four Imams[2] recommended it. It was his custom to enter *Ihram*[3] by saying: *"Allâhu Akbar"* and nothing else; and at the same time, he would raise his hands up to the lobes of his ears with his fingers extended and facing towards the *Qiblah*[4] and it has also been narrated: "up to his shoulders." Then he would place his right hand on the back of his left hand (between the wrist and the forearm, and it has not been authentically reported where he used to place them, but Abu Dawûd reported from 'Ali ؓ that he said: "When praying, the *Sunnah* is to place the (right) hand over the (left) hand below the navel."[5]

He used to begin the prayer sometimes by supplicating thus:

«اللَّهُمَّ بَاعِدْ بَيْنِي وَبَيْنَ خَطَايَايَ كَمَا بَاعَدْتَ بَيْنَ الْمَشْرِقِ وَالْمَغْرِبِ، اللَّهُمَّ اغْسِلْنِي مِنْ خَطَايَايَ بِالْمَاءِ وَالثَّلْجِ وَالْبَرَدِ، اللَّهُمَّ نَقِّنِي مِنَ

---

[1] *Tabi'ûn:* Those who heard from the Companions ؓ and died as Muslims.

[2] The four Imams: Abu Haneefah, Malik, Ash-Shafi'i and Ahmad.

[3] *Ihram:* The inviolable state of prayer in which it is not permissible to do or say anything except what is prescribed for the prayer.

[4] *Qiblah:* The direction towards which Muslims pray i.e. the *Ka'bah* in Makkah.

[5] This is an addition to the text of *'Zad Al-Ma'ad'* by the compiler and it is a weak *Hadeeth;* see *'Nail Al-Awtar'* (by Ash-Shawkani), vol. 2, pages 207-211.

الذُّنُوبِ وَالْخَطَايَا كَمَا يُنَقَّى الثَّوْبُ الأَبْيَضُ مِنَ الدَّنَسِ»

*"Allâhumma Ba'id Bainee Wa Baina Khatayaya Kama Ba'adta
Bainal-Mashriqi Wal-Maghrib, Allâhummaghsilnee Min Khatayaya
Bil-Ma'i Wath-Thalji Wal-Baradi, Allâhumma Naqqinee Minadh-
Dhunûbi Wal-Khataya Kama Yunaqqath-Thawbul-Abyadhu Minad-
Danas"*

"(Oh, Allâh! Make the distance between me and my sins as
great as You have made the distance between the east and the
west. Oh, Allâh! Cleanse me of my sins as a white garment is
cleansed of dirt. Oh, Allâh! Purify me from my sins by snow,
water and hail. Oh, Allâh! Purify me from misdeeds and sins as
a white garment is purified from dirt)."[1]

And sometimes he would say:

«وَجَّهْتُ وَجْهِيَ لِلَّذِي فَطَرَ السَّمَوَاتِ وَالأَرْضَ حَنِيفًا وَمَا أَنَا مِنَ
الْمُشْرِكِينَ، إِنَّ صَلاتِي وَنُسُكِي وَمَحْيَايَ وَمَمَاتِي للهِ رَبِّ الْعَالَمِينَ،
لَا شَرِيكَ لَهُ، وَبِذَلِكَ أُمِرْتُ وَأَنَا أَوَّلُ الْمُسْلِمِينَ»

«اللَّهُمَّ أَنْتَ الْمَلِكُ لَا إِلَهَ إِلَّا أَنْتَ، أَنْتَ رَبِّي وَأَنَا عَبْدُكَ ظَلَمْتُ
نَفْسِي، وَاعْتَرَفْتُ بِذَنْبِي، فَاغْفِرْ لِي ذُنُوبِي جَمِيعًا، إِنَّهُ لَا يَغْفِرُ
الذُّنُوبَ إِلَّا أَنْتَ، وَاهْدِنِي لِأَحْسَنِ الأَخْلَاقِ، لَا يَهْدِي لِأَحْسَنِهَا
إِلَّا أَنْتَ، وَاصْرِفْ عَنِّي سَيِّئَهَا لَا يَصْرِفُ عَنِّي سَيِّئَهَا إِلَّا أَنْتَ، لَبَّيْكَ
وَسَعْدَيْكَ، وَالْخَيْرُ بَيْنَ يَدَيْكَ، وَالشَّرُّ لَيْسَ إِلَيْكَ، أَنَا بِكَ وَإِلَيْكَ،
تَبَارَكْتَ وَتَعَالَيْتَ، أَسْتَغْفِرُكَ وَأَتُوبُ إِلَيْكَ»

*"Wajjahtu Wajhee Lilladhee Fataras-Samawati Wal-Ardha Haneefan
Wa Ma Ana Minal-Mushrikeen, Inna Salatee Wa Nusukee Wa
Mahyaya Wa Mamatee Lillahi Rabbil 'Alameen, La Shareeka Lahu
Wa Bi-Dhalika Umirtu Wa Ana Awwalul-Muslimeen.*

*Allâhumma Antal-Maliku La Ilaha Illa Anta. Anta Rabbee Wa Ana
'Abduka Zalamtu Nafsee Wa'ataraftu Bi-Dhanbee Faghfir Lee*

---

[1] Narrated by Al-Bukhari, Muslim and others.

Dhunûbee Jamee'an, Innahu La Yaghfiruz-Dhunûba Illa Anta, Wahdinee Li-Ahsanil-Akhlaqi. La Yahdee Li-Ahsaniha Illa Anta. Wasrif 'Annee Sayyi'aha, La Yasrifu 'Annee Sayyi'aha Illa Anta. Labbaika Wa Sa'daika Wal-Khairu Baina Yadaika Wash-Sharru Laisa Ilaika. Ana Bika Wa Ilaika, Tabarakta Wa Ta'alaita, Astaghfiruka Wa Atoobu Ilaika"

"I have turned my face towards the One Who created the heavens and the earth in sincere submission and I am not one of those who associates partners with Allâh [*Mushrikûn*]. Verily, my prayers, my sacrifice, my life and my death are for Allâh, the Lord of the worlds, Who has no partners. That is what I have been ordered and I am the first of those who submit [i.e. a Muslim]

Oh, Allâh! You are the Sovereign and there is no other lord besides You. You are my Lord and I am Your slave. I have wronged my soul and You are aware of my sins, so forgive me all of my sins. No one forgives sins save You Guide me to the best of characters. No one can guide to the best of it save You. Turn me away from evil character, for no one can turn me away from evil character save You. I am at Your beck and call. All good is in Your Hands and evil is not to You. I am for You and Most Blessed and Exalted are You. I seek forgiveness from You and turn to You in repentance)."[1]

But it is recorded that this was in the night prayer.

And sometimes, he would say:

«... اللَّهُمَّ رَبَّ جِبْرِيلَ وَمِيكَائِيلَ وَإِسْرَافِيلَ»

"Allâhumma Rabba Jibraila Wa Meeka'eela Wa Israfeela"

"Oh, Allâh! Lord of Jibreel, Meeka'eel and Israfeel"

– up to the end of the narration, which was mentioned previously.[2]

And sometimes, he would say:

---

[1] Narrated by Muslim, At-Tirmidhi, Abu Dawûd, Ahmad and others.
[2] Narrated by Muslim on the authority of 'A'ishah ﷺ.

«اللَّهُمَّ لَكَ الْحَمْدُ، أَنْتَ نُورُ السَّمَوَاتِ وَالْأَرْضِ وَمَنْ فِيهِنَّ»

"Allâhumma Lakal-Hamdu, Anta Nûrus-Samawati Wal-Ardi Wa Man Feehinna"

"Oh, Allâh! To You are due all praise and thanks. You are Light of the heavens and the earth and all those therein."[1]

Then he[2] mentioned two others, then he said: All of these forms have been authentically reported from him ﷺ.

And it has been narrated from him ﷺ that he used to open the prayer by saying:

«سُبْحَانَكَ اللَّهُمَّ وَبِحَمْدِكَ، وَتَبَارَكَ اسْمُكَ وَتَعَالَى جَدُّكَ، وَلَا إِلَهَ غَيْرُكَ»

"Subhanakallahumma Wa Bihamdika Wa Tabarakasmuka Wa Ta'ala Jadduka Wa La Ilaha Ghairuka"

"Glory and praise be to You, oh, Allâh and Most Blessed is Your Name and none is worthy of worship except You."

This was reported by the compilers of the *'Sunan'*, but the previous *Dhikr* is more strongly confirmed than it. But it has been reported that 'Umar ؓ used to open the prayer with it when he was in the place of the Prophet ﷺ (i.e. when he was leading the Companions ؓ in prayer) and he would say it aloud so that the people should know it. Ahmad said: "I act upon what has been related from 'Umar ؓ and if a person opens the prayer with something that has been related, then it is good."

After that, he used to say:

«أَعُوذُ بِاللهِ مِنَ الشَّيْطَانِ الرَّجِيمِ»

"A'ûdhu Billahi Minash-Shaitanir-Rajeem"

"I seek refuge from the accursed Satan", then he would recite *Sûrah Al-Fatihah*, sometimes reciting the *Basmalah*[3] aloud, but mostly, he

---

[1] Narrated by Al-Bukhari and Muslim.

[2] That is, Ibn Al-Qayyim in the original work, vol. 1, page 105.

[3] *Basmalah*: Saying: *"Bismillahir-Rahmanir-Raheem"* (In the Name of Allâh, the Most Beneficent, the Most Merciful).

would recite it quietly.[1] He used to prolong the words in his recitation, stopping at the end of each Verse and prolonging the sound of his voice.[2] Once he had completed the recitation of *Sûrah Al-Fâtihah*, he would say: *"Ameen"* (Amen) and if he was reciting aloud, he would raise his voice when pronouncing it and those behind him would repeat it.[3]

He used to observe two short silences in the prayer, one between the *"Takbeerah"*[4] and the recitation, while as for the second, there is a difference of opinion regarding it: It has been narrated that it is after *Sûrah Al-Fatihah* and it has been narrated that it is before the bowing (*Ruku*). And it has been said that in fact there are two periods of silence aside from the first, but it appears most likely that there are only two. As for the third, it is very short, in order to recover one's breath, so those who did not mention it failed to do so because of its brevity.

After he had finished reciting *Sûrah Al-Fâtihah*, he would recite another *Sûrah*, which he would sometimes prolong and sometimes shorten, because of traveling or other reasons. But most of the time, his recitation would be of medium length.

In *Fajr* prayer he would recite between sixty and a hundred Verses approximately. He would pray it sometimes by reciting *Sûrah Qâf* and sometimes by reciting *Sûrah Ar-Rûm*. At other times he would pray it by reciting *Sûrah At-Takwir*. It happened that he recited *Sûrah Az-Zalzalah* in both *Rak'ahs*. And while traveling he recited *Al-Mu'awwidhatan*[5] during the *Fajr* prayer. It also happened that he opened the prayer reading *Sûrah Al-Mu'minun* an when the mention

---

[1] What is confirmed from him ﷺ is that he used to recite it quietly, not aloud, for Al-Bukhari has narrated in his description of the prayer, on the authority of Anas ﷻ that the Prophet ﷺ, Abu Bakr and 'Umar ﷻ used to open the prayer by saying: "All praise and thanks be to Allâh, the Lord of the worlds". This was also confirmed by Muslim and At-Tirmidhi.

[2] Narrated by Al-Bukhari, Ahmad and Abu Dawûd.

[3] Narrated by Abu Dawûd and At-Tirmidhi.

[4] *Takbeerah*: Saying: *"Allâhu Akbar"* (Allâh is Most Great).

[5] *Al-Mu'awwidhatan*: *Sûrah Al-Falaq* and *Sûrah An-Nas*.

of Moses and Aaron in the first *Rak'ah* then he was seized by coughing and so he bowed.

He used to pray it on Friday by reciting *Sûrah As-Sajdah* and *Sûrah*

Ad-Dahr because they contain reminders of creation, the return to Allâh, the creation of Adam, the entry into Paradise and Hell and mention of things past and things yet to come whose occurrence is on a Friday, as he used on the days of great gatherings, such as the *'Eed* prayers and the Friday prayers to recite *Sûrah Qâf, Sûrah Al-Qamar, Sûrah Al-A'lâ* and *Sûrah Al-Ghâshiyah.*

Chapter

As for the *Zuhr* prayer, sometimes he used to prolong his recitation in it so much that Abu Sa'eed ﷺ said: "The *Zuhr* prayer would begin and a person could go to *Al-Baqee'* and take care of his affairs, return to his family, make ablution , return and still find the Prophet (ﷺ) in the first *Rak'ah* due to the length of his recital." (Narrated by Muslim)

Sometimes he would recite something of the length of *Sûrah As-Sajdah* and sometimes *Sûrah Al-A'lâ*,[1] *Sûrah Al-Lail* and *Sûrah Al-Burûj*.

As for the *'Asr* prayer, his recitation therein would be half that of the *Zuhr* prayer recitation if that recitation was long and the same as it if it was short.

As for the *Maghrib* prayer, his guidance therein contradicts the practice of the people today, for he prayed it once reciting therein *Sûrah Al-A'raf* divided between the two *Rak'ahs* and once he recited *Sûrah At-Tûr* and *Sûrah Al-Mursalât*. As for the continual practice of reciting short *Sûrahs* from *Al-Mufassal*,[2] it was a practice introduced by Marwan Ibn Al-Hakam and due to this, Zaid Ibn Thabit ﷺ reproved him.

Ibn 'Abdil Barr said: "It has been narrated that the prophet (ﷺ) recited in the *Maghrib* prayer *Sûrah Al-A'râf* divided between the two *Rak'ahs*, *Sûrah Ad-Dukhân*, *Sûrah Al-A'la*, *Sûrah At-Teen*, the *Mu'awwidhatan* and *Sûrah Al-Mursalât* and this is well known and also that he used to recite the short *Sûrahs* from *Al-Mufassal* and all of these reports are authentic and well known."

---

[1] Narrated by Ibn Khuzaimah in his *'Saheeh'*, on the authority of Anas Ibn Malik ﷺ and declared authentic by Ibn Hibban.

[2] *Al-Mufassal*: The *Sûrahs* from *Sûrah Qâf* up to the end of the Qur'ân.

As for the last *'Isha'* (the *Maghrib* prayer being known as the first *'Isha'*, he used to recite therein *Sûrah At-Teen* and he taught Mu'adh ﷺ to recite *Sûrah Ash-Shams*, *Sûrah Al-A'lâ* and *Sûrah Al-Lail* and other such *Sûrahs*, that is why he rebuked him for reciting *Sûrah Al-Baqarah* in *'Isha'* and said to him : "Are you one of those who put the people to trial, oh, Mu'adh?"[1] Peckers have concentrated on this word and they paid no attention to what came before it or what came after it (i.e. to the context).

As for the Friday prayer, he used to recite *Sûrah Al-Jumu'ah* and *Sûrah Al-Munâfiqûn*, or *Sûrah Al-A'lâ* and *Sûrah Al-Ghashiyah*. As for restricting oneself to the final Verses of the two *Sûrahs*, he never did that.

As for the *'Eed* prayers, he used to recite therein *Sûrah Qaf* and *Sûrah Al-Qamar* completely, or sometimes, he would recite *Sûrah Al-A'la* and *Sûrah Al-Ghashiyah* and he remained upon this guidance until he met Allâh, the Almighty, the All-Powerful.

Due to this, the Caliphs acted upon it and Abu Bakr ﷺ recited *Sûrah Al-Baqarah* in the *Fajr* prayer until he made the *Tasleem* just before the sun rose and 'Umar ﷺ after him recited in it *Sûrah Yûsuf* and *Sûrah An-Nahl*; and he also recited *Sûrah Hood* and *Sûrah Bani Isra'eel* and the like. As for the saying of the Prophet ﷺ: "If any of you is leading the people in prayer, he should make it light,"[2] it must be referred to the practice of the Prophet ﷺ, not to the desires of those being led in prayer.

And his guidance – and that is his habitual practice – is the judge in all matters in which there is a disagreement.

He did not designate any particular *Sûrah* which was to be read to the exclusion of all others, except in the Friday prayer and *'Eed* prayers.

It was part of his guidance ﷺ to recite a *Sûrah* and he might recite it in both *Rak'ahs*. But as for the recitation of the end of *Sûrahs* or the middle of them, that has not been recorded from him.

As for reciting two *Sûrahs* in one *Rak'ah*, he used to do that in the

---

[1] Narrated by Al-Bukhari and Muslim.
[2] Narrated by Al-Bukhari, An-Nasa'i, Ahmad and Malik.

supererogatory prayers. And as for the recitation of one *Sûrah* in both *Rak'ahs*, that is the least that he used to do.

And he would make the first *Rak'ah* longer than the second *Rak'ah* in all of his prayers. And it is possible that he may prolonged it so that he would not hear the sound of footsteps. Thus enabling late comers to catch the Prayers.

Once he had completed his recitation, he would raise his hands and say *"Allâhu Akbar"* as he bowed, and he would place the palms of his hands on his knees, as if he were grasping them[1] and he would stretch out his arms and hold them away from his sides[2] and he spread his back and kept it level[3] and he would be at ease in this position. He would neither raise his head nor let it droop,[4] but kept it level with his back.[5]

Whilst in *Ruku*, he would say: *"Subhana Rabbial-'Azeem"* (Glorified be my Lord, the Most Great) and sometimes, he would say with it or instead of it:

«سُبْحَانَكَ اللَّهُمَّ رَبَّنَا وَبِحَمْدِكَ، اللَّهُمَّ اغْفِرْ لِي»

"Subhanakallahumma Rabbana Wa Bihamdika, Allâhummaghfir Lee

"Glory be to You, oh, Allâh, our Lord, and praises are for You; forgive me."[6]

As a rule, his *Ruku* would last for as long as it takes to say *Tasbeeh*[7] ten times as was his *Sujûd*, but sometimes he would make the length of his bowing and prostration the same as that of his standing, but he only used to do that sometimes during the night prayer. So his guidance in most cases was to make his prayer balanced and even. He

---

[1] Narrated by Al-Bukhari and Abu Dawûd.

[2] Narrated by Ibn Khuzaimah and At-Tirmidhi, who declared it to be authentic.

[3] Narrated by Al-Bukhari and Al-Baihaqi.

[4] Narrated by Abu Dawûd and Al-Bukhari in *'Juz' Al-Qira'ah'* with an authentic chain of narrators.

[5] Narrated by Muslim and Abu 'Awanah.

[6] Narrated by Al-Bukhari and Muslim.

[7] *Tasbeeh*: Saying: *"Subhanallah"*.

also used to say in *Ruku:*

«سُبُّوحٌ قُدُّوسٌ رَبُّ الْمَلَائِكَةِ وَالرُّوحِ»

"*Subbûhun, Quddûsun, Rabbul-Mala'ikati War-Rûh*"

"Most Glorified, Most Holy, Lord of the angels and the Spirit (i.e. [Gabriel] Jibreel ![])."[1]

And sometimes, he would say:

«اللَّهُمَّ لَكَ رَكَعْتُ، وَبِكَ آمَنْتُ،وَلَكَ أَسْلَمْتُ، خَشَعَ لَكَ سَمْعِي وَبَصَرِي وَمُخِّي وَعَظْمِي وَعَصَبِي»

"*Allâhumma Laka Raka'tu, Wa Bika Aamantu, Wa Laka Aslamtu, Khashi'a Laka Sam'ee Wa Basaree Wa Mukhkhee Wa 'Azmee Wa 'Asabee*"

"(Oh, Allâh! To You I have bowed and in You I have believed and to You I have submitted; my hearing, my sight, my brain, my bones and my nerves are humbled before You)."[2]

But this has only been reported from him in the night prayer. Then he would raise his head, saying:

«سَمِعَ اللهُ لِمَنْ حَمِدَهُ»

"*Sami'allahu Liman Hamidah*"

"Verily Allâh listen to one who praises Him."

And he would raise his hands and he would always straighten his back when he stood up from bowing and between the two *Sajdahs* and he would say: "Prayer in which a man does not straighten his back in *Rukû'* and *Sujûd* is not accepted." (Narrated by Ibn Khuzaimah in his *'Saheeh'*).[3] Once he had straightened up from bowing, he would say:

«رَبَّنَاوَلَكَ الْحَمْدُ»

"*Rabbana Wa Lakal-Hamd*"

---

[1] Narrated by Muslim and Abu Dawûd.

[2] Narrated by Muslim on the authority of 'Ali Ibn Abi Talib ![].

[3] It was also narrated by the compilers of the *'Sunan'*.

"(Our Lord! And to You all praise and thanks are due.)"

And sometimes, he might say:

«اللَّهُمَّ رَبَّنَا لَكَ الْحَمْدُ»

"Allâhumma, Rabbana Lakal-Hamd"

"Oh, Allâh, our Lord! To You all praise and thanks are due."

But as for combining *"Allâhumma"* and the letter *"Wauw"*, this is not correct.[1]

It was a part of his guidance ﷺ that he would prolong this pillar of the prayer to a length of time equivalent to that of the *Rukû'* and it has been authentically reported from him that he would say in it:

«اللَّهُمَّ رَبَّنَا لَكَ الْحَمْدُ مِلْءَ السَّمَوَاتِ وَمِلْءَ الأَرْضِ، وَمِلْءَ مَابَيْنَهُمَا، وَمِلْءَ مَاشِئْتَ مِنْ شَيْءٍ بَعْدُ، أَهْلَ الثَّنَاءِ وَالْمَجْدِ، أَحَقُّ مَا قَالَ الْعَبْدُ، وَكُلُّنَا لَكَ عَبْدٌ، لَا مَانِعَ لِمَا أَعْطَيْتَ، وَلَا مُعْطِيَ لِمَا مَنَعْتَ، وَلَا يَنْفَعُ ذَا الْجَدِّ مِنْكَ الْجَدُّ»

"Allâhumma Rabbana Lakal-Hamdu, Mil'as-Samawati Wa Mil'al-Ardi Wa Mil'a Ma Bainahuma Wa Mil'a Ma Shi'ta Min Shay'in Badu; Ahluth-Thana'i Wal-Majdi, (- Ahaqqu Ma Qalal-'Abdu Wa Kulluna Laka 'Abd –) La Mani'a Lima A'taita Wa La Mu'tiya Lima Man'ata Wa La Yanfa'u Zal-Jaddi Minkal-Jadd"

"Oh, Allâh, our Lord! To You are due all praise and thanks, filling the heavens, filling the earth and whatever is between them and filling whatever else You wish. Lord of Glory and Majesty – This the most truthful thing that the slave may say, and we are all slaves to you – none can withhold what You give and none can give what You withhold, nor can the possessions

---

[1] In fact, that is correct, for it has been confirmed in the '*Musnad*' of Imam Ahmad and in '*Saheeh Al-Bukhari*' 2/234 in the description of the prayer, in the Chapter: What the *Imam* and Those Behind Him Should Say When He Raise His Head From *Rukû'*, in the *Hadeeth* of Abu Hurairah ﷺ and it has also been confirmed from Ibn 'Umar, Abu Sa'eed and Abu Mûsa Al-Ash'ari ﷺ.

of an owner benefit him before You."[1]

And it has been authentically reported from him that he used to say therein:

$$\text{«اللَّهُمَّ اغْسِلْنِي مِنْ خَطَايَايَ بِالْمَاءِ وَالثَّلْجِ وَالْبَرْدِ، وَنَقِّنِي مِنَ}$$
$$\text{الذُّنُوبِ وَالْخَطَايَا كَمَا يُنَقَّى الثَّوْبُ الأَبْيَضُ مِنَ الدَّنَسِ، وَبَاعِدْ بَيْنِي}$$
$$\text{وَبَيْنَ خَطَايَايَ كَمَا بَاعَدْتَ بَيْنَ الْمَشْرِقِ وَالْمَغْرِبِ»}$$

"Allâhummagh-silnee Min Khatayaya Bil-Ma'i Wath-Thalji Wal-Baradi, Allâhumma Naqqinee Minadh-Dhunûbi Wal-Khataya Kama Yunaqqath-Thawbul-Abyadu Minad-Danas Wa Ba'id Bainee Wa Baina Khatayaya Kama Ba'adta Bainal-Mashriqi Wal-Maghrib"

"Oh, Allâh! Cleanse me of my sins as a white garment is cleansed of dirt. Oh, Allâh! Purify me from my sins by ice, water and hail. Oh, Allâh! Purify me from misdeeds and sins as a white garment is purified from dirt. And make the distance between me and my sins as great as You have made the distance between the east and the west."[2]

And it has been authentically reported from him ﷺ that he used to repeat therein:

$$\text{«لِرَبِّيَ الْحَمْدُ، لِرَبِّيَ الْحَمْدُ»}$$

"Lirabbial-Hamdu, Lirabbial-Hamd"

"All praise and thanks to my Lord, all praise and thanks to my Lord"

So that it was the same length as his *Ruku*; Muslim has reported on the authority of Anas ﷺ: "When the Messenger of Allâh ﷺ said:

$$\text{«سَمِعَ اللهُ لِمِنْ حَمِدَهُ»}$$

---

[1] Narrated by Muslim, Abu Dawûd, Ahmad and Ad-Darimi.

[2] Narrated by Muslim with similar wording, without the addition: "And make the distance between me and my sins" This has only been reported as part of the opening supplication in prayer, as mentioned earlier and in general supplications, as mentioned by Al-Bukhari and Muslim.

"*Sami'allahu Liman Hamidah*"

"(Allâh listens to one who praises Him),"

he would remain standing until we would say: "He has forgotten." Then he would prostrate and sit between the two prostrations until we would say: "He has forgotten."[1] So this was the well known guidance of the Prophet ﷺ. As for the shortening of these two pillars, it was done by the leaders from among Banu Umayyah, until the people thought that it is a part of the *Sunnah*.

---

[1] Narrated by Al-Bukhari, Muslim and Ahmad.

Chapter

Then he would make the *Takbeer* and prostrate without raising his hands[1] and he used to place his knees on the ground and then his hands after them,[2] then his forehead and his nose. This is what is correct, for the part of him which was placed on the ground first was the part of him which was nearest to it, then the next nearest. The first part of him to be lifted from the ground was the highest part of him and then the next highest, so when he rose, he would lift his head first, then his hands, then his knees and this is the opposite of the action of the camel and he prohibited imitating animals in prayer: He prohibited lowering oneself to the ground in the same way that a camel does, glancing around the way a fox does, spreading the arms the way a beast of prey does, *Iq'a'*[3] in the manner of a dog, pecking

---

[1] According to Shaikh Nasir Ad-Deen Al-Albani (may Allâh have mercy on him), in 'The Prophet's Prayer Described', it is narrated by An-Nasa'i, Ad-Daraqutni and Mukhlis in '*Al-Fawa'id*' with two authentic chains of narrators that: "He would raise his hands when performing *Sajdah*." It was also the practice of a number of the Companions, including Ibn 'Umar, Ibn 'Abbas, Hasan Al-Basri, Tawoos and others ﷺ and it was done by Imam Ahmad and it was quoted from Imam Malik and Imam Ash-Shafi'i.

[2] According to Shaikh Al-Albani in 'The Prophet's Prayer Described', "He used to place his hands on the ground before his knees." (Narrated by Abu Dawûd, An-Nasa'i and others) and he quotes 'Abdul Haq in '*Kitab At-Tahajjud*' as saying: "It has a sounder chain of narrators than the previous one (i.e. the *Hadeeth* of Wa'il, which states that he used to place his knees on the ground before is hands)." Shaikh Al-Albani adds: "In fact, the latter *Hadeeth*, in addition to being contradictory to this authentic *Hadeeth* is neither authentic in its chain of narrators, nor in meaning, as I have explained in '*Silsilah Al-Ahadeeth Ad-Da'eefah Wal-Mawdû'ah*' and in '*Irwa' Al-Ghaleel*'

[3] According to Al-Baihaqi, there are two types of *Iq'a'*: (i) The above-

the ground as a crow does and raising the hands like the tails of wild horses when making the *Tasleem*.

He used to prostrate upon his forehead and his nose below the winding of his turban and it has not been reported from him that he used to prostrate on it. He used to prostrate on the earth much and on water and mud[1] and on a *Khumrah*[2] made from date palm leaves[3] and on a *Haseer*[4] made from them and on a tanned *Farwah*.[5]

When he prostrated, he would place his forehead and his nose firmly on the ground[6] and spread his palms on either side of him and he would keep his arms away from his sides until the white of his armpits could be seen.[7] He used to place his hands at the level of his shoulders and his ears and he would be at ease in his prostration and he would face the tips of his toes towards the *Qiblah* and he would place his hands and his fingers flat on the ground, without spreading them or clenching them.

(While prostrating,) he would say:

$$ \text{«سُبْحَانَ رَبِّيَ الأَعْلَىٰ»} $$

"Subhana Rabbial-A'la"

"Glorified be my Lord, Most High."[8]

---

mentioned (forbidden type) and (ii) the permissible type, which is confirmed from the Prophet ﷺ, which is sitting with the tips of the toes and knees on the ground with the buttocks resting on the heels – and that is the *Sunnah* of sitting between the two prostrations.

[1] Narrated by Al-Bukhari and Muslim.

[2] *Khumrah*: A small piece of matting just sufficient in size to place the nose and forehead on in prostration.

[3] Narrated by Al-Bukhari, the compilers of the '*Sunan*', Ahmad and Ad-Darimi.

[4] *Haseer*: A mat. This was narrated by Al-Bukhari, the compilers of the '*Sunan*' and Ahmad.

[5] *Farwah*: Animal skin, pelt or hide. This was narrated by Ahmad.

[6] Narrated by Abu Dawûd and At-Tirmidhi.

[7] Narrated by Al-Bukhari and Muslim.

[8] Narrated by Ahmad, Abu Dawûd, Ibn Majah and others.

He would also say:

«سُبْحَانَكَ اللَّهُمَّ رَبَّنَا وَبِحَمْدِكَ، اللَّهُمَّ اغْفِرْ لِي»

"Subhanakallahumma Rabbana Wa Bihamdika, Allâhummaghfir Lee"

"Oh, Allâh, our Lord glory and praise be to You. Oh, Allâh! Forgive me."[1]

And he would say:

«سُبُّوحٌ قُدُّوسٌ رَبُّ الْمَلَائِكَةِ وَالرُّوحِ»

"Subbûhun Quddûsun, Rabbul-Mala'ikati War-Rûh"

"Most Glorified, Most Holy, Lord of the angels and the Spirit [i.e. Gabriel]."[2]

And he used to say:

«اللَّهُمَّ لَكَ سَجَدْتُ، وَبِكَ آمَنْتُ، وَلَكَ أَسْلَمْتُ، سَجَدَ وَجْهِيَ لِلَّذِي خَلَقَهُ وَصَوَّرَهُ، وَشَقَّ سَمْعَهُ وَبَصَرَهُ، تَبَارَكَ اللهُ أَحْسَنُ الْخَالِقِينَ»

"Allâhumma Laka Sajadtu Wa Bika Aamantu Wa Laka Aslamtu, Sajada Wajhee Lilladhi Khalaqahu Wa Sawwarahu Wa Shaqqa Sam'ahu Wa Basarahu, Tabarakallahu Ahsanul-Khaliqeen"

"Oh, Allâh! For you I have prostrated, in You I have believed, to You I have submitted. My face has prostrated for the One Who created it and shaped it, then brought forth its hearing and sight: Blessed be Allâh, the Best of Creators."[3]

And he would say:

«اللَّهُمَّ اغْفِرْ لِي ذَنْبِي كُلَّهُ دِقَّهُ وَجُلَّهُ، وَأَوَّلَهُ وَآخِرَهُ، وَعَلَانِيَتَهُ وَسِرَّهُ»

"Allâhummaghfir Lee Dhanbee Kullahu, Diqqahu Wa Jallahu Wa Awwalahu Wa Aakhirahu Wa Alaniyatahu Wa Sirrahu"

---

[1] Narrated by Al-Bukhari and Muslim.

[2] Narrated by Muslim and Abu 'Awanah.

[3] Narrated by Muslim, Abu 'Awanah, At-Tahawi and Ad-Daraqutni.

"Oh, Allâh! Forgive me all my sins: the minor and the major, the first and the last, the apparent and the hidden."[1]

And he used to say:

«اللَّهُمَّ اغْفِرْ لِي خَطَايَايَ وَجَهْلِي وَإِسْرَافِي فِي أَمْرِي، وَمَا أَنْتَ أَعْلَمُ بِهِ مِنِّي، اللَّهُمَّ اغْفِرْ لِي جِدِّي وَهَزْلِي، وَخَطَايَايَ وَعَمْدِي وَكُلَّ ذَلِكَ عِنْدِي، اللَّهُمَّ اغْفِرْ لِي مَا قَدَّمْتُ وَمَا أَخَّرْتُ، وَمَا أَسْرَرْتُ وَمَا أَعْلَنْتُ أَنْتَ إِلَهِي لَا إِلَهَ إِلَّا أَنْتَ»

"Allâhummaghfir Lee Khatayaya Wa Jahlee Wa Israfee Fee Amree Wa Ma Anta A'lamu Bihi minee, Allâhummaghfir Lee Jiddee Wa Hazlee Wa Khatayaya Wa 'Amdee Wa Kullu dhalika 'Indee, Allâhummaghfir Lee Ma Qaddamtu Wa Ma Akhkhartu Wa Ma Asrartu Wa Ma A'lantu Anta Ilahee La Ilaha Illa Anta"

"Oh, Allâh! Forgive me my mistakes and my ignorance and my extravagance, for You know them better than I. Oh, Allâh! Forgive me my serious mistakes and those made in jest) my (unintentional) and my intentional mistakes and all of these are in me. Oh, Allâh! Forgive me my sins in the past and in the future, and those which I concealed and those which I committed openly. You are my *Ilah*[2] and none has the right to be worshipped except You".

And he ordered the Companions ﷺ to strive much in supplication when prostrating, saying: "Verily, it is most worthy to be answered for you."[3]

---

[1] Narrated by Muslim and Abu 'Awanah.
[2] *Ilah*: A deity or object of worship.
[3] Narrated by An-Nasa'i.

Chapter

Then he would raise his head, saying: *"Allâhu Akbar"*[1] without raising his hands[2] and he would sit *Muftarishan*,[3] Laying the left foot along the ground and sitting on it, with his right foot upright, and placing his hands on his thighs and placing his (right) elbow on his thigh and the edge of his (right) hand on his knee and he would make a fist with his fingers and make a circle with his thumb and forefinger and he would raise his forefinger and supplicate with it, moving it (up and down) and saying:

$$ «اللّٰهُمَّ اغْفِرْ لِي وَارْحَمْنِي وَاهْدِنِي وَارْزُقْنِي» $$

"Allâhummaghfir Lee Warhamnee Wahdinee Warzuqnee"

"Oh, Allâh! Forgive me, have mercy on me, guide me and sustain me."[4]

This was how it was described by Ibn 'Abbas ﷺ from the Prophet ﷺ.

Huzaifah ﷺ reported from him that he used to say:

$$ «رَبِّ اغْفِرْ لِي» $$

"Rabbighfir Lee"

"(My Lord! Forgive me)."[5]

---

[1] Narrated by Al-Bukhari and Muslim.

[2] It is narrated by Al-Bukhari in his *'Juz' Raf'il Yadain'*, by Abu Dawûd, Muslim and Abu 'Awanah that: "he would raise his hands with this *Takbeer* (i.e. that of rising from *Sajdah*) sometimes." Imams Ahmad, Malik and Ash-Shafi'i held that it is a *Sunnah* to raise the hands with every *Takbeer* and it has been reported from a number of Companions ﷺ and *Tabi'ûn*.

[3] Narrated by Ahmad and Abu Dawûd.

[4] Narrated by Abu Dawûd, At-Tirmidhi, Ibn Majah and Al-Hakim, who declared it to be authentic and Az-Zahabi confirmed this.

[5] Narrated by Ibn Majah.

Then he would stand up on the tips of his toes, supporting himself on his thighs.[1]

Once he was upright, he would begin reciting and he would not observe a silence as he did when opening the prayer, then he would pray the second *Rak'ah* as he did the first, except in four things: (i) The short period of silence, (ii) the opening of the prayer, (iii) the opening *Takbeerah* and (iv) the prolonging of it.

Then when he sits for the *Tashahhud*, he would place his left hand on his left thigh and his right hand on his right thigh and he would point with his (right) index finger and he would not raise it high, nor would he hold it down, but would bend it slightly and move it, clenching the little finger and the ring finger and making a circle with the middle finger and the thumb and raising the forefinger and supplicating with it, and he would fix his gaze upon it and he would spread out the left palm on his left thigh and he would rest on it. As for the description of his sitting, it was the same as that between the prostrations, as mentioned previously.

As for the *Hadeeth* of Ibn Az-Zubair narrated by Muslim: "When he sat in prayer, he would place his left foot between his thigh and his shin, laying his right foot flat," this was in the final *tashahhud*. Ibn Az-Zubair said that he used to lay the right foot flat, while Abu Humaid said that he raised it, but this – and Allâh knows better – is not a difference of opinion, because he used to sit on it, indeed, he used to push it out from his right side, so that it was between being raised and being flat. Or it was said: He used to do this and this; he used to raise it and perhaps sometimes, he laid it flat. And that is more relaxing for them (i.e. the feet).

He would always make the *Tashahhud* in this sitting and he taught his Companions ﷺ to say:

---

[1] In 'The Prophet's Prayer Described' Shaikh Muhammad Nasir Ad-Deen Al-Albani says: "As for the *Hadeeth*: "He used to get up like an arrow, not supporting himself with his hands", it is *Mawdû'* (fabricated), and all narrations of similar meaning are weak, not authentic, and I have explained this in '*Silsilah Al-Ahadeeth Ad-Da'eefah Wal-Mawdû'ah*' (562, 929, 968).

«التَّحِيَّاتُ للهِ وَالصَّلَوَاتُ وَالطَّيِّبَاتُ، السَّلَامُ عَلَيْكَ أَيُّهَا النَّبِيُّ وَرَحْمَةُ
اللهِ وَبَرَكَاتُهُ، السَّلَامُ عَلَيْنَا وَعَلَى عِبَادِ اللهِ الصَّالِحِينَ، أَشْهَدُ أَنْ لَا
إِلَهَ إِلَّا اللهُ، وَأَشْهَدُ أَنَّ مُحَمَّدًا عَبْدُهُ وَرَسُولُهُ»

*"At-Tahiyyatu Lillahi Was-Salawatu Wat-Tayyibatu, As-Salamu
'Alaika Ayyuhan-Nabiyyu Wa Rahmatullahi Wa Barakatuhu, As-
Salamu 'Alaina Wa 'Ala 'Ibadillahis-Saliheena, Ash-hadu Alla Ilaha
Illallahu Wa Ash-hadu Anna Muhammadan 'Abduhu Wa Rasuluhu"*

"All the compliments, prayers and good things are due to Allâh.
Peace be upon you, O Prophet, and Allâh's Mercy and
Blessings. Peace be upon us and upon the righteous slaves of
Allâh. I bear witness that none has the right to be worshipped
but Allâh, and I bear witness that Muhammad is His slave and
His Messenger."[1]

And he used to make it very light, as if he was praying on a hot stone.
It has not been transmitted from him in any *Hadeeth* ever that he used
to send prayers on himself and on his family in it,[2] nor did he seek
refuge in it from the punishment of the grave, nor the punishment of
the Fire, nor the trial of life and death, nor the trial of *Al-Maseeh Ad-
Dajjal*;[3] and if anyone recommended it, it was only due to his
understanding of general evidences which clearly refer to the final
Tashahhud.[4]

---

[1] Narrated by Al-Bukhari and Muslim.

[2] On the contrary, it has been narrated by Abu 'Awanah in his *'Saheeh'* and
by An-Nasa'i that he used to do so.

[3] *Al-Maseeh Ad-Dajjal*: The false messiah.

[4] According to Shaikh Muhammad Nasir Ad-Deen Al-Albani (may Allâh
have mercy on him): "They had said: "Oh, Messenger of Allâh! We have
been taught how to send peace on you (i.e. in the *Tashahhud*), but how do
we send prayers on you?" He said: "Say: "Oh, Allâh! Send prayers on
Muhammad" etc. Thus he did not specify one *Tashahhud* to the exclusion
of the other, so there is evidence here to establish sending prayers on him
in the first *Tashahhud* also Many *Ahadeeth* exist about sending prayers on
the Prophet ﷺ in *Tashahhud* and in none of them is there any such
specification mentioned. In fact, these *Ahadeeth* are general."

Then he would stand up saying: *"Allâhu Akbar"*, on the tips of his toes and on his knees, supporting himself (with his hands) on his thighs.

In *'Saheeh Muslim'* and in some routes reported by Al-Bukhari, it is mentioned that he used to raise his hands at this point, then he would recite *Sûrah Al-Fâtihah* alone, and it has not been confirmed that he used to recite anything else in the final two *Rak'ahs*.[1]

It was not a part of his guidance to look hither and thither during the prayer; and in *'Saheeh Al-Bukhari'*, it is reported that he was asked about it and he said: "It is stealing; Satan steals from the prayer of the slave." Sometimes he would do it in the prayer due to some abnormal circumstance which was not a customary action for him, such as when he looked towards the mountain pass where he who sent the reconnoiterer, – and Allâh knows better. After the *Tashahhud* and before the *Tasleem*, he would supplicate and he ordered his Companions ﷺ to do likewise in the *Hadeeth* of Abu Hurairah and the *Hadeeth* of Fadhalah ﷺ.

As for supplication after the *Tasleem* whilst facing the *Qiblah* or those who were being led in prayer, that has no basis in his guidance ﷺ. In general, he only performed the supplications connected with prayer during the prayer and he ordered his Companions ﷺ to do likewise – and that is what befits the situation of the worshipper, because he is approaching his Lord and once he makes the *Tasleem*, that is lost.

Then he would make the *Tasleem* to his right, saying:

$$\text{«السَّلَامُ عَلَيْكُمْ وَرَحْمَةُ اللهِ»}$$

"As-Salamu 'Alaikum Wa Rahmatullah".

"May the Peace of Allâh and His Mercy be upon You".

Then he would do likewise to his left. This was his customary practice, but it has been narrated from him that he used to make one *Tasleem* in

---

[1] In fact, as reported by Ahmad and Muslim: "He used to make the last two *Rak'ahs* about half as long as the first two, about fifteen Verses." And Al-Bukhari and Muslim narrated that: "sometimes he would recite only *Al-Fâtihah* in them."

front of his face, but this had not been confirmed.[1] The best *Hadeeth* which exists in this matter is that of 'A'ishah◉ which is in the '*Sunan*'[2] but it is with regard to standing in prayer at night and it has some weakness in it, because it does not clearly state that he made only one *Tasleem*.

He used to supplicate during his prayers, saying:

«اللَّهُمَّ إِنِّي أَعُوذُ بِكَ مِنْ عَذَابِ الْقَبْرِ، وَأَعُوذُ بِكَ مِنْ فِتْنَةِ الْمَسِيحِ الدَّجَّالِ، وَأَعُوذُ بِكَ مِنْ فِتْنَةِ الْمَحْيَا وَالْمَمَاتِ، اللَّهُمَّ إِنِّي أَعُوذُ بِكَ مِنَ الْمَأْثَمِ وَالْمَغْرَمِ»

"Allâhumma, Innee A'ûdhu Bika Min 'Adhabil-Qabri Wa A'ûdhu Bika Min Fitnatil Maseehid-Dajjali Wa A'ûdhu Bika Min Fitnatil-Mahya Wal-Mamati, Allâhumma Innee A'ûdhu Bika Minal-Ma'tha-mi Wal-Maghram"

"Oh, Allâh! I seek refuge with You from the punishment of the grave and I seek refuge with You from the trial of *Al-Maseeh Ad-Dajjal* and I seek refuge with You from the trial of life and death. Oh, Allâh! I seek refuge with You from sin and debt."[3]

He also used to say in his prayers:

«اللَّهُمَّ اغْفِرْ لِي ذَنْبِي، وَوَسِّعْ لِي فِي دَارِي، وَبَارِكْ لِي فِي مَا رَزَقْتَنِي»

"Allâhummaghfir Lee Dhanbee Wa Wassi' Lee Fee Daree Wa Barik Lee Feema Razaqtanee"

"Oh, Allâh! Forgive me my sins and widen for me my abode and bless me in that by which You sustain me"

And he used to say:

---

[1] In fact, this *Hadeeth* was narrated by Ahmad, Ibn Khuzaimah, Al-Baihaqi, Al-Hakim, who declared it to be authentic and Az-Zahabi concurred with this.

[2] *Sunan*: The books of *Hadeeth* compiled by At-Tirmidhi, Abu Dawûd, Ibn Majah, An-Nasa'i

[3] Narrated by Al-Bukhari and Muslim.

«اللَّهُمَّ إِنِّي أَسْأَلُكَ الثَّبَاتَ فِي الأَمْرِ، وَالْعَزِيمَةَ عَلَى الرُّشْدِ، وَأَسْأَلُكَ شُكْرَ نِعْمَتِكَ، وَحُسْنَ عِبَادَتِكَ، وَأَسْأَلُكَ قَلْبًا سَلِيمًا، وَأَسْأَلُكَ لِسَانًا صَادِقًا، وَأَسْأَلُكَ مِنْ خَيْرِ مَا تَعْلَمُ، وَأَعُوذُ بِكَ مِنْ شَرِّ مَا تَعْلَمُ وَأَسْتَغْفِرُكَ لِمَا تَعْلَمُ»

"Allâhumma Innee As'alukath-Thabata Fil-Amri Wal-'Azeemata 'Alar-Rushdi Wa As'aluka Shukra Ni'matika Wa Husna 'Ibadatika Wa As'aluka Qalban Saleeman Wa As'aluka Lisanan Sadiqan Wa As'aluka Min Khairi Ma Ta'lamu Wa A'ûdhu Bika Min Sharri Ma Ta'lamu Wa Astaghfiruka Lima Ta'lam"

"Oh, Allâh! I ask that You make me firm in the affair (i.e. of my Religion) and that You make me constant in integrity and I ask You that You make me thankful for Your Blessings and make me to worship You in the best way; and I ask You for a sound heart and I ask You for a truthful tongue and I ask You to give me from what You know to be good and I seek refuge with You from what You know to be evil and I seek forgiveness what You know."[1]

And all of the supplications (in prayer) which have been preserved are in the form of the first person singular.

When he stood in prayer, he would lower his head, according to Imam Ahmad and when making the *Tashahhud*, he would not extend his gaze beyond his pointing finger. Allâh made him find joy and peace in prayer and he used to say: "Oh, Bilal! Gladden us with the prayer."[2] But this did not prevent him from observing those whom he led in prayer, in spite of the complete presence of his heart (in the prayer).

He used to enter the prayer wishing to prolong it, but would hear the cry of a child and shorten it, fearful that he would burden his mother. Similarly, he would offer an obligatory prayer holding Umamah 🌸, his granddaughter, on his shoulder; when he stood up, he would carry her and when he bowed or prostrated, he would put her down.

---

[1] Narrated by At-Tirmidhi, An-Nasa'i and Ahmad.
[2] Narrated by Abu Dawûd and Ahmad.

And he would pray and Al-Hasan and Al-Husain ৠ would come and climb his back, so he would prolong his prostration, disliking to throw them off his back. And he would pray and 'A'ishah ৠ would come and he would open the door for her, then return to his place of prayer. And he used to return salutations of peace by indicating with his hand.

As for the *Hadeeth* which states: "Whoever indicated (with his hand) during his prayer must repeat it," it is baseless.

He used to blow during his prayer, according to Imam Ahmad, and he would cry during it and he would clear his throat when necessary. Sometimes he would pray barefoot and at other times wearing shoes.[1] And he ordered his Companions ৠ to pray in their shoes in order to be different from the Jews. Sometimes he would pray wearing a single garment and sometimes two garments – and this was more common.

He performed *Qunût*[2] in the *Fajr* prayer after the *Rukû'* for a month then he stopped it; and his *Qunût* was due to some temporary circumstances and once they had been lifted, he would stop it. His guidance was to perform *Qunût* due to some particular calamities and not to do so when there were none and he did not perform it only during the *Fajr* prayer. Indeed, most of his *Qunût* was performed during it due to its being prescribed to make it long and due to its being close to early dawn (*Sahar*)[3] and the time when supplication is answered and the time of Allâh's Descent.[4]

---

[1] This is something which few people do nowadays; indeed, most people dislike that anyone should walk in the mosque wearing shoes and some might even consider this to be one of the greatest of major sins, let alone praying in them.

[2] *Qunût*: Raising the hands and supplicating for the Muslims or against their enemies in the final *Rak'ah* of the prayer.

[3] *Sahûr*: A light meal taken before fasting commences.

[4] According to the *Hadeeth* narrated by Muslim on the authority of Abu Hurairah ৠ: "Allâh descends (in a manner befitting His Majesty) to the lowest heaven every night when half of the night or two-third of it is over and says: "Is there anyone asking who may be given? Is there anyone supplicating who may be answered?""

Chapter

It has been confirmed from him ﷺ that he said: "I am only a human being like you: I forget as you do, so if I forget, remind me."[1] And his forgetfulness was a completion of (Allâh's) Favour upon his community and the perfection of their Religion in order that they may emulate him, for he stood up after praying two *Rak'ahs* of a four *Rak'ah* prayer and when he had completed his prayer, he prostrated before making the *Tasleem*, from which it was inferred that whoever leaves a portion of the prayer which is not a pillar (*Rukn*) should prostrate for it before making the *Tasleem*. It has also been taken from some sources that if he forgot that and had begun a pillar, he would not return to it. And he made the *Tasleem* after praying two *Rak'ahs* of one of the afternoon prayers, then he spoke, then he completed it, then he made the *Tasleem*, after which, he prostrated, then made the *Tasleem* (again).

And he prayed and made the *Tasleem* and left while one *Rak'ah* remained of the prayer and Talhah ؊ said to him: "You have forgotten a *Rak'ah*," so he entered the mosque and ordered Bilal ؊ to call the *Iqamah*, then the people prayed one *Rak'ah*. (Narrated by Ahmad)

And he prayed five *Rak'ahs* in the *Zuhr* prayer and they said: "You have prayed five." So he prostrated after making the *Tasleem*."[2]

And he prayed three *Rak'ahs* in the *'Asr* prayer, then entered his house and the people reminded him, so he went out and prayed one *Rak'ah* with them, then he made the *Tasleem*, then he prostrated, then he made the *Tasleem* (again).[3]

This is the total of what has been reported from him (in this matter)

---

[1] Narrated by Al-Bukhari, Muslim, Abu Dawûd, An-Nasa'i and Ibn Majah.

[2] Narrated by Al-Bukhari, Muslim, the compilers of the *'Sunan'* and Ahmad.

[3] Narrated by Muslim.

and they are five situations.

It was not a part of his guidance to close his eyes in prayer and this was disliked by Ahmad and others, for they said: "It is one of the actions of the Jews." A number of scholars permitted it, but the correct view is that keeping them open is better if it does not detract from the required humility of prayer; but if it prevents one from achieving humility, due to the presence of ornaments and other thing (which distract the worshipper), then it is not disliked.

After making the *Tasleem*, he would seek forgiveness three times (saying: *"Astaghfirullah"* [I seek forgiveness from Allâh]), then he would say:

«اللَّهُمَّ أَنْتَ السَّلَامُ، وَمِنْكَ السَّلَامُ، تَبَارَكْتَ يَاذَا الْجَلَالِ وَالإِكْرَام»

"Allâhumma Antas-Salamu Wa Minkas-Salamu Tabarakta Ya Dhal-Jalali Wal-Ikram"

"Oh, Allâh! You are Peace and from You comes Peace, Most Blessed are You, oh, Owner of Majesty and Honour!"[1]

And he would not remain facing the *K'abah* for longer than it took to say this, but would hasten to turn towards the worshippers.

And he would turn to his right and to his left, then he would face towards the worshippers in front of him and he would not single out any particular direction in preference to the others.

When he offered the *Fajr* prayer, he would remain in the place in which he had prayed until the sun had completely risen.

At the end of his obligatory prayers, he would say:

«لَا إِلَهَ إِلَّا اللهُ وَحْدَهُ لَا شَرِيكَ لَهُ، لَهُ الْمُلْكُ، وَلَهُ الْحَمْدُ، وَهُوَ عَلَى كُلِّ شَيْءٍ قَدِيرٌ»

"La Ilaha Illallahu Wahdu La Shareeka Lahu, Lahul-Mulku Wa Lahul-Hamdu Wa Huwa 'Ala Kulli Shay'in Qadeer."

"None has the right to be worshipped except Allâh, Alone,

---

[1] Narrated by Muslim, At-Tirmidhi, Abu Dawûd, An-Nasa'i, Ibn Majah and Ahmad.

without partners, His is the Dominion and to Him are due all praise and thanks and He is Able to do all things."[1]

«اللَّهُمَّ لَا مَانِعَ لِمَا أَعْطَيْتَ، وَلَا مُعْطِيَ لِمَا مَنَعْتَ، وَلَا يَنْفَعُ ذَا الْجَدِّ مِنْكَ الْجَدُّ، وَلَا حَوْلَ وَلَا قُوَّةَ إِلَّا بِاللهِ، لَا إِلَهَ إِلَّا اللهُ، وَلَا نَعْبُدُ إِلَّا إِيَّاهُ، لَهُ النِّعْمَةُ، وَلَهُ الْفَضْلُ، وَلَهُ الثَّنَاءُ الْحَسَنُ، لَا إِلَهَ إِلَّا اللهُ مُخْلِصِينَ لَهُ الدِّينَ، وَلَوْ كَرِهَ الْكَافِرُونَ»

Allâhumma La Mani'a Lima A'taita Wa La Mu'tiya Lima Mana'ta Wa La Yanfa'u Zal-Jaddi Minka Al-Jaddu, Wa La Hawla Wa La Quwwata Illa Billahi, La Ilaha Illallahu, Wa La Na'budu Illa Iyyahu Lahun-Ni'matu Wa Lahul-Fadlu Wa Lahuth-Thana'ul Hasanu, La Ilaha Illallahu Mukhliseena Lahud-Deenu Wa Law Karihal-Kafirûn"

"Oh, Allâh! There is none who can withhold what You have given and there is none who can give what You have withheld nor can the possessions of an owner benefit him in front of You and there is no power and no strength save in Allâh; none has the right to be worshipped except Allâh and we worship none save Him. All Blessings and Bounty belong to Him and all beautiful praises are due to Him; none has the right to be worshipped except Allâh – with sincerity towards Him in Religion, even though the polytheists may detest it."[2]

And he encouraged his people to say at the end of the obligatory prayers: *"Subhanallahi"* (Glorified is Allâh) thirty-three times, *"Al-Hamdu Lillahi"* (All praise and thanks be to Allâh) thirty-three times, *"Allâhu Akbaru"* (Allâh is Most Great) thirty-three times and to complete the hundred by saying:

«لَا إِلَهَ إِلَّا اللهُ وَحْدَهُ لَا شَرِيكَ لَهُ، لَهُ الْمُلْكُ، وَلَهُ الْحَمْدُ، وَهُوَ عَلَى كُلِّ شَيْءٍ قَدِيرٌ»

"La Ilaha Illallahu Wahdahu La Shareeka Lahu, Lahul-Mulku Wa Lahul-Hamdu Wa Huwa 'Ala Kulli Shay'in Qadeer"

---

[1] Narrated by Muslim, on the authority of Abu Hurairah ﷺ.

[2] Narrated by Muslim and Abu Dawûd.

"None has the right to be worshipped except Allâh, Alone, without partners, His is the Dominion and to Him are due all praise and thanks and He is Able to do all things."[1]

Ibn Hibban reported in his '*Saheeh*', on the authority of Al-Harith Ibn Muslim ⸙ that he said: "The Messenger of Allâh ﷺ said: "If you offer the *Fajr* prayer, before speaking, say:

«اللَّهُمَّ أَجِرْنِي مِنَ النَّارِ»

"*Allâhumma Ajirnee Minan-Nar*"

"Oh, Allâh! Protect me from the Fire",

seven times and if you died during that day, Allâh will ordain for you protection from the Fire; and if you offer the *Maghrib* prayer, before speaking, say: "*Allâhumma Ajirnee Minan-Nar*" "Oh, Allâh! Protect me from the Fire" seven times and if you died during that day, Allâh will ordain for you protection from the Fire."[2]

If he prayed towards a wall, he would leave the distance sufficient for a sheep to pass between him and the wall[3] and he would not stand far from it; indeed, he ordered his Companions ⸙ to move close to the *Sutrah*.[4] If he prayed towards a stick, a pillar or a tree, he would place it slightly to his right side or his left side and he would not stand directly in front of it.[5] He would plant his spear in the ground when

---

[1] Narrated by Muslim, on the authority of Abu Hurairah ⸙.

[2] Narrated by Ibn Hibban and Abu Dawûd, but it contains in its chain of narrators a person who is unknown (*Majhûl*) and therefore, according to scholars of *Hadeeth*, it is weak.

[3] Narrated by Al-Bukhari and Muslim, on the authority of Sahl Ibn Sa'd ⸙.

[4] *Sutrah*: An obstacle of some kind, such as a wall, a pillar, a stick, another worshipper etc. It is obligatory to pray towards a *Sutrah*, as the Prophet (ﷺ) said: "Do not pray except towards a *Sutrah*." (Narrated by Ibn Khuzaimah with a good *Sanad*)

[5] Presumably, this statement is based upon the *Hadeeth* narrated by Abu Dawûd in the Chapter on Prayer, on the authority of Al-Miqdad Ibn Al-Aswad ⸙, who is reported to have said: "I did not see the Messenger of Allâh (ﷺ) praying towards a stick, a pillar or a tree except that he placed it to his right or to his left, and he did not pray directly towards it."

Traveling or in the desert and pray towards it and that would be his *Sutrah*. And he would place his riding camel and pray towards it and he would take the saddle, place it straight and pray towards the end of it. He ordered the worshipper to pray towards a *Sutrah*, even if it be an arrow or a stick and if he did not find one, he should draw a line on the ground. If there was no *Sutrah*, it has been authentically reported from him that he said: "A woman, a donkey and a black dog (passing in front of the worshipper) cuts off the prayer." Anything which contradicts this is either authentic but unclear, or clear but inauthentic. He used to pray while 'A'ishah 🌺 was sleeping in his *Qiblah* (i.e. in front of him), but this is not the same as a person passing in front of him, for it is unlawful for a man to pass in front of a worshipper, but it is not disliked for him to remain in front of a worshipper in prayer.

However its *Sanad* has a number of weaknesses, according to scholars of *Hadeeth*: (i) Abu 'Ubaidah Al-Waleed Ibn Kamil is not reliable, according to Al-Bukhari, Ibn Hajr, Ibn Al-Qattan and Al-Azadi, (ii) Al-Muhallab Ibn Hajr Al-Bahrani is unknown, according to Ibn Al-Qattan, (iii) Dhuba'ah Bint Al-Miqdad is unknown, according to Ibn Hajr and Ibn Al-Qattan.

Chapter

He would always pray ten *Rak'ahs* while he was at home and it is these regarding which Ibn 'Umar 🙏 said: "I have continued to observe the performance of ten *rak'ahs* which I learnt from the Messenger of Allâh 🕊: Two *Rak'ahs* before *Zuhr* and two *Rak'ahs* after it, two *Rak'ahs* after *Maghrib* and two *Rak'ahs* after *'Isha'* in his house and two *Rak'ahs* before the *Fajr* prayer."[1] If he missed the two *Rak'ahs* before the *Zuhr* prayer, he would make up for them during the time when it is prohibited to pray after *'Asr*. Sometimes, he used to offer four *Rak'ahs* before *Zuhr*. As for the two *Rak'ahs* before *Maghrib*, it has been authentically reported from him that he said: "Pray two *Rak'ahs* before *Maghrib* (and he repeated it three times); after the third time, he said: "For whomsoever wishes," because he disliked that the people should take them as a *Sunnah*.[2] This is the correct view, that they are recommended and not a regular *Sunnah*.

In general, he used to offer the *Sunan* and the supererogatory prayers for which there was no reason in his house, particularly the *Sunnah* of *Maghrib*, for it has not been transmitted from him that he ever performed it in the mosque, but he sometimes performed (the other *Sunan* and supererogatory prayers) in the mosque And his observation of the *Sunnah* of *Fajr* was stricter than that of all of the supererogatory prayers; likewise, he never failed to observe it and the *Witr* prayer regardless of whether he was at home or traveling, and it has not been transmitted from him that he offered any regular *Sunnah* prayers when traveling other than these.

---

[1] Narrated by Al-Bukhari, Muslim, At-Tirmidhi, Abu Dawûd, Malik and Ahmad.

[2] Narrated by Al-Bukhari, Abu Dawûd and Ahmad.

Scholars of Islamic Jurisprudence have differed as to which of them is more strongly confirmed; the *Sunnah* of *Fajr* is the first act of the day and *Witr* is the last, which is why he used to offer them by reciting therein the two *Sûrahs* of Sincerity (*Ikhlas*),[1] because they combine *Tawheed* of knowledge and *Tawheed* of action, *Tawheed* of knowledge (of Allâh) and *Tawheed* of (Allâh's) Will, *Tawheed* of belief and (the slave's) intention. So Say: "He is Allâh, One" [2] includes the Oneness which negates all manner of *Shirk*, which must be confirmed for Him, Most High and the negation of begetting or being begotten, which confirms the completeness of His Self-sufficiency and freedom from all needs and His Oneness and the negation of anything like unto Him, which includes the negation of anything similar to him or resembling Him and that includes the affirmation of every perfection and the negation of every imperfection and the invalidity of affirming anything similar, equal or comparable to Him in His Perfection and the negation of all manner of *Shirk*. These fundamental principles combine (all aspects of) *Tawheed* of knowledge by which the one who holds them differs from all of the misguided sects and the polytheists. For this reason, it is said that it (*Sûrah Al-Ikhlâs*) is equivalent to one third of the Qur'ân, for it revolves around two main points: *Khabar* (information) and *Insha'* (imperatives); *Insha'* is of three types: (i) Command, (ii) negation and (iii) permissibility, while *Khabar* is of two types: (i) Information about the Creator, Most High, His Names and Attributes and His Judgements and (ii) information about His creation (mankind, the jinn, animals, the earth, Paradise, the Hell-fire, the Universe etc.) and *Sûrah Al-Ikhlas* concentrates on information about Him and about His Names and Attributes, and so it is equivalent to one third of the Qur'ân and it purifies the one who recites it from *Shirk* in matters of knowledge just as the *Sûrah*: Say: "Oh, you disbelievers"[3] purifies him from *Shirk* in actions; and since knowledge precedes action and it is what leads him and drives him and controls him, {Say: "He is Allâh, One"} is equivalent to one third of the Qur'ân; and since *Shirk* in actions is caused by people

---

[1] That is, *Sûrah Al-Ikhlâs* and *Sûrah Al-Kâfirûn*.

[2] *Sûrah Al-Ikhlâs*: 112:1

[3] *Sûrah Al-Kâfirûn* 109:1

following their own whims and fancies, and many of them follow them even though they know that they are harmful – and eradicating it is more difficult than eradicating *Shirk* in matters of knowledge, for that may be removed by evidence and appeal to reason and it is not possible for the person who holds such ideas to know something which is clearly not so – this is the reason for the emphasis and repetition in: Say: "Oh, you disbelievers" and this is why he ﷺ used to recite them in the two *Rak'ahs* of *Tawaf*,[1] because *Hajj* is one of the signs of *Tawheed* and the day's deeds are begun with them and the deeds of the night are closed with them.

He used to lie on his right side after offering the *Sunnah* of *Fajr*[2] and regarding this action two factions held extreme views: One of them from among the *Zahiris*[3] declared it to be obligatory to do so, while another group mentioned it, saying that it is an innovation. Imam Malik and others held the middle view, considering that there is no objection if a person does it in order to rest, while disliking that anyone should do it as a *Sunnah*.

---

[1] *Tawaf*: Circumambulation of the K'abah during the rites of *Hajj* and *'Umrah*.

[2] Narrated by Al-Bukhari and Muslim, on the authority of 'A'ishah ﷺ.

[3] *Zahiris*: A sect who interpreted the Qur'ân strictly according to its literal meaning.

Chapter

Regarding His ﷺ Guidance in *Qiyam Al-Lail* (The Night Prayer)

He never abandoned the night prayer – neither when he was at home, nor when he was traveling and if sleep or illness overcame him, he would offer twelve *Rak'ahs* during the day; and I heard Shaikh Al-Islam Ibn Taimiyyah saying: "In this there is evidence that *Witr* prayers cannot be made up, since the time for them has expired, like the prayer of salutation to the mosque, eclipse prayers and rain prayers, because what is intended by it is that the last prayer of the night be the *Witr* prayer. And his night prayer used to consist of eleven or thirteen *Rak'ahs* (there is unanimity regarding the eleven *Rak'ahs* but a difference of opinion exists regarding the final two *Rak'ahs* as to whether they are the two *Rak'ahs* of *Fajr* or something else).

If this is added to the number of obligatory *Rak'ahs* and the regular *Sunan* which he habitually used to pray, the total number of *Rak'ahs* which he regularly used to offer comes to forty *Rak'ahs*; these he used to offer habitually and anything additional to these is not a regular prayer.

Therefore it is desirable that the slave be consistent in offering these prescribed prayers, continually until he dies, for how swift is the response and how quickly is the door opened to one who knocks on it every day and night forty times? And Allâh is *Al-Musta'an*.[1]

When he woke up after a night's sleep, he ﷺ would say:

«لَا إِلَهَ إِلَّا أَنْتَ سُبْحَانَكَ اللَّهُمَّ أَسْتَغْفِرُكَ لِذَنْبِي، وَأَسْأَلُكَ رَحْمَتَكَ، اللَّهُمَّ زِدْنِي عِلْمًا، وَلَا تُزِغْ قَلْبِي بَعْدَ إِذْ هَدَيْتَنِي، وَهَبْ لِي مِنْ

---
[1] *Al-Musta'an*: The One Whose Aid is sought.

«لَّدُنْكَ رَحْمَةً إِنَّكَ أَنْتَ الْوَهَّابُ»

"La Ilaha Illa Anta Subhanaka, Allâhumma Astagfhiruka Lizanbee Wa As'Aluka Rahmataka, Allâhumma, Zidnee 'Ilman Wa La Tuzigh Qalbee Ba'da Idh Hadaitanee, Wa Hab Lee Min Ladunka Rahmatan Innaka Antal-Wahhab"

"None has the right to be worshipped except You, Glory be to You. Oh, Allâh! I seek forgiveness from You for my sins and I ask You for Your Mercy. Oh, Allâh! Increase me in knowledge and do not make my heart deviate from the truth after You have guided me and grant me Mercy from You; truly, You are the Bestower".

If he awoke from sleep he would say:

«الْحَمْدُ للهِ الَّذِي أَحْيَانَا بَعْدَ مَا أَمَاتَنَا وَإِلَيْهِ النُّشُورُ»

"Al-Hamdu Lillahil-Ladhee Ahyana Ba'da Ma Amatana Wa Ilaihin-Nushûr"

"All praise and thanks be to Allâh, Who has brought us to life after he had made us to die [i.e. sleep] and to Him will be the Resurrection."

Then he would clean his teeth with the *Miswak*[1] and he might recite ten Verses from the end of *Sûrah Âl-'Imrân*, from His Words:

﴿إِنَّ فِي خَلْقِ ٱلسَّمَٰوَٰتِ وَٱلْأَرْضِ﴾

"Verily, in the creation of the heavens and the earth".

Then he would perform ablution and pray two light *Rak'ahs* and he ordered his Companions ﷺ to do likewise in the *Hadeeth* of Abu Hurairah ﷺ. He would stand up in prayer when it was halfway through the night, or a little less or a little more. Sometimes he would break them up and sometimes, he would offer all of them together – and mostly he did the latter. When he broke them up, it was in the manner described by Ibn 'Abbas ﷺ: "After offering two *Rak'ahs*, he would stop and sleep. He did this three times during six *Rak'ahs*, each time cleaning his teeth with the *Miswak* and performing Ablution and

---

[1] *Miswak*: A natural toothbrush made from the root of the *Arak* tree.

then performing a *Witr* prayer consisting of three *Rak'ahs*. His *Witr* prayer took a number of forms: Sometimes he would pray in this way and sometimes he would offer eight *Rak'ahs*, making the *Tasleem* after each two *Rak'ahs*, then he would offer a *Witr* prayer of five *Rak'ahs* in succession, uninterruptedly; and he would not sit except in the final *Rak'ah*. On other occasions, he would offer nine *Rak'ahs*, praying eight of them in succession, and he would not sit except in the eighth *Rak'ah*, when he would sit and mention Allâh, praise Him and supplicate Him, then he would rise without making the *Tasleem* and offer the ninth *Rak'ah* and then he would sit and perform the *Tashahhud* and make the *Tasleem*. After making the *Tasleem*, he would then offer two *Rak'ahs*. And sometimes he would offer seven *Rak'ahs* in the manner of the aforementioned nine *Rak'ahs*, then he would offer two *Rak'ahs* after it in a sitting position. And sometimes he would offer them two at a time and then offer a *Witr* prayer of three *Rak'ahs*, without separating between them. This was narrated by Ahmad, on the authority of 'A'ishah ☀, who said that: "He used to offer a *Witr* prayer consisting of three *Rak'ahs*, without separating between them." But there is some doubt about this. In *'Saheeh Ibn Hibban'*, it is reported on the authority of Abu Hurairah ☀ in a *marfû'* form that he ☀ said: "Do not offer *Witr* as a three *Rak'ah* prayer, but as five or seven, and do not make it resemble the *Maghrib* prayer." Ad-Daraqutni said: "All of the men in its chain of narrators (*Isnad*) are trustworthy." Harb said: "Ahmad was asked about *Witr* and he said: "One should make the *Tasleem* after two *Rak'ahs*; and if one did not make the *Tasleem*, I hope it would not harm him, although the *Tasleem* is more strongly confirmed from the Prophet ☀." And in the narration of Abu Talib, he said: "Most of the *Ahadeeth* and the strongest of them confirm that he offered one *Rak'ah* and this is what I follow."

He also used to pray as narrated by An-Nasa'i on the authority of Huzaifah ☀, who said that he prayed with the Messenger of Allâh ☀ in Ramadan prayers and he bowed and said during his *Rukû'*:

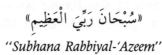

"*Subhana Rabbiyal-'Azeem*"

"Glorified be my Lord, the Most Great",

for the same length of time as his standing. It is also mentioned in the *Hadeeth* that he had only prayed four *Rak'ahs* when Bilal came and invited him to eat dinner. So he performed *Witr* at the beginning of the night, in the middle of it and in the latter part of it. And one night he stood in prayer and recited a Verse which he repeated over and over until the morning:

$$ ﴿ إِن تُعَذِّبْهُمْ فَإِنَّهُمْ عِبَادُكَ وَإِن تَغْفِرْ لَهُمْ فَإِنَّكَ أَنتَ ٱلْعَزِيزُ ٱلْحَكِيمُ ﴾ $$

"If You punish them, they are Your slaves, and if You forgive them, verily, You, only You are the All-Mighty, the All-Wise."[1]

And his prayers at night were of three types: (i) Standing (which was the most common), (ii) sitting and (iii) reciting in a sitting position and then when only a little remained of his recitation, standing and bowing in a standing position. And it has been confirmed from him that sometimes he used to offer two *Rak'ahs* after *Witr* whilst sitting and sometimes he would recite therein in a sitting position, then when he wished to bow, he would stand and bow.

This has confused many people, for they think that it contradicts the saying of the Prophet ﷺ: "Make the end of your prayers at night *Witr*." Ahmad said: "I do not do it, but I do not forbid anyone who does it." He said: "Malik disapproved of it, but the correct view is that *Witr* is a separate act of worship and so the two *Rak'ahs* after it hold the same place as the *Sunnah* of *Maghrib* and they are a completion of *Witr*.

It has not been reported from him ﷺ that he used to perform *Qunût* in *Witr* except in the *Hadeeth* narrated by Ibn Majah; Imam Ahmad said: "Nothing has been narrated from the Prophet ﷺ, but 'Umar ؓ used to perform *Qunût* from time to time.

And Ahmad and the compilers of the '*Sunan*' narrated the *Hadeeth* of Al-Hasan Ibn 'Ali ؓ, of which At-Tirmidhi said: "It is a *Hasan* (i.e. sound) *Hadeeth*; we know of no one who reports it except from this source, From the *Hadeeth* of Abu Hawra' As-Sa'di." (end of quote). *Qunût* in *Witr* has been reported from 'Umar, Ubayy and Ibn Mas'ûd

---

[1] *Sûrah Al-Mâ'idah* 5:118

&. Abu Dawûd and An-Nasa'i mentioned in the *Hadeeth* of Ubayy Ibn Ka'b & that the Messenger of Allâh 鬌 used to recite in *Witr*: "Glorify the Name of your Lord, the Most High"[1] and: "Say: 'Oh, you disbelievers'" [2] and: 'Say: "He is Allâh, One'"[3] and after he had made the *Tasleem*, he would say:

«سُبْحَانَ الْمَلِكِ الْقُدُّوسِ»

"Subhanal-Malikul-Quddûs"

"Glorified be the King, the Most Holy",

three times, prolonging his voice in the third repetition and raising it. He would recite the *Sûrah* in a slow and pleasant manner, so much so that it would be longer than normal. And what is intended by the Qur'ân is to reflect upon it, to try to comprehend it, to act upon it, to recite it and to memorize it in order to attain its meanings, as one of the *Salaf*[4] said: "The Qur'ân was revealed in order that it be acted upon, so act upon its recitation." Shu'bah said: "Abu Jamrah told us: "I said to the son of Al-'Abbas &: "I am a person who recites very quickly and I might recite the Qur'ân once or twice in a night." Ibn 'Abbas & said: "Reciting one *Sûrah* is more pleasing to me than what you do; so if you must recite, do so in a manner by which your ears may hear the recitation and your heart may retain it." Ibraheem said: "'Alqamah recited to 'Abdullah and he said: "Recite slowly and pleasantly, may my father and mother be sacrificed for you, for it is the beauty of the Qur'ân.''

And 'Abdullah (Ibn Mas'ûd & said: "Do not babble like the babbling of poetry when reciting the Qur'ân and do not let the words tumble out the way dry dates fall from the bunch when it is shaken; and stop at its miracles and move the hearts thereby and do not let the object of anyone of you be the end of the *Sûrah*." And he said: "If you heard Allâh's Words " Oh, you who believe!", then listen to it, for it is some

---

[1] *Sûrah Al-A'la* 87:1

[2] *Sûrah Al-Kafirûn* 109:1

[3] *Sûrah Al-Ikhlâs* 112:1

[4] *Salaf*: The righteous early generations of Muslims, in particular, the Companions &.

act of goodness which you are being commanded to do or some evil deed from which you are being turned away." 'Abdur-Rahman Ibn Abi Laila said: "A woman came to me while I was reciting *Sûrah Hûd* and she said to me: "Oh, 'Abdur-Rahman! Is this the way you recite *Sûrah Hûd*? By Allâh, I have been reciting it for six months and I have not yet completed the recitation of it."

Sometimes, the Messenger of Allâh ﷺ would recite the Qur'ân silently during the night prayers and sometimes, he would recite it aloud; and sometimes, he would prolong his standing and sometimes, he would make it short. He would offer voluntary prayer during the night and during the day on his riding beast when traveling, whichever way he was facing and he would bow and prostrate on it by inclining his head, making his prostration lower than his bowing.

Chapter

Al-Bukhari narrated in his *'Saheeh'* on the authority of 'A'ishah 🌸 that she said: "I did not see the Messenger of Allâh 🌸 offering any supererogatory prayers in the forenoon, but I offered them."[1] And in the *'Saheehayn'*,[2] it is reported on the authority of Abu Hurairah 🌸 that he said: "My friend (i.e. the Prophet 🌸 advised me to fast three days in every month, to pray two *Rak'ahs* in the forenoon and to offer *Witr* before lying down to sleep." And Muslim narrated on the authority of Zaid Ibn Arqam 🌸 in a *Marfû'* form: "The prayer of those who are penitent is observed when the hooves of the young camels are burnt by the intense heat of the sand." That is, the heat of the day becomes so fierce, that the young camels find the ground hot beneath their hooves. So he advised it, but he used to offer the night prayer instead of it. Masrûq said: "We used to pray in the mosque and we would remain until after Ibn Mas'ûd 🌸 stood up, then we would stand up and offer the forenoon prayer and he was informed of it and he said: "Why do you burden the slaves of Allâh with something with which Allâh did not burden them? If you must do it, then do it in your houses." And Sa'eed Ibn Jubair 🌸 said: "I have left the forenoon prayer, although I desire to pray it, out of fear that I might consider it an obligation upon me."

Part of the Prophet's guidance 🌸 and that of his Companions 🌸 was *Sujûd Ash-Shukr*[3] upon the coming of Allâh's blessings which pleased them or when some calamity was lifted. And when he recited a Verse of prostration, he would say: *"Allâhu Akbar"* (Allâh is Most Great) and prostrate; and sometimes, he might say in his

---

[1] Narrated by Al-Bukhari, Abu Dawûd and Ahmad.

[2] *Saheehayn*: The collections of *Hadeeth* compiled by Imams Al-Bukhari and Muslim, acknowledged by all Muslims to be the most authentic books of *Hadeeth* in existence.

[3] *Sujûd Ash-Shukr*: The prostration of thankfulness.

prostration:

«سَجَدَ وَجْهِيَ لِلَّذِي خَلَقَهُ وَصَوَّرَهُ، وَشَقَّ سَمْعَهُ وَبَصَرَهُ بِحَوْلِهِ
وَقُوَّتِهِ»

"Sajada Wajhee Lilladhi Khalaqahu Wa Sawwarahu Wa Shaqqa Sam'ahu Wa Basarahu Bihawlihi Wa Quwwatih"

"My face has prostrated for the One Who created it and shaped it, then brought forth its hearing and vision by His Power and His Strength."[1]

And it has not been transmitted from him that he used to say: *"Allâhu Akbar"* when he rose up from this prostration, nor that he used to perform the *Tashahhud* or make *Tasleem* – ever. And it has been authentically reported from him that he prostrated in: *"Alif-Lam-Meem,"* the Revelation[2] and in: *"Sad"*[3] and in: "Read!"[4] and in: *"An-Najm."*[5] and in: "When the heaven is split asunder"[6] Abu Dawûd reported on the authority of 'Amr Ibn Al-'As ﷺ that the Messenger of Allâh ﷺ taught him fifteen prostrations, including three in *Al-Mufassal* and two in *Sûrah Al-Hajj*. As for the *Hadeeth* of Ibn 'Abbas ﷺ, in which it is stated that the Messenger of Allâh ﷺ did not prostrate in *Al-Mufassal* after he migrated to Al-Madinah, it is a weak *Hadeeth*, containing in its chain of narrators one Abu Qudamah Al-Harith Ibn 'Ubaid, and his *Ahadeeth* may not be cited as evidence. It was declared to be *Mu'allal*[7] by Ibn Al-Qattan due to Matar Al-Warraq, of whom he said: "His faulty memory resembled that of Muhammad Ibn 'Abdur-Rahman Ibn Abi Laila. Muslim was criticized for narrating his *Ahadeeth*, because he selects from his *Ahadeeth*." But there is no sin upon Muslim in narrating his *Ahadeeth*, because he

---

[1] Narrated by Ahmad, Abu Dawûd, At-Tirmidhi and An-Nasa'i and authenticated by Al-Hakim and Az-Zahabi.

[2] *Sûrah As-Sajdah*: 32:1-2

[3] *Sûrah Sâd*: 38:1

[4] *Sûrah Al-'Alaq* 96:1

[5] *Sûrah An-Najm* 53:62

[6] *Sûrah Al-Inshiqâq*: 84:1

[7] *Mu'allal*: Defective, weak.

selected from the *Ahadeeth* of this type which he was known to have memorized correctly, just as he would abandon *Ahadeeth* narrated by a reliable person who was known to have made mistakes in them. Some of the people declare all of the *Ahadeeth* of such reliable people to be authentic, while others declare all of the *Ahadeeth* of a person with poor memory. The former is the way of Al-Hakim and his like, while the latter is the way of Ibn Hazm and his like. And the way of Muslim is the way of the *Imams* of this Religion.

Chapter

Regarding His ﷺ Guidance in Friday Prayers and a Reference to its Special Characteristics

It has been authentically reported from the Prophet ﷺ that he said:

«أَضَلَّ اللهُ عَنِ الْجُمُعَةِ مَنْ كَانَ قَبْلَنَا وَكَانَ لِلْيَهُودِ يَوْمُ السَّبْتِ، وَكَانَ لِلنَّصَارَى يَوْمُ الأَحَدِ، فَجَاءَ اللهُ بِنَا فَهَدَانَا لِيَوْمِ الْجُمُعَةِ، فَجَعَلَ الْجُمُعَةَ وَالسَّبْتَ وَالأَحَدَ، وَكَذَلِكَ هُمْ تَبَعٌ لَنَا يَوْمَ الْقِيَامَةِ، نَحْنُ الآخِرُونَ مِنْ أَهْلِ الدُّنْيَا وَالأَوَّلُونَ يَوْمَ الْقِيَامَةِ، الْمَقْضِيُّ لَهُمْ قَبْلَ الْخَلاَئِقِ»

"Allâh diverted those who were before us from Friday; for the Jews (the day set aside for prayer) was Saturday, and for the Christians it was Sunday. And Allâh turned towards us and guided us to Friday (as the day of prayer) for us. In fact, He (Allâh) made Friday, Saturday and Sunday (as days of prayer). In this order would they (Jews and Christians) come after us on the Day of Resurrection. We are the last among the people in this world and we will be the first among the created beings to be judged on the Day of Resurrection."[1]

At-Tirmidhi narrates on the authority of Abu Hurairah ﷺ in a *Marfû'* *Hadeeth* which he declared to be authentic:

«خَيْرُ يَوْمٍ طَلَعَتْ فِيهِ الشَّمْسُ يَوْمُ الْجُمُعَةِ، فِيهِ خُلِقَ آدَمُ، وَفِيهِ أُدْخِلَ الْجَنَّةَ، وَفِيهِ أُخْرِجَ مِنْهَا، وَلاَ تَقُومُ السَّاعَةُ إِلَّا فِي يَوْمِ الْجُمُعَةِ»

---

[1] Narrated by Muslim, An-Nasa'i and Ibn Majah.

"The best day on which the sun has risen is Friday: On it, Adam was created, on it, he was admitted to Paradise and on it, he was sent out of Paradise and the Hour will not be established except on Friday."

And it was narrated (by Malik) in *'Al-Muwatta"* and also authenticated by At-Tirmidhi in the words:

«خَيْرُ يَوْم طَلَعَتْ فِيهِ الشَّمْسُ، فِيهِ خُلِقَ آدَمُ، وَفِيهِ أُهْبِطَ، وَفِيهِ تِيبَ عَلَيْهِ، وَفِيهِ مَاتَ، وَفِيهِ تَقُومُ السَّاعَةُ، وَمَا مِنْ دَابَّةٍ إِلَّا وَهِيَ مُصِيخَةٌ يَوْمَ الْجُمُعَةِ مِنْ حِينَ تُصْبِحُ حَتَّى تَطْلُعُ الشَّمْسُ شَفَقًا مِنَ السَّاعَةِ، إِلَّا الْجِنُّ وَالإِنْسُ، وَمَا فِيهَا سَاعَةٌ لَا يُصَادِفُهَا عَبْدٌ مُسْلِمٌ، وَهُوَ يُصَلِّي يَسْأَلُ اللهَ شَيْئًا إِلَّا أَعْطَاهُ اللهُ إِيَّاهُ»

"The best day on which the sun has risen is Friday; on it, Adam was created and on it he was sent down (to earth), on it, his repentance was accepted (by Allâh), on it, he died and on it, the Hour will be established. And every moving creature is listening on Friday, from the time awakes in the morning, until the sun rises, due to fear of the Hour, except the jinn and mankind, and on this day, there is a time when, if a Muslim slave prays to Allâh and asks Him, He will give him what he asked for."

Ka'b said: "That is one day in every year." (Abu Hurairah ﷺ said:) but I said: "On, the contrary, it is every Friday." So he read the Torah and said: "The Messenger of Allâh ﷺ has spoken the truth." Abu Hurairah ﷺ said: "Then I met 'Abdullah Ibn Salam ﷺ and I informed him of my meeting with Ka'b and he said: "I have learned which hour it is." I said: "Then inform me of it." He said: "It is the last hour on Friday (i.e. between the *'Asr* prayer and the *Maghrib* prayer). I said: "How, when Allâh's Messenger (ﷺ) has said:

«لَا يُصَادِفُهَا عَبْدٌ مُسْلِمٌ وَهُوَ يُصَلِّي»

"There is a time when, if a Muslim slave prays to Allâh" and at that time, there is no prayer?"

Ibn Salam ﷺ said: "Did not the Messenger of Allâh ﷺ say:

«مَنْ جَلَسَ مَجْلِسًا يَنْتَظِرُ الصَّلَاةَ فَهُوَ فِي صَلَاةٍ حَتَّى يُصَلِّيَ»

"Whoever sat waiting for the prayer, he is in prayer until he offers the prayer"?"

In another version in Ahmad's *'Musnad'* in the *Hadeeth* of Abu Hurairah ﷺ, he said: "It was said to the Prophet ﷺ: "For what reason was the day called *Al-Jumu'ah*?" He said:

«لِأَنَّ فِيهَا طُبِعَتْ طِينَةُ أَبِيكَ آدَمَ، وَفِيهَا الصَّعْقَةُ وَالْبَعْثَةُ، وَفِيهَا الْبَطْشَةُ، وَفِي آخِرِهِ ثَلَاثُ سَاعَاتٍ، مِنْهَا سَاعَةٌ مَنْ دَعَا اللهَ فِيهَا اسْتُجِيبَ لَهُ»

"Because on that day, the clay was shaped from which your father, Adam was made and on that day will be *As-Sa'iqah*[1] and the Resurrection and on it will be *Al-Batshah*[2] and in the last three hours, there is an hour when whoever supplicates Allâh will be answered."

Ibn Ishaq reported on the authority of 'Abdur-Rahman Ibn Ka'b Ibn Malik that he said: "I used to lead my father when he had lost his sight and when I went out with him to the Friday prayer and he heard the *Adhan*, he would seek forgiveness for Abu Umamah As'ad Ibn Zurarah and one time, I heard this from him and I said: "I wonder if I should not ask him..." So I said: "Oh, my father! Do you consider that you should seek forgiveness for As'ad Ibn Zurarah every time you hear the *Adhan* for the Friday prayer?" He said: "Oh, my son! As'ad was the first person to gather us together in Al-Madinah (for the Friday prayers) before the arrival of the Messenger of Allâh ﷺ in Hazm An-Nabeet in the area of the tribe of Banu Bayadhah and in a *Naqee'*[3] called Naqee' Al-Khadhamat." I asked: "And how many

---

[1] *Sa'iqah*: The trump which will take place on the Day of Resurrection, which will cause all those who hear it to fall down prostrate.

[2] *Al-Batshah*: The Great Seizure, when Allâh will seize the disbelievers in His Grasp.

[3] *Naqee'*: Land which was swamp land, then when the water seeps away, grass grows.

were you in number?" He said: "Forty men."[1] Al-Baihaqi said: "Its chain of narrators is *Hasan Saheeh*."

Then the Messenger of Allâh ﷺ arrived in Al-Madinah and he stayed in Quba' on Monday, Tuesday, Wednesday and Thursday and he built their mosque, then he left on Friday and time for Friday prayer overtook him in the land of Banu Salim Ibn 'Awf and so he prayed it in the mosque which was in the middle of the valley before the building of his mosque.

Ibn Ishaq said: "It was the first sermon which he delivered; according to Abu Salamah Ibn 'Abdur-Rahman – and we seek refuge with Allâh from attributing to him anything which he did not say – he stood up among them and praised Allâh and extolled Him, then he said:

«أَمَّا بَعْدُ أَيُّهَا النَّاسُ، فَقَدِّمُوا لأَنْفُسِكُمْ، تَعْلَمُنَّ وَاللهِ لَيُصْعَقَنَّ أَحَدُكُمْ، ثُمَّ لَيَدَعَنَّ غَنَمَهُ، لَيْسَ لَهَا رَاعٍ، ثُمَّ لَيَقُولَنَّ لَهُ رَبُّهُ لَيْسَ بَيْنَهُ وَبَيْنَهُ تَرْجُمَانٌ، وَلَا حَاجِبٌ يَحْجُبُهُ دُونَهُ، أَلَمْ يَأْتِكَ رَسُولِي فَبَلَغَكَ، وَآتَيْتُك مَالًا، وَأَفْضَلْتُ عَلَيْكَ؟ فَمَا قَدَّمْتَ لِنَفْسِكَ؟ فَلْيَنْظُرَنَّ يَمِينًا وَشِمَالًا، فَلَا يَرَى شَيْئًا، ثُمَّ لَيَنْظُرَنَّ قُدَّامَهُ فَلَا يَرَى غَيْرَ جَهَنَّمَ، فَمَنِ اسْتَطَاعَ أَنْ يَقِيَ وَجْهَهُ مِنَ النَّارِ وَلَوْ بِشِقِّ تَمْرَةٍ فَلْيَفْعَلْ، وَمَنْ لَمْ يَجِدْ فَبِكَلِمَةٍ طَيِّبَةٍ، فَإِنَّ بِهَا تُجْزَى الْحَسَنَةُ بِعَشْرِ أَمْثَالِهَا إِلَى سَبْعِمائَةِ ضِعْفٍ، السَّلَامُ عَلَيْكُمْ وَرَحْمَةُ اللهِ وَبَرَكَاتُهُ»

"As for what follows, oh, you people! Send forth for yourselves (good deeds); you know for sure, by Allâh, that a person among you will be struck down unconscious and he will leave his sheep without a shepherd, then his Lord will surely say to him – and there will be neither intermediary nor screen between them: "Did not My Messenger come to you and communicate (the Message), and did I not give you wealth and favour you? And what did you send forth for yourself?" And verily, he will look right and left, but he will see nothing; then he will look in

---

[1] This *Hadeeth* was also narrated by Abu Dawûd with similar wording and by Ibn Majah, Al-Hakim and Al-Baihaqi.

front of him and he will see naught but the Hell-fire. So whoever is able to shield his face from the Fire, even if it be only by giving a piece of a date in charity, let him do so; and whoever was unable to do so, let him (shield it) by saying a good word, for the reward of a good deed is multiplied by ten times seven hundred times. And may the Peace, Mercy and Blessings of Allâh be upon you."[1]

Ibn Ishaq said: "Then the Messenger of Allâh ﷺ delivered a second sermon, saying:

«إِنَّ الْحَمْدَ لله أَحْمَدُهُ وَأَسْتَعِينُهُ، نَعُوذُ بِالله مِنْ شُرُورِ أَنْفُسِنَا، وَمِنْ سَيِّئَاتِ أَعْمَالِنَا، مَنْ يَهْدِهِ اللهُ، فَلَا مُضِلَّ لَهُ، وَمَنْ يُضْلِلِ، فَلَا هَادِيَ لَهُ، وَأَشْهَدُ أَنْ لَا إِلَهَ إِلَّا اللهُ وَحْدَهُ لَا شَرِيكَ لَهُ. إِنَّ أَحْسَنَ الْحَدِيثِ كِتَابُ الله. قَدْ أَفْلَحَ مَنْ زَيَّنَهُ اللهُ فِي قَلْبِهِ، وَأَدْخَلَهُ فِي الإِسْلَام بَعْدَ الْكُفْرِ، فَاخْتَارَهُ عَلَى سِوَاهُ مِنْ أَحَادِيثِ النَّاسِ، إِنَّهُ أَحْسَنُ الْحَدِيثِ وَأَبْلَغُهُ أَحِبُّوا مَا أَحَبَّ اللهُ، أَحِبُّوا اللهَ مِنْ كُلِّ قُلُوبِكُمْ، وَلَا تَمَلُّوا كَلَامَ الله وَذِكْرَهُ، وَلَا تَقْسُ عَنْهُ قُلُوبُكُمْ، فَإِنَّهُ مِنْ كُلِّ مَا يَخْلُقُ اللهُ يَخْتَارُ وَيَصْطَفِي، قَدْ سِمَّاهُ اللهُ خِيرَتَهُ مِنَ الأَعْمَالِ، وَمُصْطَفَاهُ مِنَ الْعِبَادِ، وَالصَّالِحَ مِنَ الْحَدِيثِ، وَمِنْ كُلِّ مَا أُوتِيَ النَّاسُ مِنَ الْحَلَالِ وَالْحَرَامِ، فَاعْبُدُوا اللهَ وَلَا تُشْرِكُوا بِهِ شَيْئًا، وَاتَّقُوهُ حَقَّ تُقَاتِهِ، وَاصْدُقُوا اللهَ صَالِحَ مَا تَقُولُونَ بِأَفْوَاهِكُمْ، وَتَحَابُّوا بِرُوح الله بَيْنَكُمْ، إِنَّ اللهَ يُبْغِضُ أَنْ يُنْكَثَ عَهْدُهُ، وَالسَّلَامُ عَلَيْكُمْ وَرَحْمَةُ الله وَبَرَكَاتُهُ»

---

[1] Mentioned by Ibn Hisham in *'As-Seerah An-Nabawiyyah'*. But according to Shu'aib Al-Arna'ût and 'Abdul Qadir Al-Arna'ût, there is some problem in its chain of narrators, because Ibn Ishaq saw Abu Salamah Ibn 'Abdir-Rahman, but he did not report from him, and the latter narrated from some of the Companions ﷺ, but he did not meet the Messenger of Allâh ﷺ. (See *'Zad Al-Ma'ad'* vol. 1, page 374 published by Maktabah Al-Manar Al-Islamiyyah).

"All praise and thanks be to Allâh, I praise Him and I seek His Aid. We seek refuge with Allâh from the evil of ourselves and from the wickedness of our deeds. Whomsoever Allâh guides, there is none can misguide him and whomsoever Allâh sends astray, there is none can guide him. And I testify that none has the right to be worshipped except Allâh, Alone, without partners. The best of speech is the Book of Allâh. He whose heart has been beautified with it by Allâh and whom He has admitted to the fold of Islam after he had disbelieved will be successful, for he has chosen it (Allâh's Speech) over that of all of mankind. Truly, it is the best of speech and the most eloquent. Love what Allâh loves; love Allâh with all of your hearts. Do not become tired of Allâh's Speech, nor of mentioning His Name and do not make your hearts hard towards it, Hence, amongst everything that Allâh creates He chooses [something]; Allâh would call it: His *Kheerah* (best) in terms of deeds; His favorite ones amongst the servants; that which is good and useful in terms of speech; So worship Allâh and do not associate anything with Him and fear Him as He should be feared and be sincere to Allâh in the righteous words which pass your lips and love one another with Allâh's Spirit between you. Verily, Allâh hates that His Covenant should be broken. And may the Peace, Mercy and Blessings of Allâh be upon you."[1]

---

[1] Mentioned by Ibn Hisham in *'As-Seerah An-Nabawiyyah'* from Ibn Ishaq, but without any chain of narrators.

It was a part of the guidance of the Prophet ﷺ to glorify this day and to honour it and to mark it in certain ways, including: That he would recite in the *Fajr* prayer on that day *Sûrah As-Sajdah* and *Sûrah Ad-Dahr*[1] for in them is mention of what has been and what is to come on that day.

Also among them is the recommendation to send many prayers upon the Prophet ﷺ during the day and during the night, because every good thing which his community have received in the life of this world and in the Hereafter came to them through his hands and the greatest favour bestowed on them was the day of *Al-Jumu'ah*: For on that day, they will be sent to their abodes in Paradise and it will be a Day of Abundance when they enter it and they will be near to their Lord on the Day of Abundance; and how much of this abundance they will receive is in accordance with their closeness to the *Imam* on Friday and how early they come to the prayer.

And among them is bathing on the day of *Al-Jumu'ah*, which is something strongly confirmed and whose obligation is greater than that of ablution due to touching the penis, nosebleed, vomiting and the obligation to send prayers on the Prophet ﷺ in the final *Tashahhud*.

And among them is the wearing of perfume and brushing the teeth with the *Miswak*; and there is a superiority in using them on this day as compared to other days.

Also among them is the *Takbeer* (saying *"Allâhu Akbar"*), occupying oneself with remembrance of Allâh, Most High and prayer until the *Imam* comes out.

And among them is listening to the sermon, which is an obligation and the recitation of *Sûrah Al-Jumu'ah* and *Sûrah Al-Munâfiqûn*, or

---
[1] Narrated by Muslim, At-Tirmidhi, Abu Dawûd and An-Nasa'i.

Sûrah Al-'Ala and *Sûrah Al-Ghashiyah.*

And among them is the wearing of one's best garments and the fact that every step which the walker takes towards it is a *Sunnah* and the reward of it is that of one who fasted on it and stood in prayer on the night of it. Also, it wipes out sins and on Friday there is an hour when one's supplications are answered.

When the Prophet ﷺ delivered the sermon, his eyes would become red and he would raise his voice and his anger would be intense, so much so that it was as if he was warning an army and he would say: "*Sabbahakum Wa Massakum*".[1] And he used to say in his sermon: "*Amma Ba'd*" (To proceed).[2] He would make the sermon short and he would make the prayer long and during the sermon, he would teach his Companions ﷺ the rules of Islam and its laws and he would command them and prohibit them, as he commanded the man who entered while he was delivering the sermon to pray two *Rak'ahs*.[3] And if he observed that one of them was in great need, he would order them to give charity and encourage them to do so.[4] And he would point with his forefinger whenever he mentioned Allâh and when he supplicated Him.[5]

And he would ask for rain during his sermon when there was a lack of rain.[6] He would come out once they were gathered and when he entered the mosque, he would greet them with salutations of peace. And when he ascended the pulpit, he would face them and greet them with salutations of peace, then he would sit and Bilal ﷺ would call the *Adhan*. When it was over, he would stand and deliver the sermon, leaning on a bow or a stick.[7] His pulpit had three steps and before he took it, he used to deliver the sermon towards a tree trunk.

---

[1] *Sabbahakum Wa Massakum*: A warning, similar to the Arabic expression: "*Ya Sabaha*".

[2] Narrated by Al-Bukhari.

[3] Narrated by Al-Bukhari, Muslim, Abu Dawûd, An-Nasâ'i and Ibn Majah.

[4] Narrated by Muslim on the authority of Jareer Ibn 'Abdillah Al-Bajli ﷺ.

[5] Narrated by Muslim, Abu Dawûd and An-Nasa'i.

[6] Narrated by Al-Bukhari and Muslim.

[7] Narrated by Abu Dawûd, on the authority of Al-Hakam Ibn Hazn Al-Kulafi ﷺ.

The pulpit was not placed in the middle of the mosque, but in the western corner of it, leaving between him and the wall a distance sufficient for a sheep to pass.[1] When he sat on it on any day other than Friday, or he delivered the sermon whilst standing on Friday, his Companions ﷺ would turn their faces towards him. And he would stand and deliver the sermon, then he would sit for a few moments, then he would stand and deliver the second sermon and once he had completed it, Bilal ﷺ would call the *Iqamah*. He ordered them to draw near and be silent and he informed us that if a man says to his companion: "Be silent," he has committed *Laghw*[2] and whoever does so has rendered his Friday prayer invalid.[3]

When he had offered the Friday prayer, he would enter his house and perform two *Rak'ahs* as the *Sunnah* of it and he ordered one who had prayed it to perform four *Rak'ahs* after it. Our *Shaikh* (i.e. Ibn Taimiyyah) said: "If he prayed it in the mosque, he would perform four *Rak'ahs* and if he prayed it in his house, he would perform two *Rak'ahs*.[4]

---
[1] Narrated by Al-Bukhari and Abu Dawûd.

[2] *Laghw*: Foolish talk, nonsense.

[3] Narrated by Ahmad with a weak *Isnad* due to the fact that the freed slave of the wife of 'Ata' Al-Khurasani is unknown, but it is supported by a similar narration of Ibn Khuzaimah in his '*Saheeh*', on the authority of 'Abdullah Ibn 'Amr ﷺ.

[4] Narrated by Abu Dawûd with a strong chain of narrators.

Chapter

He ﷺ would perform the two *'Eed* prayers in the *Musalla*,[1] which is near the eastern gate of Al-Madinah, where the luggage place for the *Hajj* pilgrims is. He did not perform the *'Eed* prayers in his Mosque, except on one occasion, when they were rained upon – assuming the *Hadeeth*, which is in Abu Dawûd's *'Sunan'* is authentic.[2] He would put on his best clothes and on *'Eed Al-Fitr*, he would consume some dates before leaving, eating an odd number (*Witr*). As for *'Eed Al-Adha*, he would not eat until he returned from the *Musalla*, when he would eat from his sacrifice. He used to bathe for the *'Eed* prayers – if the narrations to that effect are authentic – and there are two weak *Hadeeth*, but it is confirmed from Ibn 'Umar ﷺ that he used to do so – and he was very strict about following the *Sunnah*.

He would go out walking, carrying an *'Anazah*[3] in his hands and when he reached his destination, he would plant it in the ground in order to pray towards it (as a *Sutrah*), for there were no buildings in the *Musalla*.[4] He used to delay the prayer on *'Eed Al-Fitr* and he would hasten it on *'Eed Al-Adha* and Ibn 'Umar ﷺ – who was very scrupulous about adhering to the *Sunnah* – would not go out until the sun had fully risen, and he would make *Takbeer* from the time he left the house until he reached the *Musalla*.

Once he ﷺ had reached the *musalla*, he would begin the prayer without an *Adhan* or an *Iqamah* being called[5] and without saying:

---

[1] *Musalla*: A place of prayer other than a mosque, in this case a large area of ground out in the open, where *'Eed* prayers are held.

[2] Narrated by Abu Dawûd and Ibn Majah; in its chain of narrators, there is one 'Eesa Ibn 'Abdil A'la Ibn Abi Farwah, who is unknown, as is his *Shaikh*, Yahya 'Ubaidullah At-Taimi.

[3] *'Anazah*: A short stick.

[4] Narrated by Al-Bukhari and Ibn Majah.

[5] Narrated by Al-Bukhari, Muslim, Abu Dawûd and At-Tirmidhi.

"As-Salatu Jami'ah" (The prayer is convened) and neither he nor his Companions 🕸 used to offer any prayers before or after it upon reaching the *Musalla*.[1]

He used to begin by praying before the sermon, praying two *Rak'ahs* and saying *"Allâhu Akbar"* seven times consecutively in the first *Rak'ah*, beginning with the opening *Takbeer*; and he would observe a short silence between each two *Rak'ahs*, but no special *Dhikr* has been reported from him between each *Takbeer*, although it has been reported on the authority of Ibn Mas'ûd 🕸 that he used to praise Allâh and extol Him and send prayers on the Prophet 🕸; and Ibn 'Umar 🕸 used to raise his hands with each *Takbeer*.

Once he had completed the *Takbeer*, he would begin his recitation, reciting in the first *Rak'ah*: *Sûrah Al-Fâtihah* and *Sûrah Qâf*; and in the second, he would recite (after *Al-Fâtihah*): *Sûrah Al-Qamar*,[2] or sometimes, he might recite *Sûrah Al-A'lâ* in the first and *Sûrah Al-Ghashiyah* in the second;[3] and nothing other than this has been authentically reported from him. When he had completed his recitation, he would say: *"Allâhu Akbar"* and then bow. In the second *Rak'ah*, he would pronounce the *Takbeer* five times consecutively, then he would begin his recitation. Once he had completed the prayer, he would stand in front of the people while they were sitting in their rows and he would warn them and prohibit them (from sin) and if he wished to send off a military expedition or command something, he would do so; and there was no pulpit, for he used to deliver the sermon standing on the ground. As for the saying in the *Hadeeth* which is found in the 'Saheehayn': "then he descended and went to the women etc" it might be that he was standing on a raised piece of ground, but as for the pulpit in Al-Madinah, the first person to bring it out was Marwan Ibn Al-Hakam, for which he was rebuked. As for the pulpit of brick and clay, the first person to build it was Katheer Ibn As-Salt 🕸, during the rule of Marwan in Al-Madinah.

The Prophet 🕸 permitted those who had attended the *'Eed* prayer to

[1] Narrated by Al-Bukhari, An-Nasâ'i and Ibn Majah.
[2] Narrated by Muslim, At-Tirmidhi, An-Nasa'i and Ibn Majah.
[3] Narrated by Muslim, At-Tirmidhi, An-Nasâ'i and Ibn Majah.

sit down and listen to the sermon or to leave. And he permitted them, if the *'Eed* day fell on Friday, to content themselves with the *'Eed* prayer, without offering the Friday prayer.[1] And he used to take a different path when coming back from the *'Eed* prayer.[2] And it has been narrated that he used to make *Takbeer* from the *Fajr* prayer on the Day of 'Arafah (during *Hajj*) until *'Asr* time on the last day of *Tashreeq*,[3] saying:

«اللهُ أَكْبَرُ، اللهُ أَكْبَرُ، اللهُ أَكْبَرُ، لَا إِلَهَ إِلَّا اللهُ، واللهُ أَكْبَرُ، اللهُ أَكْبَرُ، وللهُ أَكْبَرُ»

"Allâhu Akbar, Allâhu Akbar, Allâhu Akbar, La Ilaha Illallah, Wallahu Akbar, Allâhu Akbar, Wa Lillahil-Hamd"

"Allâh is Most Great, Allâh is Most Great, Allâh is Most Great. None has the right to be worshipped except Allâh and Allâh is Most Great, Allâh is Most Great and to Allâh all praise and thanks are due."[4]

---

[1] Narrated by Abu Dawûd and Ibn Majah with a *Hasan* chain of narrators.

[2] Narrated by Al-Bukhari, At-Tirmidhi, Ibn Majah and Abu Dawûd.

[3] *Tashreeq*: The name given to the three days following the Day of Sacrifice (11th, 12th and 13th of Dhul-Hijjah).

[4] Narrated by Ibn Abi Shaibah with an authentic chain of narrators.

Chapter

When the sun was eclipsed, he hurried fearfully to the mosque, trailing his *Rida'*[1] behind him; the eclipse occurred at the beginning of the day, when the shadow cast by the rising sun was equivalent to the length of two or three spears and he went forth and prayed two *Rak'ahs*, reciting aloud in the first: *Sûrah Al-Fâtihah* and a long *Sûrah*, then he bowed (*Rukû'*) and he prolonged it, then he straightened up and he prolonged his standing, but it was less than the first standing (i.e. that of the recital); and when he raised his head from the *Rukû'*, he said:

«سَمِعَ اللهُ لِمَنْ حَمِدَهُ، رَبَّنَا وَلَكَ الْحَمْدُ»

"Sami'allahu Liman Hamidah, Rabbana Wa Lakal-Hamd"

"Allâh hears the one who praises Him; O, our Lord! All praise and thanks are due to You."

Then he began to recite, then he bowed and prolonged the bowing, but it was less than the first *Rukû'*; then he prostrated and prolonged the prostration, then he did in the second as he had done in the first. So he completed in the two *Rak'ahs* four bowings and four prostrations.

And in that prayer of his he saw Paradise and the Fire; he tried to pluck a bunch of grapes from it and show them to his Companions 🙵 and he saw those who were being punished in the Fire: He saw a woman who was being lacerated by a cat which she had tied up until it died of hunger and thirst and he saw 'Amr Ibn Malik dragging his intestines in the Fire – and he was the first person to change the Religion of Abraham (Ibraheem 🙵) and he saw therein a person who stole from a *Hajj* pilgrim being punished. Then he finished the prayer and delivered a most eloquent sermon. And Imam Ahmad narrated

---

[1] *Rida'*: A loose garment wrapped around the upper body

that after he had made the *Tasleem*, he would praise Allâh and extol Him and testify that none is worthy of worship except Allâh and that he is His slave and His Messenger. Then said:

«أَيُّهَا النَّاسُ أُنْشِدُكُمْ بِاللهِ إِنْ كُنْتُمْ تَعْلَمُونَ أَنِّي قَصَّرْتُ عَنْ شَيْءٍ مِنْ تَبْلِيغِ رِسَالَاتِ رَبِّي لَمَا أَخْبَرْتُمُونِي ذَلِكَ»

"Oh, you people! I implore you by Allâh, if you know that I have been deficient in conveying anything of the Messages of my Lord, will you please inform me of that, for I have conveyed the Messages of my Lord as they should be conveyed. And if you know that I have conveyed the Messages of my Lord, please inform me of that?"

Then some men stood up and said: "We testify that you have conveyed the Messages of your Lord, advised your people and fulfilled what was incumbent upon you." Then he said:

«أَمَّا بَعْدُ، فَإِنَّ رِجَالًا يَزْعُمُونَ أَنَّ كُسُوفَ الشَّمْسِ، وَخُسُوفَ هَذَا الْقَمَرِ، وَزَوَالَ هَذِهِ النُّجُومِ عَنْ مَطَالِعِهَا لِمَوْتِ رِجَالٍ عُظَمَاءَ مِنْ أَهْلِ الأَرْضِ، وَإِنَّهُمْ قَدْ كَذَبُوا، وَلَكِنَّهَا آيَاتٌ مِنْ آيَاتِ اللهِ تَبَارَكَ وَتَعَالَى، يَعْتَبِرُ بِهَا عِبَادُهُ، فَيَنْظُرُ مَنْ يَحْدُثُ لَهُ مِنْهُمْ تَوْبَةٌ، وَايْمُ اللهِ لَقَدْ رَأَيْتُ مُنْذُ قُمْتُ مَا أَنْتُمْ لَاقُوهُ مِنْ أَمْرِ دُنْيَاكُمْ وَآخِرَتِكُمْ، وَإِنَّهُ وَاللهِ لَا تَقُومُ السَّاعَةُ حَتَّى يَخْرُجَ ثَلَاثُونَ كَذَّابًا، آخِرُهُمُ الأَعْوَرُ الدَّجَّالُ، مَمْسُوحُ الْعَيْنِ الْيُسْرَى، كَأَنَّهَا عَيْنُ أَبِي تِحْيَىٰ - لِشَيْخٍ حِينَئِذٍ مِنَ الأَنْصَارِ، بَيْنَهُ وَبَيْنَ حُجْرَةِ عَائِشَةَ - وَأَنَّهُ مَتَى يَخْرُجْ، فَسَوْفَ يَزْعُمُ أَنَّهُ اللهُ، فَمَنْ آمَنَ بِهِ وَصَدَّقَهُ وَاتَّبَعَهُ، لَمْ يَنْفَعْهُ صَالِحٌ مِنْ عَمِلِهِ سَلَفَ، وَمَنْ كَفَرَ بِهِ وَكَذَّبَهُ، لَمْ يُعَاقَبْ بِسَيِّءٍ مِنْ عَمَلِهِ سَلَفَ، وَإِنَّهُ سَيَظْهَرُ عَلَى الأَرْضِ كُلِّهَا إِلَّا الْحَرَمَ وَبَيْتَ الْمَقْدِسِ، وَإِنَّهُ يَحْصُرُ الْمُؤْمِنِينَ فِي بَيْتِ الْمَقْدِسِ، فَيُزَلْزَلُونَ زِلْزَالًا شَدِيدًا، ثُمَّ يُهْلِكُهُ اللهُ عَزَّ وَجَلَّ وَجُنُودَهُ، حَتَّى إِنَّ جِذْمَ الْحَائِطِ أَوْ قَالَ: أَصْلَ

الْحَائِطِ، أَوْ أَصْلَ الشَّجَرَةِ لَيُنَادِي: يَا مُؤْمِنُ يَا مُسْلِمُ هَذَا يَهُودِيٌّ –
أَوْ قَالَ: هَذَا كَافِرٌ – فَتَعَالَ فَاقْتُلْهُ. قَالَ: وَلَنْ يَكُونَ ذَلِكَ حَتَّى تَرَوْا
أُمُورًا يَتَفَاقَمُ شَأْنُهَا فِي أَنْفُسِكُمْ، وَتَسْأَلُونَ بَيْنَكُمْ: هَلْ كَانَ نَبِيُّكُمْ
ذَكَرَ لَكُمْ مِنْهَا ذِكْرًا؟ وَحَتَّى تَزُولَ جِبَالٌ عَنْ مَرَاتِبِهَا، ثُمَّ عَلَى أَثَرِ
ذَلِكَ الْقَبْضِ»

"As for what follows: There are men who claim that the eclipse of the sun and the eclipse of the moon and the setting of the stars from their stations are due to the death of great men on earth, but they have lied, for they are signs from among the Signs of Allâh, Most Blessed, Most High, which cause His slaves to reflect and He sees which of them turns to Him in repentance. By Allâh, I have seen since I stood here what you will find in the life of this world and in the Hereafter, and by Allâh, the Hour will not be established until thirty liars have come forth, the last of them being the one-eyed Al-Maseeh Ad-Dajjal, whose left eye will be missing as if it were the eye of Abu Tahya (an old man at that time from the Ansar, who lived between the Prophet ﷺ and the chamber of 'A'ishah ﵂. And when he appears, he will claim that he is Allâh and if anyone has faith in him, believes him and follows him, none of his previous good deeds will benefit him. And whoever disbelieves in him and belies him, he will not be punished for any of his previous sins. He will enter every place in the earth except the Sacred Precincts (i.e. Makkah) and *Bait Al-Maqdis* (Jerusalem) and he will besiege the Believers in *Bait Al-Maqdis* and they will be shaken by three powerful earthquakes, then Allâh, the Almighty, the All-powerful will destroy him and his soldiers, so that even the base of the wall (or he said: the foundation of the wall, or the root of the tree) will call: "Oh, Believer! Oh, Muslim! Here is a Jew (or he said: a disbeliever) Come and kill him." Then he said: "And this will not happen until you see things which you will consider most grave. And you will ask each other: "Did your Prophet mention to you any of these things?" Even mountains will disappear from their places; after this, the souls will be taken away."[1]

It has been narrated from him 鑢 that he performed three or four bowings in each *Rak'ah* or that he performed only one bowing in each *Rak'ah*, but the most knowledgeable of the scholars do not hold this to be correct, in fact, they consider it to be a mistake.

And he 鑢 ordered that Allâh's Name be mentioned, that prayer be performed, that Allâh be supplicated and His Forgiveness sought and that charity be given and slaves be emancipated.

---

[1] This *Hadeeth* was narrated by Ahmad and contains in its chain of narrators one Tha'labah Ibn 'Ibad Al-'Abdi, who is not considered to be reliable by most scholars of *Hadeeth*; and it contradicts the authentic *Hadeeth* narrated by Al-Bukhari on the authority of Anas Ibn Malik 鑢, in which he reported that the Prophet 鑢 said: "There will be no town which Ad-Dajjal will not enter except Makkah and Al-Madinah and then Al-Madinah will shake with its inhabitants three times (i.e. three earthquakes will take place) and Allâh will expel all the disbelievers and the hypocrites from it."

Chapter

And it has been confirmed from him ﷺ that he performed the rain prayer in a number of ways:

The first was on Friday on the pulpit during the sermon.

The second was when he arranged with the people one day to go out to the *Musalla* and so he went out when the sun rose in a state of humility,[1] and when he reached the *Musalla*, he mounted the pulpit – if the narration is authentic, for one's heart feels some doubt with regard to it – and he praised and thanked Allâh and extolled Him and made *Takbeer*, and a part of what has been preserved from his sermon and his supplication is as follows:

«الْحَمْدُ لله رَبِّ الْعَالَمِينَ، الرَّحْمٰنِ الرَّحِيمِ، مَالِكِ يَوْمِ الدِّينِ، لَا إِلَهَ إِلَّا اللهُ يَفْعَلُ مَا يُرِيدُ، اللَّهُمَّ أَنْتَ اللهُ لَا إِلَهَ إِلَّا أَنْتَ تَفْعَلُ مَا تُرِيدُ، اللَّهُمَّ أَنْتَ اللهُ لَا إِلَهَ إِلَّا أَنْتَ، أَنْتَ الْغَنِيُّ وَنَحْنُ الْفُقَرَاءُ، أَنْزِلْ عَلَيْنَا الْغَيْثَ، وَاجْعَلْ مَا أَنْزَلْتَهُ عَلَيْنَا قُوَّةً لَنَا، وَبَلَاغًا إِلَى حِينٍ»

"All praise and thanks be to Allâh, the Lord of the worlds, the Most Beneficent, the Most Merciful, the Owner of the Day of Recompense, none has the right to be worshipped but Allâh and He does as He wills. Oh, Allâh! You are Allâh and none has the right to be worshipped except You and You do as You will. Oh, Allâh! You are Allâh and none has the right to be worshipped except You. You are Rich (i.e. free of All needs) and we are poor. Send down to us aid and make that which You send down a source of strength and satisfaction for a time."

Then he raised his hands and began to humbly beseech Allâh and

---

[1] Narrated by Abu Dawûd, Ibn Majah and At-Tahawi.

supplicate Him and he raised his arms so high that the whites of his armpits could be seen, then he turned his back to the people and faced the *Qiblah* and inverted his *Rida'*, while still facing the *Qiblah* and he placed the right side in place of the left and vice versa; and his *Rida'* was a black *Khameesah*.[1] He supplicated Allâh facing towards the *Qiblah* and the people did likewise, then he descended and led them in a two *Rak'ah* prayer, like the *'Eed* prayer, without an *Adhan*, reciting *Sûrah Al-A'la* in the first *Rak'ah* after *Sûrah Al-Fâtihah* and *Sûrah Al-Ghashiyah* in the second.[2]

The third was that he supplicated for rain whilst on the pulpit in Al-Madinah at a time other than during the Friday prayers, and it has not been reported from him that he offered a prayer at that time.[3]

The fourth was that he supplicated for rain whilst sitting in the mosque, raising his hands and asking Allâh, the Almighty, the All-powerful.[4]

The fifth was that he supplicated for rain at Ahjar Az-Zait, near Az-Zawra', which is outside the door of the mosque which is today known as *Bab As-Salam*, about a stone's throw to the right, outside the mosque.[5]

The sixth was that he prayed for rain during one of his battles when the polytheists reached the water before him and the Muslims were

---

[1] *Khameesah*: A square woollen blanket with marks on it.

[2] This *Hadeeth* was narrated by Abu Dawûd on the authority of 'A'ishah ﷺ. Ibn Hajr declared it to be weak, due to the presence of one Yûnus Ibn Yazeed Al-Aili in the chain of narrators, of whom he says: "He is reliable except that in his narrations from other than Az-Zuhri he makes mistakes." And this is one such narration. In spite of this, others, such as Ibn Hibban and Al-Hakim declared the *Hadeeth* to be authentic and Az-Zahabi confirmed this.

[3] See *'Sunan Ibn Majah'* (1270), The *Iqamah* of the Prayer, in the Chapter: What Has Been Said Regarding Supplication in Rain Prayers.

[4] Narrated by Abu Dawûd and Al-Baihaqi with an authentic chain of narrators, according to Al-Hakim and Az-Zahabi.

[5] Narrated by Abu Dawûd and Ahmad and declared authentic by Al-Hakim and Az-Zahabi.

afflicted by thirst and they complained to the Messenger of Allâh ﷺ and some of the hypocrites said: "If he were a Prophet, he would pray for rain for his people, as Moses did for his people." He was informed of this, so he said:

«أَوَقَدْ قَالُوهَا؟ عَسَى رَبُّكُمْ أَنْ يَسْقِيَكُمْ»

"Did they say this? Perhaps your Lord will give you water to drink."

Then he spread out his hands and supplicated and he did not lower his hands until clouds shaded them and it rained upon them; and he ﷺ was given succour every time he asked for it. On one occasion, he prayed for rain and Abu Lubabah stood up and said: "Oh, Messenger of Allâh! The dates are in *Al-Marabid*."[1] So he said:

«اللَّهُمَّ اسْقِنَا حَتَّى يَقُومَ أَبُو لُبَابَةَ عُرْيَاناً، فَيَسُدَّ ثَعْلَبَ مِرْبَدِهِ بِإِزَارِهِ»

"Oh, Allâh! Give us water until Abu Lubabah stands naked and closes up the hole in his *Mirbad* with his *Izar*."[2]

And it rained and the people gathered around Abu Lubabah and said: "It will not stop until you stand naked, so stop up the hole in your *Mirbad* with your *Izar*, as the Messenger of Allâh ﷺ said." He did so and the rain stopped.[3] And when the rain became too much, they asked him ﷺ to ask Allâh to clear away the rainclouds and he did so, saying:

«اللَّهُمَّ حَوَالَيْنَا وَلَا عَلَيْنَا، اللَّهُمَّ عَلَى الظِّرَابِ، وَالآكَامِ وَالْجِبَالِ، وَبُطُونِ الأَوْدِيَةِ، وَمَنَابِتِ الشَّجَرِ»

"Oh, Allâh! Around us and not upon us! Oh, Allâh! On the

---

[1] *Marabid*: (sing *Mirbad*) places used for the drying of dates.

[2] *Izar*: A garment worn over the lower part of the body.

[3] According to Al-Haithami, in *'Majma' Az-Zawa'id'* this *Hadeeth* was narrated by At-Tabarani in *'Al-Jami' As-Sagheer'* and it contains in its chain of narrators persons who are unknown, therefore the *Hadeeth* is not authentic. In addition, it is clear from the wording that it is not authentic, since it is forbidden in Islam for a man to reveal his *'Awrah* (i.e. the area in between his navel and his knees) in public.

plateaus, on the mountains, on the hills, at the bottom of the valleys and on the places where trees grow."[1]

Whenever he saw rain, he would say:

«صَيِّبًا نَافِعًا»

"Oh, Allâh! Let it be a useful rain."[2]

And he would remove his garment so that the rain wet him; when he was asked about this, he said:

«لِأَنَّهُ حَدِيثُ عَهْدٍ بِرَبِّهِ»

"Because it has just come from its Lord."[3]

Ash-Shafi'i said: "One whose reliability I do not doubt informed me on the authority of Yazeed Ibn Al-Had that whenever flood waters flowed, the Prophet ﷺ would say:

«اخْرُجُوا بِنَا إِلَى هَذَا الَّذِي جَعَلَهُ الله طَهُورًا، فَنَتَطَهَّرْ مِنْهُ، وَنَحْمَدِ الله عَلَيْهِ»

"Come out with us to that which Allâh has made a means of purification for us and we shall purify ourselves with it and praise and thank Allâh for it."[4]

And he said: "One whose reliability I do not doubt informed me on the authority of Ishaq Ibn 'Abdullah that when flood waters flowed, 'Umar ﷺ would go with his companions to it and say: "None passed by us except that we washed him with it.

And when the Prophet ﷺ saw clouds and wind, it could be seen in his

---

[1] Narrated by Al-Bukhari, Muslim An-Nasa'i and Malik.

[2] Narrated by Al-Bukhari.

[3] Narrated by Muslim.

[4] Narrated by Ash-Shafi'i in *'Al-Umm'* and by Al-Baihaqi in *'As-Sunan Al-Kubra'* Al-Baihaqi said: "This is *Munqati'* (a narration with a broken chain of narrators – the break may be at any point in the chain); and it has been narrated on the authority of 'Umar ﷺ, but its chain is *Munqati'*, because Yazeed Ibn 'Abdillah Ibn Al-Had did not narrate from the Messenger of Allâh ﷺ.

face, and he would become anxious and when it rained, he would be relieved, and it was because he feared that there would be a punishment in it.

Chapter

Regarding His ﷺ Guidance During His Travels and His Acts of Worship Therein

His travels fell into four categories: (i) Traveling to migrate (to Al-Madinah). (ii) Traveling for *Jihad* – and this was the most common reason for his travels, (iii) his traveling for *'Umrah* and (iv) his traveling for *Hajj*.

When he intended to undertake a journey, he would draw lots between his wives, but when he went for *Hajj*, he took all of them with him. When he traveled, he would set out at the start of the day and he preferred to leave on a Thursday[1] and he would ask Allâh to bless his people in their early departures.[2] And when he sent out a military expedition or an army, he would send them in the early part of the day. And he ordered travellers, when they are three or more to appoint one of them as the leader[3] and he forbade traveling of man alone[4] and he informed us that: "The single rider is a devil, two riders are devils and three are riders."[5] And it has been reported from him that when he started on a journey, he would say:

«اللَّهُمَّ إِلَيْكَ تَوَجَّهْتُ، وَبِكَ اعْتَصَمْتُ، اللَّهُمَّ اكْفِنِي مَا أَهَمَّنِي وَمَالَا أَهْتَمُّ لَهُ، اللَّهُمَّ زَوِّدْنِي التَّقْوَى، وَاغْفِرْ لِي ذَنْبِي، وَوَجِّهْنِي

---

[1] Narrated by Al-Bukhari, on the authority of Ka'b Ibn Malik (ﷺ).

[2] Narrated by Ad-Darimi, Abu Dawûd, At-Tirmidhi, Ibn Majah and Ahmad.

[3] Narrated by Abu Dawûd, on the authority of Abu Hurairah (ﷺ).

[4] Narrated by Al-Bukhari and At-Tirmidhi.

[5] Narrated by Malik, At-Tirmidhi and Abu Dawûd.

«لِلْخَيْرِ أَيْنَمَا تَوَجَّهْتُ»

"Allâhumma Ilaika Tawajjahtu Wa Bika'tasamtu , Allâhummakfinee Ma Ahammanee Wa Ma La Ahtammu Lahu. Allâhumma, Zawwwid-nit-Taqwa Waghfir Lee Dhanbee Wa Wajjihnee Lil-Khairi Aynama Tawajjahtu"

"Oh, Allâh! Towards You I turn and in You I seek protection. Oh Allâh! Suffice me in the things about which I am anxious and in the things to which I do not attach importance. Oh, Allâh! Equip me with the fear of You and forgive me my sins and direct me to goodness in whichever direction I may face."[1]

And when a riding beast was brought for him to mount, he would say: *"Bismillah"* as he put his foot in the stirrup and once he was mounted on its back, he would say:

«الْحَمْدُ لله الَّذِي سَخَّرَ لَنَا هَذَا وَمَا كُنَّا لَهُ مُقْرِنِينَ، وَإِنَّا إِلَى رَبِّنَا لَمُنْقَلِبُونَ»

"Al-Hamdu Lillahil-Ladhee Sakhkhara Lana Hadha Wa Ma Kunna Lahu Muqrineena, Wa Inna Ila Rabbina Lamunqalibûn"

"All praise and thanks be to Allâh, Who has subjected this to us when we could never have it by our own efforts and verily, to our Lord we shall return."

Then he would say:

«الْحَمْدُ لله، الْحَمْدُ لله، الْحَمْدُ لله»

"Al-Hamdu Lillah, Al-Hamdu Lillah, Al-Hamdu Lillah",

then he would say:

«اللهُ أَكْبَرُ، اللهُ أَكْبَرُ، اللهُ أَكْبَرُ»

"Allâhu Akbar, Allâhu Akbar, Allâhu Akbar".

Then he would say:

---

[1] Narrated by Ibn As-Sunni in *'Amal Al-Yawm Wal-Lailah'*; it contains in its chain of narrators one 'Amr Ibn Musawir, who is described as weak by scholars of *Hadeeth*.

«سُبْحَانَكَ إِنِّي ظَلَمْتُ نَفْسِي فَاغْفِرْ لِي ، إِنَّهُ لَا يَغْفِرُ الذُّنُوبَ إِلَّا أَنْتَ»

"Subhanaka Innee Zalamtu Nafsee Faghfir Lee Innahu La Yaghfir-udh-Dhunûba Illa Anta"

"Glory be to You, Verily, I have wronged myself, so forgive me, truly, there is none can forgive sins except You."

And he used to say:

«اللَّهُمَّ إِنَّا نَسْأَلُكَ فِي سَفَرِنَا هَذَا الْبِرَّ وَالتَّقْوَى، وَمِنَ الْعَمَلِ مَا تَرْضَى، اللَّهُمَّ هَوِّنْ عَلَيْنَا سَفَرَنَا هَذَا، وَاطْوِ عَنَّا بُعْدَهُ، اللَّهُمَّ أَنْتَ الصَّاحِبُ فِي السَّفَرِ، وَالْخَلِيفَةُ فِي الأَهْلِ، اللَّهُمَّ إِنِّي أَعُوذُ بِكَ مِنْ وَعْثَاءِ السَّفَرِ، وَكَآبَةِ الْمُنْقَلَبِ، وَسُوءِ الْمُنْظَرِ فِي الأَهْلِ وَالْمَالِ»

"Allâhumma Inna Nas'aluka Fee Safarina Hazal-Birra Wat-Taqwa Wa Minal-'Amali Ma Tardha, Allâhumma Hawwin 'Alaina Safarana Haza Watwi 'Anna Bu'dahu. Allâhumma Antas-Sahibu Fis-Safari Wal-Khaleefatu Fil-Ahli. Allâhumma Innee A'ûdhu Bika Min Wa'tha'is-Safari Wa Ka'abatil-Munqalibi Wa Sû'il Manzari Fil-Ahli Wal-Mal"

"Oh, Allâh! We ask You on this journey of ours to grant us righteousness and fear of You and deeds which are pleasing to You. Oh, Allâh! Make this journey of ours easy for us and make us cover the distance swiftly. Oh, Allâh! You are our Companion on the journey and the Guardian of our families. Oh, Allâh! I seek refuge with You from the hardships of travel, gloominess of the sights, and finding of evil changes in property and family on return)."[1]

When he returned from *Hajj*, he would say this and he would add:

«آيِبُونَ، تَائِبُونَ، عَابِدُونَ لِرَبِّنَا حَامِدُونَ»

"Ayibûna, Ta'ibûna, 'Abidûna Lirabbina, Hamidûn"

"[We are] returning, repentant, worshipping our Lord and praising Him."

And when he and his Companions ﷺ ascended mountain trails, they

---

[1] Narrated by Muslim in the Book of Pilgrimage.

would say: *"Allâhu Akbar"* and when they descended into valleys, they would say: *"Subhanallah"*.

And when he looked down on a village which he wished to enter, he would say:

«اللَّهُمَّ رَبَّ السَّمٰوَاتِ السَّبْعِ، وَمَا أَظْلَلْنَ، وَرَبَّ الأَرَضِينَ السَّبْعِ وَمَا أَقْلَلْنَ، وَرَبَّ الشَّيَاطِينِ وَمَا أَضْلَلْنَ، وَرَبَّ الرِّيَاحِ وَمَا ذَرَيْنَ، أَسْأَلُكَ خَيْرَ هَذِهِ الْقَرْيَةِ، وَخَيْرَ أَهْلِهَا، وَخَيْرَ مَا فِيهَا، وَأَعُوذُ بِكَ مِنْ شَرِّهَا، وَشَرِّ أَهْلِهَا، وَشَرِّ مَا فِيهَا»

"Allâhumma, Rabbas-Samawatis-Sab'i, Wa Ma Azlalna, Wa Rabbal-Ardeenas-Sab'i Wa Ma Aqlalna, Wa Rabbash-Shayateeni Wa Ma Adlalna Wa Rabbar-Riyahi Wa Ma Dharaina, As'aluka Khaira Hazihil-Qaryati Wa Khaira Ahliha Wa Khaira Ma Feeha Wa A'ûdhu Bika Min Sharri Ahliha Wa Sharri Ma Feeha"

"Oh, Allâh! Lord of the seven heavens and all that they cover, Lord of the seven earths and all that they contain, Lord of the devils and all that they misguide, Lord of the winds and all that they scatter! I ask You for the goodness of this village, the goodness of its inhabitants and all the goodness that is in it and I seek refuge with You from the evil of its inhabitants and all the evil that is in it."[1]

He used (when traveling) to shorten the four *Rak'ah* prayers; Umayyah Ibn Khalid ﷺ said: "We find mention in the Qur'ân of the prayer of the resident and the fear prayer, but we find in it no mention of the traveler's prayer." Ibn 'Umar ﷺ said: "Oh, my brother! Verily, Allâh sent Muhammad ﷺ and we knew nothing; so we only do what we saw Muhammad ﷺ doing."

It was a part of the guidance of the Prophet ﷺ to restrict himself to the obligatory prayers (when traveling) and it has not been recorded from him that he offered *Sunnah* prayers before or after them, except

[1] Narrated by Ibn As-Sunni in *'Amal Al-Yawmi Wal-Lailah'*, Ibn Hibban and Al-Hakim, who declared it to be authentic and Az-Zahabi concurred with this. Ibn Hajr said that it is *Hasan*.

the *Sunnah* of *Fajr* and *Witr*. But he did forbid the offering of supererogatory prayer before or after it and that is like the general supererogatory prayers, not that it is a regular *Sunnah* for prayer. And it has been confirmed from him that on the day of the conquest of Makkah, he offered a *Duha* prayer of eight *Rak'ahs*.

It was also a part of his guidance ﷺ to offer the voluntary prayers sitting on his riding beast, no matter which direction it took him to and he used to indicate his *Ruku'* (by inclining his head). If he wanted to set out before the sun declined, he would delay the *Zuhr* prayer until '*Asr* time and if it declined before he set out, he would perform the *Zuhr* prayer and then mount (his riding beast). If his journey impelled him, he would delay the *Maghrib* prayer and combine it with the *'Isha'* prayer. It was not a part of his guidance to combine the prayers while he was riding, nor at the time when he descended.

Regarding His ﷺ Guidance
in Reciting the Qur'ân

He would not fail to recite his regular a *Hizb*,[1] and his recitation was slow and pleasant, letter by letter; and he would cut of his recitation at the end of each Verse and he would prolong it when he recited *Madd* letters,[2] so he would prolong the recitation of the words: *Ar-Rahman* and *Ar-Raheem*. He would seek refuge with Allâh at the start of his recitation, saying:

«أَعُوذُ بِاللهِ مِنَ الشَّيْطَانِ الرَّجِيمِ»

"A'udhu Billahi Minash-Shaitanir-Rajeem"

"I seek refuge with Allâh from the accursed Satan."

and sometimes, he might say:

«اللَّهُمَّ إِنِّي أَعُوذُ بِكَ مِنَ الشَّيْطَانِ الرَّجِيمِ مِنْ هَمْزِهِ وَنَفْخِهِ وَنَفْثِهِ»

"Allâhumma, Innee A'udhu Bika Minash-Shaitanir-Rajeemi, Min Hamzihi Wa Nafkhihi Wa Nafthihi"

"Oh, Allâh! I seek refuge with You from the accursed Satan, from his prompting [his madness], from his blowing [his pride] and from his spittle [his poetry]."[3]

---

[1] *Hizb*: On sixtieth part of the Qur'ân

[2] *Madd* letters: Long vowels (*Alif*, *Wauw* and *Ya'*) whose pronunciation is drawn out when recited in the Qur'ân.

[3] Narrated by Ahmad, Abu Dawûd and Ibn Majah and declared authentic by Ibn Hibban and Al-Hakim and Az-Zahabi confirmed this.

And he used to seek refuge before the recitation. He used to love to listen to the Qur'ân recited by someone else and he commanded Ibn Mas'ûd ﷺ to recite and he did so while the Prophet ﷺ listened and he was so humbled by listening to his recitation, that his eyes filled with tears. He would recite while standing, while sitting, while lying down, while a state of ritual purity, having performed ablution and in a state of ritual impurity, but not whilst he was *Junub*.[1] He would recite it in a clear, pleasant tone and sometimes, he would cause his voice to reverberate; Ibn Al-Mughaffal reported that he made it reverberate three times thus: *"Aa-aa-aa"* – this was reported by Al-Bukhari. When this is combined with the words of the Prophet (ﷺ): "Beautify the Qur'ân with your voices,"[2] – and his words: "Allâh does not listen to a Prophet as He listens to a Prophet who recites the Qur'ân in a pleasant tone,"[3] one can see that this reverberation was deliberate on his part, not due to the shaking of his she-camel. If it were not the case, Ibn Al-Mughaffal would not have reported that it was voluntary, in order that he be emulated, for he said: "He used to cause his voice to reverberate during his recitation." And reciting pleasantly and slowly (*Taghanni*) is of two types:

The first: That which is entailed by reciting naturally, without effort; this is permissible, even though he embellished his natural voice by making it beautiful, as Abu Mûsa Al-Ash'ari ﷺ said to the Prophet ﷺ: "If I had known that you were listening, I would have beautified my recitation for you."[4] This is what the *Salaf* used to do and all of the evidences prove it.

---

[1] *Junub*: In a state of major ritual impurity, following sexual intercourse or nocturnal emission; in such a state, a person is required to perform *Ghusl* (washing of the whole body).

[2] Narrated by Al-Bukhari, An-Nas'i, Ibn Majah, Abu Dawûd, Ahmad and Ad-Darimi.

[3] Narrated by Al-Bukhari, Muslim, Abu Dawûd and An-Nasa'i.

[4] This was mentioned by Al-Haithami in *'Al-Majma"* on the authority of Abu Mûsa ﷺ and he said: "Narrated by Abu Ya'la; and in it (i.e. its *Sanad*) is Khalid Ibn Nafi' Al-Ash'ari and he is weak. Ibn Hajr mentions something similar on the authority of Anas ﷺ with a chain of narrators which conforms to the conditions laid down by Imam Muslim.

The second: That which is artificial and is the product of learning, as one learns to sing using all types of invented airs and meters, which were disliked by the *Salaf* and the evidences of its being disliked are concerning this.

Chapter

Regarding His ﷺ Guidance in Visiting the Sick

He ﷺ used to visit those of his Companions ﷺ who were sick; and he visited a boy who used to serve him from among the People of the Scripture[1] and he visited his uncle, who was a polytheist[2] and he invited them both to Islam and the Jew accepted Islam.

He would come close to the sick person and sit at his head and ask him how he was; and he would stroke the sick person with his right hand and say:

«اللَّهُمَّ رَبَّ النَّاسِ، أَذْهِبِ الْبَاسَ، وَاشْفِ أَنْتَ الشَّافِي لَا شِفَاءَ إِلَّا شِفَاؤُكَ شِفَاءً لَا يُغَادِرُ سَقَمًا»

"Allâhumma, Rabban-Nas! Adhhibil-Basa Washfi; Antash-Shafi, La Shifa' Illa Shifa'uka, Shifa'un La Yughadiru Saqman"

"Oh, Allâh, Lord of the people, take away the disease and cure him; You are the One Who cures and there is no cure except Your Cure – a cure that leaves no disease."[3]

And he used to supplicate for the sick person three times, as when he said: "Oh, Allâh! Cure Sa'd" three times.[4] And when he visited a sick person, he would say:

---

[1] Narrated by Al-Bukhari, on the authority of Anas Ibn Malik ﷺ.
[2] Narrated by Al-Bukhari and Muslim.
[3] Narrated by Al-Bukhari and Muslim.
[4] Narrated by Al-Bukhari and Muslim.

«لَا بَأْسَ، طَهُورٌ إِنْ شَاءَ اللهُ»

"La Ba'sa, Tahûrun, In Sha' Allâh"

"Don't worry, you will be purified [of your sins] if Allâh wills."[1]

And sometimes, he might say:

«كَفَّارَةٌ وطَهُورٌ»

"Kaffaratun Wa Tahûr"

"Expiation and purification."

And he used to make incantations (*Ruqyah*) if someone was afflicted by ulcer, injury or some other complaint. He would place his forefinger on the ground and then he would say:

«بِسْمِ اللهِ تُرْبَةُ أَرْضِنَا بِرِيقَةِ بَعْضِنَا يُشْفَى سَقِيمُنَا بِإِذْنِ رَبِّنَا»

"Bismillahi, Turbatu Ardina Bireeqati Ba'dina, Yushfa Saqeemuna Bi-Idhni Rabbina"

"In the Name of Allâh, the dust of our earth, and the saliva of some of us cure our patient with the permission of our Lord."

(This is in the *'Saheehayn'*) and it negates the wording of the *Hadeeth* regarding the seventy thousand, in which it is said: "They do not perform *Ruqyah*" – for this is a mistake on behalf of the narrator.

And it was not a part of his guidance to reserve a special day for visiting the sick or any special time. Indeed, he legislated visiting the sick for his people day and night. He would visit persons suffering from eye disease and other complaints and sometimes, he would place his hand on the sick person's forehead, then he would wipe over his chest and his stomach and say: *"Allâhummashfih"* (Oh, Allâh! Cure him), and he would wipe over his face as well. If he felt that the disease was terminal, he would say:

«إِنَّا للهِ وَإِنَّا إِلَيْهِ رَاجِعُونَ»

"Inna Lillahi Wa Inna Ilaihi Raji'ûn"

---

[1] Narrated by Al-Bukhari, on the authority of Ibn 'Abbas 🕭.

"Verily, we are from Allâh and to Him shall we return."[1]

His guidance in the matter of funerals was the most complete guidance, as opposed to that of the other nations, as it included acting well towards the deceased, his close kin and his relatives, establishing the acts of worship which the living person performs regarding the treatment of the dead. It was a part of his guidance to establish the worship of the Lord, Most High in the most perfect manner and to prepare the deceased for Allâh, Most High in the best way, for him and his companions to stand in rows, praising and thanking Allâh and asking forgiveness from Him, then to carry him until they reach the site where he is to be interred and then for him and his companions to stand at the graveside asking Allâh to grant him steadfastness and thereafter to make a commitment to visit his grave, delivering salutations of peace to him and supplicating for him.

The first part of this is by visiting him when is sick and reminding him of the Hereafter and ordering him to make a will and to turn in repentance to Allâh and to order those resident to make him pronounce the *Shahadah*[2] that these may be his last words. Then he ﷺ forbade (the relatives and friends of the deceased from indulging in) the practices of those who do not believe in Revelation, such as striking the cheeks, raising the voice in lament, wailing and such like.

He prescribed humility towards the dead, crying without raising the voice and sadness of the heart and he used to do these things and he said: "The eye weeps and the heart grieves, but we do not say anything except what pleases the Lord."[3] And he prescribed for his people to praise and thank Allâh, to say the words: *"Inna Lillahi Wa Inna Ilaihi Raji'ûn"* (Verily, we are for Allâh and to Him shall we

---

[1] See *Sûrah Al-Baqarah* 2:156.

[2] *Shahadah*: The testimony:

$$\text{«لَا إِلَهَ إِلَّا اللهُ مُحَمَّدٌ رَسُولُ اللهِ»}$$

"La Ilaha Illallah, Muhammadur-Ras-ûlullah"

"None has the right to be worshipped except Allâh and **Muhammad** is the Messenger of Allâh."

[3] Narrated by Al-Bukhari, Muslim and Abu Dawûd.

return) and to accept Allâh's *Qadar*.[1]

It was a part of his ﷺ guidance to hasten the preparation of the deceased for Allâh, to purify and clean him, to apply perfume to him and to shroud him in white garments, then he would be taken him and he would pray over him, while earlier, he would supplicate for him at his deathbed until he expired, then he would pray over him and accompany the body to the grave. Then the Companions ﷺ observed that this was difficult for him, so they would prepare their dead and then bring them to him and he would pray over them outside the mosque, or sometimes, he might pray over them inside the mosque, as he prayed over Suhail Ibn Baidha' and his brother ﷺ in the mosque.[2]

It was a part of his ﷺ guidance to cover the face and body of the deceased and to close his eyes. And sometimes, he might kiss the deceased, as he did to 'Uthman Ibn Maz'ûn ﷺ, and he cried.

He used to order the deceased to be washed three times, five times or more, according to what the person washing considered necessary and he ordered camphor to be used in the last wash.

He did not wash the martyrs who had been killed in battle, but used to remove the leather and armour from them and bury them in their clothing and he did not pray over them. And he ordered that the person who died in a state of *Ihram*[3] be washed and *Sidr*[4] applied to his body and that he be buried in his two *Ihram* garments, but he prohibited that perfume be applied to him or that his face be covered. He would order the person in charge of the affairs of the deceased to shroud him well and to shroud him in white. And he forbade extravagance in the matter of the shroud. If the shroud was too short to cover the whole body, he would cover his head with it and then cover his legs with some kind of grass or foliage.

When a deceased person was brought to him, he would ask: "Does he have any debts?" If he was not in debt, he would pray over him, but if

---

[1] *Qadar*: Divine Predetermination of events.

[2] Narrated by Muslim, Abu Dawûd and Ibn Majah.

[3] The state of ritual purity entered into by the *Hajj* and '*Umrah* pilgrim.

[4] *Sidr*: Essence obtained from the lotus tree.

he was in debt, he would not pray over him, but would order his Companions 🙏 to pray over him. This was because his prayer is an intercession and his intercession is answered and the slave who is pledged to pay a debt may not enter Paradise until the debt is paid for him. Then when Allâh granted him victory, he would pray over the debtor and he would assume the responsibility for his debt and he would leave his wealth for his heirs.

When he began to pray over the deceased, he would make *Takbeer* and praise and thank Allâh and extol Him. Ibn 'Abbas offered the funeral prayer over someone and after the first *Takbeer*, he recited *Sûrah Al-Fâtihah* and he recited it aloud and he said: "You should know that it is a *Sunnah*." Our *Shaikh* (i.e. Ibn Taimiyyah) said: "Its recitation is not mandatory; rather, it is a *Sunnah*."[1] And Abu Umamah reported on the authority of a number of the Companions 🙏 that they used to send prayers on the Prophet 🕌 in it.[2]

Yahya Ibn Sa'eed Al-Ansari narrated on the authority of Sa'eed Al-Maqburi, who narrated on the authority of Abu Hurairah 🙏 that he asked 'Ubadah Ibn As-Samit 🙏 about funeral prayers and he said: "By Allâh, I will inform you: You should begin by making *Takbeer*, then send prayers on the Prophet 🕌 and then say: "Oh, Allâh! Verily, Your slave, so-and-so did not use to associate partners with You and You know better concerning him. If he was righteous, then increase him in righteousness and if he was a wrongdoer, then pardon him. Oh, Allâh! Do not forbid us his reward (i.e. the reward of praying for

---

[1] Abul Khair Al-Hindi, the author of *'Fath Al-'Allam'*, an explanation of Ibn Hajr's *'Bulûgh Al-Maram'* says that while there is some difference of opinion regarding whether or not it is obligatory to recite *Sûrah Al-Fâtihah* in funeral prayers, the most authoritative view is that it is obligatory, based upon the words of the Prophet 🕌 narrated by 'Ubadah Ibn As-Samit 🙏: "There is no prayer for one who does not recite the Opening of the Book (i.e. *Sûrah Al-Fâtihah*) therein." (Narrated by Al-Bukhari and Muslim) and the funeral prayer is included in this ruling, unless some evidence can be shown that it is excepted from it.

[2] Narrated by Ash-Shafi'i in *'Al-Umm'* and by Al-Baihaqi. Al-Hakim declared it to be authentic and Az-Zahabi confirmed this.

him) and do not misguide us after him."[1]

What is meant by praying over the deceased is supplicating for him, which is why it has been recorded and transmitted from him ﷺ that he supplicated and sent prayers on himself, while it has not been transmitted from him that he recited *Sûrah Al-Fâtihah*. Included among the supplications which have been recorded from him are the following:

«اللَّهُمَّ إِنَّ فُلَانَ بْنَ فُلَانٍ فِي ذِمَّتِكَ، وَحَبْلِ جِوَارِكَ، فَقِهِ فِتْنَةَ الْقَبْرِ، وَعَذَابَ النَّارِ، وَأَنْتَ أَهْلُ الْوَفَاءِ، وَالْحَقِّ، فَاغْفِرْ لَهُ، وَارْحَمْهُ إِنَّكَ أَنْتَ الْغَفُورُ الرَّحِيمُ»

"Allâhumma, Inna Fulanabna Fulanin Fee Dhimmatika Wa Habli Jiwarika, Faqihi Min Fitnatil-Qabri Wa Min 'Adhabin-Nari, Fa-Anta Ahlul-Wafa'i Wal-Haqqi, Faghfir Lahu Warhamhu, Innaka Antal-Ghafûrur-Raheem"

"Oh, Allâh! So-and-so, the son of so-and-so is in Your Care and in Your Presence, so protect him from the trial of the grave and the punishment of the Hell-fire. You fulfill (Your Promises) and Your Word is Truth. Oh, Allâh! Forgive him and show mercy to him, for You are the Most Merciful, Most Forgiving."[2]

Another supplication recorded from him is:

«اللَّهُمَّ أَنْتَ رَبُّهَا، وَأَنْتَ خَلَقْتَهَا، وَأَنْتَ رَزَقْتَهَا، وَأَنْتَ هَدَيْتَهَا لِلْإِسْلَامِ، وَأَنْتَ قَبَضْتَ رُوحَهَا، تَعْلَمُ سِرَّهَا وَعَلَانِيَتَهَا، جِئْنَا شُفَعَاءَ فَاغْفِرْ لَهَا»

"Allâhumma, Anta Rabbuha Wa Anta Khalaqtaha Wa Anta Razaqtaha Wa Anta Hadaitaha Lil-Islami Wa Anta Qabadta Rûhaha, Ta'lamu Sirraha Wa 'Alaniyataha; Ji'na Shufa'a'a, Fighfir Laha"

"Oh, Allâh! You are her Lord and You created her and You sustained her and You guided her to Islam and You took her

---

[1] Narrated by Al-Baihaqi.
[2] Narrated by Abu Dawûd, Ibn Majah and Ahmad and authenticated by Ibn Hibban.

soul. You know her secret and her public life. We have come to plead with You on her behalf, so forgive her."[1]

And he ﷺ ordered us to be sincere when supplicating for the dead.

He used to make the *Takbeer* four times, and it has been authentically reported from him that he made it five times, while his Companions ﷺ used to make it four, five or six times. 'Alqamah said: "I said to 'Abdullah: "Some people among the companions of Mu'adh came from Ash-Sham[2] and they made *Takbeer* over one of their dead five times." He said: "There is no specific time for *Takbeer* over the dead, so make *Takbeer* as the Imam does and when he leaves, you leave."

It was said to Imam Ahmad: "Do you know of a report from any of the Companions ﷺ which states that they used to make two *Tasleems* when praying over the dead?" He said: "No, but I have heard reports on the authority of six Companions ﷺ, that they used to make one light *Tasleem* to the right." And he mentioned Ibn 'Umar, Ibn 'Abbas and Abu Hurairah ﷺ.[3]

As for raising the hands, Ash-Shafi'i said: "They should be raised according to the narration (from one of the Companions ﷺ and based upon analogy with the *Sunnah* in prayer." And what is meant by the narration is that of Ibn 'Umar and Anas ﷺ, which states that they used to raise their hands whenever they made *Takbeer* during the funeral prayers.[4] If the Prophet ﷺ missed a funeral prayer, he would

---

[1] Narrated by Abu Dawûd, on the authority of Abu Hurairah. The *Hadeeth* contains in its *Sanad* one 'Ali Ibn Shammakh, who was declared untrustworthy by some scholars of *Hadeeth*; however Ibn Hibban said that he was trustworthy and Ibn Hajr said in '*Taqreeb At-Tahzeeb*': "Acceptable." He also said regarding another narration of this *Hadeeth* by At-Tabarani: "This *Hadeeth* is *Hasan*."

[2] Ash-Sham: The area comprising present-day Syria, Jordan, Palestine and Lebanon.

[3] The others are: Wathilah Ibn Al-Asqa', Ibn Abi Awfa and Zaid Ibn Thabit; Al-Baihaqi added also 'Ali Ibn Abi Talib, Jabir Ibn 'Abdillah, Anas Ibn Malik and Abu Umamah Ibn Sahl Ibn Haneef (ﷺ). (See '*Zad Al-Ma'ad*' (vol. 1, page 511)

[4] Narrated by Al-Baihaqi.

pray over the grave.[1] Once, he prayed over the grave after a night had passed and once after three[2] and once after a month;[3] and he did not fix a time limit for it. But Malik forbade it, unless it was due to the next of kin of the deceased being absent.

And he would stand at the head of a man and in the middle of a woman's body; and he would pray over infants, but he would not pray over one who had killed himself, nor over one who had withheld anything of the booty of war. Scholars have disagreed regarding whether or not he prayed over one who had been executed for some crime, such as the adulterer, for it has been authentically reported from him that he prayed over the woman from the Juhaini tribe, whom he had stoned to death[4] and they disagreed regarding the *Hadeeth* of Mai'z Ibn Malik[5] Either it is said that there is no conflict between his words – for the prayer in it was supplication and the abandoning of prayer over him was the abandoning of funeral prayers over him, as a lesson and a warning – or it is said that if his words conflict with each other, then it should be turned away from in favour of the other *Hadeeth* (i.e. the *Hadeeth* of the woman from the Juhaini tribe).

After he had prayed over him, he would walk to the graveyard, walking in front of the body; and it is prescribed for the rider to be

---

[1] Narrated by Al-Bukhari and Muslim.

[2] Narrated by Al-Baihaqi.

[3] Narrated by Al-Baihaqi in a *Mursal* form and by Suwaid Ibn Sa'eed, who reported from 'Alqamah, on the authority of Ibn 'Abbas ﷺ in a *Mawsûl* (i.e. connected) form.

[4] Narrated by Muslim, At-Tirmidhi and Abu Dawûd.

[5] Jabir Ibn 'Abdillah reported: "A man from the tribe of Aslam came to the Prophet ﷺ and confessed that he had committed an act of illegal sexual intercourse. The Prophet ﷺ turned his face away from him till the man bore witness against himself four times. The Prophet said to him: "Are you mad?" He said "No." He said: "Are you married?" He said: "Yes." Then the Prophet ﷺ ordered that he be stoned to death, and he was stoned to death at the *Musalla*. When the stones troubled him, he fled, but he was caught and was stoned till he died. The Prophet ﷺ spoke well of him and offered his funeral prayer." (Narrated by Al-Bukhari)

behind it. If one is walking, he should be near to it, either behind it, in front of it, to the right of it or to the left of it. He used to order that it be taken with haste, even if they walked rapidly with it. When he was accompanying a funeral procession, he would walk and he said:

«لَمْ أَكُنْ لِأَرْكَبَ وَالْمَلَائِكَةُ يَمْشُونَ»

"I will not ride when the angels are walking."[1]

Once he had left, he might sometimes ride. He would not sit until the body was placed in the grave and he said:

«إِذَا تَبِعْتُمُ الْجِنَازَةَ فَلَا تَجْلِسُوا حَتَّى تُوضَعَ»

"If you accompany a funeral procession, do not sit until it has been placed in the grave."[2]

It was not from his guidance to offer funeral prayer upon every absent deceased, however it was imported that the Prophet ﷺ offered the funeral prayer for An-Najashi. (An-Najashi died in a country of disbelievers where nobody prayed upon him). It was also reported that he ordered that people should stand up when a funeral procession passes by. It was also reported that he sat down when a funeral procession was passing. So it was said, standing up was abrogated; it was also said both are permissible. It is from the guidance that the deceased should not be burried at sunrise, sunset or before noon.

It was also a part of his guidance to make a *Lahd*[3] and to dig the grave deep and to make it wide at the head and foot. And it is reported from him that when he placed the deceased in the grave, he would say:

«بِسْمِ اللهِ، وَفِي سَبِيلِ اللهِ، وَعَلَى مِلَّةِ رَسُولِ اللهِ»

"*Bismillahi Wa Fee Sabeelillahi Wa 'Ala Millati Rasûlillahi*"

"In the Name of Allâh and in Allâh's Cause and upon the

---

[1] Narrated by Abu Dawûd and authenticated by Al-Hakim and Az-Zahabi concurred with this.

[2] Narrated by Al-Bukhari, Muslim and Abu Dawûd.

[3] *Lahd*: A niche in one side of the grave, facing towards the *Qiblah*.

Religion of the Messenger of Allâh."[1]

And it is reported from him that he used to sprinkle dust over the head of the deceased three times at the time of burial and when he finished burying him, he and his Companions ﷺ would stand over the grave and he would ask Allâh to grant him steadfastness and he ordered his Companions ﷺ to do likewise. He would not sit and recite over the grave, nor would he instruct the deceased. Neither was it a part of his guidance to raise the graves, nor to build over them, nor to cover them with clay, nor to build domes over them; and he sent 'Ali Ibn Abi Talib on a mission (to Yemen) with the instruction not to leave any graven images without destroying them, nor any raised graves without levelling them.[2] So his *Sunnah* is to level all raised graves.

He forbade that graves should be plastered or built over or written on, and he taught those who wish to know where a particular grave is to mark it with a stone. He forbade taking the graves as places of worship and illuminating them with lamps and he cursed the one who does so. He also prohibited prayer towards them and making them places of celebration.

It was a part of his guidance that the grave be not treated with contempt and not be trodden on, or sat upon, or leaned on,[3] nor glorified so that they are taken as mosques, places of celebration and objects of worship.

He ﷺ used to visit the graves of his Companions ﷺ and supplicate for them and seek forgiveness for them. This is the kind of visiting which the Messenger of Allâh ﷺ prescribed; and he ordered his Companions ﷺ when they visited the graves to say:

«السَّلَامُ عَلَيْكُمْ أَهْلَ الدِّيَارِ مِنَ الْمُؤْمِنِينَ وَالْمُسْلِمِينَ، وَإِنَّا إِنْ شَاءَ

---

[1] Narrated by At-Tirmidhi, Abu Dawûd, Ibn Majah, Ahmad and it was declared authentic by Al-Hakim and Az-Zahabi agreed.

[2] Narrated by Muslim, At-Tirmidhi, Abu Dawûd, An-Nasa'i, Al-Hakim, At-Tayalisi and Ahmad.

[3] Narrated by Muslim, Abu Dawûd, An-Nasa'i, Ibn Majah, on the authority of Abu Hurairah ﷺ.

«اللهُ بِكُمْ لاحِقُونَ، نَسْأَلُ اللهَ لَنَا وَلَكُمُ الْعَافِيَةَ»

"As-Salamu 'Alaikum Ahlad-Diyari Minal-Mu'mineena Wal-Musli-meena, Wa Inna In Sha' Allâhu Bikum Lahiqûna, Nas'alullah Lana Wa Lakumul-'Afiyah"

"May Allâh's Peace be upon you, O, inhabitants of the graves, from the Believers and the Muslims; and we – Allâh Willing – will join you. We ask Allâh that He pardon us and you)."[1]

And he used to say and do the same type of things as he used to do during the prayer, but the polytheists refused except to supplicate the dead and to associate them as partners with Allâh, to ask them to fulfill their needs, to seek help from them and to turn their faces towards them, which is the opposite of the guidance of the Prophet ﷺ, for that is the guidance of *Tawheed* and acting righteously towards the dead.

It was a part of the guidance of the Prophet ﷺ to offer condolences to the family of the deceased, but it was not a part of his guidance for the people to gather and for the Qur'ân to be read for him – neither at the grave, nor anywhere else.

And it was a part of his guidance for the family of the deceased not to be burdened with the task of preparing their food for the people. Indeed, he ordered the people to prepare food for them.[2] It was a part of his guidance to refrain from publicly announcing the death of anyone and he said: "It is from the practices of the *Jahiliyyah* (days of ignorance)."[3]

---------- ❖ ❖ ❖ ----------

---

[1] Narrated by Muslim, An-Nasa'i and Ahmad.
[2] Narrated by the compilers of the *'Sunan'*, except An-Nasa'i and Ahmad.
[3] Narrated by At-Tirmidhi

Chapter

Regarding His ﷺ Guidance in the Fear Prayer (*Salah Al-Khawf*)

Allâh permitted the Prophet ﷺ to shorten pillars of the prayer and likewise their number, if it was necessary due to a combination of fear and travel and to reduce the number only, when on a journey which is not accompanied by fear and to reduce the pillars only, if there is fear but no travel. From this the wisdom of limiting the shortening mentioned in the Qur'ânic Verse[1] to traveling on the earth and fear may be seen.

If the enemy stood between him and the *Qiblah*, it was a part of his guidance during the fear prayer to arrange the Muslims in two rows behind him, then he would make *Takbeer* and they would all make *Takbeer*, then they would all bow and straighten up, then the first row behind him would prostrate alone, and the last row would stand up to face the enemy, then when the first row straighten up, the second row would prostrate twice, then they would stand up and advance to the place of the first row and the first row would retreat to take their place, so that both groups might attain the blessing of the first row and so that the second row might catch the two prostrations with him ﷺ in the second *Rak'ah* – and this is the ultimate in fairness. Then when he bowed (for a second time) the two parties would do what they did in the first *Rak'ah*. Then when he sat for the *Tashahhud*, the second row would perform its two prostrations and then they would join him in the *Tashahhud* and he would pronounce the *Tasleem* with them all together.[2]

---

[1] See *Sûrah An-Nisa'*: 4:101
[2] Narrated by Muslim, Abu Dawûd and An-Nasa'i.

If the enemy was not in the direction of the *Qiblah*, sometimes, he would split them into two groups: One facing the enemy and another praying with him; and one of the two groups would offer a *Rak'ah* with him, then they would go and complete their prayer in the place of the second group, and the latter would offer the second *Rak'ah* with him, then he would make *Tasleem* and each of the two groups would make up what they had missed after the *Imam* had made the *Tasleem*.[1] And sometimes, he ﷺ would perform a single *Rak'ah* with one of the two groups, then he would stand up and offer the second *Rak'ah*, while they would make up the second *Rak'ah* while he was standing and they would make the *Tasleem* before his *Rukû'*; then the second group would come and offer the second *Rak'ah* with him and when he sat in the *Tashahhud*, they would stand up and make up the *Rak'ah* they had missed, while waited for them in the *Tashahhud*, then when they had made the *Tashahhud*, he would make the *Tasleem* with them.[2]

And sometimes, he would offer two *Rak'ahs* with one of the two groups and make the *Tasleem* with them, then the second group would come and he would offer two *Rak'ahs* with them and make the *Tasleem* with them.[3] At other times, he would offer one *Rak'ah* with one of the two groups, then they would go and they would not make up anything and the second group would come and he would offer a *Rak'ah* with them and they would not make up anything. So he would have offered two *Rak'ahs* and they would have offered one *Rak'ah* each.[4] It is permissible to offer the prayer in all of these ways.

Ahmad said: "Six or seven ways have been narrated regarding it (i.e. the fear prayer) and all of them are permissible." And it is apparent from this that he ﷺ permitted each group to pray one *Rak'ah* and not to make up anything and this was the way of Jabir, Ibn 'Abbas, Tawûs, Mujahid, Al-Hasan, Qatadah, Al-Hakim and Ishaq.

---

[1] Narrated by Al-Bukhari, At-Tirmidhi, Abu Dawûd and An-Nasa'i.

[2] Narrated by Muslim, Abu Dawûd and Malik in *'Al-Muwatta'*.

[3] Narrated by An-Nasa'i and Ad-Daraqutni.

[4] Narrated by An-Nasa'i, Ahmad, At-Tahawi and Al-Hakim, who declared it authentic and Az-Zahabi confirmed this.

Other descriptions have been narrated, but all of them return to these. Some of them have mentioned that there are ten and Ibn Hazm mentioned fifteen descriptions, but the correct forms are those which we have mentioned and whenever those people noted a difference among the narrators in a narrative, they would declare it to be a form practised by the Prophet ﷺ.

Chapter

Regarding His ﷺ Guidance in *Zakah*

His guidance was the most perfect regarding the timing of it, the amount of it, (the *Nisab*)[1] and upon whom it is incumbent and upon what it may be spent. And he kept in mind the interests of both the owners of the wealth and the poor and needy. And Allâh has made it a means of purification for both the wealth and its owner and he restricted the blessing of it to the rich and the blessing of the wealth of those who give *Zakah* does not cease; indeed, Allâh preserves it and increases it.

And He has made *Zakah* incumbent upon four types of wealth, which account for most of the wealth circulating among the people and their need for them is indispensable.

The First: Plants and fruits.

The Second: Cattle: Camels, cows and sheep.

The Third: The two precious metals which are the mainstay of the world's economy and they are: Gold and silver.

The Fourth: Trading goods in all their different forms.

He has made it incumbent every year and He has made the *Hawl*[2] of fruits and crops when they become mature and ripe and nothing could be fairer than this, since, if it were obligatory every month or every Friday, it would be prejudicial to the owners of the wealth, while if it were only obligatory once in a lifetime, it would be

---

[1] *Nisab*: The minimum amount of wealth or property which makes one liable to pay *Zakah*.

[2] *Hawl*: The minimum period of time after which *Zakah* becomes due upon property.

prejudicial to the poor and needy. He has also made the rates of *Zakah* different according to the effort put into earning the wealth, for He has made one fifth incumbent upon the whole of the wealth which a person finds – and that is buried treasure *(Rikaz)*[1] and it is not deemed that there is any *Hawl* for it. And He has made the payment of half of it, i.e. one tenth, for that which requires effort to acquire it; and that is with regard to fruits and crops which grow unaided and whice irrigation is undertaken by Allâh, without any effort on the part of the slave. And He has made the payment of half of one tenth for produce whose irrigation is undertaken by the slave, and which requires effort to irrigate, or which is watered by irrigation wheels or sprinklers or the like. And he has made incumbent a half of that, i.e. a quarter of one tenth on wealth whose growth depends upon work on the part of the owner of the wealth, which is sometimes connected with travel through the land, or sometimes management, or sometimes waiting (for income). Since charity is not due upon all forms of property, He has fixed *Nusub*[2] for those forms of wealth upon which *Zakah* is due which are not injurious to the owners of the wealth and which are shared by the poor and needy: He fixed for silver two hundred *Dirhams*[3] and for gold twenty *Mithqals*[4] For grains and fruits, it is five *Wasqs* – and that is five loads of the Arabian camel.[5] For sheep, it is forty sheep, for cows, it is thirty cows and for camels, it is five camels. However if the *Nisab* does not necessitate *Muwasah*[6] from the same species of animal, the owner is obliged to pay one sheep. And if the five is repeated five times and the number of camels reaches twenty-five, the *Nisab* due is one of them.[7] Also, He has fixed the ages of these obligatory animals in accordance with

---

[1] Narrated by Al-Bukhari, Muslim, At-Tirmidhi, Abu Dawûd, An-Nasa'i and Malik.

[2] *Nusub*: Plural of *Nisab*.

[3] Narrated by At-Tirmidhi, Abu Dawûd and Ibn Majah.

[4] *Mithqal*: A measure of gold equivalent to a gold *Deenar*.

[5] Narrated by Al-Bukhari, Muslim and Malik.

[6] *Muwasah*: Charity given by the rich to the poor, which does not cause hardship to either of them.

[7] For each five camels up to twenty-five, one sheep must be given.

their increase or decrease and according to the greatness or smallness of their numbers, such as *Ibn Makhadh* and *Bint Makhadh*[1] and above that, *Ibn Labûn* and *Bint labûn*[2] and above that, *Al-Hiqq* and *Al-Hiqqah*[3] and above that *Al-Jaza'* and *Al-Jaza'ah*[4] and the more the number of camels increases, the greater the age – up to the end, after which, He has made the increase in the number which must be given in accordance with the number of the animals owned. So His Wisdom necessitates that He designate a fixed amount on property which is liable to *Muwasah*, which does not cause hardship to the owner and which is sufficient for the poor and needy. And it happens that injustice is perpetrated by the two parties: The rich person when he refuses to pay what is obligatory for him and the recipient when he takes what he does not deserve, which results in great harm from the two parties to the poor and needy.[5]

And Allâh, Most High has assumed the Responsibility Himself for the division of charity and He has divided it into eight categories, all of which fall under two types:

The First: Those who take what they need and they take in accordance with the severity or weakness of their need, or the greatness or smallness of the amount; and they are the poor and needy, for the manumission of slaves and the wayfarers.

The Second: Those who take from it in order to benefit (others) thereby; and they are those whose work it is to collect it, distribute it etc., those whose hearts are inclined towards Islam, the debtors, in order to resolve disputes and the warriors who fight in Allâh's Cause. If the one who takes it is not in need and does not benefit the Muslims with it, then he has no share in *Zakah*.

---

[1] *Ibn Makhadh* and *Bint Makhadh*: A male and female camel which is one year old.

[2] *Ibn Labûn* and *Bint Labûn*: A male and female camel which is two years old.

[3] *Al-Hiqq* and *Al-Hiqqah*: A male and female came which is three years old.

[4] *Al-Jaza'* and *Al-Jaza'ah*: A male and female camel which is four years old.

[5] This is the case with many people and it is corruption which causes injustice.

Chapter

If he ﷺ knew that a man had a right to it, he would give him and if he was asked for it by those whose circumstances he did not know, he would give him after informing him that the rich have no share in it, nor does the strong person who is able to earn a living.[1]

It was a part of his guidance to distribute it among those who had a right to it in the country in which it was collected, and anything which remained was brought to him and he ﷺ would distribute it personally. For this reason, he used to send his collectors to the countryside and he would not send them to the towns and villages; indeed, he ordered Mu'adh ﷺ to take it from the wealthy in Yemen and to give it to their poor.[2]

It was not a part of his guidance to send his collectors except to those who clearly had property, such as cattle, crops and fruits; and he used to send the assessor to assess the amount of dates held by the owners of the date-palms (and to the owners of the orchards to assess their fruit-trees)[3] and to estimate how many *Wasqs* they would yield and then calculate accordingly how much *Zakah* was incumbent upon them.[4] And he would order the assessor to leave for them a third or a quarter and not to assess it, due to the unforeseen disasters which may afflict the date-palms.[5] The purpose of this assessment was to estimate the amount of *Zakah* before the yield was eaten or distributed and so that their owners could dispose of them as they wished and they could set aside the amount which had been fixed for *Zakah*.

---

[1] Narrated by Muslim, Abu Dawûd and An-Nasa'i.
[2] Narrated by Ibn Majah.
[3] This addition is not found in the original complete 'Zad Al-Maad'.
[4] Narrated by Ash-Shafi'i in his 'Musnad' and by At-Tirmidhi, Ibn Majah, Abu Dawûd and Al-Baihaqi.
[5] Narrated by the compilers of the 'Sunan'.

It was not part of his guidance to take *Zakah* from horses, nor from slaves, nor mules, nor donkeys, nor vegetables, nor melon patches, nor cucumber patches, nor fruits which cannot be stored or measured by capacity – except grapes and dates – and he did not distinguish between fresh ones and dried ones. And if a man came to him with *Zakah* money, he would supplicate for him, and sometimes, he would say:

«اللَّهُمَّ بَارِكْ فِيهِ وَفِي إِبِلِهِ»

"Allâhumma, Barik Feehi Wa Fee Iblihi"[1]

"Oh, Allâh! Bless him and bless his camels."

And at other times, he would say:

«اللَّهُمَّ صَلِّ عَلَيْهِ»

"Allâhumma, Salli 'Alaihi"

"Oh, Allâh! Bless him."[2]

It was not part of his guidance to take the person's most valuable possessions, but those of medium quality. And he prohibited the one who gives *Sadaqah* (i.e. *Zakah*) from purchasing that which he had given,[3] but he permitted the wealthy person to eat from his *Zakah*, if it was given to him by the poor person who had received it.[4] And sometimes, he would borrow against *Sadaqah* (i.e. *Zakah*), when there was some benefit for the Muslims in doing so and he would mark the camels of *Sadaqah* with his own hand and if something unforeseen happened, he would borrow the *Sadaqah* animals from their owners, as he once did with two years' *Sadaqah*.[5]

And he declared *Zakah Al-Fitr* to be incumbent upon the Muslim and upon those whom he provides for, including the children and adults –

---

[1] Narrated by A-Nasa'i, on the authority of Wa'il Ibn Hajr ﷺ.

[2] Narrated by Al-Bukhari, Muslim and Abu Dawûd.

[3] Narrated by Al-Bukhari, Muslim and Malik.

[4] Narrated by Al-Bukhari, Muslim, Ahmad and Malik.

[5] Narrated by the compilers of the *'Sunan'* except An-Nasa'i, Ahmad, Ad-Daraqutni and Al-Baihaqi.

a *Sa'*[1] of dates, barley, cottage cheese or raisins;[2] and it has been reported from him that he permitted a *Sa'* of flour;[3] and it has been reported from him that he permitted half a *Sa'* of wheat,[4] in place of a *sa'* of these other things. This was reported by Abu Dawûd and in the *'Saheehayn'*, it was said that it was Mu'awiyah ﷺ who fixed this.

It was a part of his guidance to pay it before the *'Eed* prayer; and in the *'Saheehayn'*, it is reported on the authority of Ibn 'Umar ﷺ that he said: "The Messenger of Allâh ﷺ ordered us to pay *Zakah Al-Fitr* before the people went out to the prayer." And in the *'Sunan'*, it is reported from him that he said:

«مَنْ أَدَّاهَا قَبْلَ الصَّلَاةِ، فَهِيَ زَكَاةٌ مَقْبُولَةٌ، وَمَنْ أَدَّاهَا بَعْدَ الصَّلَاةِ، فَهِيَ صَدَقَةٌ مِنَ الصَّدَقَاتِ»

"Whoever gave it before the prayer, it will be an accepted *Zakah* for him, while whoever gave it after the prayer, it would be simply a voluntary charity for him ."

According to these two *Hadeeths*, it is not permissible to delay it until after the *'Eed* prayer and when the people leave the prayer, the opportunity to give it is lost. And this is correct. Similar to this is arranging the slaughter of the sacrificial animal after the *Imam* has prayed, not at the time of the prayer, and whoever slaughters before the prayer of the *Imam*, his slaughter will simply be mutton.

And it was a part of his guidance to favour the poor with it, but he did not distribute it among the eight categories (mentioned in the Qur'ân)[5] nor did any of his Companions ﷺ did so after him.

---

[1] *Sa'*: Approximately three kilograms.

[2] Narrated by Al-Bukhari, Muslim and Malik.

[3] Narrated by An-Nasa'i and Abu Dawûd.

[4] Narrated by Abu Dawûd and An-Nasa'i.

[5] See *Sûrah At-Tawbah* 9:60.

Regarding His ﷺ Guidance in Voluntary Charity (*Sadaqah At-Tatawwu'*)

He was the greatest of the people in giving charity with whatever was in his hands and he did not overestimate the value of anything which Allâh gave him, nor did he underestimate it (i.e. nothing in his possession was considered to much or too little by him to be given in charity). If anyone asked him for something, he would give it to him, whether it was little or much and his happiness and joy in giving were greater than that of the receiver!. And when a person in need submitted his case to him, he would give preference to his needs over his own, sometimes with his food and sometimes with his clothes.

His giving and charity were of different types: Sometimes, it took the form of a gift, sometimes charity and sometimes a grant; and sometimes, he would buy something and then give it to the seller along with its price. At other times, he would borrow something and then return more than he had borrowed. He would accept a gift and in return, he would give something of greater value,[1] out of kindness and in order to express all diverse forms of charitable deeds to the utmost of his ability. His benevolence was expressed with his property, his actions and his words. He would give whatever he had, he would order the giving of charity and he would encourage it, so that if a miserly person saw him, his behaviour would call upon him to be giving.

Anyone who associated with him could not help but be kind and generous. For this reason, he was the most open-hearted of people and the finest soul among them; for charity and righteous deeds have

---
[1] Narrated by Al-Bukhari.

an amazing ability to open the heart – and this was in addition to the things by which Allâh had distinguished him, such as His opening his heart by the Message, its special characteristics and its consequences and the opening of his heart to compassion and the removal of Satan's portion (i.e. influence) from it.

And the greatest cause of open-heartedness is monotheism, *Tawheed*; and in accordance with its completeness, its strength and its increase, a person's heart will be opened; Allâh, Most High says:[1]

$$﴿أَفَمَن شَرَحَ ٱللَّهُ صَدْرَهُ لِلْإِسْلَـٰمِ فَهُوَ عَلَىٰ نُورٍ مِّن رَّبِّهِۦ﴾$$

"Is he whose breast Allâh has opened to Islam, so that he is in light from his Lord (as he who is a non-Muslim)?"

$$﴿فَمَن يُرِدِ ٱللَّهُ أَن يَهْدِيَهُ يَشْرَحْ صَدْرَهُ لِلْإِسْلَـٰمِ وَمَن يُرِدْ أَن يُضِلَّهُ يَجْعَلْ صَدْرَهُ ضَيِّقًا حَرَجًا﴾$$

"And whomsoever Allâh wills to guide, He opens his breast to Islam; and whomsoever He wills to send astray, He makes his breast closed and constricted."[2]

Another cause is the Light which Allâh places in the heart, and that is the Light of Faith (*Iman*). It is reported in 'Sunan At-Tirmidhi' in a *Marfû'* form:

$$«إِذَا دَخَلَ النُّورُ الْقَلْبَ انْفَسَحَ وانْشَرَحَ»$$

"When the Light enters the heart, it is expanded and opened."[3]

Another cause is knowledge, for it opens the heart and expands it;

---

[1] *Sûrah Az-Zumar* 39:22

[2] *Sûrah Al-An'am* 6:125

[3] According to Shu'aib and 'Abdul Qadir Al-Arna'ût, who checked the *Ahadeeth* of the full version of 'Zad Al-Ma'ad', it was not narrated by At-Tirmidhi, as Ibn Al-Qayyim states, but by At-Tabari, on the authority of Ibn Mas'ood ﷺ and it was mentioned by As-Suyûti in 'Ad-Darr Al-Manthûr' and by Ibn Katheer, who related it from Ibn Abi Hatim and Ibn Jareer (At-Tabari). Some of its chains of narrators are connected (*Muttasil*) and some of them are broken (*Mursal*) and they all strengthen each other.

but this is not true for all knowledge – only for that which we have inherited from the Prophet 鑑.

Still another cause is turning in repentance to Allâh and loving Him with all one's heart. And love has an amazing effect in opening the heart and in bringing about goodness of the soul. And the more love for Him grows stronger, the more the heart is opened and it is not straitened except by the idle ones.

And another cause is being constant in remembrance of Allâh, for *Dhikr* has an amazing effect in opening the heart.

Also among them is acting righteously (*Ihsan*) towards all created beings and benefitting them to the best of one's ability, through one's wealth and status and by physically helping them with all sorts of righteous deeds.

As for spiritual happiness and bliss, it is forbidden to every coward, as it is forbidden to every miser and every person who turns away from Allâh, unmindful of remembrance of Him and ignorant of Him and His Religion and whose heart is attached to other than Him; and no heed should be paid to the opening of the heart of such a person due to something which befalls him, nor to the anguish of his heart caused by some mishap befalling him for verily, the things which affect the heart are removed by removing their causes (i.e. if happiness is dependent on some material thing, then the removal of that material thing will cause unhappiness); what is relied upon is the quality of the heart that makes it open or straitened for it is the measure of the heart.

Another cause – indeed, the greatest of them – is the removal of corruption in the heart caused by reprehensible characteristics.

And also among them is abandoning looking into undesirable things, vain speech, listening to undesirable things, mixing with undesirable people, eating bad things and sleeping excessively.

Regarding His ﷺ Guidance in Fasting

Since the intention behind fasting is to restrain oneself from desires in order to prepare oneself for seeking that wherein lies the utmost happiness and the acceptance of that which purifies the heart and reduces the sharpness of hunger and thirst and reminds one of the hunger felt by the needy and narrows the courses of Satan by narrowing the courses of food and drink. It is the bridle of *Al-Muttaqûn*[1] the shield of the warriors and the (spiritual) exercise of the righteous, who are near to Allâh. And out of all acts, it is for the Lord of the worlds, for the fasting person does not do anything; he only refrains from following his desire – and that is abandoning the things which he loves for love of Allâh and it is a secret between the slave and his Lord, for the slaves might observe one abstaining from the things which clearly break the fast, but as for him abstaining from them for the sake of the One Whom he worships, that is something that mankind cannot see and that is the reality of fasting.

Fasting has an amazing effect on protecting the limbs (from sin) and the internal urges from attraction to corrupting elements and in removing the harmful substances from the body which prevent it from attaining good health. It is one of the greatest forces in helping one to achieve *Taqwa*,[2] as Allâh, Most High says:

$$﴿يَٰٓأَيُّهَا ٱلَّذِينَ ءَامَنُوا۟ كُتِبَ عَلَيْكُمُ ٱلصِّيَامُ كَمَا كُتِبَ عَلَى ٱلَّذِينَ مِن قَبْلِكُمْ لَعَلَّكُمْ تَتَّقُونَ﴾$$

"O you who believe! Observing *As-Saum* (the fasting) is

---

[1] *Al-Muttaqûn*: The pious and righteous, who fear Allâh much.
[2] *Taqwa*: Fear of Allâh, piety, righteousness.

prescribed for you as it was prescribed for those before you, that you may become *Al-Muttaqûn* (the pious)."[1]

And the Prophet 鑾 ordered those whose desire for marriage is intense, but who are unable to do so, to fast and he declared it to be a means of controlling these desires.[2]

The guidance of the Prophet 鑾 was the most perfect of guidance and the greatest in achieving the goal of fasting and the easiest for human beings to follow. And since weaning people away from their desires and the things to which they are accustomed is one of the most difficult things, the injunction to fast was delayed until after the *Hijrah*;[3] and at first its obligation was in the form of a choice between fasting and feeding a needy person for each day, then fasting was made compulsory and feeding a needy person was granted for the old man and the woman, if they are unable to bear fasting. And it was permitted for the sick person and the traveller to break their fast and to make up for it; likewise, it was permitted for the pregnant woman and the breast-feeding woman, if they fear for their health. And if they fear for the safety of their children, then in addition to making up for the fast, they must feed a needy person for each day.[4] This is because their breaking the fast is not due to fear of illness, but it is done in spite of the woman being in good health and so she must feed a needy person, as was the case with a person who broke his fast in the early days of Islam.

It was a part of his guidance 鑾 in the month of Ramadan to perform many acts of worship of various types, and Gabriel (peace be upon him) used to go over the Qur'ân with him in the month of Ramadan. He also used to perform many acts of charity and benevolence, recite the Qur'ân and pray, mention Allâh's Name (*Dhikr*) and perform *I'tikaf*.[5] He used to favor Ramadan with more acts of worship than

---

[1] *Sûrah Al-Baqarah* 2:183

[2] Narrated by Al-Bukhari, Muslim, At-Tirmidhi, Abu Dawûd and An-Nasa'i.

[3] *Hijrah*: The migration of the Prophet 鑾 and his Companions 鑾 from the persecution of Makkah to the freedom and security of Al-Madinah.

[4] Narrated by the compilers of the '*Sunan*' and Ahmad, At-Tahawi and At-Tabari.

[5] *I'tikaf*: Seclusion in the mosque during the last ten days of Ramadan for the purpose of devoting oneself to the worship of Allâh, Most High.

other times. So that he would sometimes fast continuously for two days or more without breaking the fast (*Al-Wisal*), in order to devote the hours of the day and night to worship. But he forbade his Companions ﷺ from practising *Al-Wisal*. They said to him: "But you practise *Al-Wisal*." He said: "I am not as you." I stay with my Lord and he sustains me."[1] He prohibited it out of compassion for his people and he permitted it up to the predawn.

---

[1] Narrated by Malik in '*Al-Muwatta*".

Chapter

It was a part of his ﷺ guidance that he would not begin fasting the month of Ramadan until he had sighted the new moon or someone testified that he had seen it. If he did not sight it and no one testified to having sighted it, he would complete thirty days of Sha'ban.[1] Then on the night of the thirtieth, if he had not sighted the new moon due to clouds, he would complete thirty days of Sha'ban and he would not fast on a day when it was cloudy, nor did he order his Companions ﷺ to do so. Instead, he ordered them to complete thirty days of Sha'ban; and this does not contradict his words:

«فَإِنْ غُمَّ عَلَيْكُمْ فَاقْدُرُوا لَهُ»

"If it is hidden from you, then calculate (when it should appear)."[2]

The Arabic word *"Qadr"* (used in the *Hadeeth*) means the estimated account and what is intended by its completion.

It was a part of his guidance to end the fast of Ramadan based upon the testimony of two persons.[3] And if two witnesses testified that they had seen it after the time for *'Eed* had gone, he would break his fast and order his Companions ﷺ to break their fast and he offered the *'Eed* prayer the next day at its time (the previous day).[4]

He used to hasten to break his fast and he encouraged his Companions ﷺ to do likewise and he used to partake of *Sahûr*[5]

---

[1] *Sha'ban*: The month preceding Ramadan.
[2] Narrated by Al-Bukhari and Muslim.
[3] Narrated by An-Nasa'i and Ahmad.
[4] Narrated by Abu Dawûd and Ahmad.
[5] *Sahûr*: A simple repast taken shortly before dawn during fasting.

and he encouraged them to do the same and he used to delay it and he would urge them to delay it. He encouraged them to break the fast with dates, or water if none were available.[1]

And he forbade the fasting person from sexual relations, raising the voice (in anger), reviling people and answering the insults of one who does so; and he ordered the one who is abused to respond by saying: "I am fasting."[2]

He traveled during Ramadan and he fasted and broke his fast and he left it to his Companions ☙ to decide which they preferred. He would order them to break their fast if they were near to the enemy, but it was not a part of his guidance to define the distance which a fasting person must travel. When the Companions ☙ started out on a journey, they would break their fast, without consideration as to whether or not they had left behind their houses; and they informed us that that was the *Sunnah* of the Prophet ﷺ.[3]

Fajr time would come upon him while he was in a state of *Janabah* due to having sexual intercourse with his wife and he would perform *Ghusl* after *Fajr* and then fast.[4] He used to kiss some of his wives when he was fasting[5] and he compared the kissing of a fasting person to rinsing the mouth with water (during ablution).[6] And it has not been authentically reported from him that he discriminated between an elderly man and a young man (in this matter).

It was a part of his guidance to waive the ruling on one who ate or drank forgetfully and he said that it was Allâh who fed him and gave him drink.[7] The things which have been authentically reported from him that nullify fasting are: Eating and drinking (intentionally),

---

[1] Narrated by At-Tirmidhi, Abu Dawûd, Ahmad and Ibn Khuzaimah.
[2] Narrated by Al-Bukhari, Muslim, the compilers of the '*Sunan*', Ahmad, Malik and Ad-Daraqutni.
[3] Narrated by At-Tirmidhi, Ad-Daraqutni and Al-Baihaqi.
[4] Narrated by Al-Bukhari, Muslim and Malik.
[5] Narrated by Al-Bukhari, Muslim and Malik.
[6] Narrated by Abu Dawûd and declared authentic by Ibn Khuzaimah, Ibn Hibban and Al-Hakim and this was confirmed by Az-Zahabi.
[7] Narrated by Al-Bukhari and At-Tirmidhi.

cupping[1] and vomiting.[2] The Qur'ân also proves that sexual intercourse invalidates fasting. Nothing authentic has been reported from him 🖼 regarding the use of kohl.

It has been authentically reported from him that he used a *Miswak* while he was fasting.[3] Imam Ahmad reported that he used to pour water on his head while he was fasting and he used to rinse his mouth (*Madmadah*) and sniff water into his nose (*Istinshaq*) while he was fasting, but he forbade the fasting person from sniffing the water up high into the nose.[4] It is not correct that he performed cupping while he was fasting;[5] Ahmad said: "It has been narrated from him that he said regarding antimony: "The fasting person should avoid it," but this is not correct; Ibn Ma'een said: "This *Hadeeth* is *Munkar*."[6]

---

[1] Narrated by Abu Dawûd, Ibn Majah, Al-Hakim, Ash-Shafi'i, At-Tahawi and Al-Baihaqi and declared authentic by Ibn Hibban and Al-Hakim.

[2] That is, if the vomiting was induced. It is reported on the authority of Abu Hurairah 🖼 that the Prophet 🖼 said: "Whoever was afflicted by vomiting, there is no need for him to make up for it; but whoever intentionally vomited, he should make up for it." (Narrated by At-Tirmidhi, Abu Dawûd, Ibn Majah and Ad-Daraqutni and declared authentic by Ibn Khuzaimah, Ibn Hibban and Al-Hakim)

[3] It is reported on the authority of 'Amir Ibn Rabee'ah 🖼 that he said: "I saw the Prophet 🖼 cleaning his teeth with *Miswak* while he was fasting more times than I can count." (Narrated by Al-Bukhari)

[4] Narrated by Abu Dawûd, Ibn Majah, An-Nasa'i, Ahmad and Ash-Shafi'i.

[5] On the contrary, it was narrated by Al-Bukhari on the authority of Ibn 'Abbas 🖼 that he said: "The Prophet 🖼 performed cupping while he was fasting."

[6] *Munkar*: Disparaged by scholars of *Hadeeth* due to the presence in its *Sanad* of a narrator deemed to have made excessive mistakes, to have been extremely careless, or to have been known as a dissolute person. Or, it was said that a *Munkar* narration is one in whose chain of narrators there is a person deemed weak who narrates something which contradicts what has been authentically reported.

He would fast so much that it would be said: "He will not break his fast," and he would break his fast until it would be said: "He will not fast."[1] He did not fast a whole month except for the month of Ramadan; and he did not fast in any month more than he did in the month of Sha'ban.[2] And he did not let any month pass without fasting in it. He used to observe fasting on Mondays and Thursdays.[3] Ibn 'Abbas 🙞 said: "The Messenger of Allâh did not leave fasting on the days of the full moon – neither when he was at home, nor when he was traveling." This was mentioned by An-Nasa'i.[4] And he used to encourage his Companions 🙞 to do likewise.[5]

As for fasting the 10th day of *Dhul Hijjah*, scholars disagree on it.[6] But as for fasting six days in Shawwal, it has been authentically reported from him ﷺ that he said:

$$ \text{«صِيَامُهَا مَعَ رَمَضَانَ يَعْدِلُ صِيَامَ الدَّهْرِ»} $$

"Fasting it along with Ramadan is equivalent (in reward) to a perpetual fast."[7]

---

[1] Narrated by Al-Bukhari.

[2] Narrated by Al-Bukhari, Muslim and Malik.

[3] Narrated by At-Tirmidhi, An-Nasa'i and Ibn Majah, on the authority of 'A'ishah 🙞.

[4] Narrated by An-Nasa'i, it contains in its chain of narrators one Ya'qûb Ibn 'Abdillah Al-Qummi, who is described by scholars of *Hadeeth* as weak: Ibn Hajr says: "Truthful, but he makes mistakes." The person who narrated from him, Ja'far Ibn Abil Mugheerah Al-Qummi is also weak; Ibn Hajr also says of him: "Truthful, but he makes mistakes."

[5] Narrated by An-Nasa'i and Ahmad.

[6] 'A'ishah 🙞 reported: "I never saw the Messenger of Allâh ﷺ fasting ten days in Dhul Hijjah.

[7] Narrated by Muslim, the compilers of the 'Sunan' (except An-Nasa'i) and Ahmad.

Regarding fasting on the day of '*Ashûra*', he used to observe fasting on that day more than any other day; and when he arrived in Al-Madinah, he found the Jews fasting on it and revering it and he said:

«نَحْنُ أَحَقُّ بِمُوسَى مِنْكُمْ»

"We have more right to Moses than you."

So he fasted it and he ordered his Companions 🙵 to do likewise.[1] That was before the fasting of Ramadan became obligatory; then when Ramadan was made obligatory, he said:

«مَنْ شَاءَ صَامَهُ وَمَنْ شَاءَ تَرَكَهُ»

"Whoever wishes may fast it and whoever wishes may leave it."[2]

It was a part of his guidance to break his fast on the Day of '*Arafah* when he was in '*Arafah*. This is confirmed from him in the '*Saheehayn*'. It has also been narrated from him that he prohibited fasting on the Day of 'Arafah for those in 'Arafah. This was narrated by the compilers of the '*Sunan*'. And it has been authentically reported from him that he said:

«صِيَامُهُ يُكَفِّرُ السَّنَةَ الْمَاضِيَةَ وَالْبَاقِيَةَ»

"Fasting it wipes out (the sins of) the previous year and the remaining year."

This was mentioned by Muslim.

It was not a part of his guidance to fast continuously; indeed, he said:

«مَنْ صَامَ الدَّهْرَ لَا صَامَ وَلَا أَفْطَرَ»

"Whoever fasted continuously has neither fasted nor broken his fast."[3]

He would visit his wives and say:

---

[1] Narrated by Al-Bukhari and Muslim.

[2] Narrated by Al-Bukhari and Muslim.

[3] Narrated by An-Nasa'i, Ibn Majah and Ahmad and authenticated by Al-Hakim and Ibn Khuzaimah.

«هَلْ عِنْدَكُمْ شَيْءٌ؟»

"Do you have anything (to eat)?"

If they said: "No," he would say:

«إِنِّي إِذَا صَائِمٌ»

"Then I am fasting."[1]

Sometimes he would intend to perform a voluntary fast, then he would break it. As for the *Hadeeth* of 'A'ishah ☙, in which it is stated that he ﷺ said to her and Hafsah ☙: "

«اقْضِيَا يَوْمًا مَكَانَهُ»

"Make up for it by fasting another day in its place,"[2]

it is a *Hadeeth* with some defect in it.[3] If he visited some people while he was fasting, he would complete his fast, as he did when he visited Umm Sulaim,[4] but he considered Umm Sulaim as his family. And it is authentically reported from him that he said:

«إِذَا دُعِيَ أَحَدُكُمْ إِلَى طَعَامٍ وَهُوَ صَائِمٌ، فَلْيَقُلْ: إِنِّي صَائِمٌ»

"If any of you is invited to eat when he is fasting, he should say: "I am fasting."[5]

And it was a part of his guidance that he disliked singling out Friday for fasting.[6]

---

[1] Narrated by Muslim, on the authority of 'A'ishah ☙.

[2] Narrated by At-Tirmidhi and Ahmad.

[3] According to Shu'aib and 'Abdul Qadir Al-Arna'ût, it was also narrated by At-Tahawi and Ibn Hibban with an authentic chain of narrators.

[4] Narrated by Al-Bukhari and Ahmad.

[5] Narrated by Muslim, Abu Dawûd, Ibn Majah, Ahmad and Ad-Darami.

[6] It is reported on the authority of Jabir Ibn 'Abdillah ☙ that the Prophet ﷺ said: "Do not fast on Friday unless you fast the day before it or the day after it as well." (Narrated by Al-Bukhari and Muslim)

Chapter

Regarding His ﷺ Guidance in *I'tikaf*

Since righteousness of the heart and its going straight upon the path which leads to Allâh, Most High is dependent upon its being totally dedicated to Allâh and completely focused on approaching Allâh – for the muddled affairs of the heart cannot be set in order except by approaching Allâh – and since excessive eating and drinking, socializing with people, sleeping and talking are things which increase the confusion in his heart and distract him in every way and prevent him from proceeding on the path to Allâh, Most High and weaken him or hinder him and stop him, the Wisdom of the Almighty, the Most Merciful necessitated that He legislate for His worshippers fasting which will remove the desire for of food and drink and empty the heart of the distraction of desires, which are obstacles to its reaching Allâh. And so He has legislated in accordance with what is beneficial, so that the worshippers might benefit thereby in this world and in the Hereafter and not be harmed by it. And He legislated *I'tikaf* for them, the purpose and spirit of which is to cause the heart to be devoted to Allâh and to cut it off from material affairs and to uccupy it with (worshipping) Him, Alone, so that his intimacy is with Allâh and not with people, which will prepare him for his intimacy with Him on the day of loneliness when he is in his grave.

And since this goal is only achieved when it is accompanied by fasting, *I'tikaf* was legislated during the best days of fasting – and they are the last ten days of Ramadan; and Allâh, Most High has not mentioned *I'tikaf* except with fasting and the Messenger of Allâh ﷺ did not perform it except while fasting. As for speech, He has legislated for the (Muslim) community that they check their tongues from all speech except that which benefits them in the Hereafter. As for excess of sleep, He has legislated the night prayer for them, which is the best form of wakefulness, with the most benign result. And it is the middle form (i.e. neither too much nor too little) of wakefulness, which benefits the heart and the body and does not prevent the worshippers from attaining his needs (i.e. working during the day), nor from spiritual exercises, nor from practising these four pillars (i.e. prayer, *Zakah*, fasting and *Hajj*). And the happiest of people are those who perform them in the manner prescribed by Muhammad ﷺ and do not deviate in the way that most people do, nor fall short in the way that those who are careless do. And we have already mentioned his guidance in fasting, the night prayer and in speech, so now we shall speak of his guidance in *I'tikaf* :

He used to perform *I'tikaf* during the last ten days of Ramadan until Allâh, the Almighty, the All-powerful caused him to die. One time, he did not perform it and so he made it up in Shawwal. And once, he performed *I'tikaf* in the first ten days of Ramadan, then in the middle and then in the last ten days. He was in search of *Lailah Al-Qadr* (the Night of Decree); then it became clear to him that it was in the last ten days and thenceforth, he continued to observe *I'tikaf* until he met his Lord, the Almighty, the All-powerful. He would order a tent and it would be erected for him in the mosque, then he would seclude himself in it for his Lord, the Almighty, the All-powerful. And when he wished to perform *I'tikaf*, he would offer the *Fajr* prayer and then enter it. On one occasion, he order it and it was erected for him, then his wives ordered their tents to be erected and so they were erected for them. When he offered the *Fajr* prayer, he saw those tents and he ordered his tent to be taken down and he left *I'tikaf* in Ramadan and offered it in the first ten days of Shawwal.[1] He used to perform *I'tikaf* every year for ten days, but in the year in which he died, he performed *I'tikaf* for twenty days; and Jibreel ﷺ, who used to recite the Qur'ân with him once a year, recited it with him twice in that year; and he also used to present the Qur'ân to him every year once, but in that year, he presented it to him twice. When he was in *I'tikaf*, he would enter his tent alone and he would not enter his house except for some human necessity and he would put his head out to

---

[1] Narrated by Al-Bukhari, on the authority of 'A'ishah ﷺ.

the house of 'A'ishah ☙ and she would comb his hair while she was menstruating;[1] and one of his wives visited him while he was in *I'tikaf* and when she got up to leave, he got up with her and accompanied her and that was at night.[2] He did not have intimate relations with his wives while he was in *I'tikaf*, neither kissing them, nor anything else. And when he made *I'tikaf*, his mattress and his bed would be put for him in the place of his seclusion.

And when leaving to fulfill some need, he might pass by a sick person on his way and he would not visit him.[3] One time, he performed *I'tikaf* in a Turkish tent and he placed at its threshold a straw mat[4] – all of this was to attain what is intended by *I'tikaf* – the opposite of what the ignorant people do, which is for the person performing *I'tikaf* to take a place big enough for ten people and a *Majlabah*[5] for visitors. This is something else and the *I'tikaf* of Prophet ﷺ is something else.

---

[1] Narrated by Al-Bukhari, Muslim and Malik.

[2] Narrated by Al-Bukhari and Muslim, on the authority of Safiyyah Bint Huyay ☙.

[3] Narrated by Abu Dawûd, this *Hadeeth* contains in its chain of narrators a man named Al-Laith Ibn Abi Sulaim Ibn Zunaim, of whom Ibn Hajr said: "He is honest, but he mixes things up a great deal and his *Hadeeth* are not clear and so he is abandoned.

[4] Narrated by Muslim, on the authority of Abu Sa'eed Al-Khudri.

[5] *Majlabah*: A cause to get.

Regarding His ﷺ Guidance
in *Hajj* and *'Umrah*

He ﷺ performed *'Umrah* four times after the migration to Al-Madinah (*Hijrah*), all of them in the month of Dhul Qa'dah.

The First: The *'Umrah* of Hudaibiyyah, in the sixth year following the Hijrah, when the pagans prevented him from entering the House (of Allâh), so he and his Companions ؓ slaughtered a camel and shaved their heads at the place where they were stopped and left their state of ihram.[1]

The Second: *'Umrah Al-Qadhiyyah* in the following year; he remained for three days and then left.

The Third: The *'Umrah* that he performed along with his *Hajj*.

The Fourth: The *'Umrah* which he performed from Al-Ji'ranah. And not a single one of his *'Umrahs* was performed by leaving Makkah, as many of the people do nowadays. All of his *'Umrahs* were performed by him upon entering Makkah; and he remained a resident of Makkah for thirteen years after the Revelation started, but it has not been transmitted from him that he performed *'Umrah* by leaving Makkah, neither did anyone ever do so during his lifetime, except 'A'ishah ؓ, because she had set out to perform *'Umrah* and then she started her menstruation and so he ﷺ ordered her to combine *Hajj* with *'Umrah* (*Qiran*) and he informed her that the requirement to perform circumambulation (*Tawaf*) and Sa'ee between As-Safa and Al-Marwah had been lifted from her *Hajj* and *'Umrah*. And she felt some

---

[1] Narrated by Al-Bukhari, on the authority of Al-Bara' ؓ and of Ibn 'Umar ؓ.

sadness in her heart upon seeing her female companions returning to perform *Hajj* and *'Umrah* separately, for they were performing *Hajj At-Tamattu'*[1] and they were not menstruating and so did not perform *Qiran* – while she was returning to perform *'Umrah* as part of her *Hajj*. So the Prophet ﷺ ordered her brother, 'Abdur-Rahman to perform *'Umrah* with her from *At-Tan'eem*, in order to conciliate her heart. All of his 'Umrahs were performed in the months of *Hajj*, in contradiction to the practice of the polytheists, for they disliked that *'Umrah* be performed during them; and this is evidence that performing *'Umrah* in the months of *Hajj* is without doubt preferable to performing it in the month of Rajab. As for performing it in the month of Ramadan, it is a matter for debate (whether it is equivalent to or better than *'Umrah* with *Hajj* or not). It has been authentically reported from him ﷺ that:

$$\text{«عُمْرَةٌ فِي رَمَضَانَ تَعْدِلُ حَجَّةً»}$$

"*Umrah* in Ramadan is equivalent (in reward) to *Hajj*."[2]

And it might be said that the Messenger of Allâh ﷺ was occupied in Ramadan with acts of worship which were more important than *'Umrah*, in addition to the fact that his not performing it was a mercy for his people, for had he done it, the people would have rushed to do so, and combining *'Umrah* with fasting would have been a hardship for them. And he used to avoid many acts which he should have performed due to fear that they would be a burden to them.

It has not been recorded from him that he performed *'Umrah* more than once in a year and there is no disagreement that he did not perform *Hajj* after the migration to Al-Madinah except once in the tenth year following the *Hijrah*. And when the obligation of *Hajj* was revealed, the Messenger of Allâh ﷺ hastened to perform it without delay, for the obligation to perform it was only revealed in the ninth or tenth year. As for the Words of Allâh, Most High:

$$\text{﴿وَأَتِمُّوا۟ ٱلْحَجَّ وَٱلْعُمْرَةَ لِلَّهِ﴾}$$

---

[1] *Hajj At-Tamattu'*: Combining *Hajj* and *'Umrah* with a break in between.
[2] Narrated by At-Tirmidhi, Ibn Majah, Ahmad and Ad-Darimi.

"And perform properly (i.e. all the ceremonies according to the ways of Prophet Muhammad ﷺ), the *Hajj* and *'Umrah* (i.e. the pilgrimage to Makkah) for Allâh."[1]

Even though they were revealed in the sixth year following the *Hijrah*, there is no enjoinment in them to perform *Hajj*, only an order to complete it and to complete *'Umrah* once they are begun.

Once he had decided to perform *Hajj*, he announced to the people that he intended to perform *Hajj* and they prepared themselves to leave with him.

Those living around Al-Madinah heard of this and they went out, desiring to perform *Hajj* with the Messenger of Allâh ﷺ and he was joined on the road by a crowd of people whose numbers cannot be estimated: They were in front of him, behind him, to his right and to his left, as far as the eye could see. He left Al-Madinah during the day, in the afternoon, with six days remaining of Dhul Qa'dah, after offering the *Zuhr* prayer of four *Rak'ahs*. And he delivered a sermon to them before that, in which he taught them about *Ihram* and its obligations and its *Sunnah* acts, after which he performed the *Zuhr* prayer, then he combed his hair, applied oil to himself, then donned his upper and lower garments. Then he departed and stopped at Dhul Hulaifah and offered the *'Asr* prayer of two *Rak'ahs*.

Then he spent the night there[2] and performed the *Maghrib*,*'Isha'*, *Fajr* and *Zuhr* prayers.[3] All of his wives were with him and he went round (i.e. had sexual relations with) all of them that night.[4] Then when he wished to enter the state of *Ihram*, he performed a second *Ghusl* for *Ihram* (in addition to the *Ghusl* which he had performed due to having intimate relations with his wives),[5] then 'A'ishah ﭪ scented his head and body with her own hand, using *Zareerah*[6] and

---

[1] *Sûrah Al-Baqarah* 2:196.
[2] Narrated by Al-Bukhari, on the authority of Anas ﭪ.
[3] Narrated by An-Nasa'i on the authority of Anas ﭪ.
[4] Narrated by Al-Bukhari and Muslim on the authority of 'A'ishah ﭪ.
[5] Narrated by At-Tirmidhi, who declared it to be *Hasan*, Ad-Darimi and Al-Baihaqi.
[6] *Zareerah*: A scented powder.

perfume containing musk, until the gleaming of musk could be seen in the parting of his hair and in his beard,[1] then he continued it and he did not wash it. After that, he donned his upper and lower garments and offered the *Zuhr* prayer of two *Rak'ahs*, then he made the *Ihlal*[2] to perform *Hajj* and *'Umrah* in his prayer place. It has not been transmitted from him that he performed a two *Rak'ah* prayer for entering the state of *Ihram*.[3] Before assuming *Ihram*, he hung two shoes around the neck of his camel and marked it on its right side, cutting the side of its hump and then removing the blood from it.[4]

The reason we said that he 鐃 assumed *Ihram* for *Hajj Al-Qiran* was due to more than twenty clear and authentic *Hadeeths* to that effect. The Messenger of Allâh 鐃 soaked his head with *Ghisl*, which is used for washing the head and it is made from the marshmallow flower or the like and which causes the hair to stick, so that it does not fall down. He made the *Ihlal* to perform *Hajj* in his prayer place and mounted his she-camel and made the *Ihlal* again when it stood up with him and again when he looked down upon the mountain known as Al-Baida'.[5] Sometimes, he would make the *Ihlal* to perform *Hajj* and *'Umrah* and sometimes, he would make the *Ihlal* to perform *Hajj* (only); this is because *'Umrah* is a part of *Hajj*. Due to this, it was said that he performed *Hajj Al-Qiran*, and it was said that he performed *Hajj At-Tamattu'* and that he performed *Hajj Al-Ifrad*[6] As regards the saying of Ibn Hazm: "That was just before the *Zuhr* prayer," it is surmise on his part; what has been recorded from him is that he made the intention after *Zuhr*, and no one has ever said that he assumed *Ihram* before *Zuhr*, so I do not know from where he got this.

---

[1] Narrated by Al-Bukhari and Muslim, on the authority of 'A'ishah 鐃.

[2] *Ihlal*: To say: *"Labbaikallahumma Bil Hajji Wal-'Umrah"* (Oh, Allâh! I respond to Your Call with *Hajj* and *'Umrah*)

[3] As for the *Hadeeth* narrated by Muslim, on the authority of 'Abdullah Ibn 'Umar 鐃, in which he said: "The Messenger of Allâh 鐃 used to perform two *Rak'ahs* in Dhul –Hulaifah," what is meant by it is the two *Rak'ahs* of *Zuhr*.

[4] Narrated by Muslim, on the authority of Ibn 'Abbas 鐃.

[5] Narrated by Abu Dawûd, on the authority of Sa'd Ibn Abi Waqqas 鐃 and by Ahmad, on the authority of 'Abdulllah Ibn 'Abbas 鐃.

[6] *Hajj Al-Ifrad*: Performing only *Hajj*, without *'Umrah*.

Then he made the *Talbiyyah*, saying:

«لَبَّيْكَ اللَّهُمَّ لَبَّيْكَ، لَا شَرِيكَ لَكَ لَبَّيْكَ، إِنَّ الْحَمْدَ وَالنِّعْمَةَ لَكَ وَالْمُلْكَ، لَا شَرِيكَ لَكَ»

"Labbaik Allaahumma Labbaik, Labbaika Laa Shareeka Laka Labbaik, Innal-Hamda Wan-Ni'mata Laka Wal-Mulka, Laa Shareeka Lak"

"Oh, Allâh! I respond to Your call! I respond to Your call! I respond to Your call! You have no partners, I respond to Your call! Verily, all praise and thanks are due to You and all Grace is Yours, as is the Dominion! You have no partners."

And he raised his voice during this *Talbiyyah* until his Companions ﷺ heard it. He went to *Hajj* on a riding camel, not on a litter and his baggage was beneath it. Scholars have disagreed as to whether or not it is permissible for a person in the state of *Ihram* to ride in a litter, a sedan or the like.

At the time of assuming *Ihram*, the Prophet ﷺ allowed them to choose which of the three types of *Hajj* they wished to perform, then when they were close to Makkah, he advised them to cancel *Hajj* and *Qiran* in favour of *'Umrah* for those who did not have a sacrificial animal with them. Then he ordered them to do that when they were at Al-Marwah.

Asma' Bint 'Umais ﷺ gave birth to Muhammad Ibn Abi Bakr ﷺ on the journey and so the Prophet ﷺ ordered her to perform *Ghusl* and to bandage her private parts, assume her *Ihram* and make the *Ihlal* to perform *Hajj*.[1]

And in this *Hadeeth* there is a permission for the person in a state of *Ihram* to perform *Ghusl* and it informs us that the menstruating women may perform *Ghusl* and that a menstruating woman's *Ihram* is valid.

Then he proceeded, making the *Talbiyyah* which we mentioned earlier as he went and the people did so with him, adding to it and subtracting from it – and he approved of what they said.[2]

---

[1] Narrated by Muslim, Abu Dawûd and Ibn Majah.
[2] Narrated by Al-Bukhari, Muslim, Malik and others.

When they reached Ar-Rawha', they saw a wounded wild ass and he 🕮 said:

$$«دَعُوهُ، فَإِنَّهُ يُوشِكُ أَنْ يَأْتِيَ صَاحِبُهُ»$$

"Leave it, for its owner will be along shortly."

The owner then appeared and he said: "Oh, Messenger of Allâh! You may do with it as you wish." So the Messenger of Allâh 🕮 told Abu Bakr 🕮 to divide it up among the company.[1] In this *Hadeeth* there is a permission for the person in a sate of *Ihram* to eat game whose meat is lawful, if it was not killed for him; and it proves that the ownership of game is proven by evidence.

Then they continued until they came to the well of Al-Uthabah, which was between Ar-Ruwaythah and Al-'Arj (on the road from Makkah to Al-Madinah), where they unexpectedly came upon a gazelle with an arrow in it, lying on its side in some shade. He claimed that the Messenger of Allâh, may Allâh bless him and grant him peace, told someone to stand by it to make sure no one disturbed it until everyone had passed by.[2]

Then they continued on until they reached Al-'Arj, and the luggage of the Prophet 🕮 and Abu Bakr 🕮 were both held by a servant boy of Abu Bakr 🕮. The boy arrived, but he did not have the camel with him. Abu Bakr 🕮 said to him: "Where is your camel?" He said: "I lost it yesterday." Abu Bakr 🕮 said: "One camel and you lost it!" He began to beat him and the Messenger of Allâh 🕮 was smiling and saying:

$$«انْظُرُوا إِلَى هَذَا الْمُحْرِمِ مَا يَصْنَعُ»$$

"Look at this man in a state of *Ihram*, how he is behaving."[3]

Then they went on until they reached Al-Abwa' and As-Sa'b Ibn Jaththamah presented the Prophet 🕮 with a wild ass as a gift, but he was unable to accept it and he returned it. (Seeing the signs of disappointment on the man's face) the Prophet 🕮 said:

---

[1] Narrated by Imam Malik, in *'Al-Muwatta"*, on the authority of Al-Bahzi.

[2] Narrated by Imam Malik in *'Al-Muwatta"*, on the authority of Al-Bahzi.

[3] Narrated by Abu Dawûd, Ibn Majah and Ahmad.

«إِنَّا لَمْ نَرُدَّهُ عَلَيْكَ إِلَّا أَنَّا حُرُمٌ»

"We would not return it except for the fact that we are in a state of *Ihram*."[1]

When they passed by Wadi 'Usfan, the Prophet ﷺ said:

«يَا أَبَا بَكْرٍ أَيُّ وَادٍ هَذَا؟»

"O, Abu Bakr! Which valley (i.e. *Wadi*) is this?"

He said: "Wadi 'Usfan." The Prophet ﷺ said:

«لَقَدْ مَرَّ بِهِ هُودٌ وَصَالِحٌ عَلَى بِكْرَيْنِ أَحْمَرَيْنِ خُطُمُهُمَا اللِّيفُ،
وَأُزْرُهُمَا الْعَبَاءُ، وَأَرْدِيَتُهُمَا النِّمَارُ يُلَبُّونَ يَحُجُّونَ الْبَيْتَ الْعَتِيقَ»

"Prophets Hûd and Salih ﷺ passed through it on two red camels; their reins were made of palm fibre, their upper garments were woolen wraps and their lower garments were of striped material and they were making the *Talbiyyah* on their way to perform *Hajj* to the Ancient House (i.e. the House of Allâh in Makkah)."[2]

When they reached Sarif, 'A'ishah ﷺ began menstruating; and at Sarif, the Prophet ﷺ said:

«مَنْ لَمْ يَكُنْ مَعَهُ هَدْيٌ، فَأَحَبَّ أَنْ يَجْعَلَهَا عُمْرَةً، فَلْيَفْعَلْ، وَمَنْ
كَانَ مَعَهُ هَدْيٌ فَلَا»

"Anyone who has not brought a sacrificial animal and would like to make his pilgrimage *'Umrah*, (i.e. to perform *Hajj At-Tamattu'*) he should do so and anyone who has with him a sacrificial animal should not do so (i.e. he should perform *Hajj Al-Qiran*)."

This is another level, above that of the choice which he gave them at

---

[1] Narrated by Al-Bukhari, Muslim, An-Nasa'i, Ahmad and Malik.

[2] Narrated by Ahmad in his '*Musnad*', on the authority of Ibn 'Abbas ﷺ, it contains in its chain of narrators one Zam'ah Ibn Salih, who is considered weak by scholars of *Hadeeth*, including Ahmad himself, Yahya Ibn Ma'een and Al-Bukhari.

the *Meeqat* (i.e. Dhul Hulaifah). And when they were in Makkah, he made a definite order that whoever did not have a sacrificial animal with him must perform *'Umrah* and leave his state of *Ihram* (until it was time to perform *Hajj*) while whoever had a sacrificial should remain in his state of *Ihram* – and nothing has ever abrogated this; indeed, Suraqah Ibn Malik ﷺ asked him about this *'Umrah* which he had ordered them to perform: "Is it for this year only, or is it for all time?" He replied: "Indeed, it is for all time."[1]

Then they continued until the Prophet (ﷺ) descended at Dhu Tuwa, which is known today as Abar Az-Zahir and he stayed there on a Sunday night when four days of Dhul Hijjah had passed and he offered the *Fajr* prayer there. Then he performed *Ghusl* on that day and went on to Makkah, entering it during the day from above by way of the high mountain pass which overlooks Al-Hajûn – when he was in *'Umrah*, he would enter from below – and then he continued until he entered the mosque, and that was before noon. At-Tabari has reported that he (ﷺ) entered through the gate known as *Bab 'Abdi Manaf*, which is now known as *Bab Bani Shaibah*. Ahmad reported that when he entered a place in Dar Ya'la, he faced towards the House (of Allâh) and supplicated. At-Tabari said that when he looked towards the House (of Allâh), he said:

«اللَّهُمَّ زِدْ هَذَا الْبَيْتَ تَشْرِيفًا وَتَعْظِيمًا وَتَكْرِيمًا وَمَهَابَةً»

"Allâhumma, Zid Hadhal-Baita Tashreefan, Wa Ta'zeeman Wa Takreeman Wa Mahabatan"

"Oh, Allâh! Increase this House in honour, greatness, reverence and dignity."

And it has been reported from him ﷺ that when he saw it, he would raise his hands, make *Takbeer* and say:

«اللَّهُمَّ أَنْتَ السَّلَامُ وَمِنْكَ السَّلَامُ، حَيِّنَا رَبَّنَا بِالسَّلَامِ، اللَّهُمَّ زِدْ هَذَا الْبَيْتَ تَشْرِيفًا وَتَعْظِيمًا، وَتَكْرِيمًا وَمَهَابَةً، وَزِدْ مَنْ حَجَّهُ أَوِ اعْتَمَرَهُ تَكْرِيمًا وَتَشْرِيفًا وَتَعْظِيمًا وَبِرًّا»

---

[1] Narrated by Al-Bukhari, Ahmad and Abu Dawûd.

"Allâhumma, Antas-Salamu Wa Minkas-Salamu, Hayyana Rabbana Bis-Salami, Allâhumma, Zid Hadhal-Baita Tashreefan, Wa Ta'zeeman Wa Takreeman Wa Mahabatan, Wa Zid Man Hajjahu Awi'tamarahu Takreeman Wa Tashreefan Wa Ta'zeeman Wa Birran"

"Oh, Allâh! You are Peace and from You comes Peace. Greet us with Peace. Oh, Allâh! Increase this House in honour, greatness, reverence and dignity and increase whoever perform *Hajj* or *'Umrah* to it in honour, greatness, reverence and dignity)." But it is *Mursal.*[1]

When he entered the Mosque, he headed towards the House (of Allâh) and he did not offer a prayer of salutation to the Mosque, because the prayer of salutation to the Sacred Mosque is circumambulation of the *Ka'bah* (*Tawaf*). When he drew level with the Black Stone, he touched it, but he did not push and jostle in order to do so and he did not pass by and head towards the direction of the Yemeni Corner, nor did he raise his hands and say: "I have made the intention by my *Tawaf* this week to do such-and-such," nor did he begin it by making *Takbeer* as those who have no knowledge to do. Neither did he touch the Black Stone with his whole body, then turn away from it and place it on his right side; rather, he would face it and touch it, then turn right; and he did not supplicate at the door, nor under the *Meedab,*[2] nor behind the *Ka'bah*, nor at its corners, nor did he specify any special *Dhikr* when performing *Tawaf*. What has been recorded from him is that he said between the two corners:

$$\text{﴿رَبَّنَآ ءَاتِنَا فِى ٱلدُّنْيَا حَسَنَةً وَفِى ٱلْأَخِرَةِ حَسَنَةً وَقِنَا عَذَابَ ٱلنَّارِ﴾}$$

"Our Lord! Give us in this world that which is good and in the Hereafter that which is good, and save us from the torment of the Fire!"[3]

---

[1] *Mursal*: A chain of narrators in which the Companion's name is not mentioned, in which a *Tabi'i* reports some saying or action of the Prophet 🕌; such a narration is weak, since the *Tabi'i* could not have seen the Prophet 🕌 himself.

[2] *Meedab*: Drain.

[3] *Sûrah Al-Baqarah* 2:201

In his first three circuits, he trotted around the *Ka'bah*, taking short steps and wrapped his upper garment around him so that it was around one shoulder (the left) and revealed the other (i.e. the right) shoulder.[1] And whenever he drew level with the Black Stone, he pointed towards it and touched it with his *Mihjan*[2] and kissed the *Mihjan* – and a *Mihjan* is a stick with a curved head.

It has been confirmed from him ﷺ that he touched the Yemeni Corner, but it has not been confirmed from him ﷺ that he kissed it, nor that he kissed his hand when touching it. But it has been confirmed from him ﷺ that he kissed the black stone, that he touched it with his hand and that he touched it with his *Mihjan*; these are three descriptions (of his actions regarding the Black Stone); and At-Tabari has reported, with a good *Isnad*, that when he touched the Corner, he said:

$$ \text{«بِسْمِ اللهِ وَاللهُ أَكْبَرُ»} $$

"Bismillahi Wallahu Akbar"

"In the Name of Allâh and Allâh is Most Great",[3]

and each time he reached the Black Stone, he said:

$$ \text{«اللهُ أَكْبَرُ»} $$

"Allâhu Akbar"[4]

and he did not touch or handle any corner except the two Yemeni Corners.

When he had completed his *Tawaf*, he went behind *Maqam Ibraheem*,[5] and recited:

---

[1] Narrated by Abu Dawûd and Ahmad.

[2] According to Muslim, Abu Dawûd, An-Nasa'i and Ibn Majah, this was in the Farewell Pilgrimage, when he was riding his camel.

[3] Narrated by by At-Tabarani in a *Mawqûf* form from Ibn 'Umar ﷺ.

[4] Narrated by Al-Bukhari, on the authority of Ibn 'Abbas ﷺ.

[5] *Maqam Ibraheem*: The place where Ibraheem ﷺ stood while building the *Ka'bah*.

$$﴾ وَٱتَّخِذُوا۟ مِن مَّقَامِ إِبْرَٰهِـۧمَ مُصَلًّى ﴿$$

"And take you *Maqam Ibraheem* as a place of prayer."[1]

And he performed a two *Rak'ah* prayer with the *Maqam* between him and the House, reciting in them *Sûrah Al-Fâtihah* with *Sûrah Al-Kâfirûn* (in the first) and *Sûrah Al-Ikhlas* (in the second). His recitation of the above Verse is an explanation by him of the meaning of Allâh's Words via his action. When he had completed his prayer, he approached the Stone and touched it, then he headed towards As-Safa via the gate which was in front of him and when he was close to it, he recited:

$$﴾ إِنَّ ٱلصَّفَا وَٱلْمَرْوَةَ مِن شَعَآئِرِ ٱللَّهِ ﴿$$

"Verily, As-Safa and Al-Marwah (two mountains in Makkah) are from among the Symbols of Allâh."[2]

Then he said: "I begin with that with which Allâh began (i.e. he began his *Sa'ee* from As-Safa, as this is what Allâh has mentioned first). And in An-Nasa'i's version: "Begin with that with which Allâh began."

Then he ascended it until he could see the House and he faced towards the *Qiblah* and declared Allâh's Oneness and His Greatness and said:

«لَا إِلَهَ إِلَّا اللهُ وَحْدَهُ لَا شَرِيكَ لَهُ ، لَهُ الْمُلْكُ، وَلَهُ الْحَمْدُ، وَهُوَ عَلَى كُلِّ شَيْءٍ قَدِيرٌ، لَا إِلَهَ إِلَّا اللهُ وَحْدَهُ، أَنْجَزَ وَعْدَهُ، وَنَصَرَ عَبْدَهُ، وَهَزَمَ الْأَحْزَابَ وَحْدَهُ»

"La Ilaha Illallahu Wahdahu La Shareeka Lahu, Lahul-Mulku Wa Lahul-Hamdu Wa Huwa 'Ala Kulli Shay'in Qadeer. La Ilaha Illallahu Wahdahu, Anjaza Wa'dahu Wa Nasara 'Abdahu Wa Hazamal-Ahzaba Wahdahu"

"None has the right to be worshipped except Allâh, Alone, without partners. To Him belongs the Dominion and to Him are due all praise and thanks and He is Able to do all things. None

---

[1] *Sûrah Al-Baqarah* 2:125
[2] *Sûrah Al-Baqarah* 2:158

has the right to be worshipped except Allâh, Alone; He fulfilled His Promise and aided His slave and vanquished the confederates Alone."[1]

Then he supplicated between As-Safa and Al-Marwah and he repeated this three times. Then he descended and walked towards Al-Marwah and when his feet reached the bottom of the valley, he ran until he had crossed the valley and reached elevated ground, then he walked again and that is before the two green markers at the beginning and end of the *Sa'ee* (i.e. that he walked). And it would seem that the valley has not changed since then.

When he reached Al-Marwah, he ascended it and faced towards the House and declared Allâh's Greatness and His Oneness and then did the same as he had done at As-Safa. When he had completed his *Sa'ee*, at Al-Marwah, he decisively ordered all of those who had not brought a sacrificial animal with them to leave their state of *Ihram* and he ordered them to do so completely and to remain thus until *Yawm At-Tarwiyah*,[2] but he did not do so himself, due to the fact that he had brought a sacrificial animal with him; and there, he said:

«لَوِ اسْتَقْبَلْتُ مِنْ أَمْرِي مَا اسْتَدْبَرْتُ لَمَا سُقْتُ الْهَدْيَ، وَلَجَعَلْتُهَا عُمْرَةً»

"If I had known before what I know now, I would have not have brought the sacrificial animal with me and I would have changed it into *'Umrah* (i.e. *Hajj Tamattu'*)."[3]

And there he supplicated for those who shaved their heads three times and for those who shortened their hair once.[4]

---

[1] Narrated by Al-Bukhari, Muslim, the compilers of the *'Sunan'*, Ahmad, Malik and Ad-Darimi.

[2] *Yawm At-Tarwiyah*: The Day of Quenching the Thirst, i.e. the 8th of Dhul Hijjah. According to the author of *'Fath Al-'Allam'*, Abul Khair Al-Hindi, it was so called due to the fact that they used to quench their thirst then, since there was no water at 'Arafah, but they were able to drink once they arrived in Mina.

[3] Narrated by Al-Bukhari, Muslim, Abu Dawûd, An-Nasa'i, Ahmad and Ad-Darimi.

[4] Narrated by Al-Bukhari and Muslim on the authority of Ibn 'Umar and Abu Hurairah ﷺ.

As for his wives, they left their state of *Ihram* and they were performing *Hajj Al-Qiran*, except 'A'ishah 🌸, who did not leave her state of *Ihram*, for she was excused from doing so due to her having her menstrual period. And he ordered those who had made the same *Ihlal* as he, to remain in their state of *Ihram* if they had their sacrificial animals with them and to leave their state of *Ihram* if they did not have a sacrificial animal with them.[1]

During the time he remained, until *Yawm At-Tarwiyah*, he would pray in the place where he was staying with the Muslims on the outskirts of Makkah; he continued for four days to shorten his prayers,[2] then when it was Thursday, in the forenoon, he turned with those Muslims who were accompanying him towards Mina, and those of them who had left their *Ihram* entered the state of *Ihram* for *Hajj* from their riding camels and they did not enter the mosque; instead, they entered *Ihram* while Makkah was behind them.

When he arrived in Mina, he descended and offered the *Zuhr* and *'Asr* prayers there and stayed the night there. When the sun rose, he went on to 'Arafah and he took the Dhabb road, which lies to the right of the road which the people use today. Among the Companions 🌸 were those making *Talbiyyah* and among them were those making *Takbeer* and he 🌺 heard them, but he did not reproach them.[3] and he found that a tent had been erected for him by his order at Namirah, which is a village to the east of 'Arafat, but it is in ruins today. There he stayed until the sun had descended, then he ordered his she-camel, Al-Qaswa' to be brought and saddled for him and he went on until he came to the bottom of the valley in the land of 'Uranah.

There he addressed the people while sitting on his camel, delivering a

---

[1] Narrated by Al-Bukhari, Muslim, the compilers of the '*Sunan*', except At-Tirmidhi, Ahmad, Malik and Ad-Darimi.

[2] It is narrated in '*Saheeh Al-Bukhari*', on the authority of Ibn 'Abbas 🌸 that the Messenger of Allâh 🌺 arrived in Makkah with his Companions 🌸 on the morning of the 4th of Dhul Hijjah, making the *Talbiyyah* for *Hajj*; so the period of his stay in Makkah before he went out to Mina and then to 'Arafah was four days, because he arrived on the 4th and left on the 8th.

[3] Narrated by Al-Bukhari and Muslim on the authority of Anas Ibn Malik.

powerful sermon to them, in which he set forth the foundations of Islam and demolished the foundations of *Shirk* and the *Jahiliyyah*; and he established in it the sanctity of those things whose inviolability is agreed upon by all religions, and they are blood, property and honour. And in it, he placed everything pertaining to the *Jahiliyyah* under his feet, and he placed all of the usury of the *Jahiliyyah* (under his feet) and cancelled it. He advised them to treat their women well and he mentioned their rights and the duties incumbent upon them and he declared that it is an obligation upon men to provide for them and to clothe them in fairness and justice, but he did not fix the amount. And he permitted husbands to beat their wives (but not severely) if they allowed someone whom they dislike to enter their house. And he advised the people in it to adhere closely to the Book of Allâh and he informed them that they would not go astray so long as they held fast to it. Then he informed them that they will be questioned about him and he instructed them as to what they should say and to what they should bear witness, and they said: "We witness that you have conveyed the Message, discharged the duty of Prophethood and given wise counsel." Then he raised his finger to the heaven and called upon Allâh three times to witness what they had said. And he ordered those who were present to inform those who were absent about what he had said.[1] He delivered one sermon and not two in between which he sat.

When he had completed it, he ordered Bilal ⬥, who called the *Adhan*, then the *Iqamah* and he offered the *Zuhr* prayer as two *Rak'ahs* in which he recited quietly; and it was a Friday. This proves that the traveller does not perform the Friday prayer. Then he (i.e. Bilal ⬥ called the *Iqamah* and the Prophet ﷺ offered the *'Asr* prayer as two *Rak'ahs* also and the people of Makkah were with him, and they prayed the same prayers as he, shortening them and combining them, which is the clearest proof that the shortening of prayer by the traveller is not bound to a fixed distance.

When he had completed the prayers, he mounted his camel and rode until he reached the stopping place at the foot of the mountain (i.e.

---

[1] Narrated by Muslim.

'Arafah) near to the rocks and he turned to face the *Qiblah*, having the
path taken by those who went on foot in front of him – and he was
(still) on his camel – and he began to supplicate, implore and beseech
Allâh until the sun had set. And he ordered the people to ascend from
the middle of 'Uranah and he informed them

«عَرَفَةُ كُلُّهَا مَوْقِفٌ»

"that all of 'Arafah is a stopping place."[1]

And he sent out to inform the people to keep to their *Hajj* stations and
to stop in them, for they are from the heritage of their father,
Ibraheem ﷺ.[2] When he supplicated, he would raise his hands to
the level of his chest, in the manner in which a needy person asks for
food and he informed them

«أَنَّ خَيْرَ الدُّعَاءِ يَوْمَ عَرَفَةَ»

"that the best supplication is that which is made on the day of
'Arafah."[3]

And it was mentioned that in his supplication, he said:

«اللَّهُمَّ لَكَ الْحَمْدُ كَالَّذِي تَقُولُ، وَخَيْرًا مِمَّا نَقُولُ، اللَّهُمَّ لَكَ
صَلَاتِي وَنُسُكِي وَمَحْيَايَ وَمَمَاتِي، وَإِلَيْكَ مَآبِي، وَلَكَ رَبِّ تُرَاثِي،

---

[1] Narrated by Muslim, Malik and At-Tabarani.

[2] Narrated by the compilers of the '*Sunan*' and Imam Ash-Shafi'i, on the
authority of Ibn Mirba' Al-Ansari and declared authentic by Al-Hakim
and Az-Zahabi concurred with this.

[3] Narrated by Malik, on the authority of Talhah Ibn 'Ubaidillah Ibn Kareez,
it is a *Mursal* narration, since Talhah was a *Tabi'i* and could not have
related from the Prophet ﷺ; however, it is supported by the *Hadeeth* of
'Amr Ibn Shu'aib, who reported from his father, who reported from his
grandfather that the Messenger of Allâh ﷺ said: "The best supplication is
(that of) 'Arafah and the best thing which I and the (other) Prophets
have said from the heart is: "*La Ilaha Illallahu Wahdau La Shareeka Lahu,
Lahul-Mulku Wa Lahul-Hamdu Wa Huwa 'Ala Kulli Shay'in Qadeer*" (None
has the right to be worshipped except Allâh, Alone, without partners. His
is the Dominion and to Him is due all praise and He is Able to do all
things). (Narrated by At-Tirmidhi).

اللَّهُمَّ إِنِّي أَعُوذُ بِكَ مِنْ عَذَابِ الْقَبْرِ، وَوَسْوَسَةِ الصَّدْرِ، وَشَتَاتِ
الأَمْرِ، اللَّهُمَّ إِنِّي أَعُوذُ بِكَ مِنْ شَرِّ مَا تَجِيءُ بِهِ الرِّيحُ»

*"Allâhumma, Lakal-Hamdu Kalladhee Naqûlu Wa Khairan Mimma
Naqûlu. Allâhumma, Laka Salatee Wa Nusukee Wa Mahyaya Wa
Mamatee Wa Ilaika Ma'abee Wa Laka Rabbee Turathee. Allâhumma,
Innee A'ûdhu Bika Min 'Adhabil-Qabri Wa Waswasatis-Sadri Wa
Shattatil-Amri. Allâhumma, Innee A'ûdhu Bika Min Sharri Ma
Tajee'u Bihir-Reeh"*

"Oh, Allâh! To You all praise and thanks are due, which we
express and better than we can express. Oh, Allâh! My prayers,
my sacrifice, my life, my death and my final destination are for
You. And to You, my Lord, belong my deeds. Oh, Allâh! I seek
refuge with You from the punishment of the grave, from the
whispering in my breast and from confusion in my affairs. Oh,
Allâh! I seek refuge with You from the evil which is brought by
the wind."[1]

Other supplications which have been reported from him ﷺ at the
stopping place include:

«اللَّهُمَّ إِنَّكَ تَسْمَعُ كَلَامِي، وَتَرَى مَكَانِي، وَتَعْلَمُ سِرِّي وَعَلَانِيَتِي
وَلَا يَخْفَى عَلَيْكَ شَيْءٌ مِنْ أَمْرِي، أَنَا الْبَائِسُ الْفَقِيرُ، الْمُسْتَغِيثُ
الْمُسْتَجِيرُ، الْوَجِلُ الْمُشْفِقُ، الْمُقِرُّ الْمُعْتَرِفُ بِذُنُوبِهِ، أَسْأَلُكَ مَسْأَلَةَ
الْمِسْكِينِ، وَأَبْتَهِلُ إِلَيْكَ ابْتِهَالَ الْمُذْنِبِ الذَّلِيلِ، وَأَدْعُوكَ دُعَاءَ
الْخَائِفِ الضَّرِيرِ مَنْ خَضَعَتْ لَكَ رَقَبَتُهُ، وَفَاضَتْ لَكَ عَيْنَاهُ، وَذَلَّ
جَسَدُهُ، وَرَغِمَ أَنْفُهُ لَكَ، اللَّهُمَّ لَا تَجْعَلْنِي بِدُعَائِكَ رَبِّ شَقِيًّا، وَكُنْ
بِي رَؤُوفًا رَحِيمًا يَا خَيْرَ الْمَسْؤُولِينَ، وَيَاخَيْرَ الْمُعْطِينَ»

"Allâhumma, Innaka Tasma'u Kalamee Wa Tara Makanee Wa

[1] Narrated by At-Tirmidhi, on the authority of 'Ali Ibn Abi Talib, it contains
in its *Sanad* one Qais Ibn Ar-Rabee', who has been declared weak by
scholars of *Hadeeth*, including Ad-Daraqutni, Yahya Ibn Ma'een, Ahmad
and others.

Ta'lamu Sirree Wa 'Alaniyatee Wa La Yukhfa 'Alaika Shay'un Min Amree. Anal-Ba'isul-Faqeeru, Al-Mustagheethu, Al-Mustajeeru Wal-Wajilul-Mushfiqu, Al-Muqirrul-Mu'tarifu Bidhunûbee. As'aluka Mas'alatal-Miskeeni, Wa Abtahilu Ilaikabtihalal-Mudhnibidh-Dhaleeli, Wa Ad'ûka Du'aa'l-Kha'ifid-Dareeri Man Khada'at Laka Raqabatuhu Wa Fadat Laka 'Ainahu Wa Dhalla Jasaduhu Wa Raghima Anfuhu Laka, Allâhumma, La Taj'alnee Bidu'a'ika Rabbi Shaqiyan, Wa Kun Bee Ra'ûfan Raheeman, Ya Khairal-Mas'ûleena Wa Ya Khairal-Mu'teena''

"Oh, Allâh! You hear my words, You see my place, you know my secrets and the things which I do openly and nothing of my affairs is hidden from You. I am wretched and poor and I am a seeker of aid and a seeker of protection [from You], apprehensive and fearful [of Your Wrath]; I acknowledge and admit my sins. I ask You as a needy person does and I pray with the humility of a wretched sinner and I supplicate to You with the supplication of a fearful blind man, whose neck is bowed to You and whose eyes overflow [with tears] to You and whose will is subordinate to You. O, Allâh! Do not make me wretched due to this supplication to you, my Lord. And be Kind and Merciful to me, O You, the Best of those who are asked and O, You, the Best of givers" This was mentioned by At-Tabarani.[1]

And most of the supplications of the Prophet ﷺ on the day of 'Arafah consisted of:

«لَا إِلَهَ إِلَّا اللهُ وَحْدَهُ لَا شَرِيكَ لَهُ ، لَهُ الْمُلْكُ، وَلَهُ الْحَمْدُ، بِيَدِهِ الْخَيْرُ، وَهُوَ عَلَى كُلِّ شَيْءٍ قَدِيرٌ»

"La Ilaha Illallahu Wahdahu La Shareeka Lahu, Lahul-Mulku Wa Lahul-Hamdu, Biyadihil-Khairu Wa Huwa 'Ala Kulli Shay'in Qadeer''

"None has the right to be worshipped except Allâh, Alone,

---

[1] Narrated by At-Tabarani in *'Al-Mu'jam As-Sagheer'* and by Al-Haithami in *'Al-Majma''*, on the authority of Ibn 'Abbas ﷺ, it contains in its chain of narrators one Yahya Ibn Salih Al-Aili, of whom Al-'Uqaili said: "Yahya Ibn Bakeer narrated *Ahadeeth* which are *Munkar*.

without partners; to Him belongs the Dominion and to Him are due all praise and thanks. All goodness is in His Hand and He is Able to do all things."[1]

And all of these narrations contain some weakness.

And here (at 'Arafah) this Verse was revealed to him:

﴿الْيَوْمَ أَكْمَلْتُ لَكُمْ دِينَكُمْ وَأَتْمَمْتُ عَلَيْكُمْ نِعْمَتِى وَرَضِيتُ لَكُمُ الْإِسْلَامَ دِينًا﴾

"This day, I have perfected your religion for you, completed My Favour upon you, and have chosen for you Islam as your religion."[2]

And it was here that a man fell from his riding beast and was killed, so the Messenger of Allâh ﷺ ordered that he be wrapped in his two garments and that perfume be not applied to him, but that he be washed with water containing *Sidr* and that neither his head nor his face be covered. And he informed them that on the Day of Resurrection, Allâh, Most High will bring him forth making the *Talbiyyah*. In this there are twelve rulings:

The First: The obligation to wash the body of the deceased.

The Second: That a Muslim does not become unclean due to death, for if he did, the washing would increase him in naught but uncleanness.

The Third: That the deceased is washed with water and *Sidr*.

The Fourth: That water being altered by something clean (such as *sidr* or camphor) does not cause it to lose its pure nature.

The Fifth: The permissibility of a person in a state of *Ihram* washing a dead body.

The Sixth: That a person in the state of *Ihram* is not forbidden to use

---

[1] Narrated by Ahmad on the authority of 'Amr Ibn Shu'aib, on the authority of his father, on the authority of his grandfather; in its *Sanad* there is one Muhammad Ibn Abi Humaid and he is weak, according to scholars of *Hadeeth*, such as Ibn Hajr, Yahya Ibn Ma'een, Al-Bukhari and Ahmad himself. Imam Malik narrated something similar in '*Al-Muwatta*'' but it is *Mursal*.

[2] *Sûrah Al-Ma'idah* 5:3

water and *Sidr.*

The Seventh: That the shroud takes precedence over the inheritance of his estate and his debts, because the Prophet ﷺ ordered that he be shrouded in his two garments and he did not ask about his heirs, nor if there were any debts incumbent upon him.

The Eighth: The permissibility of limiting the shroud to two garments.

The Ninth: That a person in a state of *Ihram* is not allowed to use perfume.

The Tenth: That the person in a state of *Ihram* is not allowed to cover his head.

The Eleventh: That it is prohibited for a person in a state of *Ihram* to cover his or her face, although six of the Companions ﷺ permitted it and those who permit it cite as evidence the sayings of these Companions ﷺ and they replied his words:

«لَا تُخَمِّرُوا وَجْهَهُ»

"Do not cover his face,"

by saying that these words are not confirmed by him.

The Twelfth: That a person remains in a state of *Ihram* even after death.

When the sun had set and its setting was completed by its yellowness having departed, he left 'Arafah and he seated Usamah Ibn Zaid ﷺ behind him. He left calmly and pulled the reins of his camel so tightly that its head was near to his saddle (in order to control it) and he was saying:

«أَيُّهَا النَّاسُ عَلَيْكُمُ السَّكِينَةُ، فَإِنَّ الْبِرَّ لَيْسَ بِالإيضَاعِ»

"Oh, people! Be calm, for righteousness is not attained through hurrying."[1]

He departed 'Arafah by way of *Al-Ma'ziman*[2] having arrived there by way of Dhabb; and this was his custom ﷺ during any *'Eed*: He would take a different route coming and going. Then he began move at a

---
[1] Narrated by Al-Bukhari, Muslim and An-Nasa'i.
[2] *Al-Ma'ziman*: A well known place between 'Arafah and Muzdalifah.

trotting pace and whenever he came upon a *Fajwah* – and that is open ground – he increased his pace. And whenever he came upon a *Rubwah* – and that is a hill – he would loosen the reins of his camel slightly, so that it could climb.

During his journey, he made the *Talbiyyah* without ceasing and then on the way, he descended and urinated and then made a light ablution and Usamah ؊ said to him: "The prayer, oh, Messenger of Allâh." He replied:

«الْمُصَلَّى أَمَامَكَ»

"The place of prayer is ahead (at Muzdalifah) of you."

And he rode on until he reached Muzdalifah, where he performed ablution for prayer, then he ordered the *Adhan* to be called and the *Mu'adhdhin* did so and then he called the *Iqamah* and he offered the *Maghrib* prayer before they had unsaddled their riding beasts and before the camels had been made to kneel down. So after they had unsaddled their riding beasts, he ordered the *Iqamah* to be called, then he offered the *'Isha'* prayer – with an *Iqamah* and without an *Adhan* – and he did not offer any prayer in between them; then he slept until dawn.

He did not spend that night in prayer and it has not been authentically reported from him that he spent the two nights of *'Eed* in prayer. He permitted the weaker members of his family ؊ that night to go on to Mina before sunrise. It was at night, when the moon had disappeared and he ordered them not to stone the *Jamrah* until after sunrise.[1] As for the *Hadeeth* in which it is mentioned that Umm Salamah ؊ stoned the *Jamrah* before *Fajr*, it is a *Munkar* narration and it was declared so by Imam Ahmad and others; then he (i.e. Imam Ahmad) mentioned the *Hadeeth* of Sawdah ؊ and other (like) *Ahadeeth* and he said: "We looked into it and we found that there is no contradiction between these *Ahadeeth*, for he ordered the youths not to stone the *Jamrah* before sunrise, so there is no excuse for them to bring forward the stoning. As for those among the women who brought it forward and stoned before sunrise due to an excuse and

---

[1] Narrated by Al-Bukhari, Muslim, Abu Dawûd, Ibn Majah and An-Nasa'i.

the fear for them of being harmed by the crowding of the people, this is what is proven by the *Sunnah*: The permissibility of stoning before sunrise due to an excuse, such as illness, or advanced age. But as for the one who is able and in good health, it is not permissible for him to do so. And what is proven by the *Sunnah* is the permissibility of advancing it after the moon has disappeared – not in the middle of the night; and those who fix it in the middle of the night have no evidence.

So once *Fajr* had begun, he prayed it at the start of its time – never before it – with an *Adhan* and an *Iqamah*, then he mounted his camel and rode until he reached his stopping place in Muzdalifah and there he turned to face the *Qiblah* and he began to supplicate Allâh, implore Him, declare His Greatness and His Oneness and make *Dhikr*, until it was completely light, and he remained in his stopping place and he informed the people that all of Muzdalifah is a stopping place and Usamah 🙵 went on foot with Quraish, who had gone ahead.

On his way, the Prophet 🙵 ordered Ibn 'Abbas 🙵 to pick up seven pebbles for him for the purpose of stoning the *Jamrah*; and he did not break them from the mountain on that night as those with no knowledge do, nor did he pick them up at night. Ibn 'Abbas 🙵 picked up seven small stones for him and he began to shake them in his hand and he was saying:

«أَمْثَالُ هَؤُلَاءِ فَارْمُوا، وَإِيَّاكُمْ وَالْغُلُوَّ فِي الدِّينِ، فَإِنَّمَا أَهْلَكَ مَنْ كَانَ قَبْلَكُمُ الْغُلُوُّ فِي الدِّينِ»

"Throw the likes of these and I warn you against immoderation in religious matters, for it was immoderation in religious matters that destroyed those who came before you."[1]

When he reached the bottom of Muhassir, he urged his camel and went along quickly; and this was his custom when he arrived at places in which Allâh's Punishment fell upon His enemies, for it was in this place that the people of the Elephant were stricken with the punishment which Allâh has related (in *Sûrah Al-Feel*), which is why

---

[1] Narrated by An-Nasa'i, Ibn Majah, Ahmad and Malik.

it was called Wadi Muhassir, because the elephant became tired and refused to move there: That is, it became recalcitrant and broke off its journey to Makkah. And this was what he 鏐 did in Al-Hijr, the abode of Thamûd. And Muhassir is a barrier between 'Arafah and Muzdalifah – it is neither a part of the former, nor the latter. And 'Arunah is a barrier between 'Arafah and *Al-Mash'ar Al-Haram* (The sacred monument) and between every two monuments there is a barrier which is not a part of either of them. Mina is a part of the sacred precincts (of Makkah) and it is a monument; and Muhassir is a part of the Sacred Precincts, but it is not a Monument. Muzdalifah is Sacred and it is a Monument, but 'Arunah is not a Monument and it is part of the area which is not sacred. 'Arafah is not sacred, but it is a monument.

He 鏐 took the middle way between the two roads – which is the one which leaves from *Al-Jamrah Al-Kubra* – until he reached Mina, then he went to *Al-Jamrah Al'Aqabah* and he stopped at the bottom of the valley, placing the House (of Allâh) on his left and Mina on his right. Then he faced the *Jamrah* while he was seated on his camel and stoned it after the sun had risen, throwing the stones one at a time and making *Takbeer* as he threw each one; and at this point, he stopped making the *Talbiyyah*. Bilal and Usamah 鏐 were both with him, one of them holding the bridle of his camel and the other sheltering him from the heat with his garment.[1] From this may be derived the permissibility of sheltering a person in the state of *Ihram* in a litter or the like.

---

[1] Narrated by Muslim and Ahmad.

Chapter

Then he ﷺ returned to Mina and delivered an eloquent sermon, in which he informed them about the sacredness of *Yawm An-Nahr* (the Day of Sacrifice) and its inviolability and its virtue and that the sanctity of Makkah is greater than any other city. And he ordered them to hear and to obey those who lead them according to the Book of Allâh. And he ordered the people to take their manner of performing *Hajj'* rites from him, saying:

«لَعَلِّي لَا أَحُجُّ بَعْدَ عَامِي هَذَا»

"It may be that I will not perform *Hajj'* after this year."[1]

And he taught them their *Hajj'* rites and he declared the statuses of the *Muhajirûn* and the *Ansar* and he ordered the people not to return to disbelief after him by striking each other's necks (i.e. by killing each other). And he ordered them to convey what they had heard to others, saying:

«رُبَّ مُبَلَّغٍ أَوْعَى مِنْ سَامِعٍ»

"It may be that the one who is informed about it will be more heedful than the one who heard it."[2]

And he said in this sermon:

«لَا يَجْنِي جَانٍ إِلَّا عَلَى نَفْسِهِ»

"The criminal inflicts harm on no one but himself."[3]

And he placed the *Muhajirûn* to the right of the *Qiblah* and the *Ansar* to

---

[1] Narrated by Muslim, An-Nasa'i, Abu Dawûd and Ahmad.

[2] Narrated by Al-Bukhari, At-Tirmidhi, Ahmad and Ad-Darimi.

[3] Narrated by Ahmad, on the authority of 'Amr Ibn Al-Ahwas ﷺ.

the left of the *Qiblah*' and the people were around them; and Allâh opened for him the ears of the people, so that the people of Mina heard him from their homes. And he said in this sermon:

«اعْبُدُوا رَبَّكُمْ، وَصَلُّوا خَمْسَكُمْ، وَصُومُوا شَهْرَكُمْ، وَأَطِيعُوا ذَا أَمْرِكُمْ تَدْخُلُوا جَنَّةَ رَبِّكُمْ»

"Worship your Lord and offer your five prayers and fast your month (i.e. Ramadan) and obey those placed in authority over you and you will enter the Paradise of your Lord."[1]

With that, he bade farewell to the people and so they said: "This is the Farewell Pilgrimage."

Then he departed for the place of slaughter and he slaughtered sixty-three camels with his own hand. And he slaughtered them standing, with their left forelegs tethered[2] and their number was that of his age. Then he stopped and ordered 'Ali ؤ to slaughter the remainder of the hundred, then he ordered him to give their *Jilal*,[3] their skins and their meat as charity to the needy.[4] And he ordered him not to give the butcher anything of them, saying:

«نَحْنُ نُعْطِيهِ مِنْ عِنْدِنَا»

"We will give him something from what is with us."

And he said:

«مَنْ شَاءَ اقْتَطَعَ»

"Anyone who wants, can cut off a piece."[5]

And if it is said that in the *'Saheehayn'*, it is reported on the authority of Anas ؤ in his *Hajj*: "And he slaughtered seven camels while standing," it may be said that there are three possible explanations for this:

---

[1] Narrated by Ahmad and At-Tirmidhi and declared authentic by Ibn Hibban and Al-Hakim and Az-Zahabi concurred with this.

[2] Narrated by Abu Dawûd, on the authority of Jabir ؤ.

[3] *Jilal*: Blankets, cloths etc. thrown on the backs of the camels.

[4] Narrated by Al-Bukhari, on the authority of 'Ali Ibn Abi Talib ؤ.

[5] Narrated by Abu Dawûd, on the authority of 'Abdullah Ibn Qurt ؤ.

The First: That he did not slaughter more than seven camels with his own hand and that he ordered someone to complete the slaughter of the sixty-three camels, then he left that place and ordered 'Ali ☺ to slaughter the remainder.

The Second: That Anas ☺ only witnessed him slaughtering seven camels, while Jabir ☺ witnessed him slaughtering the remainder.

The Third: That he slaughtered seven alone, and that then he and 'Ali ☺ took the spear together and slaughtered the remainder of the sixty-three camels in this way, as 'Ghurfah bin Al-Harith Al-Kindi[1] said: That he witnessed the Prophet ﷺ on that day: He had taken the upper part of the spear and he ordered 'Ali ☺ to take the lower part of it and they both slaughtered the camels with it, then 'Ali ☺ slaughtered the remainder of the hundred alone. And Allâh knows better.

And no one has reported from him ﷺ or his Companions ☺ that they combined the slaughter of their sacrificial animals (*Hadi*) with the animals which they slaughtered for '*Eed Al-Adha* (*Udhiyah*). On the contrary, their *Hadi* was their *Udhiyah* and that was the sacrifice in Mina and the animals slaughtered for '*Eed* were slaughtered elsewhere. As for the saying of 'A'ishah ☺: "The Prophet slaughtered cows on behalf of his wives,"[2] they were sacrificial animals (*Hadi*) to which the word (*Udhiyah*) was applied, for they were performing *Hajj At-Tamattu'*, so they were obliged to sacrifice an animal – and that is what he slaughtered on their behalf. However, in the account of the slaughter of the cow on their behalf – and they were nine in number – there is a problem; and that is: The sharing of this cow by more than seven; and this *Hadeeth* has been reported with three different wordings:

The First: That it was one cow between them.

The Second: That on that day, he slaughtered a number of cows on their behalf.

---

[1] In the two documents from which this book was compiled, it says: 'Urwah Ibn Mudharris ☺ and this is incorrect; the correction is from the original '*Zad Al-Ma'ad*' and from Abu Dawûd's '*Sunan*'.

[2] Narrated by Al-Bukhari and Muslim.

The Third: "Some beef was brought to us on the Day of Sacrifice and I said: "What is this?" It was said: "The Messenger of Allâh ﷺ has slaughtered on behalf of his wives."

Scholars have differed as to how many people a camel and a cow suffice; it has been said seven,[1] and it has been said ten – and this (latter) is the view of Ishaq, then he quoted some *Ahadeeth*, then he said: "These *Ahadeeth* are interpreted in one of three ways: (i) Either it is said that the *Ahadeeth* which prove that it is seven are more numerous and more authentic, or (ii) it is said that a camel is equivalent to ten sheep when dividing the spoils of war, in order to be just in sharing them out. But as for sacrificial animals (*Hadi*) and animals slaughtered on the Day of Sacrifice (*Udhiyah*) and that is a legal estimate, or (iii) it is said that it differs according to different times and places and different animals. And Allâh knows better.

And he slaughtered in the place of sacrifice in Mina and he informed them that:

$$«مِنَّى كُلُّهَا مَنْحَرٌ»$$

"All of Mina is a place of sacrifice."[2]

And he said that:

$$«فِجَاجُ مَكَّةَ طَرِيقٌ وَمَنْحَرٌ»$$

"The mountain paths of Makkah are a way and a place of slaughter."[3]

This is proof that slaughtering is not exclusive to Mina; indeed, since he slaughtered in the mountain passes of Makkah, it is counted, according to the words of the Prophet ﷺ:

$$«وَقَفْتُ هَاهُنَا وَعَرَفَةُ كُلُّهَا مَوْقِفٌ»$$

"I have stopped here, but all of 'Arafah is a stopping place."[4]

---

[1] This was the view of Ash-Shafi'i and Ahmad.

[2] Narrated by Muslim, At-Tirmidhi, Abu Dawûd, Ibn Majah, Ahmad and Ad-Darimi.

[3] Narrated by Abu Dawûd, Ibn Majah, Ahmad and Ad-Darimi.

[4] Narrated by Muslim and Ahmad.

And he was asked if they should build a shelter from the heat for him in Mina, but he said:

«لَا مِنَى مُنَاخُ مَنْ سَبَقَ»

"No, Mina is a place for the one who reaches it earlier (i.e. no one may reserve a place there)."[1]

In this there is evidence that the Muslims should cooperate with each other there and that whoever arrived at a place there first has the greater right to it, until he should leave it and he does not possess it thereby.

After he had completed his sacrifice in Mina and he had informed them that: "All of Mina is a place of sacrifice," he shaved his head and he said (to the man shaving him):

«يَا مَعْمَرُ أَمْكَنَكَ رَسُولُ الله مِنْ شَحْمَةِ أُذُنِهِ، وَفِي يَدِكَ الْمُوسَى»

"Oh, Ma'mar! Allâh's Messenger has made it possible for you (to cut) his earlobes and in your hand is the razor."

Ma'mar ☀ replied: "By Allâh, oh, Messenger of Allâh! That is from Allâh's Blessing and His Grace upon me." He (☀) replied: "Yes." This was mentioned by Ahmad.[2] And he said to him: "Take (from here)," and he indicated the right side of his head, then he shared it (his hair) between those who were in front of him. Then he pointed to him and he shaved the left side. Then he said: "Is Abu Talhah here?" And he gave it to him (to distribute among the people). This is how it was narrated in 'Saheeh Muslim'[3]

And in 'Saheeh Al-Bukhari', it is reported on the authority of Ibn Seereen, that he reported on the authority of Anas ☀ that when the Messenger of Allâh ☀ shaved his head, Abu Talhah ☀ was the first to take some of his hair.[4] And he supplicated Allâh for forgiveness for

---

[1] Narrated by At-Tirmidhi, Abu Dawûd, Ibn Majah, Ahmad and Ad-Darimi.

[2] Narrated by Ahmad, on the authority of Ma'mar Ibn 'Abdillah ☀, it contains in its chain of narrators one 'Abdur-Rahman Ibn 'Uqbah, who is unknown, according to Ibn Hazm.

[3] Narrated by Muslim, on the authority of Anas ☀.

[4] Narrated by Al-Bukhari, on the authority of Anas ☀.

those who shave their hair three times and for those who cut it once. This is an evidence that shaving is a rite and is not prohibited in all circumstances.

Then the Prophet ﷺ set out on his camel for Makkah before *Zuhr*, where he performed *Tawaf Al-Ifadah*[1] and he did not make any other *Tawaf* with it, nor did he perform *Sa'ee*. This is what is correct. And he did not trot in it,[2] nor in *Tawaf Al-Wada'*[3] - he only trotted in *Tawaf Al-Qudûm*.[4]

Then he went to Zamzam and found the people drinking there and he said:

«لَوْلَا أَنْ يَغْلِبَكُمُ النَّاسُ لَنَزَلْتُ فَسَقَيْتُ مَعَكُمْ»

"Were it not that the people would inundate you, I would have descended and drunk with you."

So they passed him a bucket and he drank from it while he was standing.[5] It was said: "Because the prohibition of drinking standing is one of preference." And it was said: "He did so out of necessity," and this is more obvious.

And it is authentically reported on the authority of Ibn 'Abbas that he said: "The Messenger of Allâh ﷺ performed *Tawaf* during the

---

[1] *Tawaf Al-Ifadah*: The Circumambulation of Departure (from Mina) of the Ka'bah performed by the pilgrims after their return from Mina, it is one of the essential pillars of the *Hajj*.

[2] Narrated by Abu Dawûd and Ibn Majah, on the authority of Ibn 'Abbas and declared authentic by Al-Hakim, and Az-Zahabi agreed with this.

[3] *Tawaf Al-Wada'*: The Farewell Circumambulation, performed by all pilgrims prior to departing from Makkah.

[4] *Tawaf Al-Qudûm*: The Circumambulation of Arrival (in Makkah) performed by all *Hajj* and *'Umrah* pilgrims, for whom it is an essential rite.

[5] Narrated by Muslim, without the words: "while he was standing." At-Tirmidhi, Ibn Majah, Abu Dawûd and Ahmad.

Farewell Pilgrimage on a camel, touching the Corner with a *Mihjan*[1] and something similar is reported in the *Hadeeth* of Jabir 🕮 and in it is: "so that the people could see him and so that he could supervise them and they could ask him questions, because the people were crowding around him."[2] But this was not *Tawaf Al-Wada'*, because he performed it at night, nor was it *Tawaf Al-Qudûm*, because he trotted in it; and no one said that his camel trotted with him. Then he returned to Mina.

Scholars have disagreed as to whether he offered the *Zuhr* prayer there or in Makkah. 'A'ishah 🕮 performed one *tawaf* that day and she performed one *Sa'ee*, which sufficed her for her *Hajj'* and her *'Umrah*. And Safiyyah 🕮 performed *Tawaf* that day, then her menstruation started and that *Tawaf* sufficed her for *Tawaf Al-Wada'*. So the *Sunnah* of the Prophet 🕮 established for the woman who menstruates before the *Tawaf*, that her *Hajj* be *Hajj Al-Qiran* and that she content herself with one *Tawaf* and one *Sa'ee*. And if she menstruates after *Tawaf Al-Ifadah*, it is sufficient for her without *Tawaf Al-Wada'*.

Then he returned to Mina on that day and stayed the night there. When he awoke in the morning, he waited for the sun to pass its zenith, then he walked – didn't ride – to the *Jamrah*, and he began with the first *Jamrah* , which is in front of Al-Khaif Mosque, and he stoned it with seven stones, one after another, saying as he threw each stone: *"Allâhu Akbar"*; He then would go ahead till he reached the level ground; and he stood facing the *Qiblah*; then he raised his hands and made a long supplication, equivalent in length to *Sûrah Al-Baqarah*. Then he proceeded to *Al-Jamrah Al-Wusta* (the Middle *Jamrah*) and he stoned it in the same way. Then he descended leftwards to a place beside the valley and he stood facing the *Qiblah*, and he raised his hands for a time almost as long as the first standing, then he went to *Jamrah Al-'Aqabah* and he stood in the middle of the valley and kept the House (of Allâh) to his left and stoned the *Jamrah* with seven pebbles also. Then he returned and he did not stop at them, it has been said, due to the limited space, and it has been said – and this is

---

[1] Narrated by Al-Bukhari and Muslim.
[2] Narrated by Muslim, on the authority of Jabir Ibn 'Abdillah 🕮.

more correct – that his supplication was during the selfsame act of worship, so when he had stoned them, he stopped stoning. And supplication whilst performing an act of worship is better. But to me, the question remains: Did he perform the stoning before the prayer, or after it? And what seems most likely is that it was before it, because Jabir  and others said that he stoned once the sun had passed its zenith.

---------- ❖ ❖ ❖ ----------

Chapter

The *Hajj* of the Prophet ﷺ included six stops for supplication: On Mount Safa, on Mount Marwah, on Mount 'Arafah, at Muzdalifah, at the first *Jamrah* and at the second *Jamrah*.

At Mina, he delivered two sermons: One on the Day of Sacrifice – and this has been mentioned previously – and the second in the middle of the Days of *Tashreeq*.[1]

Al-'Abbas ؓ sought permission to remain in Makkah on the nights of Mina, in order to provide pilgrims with drinking water and so the Prophet ﷺ permitted him to do so.[2] And the camel herders sought permission from him to stay outside Mina with their camels and he allowed them to stone the *Jamarat* on the Day of Sacrifice, then to combine two days of stoning after the Day of Sacrifice in one of the two remaining days.[3] Malik said: "I thought that he said: "On the first of them, then to stone on the Day of *An-Nafr*.[4] Ibn 'Uyainah said, regarding this *Hadeeth*: He permitted the camel herders to stone in one day and to supplicate for one day." And it is permissible for both parties, according to the *Sunnah*, to be excused from remaining, but as for the stoning, they may not abandon it, but they may delay it until the night. And they may combine the stoning of two days in one day.

Whoever has money which he fears will be lost, or has a sick person with him whom he fears to leave behind, or he is ill and it

---

[1] Days of *Tashreeq*: The three days after the Day of Sacrifice (11th, 12th and 13th of Dhul Hijjah).

[2] Narrated by Al-Bukhari and Muslim.

[3] Narrated by the compilers of the '*Sunan*' and Malik.

[4] Day of *An-Nafr*: The day of departure from Mina, after performing the rites.

is impossible for him to stay, then the obligation is lifted from him, in accordance with the evidence of those people. He did not hasten to leave in two days, but remained until he had completed the stoning in the three days and then he departed on Tuesday after *Zuhr* for Al-Muhassab and that is Al-Abtah and it is Khaif Bani Kinanah. There he found Abu Rafi' – who was in charge of his baggage – and he had pitched his tent for him;[1] and Allâh, the Almighty, the All-powerful granted success to his efforts, for the Messenger of Allâh 鑑 did not order him to do so, but he offered the *Zuhr, 'Asr, Maghrib* and *'Isha* prayers and then slept the night there, after which, he set out for Makkah and performed *Tawaf Al-Wada'* at night, just before dawn.

And that night, 'A'ishah 鑑 requested him to take her for *'Umrah* by itself, but he informed her that her circumambulation of the House and her *Sa'ee* between As-Safa and Al-Marwah sufficed for her *Hajj* and her *'Umrah*. But she insisted on performing *'Umrah* by itself and so he ordered her brother ('Abdur-Rahman) to take her to perform *'Umrah* from At-Tan'eem and so she completed her *'Umrah* by night, then she arrived at Al-Muhassab with her brother in the middle of the night and he 鑑 said: "Have you completed it?" She said: "Yes." Then he announced their departure and the people departed.

And in the authentic *Hadeeth* of Al-Aswad 鑑, it is reported from 'Aishah 鑑 that she said: "The Messenger of Allâh 鑑 met me when he was ascending from Makkah and I was descending to it, (or she said:) I was ascending and he was descending from it" and it is mentioned in the *Hadeeth* that they met and at the beginning of the *Hadeeth*, it is mentioned that he waited for her at his stopping place (above Makkah).[2] And although the *Hadeeth* of Al-Aswad 鑑 may be recorded (thus), the correct wording is: "He met me while I was ascending from Makkah and he was descending to it," because she had completed her *'Umrah*, then ascended to the appointed meeting place and she met him while he was descending to Makkh for Tawaf Al-Wada'. And it is reported from a source other than this. And

---

[1] Narrated by Muslim and Abu Dawûd, on the authority of Abu Rafi' 鑑.
[2] Narrated by Al-Bukhari, on the authority of 'A'ishah 鑑.

scholars have differed regarding whether the *Tahseeb* [1] is a *Sunnah* or something on which scholars are agreed.

---

[1] *Tahseeb*: Staying the night in Al-Muhassab during the Days of *Tashreeq*.

Many people consider that entering the House (of Allâh) is one of the *Sunan* of *Hajj*, following the example of the Prophet ﷺ, but what is proven by his *Sunnah* is that he did not enter it during his *Hajj*, nor during his *'Umrah*; he only entered it in the year of the conquest of Makkah. Likewise, standing at Al-Multazam[1] which he was reported to have observed on the day of the conquest. As for the *Hadeeth* narrated by Abu Dawûd on the authority of 'Amr Ibn Shu'aib 🙏, who narrated from his father, who narrated from his grandfather, that he placed his chest, his face, his arms and the palms of his hands and spread them and said: "I saw the Messenger of Allâh ﷺ doing thus," it is possible that this was at the time of *Tawaf Al-Wada'* and it is possible that it was at some other time, but Mujahid and others said: "It is recommended to stand at Al-Multazam after performing *Tawaf Al-Wada'*." And Ibn 'Abbas 🙏 used to hold onto what is between the corner (in which the Black Stone is situated) and the door.

And it is reported in *'Saheeh Al-Bukhari'* that when the Prophet ﷺ wished to leave and Umm Salamah 🙏 had not performed *Tawaf* of the House as she was ill and wished to leave, he said to her:

$$\text{«إِذَا أُقِيمَتْ صَلَاةُ الصُّبْحِ، فَطُوفِي عَلَى بَعِيرِكَ وَالنَّاسُ يُصَلُّونَ»}$$

"Once the *Iqamah* for the *Fajr* prayer is called, circumambulate the House on your camel while the people are praying."

She did so and she did not pray until she left. It is impossible that this was on the Day of Sacrifice; without doubt, it was *Tawaf Al-Wada'*. So it is apparent that he offered the *Fajr* prayer on that day in Makkah and

---

[1] Al-Multazam: Part of the House of Allâh, between the door and the Black Stone.

Umm Salamah 🌸 heard him reciting *Sûrah At-Tûr*. Then he set out on the return journey to Al-Madinah.

When he was in Ar-Rawha', he met some riders and he greeted them with salutations of peace and he asked: "Who are (you) people?" They said: "Muslims." Then they asked: "And who are (you) people?" He replied: "The Messenger of Allâh." Then a woman raised her baby to him from a litter and said: "Oh, Messenger of Allâh! Is there any *Hajj* for this?" He 🌸 replied:

$$\text{«نَعَمْ وَلَكِ أَجْرٌ»}$$

"Yes; and you will be rewarded for it."[1]

When he reached Dhul Hulaifah, he spent the night there and when he saw Al-Madinah, he made *Takbeer* three times and he said:

$$\text{«لَا إِلَهَ إِلَّا اللهُ وَحْدَهُ لَا شَرِيكَ لَهُ، لَهُ الْمُلْكُ، وَلَهُ الْحَمْدُ، وَهُوَ}$$
$$\text{عَلَى كُلِّ شَيْءٍ قَدِيرٌ آيِبُونَ تَائِبُونَ عَابِدُونَ سَاجِدُونَ، لِرَبِّنَا حَامِدُونَ،}$$
$$\text{صَدَقَ اللهُ وَعْدَهُ، وَنَصَرَ عَبْدَهُ، وَهَزَمَ الْأَحْزَابَ وَحْدَهُ»}$$

"La Ilaha Illallahu Wahdahu La Shareeka Lahu, Lahul-Mulku Wa Lahul-Hamdu Wa Huwa 'Ala Kulli Shay'in Qadeer. Ayibûna, Ta'ibûna, 'Abidûna, Sajidûna Lirabbina Hamidûn. Sadaqallahu Wa'dahu Wa Nasara 'Abdahu Wa Hazamal-Ahzaba Wahdahu"

"None has the right to be worshipped except Allâh, Alone, without partners. To Him belongs the Dominion and to Him are due all praise and thanks and He is Able to do all things. [We are] returning, repentant, worshipping our Lord and praising Him. Allâh fulfilled His Promise and aided His slave and vanquished the tribes Alone.

Then he entered Al-Madinah during the day via Al-Mu'arras, having departed via *Ash-Shajarah*."[2]

---

[1] Narrated by Muslim, Abu Dawûd, Ahmad and Ash-Shafi'i.
[2] Narrated by Al-Bukhari and Muslim.

Chapter

Regarding His ﷺ Guidance in Sacrificial Animals for *Hajj* (*Hadi*), Slaughtering for *'Eed* (*Udhiyah*) and Sacrifice on the Occasion of a Child's Birth (*'Aqeeqah*)

It refers specifically to the eight pairs mentioned in *Sûrah Al-An'am*; and this is taken from four Verses in the Qur'ân (the first):

﴿أُحِلَّتْ لَكُم بَهِيمَةُ ٱلْأَنْعَٰمِ﴾

"Lawful to you (for food) are all the beasts of cattle except that which will be announced to you (herein),"[1]

and the second is:

﴿لِّيَذْكُرُوا۟ ٱسْمَ ٱللَّهِ عَلَىٰ مَا رَزَقَهُم مِّنۢ بَهِيمَةِ ٱلْأَنْعَٰمِ﴾

"that they may mention the Name of Allâh over the beast of cattle that He has given them for food."[2]

The third is:

﴿وَمِنَ ٱلْأَنْعَٰمِ حَمُولَةً وَفَرْشًا﴾

"And of the cattle (are some) for burden (like camel) and (some are) small (unable to carry burden like sheep and goats for food, meat, milk and wool)." [3]

---

[1] *Sûrah Al-Ma'idah* 5:1

[2] *Sûrah Al-Hajj* 22:34

[3] *Sûrah Al-An'am* 6:142

And the Verse which follows it; and the fourth is the Words of Allâh:

$$\text{﴿هَدْيًا بَٰلِغَ ٱلْكَعْبَةِ﴾}$$

"The penalty is an offering, brought to the *Ka'bah*,"[1]

This proves that the offering brought to the *Ka'bah* is these eight pairs; and this is the deduction of 'Ali Ibn Abi Talib ﷺ.

And the slaughtered animals which are acts of worship are three: *Hadi*, *Udhiyah* and *'Aqeeqah*. The Prophet ﷺ slaughtered sheep and camels as a *Hadi* and he slaughtered a cow as a *Hadi* on behalf of his wives and the *Hadi* was in his stay, during his *Hajj* and during his *'Umrah*. His *Sunnah* was to garland the sheep, without marking them; and if he sent his *Hadi* when he was resident, nothing was unlawful to him which had previously been lawful. When he offered a camel as a *Hadi*, he would both garland it and mark it by cutting it slightly on the right side of its hump until the blood flowed. And if he sent a *Hadi*, he would inform his messenger that if he observed an injury to any of them while it was in his charge, to slaughter it and dip its hooves in its blood and imprint it on the side of its hump, but not to eat from it, nor allow any of his companions to do so, then to divide up its meat. And the forbiddance of eating its meat was to prevent any means which might lead to his being deficient in his guardianship of it. And he allowed participation in the *Hadi* by his Companions ﷺ as follows: The camel for seven persons and the cow for seven persons; and he permitted the man driving the *Hadi* to ride it if it was necessary, until he finds an alternative riding beast. 'Ali ﷺ said: "He may drink of its milk anything that is surplus to the requirements of its young." It was a part of his guidance to slaughter the camel in a standing position, with its left foreleg tied, and he used to invoke Allâh's Name when he slaughtered it and make *Takbeer* and he used to slaughter sacrificial animals by hand, but he might appoint another to slaughter some of them. When he slaughtered sheep, he would place his foot on its side, then he would invoke Allâh's Name and make *Takbeer*, then slaughter it. And he permitted the people of his community to eat from the meat of their sacrificial animals (*Hadi*)

---

[1] *Sûrah Al-Ma'idah* 5:95

and the animals which they slaughter for *'Eed Al-Adha* (*Udhiyah*) and
to take provision from it, but he forbade them from storing anything
of it after three days due to a large influx of needy people that year.[1]
And sometimes, he might divide up the meat of the *Hadi* and
sometimes, he might say: "Whoever wishes may cut something from
it."[2] Some scholars have cited this as evidence that it is permissible
to throw (money, sweets, gifts etc.) to be caught by the guests in
weddings and such like. And a distinction was made between them
(by some scholars), but it is based upon some difference which is
unclear. And it was a part of his guidance to slaughter the sacrificial
animal for *'Umrah* at Al-Marwah and the sacrificial animal for *Hajj Al-
Qiran* in Mina; and he never slaughtered his sacrificial animal until
after he left the state of *Ihram*, nor did he slaughter it until after the
sun had risen and after the stoning. The four things must be
performed in order on the Day of Sacrifice: (i) The stoning, then (ii)
the slaughter, then (iii) the shaving, then (iv) the *Tawaf*; and he did
not permit anyone ever to slaughter before sunrise.

---

[1] Narrated by Muslim, on the authority of 'A'ishah 🙵.
[2] Narrated by Al-Bukhari and Muslim, on the authority of 'Ali Ibn Abi
   Talib 🙵.

Chapter

As for his 壄 guidance in the slaughter for *'Eed Al-Adha*, he never failed to slaughter for it; he would slaughter two sheep after the prayer and he informed us that one who slaughters before it has not performed the rite, it is only meat which he has presented to his family."[1] And this is what we submit ourselves to Allâh with. It is not dependent upon the time of the prayer. He ordered them to slaughter a sheep which is between six months and one year, or any other which is in its third year. And it has been reported from him 壄 that he said:

«كُلُّ أَيَّامِ التَّشْرِيقِ ذَبْحٌ»

"All of the Days of *Tashreeq* are for slaughtering."

However, the chain of narrators is *Munqati'*.[2] And that is the *Mazhab* of 'Ata, Al-Hasan and Ash-Shafi'i and it was the preferred view of Ibn Al-Munzir.

It was a part of his guidance to select the sacrificial animals for *'Eed Al-Adha* and to do it well and to choose the best of them, those free from defects; and he prohibited slaughtering those with torn ears or half or more of their horns broken. This was mentioned by Abu Dawûd. And he 壄 ordered that the eye and ear be examined, i.e. that their health be ascertained. And he ordered that a one-eyed animal should not be slaughtered, nor one the front of which ear is cut, nor one the back of which ear is cut, nor one which ear is slit or one which ear is pierced. This was mentioned by Abu Dawûd.

It was also a part of his guidance to slaughter in the prayer place; and

---

[1] Narrated by Al-Bukhari and Muslim.

[2] *Munqati'*: Broken; such a *Hadeeth* is weak.

Abu Dawûd reported from him that on the Day of Sacrifice, he slaughtered two horned sheep whose colour was more white than black and which had been castrated, and when he faced them, he said:

«وَجَّهْتُ وَجْهِيَ لِلَّذِي فَطَرَ السَّمَوَاتِ وَالأَرْضَ حَنِيفًا وَمَا أَنَا مِنَ الْمُشْرِكِينَ، إِنَّ صَلَاتِي وَنُسُكِي وَمَحْيَايَ وَمَمَاتِي للهِ رَبِّ الْعَالَمِينَ، لَا شَرِيكَ لَهُ، وَبِذَلِكَ أُمِرْتُ وَأَنَا أَوَّلُ الْمُسْلِمِينَ، اللَّهُمَّ مِنْكَ وَلَكَ عَنْ مُحَمَّدٍ وَأُمَّتِهِ، بِسْمِ اللهِ وَاللهُ أَكْبَرُ»

"Wajjahtu Wajhee Lilladhee Fataras-Samawati Wal-Arda Haneefan Wa Ma Ana Minal-Mushrikeen, Inna Salatee Wa Nusukee Wa Mahyaya Wa Mamatee Lillahi Rabbil 'Alameen, La Shareeka Lahu Wa Bi-Dhalika Umirtu Wa Ana Awwalul-Muslimeen. Allâhumma, Minka Wa Laka 'An Muhammadin Wa Ummatihi, Bismillahi Wallahu Akbar"

"I have turned my face to the One Who created the heavens and the earth in sincere submission and I am not one of those who associates partners with Allâh [*Mushrikûn*]. Verily, my prayers, my sacrifice, my life and my death are for Allâh, the Lord of mankind, Who has no partners. That is what I have been ordered and I am the first of those who submit [i.e. a Muslim] Oh, Allâh! This from You and to You, from Muhammad and his people."

And he ordered the people to slaughter well when they slaughter and to kill well when they kill, and he said:

«إِنَّ اللهَ كَتَبَ الْإِحْسَانَ عَلَى كُلِّ شَيْءٍ»

"Verily, Allâh has ordained *Ihsan* upon everything."[1]

And it was a part of his guidance that a sheep is sufficient for a man and his family.[2]

---

[1] Narrated by Muslim, the compilers of the '*Sunan*', Ahmad and Ad-Darimi.

[2] Narrated by At-Tirmidhi, Ibn Majah and Malik.

Chapter

Regarding His ﷺ Guidance in Slaughtering on the Occasion of a Child's Birth ('*Aqeeqah*)

It is reported in '*Al-Muwatta*' that the Prophet ﷺ was asked about it and he said: "I do not like *Al-'Uqûq*." And it was as if he did not like the name (i.e. calling the '*Aqeeqah* '*Uqûq*, not the action).[1] And it has been authentically reported on the authority of 'A'ishah ﷺ that the Prophet ﷺ said:

«عَنِ الْغُلَامِ شَاتَانِ، وَعَنِ الْجَارِيَةِ شَاةٌ»

"For a boy, (slaughter) two sheep and for a girl (slaughter) one sheep."[2]

And he said:

«كُلُّ غُلَامٍ رَهِينَةٌ بِعَقِيقَتِهِ، تُذْبَحُ عَنْهُ يَوْمَ السَّابِعَ، وَيُحْلَقُ رَأْسُهُ وَيُسَمَّى»

"Every boy is in pledge for his '*Aqeeqah*: (Two sheep) should be sacrificed on his behalf on the seventh day and his head should be shaved and he should be named."[3]

And the word *Rahn* (used in the *Hadeeth*) means linguistically pledge. It was said that he is prevented from seeking intercession for his parents. But what is apparent is that he is pledged by himself and that he is prevented from some desirable goodness. It does not

---

[1] Narrated by Imam Malik and Imam Ahmad.
[2] Narrated by An-Nasa'i, Abu Dawûd and Ahmad.
[3] Narrated by Abu Dawûd, Ahmad and Ad-Darimi.

necessarily mean that he will be punished in the Hereafter, but the
boy might lose some goodness due to the neglect of his parents, such
as failing to invoke Allâh's Name at the time of having sexual
intercourse. Abu Dawûd mentioned in *'Al-Maraseel'*, on the authority
of Ja'far Ibn Muhammad, on the authority of his father, that the
Prophet ﷺ said in the *'Aqeeqah* of Al-Hasan and Al-Husain ﵂:

«أَنْ يَبْعَثُوا إِلَى بَيْتِ الْقَابِلَةِ بِرَجُلٍ، وَكُلُوا وَأَطْعِمُوا وَلَا تَكْسِرُوا مِنْهَا
عَظْمًا»

"They should send a leg (of mutton) to the midwife, and eat
and give others to eat and do not break any of its bones."[1]

Al-Maimûni said: "Can you recall for us after how many days the
child should be named?" Abu 'Abdillah said: "It is narrated on the
authority of Anas ﵁ that he should be named after three days, but as
for Samurah ﵁, he said: "He should be named on the seventh day."

---

[1] Narrated by Al-Baihaqi, but its *Sanad* is broken (*Munqati'*).

Chapter

Regarding His ﷺ Guidance in Names and Agnomens

It has been confirmed from the Prophet ﷺ that he said:

«إِنَّ أَخْنَعَ اسْم عِنْدَ اللهِ يَوْمَ الْقِيَامَةِ رَجُلٌ تَسَمَّى بِمَلِكِ الْأَمْلَاكِ،
لَا مَالِكَ إِلَّا اللهُ»

"Verily, the most wretched of names in Allâh's Sight on the Day of Resurrection will be that of a man who calls himself *Malik Al-Amlak* (King of Kings); there is no King except Allâh."[1]

And it has been confirmed from him ﷺ that he said:

«إِنَّ أَحَبَّ الْأَسْمَاءِ إِلَى اللهِ عَبْدُ اللهِ وَعَبْدُ الرَّحْمٰنِ، وَأَصْدَقَهَا
حَارِثٌ وَهَمَّامٌ وَأَقْبَحَهَا حَرْبٌ وَمُرَّةُ»

"Verily, the names most beloved by Allâh are 'Abdullah and 'Abdur-Rahman, and the most truthful of them are Harith and Hammam and the ugliest of them are Harb and Murrah."[2]

And it is confirmed that he said:

«لَا تُسَمِّيَنَّ غُلَامَكَ يَسَارًا وَلَا رَبَاحًا وَلَا نَجِيحًا وَلَا أَفْلَحَ، فَإِنَّكَ

---

[1] Narrated by Al-Bukhari, Muslim, At-Tirmidhi, Abu Dawûd and Ahmad.

[2] Narrated Al-Bukhari, Muslim and At-Tirmidhi, without the addition: "and the most truthful of them are Harith and Hammam and the ugliest of them are Harb and Murrah." This was narrated by Imam Ahmad, on the authority of Abu Wahb Al-Jushami ﷺ, but it contains in its *Sanad* one 'Aqeel Ibn Shabeeb, who is unknown, according to Ibn Hajr, Abu Hatim Ar-Razi and Ibn Al-Qattan.

«تَقُولُ: أَثَمَّ هُوَ؟ فَلَا يَكُونُ، فَيَقُولُ: لَا»

"Do not name your child Yasar (Ease), nor Rabah (Profit), nor Najeeh (Successful), nor Aflah (Fortunate), as you nay call him so and he would not be (as named), so it will be said: "No."[1]

And it has been confirmed from him ﷺ that he changed the name of 'Asiyah, saying: "You are Jameelah."[2] And Juwairiyah's name was Barrah and he changed it to Juwairiyah."[3]

Zainab Bint Umm Salamah ﷻ said: "The Messenger of Allâh ﷺ prohibited a person to be called by this name (i.e. *Barrah* righteous) and he said:

«لَا تُزَكُّوا أَنْفُسَكُمْ اللهُ أَعْلَمُ بِأَهْلِ الْبِرِّ مِنْكُمْ»

"Do not bear witness to your own righteousness, for Allâh knows better who are the righteous ones."[4]

And he changed the name of Abul Hakam to Abu Shuraih.[5] And he changed the name of Asram (cut tree) to Zur'ah (growing).[6] And he changed the name of Hazn (Rugged), the grandfather of Ibn Al-Musayyib, to Sahl (Smooth), but he refused, saying: "Sahl is downtrodden and disgraced."

Abu Dawûd said: "The Prophet ﷺ changed the names Al-'As, 'Azeez, 'Atalah, Shaitan, Al-Hakam, Ghurab, Hubab, and Shihab and called him Hisham. He changed the name Harb (War) and called him Salm (Peace). He changed the name Al-Mudtaji' (One who lies down) and called him Al-Munba'ith (One who stands up). He changed the name of a land called 'Afirah (Barren) and called it Khadirah (Green). He

---

[1] That is, the Prophet ﷺ wished to avoid them falling into pessimism and thinking badly of Allâh, its being said: "There is no success, profit, ease etc."

[2] Narrated by Muslim and Abu Dawûd, on the authority of Ibn 'Umar ﷻ.

[3] Narrated by Muslim, on the authority of Ibn 'Abbas ﷻ.

[4] Narrated by Muslim, on the authority of Zainab Bint Umm Salamah ﷻ.

[5] Narrated by Abu Dawûd and An-Nasa'i and by Al-Bukhari in *'Al-Adab Al-Mufrad.'*

[6] Narrated by Abu Dawûd, on the authority of Usamah Ibn Akhdari.

changed the name Shi'b Ad-Dalalah (the Mountain Path of Error) and called it Shi'b Al-Huda (the Mountain Path of Guidance). He changed the name Banu Az-Zinyah (Children of Fornication) and called them Banu Ar-Rishdah (Children of Those Who are Rightly Guided), and he changed the name of Banu Mughwiyah (Children of a Woman who Allures and Goes Astray), and called them Banu Rishdah (Children of a Rightly Guided Woman)."[1]

And because these names are vessels for the meanings which they indicate, logic dictates that there must be some connection and some relation between the names and their meanings and that the meanings should not be divorced from the names, because wisdom rejects this and reality testifies to the opposite. In fact, names have an effect on the things which are named and the things which are named are affected by the goodness or badness of their names, by their lightness or their weight (i.e. ease or difficulty of pronunciation) and by their delicateness or thickness, as it said (by the poet):

'And rarely do one's eyes behold the bearer of a nickname, Whose description does not tally with the meaning – when one thinks about it.'

He loved good names and he ordered that if a messenger was sent to him, that he should have a good name and a pleasant face. And he used to take the meanings from names during sleep and wakefulness, as when he dreamt that he and his Companions ﷺ were in the house of 'Uqbah Ibn 'Rafi' and they brought him dates from the dates of Ibn Tab, and he interpreted it as meaning sublimity in the life of this world and that the end result was for them in Hereafter and that the Religion which Allâh has chosen for them was both complete and good.[2] And he interpreted the arrival of Suhail (Ibn 'Amr) as meaning ease in their affairs on the Day of Hudaibiyyah.[3] And he delegated a group to milk a sheep and a man stood up to milk it and he said to him: "What is your name?" He said; "Murrah (Bitterness)"

---

[1] Narrated by Abu Dawûd in his *'Sunan'* and he said: "I omitted their chains of narrators for the sake of brevity.

[2] Narrated by Muslim, Abu Dawûd and Ahmad.

[3] Narrated by Al-Bukhari.

The Prophet ﷺ said to him: "Sit." Then another stood and he said to him: "What is your name?" He said: "Harb (War)." The Prophet ﷺ said: "Sit." Another man stood up and he asked him: "What is your name?" He replied: "Ya'eesh (Living)." The Prophet ﷺ said: "Milk it."[1]

He disliked places with objectionable names and hated to pass through them, such as on one occasion, when he passed between two mountains and he asked about their name and they said: "Fadhih (Disgraceful) and Mukhzin (Shameful), so he avoided them.

And since there is a connection and a relation between names and things named and closeness, such as there is between the vessels[2] of things and their reality, and such as there is between spirits and bodies, the mind makes a connection between one and the other, as when Iyyas Ibn Mu'awiyah and others used to see a person and say: "His name should be such-and-such." And he was almost never wrong. And the opposite of this is making a connection between his name and its meaning, as when 'Umar ؓ asked a man about his name and he said: "Jamrah (Firebrand)." So he asked him: "What is your father's name?" He replied: "Shihab (Flame)." 'Umar ؓ asked: "And your house?" He said: "(It is in) Harrah An-Nar (The Lava Field of Fire)." He inquired: "Then where is your abode?" He answered: "In Zat Laza (The Place of the Raging Fire)." 'Umar ؓ said to him: "Go, for your abode has burnt down." And he left and found it to be so.[3]

Likewise, the Prophet ﷺ made a connection between the name of Suhail and ease in their affairs. And he ordered his people to choose their names well and he informed them that on the Day of Resurrection, they will be called forth by them. And consider how two fitting names of the Prophet ﷺ are derived from his attributes; and they are Ahmad and Muhammad, for he is – due to the

---

[1] Narrated by Malik, in 'Al-Muwatta".

[2] That is, outward appearance.

[3] Narrated by Malik in 'Al-Muwatta", its *Sanad* is described as *Munqati'* (broken) since the narrator, Yahya Ibn Sa'eed Al-Ansari did not hear from 'Umar ؓ. According to Shu'aib and 'Abdul Qadir Al-Arna'ût, it also has a connected chain, narrated by Abul Qasim Ibn Bishran, in his book 'Al-Fawa'id'. And Allâh knows better.

numerous praiseworthy attributes which he possesses and their
nobility and virtue – compared to the attributes of others Ahmad (i.e.
more praised). Likewise his nicknaming Abul Hakam (Owner of
Wisdom) Abu Jahl (Owner of Ignorance) and likewise Allâh, the
Almighty, the All-Powerful's nicknaming 'Abdul 'Uzza (Slave of Al-
'Uzza[1]) Abu Lahab (Owner of Flame), due to the fact that his
destination was the Hell-fire. And when the Prophet ﷺ arrived in Al-
Madinah, its name was Yathrib (Censure). And because a good name
necessitates that the person or thing so named is also good, the
Prophet ﷺ said to some Arabs:

«يَا بَنِي عَبْدِاللهِ إِنَّ اللهَ قَدْ أَحْسَنَ اسْمَكُمْ وَاسْمَ أَبِيكُمْ»

"O, Banu 'Abdillah! Verily, Allâh has given you and your father
a good name."

See how he called them to the worship of Allâh thereby!

And consider the names of the six who went forth in single combat
on the day of the Battle of Badr: Al-Waleed (whose name means
newborn) was the first, and a newborn is at the start of his life, and
Shaibah (whose name means old man) was the last, and an old man
is at the end of his life. And 'Utbah means censure and rebuke. And
their opponents were 'Ali, 'Ubaidah and Al-Harith: Exaltedness,
Worship and Striving – which is the meaning of *Harth* – This is why
the most beloved names to Allâh are those which necessitate the
most beloved attributes to Him; and adding worship to the Name
Allâh and to the Name Ar-Rahman (the Most Beneficent) is more
beloved by Him that adding it to the Name Al-Qadir (Most Able) and
Al-Qahir (the Irresistable) and others; this is because the connection
between the slave and his Lord is only that of pure and sincere
worship and the connection between Allâh and the slave is pure
Mercy and Compassion (*Rahmah*). By His Mercy and Compassion,
the slave exists and is made in the most perfect of forms. And the
purpose for which he was brought into being is to worship Him
Alone, with love, fear (of His Punishment) and hope (of His Reward).

---

[1] Al-'Uzza: The name of one of the deities worshipped by the pagan
Quraish.

And because every slave acts in accordance with his desires – and every desire begins with an intention – and the result of his desire is striving and acquisition, the truest names are: Hammam (Intending) and Al-Harith (the Striver) And since the name: Al-Malik (the King) is the right of Allâh Alone, it is the most wretched of names in Allâh's Sight; and even more vexing to Him is the name: *Shahan Shah* i.e. King of Kings and Sultan of Sultans, because none has the right to such names except Allâh, the Almighty, the All-Powerful. Therefore calling anyone other than Him by these names is false and invalid and Allâh loves not that which is false and invalid. And some have added to this the title: *Qadi Al-Qudah* (Judge of Judges) and it is followed (in the list of hateful names) by the ugly appellation: *Sayyid An-Nas* (Master of the People), because this belongs to no one except the Messenger of Allâh ﷺ.

And because war and bitterness are the most detested things in the eyes of the people, the names: Harb and Murrah are the ugliest names to them. Similar to them are the names: Hanzalah (A bitter tasting fruit) and Hazn (Rugged) and others like them. And since the characters of the Prophets are the noblest of characters, their names are the best of names, so the Prophet ﷺ recommended his people to take their names, as reported from the Prophet ﷺ in Abu Dawûd's '*Sunan*' and An-Nasa'i's '*Sunan*': "Call yourselves (i.e. your children) by the names of the Prophets."[1] And if it were only that the name reminds us of the one who bore it and necessitates a connection (in the mind) with its meaning, it would be sufficient benefit.

As for the prohibition of naming a child Yasar and the like, it is due to another reason which was indicated in the *Hadeeth*, and that is his words: "It will be said: "Is he there?" up to the end of the *Hadeeth*. And Allâh knows better whether they are a part of the *Hadeeth* or whether they have been added (i.e. whether they are the words of the narrator), but since these names might cause people to regard them

---

[1] Narrated by Abu Dawûd, An-Nasa'i, Al-Bukhari in '*Al-Adab Al-Mufrad*'. And Muslim narrated on the authority of Al-Mugheerah Ibn Shu'bah ﷺ: "They used to call themselves by the names of the Prophets and the righteous folk before them."

as omens and the things which they apprehend from them might actually occur, the wisdom of the most kind to his people (i.e. the Prophet 鷐 dictates that He forbid them from things which cause them to hear what is disliked, or cause it to occur. In addition to this, the opposite of the name may be connected with him, as when a person is called Yasar (Ease), when he is the most difficult of people, or being called Najeeh (Successful) when he has no success, or Rabah (Profit), when he is one of the losers. In that case, he would have fallen into lying upon him and upon Allâh. And there is another matter, which is that he might be called by his given name and he is not so, which causes him to be maligned by someone saying: "Out of their ignorance, they called you Sadeed (Correct), but by Allâh, there is no correctness in you." Likewise, some praises may result in blame or rebuke to the one praised (i.e. the one bearing the name), causing people to be critical of him, for he is being praised for some attribute which he does not possess and people expect him to have the virtue for which he is praised and they believe him to have it, but then they find that he does not, and so the praise turns to rebuke. So if this praise had been abandoned, this cause of evil could have been avoided. And there is another matter, which is the belief of the person named that he possesses this attribute and so he falls into self praise, which is why the Prophet 鷐 prohibited Juwairiyah 鷐 from calling herself Barrah (Righteous). Based upon this, it is disliked to called oneself Ar-Rasheed (the Rightly Guided), Al-Mutee' (the Submissive) At-Ta'i (the Obedient) and the like.

As for the disbelievers calling themselves by such names, it is not permissible to allow them to do so, nor is it permissible to address them by any of these names.

As for the *Kunyah*,[1] it is a form of honouring someone; and the Prophet 鷐 bestowed the *Kunyah*: Abu Yahya on Suhaib 鷐 and upon 'Ali 鷐 the *Kunyah*: Abu Turab and upon the brother of Anas 鷐 the *Kunyah*: Abu 'Umair while he was still a small child. It was a part of his guidance to bestow a *Kunyah* upon a person who had a son and

---

[1] *Kunyah*: A nickname which contains the appellation: 'Abu', such as Abu Bakr, Abu Hurairah etc.

upon one who had no son. And it has not been confirmed from him that he prohibited any *Kunyah* except Abul Qasim;[1] scholars have disagreed regarding it: Some said that it is totally impermissible, while others said that it is not permissible to combine it with his name (i.e. Abul Qasim Muhammad); and there is a *Hadeeth* to that effect which was declared authentic by At-Tirmidhi. And it was said that it is permissible to combine them, based upon the *Hadeeth* of 'Ali ﷺ, in which he said (to the Prophet ﷺ: "If another son is born to me after you (die), may I call him by your name and bestow upon him your *Kunyah*?" He ﷺ said: "Yes."[2] This was declared authentic by At-Tirmidhi. And it was said that the prohibition was only during his lifetime.

The correct opinion is that bestowing his *Kunyah* on anyone is forbidden; and it was more strictly prohibited during his lifetime. Also combining them is prohibited, for the authenticity of the *Hadeeth* of 'Ali ﷺ is questionable[3] and At-Tirmidhi was not strict regarding the authentication of *Ahadeeth*. And 'Ali ﷺ said that it was a license for him, which proves that the prohibition remains for others. As for the *Hadeeth* of 'A'ishah ﷺ: "What could make my name lawful and my *Kunyah* unlawful?" – it is *Ghareeb*.[4] An authentic *Hadeeth* may not be contradicted by such a narration.

A group of the *Salaf* disliked that the *Kunyah*: Abu 'Eesa be applied to anyone, while others permitted it. Abu Dawûd narrated on the authority of Zaid Ibn Aslam ﷺ that 'Umar ﷺ struck one of his sons who took for himself the *Kunyah*: Abu 'Eesa and that Al-Mugheerah ﷺ took for himself the *Kunyah*: Abu 'Eesa and 'Umar ﷺ said: "Is it not enough for you to take the name Abu

---

[1] That is, the Prophet's own *Kunyah*.

[2] Narrated by Abu Dawûd and At-Tirmidhi and declared *Hasan-Saheeh* by At-Tirmidhi.

[3] All of the narrators in the *Sanad* are described by scholars of *Hadeeth* as reliable.

[4] *Ghareeb*: A *Hadeeth* reported at some point(s) in its *Sanad* by a single narrator; such a *Hadeeth* is not necessarily weak, but obviously Ibn Al-Qayyim means to suggest that it is so here. However, all of the narrators are described as reliable by scholars of *Hadeeth*.

'Abdillah as a *Kunyah*?" Al-Mugheerah ⁓ replied: "The Messenger of Allâh ﷺ bestowed this *Kunyah* upon me." 'Umar ⁓ responded: "The Messenger of Allâh ﷺ has had all of his sins, past and future been forgiven by Allâh, while we are in our *Jaljah*."[1] (After this,) he continued to use the *Kunyah*: Abu 'Abdillah until he died."

He forbade that grapes be called *Karm*, and he said:

$$«الْكَرَمُ قَلْبُ الْمُؤْمِنِ»$$

"*Al-Karm* is the heart of a Believer."[2]

This is because the wording indicates much goodness and benefits (and the heart of a Believer has more right to be so described than do grapes). And he said:

$$«لَا يَغْلِبَنَّكُمُ الْأَعْرَابُ عَلَى اسْمِ صَلَاتِكُمْ أَلَا وَإِنَّهَا الْعِشَاءُ، وَإِنَّهُمْ يُسَمُّونَهَا الْعَتَمَةَ»$$

"Do not be influenced by Bedouins regarding the name of your prayer which is called '*Isha*', but they call it *Al-'Atamah* (darkness)."[3]

And he said:

$$«لَوْ يَعْلَمُونَ مَا فِي الْعَتَمَةِ وَالصُّبْحِ لَأَتَوْهُمَا وَلَوْ حَبْوًا»$$

"If they knew what (virtue) there is in *Al-'Atamah* and the *Fajr* prayer, they would come to it even crawling on their hands and knees."[4]

So the correct view is that he did not totally prohibit this name, he only forbade that it should replace the name '*Isha*'. And this is

---

[1] In our *Jaljah*: That is, we still remain amongst a number of Muslims like us, and we do not know what Allâh will do with us. All of the narrators are described as reliable by scholars of *Hadeeth*.

[2] Narrated by Al-Bukhari, Muslim, Abu Dawûd and Ahmad.

[3] Narrated by Abu Dawûd and Ahmad. The Bedouins called the '*Isha*' prayer *Al-'Atamah* because they used to delay performing it until it was very dark, at which time they used to milk their camels.

[4] Narrated by Al-Bukhari and Muslim, on the authority of Abu Hurairah ⁓.

preserving the name which Allâh has given to this act of worship. So it should neither be replaced or affected by any other name, as was done by the later generations and it caused corruption of which Allâh is fully Aware. And thereby, he was preserving a preference for that which Allâh has preferred.

And he began the *'Eed* with the prayer, then he slaughtered. And he began his ablution by washing the face, then the hands, then the head, then the feet. And he gave *Zakat Al-Fitr* before the *'Eed* prayer, in accordance with the Words of Allâh:

"Indeed whosoever purifies himself (by avoiding polytheism and accepting Islamic Monotheism) shall achieve success. And remembers (glorifies) the Name of his Lord (worships none but Allâh), and prays (five compulsory prayers and *Nawafil* — additional prayers)."[1]

And examples of this are numerous.

---------- ❖ ❖ ❖ ----------

---

[1] *Sûrah Al-A'la* 87:14-15

> **Chapter**

Regarding His ﷺ Guidance in Guarding His Words and Choosing His Expressions With Care

He used to choose his words carefully in his public addresses, selecting for his people the best terms, and he used to avoid the expressions of the coarse folk and obscenities. He was neither obscene in speech, nor in deed, nor did he bellow, nor did he speak crudely or coarsely. And he disliked that noble words should be used regarding a person who did not deserve it and he disliked that hated expressions be used regarding one who did not deserve it.

From the first category, he forbade that a hypocrite should be addressed as *Sayyid* (Master) and he prohibited that grapes should be called *Karm* and he forbade that Abu Jahl should be called Abul Hakam and he also changed the name of one of the Companions ﷺ from Abul Hakam and he said:

"Verily, Allâh is *Al-Hakam* and to Him belongs *Al-Hukm* (the Judgement)."[1]

He also forbade that the bonded slave should call his master: *"Rabbee"* (My Lord) and that the master should say to his slave: *"Abdee"* (My slave) and: *"Amatee"* (My slave-girl). And to a person who claimed that he was a physician, he said:

---

[1] Narrated by Abu Dawûd and An-Nasa'i, on the authority of Hani'.

«أَنْتَ رَفِيقٌ، وَطَبِيبُهَا الَّذِي خَلَقَهَا»

"You are a companion and the One Who created her is her Physician)."[1]

The ignorant people refer to a disbeliever who has some knowledge of medicine as: *"Hakeem"* (Wise). And to a person who said: "And whoever disobeys them (i.e. Allâh and His Messenger 鐐 has gone astray," he 鐐 said:

«بِئْسَ الْخَطِيبُ أَنْتَ»

"What a bad speaker you are;

say: "He who disobeys Allâh and His Messenger." Ibn Numair added: "He (the speaker) in fact went astray."[2] Also in this first category is his saying: "Do not say: "As Allâh wills and so-and-so wills."[3] — and carrying the same meaning is the saying of one who does not guard himself against *Shirk*: "I (seek help) with Allâh and with you" And: "Allâh and you are sufficient for me." And: "I have no one except Allâh and you." And: "I place my trust and dependence in Allâh and you." And: "This is from Allâh and from you." And: "By Allâh and by your life." – and other such sayings in which the one who says them assigns partners to Allâh; these sayings are more strictly forbidden and uglier than the saying: "As Allâh wills and as you will."

But if a person said: "I (seek help) with Allâh and then with you," or: "As Allâh wills, then as you will," then there is no objection to it, as in the *Hadeeth* of the three (from Banu Isra'eel):

«لَا بَلَاغَ لِيَ الْيَوْمَ إِلَّا بِاللهِ ثُمَّ بِكَ»

"There is no sufficiency for me (to complete my journey) this day except with Allâh and then with you."[4]

As for the second category, it is to emit expressions of censure and

---

[1] Narrated by Abu Dawûd and Ahmad.

[2] Narrated by Muslim, on the authority of 'Adi Ibn Hatim 鐐.

[3] Narrated by Abu Dawûd and Ahmad, on the authority of Huzaifah 鐐.

[4] Narrated by Muslim, on the authority of Abu Hurairah 鐐.

rebuke to those who do not deserve them; and it is like his prohibition of reviling *Ad-Dahr* (Time), saying:

«إِنَّ اللهَ هُوَ الدَّهْرُ»

"Do not revile *Ad-Dahr*, for Allâh is *Ad-Dahr*."[1]

And in this there are three evils:

The First: Maligning that which does not deserve it.

The Second: That maligning it implies *Shirk*, since he only maligns it because of his belief that it harms or benefits and that it is unjust and the poems in which these people malign it are very numerous, and many of the ignorant openly curse it.

The Third: That such revilement is only committed by those who do those deeds in which if the truth were subordinate to their vain desires, the heavens and the earth would have been corrupted; and if it coincides with their vain desires, they praise time and extol it.

Included in this is the saying of the Prophet ﷺ:

«لَا يَقُولَنَّ أَحَدُكُمْ، تَعِسَ الشَّيْطَانُ، فَإِنَّهُ يَتَعَاظَمُ حَتَّى يَكُونَ مِثْلَ البَيْتِ، وَيَقُولُ: صَرَعْتُهُ بِقُوَّتِي، وَلَكِنْ لِيَقُلْ: بِاسْمِ اللهِ، فَإِنَّهُ يَتَصَاغَرُ حَتَّى يَكُونَ مِثْلَ الذُّبَابِ»

"None of you should say: "May Satan perish," for if you say that, he will swell so much so that he will be like a house and he will say: "By my power I have vanquished him by my power." But say: "In the Name of Allâh," for when you say that, he will diminish so that he will be like a fly."[2]

And in another *Hadeeth*:

«إِنَّ الْعَبْدَ إِذَا لَعَنَ الشَّيْطَانَ يَقُولُ: إِنَّكَ لَتَلْعَنُ مَلْعَنًا»

"Verily, when the slave curses Satan, he says: "Verily, you are cursing one who is (already) cursed."

Similar to this is the saying: "May Allâh humiliate Satan," and: "May

---

[1] Narrated by Al-Bukhari, Muslim, Ahmad and Malik.

[2] Narrated by Abu Dawûd and Ahmad.

Allâh disgrace Satan," for all of these things make him happy and he says: "The son of Adam knows that I have defeated him by my power." And this lends support to him in his misguidance; this is why the Prophet ﷺ advised a person who is touched by something from Satan to mention Allâh and to recite his Name and seek refuge with Him from Satan, for that is more beneficial for him and more exasperating for Satan.

He ﷺ also prohibited that a person should say: "*Khabuthat Nafsee*," and that he should say instead: "*Lasiqat Nafsee*."[1] And their meaning is one, that is: My soul has become sickened and it has become straitened.[2] But the Prophet (ﷺ) disliked for them to use the verb "*Khabutha*" due to the meanings of wickedness and disgracefulness which it connotes.

And he ﷺ also forbade that a person should say, after missing something: "If only I had done such-and-such" and he said:

$$\text{«إِنَّهَا تَفْتَحُ عَمَلَ الشَّيْطَانِ»}$$

"Verily, it opens up (the door to) the deeds of Satan."[3]

And he ﷺ guided us to what is more beneficial than that, which is to say: "*Qaddarallahu Wa Ma Sha'a Fa'ala*" (Allâh has ordained and as He willed, He has done).[4] This is because his saying: "If I had done such-and-such, I would not have lost the thing which I lost," or: "I would not have done that thing which I did," does not benefit anything, for it does not change what has already occurred, nor does the word "*Lauw*" (if) solve his problem. And implied in it is that if the matter had been as he planned to himself, it would have been other than as Allâh decreed; and the occurrence of something other than what has been decreed is impossible, so his speech includes untruth,

---

[1] Narrated by Al-Bukhari, Muslim, Abu Dawûd and Ahmad.

[2] Both expressions carry the same meaning, but "*Khabuthat Nafsee*" also means: "I have become wicked," whereas "*Laqisat Nafsee*" means only: "I am annoyed," which is why the Prophet ﷺ preferred it over the former expression.

[3] Narrated by Muslim and Ibn Majah.

[4] Narrated by Muslim and Ibn Majah.

ignorance and impossibility. And if it is free from denial of (Allâh's) *Qadar*, it is not free from opposing it by saying "*Lauw*". And if it is said: "But the things which he wished for are also a part of *Qadar*," it may be said: "That is true, but that is of benefit before something disliked which Allâh ordained occurs, and once it occurs, there is no way to avoid it or lessen it. Rather, what he should do in these circumstances is to face the deeds necessary to remove or limit the damage resulting from the *Qadar* and not to wish for something whose occurrence is not to be hoped for, for that is simply helplessness and Allâh censures helplessness, but he loves intelligence and resourcefulness, which is to undertake the means (of achieving one's aims) and this opens up the door to goodness, while helplessness opens up the door to Satan, for if a person fails to do what is of benefit to him, it becomes a vain desire, which is why the Prophet ﷺ sought refuge with Allâh from helplessness and laziness, for they are the key to every evil – and anxiety, depression, cowardice, miserliness, the burdensome debt and the oppression of men result from them – all of these things result from helplessness and laziness[1] and the sign of it is "*Lauw*", for the one who wishes (that Allâh's *Qadar* were different) is among the most helpless of people and the most bankrupt. And the root of all sins is weakness or helplessness, because the slave is unable to undertake the means of achieving obedience and the means which keep him far away from acts of disobedience and form a barrier between him and them; and in this noble *Hadeeth*, all of the roots and branches of evil are mentioned, along with its origins and its end results and its causes and its sources. And it comprises eight characteristics, each two of which are similar in meaning: He (ﷺ) said:

$$ «أَعُوذُ بِكَ مِنَ الهَمِّ وَالْحُزْنِ» $$

---

[1] These words are taken from a *Hadeeth* reported on the authority of Anas ﷺ, who said that the Prophet ﷺ said: "O Allâh! I seek refuge with You from anxiety and sorrow, from helplessness and laziness, from miserliness and cowardice, from being heavily in debt and from being overcome by men." (Narrated by Al-Bukhari, At-Tirmidhi, An-Nasa'i, Abu Dawûd and Ahmad.

"I seek refuge with You from *"Al-Hamm"* (anxiety) and *"Al-Hazn"* (sorrow).

and they are both near to each other in meaning, because when something which is disliked afflicts the heart, the cause of it is either something which has already occurred, in which case, it results in sorrow, or else, it is expected to occur in the future, in which case, it gives rise to anxiety – and both of them are from helplessness, because that which has already occurred cannot be dispelled by sorrow; but rather by acceptance, praise and thanks (to Allâh), patient perseverance, belief in Allâh's *Qadar* and the saying of the slave:

$$\text{«قَدَّرَ اللهُ وَمَا شَاءَ فَعَلَ»}$$

"Qaddarallahu Wa Ma Sha'a Fa'l"

"Allâh has ordained and as He willed, He has done."

And that which has yet to happen cannot be repelled by anxiety, for either there is a solution for it, in which case, he is able to do it, or there is no solution, in which case, he is unable to do it; and he should don the garments of *Tawheed* and *Tawakkul*[1] and display acceptance of Allâh as his Lord, regarding the things which he loves and the things which he hates. And anxiety and sorrow weaken the will and enfeeble the heart and form a barrier between the slave and striving to achieve what is beneficial for him and so they are a heavy burden on the wayfarer's back.

And it is from the Wisdom of the Almighty, the Most Wise that he inflicts these two things upon the hearts which reject Him, in order to turn them away from many of the acts of disobedience which they commit; and these hearts remain in this prison until they reach a state of pure, unadulterated acceptance and affirmation of Allâh's Oneness and draws near to Allâh; and there is no way to purify the hearts from that (imprisonment) except this, and there is no recourse except to Allâh, Alone, for nothing leads to Allâh except Allâh and nothing guides to Him but He. And whatever situation the slave finds

---

[1] *Tawakkul*: Depending upon Allâh, but at the same time, undertaking the necessary steps to achieve one's objective.

himself in, it is Allâh Who placed him in it and it is thanks to Him and His Wisdom. And He does not forbid the slave from any right which is his; rather, he prevents him in order that he may implore Allâh through the deeds which He loves and then He gives him; and (He prevents him) in order that he may return to Him and strengthen him through humility towards Him, to make him independent (of people) through his need for Allâh, to restore him by submission before Allâh, to raise him to the noblest position and to show him the Wisdom in His Ability and the Mercy in His Might. And truly, when His Forbiddance is in fact giving and His Punishment is in fact Discipline. And when He causes an enemy to be victorious over him, it is in order that he be guided to Allâh; And Allâh knows better where and to whom, He gives His Bounty and He knows better where and with whom He places His Message:

﴿وَكَذَٰلِكَ فَتَنَّا بَعْضَهُم بِبَعْضٍ لِّيَقُولُوٓاْ أَهَٰٓؤُلَآءِ مَنَّ ٱللَّهُ عَلَيْهِم مِّنۢ بَيْنِنَآ أَلَيْسَ ٱللَّهُ بِأَعْلَمَ بِٱلشَّٰكِرِينَ﴾

"Thus We have tried some of them with others, that they might say: 'Is it these (poor believers) whom Allâh has favoured from amongst us?' Does not Allâh know best those who are grateful?"[1]

So He, Most Glorified knows better whom He should choose. Therefore, when a person is prevented from something, it becomes a gift bestowed on him, while whoever busied himself with what was bestowed upon him, it becomes a prevention for him (from the reward of the Hereafter). What He, Most Glorified, Most High requires of us is that we be upright and take the Path which leads to Him; and He informed us that this desire cannot be achieved until a person wills as Allâh wills, as He, Most High says:

﴿وَمَا تَشَآءُونَ إِلَّآ أَن يَشَآءَ ٱللَّهُ رَبُّ ٱلْعَٰلَمِينَ ۝﴾

"And you cannot will unless (it be) that Allâh wills — the Lord of the 'Alamın (mankind, jinn and all that exists)."[2]

---

[1] *Sûrah Al-An'am* 6:53
[2] *Sûrah At-Takweer* 81:29

For if the slave possessed a second soul, its relationship to the first soul would be as that of the first soul to his body, with which he seeks to do Allâh's Will; If he does not, then his situation does not merit that he be given; and he has no vessel in which the gift may be placed, for whoever comes with no vessel will return with nothing and he has no one to blame but himself.

And what is meant is that he ﷺ sought refuge from worry and sorrow – and they are connected to each other and they are due to helplessness and laziness, which are also connected, so if the slave delayed performing righteous deeds or performed them imperfectly, it would be either due to inability on his part, and that is helplessness, or it would be that he was able to do it, but he did not want to, and that is laziness. And the result of these two characteristics is that he would miss every good thing and attain every evil. And included in this evil is his failing to perform physical acts which are beneficial, and this is cowardice, and to use his wealth, and this is miserliness. The result of this is that he is oppressed by two things: One of them rightfully, and that is the oppression of being in debt and one of them falsely, which is the oppression of men. And all of these things are the result of helplessness and laziness. And from this is the saying in the authentic *Hadeeth* of the man against whom a judgement was made:

$$\text{«حَسْبِيَ اللهُ وَنِعْمَ الْوَكِيلُ»}$$

"Hasbiyallahu Wa Ni'mal-Wakeel"

"Allâh is sufficient for me and He is the Best Disposer of Affairs."

Verily, Allâh censures helplessness and weakness, but you must be intelligent and resourceful, then if something gets the better of you, you should say:

$$\text{«حَسْبِيَ اللهُ وَنِعْمَ الْوَكِيلُ»}$$

"Hasbiyallahu Wa Ni'mal-Wakeel"[1]

This man said it after he failed to do all that was required of him in

---

[1] Narrated by Abu Dawûd and Ahmad, on the authority of 'Awf Ibn Malik ﷺ.

order to win his case, which if he had done, the case would have been decided in his favour. And if he had undertaken the necessary measures to achieve his aim, then he had been defeated, he should have said it and it would have had its effect, as when Abraham (Ibraheem 🕮), Allâh's *Khaleel*, said, when he had undertaken the necessary means to reach his goal which he was commanded to do, and he did not fail to do any of them; then the enemy overcame him and they threw him in the fire and he said: *"Hasbiyallahu Wa Ni'mal-Wakeel"*. And so the words were spoken in their proper place and they had their effect.

Likewise, when it was said to the Messenger of Allâh 🕮 and his Companions 🕮 on the day of the Battle of Uhud after they had departed from there:

$$﴿إِنَّ ٱلنَّاسَ قَدْ جَمَعُوا۟ لَكُمْ فَٱخْشَوْهُمْ﴾$$

"Verily, the people (i.e. the pagans) have gathered against you (a great army), so fear them."[1]

They prepared themselves and went out to meet them, then they said the words (*Hasbunallahu Wa Ni'mal-Wakeel*) and they had their effect. This is why Allâh, Most High says:

$$﴿وَمَن يَتَّقِ ٱللَّهَ يَجْعَل لَّهُۥ مَخْرَجًا ۝ وَيَرْزُقْهُ مِنْ حَيْثُ لَا يَحْتَسِبُ ۚ وَمَن يَتَوَكَّلْ عَلَى ٱللَّهِ فَهُوَ حَسْبُهُۥٓ﴾$$

"And whosoever fears Allâh and keeps his duty to Him, He will make a way for him to get out (from every difficulty). And He will provide him from (sources) he never could imagine. And whosoever puts his trust in Allâh, then He will suffice him."[2]

And He, Most High says:

$$﴿وَٱتَّقُوا۟ ٱللَّهَ ۚ وَعَلَى ٱللَّهِ فَلْيَتَوَكَّلِ ٱلْمُؤْمِنُونَ﴾$$

"So fear Allâh. And in Allâh let the believers put their trust."[3]

---

[1] *Sûrah Âl 'Imrân:* 3:173
[2] *Sûrah At-Talâq:* 65:2-3
[3] *Sûrah Al-Ma'idah:* 5:11

So *Tawakkul* (dependence on Allâh) and *Al-Hasb* (declaring that Allâh is Sufficient) without undertaking the measures which have been commanded is pure weakness and helplessness, even though there may be an element of *Tawkkul* in it. It is not fitting that the slave should let his *Tawakkul* be in the form of helplessness, nor that he should claim that his helplessness was in fact *Tawakkul*; instead, he should make his *Tawakkul* one of the necessary measures, without which one's aim will not be achieved.

On this point, two groups have gone astray: One of them claimed that *Tawakkul* alone is an independent means, so they denied the means which are necessitated by Allâh's Wisdom. The second undertook the means and rejected *Tawakkul* as having no role in the matter. And what is meant (by this *Hadeeth*) is that the Prophet 鑑 guided the slave to that wherein lies his utmost perfection, that he takes care to do what is beneficial for him and to strive hard; in that case his declaring that Allâh is Sufficient for him will benefit him, as opposed to one who is neglectful and then says: *"Hasbiyallahu Wa Ni'mal-Wakeel"*. Allâh will blame him for this and He will not be Sufficient for him in that case, for He is only Sufficient for those who fear Him, then place their trust and dependence on Him.

Chapter

Regarding His ﷺ Guidance in *Dhikr* (Mentioning Allâh's Name)

He ﷺ was the most perfect of people in remembrance of Allâh, the Almighty, the All-Powerful; indeed, all of his speech was remembrance of Allâh and the Help which He gave to him. And his command, his prohibition and his legislation were all remembrance of Allâh from him. And his informing us of the Lord's Names and His Attributes, His Judgements, His Actions, His Promise and His Threat were all forms of remembrance of Him. And his extolling Him by His Signs, exalting Him, glorifying Him and praising Him were remembrance of Him, as was his silence a form of remembrance of Him in his heart. His remembrance of Allâh flowed with his breath, whether he was standing, sitting, lying on his side, walking or riding, upon his departure and upon his arrival, when he was traveling and when he was residing.

And when he awoke, he would say:

«الْحَمْدُ لله الَّذِي أَحْيَانَا بَعْدَ مَا أَمَاتَنَا وَإِلَيْهِ النُّشُورُ»

"Al-Hamdu Lillahil-Ladhee Ahyana Ba'da Ma Amatana Wa Ilaihin-Nushûr"

"All praise and thanks be to Allâh, Who brought us to life after He had brought death [i.e. sleep] to us, and to Him will be the Resurrection."[1]

Then he (i.e. Ibn Al-Qayyim) mentioned *Ahadeeth* that had been narrated regarding what a person should say when he wakes up, when he opens the prayer, when he leaves his house and when he

---

[1] Narrated by Al-Bukhari, Muslim, Ibn Majah, Ahmad and Ad-Darimi.

enters the mosque and what he should say in the evening and in the morning, when he dons his clothes, when he enters the house, when he enters the privy, when ablution is made, when the call to prayer is made, when the new moon is sighted, when eating and when sneezing.

---------- ❖ ❖ ❖ ----------

Regarding His ﷺ Guidance Upon Entering His House

He never used to take his family by surprise by entering upon them all of a sudden, which might cause harm to them; rather, he would enter upon his family with their knowledge that he was going to do so and he would deliver salutations of peace to them. And when he entered, he would begin by asking how they were, or he would ask of them. And he might say:

«هَلْ عِنْدَكُمْ مِنْ غَدَاءٍ»؟

"Do you have anything to eat?"[1]

And he might remain silent until whatever was available was brought before him.

And it has been authentically reported from him that a man delivered salutations of peace to him while he was urinating, but he did not reply to him, and he informed that Allâh, Most Glorified, Most High abhors that a person should speak while defecating. He would not face towards the *Qiblah*, nor turn his back to it when he was defecating or urinating and he forbade others to do so.

---

[1] Narrated by Muslim, on the authority of 'A'ishah ﵂.

Chapter

It has been authentically reported from him ﷺ that he legislated the calling of the *Adhan* with reverberation and without reverberation in the voice and he legislated that the *Iqamah* be called reciting each phrase twice and reciting each phrase only once; however, single recitation of the phrase:

«قَدْ قَامَتِ الصَّلَاةُ»

"Qad Qamatis-Salah"

"The prayer has commenced" has never been authentically reported from him ﷺ. Similarly, what has been authentically reported from him is repetition of the words of *Takbeer* at the start of the *Adhan*, but it has not been authentically reported from him that it may not be recited more than twice; and he legislated five ways for responding to the *Adhan* for his community (i.e. the Muslims):

The First: That they should say as the *Mu'adhdhin* does, except for the words: *"Hayya 'Alas-Salah"* (Hurry to prayer) and: *"Hayya 'Alal-Falah"* (Hurry to success); instead, he instructed that they should say:

«لَا حَوْلَ وَلَا قُوَّةَ إِلَّا بِاللهِ»

"La Hawla Wa La Quwwata Illa Billah"

"There is no power and no strength save in Allâh."[1]

And it has not been transmitted to us that he combined them, nor limiting oneself to saying: *"Hayya 'Alas-Salah, Hayya 'Alal-Falah"*, and this is dictated by the wisdom behind this, since the words of the *Adhan* are *Dhikr*, while the words: *"Hayya 'Alas-Salah, Hayya 'Alal-Falah"* are an invitation to prayer; therefore, it is legislated for one who hears the *Adhan* to seek help (from Allâh) by the words of

---

[1] Narrated by Al-Bukhari, Muslim and Malik.

seeking help (*La Hawla Wa La Quwwata Illa Billah*).

The Second: That they should say:

«رَضِيتُ بِاللهِ رَبًّا، وَبِالإِسْلَامِ دِينًا، وَبِمُحَمَّدٍ رَسُولًا»

"*Radeetu Billahi Rabban Wa Bil-Islami Deenan Wa Bimuhammadin Rasûla*"

"I am well pleased with Allâh as my Lord, with Islam as my Religion and with Muhammad as a Messenger."

And he informed us that who said that: "His sins will be forgiven."[1]

The Third: That they should send prayers on the Prophet ﷺ upon completing the reply to the *Mu'adhdhin*, and the most perfect is that which he taught to his people, even though those who feign knowledge may claim to know better.

The Fourth: That they should say after sending prayers upon him:

«اللَّهُمَّ رَبَّ هَذِهِ الدَّعْوَةِ التَّامَّةِ، وَالصَّلَاةِ الْقَائِمَةِ، آتِ مُحَمَّدًا الْوَسِيلَةَ وَالْفَضِيلَةَ، وَابْعَثْهُ مَقَامًا مَحْمُودًا»

"*Allâhumma, Rabba Hazihid-Da'watit-Tammati, Was-Salatil-Qa'imati, Ati Muhammadan Al-Waseelata Wal-Fadheelata Wab'athhu Maqaman Mahmûda*"

"Oh, Allâh! Lord of this most complete supplication and of the established prayer, grant Muhammad the place of intercession, the most virtuous place and raise him to a praiseworthy position."

The Fifth: That they supplicate for themselves after that; and in the '*Sunan*', it is reported from him ﷺ that he said:

«الدُّعَاءُ لَا يُرَدُّ بَيْنَ الأَذَانِ وَالإِقَامَةِ»

"Supplication between the *Adhan* and the *Iqamah* is not rejected."

They said: "What should we say, O, Messenger of Allâh?" He ﷺ replied:

---

[1] Narrated by Muslim, the compilers of the '*Sunan*' and Ibn Khuzaimah.

«سَلُوا اللهَ الْعَافِيَةَ فِي الدُّنْيَا وَالآخِرَةِ»

"Ask Allâh for well-being in the life of this world and in the
Hereafter." (An authentic *Hadeeth*)[1]

He used to supplicate much on the tenth of Dhul Hijjah and he
ordered his Companions ☀ thereon to declare Allâh's Oneness and to
glorify Him and praise Him; and it is reported from him ﷺ that he
used to make *Takbeer* from the *Fajr* prayer on the Day of *'Arafah*, until
the *'Asr* prayer on the last Day of *Tashreeq*; and he would say:

«اللهُ أَكْبَرُ، اللهُ أَكْبَرُ، لَا إِلَهَ إِلَّا اللهُ، وَاللهُ أَكْبَرُ، اللهُ أَكْبَرُ، وَللهِ
الْحَمْدِ»

"*Allâhu Akbar, Allâhu Akbar, La Ilaha Illallah, Wallahu Akbar,
Allâhu Akbar, Wa Lillahil-Hamd*"

"Allâh is Most Great, Allâh is Most Great, None has the right to
be worshipped except Allâh, and Allâh is Most Great, Allâh is
Most Great, and to Allâh are due all praise and thanks."

And although the *Sanad* of this may not be authentic, it may be acted
upon; and its wording is thus, with the *Takbeer* pronounced twice. As
for it being pronounced three times, it has only been reported on the
authority of Jabir and Ibn 'Abbas ☀ that they did so but three times
in succession and both narrations are *Hasan*. Ash-Shafi'i said: "If a
person adds to it, saying:

«اللهُ أَكْبَرُ كَبِيرًا، وَالْحَمْدُ للهِ كَثِيرًا، وَسُبْحَانَ اللهِ بُكْرَةً وَأَصِيلًا»

"*Allâhu Akbaru Kabeeran, Wal-Hamdu Lillahi Katheeran, Wa
Subhanallahi Bukratan Wa Aseelan*", it is good."

---

[1] Narrated by At-Tirmidhi, on the authority of Anas Ibn Malik ☀. It
contains in its *Sanad* one Yahya Ibn Yaman, of whom Ibn Hajr says: "He
was a righteous man, but they (i.e. the scholars of *Hadeeth*) are agreed
that he used to make many mistakes, especially in the *Hadeeth* of (Sufyan)
Ath-Thawri." It was also reported by Imam Ahmad as: "Supplication
between the *Adhan* and the *Iqamah* is not rejected, so supplicate." Its
Sanad was declared to be authentic by Ibn Khuzaimah and Ibn Hibban.

Chapter

When the Prophet ﷺ placed his hand in the food, he would say: *"Bismillah"* (In the Name of Allâh) and he ordered his Companions ﷺ to do likewise. If he forgot to do so, he would say when he remembered:

«بِسْمِ اللهِ أَوَّلَهُ وَآخِرَهُ»

"Bismillahi Awwalahu Wa Akhirahu

"In the Name of Allâh, in the beginning and in the end)." (An authentic *Hadeeth*)[1]

And the correct view is that it is obligatory to invoke Allâh's Name when starting to eat; and when a person fails to do so, the devil shares his food and drink with him. And the *Ahadeeth* which enjoin this are authentic and clear and there is nothing which contradicts them, nor is there any consensus which would warrant disagreement with them.

But does the invocation of one member of a group prevent the participation of the devil? Ash-Shafi'i has determined that the invocation of Allâh's Name by each individual is effective. It might be said that the participation of Satan with an eater is not interdicted except by his personal invocation of Allâh's Name, but it is narrated by At-Tirmidhi – and he declared it to be authentic – on the authority of 'A'ishah ﷺ that (she said): "The Messenger of Allâh ﷺ was eating with six of his Companions ﷺ and a Bedouin man came and ate a couple of bites and the Messenger of Allâh ﷺ said:

«أَمَا إِنَّهُ لَوْ سَمَّى لَكَفَاكُمْ»

"If he had said: *"Bismillah"*, it would have sufficed you all (i.e. it would have prevented the devil from eating any of the food)."

---

[1] Narrated by At-Tirmidhi and Abu Dawûd and declared authentic by Ibn Hibban and Al-Hakim and Az-Zahabi confirmed this.

And it is well known that the Prophet ﷺ and his Companions ﷺ used to invoke Allâh's Name. This is why it was reported in the *Hadeeth* of Huzaifah ﷺ: "We came to eat and a girl came as if she was impelled forward, and went to put her hand in the food, but the Messenger of Allâh ﷺ grabbed her hand. Then a Bedouin man came and it was as if he was impelled forward, but the Prophet ﷺ seized his hand and he said:

«إِنَّ الشَّيْطَانَ يَسْتَحِلُّ الطَّعَامَ أَنْ لَا يُذْكَرَ اسْمُ اللهِ عَلَيْهِ، وَإِنَّهُ جَاءَ بِهَذِهِ الْجَارِيَةِ لِيَسْتَحِلَّ بِهَا، فَأَخَذْتُ بِيَدِهَا، فَجَاءَ بِهَذَا الْأَعْرَابِيِّ لِيَسْتَحِلَّ بِهِ، فَأَخَذْتُ بِيَدِهِ، وَالَّذِي نَفْسِي بِيَدِهِ إِنَّ يَدَهُ لَفِي يَدِي مَعَ يَدَيْهِمَا»

"Verily, Satan considers it permissible for him to eat of food over which the Name of Allâh is not invoked, and he brought this girl in order to make it permissible for him, but I seized her hand and so he brought this Bedouin man in order to make it permissible for him, but I grabbed his hand. By Him in Whose Hand is my soul, Verily, his (i.e. the devil's) hand is in my hand with their hands."

Then he mentioned Allâh's Name and ate.[1] However, it might be said in reply that the Prophet ﷺ had not yet placed his hand in the food when the girl started eating. As for the matter of responding to salutations of peace and invoking Allâh's Blessings on a person who sneezes, there is some doubt about them; and it has been authentically reported from him ﷺ that he said:

«إِذَا عَطِسَ أَحَدُكُمْ فَحَمِدَ اللهَ، فَحَقٌّ عَلَى كُلِّ مَنْ سَمِعَهُ أَنْ يُشَمِّتَهُ»

"If any of you sneezes and then says: "*Al-Hamdu Lillah*" (All praise and thanks be to Allâh), then it is incumbent upon everyone who hears him to invoke Allâh's Mercy on him."[2]

---

[1] Narrated by Muslim, Abu Dawûd and Ahmad, on the authority of Huzaifah ﷺ. The addition: "Then he mentioned Allâh's Name and ate" is in Muslim's version.

[2] Narrated by Al-Bukhari, Muslim and Ahmad.

But even though the ruling in them is established, the difference between them and the matter of a person eating is obvious, for the devil is only able to partake of food with him (the one who did not invoke Allâh's Name) and if someone else invokes His Name, the participation of Satan is diminished for him, but his participation remains with those who did not mention Allâh's Name. And it is reported that when the Prophet ﷺ drank from a cup, he would take three breaths while drinking from it (i.e. he would not drink it all in one gulp), praising Allâh with every breath and thanking Him with the last breath.[1] He never criticized food; rather, if he disliked it, he would not eat it, but he would remain silent about it,[2] or he might say:

$$«أَجِدُنِي أَعَافُهُ»$$

"I find that I do not desire it."[3]

He would sometimes praise food, by saying for example, when it was said to him:

$$«نِعْمَ الإِدَامُ الْخَلُّ»$$

"We have nothing but vinegar."

"The best condiment is vinegar."[4] He said it in order to placate the one who offered it to him (i.e. his wife), not to say that vinegar is preferable to all other condiments.[5] When food was brought to him

---

[1] Narrated by Ibn As-Sunni, on the authority of Ibn Mas'ûd ☺, it contains in its chain of narrators a person known as Al-Ma'la Ibn 'Irfan, of whom Az-Zahabi said in '*Al-Meezan*': "(Yahya) Ibn Ma'een said: "He is nothing." Al-Bukhari said of him: "His *Ahadeeth* are *Munkarah*." An-Nasa'i said: "His *Ahadeeth* are abandoned." However, the fundamental principle of taking three breaths while drinking is established by *Ahadeeth* narrated by Al-Bukhari, Muslim and Abu Dawûd, but without the mention of praising Allâh and thanking Him.

[2] Narrated by Al-Bukhari and Muslim.

[3] Narrated by Al-Bukhari and Muslim, on the authority of Khalid Ibn Al-Waleed ☺.

[4] Narrated by Muslim, At-Tirmidhi, Abu Dawûd, Ahmad and Ad-Darimi.

[5] This is Ibn Al-Qayyim's opinion.

and he was fasting, he would say:

«إِنِّي صَائِمٌ»

"I am fasting."[1]

And he ordered whoever is presented with food while he is fasting to pray, i.e. to supplicate Allâh for the one who brought it and if he is not fasting, to eat from it.[2]

When he was invited to eat and he had someone with him, he would inform the owner of the house, saying:

«إِنَّ هَذَا تَبِعَنَا، فَإِنْ شِئْتَ أَنْ تَأْذَنَ لَهُ، وَإِنْ شِئْتَ رَجَعَ»

"This person is with us, if you wish, you may permit him and if you wish, he will return."[3]

He used to speak while he was eating, as when he said to his step-son ('Umar Ibn Abi Salamah :

«سَمِّ اللهَ، وَكُلْ مِمَّا يَلِيكَ»

"Invoke Allâh's Name and eat from what is in front of you."[4]

And sometimes he might repeatedly urge his guests to partake of the food, as hospitable people do, like in the *Hadeeth* of Abu Hurairah , in which he urged him to drink milk until he was full. And when he ate with a people, he would not leave without supplicating Allâh for them. Abu Dawûd reported from him in the story of Abul Haitham : "They ate, and when they had finished, he said:

«أَثِيبُوا أَخَاكُمْ»

"Reward your brother."

They said: "Oh, Messenger of Allâh! What is his reward?" He said:

«إِنَّ الرَّجُلَ إِذَا دُخِلَ بَيْتُهُ، فَأُكِلَ طَعَامُهُ، وَشُرِبَ شَرَابُهُ فَدَعَوْا لَهُ،

---

[1] Narrated by Al-Bukhari, on the authority of Anas Ibn Malik .

[2] Narrated by Muslim, on the authority of Abu Hurairah .

[3] Narrated by Muslim, on the authority of Abu Mas'ûd Al-Ansari

[4] Narrated by Al-Bukhari, Muslim, the compilers of the '*Sunan*', Ahmad, Malik and Ad-Darimi.

«فَذَلِكَ إِثَابَتُهُ»

"When a man's house is entered, his food eaten and his beverage drunk, and then they supplicate Allâh for him, that is his reward."[1]

And it has been authentically reported from him ﷺ that he entered his house at night and looked for food, but he did not find it, so he said:

«اللَّهُمَّ أَطْعِمْ مَنْ أَطْعَمَنِي، وَاسْقِ مَنْ سَقَانِي»

"Oh, Allâh! Feed the one who fed me and give drink to the one who gave drink to me."[2]

He also used to supplicate for those who gave hospitality to the poor and needy and he would praise them. He would not disdain eating with anyone, whether an eminent person or an insignificant one, whether a free man or a slave. And he ordered us to eat with the right hand and prohibited eating with the left, saying:

«إِنَّ الشَّيْطَانَ يَأْكُلُ بِشِمَالِهِ، وَيَشْرَبُ بِشِمَالِهِ»

"Verily, Satan eats with his left hand and drinks with his left hand."[3]

Accordingly, eating with it is unlawful – and that is the correct opinion. And he ordered those who complained to him that they were not satisfied by what they ate together and not to separate and to

---

[1] Narrated by Abu Dawûd, on the authority of Jabir Ibn 'Abdillah, it contains in its *Sanad* a narrator identified only as "a man", thus the chain is weak. It also contains one Abu Ahmad, who, according to Imam Ahmad: "made a lot of mistakes when he narrated from Sufyan (Ath-Thawri)," – as in this case.

[2] Narrated by Muslim, on the authority of Al-Miqdad ﷺ. This is a long *Hadeeth*, in which it is reported that Al-Miqdad ﷺ, who was staying with the Prophet ﷺ drank his milk while he was absent; upon his return, he made the above supplication and so Miqdad ﷺ went and milked the Prophet's goats and gave him to drink.

[3] Narrated by Muslim, on the authority of Ibn 'Umar ﷺ.

mention Allâh's Name over it."[1] And it has been narrated from him:

«أَذِيبُوا طَعَامَكُمْ بِذِكْرِ اللهِ عَزَّ وَجَلَّ وَالصَّلَاةِ، وَلَا تَنَامُوا عَلَيْهِ،
فَتَقْسُوَ قُلُوبُكُمْ»

"Consume your food by mentioning Allâh, the Almighty, the All-Powerful and prayer and do not sleep on it and harden your hearts thereby."[2]

It deserves to be considered authentic and experience supports it.

---

[1] Narrated by Abu Dawûd, Ibn Majah and Ahmad, on the authority of Wahshi Ibn Harb ◈; his son, Harb Ibn Wahshi Ibn Harb was, according to Al-Bazzar, known as the son of Wahshi ◈, however his reliability as a narrator was unknown. Likewise, his son (who narrated from him), whose name was Wahshi, was, according to Az-Zahabi: "Lax in reporting *Hadeeth*." There are however, a number of authentic *Ahadeeth* which support its meaning, according to Shu'aib and 'Abdul Qadir Al-Arna'ût.

[2] Narrated by Ibn As-Sunni in '*Amalul-Yawmi Wal-Lailah*' and by Ibn Hibban in '*Ad-Du'afa*", it contains in its chain of narrators one Bazeegh Ibn Hassan, who was declared a liar by scholars of *Hadeeth*, including Ibn Hibban and Ibn Hajr Al-'Asqalani. As for Ibn Al-Qayyim's comment: "Experience supports it," experience does not confirm the authenticity of a *Hadeeth*, according to the consensus of scholarly opinion.

Chapter

Regarding His ﷺ Guidance in Delivering Salutations of Peace, Asking Permission and Invoking Blessings on the Sneezer

It is reported in the 'Saheehayn' from the Prophet ﷺ that he said:

«إِنَّ أَفْضَلَ الْإِسْلَامِ إِطْعَامُ الطَّعَامِ، وَأَنْ تَقْرَأَ السَّلَامَ عَلَى مَنْ عَرَفْتَ وَمَنْ لَمْ تَعْرِفْ»

"The best Islam is to feed (others) and to greet those whom you know and those whom you do not know."[1]

And it is also mentioned in the 'Saheehayn' that he ﷺ said:

«إِنَّ آدَمَ لَمَّا خَلَقَهُ اللهُ قَالَ لَهُ: اذْهَبْ إِلَى أُولَئِكَ النَّفَرِ مِنَ الْمَلَائِكَةِ فَسَلِّمْ عَلَيْهِمْ، وَاسْتَمِعْ مَا يُحَيُّونَكَ، فَإِنَّهَا تَحِيَّتُكَ وَتَحِيَّةُ ذُرِّيَّتِكَ. فَقَالَ: السَّلَامُ عَلَيْكُمْ. فَقَالُوا: السَّلَامُ عَلَيْكُمْ وَرَحْمَةُ اللهِ. فَزَادُوهُ: وَرَحْمَةُ اللهِ»

"Verily, when Allâh created Adam, He said to him: "Go to those individuals from among the angels and give salutations of peace to them and listen to what they inform you, for it is your salutation and that of your descendants." So he said: "As-Salamu 'Alaikum" (May the Peace of Allâh be upon you)." And they replied: "Wa 'Alaikumus-Salamu Wa Rahmatullah" (May the Peace of Allâh and His Mercy be upon you). So they added: "Wa

---

[1] Narrated by Al-Bukhari and Muslim.

Rahmatullah" (and His Mercy)."[1]

It is also reported in the *'Saheehayn'* that he ﷺ ordered his Companions ﷺ to spread salutations of peace among themselves, and he told them that if they did so, it would cause them to love one another and that they would not enter Paradise until they had complete faith and that they would not have complete faith until they loved one another.[2] He also said that faith consists of three things: To be just towards oneself, to give salutations of peace to the world and to give in charity when one is in straitened circumstances.[3]

These three basic principles include goodness and all its branches, for justice necessitates that a person perform all the rights of Allâh in full and all of the rights of mankind as well, and to treat them in the way that he would like to be treated by them. It also includes justice towards oneself, so he should not claim for himself that which is not his, nor should he soil his soul through the perpetration of acts of disobedience.

What is meant by this is that acting with justice towards his own self enjoins upon a person knowledge of his Lord and knowledge of himself and that he vie not with its Owner for it and that he divide not his desire between the Will of his Master and his own will, for that is a most unfair division, like the division of those who said:

﴿هَٰذَا لِلَّهِ بِزَعْمِهِمْ وَهَٰذَا لِشُرَكَآئِنَا فَمَا كَانَ لِشُرَكَآئِهِمْ فَلَا يَصِلُ إِلَى اللَّهِ وَمَا كَانَ لِلَّهِ فَهُوَ يَصِلُ إِلَىٰ شُرَكَآئِهِمْ سَآءَ مَا يَحْكُمُونَ ۝﴾

"This is for Allâh" according to their claim, "and this is for our (Allâh's so-called) partners." But the share of their (Allâh's so-called) "partners" reaches not Allâh, while the share of Allâh reaches their (Allâh's so-called) "partners"! Evil is the way they

---

[1] Narrated by Al-Bukhari, on the authority of Abu Hurairah ﷺ.

[2] Narrated by Muslim, on the authority of Abu Hurairah ﷺ. It was not narrated by Al-Bukhari in his *'Saheeh'*, as the author says, but in *'Al-Adab Al-Mufrad'*. It was also narrated by Ibn Majah and others.

[3] Narrated by Al-Bukhari, in a *Mu'allaq* form.

judge!"[1]

So the slave should make sure that he is not one of those who make this unfair division without him realizing it, for he was created unjust and ignorant. So how may justice be sought from one whose nature is injustice and ignorance? And how may one who is unjust to his Lord be just towards the creation? As Allâh says in the (*Qudsi*) narration: "Son of Adam! You have not been just to Me: I created you and you worship another and I sustain you and you thank other than Me."[2] So how can one who is unjust to himself act with justice towards others, but instead is guilty of the worst kind of injustices towards his own self, while he thinks that he is honouring it?!

And conveying greetings of peace implies humility, that a person should not behave arrogantly towards anyone; and charity will not emanate from a person who is in straitened circumstances unless he trusts firmly in Allâh and has strong certainty (that Allâh will not let harm come to him thereby) and who has compassion (towards his fellow man), asceticism and a generous soul and rejects the warning of those who warn him of poverty and order him to commit abominable sins.

And it has been authentically reported from him ﷺ that he passed by some young boys and he greeted them with salutations of peace.[3] And At-Tirmidhi reported that he passed by a group of women and he waved his hand in greeting of peace. And Abu Dawûd reported on the authority of Asma' Bint Yazeed that: "The Prophet ﷺ passed by us when we were sitting among a group of women and he greeted us with salutations of peace." And this is the narration of the *Hadeeth* of At-Tirmidhi, so it is apparent that they both relate to the same incident and that he gave salutations to them with his hand. And in Al-Bukhari, it is reported that the Companions ﷺ were leaving the Friday prayer and they passed by an old woman on their way and they greeted her with salutations of peace and she gave them food

---

[1] *Sûrah Al-An'am* 6:136

[2] Narrated by Ad-Dailami and Ar-Rafi'i, on the authority of Ali ﷺ, according to Shu'aib and 'Abdul Qadir Al-Arna'ût, it is weak.

[3] Narrated by Al-Bukhari and Muslim.

from the roots of *Salq*[1] and barley.[2] And this is the correct opinion regarding the question of greeting women, that one should greet old women and women for whom one is a *Mahram*, but not others (i.e. unrelated marriageable women).[3]

And in '*Saheeh Al-Bukhari*', it is reported that the Prophet ﷺ said:

«يُسَلِّمُ الصَّغِيرُ عَلَى الْكَبِيرِ، وَالْمَارُّ عَلَى الْقَاعِدِ، وَالرَّاكِبُ عَلَى الْمَاشِي، وَالْقَلِيلُ عَلَى الْكَثِيرِ»

"The young person should give salutations of peace to the older person, the passerby to the one sitting, the rider to the walker and those few in number to those greater in number."[4]

And in (the compilation of) At-Tirmidhi:

«يُسَلِّمُ الْمَاشِي عَلَى الْقَائِمِ»

"The walker should give salutations of peace to the standing person."

And in Al-Bazzar's '*Musnad*', it is reported from the Prophet ﷺ that he said:

«وَالْمَاشِيَانِ أَيُّهُمَا بَدَأَ فَهُوَ أَفْضَلُ»

"And two walkers, whichever of them begins (with salutation) first is the best of them."[5]

It was a part of his guidance ﷺ to deliver salutations of peace when he visited a people and to do so upon leaving them; and it has been

---

[1] *Salq*: Chard, a kind of green vegetable, whose leaves are often chopped up and eaten in salad or as a side dish.

[2] Narrated by Al-Bukhari, on the authority of Sahl ﷺ.

[3] This is Ibn Al-Qayyim's opinion. However, it is reported in '*Saheeh Al-Bukhari*' that in the time of the Prophet ﷺ, men used to give greetings of peace to women and women to men.

[4] Narrated by Al-Bukhari and Muslim, on the authority of Abu Hurairah ﷺ.

[5] Mentioned by Al-Haitahmi, in '*Al-Majma*", on the authority of Jabir ﷺ and he attributed it to Al-Bazzar, saying: "All of the narrators are narrators of authentic *Hadeeth*."

confirmed from him ﷺ that he said:

«إِذَا قَعَدَ أَحَدُكُمْ فَلْيُسَلِّمْ، وَإِذَا قَامَ، فَلْيُسَلِّمْ، فَلَيْسَتِ الأُولَى بِأَحَقَّ
مِنَ الآخِرَةِ»

"When any of you sits, he should give salutations of peace and when he stands up, he should do so; and the first salutation is not a greater obligation than the second."[1]

And Abu Dawûd has reported from him ﷺ that he said:

«إِذَا لَقِيَ أَحَدُكُمْ صَاحِبَهُ، فَلْيُسَلِّمْ عَلَيْهِ، فَإِنْ حَالَ بَيْنَهُمَا شَجَرَةٌ أَوْ
جِدَارٌ، ثُمَّ لَقِيَهُ، فَلْيُسَلِّمْ عَلَيْهِ أَيْضًا»

"If any of you meets his companion, he should greet him with salutations of peace; and if a tree or a wall intervenes between them, then he meets up with him gain, he should greet him with salutations of peace also."[2]

And Anas ؓ said: "When the Companions of the Messenger of Allâh ﷺ were walking, if they encountered a tree or a hill, they would split up to the right and left of it, then when they met beyond it, they would greet each other with salutations of peace."[3]

It was also a part of his guidance that the person who entered the mosque should begin by offering a two *Rak'ah* prayer, then come and greet the worshippers with salutations of peace; so the salutation to the mosque should be before the salutation of those present therein, for that is an obligation towards Allâh, while greeting them is an obligation towards them; and an obligation to Allâh in such circumstances as these is more worthy to be fulfilled first, as opposed to financial obligations, for there is disagreement among scholars regarding them. And the difference between them both is the need of a person and the insufficiency of the money to fulfill both obligations.

---

[1] Narrated by Abu Dawûd, At-Tirmidhi, Al-Bukhari in '*Al-Adab Al-Mufrad*' and Ahmad, on the authority of Abu Hurairah ؓ.

[2] Narrated by Abu Dawûd, on the authority of Abu Hurairah ؓ.

[3] Narrated by Ibn As-Sunni and Al-Bukhari in '*Al-Adab Al-Mufrad*', on the authority of Anas ؓ.

So based upon this, it is prescribed for one who enters the mosque, if there are a number of people there, to perform three greetings, in order: (i) The first is that he says upon entering the mosque:

$$«بِسْمِ اللهِ وَالصَّلَاةُ وَالسَّلَامُ عَلَى رَسُولِ اللهِ»$$

"Bismillahi Was-Salatu Was-Salamu 'Ala Rasûlillah"

"In the Name of Allâh and may the Peace and Blessings of Allâh be upon the Messenger of Allâh,"

then (ii) he should offer the prayer of salutation to the mosque and then (iii) he should greet the people with salutations of peace.

When he entered the house of his family at night, he would Say: *"As-Salamu 'Alaikum"* in a manner which did not awaken a sleeper, but which would be heard by a wakeful person. This was narrated by Muslim.[1]

At-Tirmidhi reported from him ﷺ that he said:

$$«السَّلَامُ قَبْلَ الْكَلَامِ»$$

"Give salutations of peace before speaking."[2]

And Abu Ahmad has reported on the authority of Ibn 'Umar ﷺ in a *Marfû'* form:

$$«السَّلَامُ قَبْلَ السُّؤَالِ»$$

"Greetings of peace should be given before asking a question."

So whoever asks a question before giving greetings of peace, do not answer him."[3] It is also reported from him ﷺ that he said:

---

[1] Narrated in the Book of Drinks, in the Chapter on Hospitality Towards a Guest, on the authority of Al-Miqdad ﷺ.

[2] Narrated by At-Tirmidhi, on the authority of Jabir Ibn 'Abdillah ﷺ, it contains in its chain of narrators one 'Anbasah Ibn 'Abdir-Rahman, who is abandoned by scholars of *Hadeeth* and who was accused by Abu Hatim of having fabricated *Ahadeeth* and his Shaikh (from whom he narrates) is Muhammad Ibn Zazan, who is also abandoned, so the *Hadeeth* is not authentic.

[3] Narrated by Ibn 'Adiyy in *'Al-Kamil'*, it contains in its *Sanad* one Hafs Ibn

«لَا تَأْذَنُوا لِمَنْ لَمْ يَبْدَأْ بِالسَّلَام»

"Do not give permission (to speak) to one who does not begin with greetings of peace."[1]

When he came to someone's door, he would not stand directly facing it, but to the right or left side of it and he would say:

«السَّلَامُ عَلَيْكُمْ»

"As-Salamu 'Alaikum".[2]

And he would give salutations himself to a person who stood before him and he would send greetings to one who was absent[3] and he would bear the responsibility of conveying them, as he did to Khadeejah (from Allâh)[4] and he said to the second *Siddeeqah* (i.e. 'A'ishah) ﷺ:

«هَذَا جِبْرِيلُ يَقْرَأُ عَلَيْكِ السَّلَامُ»

"This is Jibreel greeting you."[5]

It was also a part of his guidance to add to his greeting: "*Wa Rahmatullahi Wa Barakatuh*" (and His Mercy and Blessings). And it was a part of his guidance to give salutations of peace three times, as reported in '*Saheeh Al-Bukhari*', on the authority of Anas ﷺ. Most likely, this was his practice when giving salutations of peace to a lot of people who were not reached by one greeting, or if he thought that the first or second had not been heard. And anyone who studies his

---

'Umar, of whom 'Ibn 'Adiyy said; "All of his *Ahadeeth* are *Munkarah*, either in their content or in their chains of narrators." However, Ibn As-Sunni narrated something similar, with a *Hasan* chain of narrators, according to Shu'aib and 'Abdul Qadir Al-Arna'ût. And Allâh knows better.

[1] Narrated by Abu Na'eem in '*Akhbar Asbahan*', it contains an unknown person in its *Sanad*, according to Al-Haithami.

[2] Narrated by Abu Dawûd, on the authority of 'Abdullah Ibn Busr ﷺ

[3] Narrated by Muslim, on the authority of Anas ﷺ.

[4] Narrated by Al-Bukhari and Muslim, on the authority of Abu Hurairah ﷺ.

[5] Narrated by Al-Bukhari and Muslim, on the authority of 'A'ishah ﷺ.

guidance knows that repetition (otherwise) is something contrary (to the *Sunnah*). He would begin by giving salutations to the people whom he met, and if anyone greeted him, he would immediately reply to him with the same greeting or better, unless there was some reason for not doing so, such as answering the call of nature. He would not answer with his hand, nor with his head, nor with his finger, except when he was praying; in that case, it has been authentically reported from him that he answered salutations of peace by indicating.

When he began first with greetings of peace, he would say:

«السَّلَامُ عَلَيْكُمْ وَرَحْمَةُ اللهِ»

"As-Salamu 'Alaikum Wa Rahmatullah."

And he disliked for the one who began first with salutations to say: "Alaikas-Salam" (Upon you be (Allâh's) Peace). To the Muslim, he would reply: *"Wa 'Alaikumus-Salam"* (And may [Allâh's] Peace be upon you) with letter '*Wauw*' (and). Some groups have said that if the person who replies does not pronounce the '*Wauw*', he has not fulfilled the obligation of reply, because he has contradicted the *Sunnah* and because it is not known if it is a reply or initiation of the salutation. Another group holds that the reply is correct; this was determined by Ash-Shafi'i, and he cited as evidence for it the Words of Allâh, Most High:

﴿فَقَالُوا۟ سَلَـٰمًۭا قَالَ سَلَـٰمٌۭ﴾

"And said: "*Salam* (peace be upon you)!" He answered: "*Salam* (peace be upon you)."[1]

That is, it must be said: *"Salamun 'Alaikum"* May [Allâh's] Peace be upon you all), but it is good to remove the '*Wauw*' in the reply due to its having been removed in the first *Tasleem*; and they cited as evidence for this the aforementioned reply of the angels to Adam (عليه السلام).

---------- ❖ ❖ ❖ ----------

---
[1] *Sûrah Adh-Dhariyat* 51:25

Chapter

Regarding His ﷺ Guidance in Giving Salutations of Peace to the People of the Scripture

It has been authentically reported from the Prophet ﷺ that he said:

«لَا تَبْدَؤُوهُمْ بِالسَّلَامُ، وِإِذَا لِقِيتُمُوهُمْ فِي الطَّرِيقِ، فَاضْطَرُّوهُمْ إِلَى أَضْيَقِ الطَّرِيقِ»

"Do not anticipate them in offering salutations of peace; and if you meet them in the road, force them to the narrowest part of it."[1]

However, it has been said: That was in special circumstances, when he ﷺ went out to Banu Quraizah and he said: "Do not anticipate them in offering salutations of peace." The question is, is that general for all of *Ahl Adh-Dhimmah*,[2] or is it specific to those who are in the same situation those people? But in '*Saheeh Muslim*', it says:

«لَا تَبْدَؤُوا الْيَهُودَ وَلَا النَّصَارَىٰ بِالسَّلَامِ، وَإِذَا لَقِيتُمْ أَحَدَهُمْ فِي الطَّرِيقِ فَاضْطَرُّوهُ إِلَى أَضْيَقِهِ»

"Do not anticipate the Jews and Christians in offering salutations of peace; and if you meet one of them in the road, force him to the narrowest part of it."[3]

---

[1] Narrated by At-Tirmidhi, Abu Dawûd and Ahmad.

[2] *Ahl Adh-Dhimmah*: Those Jews and Christians living under Muslim protection in an Islamic State.

[3] Narrated by Muslim, on the authority of Abu Hurairah ﷺ.

And it would appear that this is general.

There is also disagreement among scholars regarding the reply to them, but the correct opinion is that it is obligatory. And the difference between them and the innovators is that we are commanded to desert them, unlike the People of the Scripture. And it has been confirmed from him ﷺ that he passed by a mixed group of Muslims and polytheists and he gave salutations of peace to them.[1] And he wrote to Heraclius and others:

$$«السَّلَامُ عَلَى مَنِ اتَّبَعَ الْهُدَى»$$

"May the Peace of Allâh be upon those who follow the guidance."[2]

And it is reported from him ﷺ that he said: '

$$«يُجْزِىءُ عَنِ الْجُلُوسِ أَنْ يَرُدَّ أَحَدُهُمْ»$$

"It is sufficient for an assembly that one of them reply."[3]

This is the opinion of those who hold that the reply is *Fardh Kifayah*,[4] sufficiency duty. But how good this would be if it were confirmed, for in it there is Sa'eed Ibn Khalid, of whom Abu Zur'ah (Ar-Razi) said: "Weak," and Abu Hatim said likewise.

It was also a part of his ﷺ guidance that if anyone conveyed salutations of peace to him from another, he would reply to him and to the bearer of the greetings. And it was a part of his guidance not to begin with greetings of peace or reply to a person who had committed a bad deed until he repented.

---

[1] Narrated by Al-Bukhari, Muslim and Ahmad.

[2] Narrated by Al-Bukhari and Muslim.

[3] Narrated by Abu Dawûd, on the authority of 'Ali Ibn Abi Talib ؓ, it contains in its *Isnad* one Sa'eed Ibn Khalid, of whom Al-Bukhari said: "There is doubt about him," while Abu Hatim Ar-Razi said: "Weak," and Ibn Hibban said: "Makes atrocious mistakes." Imam Malik narrated something similar in '*Al-Muwatta*", on the authority of Zaid Ibn Aslam, however Zaid is a Tabi'i, thus the *Hadeeth* is *Mursal*.

[4] *Fard Kifayah*: An obligation upon the Muslim community which is considered to have been fulfilled if some of them undertake it.

Chapter

Regarding His ﷺ Guidance in Asking Permission

It has been authentically reported from the Prophet ﷺ that he said;

«الاِسْتِئْذَانُ ثَلَاثًا، فَإِنْ أُذِنَ لَكَ، وَإِلَّا فَارْجِعْ»

"Seek permission (to enter) three times, then if it was permitted for you, (enter); if not, then return."[1]

And it was authentically reported from him that he said:

«إِنَّمَا جُعِلَ الاِسْتِئْذَانُ مِنْ أَجْلِ الْبَصَرِ»

"Seeking permission has only been made incumbent for the sake of (guarding) the eyes (from seeing what it is forbidden to look at)."[2]

And it has been authentically reported from him that he used to make *Tasleem* before seeking permission and that he taught his Companions ؆ to do likewise. And it has been reported that a man sought permission from him, saying: "May I enter?" The Messenger of Allâh ﷺ said to a man:

«اخْرُجْ إِلَى هَذَا فَعَلِّمْهُ الاِسْتِئْذَانَ، فَقُلْ لَهُ: قُلِ السَّلَامُ عَلَيْكُمْ أَأَدْخُلُ»

---

[1] Narrated by Al-Bukhari, Abu Dawûd and Malik, on the authority of Abu Sa'eed Al-Khudri ؆.

[2] Narrated by Al-Bukhari, Muslim, An-Nasa'i and Ahmad.

"Go out to this man and teach him how to seek permission and say to him: "Say: "*As-Salamu 'Alaikum*", may I enter?"

The man heard him and said this and the Prophet ﷺ permitted him to enter and he did so.[1] In this *Hadeeth* there is a reply to those who said that one should seek permission first and to those who said that if his eye fell upon the owner of the house before he entered it, he should begin by saying "*As-Salamu 'Alaikum*", but if not, he should seek permission.

And it was a part of his ﷺ guidance that if he sought permission three times and permission was not given to him, he would leave. And this is a reply to those who say that if he thinks that they did not hear him, he may seek permission more than three times. And it is a reply to those who say that he may repeat his request using different words.

It was also a part of his guidance that if it was said to the person seeking permission: "Who are you?" he should reply: "So-and-so, the son of so-and-so," or he should mention his *Kunyah*, but he should not say: "It is I." Abu Dawûd narrated from the Prophet ﷺ that:

«أَنَّ رَسُولَ الرَّجُلِ إِلَى الرَّجُلِ إِذْنُهُ»

"The messenger of a man to a man is his permission."[2]

This was also reported by Al-Bukhari in a *Mu'allaq* form, then he mentioned what proves that permission has been granted after one is invited, which is the *Hadeeth* of the invitation of *Ahl As-Suffah*[3] and the saying of Abu Hurairah ؓ: "So I invited them and they approached and sought permission (to enter)." Some said that these two *Hadeeths* relate to two situations and that if the person invited comes along with the messenger immediately, he does not need to

---

[1] Narrated by Abu Dawûd and Ahmad.

[2] Narrated by Abu Dawûd, on the authority of Abu Rafi' ؓ. This means that if someone sends a message to a person inviting him to his house and he arrives with the bearer of the message, it is permissible for him to enter with the messenger.

[3] *Ahl As-Suffah*: A group of poor people who slept in the Prophet's Mosque during the time of the Prophet ﷺ.

ask permission, but if he delayed, he is required to do so. Others said if there is someone with the person inviting who had been given permission to enter before the person invited arrives, then he does not need to ask permission to enter, but otherwise, he should ask permission.

And when the Prophet ﷺ entered a place in which he wished to be alone, he would appoint someone to guard the door and no one could enter without permission.

As for the seeking of permission which Allâh enjoined upon slaves and minors at the three times when a person's *'Awrah*[1] may be uncovered, they are: (i) before *Fajr*, (ii) at *Zuhr* time (when it is a *Sunnah* to take rest) and (iii) when sleeping (at night). Ibn 'Abbas ﷺ used to order the people to act upon it and he said: "The people have abandoned acting upon it." One group said that the Verse[2] has been abrogated, but they did not bring any evidence to support their claim. Another group said that the order is one indicating preference, but they have no evidence for changing the meaning of the command from its apparent meaning. Another group said that the command is only for women, and this is clearly false. Another group said the opposite (i.e. that it is only for men) based upon the wording: *Al-Ladheena* (i.e. those [masc.] who), but this is rejected by the context of the Verse, so reflect on it. Another group said that the command is only applicable when a certain cause exists and that when the cause is removed, so is the command – and that cause is need: Abu Dawûd has reported in his *'Sunan'* that some people said to Ibn 'Abbas ﷺ: "What is your opinion regarding this Verse, when no one acts upon it?" He said: "Verily, Allâh is Most Forbearing and Full of Kindness

---

[1] *'Awrah*: The portion of the body which must remain covered from public gaze.

[2] The Verse referred to is the Saying of Allâh, Most High:

$$﴿يَـٰٓأَيُّهَا ٱلَّذِينَ ءَامَنُوا۟ لِيَسْتَـٔذِنكُمُ ٱلَّذِينَ مَلَكَتْ أَيْمَـٰنُكُمْ وَٱلَّذِينَ لَمْ يَبْلُغُوا۟ ٱلْحُلُمَ مِنكُمْ ثَلَـٰثَ مَرَّٰتٍ﴾$$

"Oh, you who believe! Let those whom your right hands possess (i.e. slaves and slave-girls) and those among you who have not reached the age of puberty ask your permission (before they come into your presence) on three occasions." (*Sûrah An-Nûr* 24:58)

towards the Believers and He loves them to screen themselves, but the people did not have screens or curtains, and so the servant or the child might enter while a man was having sexual intercourse with his wife and so Allâh ordered them to ask permission at these times of undress. Then Allâh, Most High gave them screens and goodness (i.e. wealth) and so I have not seen anyone acting upon this since. Some have doubted the authenticity of this narration, maligning 'Ikrimah, saying that he did not do anything and they also disparaged 'Amr Ibn Abi 'Amr, but the compilers of the *'Saheehayn'* (i.e. Al-Bukhari and Muslim) both asserted his reliability, therefore, disparaging him is mere obstinacy without reason. Another group said that the Verse is valid and there is nothing to invalidate it.

The correct opinion is that the ruling is dependent upon the existence of a cause, which was indicated by the Verse, so if there is something to take the place of asking permission, such as opening a door, then opening it is an evidence for entering, or lifting a screen, or hesitation on the part of the person entering or the like and it is unnecessary to ask permission. But if there is nothing to take its place, then permission must be asked, for if the cause is present, the ruling must also be present and if it is absent, then the ruling must also be absent.

Chapter

It has been confirmed from the Prophet ﷺ that he said:

«إِنَّ اللهَ يُحِبُّ الْعُطَاسَ، وَيَكْرَهُ التَّثَاؤُبَ، فَإِذَا عَطِسَ أَحَدُكُمْ وَحَمِدَ
اللهَ كَانَ حَقًّا عَلَى كُلِّ مُسْلِمٍ سَمِعَهُ أَنْ يَقُولَ لَهُ: يَرْحَمُكَ اللهُ، وَأَمَّا
التَّثَاؤُبُ فَإِنَّمَا هُوَ مِنَ الشَّيْطَانِ، فَإِذَا تَثَاءَبَ أَحَدُكُمْ، فَلْيَرُدَّهُ مَا
اسْتَطَاعَ، فَإِنَّ أَحَدَكُمْ إِذَا تَثَاءَبَ ضَحِكَ الشَّيْطَانُ»

"Verily, Allâh loves sneezing and He dislikes yawning, so if any of you sneezes and praises and thanks Allâh (by saying: "*Al-Hamdu Lillah*"), it is incumbent upon every Muslim who hears him to say to him: "*Yarhamukallah*" (May Allâh have mercy on you). But as for yawning, it is only from Satan, so if one of you yawns, he should try to suppress it as much as he can, because when one of you yawns, Satan laughs at him."

This was mentioned by Al-Bukhari.[1] Also in his '*Saheeh*', it is reported that he ﷺ said:

«إِذَا عَطِسَ أَحَدُكُمْ، فَلْيَقُلْ: الْحَمْدُ لله، وَلْيَقُلْ لَهُ أَخُوهُ أَوْ صَاحِبُهُ:
يَرْحَمُكَ اللهُ. فَإِذَا قَالَ لَهُ: يَرْحَمُكَ اللهُ. فَلْيَقُلْ: يَهْدِيكُمُ اللهُ
وَيُصْلِحُ بَالَكُمْ»

"If any of you sneezes, he should say: "*Al-Hamdu Lillah*" and those who hear him should say: "*Yarhamukallah*". And if it is said to him: "*Yarhamukallah*", he should reply: "*Yahdeekumulla-*

---

[1] Narrated by Al-Bukhari and At-Tirmidhi, on the authority of Abu Hurairah ﷺ.

hu Wa Yuslihu Balakum" (May Allâh guide you and improve your condition)."[1]

And in '*Saheeh Muslim*', it is reported that he ﷺ said:

«إِذَا عَطِسَ أَحَدُكُمْ، فَحَمِدَ اللَّهَ، فَشَمِّتُوهُ، وَإِنْ لَمْ يَحْمَدِ اللَّهَ، فَلَا تُشَمِّتُوهُ»

"If any of you sneezes and praises and thanks Allâh, invoke Allâh's Mercy on him; but if he does not praise and thank Allâh, then do not invoke Allâh's Mercy on him."[2]

It is also narrated in his '*Saheeh*' that the Prophet (ﷺ) said:

«حَقُّ الْمُسْلِمِ عَلَى الْمُسْلِمِ سِتٌّ: إِذَا لَقِيتَهُ، فَسَلِّمْ عَلَيْهِ، وَإِذَا دَعَاكَ فَأَجِبْهُ، وَإِذَا اسْتَنْصَحَكَ، فَانْصَحْ لَهُ، وَإِذَا عَطِسَ وَحَمِدَ اللَّهَ فَشَمِّتْهُ، وَإِذَا دَعَاكَ فَأَجِبْهُ، وَإِذَا مَاتَ فَاتَّبِعْهُ، وَإِذَا مَرِضَ فَعُدْهُ»

"The rights of a Muslim upon another Muslim are six: (i) When you meet him, greet him with salutations of peace, (ii) if he invites you, accept his invitation, (iii) if he asks your advice, advise him, (iv) if he sneezes and praises and thanks Allâh, invoke Allâh's Mercy upon him, (v) if he is sick visit him and (vi) if he dies, follow him (to the place of burial)."[3]

At-Tirmidhi has narrated on the authority of Ibn 'Umar ﷺ that he said: "The Messenger of Allâh ﷺ taught us to say upon sneezing:

«الْحَمْدُ للهِ عَلَى كُلِّ حَالٍ»

"*Al-Hamdu Lillahi 'Ala Kulli Hal*"

"All praise and thanks be to Allâh in all circumstances."[4]

---

[1] Narrated by Al-Bukhari and Ahmad, on the authority of Abu Hurairah ﷺ.

[2] Narrated by Muslim and Ahmad, on the authority of Abu Mûsa Al-Ash'ari ﷺ.

[3] Narrated by Al-Bukhari, Muslim and Ibn Majah.

[4] Narrated by At-Tirmidhi, in the 'Book of Good Manners' and according to Shu'aib and Ibraheem Al-Arna'ût, all of the narrators in its *Sanad* are trustworthy.

And Malik has reported on the authority of Nafi' Ibn 'Umar 🞜: "If any of you sneezes and it is said to him: *"Yarhamukallah"*, he should say:

«يَرْحَمُنَا اللّٰهُ وَإِيَّاكُمْ، وَيَغْفِرُ لَنَا وَلَكُمْ»

"Yarhamunallahu Wa Iyyakum Wa Yaghfiru Lana Wa Lakum"

"May Allâh have mercy upon us and you and may He forgive us and you."

It is apparent from the *Hadeeth* with which the chapter began that invoking Allâh's Mercy is *Fardh 'Ain;*[1] this was the view Ibn Abi Zaid and there is no contradiction to it.

And since the sneezer obtains blessing and benefit through the expulsion of congested mucus from his nose, it was legislated for him 🞜 to praise and thank Allâh for this blessing, in addition to his organs remaining in their place after this convulsion, which to the body is like an earthquake to the earth. And when he sneezed, he would place his hand or his garment over his mouth and thereby suppress his voice;[2] and it is reported from him 🞜 that: "Loud yawning and severe sneezing are from Satan."[3]

And it has been authentically reported from him 🞜 that a man sneezed in his presence and he said:

«يَرْحَمُكَ اللّٰهُ»

"Yarhamukallah",

then the man sneezed again and he said:

«الرَّجُلُ مَزْكُومٌ»

"The man is suffering from a cold."

This is the wording of Muslim. According to At-Tirmidhi's version, he

---

[1] *Fardh 'Ain*: An obligation upon every Muslim individual.

[2] Narrated by Abu Dawûd, At-Tirmidhi, An-Nasa'i and Ahmad and authenticated by Al-Hakim.

[3] Narrated by Ibn As-Sunni, on the authority of Umm Salamah 🞜, according to Shu'aib and 'Abdul Qadir Al-Arna'ût, it is a weak *Hadeeth*.

said it after the third sneeze and he (At-Tirmidhi) said: "It is an authentic *Hadeeth*." Abu Dawûd reports on the authority of Abu Hurairah 🙵 in a *Mawqûf* form that he said: "Invoke Allâh's Mercy for your brother three times, then anything more than this is a cold."[1] And if it is said: "The one who is suffering from a cold is more worthy to be supplicated for," it may be said: "Supplication is made for him as it is made for the sick person, but as for the *Sunnah* of sneezing which Allâh loves, it is a blessing and it is up until a third sneeze has been made. As for his words: "The man is suffering from a cold," it is to apprise the people of the necessity to supplicate Allâh for his good health and implicit is an excuse for leaving off invoking Allâh's Mercy for him.

If he praises and thanks Allâh and some of them hear him while others do not, then the correct position is that those who did not hear him should invoke Allâh's Mercy for him, if it is ascertained that he praised and thanked Allâh, for the Prophet 🙴 said:

«فَإِنْ حَمِدَ اللهَ، فَشَمِّتُوهُ»

"If he praises and thanks Allâh, then invoke Allâh's Mercy for him."

And if he forgot to say: *"Al-Hamdu Lillah"* Ibn Al-'Arabi said: "He should not be reminded to do so." And it is apparent from the *Sunnah* that this is a strong opinion, because the Prophet 🙴 did not remind anyone who forgot and he was the best in applying the *Sunnah* and teaching it. And it has been authentically reported from him 🙴 that the Jews used to sneeze in his presence, hoping that he would say: *"Yarhamukumullah"* (May Allâh have mercy on all of you), but he would say:

«يَهْدِيكُمُ اللهُ وَيُصْلِحُ بَالَكُمْ»

"Yahdeekumullahu Wa Yuslihu Balakum".[2]

---

[1] Abu Dawûd narrated this *Hadeeth* in both a *Mawqûf* and a *Marfû'* form and all of its narrators are trustworthy.

[2] Narrated by Abu Dawûd, At-Tirmidhi, Ahmad and Al-Bukhari in '*Al-Adab Al-Mufrad*', it was declared authentic by At-Tirmidhi, An-Nawawi and Al-Hakim.

Regarding His ﷺ Guidance in the Manners of Traveling

It has been authentically reported from the Prophet ﷺ that he said:

«إِذَا هَمَّ أَحَدُكُمْ بِالأَمْرِ، فَلْيَرْكَعْ رَكْعَتَيْنِ»

"If any of you is concerned about some matter, he should offer two *Rak'ahs*."[1]

So he replaced thereby for his people the practice which they had followed in the days of ignorance, which was holding back from embarking on a journey due to *At-Tair*,[2] seeking decision through *Al-Azlam*,[3] and that is similar to *Al-Qar'ah*,[4] which the brothers of the polytheists used to employ in order to seek knowledge of what was apportioned to them in the unseen, which is why it is known as *Istiqsam*.[5] He replaced seeking omens, astrology, the movements of celestial bodies and the like for them with supplication, which is *Tawheed* and *Tawakkul* and asking the One aside from Whom none makes it possible for us to earn *Hasanat* and aside from Whom none

---

[1] Narrated by Al-Bukhari, At-Tirmidhi, An-Nasa'i, Abu Dawûd, Ibn Majah and Ahmad.

[2] *At-Tair*: In pre-Islamic times, the Arabs believed that the movements of certain birds were good or bad omens.

[3] *Al-Azlam*: Divining arrows.

[4] *Al-Qar'ah*: Casting lots.

[5] *Istiqsam*: From the Arabic root *Qasama*, which means to distribute or share something out.

removes *Sayyi'at*. And this supplication is the good fortune of the successful people, as opposed to the people of *Shirk*

$$\text{﴿ ٱلَّذِينَ يَجْعَلُونَ مَعَ ٱللَّهِ إِلَٰهًا ءَاخَرَ فَسَوْفَ يَعْلَمُونَ ﴿٩٦﴾ ﴾}$$

"Who set up along with Allâh another *Ilah* (god); but they will come to know."[1]

And implicit in this supplication is the affirmation of His Existence and of His Attributes of Perfection, including His Perfect Knowledge, His Ability to do all things and His Will, and implicit in it also is the affirmation of His Lordship, trust in Him and dependence on Him (*Tawakkul*) and the slave's acknowledgement of his own inability to know what is beneficial for him and the lack of his ability to achieve it or will it. It is narrated by Ahmad on the authority of Sa'd Ibn Abi Waqqas ☀ in a *Marfû'* form that the Prophet ﷺ said:

$$\text{«إِنَّ مِنْ سَعَادَةِ ابْنِ آدَمَ اسْتِخَارَةَ اللهِ وَرِضَاهُ بِمَا قَضَى اللهُ، وَإِنَّ مِنْ}$$
$$\text{شَقَاوَةِ ابْنِ آدَمَ تَرْكَ اسْتِخَارَةِ اللهِ وَسُخْطَهُ بِمَا قَضَى اللهُ»}$$

"Among the means of (achieving) happiness for the son of Adam is to seek Allâh's Guidance (*Istikharah*) and his acceptance of what Allâh has decreed; and one of the causes of wretchedness for the son of Adam is his not seeking Allâh's Guidance and his rejection of what Allâh has decreed."[2]

Observe how that which has been ordained takes place in accordance with two things: (i) *Tawakkul*, which consists of *Istikharah* before it, and (ii) acceptance of what Allâh has decreed after it.

When he ﷺ mounted his riding camel, he would make *Takbeer* three times, then he would say:

$$\text{﴿ سُبْحَٰنَ ٱلَّذِى سَخَّرَ لَنَا هَٰذَا وَمَا كُنَّا لَهُ مُقْرِنِينَ ﴿١٣﴾ وَإِنَّآ إِلَىٰ رَبِّنَا}$$

---

[1] *Sûrah Al-Hijr* 15:96

[2] Narrated by Ahmad in his '*Musnad*' and by At-Tirmidhi, in its chain of narrators is one Muhammad Ibn Abi Humaid, who is weak; according to Ahmad, Al-Bukhari, Yahya Ibn Ma'een, Ibn Hajr and others, he narrated *Ahadeeth* which were *Munkarah*. In spite of this, Ibn Hajr declared the *Hadeeth* to be *Hasan*. And Allâh knows better.

"Subhanalladhee Sakhkhara Lana Hadha Wa Ma Kunna Lahu Muqrineena Wa Inna Ila Rabbina Lamunqalibûn"

"Glory be to Him Who granted this [journey] to us and we were not able to do it and to our Lord we are turning back)."[1]

Then he would say:

«اللَّهُمَّ إِنِّي أَسْأَلُكَ فِي سَفَرِي هَذَا الْبِرَّ وَالتَّقْوَى، وَمِنَ الْعَمَلِ مَا تَرْضَى، اللَّهُمَّ هَوِّنْ عَلَيْنَا السَّفَرَ، وَاطْوِ عَنَّا بُعْدَهُ، اللَّهُمَّ أَنْتَ الصَّاحِبُ فِي السَّفَرِ، وَالْخَلِيفَةُ فِي الأَهْلِ اللَّهُمَّ اصْحَبْنَا فِي سَفَرِنَا، وَاخْلُفْنَا فِي أَهْلِنَا»

"Allâhumma, Innee As'aluka Fee Safaree Hazal-Birra Wat-Taqwa Wa Minal-'Amali Ma Tarda. Allâhumma, Hawwin 'Alainas-Safara Watwai 'Anna Bu'dah. Allâhumma, Antas-Sahibu Fis-Safari Wal-Khaleefatu Fil-Ahli. Allâhummas-habna Fee Safarina Wakhlufna Fee Ahlina"

"Oh, Allâh! I ask You in this journey of mine righteousness and piety and deeds which are pleasing to You. Oh, Allâh! Make this journey easy for us and cause us to cover the distance [quickly]. You are our Companion on the journey and the One in Whose Charge we leave our families. Oh, Allâh! Accompany us on our journey and take charge of our families in our absence."[2]

When he returned, he would say the same thing, adding:

«آيِبُونَ تَائِبُونَ إِنْ شَاءَ اللهُ عَابِدُونَ لِرَبِّنَا حَامِدُونَ»

"Ayibûna Ta'ibûna, In sha' Allâhu 'Abidûna Lirabbina Hamidûn"

"We are returning, turning to Allâh in repentance, if Allâh wills, worshipping our Lord and praising and thanking Him).[3]

And Ahmad has reported from him ﷺ that when he returned home

---

[1] Narrated by Muslim, At-Tirmidhi, Abu Dawûd, Ahmad and Ad-Darimi.

[2] Narrated by At-Tirmidhi, Ahmad and Ad-Darimi.

[3] Narrated by Al-Bukhari, Muslim, At-Tirmidhi, Abu Dawûd, Ahmad and Malik.

to his family, he would say:

«تَوْبًا تَوْبًا، لِرَبِّنَا أَوْبًا، لَا يُغَادِرُ عَلَيْنَا حَوْبًا»

"Tawban, Tawban Lirabbina Awban, La Yughadiru 'Alaina Hawban"

"Repenting, repenting to our Lord, we return [home]; may He not leave us as sinners."[1]

And when he placed his foot in the stirrup in order to mount his riding beat, he would say: "Bismillah" and once he had sat on its back, he would say: "Al-Hamdu Lillah" (three times), then he would say:

﴿سُبْحَٰنَ ٱلَّذِى سَخَّرَ لَنَا هَٰذَا وَمَا كُنَّا لَهُ مُقْرِنِينَ﴾

"Subhanalladhee Sakhkhara Lana Hadha Wa Ma Kunna Lahu Muqrineen"

"Glory be to Him Who granted this [journey] to us and we were not able to do it."

And when he bade farewell to his Companions ﷺ before setting off on a journey, he would say:

«أَسْتَوْدِعُ اللهَ دِينَكَ وَأَمَانَتَكَ وَخَوَاتِيمَ عَمَلِكَ»

"Astawdi'ullaha Deenaka Wa Amanataka Wa Khawateema 'Amalik"

"I commend to Allâh your Religion, what you are responsible for and your final deeds."[2]

And a man said to him: "I wish to undertake a journey." So he ﷺ said to him:

«أُوصِيكَ بِتَقْوَى اللهِ، وَالتَّكْبِيرِ عَلَى كُلِّ شَرَفٍ»

"I advise you to fear Allâh and to make Takbeer in every elevated place."[3]

---

[1] Narrated by Imam Ahmad, on the authority of Ibn 'Abbas ﷺ.

[2] Narrated by At-Tirmidhi and Abu Dawûd on the authority of Ibn 'Umar ﷺ and At-Tirmzi and Ahmad graded it Hasan-Saheeh, while Ibn Hibban and Al-Hakim declared it authentic and Az-Zahabi confirmed this.

[3] Narrated by At-Tirmidhi and Ibn Majah, on the authority of Abu Hurairah ﷺ and declared authentic Ibn Hibban and Al-Hakim and Az-Zahabi confirmed it.

And when the Prophet ﷺ and his Companions ﷺ ascended the mountain paths, they would say: *"Allâhu Akbar"* and if they descended, they would say: *"Subhanallah"* (Glory be to Allâh) and the prayer was erected upon that.[1] Anas ﷺ said: "When the Prophet ﷺ ascended an elevated piece of ground, he would say:

«اللَّهُمَّ لَكَ الشَّرَفُ عَلَى كُلِّ شَرَفٍ، وَلَكَ الْحَمْدُ عَلَى كُلِّ حَالٍ»

"Allâhumma, Lakash-Sharafu 'Ala Kulli Sharaf Wa Lakal-Hamdu 'Ala Kulli Halin"

"Oh, Allâh! High above every elevation are You and all praise and thanks are due to You in all circumstances."[2]

And he said:

«لَا تَصْحَبُ الْمَلَائِكَةُ رُفْقَةً فِيهَا كَلْبٌ وَلَا جَرَسٌ»

"The angels do not accompany a group of travellers which includes a dog or a bell."[3]

He disliked that a person traveling alone should set out at night and he said:

«لَوْ يَعْلَمُ النَّاسُ مَا فِي الْوَحْدَةِ مَا سَارَ أَحَدٌ وَحْدَهُ بِلَيْلٍ»

"If the people knew what is entailed by traveling alone, no one would set out on his own at night."[4]

Indeed, he disliked that anyone should travel alone and he informed us that:

«الْوَاحِدُ شَيْطَانٌ وَالِاثْنَانِ شَيْطَانَانِ، وَالثَّلَاثَةُ رَكْبٌ»

---

[1] Narrated by Muslim without the words: "and the prayer was erected upon that." This is in Abu Dawûd's version and it is *Mudraj* (something inadvertently included in the *Hadeeth* from the words of the narrator), according to Shu'aib and 'Abdul Qadir Al-Arna'ût.

[2] Narrated by Ahmad, on the authority of Anas Ibn Malik ﷺ.

[3] Narrated by Muslim, Abu Dawûd, At-Tirmidhi, Ahmad and Ad-Darimi.

[4] Narrated by Al-Bukhari, Ahmad and Ad-Darimi, on the authority of Ibn 'Umar ﷺ.

"One is a devil and two are two devils, but three are a group."[1]

And he ﷺ said:

«إِذَا نَزَلَ أَحَدُكُمْ مَنْزِلًا فَلْيَقُلْ : أَعُوذُ بِكَلِمَاتِ اللهِ التَّامَّاتِ مِنْ شَرِّ مَا
خَلَقَ . فَإِنَّهُ لَا يَضُرُّهُ شَيْءٌ حَتَّى يَرْتَحِلَ مِنْهُ»

"When any one of you stays at a place, he should say: "I seek
refuge in the Perfect Word of Allâh from the evil of that which
He created," nothing would then do him any harm until he
moves from that place."[2]

And he ﷺ said:

«إِذَا سَافَرْتُمْ فِي الْخِصْبِ، فَأَعْطُوا الإِبِلَ حَظَّهَا مِنَ الأَرْضِ، وَإِذَا
سَافَرْتُمْ فِي السَّنَةِ، فَأَسْرِعُوا عَلَيْهَا السَّيْرِ، وَإِذَا عَرَّسْتُمْ، فَاجْتَنِبُوا
الطَّرِيقَ، فَإِنَّهَا طُرُقُ الدَّوَابِّ، وَمَأْوَى الْهَوَامِّ بِاللَّيْلِ»

"When you travel through a fertile land, you should (go slow
and) give the camels a chance to graze in the land. When you
travel in an arid land where there is scarcity of vegetation, you
should quicken their pace (lest your camels grow feeble and
emaciated for lack of fodder). When you halt for the night,
avoid (pitching your tent on) the road, for it is the path of
riding beasts and the abode of harmful small creatures (such as
scorpions, centipedes etc.) at night."[3]

He prohibited traveling to the land of the enemy with the Qur'ân,
fearful that the enemy would get hold of it.[4] And he forbade a
woman from traveling even a short distance without a *Mahram*. And
he ordered the traveller upon completing his business to hasten to
return to his family. And he forbade a man from awakening his family

---

[1] Narrated by Abu Dawûd, At-Tirmidhi, Ahmad and Malik.

[2] Narrated by Muslim, on the authority of Khawlah Bint Hakeem As-
Sulamiyyah ﷺ.

[3] Narrated by Muslim, At-Tirmidhi, Abu Dawûd and Ahmad, on the
authority of Abu Hurairah ﷺ.

[4] Narrated by Al-Bukhari, Muslim, Abu Dawûd, Ibn Majah, Malik and
Ahmad.

at night, if his absence from them had been prolonged.[1] And when he returned from a journey, he would meet his children[2] and he would embrace the person who had returned from a journey and kiss him if he was a member of his family.[3]

Ash-Sha'bi said: "When the Companions of the Messenger of Allâh ﷺ returned from a journey, they used to embrace one another and when he ﷺ returned from a journey, he would go first to the mosque and offer a two *Rak'ah* prayer there.

---

[1] Narrated by Al-Bukhari, Muslim, At-Tirmidhi, Ahmad and Ad-Darimi.
[2] Narrated by Muslim, on the authority of 'Abdullah Ibn Ja'far ﷺ.
[3] Narrated by At-Tabarani, Al-Bukhari in '*Al-Adab Al-Mufrad*' and Ahmad.

Chapter

It has been authentically reported from the Prophet ﷺ that he taught the Companions ؓ the *Khutbah*[1] of need thus:

«إِنَّ الْحَمْدَ لِلهِ نَحْمَدُهُ وَنَسْتَعِينُهُ وَنَسْتَغْفِرُهُ وَنَعُوذُ بِاللهِ مِنْ شُرُورِ أَنْفُسِنَا – وَفِي لَفْظٍ –: وَسَيِّئَاتِ أَعْمَالِنَا، مَنْ يَهْدِهِ اللهُ فَلَا مُضِلَّ لَهُ، وَمَنْ يُضْلِلْ، فَلَا هَادِيَ لَهُ، وَأَشْهَدُ أَنْ لَا إِلَهَ إِلَّا اللهُ وَأَشْهَدُ أَنَّ مُحَمَّدًا عَبْدُهُ وَرَسُولُهُ»

"All praise and thanks be to Allâh, we praise Him and we seek His Aid and we ask His Forgiveness and we seek shelter with Allâh from the evil of ourselves (and in one narration: and the wickedness of our deeds); whomsoever Allâh guides, there is none can misguide him and whomsoever Allâh sends astray, there is none can guide him. And I testify that none is worthy of worship except Allâh and I testify that Muhammad is His slave and His Messenger."[2]

Then he would recite these three Verses:

﴿يَٰٓأَيُّهَا ٱلَّذِينَ ءَامَنُوا۟ ٱتَّقُوا۟ ٱللَّهَ حَقَّ تُقَاتِهِۦ وَلَا تَمُوتُنَّ إِلَّا وَأَنتُم مُّسْلِمُونَ ۝﴾

"O you who believe! Fear Allâh (by doing all that He has ordered and by abstaining from all that He has forbidden) as He should be feared. (Obey Him, be thankful to Him, and remember Him always,) and die not except in a state of Islam [as Muslims (with complete submission to Allâh)].[3]

﴿يَٰٓأَيُّهَا ٱلنَّاسُ ٱتَّقُوا۟ رَبَّكُمُ﴾

---

[1] *Khutbah*: Sermon, address.

[2] Narrated by Abu Dawûd, and At-Tirmidhi on the authority of Abdullah bin Masûd.

[3] *Sûrah Âl-'Imrân* 3:102

"O mankind! Be dutiful to your Lord",[1]

and

﴿يَـٰٓأَيُّهَا ٱلَّذِينَ ءَامَنُوا۟ ٱتَّقُوا۟ ٱللَّهَ وَقُولُوا۟ قَوْلًا سَدِيدًا ۝ يُصْلِحْ لَكُمْ أَعْمَـٰلَكُمْ﴾

"O you who believe! Keep your duty to Allâh and fear Him, and speak (always) the truth. He will direct you to do righteous good deeds."[2]

Shu'bah said: "I said to Abu Ishaq: "Is this in the *Khutbah* of marriage or another?" He said: "It is for every need." And the Prophet ﷺ said:

«إِذَا أَفَادَ أَحَدُكُمُ امْرَأَةً أَوْ خَادِمًا أَوْ دَابَّةً، فَلْيَأْخُذْ بِنَاصِيَتِهَا، وَلْيَدْعُ اللهَ بِالْبَرَكَةِ، وَبِسْمِ اللهِ عَزَّ وَجَلَّ، وَلْيَقُلْ: اللَّهُمَّ إِنِّي أَسْأَلُكَ خَيْرَهَا وَخَيْرَ مَا جُبِلَتْ عَلَيْهِ، وَأَعُوذُ بِكَ مِنْ شَرِّهَا وَشَرِّ مَا جُبِلَتْ عَلَيْهِ»

"If any of you acquired a wife, a servant or a riding beast, he should take her (him or it) by the forelock and invoke Allâh's Blessing and invoke the Name of Allâh, the Almighty, the All-powerful, then say: *Allâhumma, Innee As'aluka Khairaha Wa Khaira Ma Julibat 'Alaihi Wa A'ûdu Bika Min Sharriha Wa Sharri Ma Julibat 'Alaihi* "Oh, Allâh! I ask You for the good in her, and in the disposition which You have given her; and I seek refuge in You from the evil in her, and in the disposition which You have given her."[3]

And he used to say to the (newly) married person:

«بَارَكَ اللهُ لَكَ، وَبَارَكَ عَلَيْكَ، وَجَمَعَ بَيْنَكُمَا فِي خَيْرٍ»

"May Allâh bless (your marriage) for you and may He bless you and join you both in goodness."[4]

And it has been authentically reported from him ﷺ that he said:

---

[1] *Sûrah An-Nisa'* 4:1

[2] *Sûrah Al-Ahdhab* 33:70-71

[3] Narrated by Ibn Majah and Abu Dawûd, on the authority of 'Amr Ibn Shu'aib, from his father, who reported from his grandfather.

[4] Narrated by Abu Dawûd, At-Tirmidhi, Ibn Majah and Ahmad, on the authority of Abu Hurairah ﷺ.

«مَا مِنْ رَجُلٍ رَأَى رَجُلًا مُبْتَلًى، فَقَالَ: الْحَمْدُ لِلهِ الَّذِي عَافَانِي مِمَّا ابْتَلَاكَ
بِهِ، وَفَضَّلَنِي عَلَى كَثِيرٍ مِمَّنْ خَلَقَ تَفْضِيلًا . إِلَّا لَمْ يُصِبْهُ ذَلِكَ الْبَلَاءُ
كَائِنًا مَا كَانَ»

"If any man sees someone who is put to trial and says: *Al-
Hamdu Lillahil-Ladhee 'Afanee Mimmabtalaka Bihi Wa Fadhdhala-
nee 'Ala Katheerin Mimman Khalaqa Tafdeelan* (All praise and
thanks be to Allâh, Who spared me from what has afflicted you
and greatly preferred me to many of his creatures), he will not
be affected by that affliction, whatever it was."[1]

And it is reported from him 饜 that belief in omens was mentioned in
his presence and he said:

«أَحْسِنُهَا الْفَأْلُ، وَلَا تَرُدُّ مُسْلِمًا، فَإِذَا رَأَيْتَ مِنَ الطِّيَرَةِ مَا تَكْرَهُ،
فَقُلْ: اللَّهُمَّ لَا يَأْتِي بِالْحَسَنَاتِ إِلَّا أَنْتَ، وَلَا يَدْفَعُ السَّيِّئَاتِ إِلَّا
أَنْتَ، وَلَا حَوْلَ وَلَا قُوَّةَ إِلَّا بِكَ»

"The best of it is optimism; it should not cause a Muslim to be
undecided, so if you see some omen which you dislike, say:
*Allâhumma, La Ya'tee Bil-Hasanati Illa Anta Wa La Yadfa'us-Sayyi'ati
Illa Anta Wa La Hawla Wa La Quuwwata Illa Bik.* (Oh, Allâh! None
makes it possible for us to earn *Hasanat* except You and none
removes *Sayyi'at* except You and there is no power and no might
except with You.)"[2]

---

[1] Narrated by At-Tirmidhi, on the authority of Abu Hurairah 饜.

[2] Narrated by Abu Dawûd, on the authority of 'Urwah Ibn 'Amir, it is a
weak *Hadeeth* due to the *Tadlees* (making it appear that he heard directly
from someone, when in fact, he only heard it through a third party, who is
not mentioned and who might or might not be reliable, or covering up the
fact that a reporter was weak by not referring to him by his known name,
or by referring to him only by his *Kunyah*)of Habeeb Ibn Abi Thabit; also,
scholars differ regarding whether or not 'Urwah Ibn 'Amir was a
Companion. Ibn Hibban mentioned him as a reliable reporter from
among the *Tabi'ûn*. Something similar was narrated by Al-Bukhari and
Muslim, on the authority of Abu Hurairah 饜 but without mentioning the
supplication: "Oh, Allâh! None makes it possible" etc.

Chapter

It has been authentically reported from the Prophet ﷺ that he said:

«الرُّؤْيَا الصَّالِحَةُ مِنَ اللهِ، وَالرُّؤْيَا السَّوْءُ مِنَ الشَّيْطَانِ، فَمَنْ رَأَى
رُؤْيَا يَكْرَهُ مِنْهَا شَيْئًا، فَلْيَنْفُثْ عَنْ يَسَارِهِ، وَلْيَتَعَوَّذْ بِاللهِ مِنَ
الشَّيْطَانِ، فَإِنَّهَا لَا تَضُرُّهُ، وَلَا يُخْبِرْ بِهَا أَحَدًا، فَإِنْ رَأَى رُؤْيَا
حَسَنَةً، فَلْيَسْتَبْشِرْ وَلَا يُخْبِرْ بِهَا إِلَّا مَنْ يُحِبُّ»

"A righteous vision comes from Allâh and a bad dream (*Hulm*) from Satan. So when one of you sees a bad dream in which there is something that he does not like, he should spit on his left side three times and seek refuge with Allâh from the devil, then it will not harm him; and he should not tell anyone about it; and if he sees a righteous vision, he should feel pleased, but he should not disclose it to anyone except those whom he loves."[1]

And he ordered one who sees something which dislikes to change the side on which he was lying and he ordered him to pray.[2] So he ordered him to do five things: (i) To spit on his left side, (ii) to seek refuge with Allâh from Satan, (iii) not to inform anyone of it, (iv) to change the side on which he had been lying and (v) to stand up and pray. And he ﷺ said:

«الرُّؤْيَا عَلَى رِجْلِ طَائِرٍ مَالَمْ تُعَبَّرْ، فَإِذَا عُبِّرَتْ وَقَعَتْ، وَلَا يَقُصَّهَا
إِلَّا عَلَى وَادٍّ أَوْ ذِي رَأْيٍ»

---

[1] Narrated by Al-Bukhari, Muslim and At-Tirmidhi, on the authority of Abu Qatadah ؓ and this is the wording of Muslim.

[2] Narrated by Muslim, on the authority of Jabir and Abu Hurairah ؓ.

"A vision (flies away) on the leg of a bird, so long as it is not interpreted, but if it is interpreted, it settles." (Abu Razeen said:) "And I think he said: "Do not tell it except to one whom you love or one who has judgment."[1]

And it is also reported that he ﷺ said to the one who had had a vision:

"You have seen something good,"

then he interpreted it.[2]

---------- ❖ ❖ ❖ ----------

---

[1] Narrated by Abu Dawûd, Ibn Majah and Ahmad, on the authority of Abu Razeen ﷺ.

[2] Narrated by Ibn Majah, on the authority of Umm Al-Fadl ﷺ.

Chapter

Regarding What Should be Said and Done by a Person Who is Afflicted by Whispering

It is reported on the authority of 'Abdullah Ibn Mas'ûd 🙵, who declared that he heard it from the Prophet ﷺ:

»إِنَّ لِلْمَلَكِ بِقَلْبِ ابْنِ آدَمَ لَمَّةً، وللشَّيْطَانِ لَمَّةً، فَلَمَّةُ الْمَلَكِ إِيعَادٌ بِالْخَيْرِ، وَتَصْدِيقٌ بِالْحِقِّ، وَرَجَاءُ صَالِحِ ثَوَابٍ، وَلَمَّةُ الشَّيْطَانِ إِيعَادٌ بِالشَّرِّ، وَتَكْذِيبٌ بِالْحَقِّ، وَقُنُوطٌ مِنَ الْخَيْرِ، فَإِذَا وَجَدْتُمْ لَمَّةَ الْمَلَكِ، فَاحْمَدُوا اللهَ، وَاسْأَلُوهُ مِنْ فَضْلِهِ، وَإِذَا وَجَدْتُمْ لَمَّةَ الشَّيْطَانِ، فَاسْتَعِيذُوا بِالله وَاسْتَغْفِرُوهُ«

"The appointed angel whispers into the heart of the son of Adam and Satan whispers into his heart; the whispering of the angel is a promise of goodness, an affirmation of the truth, the hope of a goodly reward, while the whispering of Satan is a promise of evil, denial of the truth and despair of goodness. So if you find the whispering of the angel, praise and thank Allâh and ask Him to give you from His Bounty; but if you found the whispering of Satan, seek refuge with Allâh and ask His Forgiveness."[1]

---

[1] Narrated by Salih Ibn Kaisan, on the authority if Ibn Mas'ûd 🙵, its *Sanad* is *Munqati'* (broken), because 'Ubaidillah Ibn 'Abdillah did not meet his father's uncle, Ibn Mas'ûd 🙵. It was also narrated by At-Tirmidhi, Ibn Hibban and At-Tabari, on the authority of Ibn Mas'ûd 🙵, in a *Marfû'* form, but its *Sanad* is weak, because it contains one 'Ata' Ibn As-Sa'ib,

'Uthman Ibn Abil-'As said to the Prophet ﷺ: "Oh, Messenger of Allâh! Satan intervenes between me and my prayer and my recitation (of the Qur'ân) and he confounds me." Thereupon, the Messenger of Allâh ﷺ said:

$$ \text{«ذَاكَ شَيْطَانٌ يُقَالُ لَهُ: خِنْزَبٌ، فَإِذَا أَحْسَسْتَهُ، فَتَعَوَّذْ بِاللهِ، وَاتْفُلْ عَنْ يَسَارِكَ ثَلَاثًا»} $$

"That is (the doing of) a devil who is known as Khinzab; so when you perceive his effect, seek refuge with Allâh from it and spit three times to your left."[1]

And the Companions ؓ complained to him that a person among them finds within himself something which he would rather be burnt to a cinder than to speak about; and the Prophet ﷺ said:

$$ \text{«اللهُ أَكْبَرُ، اللهُ أَكْبَرُ، الْحَمْدُ للهِ الَّذِي رَدَّ كَيْدَهُ إِلَى الْوَسْوَسَةِ»} $$

"Allâh is Most Great, Allâh is Most Great, Allâh is Most Great! All praise and thanks be to Allâh, Who repels his (Satan's) plot and reduces it to whispering."[2]

And he ﷺ advised one who is afflicted by any kind of whispering of association of ideas regarding the doers of actions, if it is said to him: "This is Allâh, Who created all things in creation; then who created Allâh?" – that he should say:

$$ \text{﴿هُوَ ٱلْأَوَّلُ وَٱلْآخِرُ وَٱلظَّاهِرُ وَٱلْبَاطِنُ وَهُوَ بِكُلِّ شَيْءٍ عَلِيمٌ﴾} $$

"He is the First (nothing is before Him) and the Last (nothing is after Him), the Most High (nothing is above Him) and the Most Near (nothing is nearer than Him). And He is the All-Knower of every thing."[3]

---

who used to mix up his narrations in his later years, according to Ahmad, Abu Hatim Ar-Razi and others. It was also narrated by At-Tabari as a saying of Ibn Mas'ûd ؓ with an authentic chain of narrators.

[1] Narrated by Muslim and Ahmad on the authority of 'Uthman Ibn Al-'As ؓ.

[2] Narrated by Abu Dawûd and Ahmad, on the authority of 'Abdullah Ibn 'Abbas ؓ.

[3] *Sûrah Al-Hadeed* 57:3

Likewise, Ibn 'Abbas ﷺ said to Abu Zameel, when he asked about some thought which he found in his heart: What is it?" Abu Zameel said: "By Allâh, I will not speak of it." Ibn 'Abbas ﷺ asked: "Is it some form of doubt?" Abu Zameel said: "Yes." He laughed and said: "No one is free from that; if you find such a thing within yourself, say:

﴿هُوَ ٱلْأَوَّلُ وَٱلْآخِرُ وَٱلظَّاهِرُ﴾

"He is the First (nothing is before Him) and the Last (nothing is after Him), the Most High (nothing is above Him)."[1]

So he showed them through this Verse the falseness of logical association of ideas and that the chain of creation begins with the Creator and there is nothing before Him, just as it ends with the last creation, after which there is nothing, and just as His Highness is that above which there is nothing and His Nearness is that more than which there is nothing more encompassing. And if there had been anything before him which had affected Him, that would be the Lord, the Creator, therefore there can be nothing before the Creator, Who is Independent of all others, while everything else is in need of Him. He is the Self-existent, while all others exist through Him. He exists with His Self and He is Eternal, and none existed before Him, while everything else existed having formerly been non-existent. He is Eternal and Everlasting, while everything else remains in existence through Him. The Prophet ﷺ said:

«لَا يَزَالُ النَّاسُ يَتَسَاءَلُونَ حَتَّى يَقُولَ قَائِلُهُمْ: هَذَا اللهُ خَلَقَ الْخَلْقَ، فَمَنْ خَلَقَ اللهَ؟ فَمَنْ وَجَدَ مِنْ ذَلِكَ شَيْئًا، فَلْيَسْتَعِذْ بِاللهِ، وَلْيَنْتَهِ»

"The people will keep on asking until one of them says: "This is Allâh, Who created the whole of creation; then who created Allâh?" So whoever finds any such thing (within himself) should seek refuge with Allâh and it will cease."[2]

And Allâh, Most High says:

---

[1] *Sûrah Al-Hadeed* 57:3.
[2] Narrated by Al-Bukhari, Muslim, Abu Dawûd and Ahmad, on the authority of Abu Hurairah ﷺ.

﴿وَإِمَّا يَنزَغَنَّكَ مِنَ ٱلشَّيْطَٰنِ نَزْغٌ فَٱسْتَعِذْ بِٱللَّهِ﴾

"And if an evil whisper from *Shaitan* (Satan) tries to turn you away (from doing good), then seek refuge in Allâh."[1]

And because the devil is of two types: One which is seen by the eye – and that is the human type – and one which is not seen and that is the jinn – Allâh, Most High has commanded His Prophet ﷺ to suffice himself against the evil of the human devil by avoiding him and by pardoning him and by opposing him with that which is better; and to suffice himself against the evil of the jinn by seeking refuge from him with Allâh and He has combined the two in *Sûrah Al-A'raf* and *Sûrah Al-Mu'minûn*.

For what is it but seeking refuge (with Allâh) in humility, or to repel it with that which is better, they are both good and desirable.

This is the cure for the disease of the evil that is seen. And that is the cure for the disease of the evil that is unseen.

Chapter

He ﷺ ordered the person whose anger is intense to extinguish the burning embers of his wrath by performing ablution and by sitting if he was standing and by lying down if he was sitting and by seeking refuge with Allâh from Satan. And because anger and desire are two embers of fire in the heart of the son of Adam, he ordered him to extinguish them in the aforementioned manner, as in the Words of Allâh, Most High:

﴿أَتَأۡمُرُونَ ٱلنَّاسَ بِٱلۡبِرِّ وَتَنسَوۡنَ أَنفُسَكُمۡ﴾

"Enjoin you *Al-Birr* (piety and righteousness and every act of obedience to Allâh) on the people and you forget (to practise it) yourselves."[1]

And this was due only to intensity of desire, so He commanded them to employ the means to extinguish the burning ember of it, which is to seek help from Allâh with patience and prayer and He, Most High commanded them seek refuge with Him from Satan when he whispers evil thoughts to him.

And since all sins are generated by anger and desire and the result of intense anger is murder and the result of intense desire is unlawful sexual intercourse, Allâh has linked them together in *Sûrah Al-An'am* and *Sûrah Al-Isra'* and *Sûrah Al-Furqân*.

When the Prophet ﷺ saw something that he loved, he would say:

«الْحَمْدُ للهِ الَّذِي بِنِعْمَتِهِ تَتِمُّ الصَّالِحَاتُ»

"*Al-Hamdu Lillahil-Ladhee Bini'matihi Tatimmus-Salihat*"

"All praise and thanks be to Allâh, by Whose Grace good deeds are accomplished."

---

[1] *Sûrah Al-Baqarah* 2:44

And if he saw something which he disliked, he would say:

$$«الْحَمْدُ للهِ عَلَى كُلِّ حَالٍ»$$

"Al-Hamdu Lillahi 'Ala Kulli Hal"

"All praise and thanks be to Allâh in all circumstances."[1]

He would supplicate Allâh for those who approached him with something which he loved, so when Ibn 'Abbas 🙾 placed water for him to perform ablution, he said:

$$«اللَّهُمَّ فَقِّهْهُ فِي الدِّينِ، وَعَلِّمْهُ التَّأْوِيلَ»$$

"Oh, Allâh! Grant him knowledge in the Religion and teach him interpretation."[2]

And when Abu Qatadah supported him when he slipped from his riding beast, he said to him:

$$«حَفِظَكَ اللهُ بِمَا حَفِظْتَ بِهِ نَبِيَّهُ»$$

"May Allâh protect you by that with which you have protected His Prophet."[3]

And he ﷺ said:

---

[1] Narrated Ibn Majah and Ibn A-Sunni, on the authority of 'A'ishah 🙾, its *Sanad* is weak, containing one Zuhair Ibn Muhammad, who, according to Ad-Darimi: "He commits many mistakes." It also contains one Mansûr Ibn 'Abdir-Rahman, of whom Ibn Hajr Al-'Asqalani said: "He is not strong." Abu Na'eem narrated it in '*Al-Hilyah*' with another chain, on the authority of Abu Hurairah 🙾, as did Ibn Majah, but its *Sanad* is also weak, containing in its chain of narrators one Moosa Ibn 'Ubaidah Ibn Nasheet, of whom Imam Ahmad said: "It is not permissible to quote his *Hadeeth*," and Abu Hatim Ar-Razi said: "He narrates *Ahadeeth* which are *Munkarah*." It also contains one Muhammad Ibn Thabit, who, according to Yahya Ibn Ma'een, Az-Zahabi, Abu Hatim Ar-Razi and others, is unknown. Thus it cannot support the first *Hadeeth*.

[2] Narrated by Al-Bukhari, Muslim and Ahmad, on the authority of Ibn 'Abbas 🙾, this is the wording of Ahmad.

[3] Narrated by Muslim and Abu Dawûd, on the authority of Abu Qatadah 🙾.

«مَنْ صُنِعَ إِلَيْهِ مَعْرُوفٌ فَقَالَ لِفَاعِلِهِ: جَزَاكَ اللهُ خَيْرًا . فَقَدْ أَبْلَغَ فِي الثَّنَاءِ»

"Whoever had a good deed done for him and said to the doer of the deed: "May Allâh reward you with goodness," he has attained the highest level of praise."[1]

And he said to the man ('Abdullah Ibn Abi Rabee'ah 🙵 who lent him money when he repaid it:

«بَارَكَ اللهُ لَكَ فِي أَهْلِكَ وَمَالِكَ، إِنَّمَا جَزَاءُ السَّلَفِ الْحَمْدُ وَالأَدَاءُ»

"May Allâh bless you in your family and your wealth; the only reward of a loan is praise and payment."[2]

And if he was given a gift and he accepted it, he would give something even better in return for it.[3] If he did not want it, he would apologize to the giver, such as his saying to As-Sa'b Ibn Jathamah 🙵:

«إِنَّا لَمْ نَرُدَّهُ عَلَيْكَ إِلَّا أَنَّا حُرُمٌ»

"We only return it because we are in a state of *Ihram*."[4]

And he ordered his people to seek refuge with Allâh from the accursed Satan when they hear the braying of a donkey and when they hear a cockerel crowing, to seek Allâh's Bounty.[5] And it is narrated that he ordered them to make *Takbeer* when there is a fire, for it extinguishes it.[6] And he disliked for a group of people sitting

---

[1] Narrated by At-Tirmidhi, on the authority of Usamah Ibn Zaid 🙵, it was declared authentic by Ibn Hibban.

[2] Narrated by An-Nasa'i, Ibn Majah and Ahmad, on the authority of 'Abdullah Ibn Rabee'ah 🙵.

[3] Narrated by Al-Bukhari, Abu Dawûd and At-Tirmidhi, on the authority of 'A'ishah 🙵.

[4] Narrated by Al-Bukhari, At-Tirmidhi and Ibn Majah, on the authority of Ibn 'Abbas 🙵.

[5] Narrated by Al-Bukhari and Muslim, on the authority of Abu Hurairah 🙵.

[6] Narrated by Ibn As-Sunni, Al-'Uqaili in *'Ad-Du'afa'* (The Weak Narrators) and Ibn 'Adi in *'Al-Kamil'*, on the authority of 'Amr Ibn Shu'aib, on the authority of his father, on the authority of his grandfather; and it is a weak *Hadeeth*, according to Shu'aib and 'Abdul Qadir Al-Arna'ût.

together that their meeting should be empty of mention of Allâh, the Almighty, the All-Powerful; and he said:

«مِنْ قَعَدَ مَقْعَدًا لَمْ يَذْكُرِ اللهَ فِيهِ كَانَتْ عَلَيْهِ مِنَ اللهِ، تِرَةً، وَمَنِ اضْطَجَعَ مَضْجَعًا لَا يَذْكُرُ اللهَ فِيهِ كَانَتْ عَلَيْهِ مِنَ اللهِ تِرَةً»

"Whoever sat in a place in which he did not mention Allâh's Name, *Tirah* from Allâh will befall him; and whoever lay down without mentioning Allâh's Name, *Tirah* will befall him from Allâh."[1]

Tirah means grief. And he said: "Whoever sat in a gathering in which there is much clamour and shouting and he said before standing up from the gathering:

«سُبْحَانَكَ اللَّهُمَّ وَبِحَمْدِكَ، أَشْهَدُ أَنْ لَا إِلَهَ إِلَّا أَنْتَ، أَسْتَغْفِرُكَ، وَأَتُوبُ إِلَيْكَ إِلَّا غُفِرَ لَهُ مَا كَانَ فِي مَجْلِسِهِ ذَلِكَ»

"Subhanakallahumma Wa Bihamdika, Ashhadu Alla Ilaha Illa Anta, Astaghfiruka Wa Atûbu Ilaik"

"Glory and praise be to You, O, Allâh! I testify that none is worthy of worship except You; I seek forgiveness from You and I turn to You in repentance), whatever happened during his sitting there will be forgiven for him."[2]

And in Abu Dawûd's '*Sunan*', it is reported that he used to say it when he wished to stand up from a gathering and he was asked about it and he said:

«ذَلِكَ كَفَّارَةٌ لِمَا يَكُونُ فِي الْمَجْلِسِ»

"It is an expiation for what takes place during the gathering."

---

[1] Narrated by Abu Dawûd, Ibn As-Sunni and Al-Humaidi, on the authority of Abu Hurairah 🙵.

[2] Narrated by At-Tirmidhi and Abu Dawûd, on the authority of Abu Hurairah 🙵. It was declared authentic Ibn Hibban and Al-Hakim and this was confirmed by Az-Zahabi.

Chapter

Regarding Expressions Which He ﷺ Disliked[1] to Hear Spoken

Such expressions included: *"Khabutah Nafsee"*[2] or: *"Jashat Nafsee"* (My soul has become agitated). He also disliked that grapes be called *Karm* and that a person should say: *"Halakan-Nas"* (The people are ruined [i.e. they will all enter the Hell-fire])." And he said: "If he said that, he is the first of them to be ruined."[3] And bearing the same meaning is the expression: *"Fasadan-Nas"* (the people have become evil) and: *"Fasadaz-Zaman"* (The time is evil) and other similar expressions. He forbade that it be said: "We have received rain due to the position of such-and-such a heavenly body."[4] He also forbade that it be said: "As Allâh and you will."[5] Also among the things which he detested is swearing by other than Allâh[6] and saying in one's oath: "He is a Jew, or the like, if he does such-and-such a thing."[7] Also among the things which he hated is saying about a

---

[1] Although Ibn Al-Qayyim has used the word disliked, it should be understood that some of these expressions are prohibited. It is not uncommon among scholars of Islamic Jurisprudence to describe something which is prohibited as *'Makrûh'* (disliked).

[2] See Chapter: Regarding His ﷺ Guidance in Guarding His Words and Choosing His Expressions With Care.

[3] Narrated by Muslim and Ahmad, on the authority of Ibn 'Abbas ﷺ.

[4] Narrated by Muslim, At-Tirmidhi, Abu Dawûd, An-Nasa'i, Ahmad, Malik and Ad-Darimi.

[5] Narrated by Ahmad, on the authority of Ibn 'Abbas ﷺ.

[6] Narrated by At-Tirmidhi, Abu Dawûd and Ahmad, on the authority of Ibn 'Umar ﷺ.

[7] Narrated by Abu Dawûd, An-Nasa'i, And Ibn Majah, on the authority of Buraidah ﷺ.

ruler: "King of Kings"[1] and a master referring to his slave as : *"Abdee"* or: *"Amatee"*.[2] He also hated that anyone should malign the wind,[3] fever[4] and the cockerel (when it crows)[5] and he hated that anyone should call people with the calls of the *Jahiliyyah*, such as calling people to tribalism and fanatical allegiance to it.[6] Similar to it is the fanatical following of schools of Islamic Jurisprudence, methodologies and scholars. He also disliked that *'Isha'* should commonly be referred to as *"Al-'Atamah"*, ignoring thereby the term *'Isha'*.[7] He also prohibited that a Muslim should revile another Muslim[8] and that two people should whisper to each other and exclude the third.[9] He also forbade that a woman should inform her husband about the charms of another woman[10] and that a person should say: "Oh, Allâh! Forgive me, if You wish."[11] He also prohibited frequent swearing[12] and he forbade that a person should refer to a rainbow as *Qaws Qudah* (Qudah's bow)[13] And he

---

[1] Narrated by Al-Bukhari, Muslim, Abu Dawûd and At-Tirmidhi, on the authority of Abu Hurairah ﷺ.

[2] Narrated by Al-Bukhari and Muslim, on the authority of Abu Hurairah ﷺ.

[3] Narrated by At-Tirmidhi, on the authority of Ubayy Ibn Ka'b ﷺ and he declared it *Hasan-Saheeh*. It was also narrated by Ahmad, Abu Dawûd and Al-Bukhari in *'Al-Adab Al-Mufrad'*.

[4] Narrated by Muslim, on the authority of Jabir Ibn 'Abdillah ﷺ.

[5] Narrated by Abu Dawûd and Ahmad, on the authority of Zaid Ibn Khalid Al-Juhani ﷺ.

[6] Narrated by Ahmad, Al-Bukhari in *'Al-Adab Al-Mufrad'* and At-Tabarani, on the authority of Ubayy Ibn Ka'b ﷺ.

[7] Narrated by Muslim, on the authority of Ibn 'Umar ﷺ.

[8] Narrated by Al-Bukhari, on the authority of Ibn Mas'ûd ﷺ.

[9] Narrated by Al-Bukhari and Muslim, on the authority of Ibn 'Umar ﷺ.

[10] Narrated by Al-Bukhari, on the authority of Ibn Mas'ûd ﷺ.

[11] Narrated by Al-Bukhari and Muslim, on the authority of Abu Hurairah ﷺ.

[12] Narrated by Muslim, on the authority of Abu Qatadah ﷺ.

[13] Narrated by Abu Na'eem in *'Hilyah Al-Awliya'*, on the authority of Ibn 'Abbas ﷺ, it contains in its *Sanad* one Zakariyyah Ibn Hakeem, who is weak, according to scholars of *Hadeeth*. Qudah was the pre-Islamic god of storms and thunder. He was believed to carry a bow and arrows which,

forbade that anyone should ask another by Allâh's Countenance[1] and that Al-Madinah should be referred to as Yathrib[2] and he forbade that a man should be asked for what reason he had beaten his wife, unless there was some pressing need for it. He also disliked that a person should say: "I have fasted all of Ramadan," or: "I have stood the whole night in prayer."[3]

Also disliked is to speak clearly about things which should be alluded to indirectly (such as sexual intercourse, answering the call of nature etc.) and to say: "May Allâh prolong your existence" and other such expressions. Also hated is the saying of the fasting person: "By the right of the One Who has sealed my mouth," for it is only the mouth of the disbeliever which is sealed. It is also hated to describe taxes as "rights", or to describe what has been spent in obedience to Allâh as "lost". And it is hated to say: "I have spent much money in this world." And it is hated for the scholar delivering a legal ruling to say in matters where juristic reasoning (*Ijtihad*) is exercised: "Allâh has made such-and-such lawful," or: "Allâh has made such-and-such unlawful." It is also hated to describe evidences from the Qur'ân and *Sunnah* as metaphorical or figurative, especially if the doubts expressed by free thinkers and philosophers are presented as irrefutable facts, for (I swear that) none is worthy of worship except Allâh – how much corruption has occurred in the Religion and in worldly matters due to these two expressions! It is also detested for a man to speak of what occurs between him and his wife, as the villains do.

Another expression which is hated is to say: "They claim"[4] or:

---

when fired, causes hailstorms. In ancient Arabia, the center of his cult was near Makkah.

[1] Narrated by Abu Dawûd, on the authority of Jabir Ibn 'Abdillah ﷺ, it contains in its *Sanad* one Sulaiman Ibn Mu'adh At-Tameemi, who is maligned by more than one scholar of *Hadeeth*, including Ibn Hajr, who said: "A poor memory and has Shiite leanings."

[2] Narrated by Al-Bukhari, on the authority of Abu Hurairah ﷺ.

[3] Narrated by Abu Dawûd, on the authority of Abu Bakrah ﷺ.

[4] Narrated by Abu Dawûd, Al-Bukhari in '*Al-Adab Al-Mufrad*' and At-Tahawi by routes on the authority of Al-Awza'i, on the authority of Yahya

"They mentioned" or: "They say" or other such like expressions. It is also hated for the Sultan to be called Allâh's *Khaleefah*, because a *Khaleefah* is only one who takes the place of someone who is absent and Allâh is the *Khaleefah* of a person's family during his absence.

And one should be extremely careful regarding the oppression incumbent in few words: "I", "mine" and "I have". For by these words *Iblees* (Satan), Pharaoh and Qârûn[1] were put to trial, for *Iblees* said: {I am better than he},[2] Pharaoh said: {Is not mine the dominion of Egypt? }[3] and Qârûn said: { This has been given to me because of the knowledge I possess}[4] The best use of the word "I" is in the saying of the slave: "I am the sinning slave, who acknowledges his sins and seeks forgiveness" and other similar expressions (of humility). As for the word "mine", the best use of it is as in the saying: "Mine is the sin, mine is the transgression, mine is the dire need (for Allâh) and mine is the humility." As for the words: "I have", the best use of them is as in the words: "Forgive me my seriousness, my jesting, my mistakes and the things which I do intentionally – and all of these (failings) are in me."[5]

Ibn Abi Katheer, on the authority of Abu Qilabah, who said that Ibn Mas'ûd said to 'Abu 'Abdillah, or 'Abdullah said to Abu Mas'ûd: "What have you heard the Messenger of Allâh saying with regard to the expression: "They claim"? He said: "I heard the Messenger of Allâh (ﷺ) saying: "It is a bad riding-beast for a man (to say): "They claim" Abu 'Abdillah is Hudhaifah ☀. According to scholars of *Hadeeth*, all of the narrators are trustworthy, however, Abu Qilabah did not hear from Abu Mas'ûd Al-Ansari, according to *Al-Hafiz* Al-Munziri, so if he narrates on the authority of Huzaifah ☀, it is *Mursal*.

[1] Qârûn: One of the people of Moses ﷺ, he was reputed to have been a very wealthy man, which caused him to be proud and arrogant, for which reason Allâh destroyed him.

[2] *Sûrah Al-A'raf* 7:12

[3] *Sûrah Az-Zukhruf* 43:51

[4] *Sûrah Al-Qasas* 28:78

[5] Narrated by Muslim and Ahmad, on the authority of Abu Mûsa Al-Ash'ari ☀.

Chapter

Regarding His ﷺ Guidance in *Jihad* and Battles

Because *Jihad* is the apex of Islam and the positions of those who perform it are the loftiest positions in Paradise and likewise, they have a high status in the life of this world, the Messenger of Allâh was at the highest peak of it, for he mastered all types of it: He struggled (*Jihad*) with his heart and soul, by calling (to Islam) and proclaiming (the truth), with the sword and the spear. His hours were devoted to *Jihad*, which is why he was the best in all the worlds in remembering Allâh and the greatest in Allâh's Estimation.

Allâh, Most High commanded him to perform *Jihad* from the time when He sent him, for He said:

$$﴿فَلَا تُطِعِ ٱلۡكَٰفِرِينَ وَجَٰهِدۡهُم بِهِۦ جِهَادٗا كَبِيرٗا ۝﴾$$

"So obey not the disbelievers, but strive against them (by preaching) with the utmost endeavour with it (the Qur'ân)."[1]

– And this is a Makkan *Sûrah* in which he ordered him to make *Jihad* by proclaiming (the truth). Likewise, *Jihad* against the hypocrites is only by convincing argument and is more difficult than *Jihad* against the disbelievers and it is the *Jihad* of the special and unique people (the Prophets and the righteous) and those who help them; and even though they may be small in numbers, they are greater in Allâh's Sight.

---

[1] *Sûrah Al-Furqân* 25:52

And because the best form of *Jihad* is speaking the truth in spite of the severest opposition, such as when one speaks it while he fears the power of another, the Messenger ﷺ had an abundant share of that and he was the most perfect and complete among mankind in doing so. And since making *Jihad* against an enemy is secondary to *Jihad* of oneself, as the Prophet ﷺ said:

«الْمُجَاهِدُ مَنْ جَاهَدَ نَفْسَهُ فِي ذَاتِ اللهِ»

"The *Mujahid* is one who performs *Jihad* of his self in obedience to Allâh."[1]

Jihad of the self takes precedence. These are two enemies by which the slave's *Jihad* is tested. And between them there is a third enemy which, if he does not struggle against it, he will be unable to make *Jihad* of the other two and it stands between them, hindering the performance of *Jihad* against them and that is Satan; Allâh, Most High says:

﴿إِنَّ ٱلشَّيۡطَٰنَ لَكُمۡ عَدُوّٞ فَٱتَّخِذُوهُ عَدُوًّاۚ﴾

"Surely, *Shaitan* (Satan) is an enemy to you, so take (treat) him as an enemy."[2]

And the command to treat him as an enemy is an exhortation to strive to the utmost of one's ability to fight against him. So the slave is commanded to fight against these three enemies and they have been sent to him as a test from Allâh, and the slave has been given support and strength. And each of the two sides is tested by the other and some of them are made a trial for the others, in order to see what they will do. And Allâh has given His slaves hearing, sight, reason and strength. And has sent down His Books and His Messengers to them and supported them with His angels. He commanded them to do that which is the greatest support for them in their fight against their enemy, and informed them that if they fulfill what He has commanded them to do, they will continue to be supported; and that

---

[1] Narrated by Ahmad, on the authority of Fadalah Ibn 'Ubaid ﷺ, it was declared authentic by Ibn Hibban and Al-Hakim and Az-Zahabi confirmed this.

[2] *Sûrah Fâtir* 35:6

if they are overcome, it will be because of their having abandoned a part of what they were commanded to do. But He did not cause them to despair; rather, He informed them that they should treat their wounds and go back and fight their enemies with patient perseverance. And He informed them that He is with the God-fearing among them, with those among them who do righteous deeds, with those among them who patiently persevere and with the believers. And He defends the believers from that from which they are unable to defend themselves; indeed, it is by His defence that they are victorious and were it not for that, their enemy would have vanquished them.

And this defence is in accordance with their belief: If their belief is strong, the defence is strong, so whoever finds something good, he should praise and thank Allâh and whoever finds something other than that, he should not blame anyone except himself. He commanded them to strive in his cause in the manner in which they ought to strive,[1] just as He commanded them to fear Him in the manner in which they ought to fear Him.[2] So just as fearing Him in the manner in which He should be feared means to obey Him and not to disobey Him, to remember Him and not to forget Him, to thank Him and not to be ungrateful to Him. So *Jihad* in His cause in the manner in which it should be performed means to make *Jihad* of his own self in order that his heart, his tongue and his limbs submit to Allâh and by Allâh, not to himself and by himself. And he should struggle against his devil by disbelieving in his promises and disobeying his commands, for he promises to fulfill their vain desires and he incites deception and commands the commission of evil deeds (adultery, fornication etc.) and he forbids guidance and all characteristics of faith and belief. So oppose him by belying his promises and disobeying his commands and from these two *Jihads*, strength and preparedness will result for him by which he may struggle against the enemies of Allâh with his heart, his tongue, his hand and his wealth, in order that Allâh's Word be exalted.

---

[1] *Sûrah Al-Hajj* 22:78
[2] *Sûrah Âl 'Imrân* 3:102

The explanations of the *Salaf* differ regarding the meaning of striving (*Jihad*) in the required manner; Ibn 'Abbas ﷺ said: "It is to strive to the utmost of one's ability in Allâh's Cause and not to fear the rebuke of the censurers. But those people are incorrect who say that the two Verses are abrogated, due to their (erroneous) belief that they contain a command to do something which is not possible, for fearing Allâh as He should be feared and performing *Jihad* as it should be performed means to the best of each individual slave's personal ability – and that varies according to the circumstances of the *Mukallafûn*.[1] Now observe how Allâh has followed the command to do that with His Words:

$$\text{﴿هُوَ ٱجْتَبَنكُمْ وَمَا جَعَلَ عَلَيْكُمْ فِى ٱلدِّينِ مِنْ حَرَجٍ﴾}$$

"He has chosen you (to convey His Message of Islamic Monotheism to mankind by inviting them to His religion of Islam), and has not laid upon you in religion any hardship:"[2]

And the word "*Haraj*" means hardship. And the Prophet ﷺ said: "I was sent with *Al-Haneefiyyah, As-Samhah.*"[3] *Al-Haneefiyyah* is in *Tawheed* and *As-Samhah* is in actions. And Allâh, Most Glorified has made His Religion easy for the slaves to the utmost degree, and likewise His Sustenance, His Pardon and His Forgiveness and He has made repentance simple for them, as long as the soul remains in the body. And He has made an atonement for every sin and He has made a lawful substitute for everything which He has declared unlawful and He has made for every hardship by which He tests them ease before it and ease after it, so how can He make something incumbent upon them which it is not possible for them to do, let alone something which they have no power to do?

---

[1] *Mukallafûn*: (sing. *Mukallaf*) Those who are legally required to observe the precepts of the Religion.

[2] *Sûrah Al-Hajj* 22:78

[3] Narrated by Ahmad, on the authority of Abu Umamah ﷺ, it contains in its chain of narrators one 'Ali Ibn Yazeed Ibn Hilal, who was declared weak by Ahmad Ibn Hanbal, Yahya Ibn Ma'een and Al-Bukhari.

Chapter

When this is known, then (it is clear that) *Jihad* is on four levels:

(1) *Jihad* of the self, and this is also on four levels:

The First: That he struggles against it by learning guidance.

The Second: That he struggles against it by acting upon that guidance once he has learnt it.

The Third: That he struggles against it by calling people to the guidance, for if he does not, he will be one of those who hides what Allâh has revealed.

The Fourth: That he does so with patient perseverance in the face of the hardships which afflict one who is calling to Allâh and that he bears all of this for Allâh.

If all of these four are fulfilled, he will be one of the *Rabbaniyyûn*,[1] for the *Salaf* are in agreement that a scholar is not one of the *Rabbaniyyûn* until he knows the truth, acts upon it and teaches it.

(2) Struggling against Satan; and this is at two levels:

The First: Struggling against him by repelling the doubts which may afflict him.

The Second: By repelling the desires which assail him.

The first is with the weapon of certainty and the second is with the weapon of patience; Allâh, Most High says:

﴿وَجَعَلْنَا مِنْهُمْ أَئِمَّةً يَهْدُونَ بِأَمْرِنَا لَمَّا صَبَرُوٓاْ وَكَانُواْ بِـَٔايَٰتِنَا يُوقِنُونَ ۝٢٤﴾

---

[1] *Rabbaniyyûn*: Learned men of Religion, who practise what they know and teach it to others.

"And We made from among them (Children of Israel), leaders, giving guidance under Our Command, when they were patient and used to believe with certainty in Our *Âyat* (proofs, evidences, verses, lessons, signs, revelations, etc.)."[1]

(3) Struggling (i.e. *Jihad*) against the disbelievers and the hypocrites; and this is on four levels: (i) With the heart, (ii) with the tongue (i.e. by preaching), (iii) with one's wealth and (iv) with the body (i.e. by fighting). And *Jihad* against the disbelievers is more particularly by the hand, while *Jihad* against the hypocrites is more particularly by the tongue.

(4) *Jihad* against the perpetrators of injustice, evil deeds and innovations; and that is at three levels:

The First: With one's hand, if one is able to do so; if he is unable to do so, he proceeds to the second.

The Second: With one's tongue (i.e. to speak against it). If he is unable to do that, he must proceed to the third.

The Third: With one's heart (i.e. to hate the deed in one's heart).

These are thirteen levels of *Jihad* and

$$\text{«مَنْ مَاتَ وَلَمْ يَغْزُ، وَلَمْ يُحَدِّثْ نَفْسَهُ بِالْغَزْوِ، مَاتَ عَلَى شُعْبَةٍ مِنَ النِّفَاقِ»}$$

"Whoever died without fighting in Allâh's Cause and without expressing any desire (or determination) for *Jihad* has died upon a type of hypocrisy."[2]

And *Jihad* is not complete without *Hijrah*,[3] nor are *Hijrah* and *Jihad* complete without faith and belief (*Eeman*). And those who hope for Allâh's Mercy are those who do these three (i.e. *Jihad*, *Hijrah* and *Eeman*); Allâh, Most High says:

$$\text{﴿إِنَّ الَّذِينَ ءَامَنُوا وَالَّذِينَ هَاجَرُوا وَجَهَدُوا فِي سَبِيلِ اللَّهِ أُوْلَٰئِكَ يَرْجُونَ}$$

---

[1] *Sûrah As-Sajdah* 32:24

[2] Narrated by Muslim, Abu Dawûd and An-Nasa'i, on the authority of Abu Hurairah ﷺ.

[3] *Hijrah:* Migration for the sake of one's Religion.

$$\text{رَحْمَتَ ٱللَّهِ وَٱللَّهُ غَفُورٌ رَّحِيمٌ} \text{ ﴿٢٧٨﴾}$$

"Verily, those who have believed, and those who have emigrated (for Allâh's religion) and have striven hard in the way of Allâh, all these hope for Allâh's Mercy. And Allâh is Oft-Forgiving, Most-Merciful."[1]

And just as *Eeman* is incumbent upon every individual, two *Hijrahs* are incumbent upon him at all times: (i) Fleeing to Allâh, the Almighty, the All-Powerful with sincerity and (ii) fleeing to His Messenger ﷺ by conforming (to his *Sunnah*). And *Jihad* of his own self and of his devil has been enjoined upon him, and no one can take the place of another in this.

As for *Jihad* against the disbelievers and the hypocrites, it might be sufficient for a part of the Muslim community to take part in it.

Chapter

The most perfect human being in Allâh's Sight is the one who completes all levels of *Jihad*; this is why the most perfect and the most noble of them in Allâh's Sight is the Seal of His Prophets, Muhammad, the Messenger of Allâh ﷺ. For he completed all of its levels and struggled in Allâh's Cause in the manner in which it should be carried out; and he undertook it from the time Allâh sent him until He took him unto Him, for when it was revealed to him:

"O you (Muhammad ﷺ) enveloped in garments! Arise and warn! And magnify your Lord (Allâh)! And purify your garments!"[1]

He buckled down to the task of calling people to Islam and performed it in the most complete way and he called to Allâh night and day, openly and in secret. And when it was revealed to him:

$$\text{﴾فَٱصْدَعْ بِمَا تُؤْمَرُ﴿}$$

"Therefore proclaim openly (Allâh's Message — Islamic Monotheism) that which you are commanded,"[2]

he acted in accordance with Allâh's Command and he cared not for the rebuke of the censurer. He called to Allâh both the old and the young, the free man and the slave, male and female, jinn and human.

And when he acted upon Allâh's Command and called his people to Islam, beginning by reviling their (false) deities and maligning their religion, their enmity towards him and those who answered his call increased; and this is Allâh, the Almighty, the All-powerful's way

---

[1] *Sûrah Al-Muddaththir* 74:1-4

[2] *Sûrah Al-Hijr* 15:94

with regard to His creatures, as He, Most High says:

﴿مَّا يُقَالُ لَكَ إِلَّا مَا قَدْ قِيلَ لِلرُّسُلِ مِن قَبْلِكَ﴾

"Nothing is said to you (O Muhammad ﷺ) except what was said to the Messengers before you."[1]

And He, Most High says:

﴿وَكَذَٰلِكَ جَعَلْنَا لِكُلِّ نَبِيٍّ عَدُوًّا شَيَٰطِينَ ٱلْإِنسِ وَٱلْجِنِّ﴾

"And so We have appointed for every Prophet enemies — *Shayatin* (devils) among mankind and jinn."[2]

And He, Most High says:

﴿كَذَٰلِكَ مَآ أَتَى ٱلَّذِينَ مِن قَبْلِهِم مِّن رَّسُولٍ إِلَّا قَالُوا۟ سَاحِرٌ أَوْ مَجْنُونٌ ۝ أَتَوَاصَوْا۟ بِهِۦ بَلْ هُمْ قَوْمٌ طَاغُونَ ۝﴾

"Likewise, no Messenger came to those before them but they said: "A sorcerer or a madman!" Have they (the people of the past) transmitted this saying to these (Quraish pagans)? Nay, they are themselves a people transgressing beyond bounds (in disbelief)!"[3]

So Allâh, Most Glorified strengthened His Prophet thereby and informed him that he has an example in those (Prophets) who came before him. And He strengthened his followers with His Words:

﴿أَمْ حَسِبْتُمْ أَن تَدْخُلُوا۟ ٱلْجَنَّةَ وَلَمَّا يَأْتِكُم مَّثَلُ ٱلَّذِينَ خَلَوْا۟ مِن قَبْلِكُم﴾

"Or think you that you will enter Paradise without such (trials) as came to those who passed away before you?"[4]

And His Words:

﴿الٓمٓ ۝ أَحَسِبَ ٱلنَّاسُ أَن يُتْرَكُوٓا۟ أَن يَقُولُوٓا۟ ءَامَنَّا وَهُمْ لَا يُفْتَنُونَ ۝﴾

"*Alif-Lam-Mim.* [These letters are one of the miracles of the

---

[1] *Sûrah Fussilat* 41:43
[2] *Sûrah Al-An'am* 6:112
[3] *Sûrah Adh-Dhariyat* 51:52-53
[4] *Sûrah Al-Baqarah* 2:214

Qur'ân, and none but Allâh (Alone) knows their meanings.] Do people think that they will be left alone because they say: "We believe," and will not be tested."

Up to His Words:

$$\text{﴿} \text{أَوَ لَيْسَ ٱللَّهُ بِأَعْلَمَ بِمَا فِى صُدُورِ ٱلْعَٰلَمِينَ} \text{(10)} \text{﴾}$$

"Is not Allâh Best Aware of what is in the breasts of the *'Alamin* (mankind and jinn)?"[1]

Let the slave observe the context of these Verses and the admonitions and treasures of wisdom they contain, for when Messengers are sent to the people, they respond in one of two ways: Either one of them will say: "We have believed," or he will not, but continue to commit sins. And whoever says: "We have believed" is tested by his Lord and testing means trying him by afflictions and giving him choices, in order to make clear the truthful person from the liar. And whoever did not say: "We have believed" should not imagine that he will evade Allâh or outstrip Him; and whoever believed in the Messengers, their enemies will become enemies to him and will seek to harm him, so he will be put to trial by what causes him pain. But as for those who do not obey them (i.e. the Messengers), they will be punished in the life of this world and in the Hereafter.

Every person must experience pain, but the believer experiences pain at the beginning, but then the final outcome is in his favour. The rejecter, on the other hand experiences pleasure at the beginning, but later he will experience unending pain. Ash-Shafi'i – may Allâh have mercy on him – was asked: "What is better for a man, to be established (in the earth) or to be tried by affliction?" He replied: "He will not be established until he has been tried by affliction. Allâh, the Almighty, the All-Powerful tried *Ulul-'Azm*[2] from among His Messengers; and when they were patient, He established them (in the earth)." So no one should imagine that he will completely escape pain. And the most intelligent of them are those who endured

---

[1] *Sûrah Al-'Ankabût* 29:1-10

[2] *Ulul-'Azm*: The Possessors of Firm Will: Noah, Abraham, Moses, Jesus and Muhammad 鑢. See *Sûrah Al-Ahqâf* 46:35.

unending pain in return for pain which will cease, while the most foolish of them are those who endured pain which will cease in return for severe, unending pain.

And if it is said: How can an intelligent person choose this? It may be said in reply what causes him to do this is (fear of) censure and the fact that the reward (of bearing temporary pain) is delayed; and the human soul craves that which is present now:

$$ ﴿ كَلَّا بَلْ تُحِبُّونَ ٱلْعَاجِلَةَ ۝ وَتَذَرُونَ ٱلْأَخِرَةَ ۝ ﴾ $$

"Not [as you think, that you (mankind) will not be resurrected and recompensed for your deeds], but you (men) love the present life of this world, And neglect the Hereafter."[1]

$$ ﴿ إِنَّ هَـٰٓؤُلَآءِ يُحِبُّونَ ٱلْعَاجِلَةَ ﴾ $$

"Verily, these (disbelievers) love the present life of this world."[2]

So this happens to everyone, because a person must live among the people and there are things which they require him to agree to; and if he does not, they will seek to harm him and punish him, whereas, if he does agree to them, he will (still) be afflicted by harm and punishment, sometimes from them and sometimes from others. Like one who is religious and pious and who lives among an unjust people and they are unable to perform their acts of injustice without his consent, or his silence regarding them. If he does so, he will escape their evil at first, but then they will cause him humiliation and hurt, much more than he feared from them, if he had criticized them at the outset. And if he escapes from them, he will certainly be humiliated by others.

Therefore he should resolve firmly to act upon the words of 'A'ishah ﷺ to Mu'awiyah ﷺ: "Whoever pleased Allâh by incurring the anger of the people, Allâh will suffice against (relying on) the provision of people; but whoever pleased the people by incurring Allâh's Anger, they will avail him nothing against Allâh."[3]

---

[1] *Sûrah Al-Qiyamah* 75:20-21

[2] *Sûrah Ad-Dahr* 76:27

[3] Narrated by At-Tirmidhi, on the authority of 'A'ishah ﷺ, who attributed it to the Prophet ﷺ.

And whoever observes the affairs of this world will see this much among those who support leaders and innovators out of fear of being punished by them. And whomsoever Allâh protected from the evil of himself will refuse to agree to what is unlawful and will patiently persevere in the face of their enmity; then the end result in the life of this world and in the Hereafter will be in his favour, as it was for those among the scholars and others who were tried by affliction.

And because there can be no complete freedom from pain, Allâh, Most Glorified has consoled those who choose temporary pain by His Words:

$$ \text{﴿مَن كَانَ يَرْجُوا۟ لِقَآءَ ٱللَّهِ فَإِنَّ أَجَلَ ٱللَّهِ لَءَاتٍ وَهُوَ ٱلسَّمِيعُ ٱلْعَلِيمُ ۝﴾} $$

"Whoever hopes for the Meeting with Allâh, then Allâh's Term is surely coming, and He is the All-Hearer, the All-Knower."[1]

So He has fixed for this temporary pain a limit which is the Day on which he will meet with Him, so the slave will enjoy the greatest pleasure due to the pain which he bore for His sake and He has added to this consolation the hope of the meeting with Him, so that the slave's desire to meet his Lord may cause him to bear the present pain; indeed, his desire to see his Lord might even cause him to be unaware of the pain and not to feel it. This is why the Prophet ﷺ asked his Lord to make him desire the meeting with Him (in the Hereafter); and the desire for this is one of the greatest blessings. However, in order to attain this great blessing, one is required to say certain things (supplication, *Dhikr* etc.) and do certain things (acts of worship, kindness etc.), which are the means of his achieving it; and Allâh, Most Glorified hears these words and knows of these actions and He knows which of them deserve this blessing, as He, Most High says:

$$ \text{﴿وَكَذَٰلِكَ فَتَنَّا بَعْضَهُم بِبَعْضٍ﴾} $$

"Thus We have tried some of them with others."[2]

And if the slave loses some blessing, he should recite to himself:

---

[1] *Sûrah Al-'Ankabût* 29:5

[2] *Sûrah Al-An'am* 6:53

﴾ أَلَيْسَ اللَّهُ بِأَعْلَمَ بِالشَّاكِرِينَ ۝ ﴾

"Does not Allâh know best those who are grateful?"[1]

And Allâh, Most High has comforted them with another solace, which is that their *Jihad* in His Cause is only for themselves and that He is Independent of all creation, so the benefit of this *Jihad* returns to them, not to Him, Most Glorified. And He informed them that because of their *Jihad*, He will admit them among the party of the righteous. And He also informed us about the situation of one who enters into faith without knowledge, that he thinks that the trial which befalls him from the people, i.e. the harm and the pain – which there is no avoiding – that they inflict upon him, is like the punishment of Allâh from which the believers flee with faith and belief; then when the Help of Allâh comes to His Army, he says to them: "I am with you." And Allâh knows better the hypocrisy which he conceals in his heart.

And what is meant is that the Wisdom (of Allâh) dictates that He, Most Glorified must test the souls of the people, in order that the righteous ones stand out clearly from the evil ones, since essentially the soul is ignorant and unjust and due to this, it garners evil, the purification of which is required in order to remove it. And if it is removed in the life of this world (all well and good), but if it is not, then it will be removed in the furnace of the Hell-fire; then once the slave is purified, he is permitted to enter Paradise.

---
[1] *Sûrah Al-An'am* 6:53

When the Prophet ﷺ called the people to Allâh, slaves of Allâh from
every tribe responded to his call and the first of them was the *Siddeeq*
of this nation, Abu Bakr ؓ and he supported him in (spreading) the
Religion and he called the people to Allâh with him; and among those
who responded to Abu Bakr's call were 'Uthman, Talhah and Sa'd ؓ.
And the *Siddeeqah* of the women, Khadeejah ؓ rushed to answer his
call and she fulfilled the duties incumbent upon her. and he said to
her:

«لَقَدْ خَشِيتُ عَلَى نَفْسِي»

"I feared for myself."

She said to him: "Be of good cheer, for by Allâh, Allâh will never
disgrace you." Then she cited as evidence of this the virtuous
attributes which he possessed, saying that whoever possessed such
attributes would never be disgraced by Allâh,[1] for she knew by her
own natural state of belief in Allâh (*Fitrah*) and her unimpaired
intellect that righteous deeds and virtuous attributes are befitting of
Allâh's Generosity and His Benevolence, not disgrace.

And because of this intellect, she was deemed deserving of being sent
salutations of peace from her Lord through His two Messengers,
Jibreel and Muhammad ﷺ.[2]

Also among those who hastened to submit to Allâh was 'Ali Ibn Abi
Talib ؓ, when he was a boy of eight years old, or move. He was under
the guardianship of the Messenger of Allâh ﷺ, who had taken him
from his uncle, in order to help him in a year of drought.

---

[1] Narrated by Al-Bukhari, Muslim and Ahmad, on the authority of
'A'ishah ؓ.

[2] Narrated by Al-Bukhari and Muslim, on the authority of Abu Hurairah ؓ.

Another who hastened to embrace Islam was Zaid bin Harithah, the dear one of the Messenger of Allâh ﷺ; he was a servant of Khajeedah ؓ and she gave him to the Prophet ﷺ. His father and uncle came to him to ransom the boy, and the Messenger of Allâh ﷺ said:

«فَهَلَّا غَيْرَ ذَلِكَ»

"Why do you not ask something else?"

So he allowed him to choose, saying:

«فَإِنِ اخْتَارَكُمْ فَهُوَ لَكُمْ، وَإِنِ اخْتَارَنِي، فَوَاللهِ مَا أَنَا بِالَّذِي أَخْتَارُ عَلَى مَنِ اخْتَارَنِي أَحَدًا»

"If he chooses you, then he is yours, but if he chooses me, by Allâh, I will not choose another than one who has chosen me."

They said: "You have answered us by meeting us halfway and you have behaved well." So he called him and gave him the choice and he said: "I will not choose anyone besides you." They said: "Shame on you, Zaid! Would you choose slavery over freedom and over your family?" He said: "Yes. I have seen something of this man and I will never choose another over him." When the Messenger of Allâh ﷺ saw this, he took him out to Hijr Isma'eel[1] and said:

«أُشْهِدُكُمْ أَنَّ زَيْدًا ابْنِي أَرِثُهُ وَيَرِثُنِي»

"I call upon you as witnesses that Zaid is my son; I am his heir and he is my heir."

When his father and uncle hear this, they became happy and left. He was called Zaid Ibn Muhammad until Islam came and the following Verse was revealed:

﴿ٱدْعُوهُمْ لِءَابَآئِهِمْ هُوَ أَقْسَطُ عِندَ ٱللَّهِ﴾

"Call them (adopted sons) by (the names of) their fathers, that is more just with Allâh."[2]

---

[1] Hijr Isma'eel: A place near to the Ka'bah which was commonly used to make public announcements in the time of the Prophet ﷺ.

[2] *Sûrah Al-Ahzâb* 33:5

After which he was known as Zaid bin Harithah.[1] Ma'mar narrated on the authority of Az-Zuhri that he said: "We do not know of anyone who embraced Islam before Zaid."[2]

Waraqah bin Nawfal embraced Islam; and in At-Tirmidhi's 'Jami", it is reported that the Messenger of Allâh ﷺ saw him in a dream in a good condition.[3]

The people entered Islam one after another and Quraish did not object to that, until he began to malign their religion and revile their (false) deities. At that point, they began to exhibit serious enmity to him and his Companions. Allâh protected His Messenger ﷺ with Abu Talib, because he was respected and highly regarded by them. And it was from the Wisdom of the Most Just of judges that he should remain upon the religion of his people due to the benefits which are obvious to those who think about them.

As for his Companions, those of them who belonged to a tribe which could protect them were safe; but the rest of them were tortured, including 'Ammar, his mother and his family members. They were tortured for their belief in Allâh and when the Messenger of Allâh ﷺ passed by them while they were being subjected to torture, he said:

$$ «صَبْرًا يا آلَ يَاسِرٍ . فَإِنَّ مَوْعِدَكُمُ الْجَنَّةُ» $$

"Have patience, O, family of Yasir, for verily, you are promised a place in Paradise."[4]

Another one was Bilal, who was tortured with the most severe torment, for they cared little for him, while he cared little for himself due to his belief in Allâh, and whenever the torment increased he would cry: "(Allâh is) One! One!" And Waraqah bin Nawfal passed by and said: "Yes, by Allâh, oh, Bilal! (He is) One, One! But should you kill him, I will take him as a mercy."[5]

---

[1] Narrated by Al-Bukhari, on the authority of Ibn 'Umar ﷺ.
[2] Narrated by 'Abdur-Razzaq in 'Al-Musannaf'.
[3] Narrated by At-Tirmidhi and Ahmad.
[4] Narrated by Ibn Ishaq and At-Tabarani.
[5] Narrated by Az-Zubair Ibn Bakkar, it is a Mursal narration and it contains in its chain a narrator identified as 'Uthman, who is weak, according to Shu'aib and 'Abdul Qadir Al-Arna'ût.

When the harm they inflicted on the believers increased in intensity and some of them were put to trial, Allâh permitted them to make the first *Hijrah* to the land of Abyssinia; and the first of those who migrated there was 'Uthman ﷺ and with him went his wife Ruqayyah ﷺ, the daughter of the Messenger of Allâh ﷺ. They were twelve men and four women and they slipped away in secret and Allâh caused it to come about that when they arrived at the coast, they found two boats which carried them. They left in the month of Rajab in the fifth year after the Prophet ﷺ was sent with the Revelation. Quraish set out in pursuit of them until they reached the sea coast, but they did not catch them. Then news came to the migrants that Quraish had ceased their persecution of the Prophet ﷺ and so they returned, but when they were an hour away from Makkah, news reached them that Quraish's enmity was now worse than ever. Some of them entered under the protection of others. It was on this occasion that Ibn Mas'ûd (one of the migrants) entered and gave greetings of peace to the Prophet ﷺ while he was praying and he did not respond. And this is correct; it was reported by Ibn Ishaq, who said that when they were informed that it was false (that Quraish had ceased their persecution), none of them entered Makkah except under protection or in secret and he was one of those who arrived and remained resident there until the *Hijrah* to Al-Madinah, after which he took part in the Battles of Badr and Uhud. And Ibn Mas'ûd ﷺ was mentioned as being among them. The *Hadeeth* of Zaid bin Arqam ﷺ may be answered in two ways:

The First: That the prohibition of speaking during the prayer was confirmed in Makkah, then he ﷺ permitted it in Al-Madinah, then he forbade it.

The Second: That Zaid was one of the minors among the Companions ﷺ and he and his group used to talk to one another during the prayer in accordance with their custom and they had not been informed that it was prohibited to do so, but once they were informed that it was not permissible, they ceased doing so. Then the severity of the trials inflicted by Quraish on those who had returned from Abyssinia and others increased and their tribes turned upon them and so the Messenger of Allâh ﷺ permitted them to leave for the land of

Abyssinia once more. Their second departure was more difficult for them and they encountered severe harm from Quraish and it was hard upon them to be informed of the asylum offered to them by the Negus of Abyssinia.

The number of those who departed this time was eighty-three men – assuming that 'Ammar bin Yasir was one of them and nineteen women. I say: 'Uthman and a number of those who took part in the Battle of Badr were mentioned as being included in this second migration. Either this is conjecture, or they returned once again before Badr, which would mean that they returned three times. This is why Ibn Sa'd and others said that when they heard of the migration of the Messenger of Allâh ﷺ, thirty-three men and eight women from among them returned and that two men from among them died in Makkah and seven of them were imprisoned, while twenty-four men from among them took part in the Battle of Badr. Then, in the month of Rabee' Al-Awwal, in the seventh year after the migration to Al-Madinah, the Messenger of Allâh ﷺ wrote a letter with 'Amr Ibn Umayyah ﷺ to the Negus, calling him to Islam and he embraced Islam. He said: "Were I able to come to him, I would do so."[1] And he wrote to him requesting him to marry Umm Habeebah ﷺ to him, for she was one of those who had migrated to Abyssinia, along with her husband, 'Ubaidullah Ibn Jahsh, and he had converted to Christianity there and died a Christian. So the Negus married him to her and gave her as a dowry on his behalf the sum of four hundred *Deenars*. And the person who acted as her guardian was Khalid Ibn Sa'eed Ibn Al-'As ﷺ. And the Prophet ﷺ wrote asking the Negus to send those of his Companions ﷺ who remained in Abyssinia back to him and to provide transport for them and he did so in two boats with 'Amr Ibn Umayyah ﷺ and they approached the Messenger of Allâh ﷺ in Khaibar, arriving after he had conquered it. Based upon this, any doubt or contradiction between the *Hadeeth* of Ibn Mas'ûd ﷺ and the *Hadeeth* of Zaid Ibn

---

[1] Narrated by Ibn Sa'd in '*At-Tabaqat*' from Al-Waqidi (who was well known for reporting fabricated *Ahadeeth*) and it is weak; but the Islam of the Negus is confirmed, because the Prophet (ﷺ) offered the funeral prayer for him when he died.

Arqam  is removed and it becomes clear that the prohibition of speaking during the prayers took place in Al-Madinah.

And if it is said: What a good saying this would be were it not for the fact that Ibn Ishaq has said what you have related from him, which is that Ibn Mas'ûd  stayed in Makkah – it may be said in reply: Ibn Sa'd has said that he stayed in Makkah for a short period of time, then returned to the land of Abyssinia. And this is what appears most likely, since he had no one in Makkah to protect him. So it is implied that this extra information was unknown to Ibn Ishaq; and Ibn Ishaq has not mentioned who informed him, while Ibn Sa'd has attributed it to Al-Muttalib Ibn 'Abdillah Ibn Hantab, so any doubt is dispelled, all praise and thanks be to Allâh.

And Ibn Ishaq has mentioned that Abu Mûsa Al-Ash'ari took part in this *Hijrah*, but this has been rejected by Al-Waqidi and others; they asked how this could be unknown to other than him. I say: This is not something which was unknown to other than him, for the erroneous belief has arisen that Abu Mûsa migrated from Yemen to Ja'far and his companions in (Abyssinia), then proceeded with them (to Khaibar); and Ibn Ishaq considered this to be a *Hijrah*, but he did not say that he migrated from Makkah, as this would have been rejected from him.

---------- ❖ ❖ ❖ ----------

Chapter

The Muslims joined the Negus in Abyssinia, where they lived in safety. Quraish sent after them 'Abdullah bin Abi Rabee'ah and 'Amr Ibn Al-'As with gifts for the Negus, so that he would send them back to them and they sought intercession from the highest ranking officers in his army, but he refused, so they lied to him that they (i.e. the Muslims) say terrible things about Jesus ('Isa ﷺ), saying: "They say that he is a slave." So he called for them and their leader was Ja'far Ibn Abi Talib ﷺ. When they wanted to enter his presence, Ja'far ﷺ said: "The Party of Allâh seeks permission to enter your presence." He said to the one who admitted people: "Tell him to repeat his request to enter." And he did so, then when they entered, he asked them: "What do you say about Jesus?" In reply, Ja'far ﷺ recited to him from the beginning of *Sûrah Maryam*; the Negus took a stick from the ground and said: "Jesus does not exceed what you have said, even by the length of this stick." His bishops around him snorted when he said this, but he said: "Even though you snort, even though you snort." He said (to the Muslims): "Go, for you are *Suyûm* in my land and whoever abuses you will be fined." *Suyûm* in their language means safe. Then he said to the two messengers (from Quraish): "Even if you were to give me a *Dabr* (the narrator said: a mountain) of gold, I would not deliver them to you." Then he ordered that their gifts be returned to them and they returned in ignominy.

Then Hamzah and a large group embraced Islam, after which Quraish saw that the Religion of the Messenger of Allâh ﷺ was in the ascendant, so they agreed to ostracize the tribes of Banu Hashim and Banu 'Abdil Muttalib, agreeing not to trade with them, nor to contract marriages with them, nor to speak to them, nor to sit with them until they delivered the Messenger of Allâh ﷺ to them. They wrote all of this in a document and they attached it to the ceiling of the *Ka'bah*. It was written by Bagheedh Ibn 'Amir Ibn Hashim and the Messenger of Allâh ﷺ invoked Allâh against him and his hand became paralyzed. The believers and the disbelievers among them moved to the ravine (to which they had been ostracized) except Abu Lahab, for he supported Quraish against them. This happened in the seventh year after the Prophet ﷺ was sent to deliver the Message of Islam and they remained isolated and extremely oppressed for about three years until they suffered greatly and the voices of their crying children could be heard from beyond the ravine. There Abu Talib wrote his well known poem whose verse all end with the Arabic letter (*Lam*), while Quraish remained divided between approval and condemnation and all of those who condemned the boycott tried to have it annulled and Allâh informed His Messenger regarding the condition of the document and that Allâh had sent termites and that they had eaten all of the words of boycott and oppression and left nothing except the mention of Allâh, the Almighty, the All-Powerful. He informed his uncle of this and he went out to Quraish and informed them that his nephew had said such-and-such and he said: "If he is lying, we shall let the boycott between you and him remain, but if he is truthful, you must go back upon it (i.e. the boycott)." They said: "You have spoken fairly." So they took it down and when they found that the matter was as he had said, they increased their disbelief.

The Messenger of Allâh ﷺ and those with him left the ravine and Abu Talib died six months later, while Khadeejah ﷺ died three days after him and it was said that she died at other times. The trials inflicted upon the Messenger of Allâh ﷺ by the foolish among his people increased in severity and so he went to Ta'if, hoping that they would help him against them and he called them to believe in Allâh, but he did not find anyone among them who would give him shelter, nor did he find any helper. Instead, they hurt him and treated him in a manner worse than that of his own people. With him was Zaid Ibn Harithah ﷺ and he remained among them for ten days, during which time he did not leave any of their leaders without talking to him, but they said: "Leave our city." And they incited the foolish among them to stand in wait for him and throw stones at him, until

his feet were bleeding and Zaid shielded him with his body until his
skull was fractured and he returned to Makkah dejected.

On his return, he made that well known supplication:

«اللَّهُمَّ إِلَيْكَ أَشْكُو ضَعْفَ قُوَّتِي، وَقِلَّةَ حِيلَتِي» إلخ . . .

"Allâhumma, Ilaika Ashkû Da'fa Quwwatee Wa Qillata Heelatee" etc.

"Oh, Allâh! I complain to You of the weakness of my ability and
my lack of my means to accomplish."[1]

At which, his Lord, the Most Blessed, Most High sent the angel of the
mountains to him, to ask him if he would order that *Al-Akhshaban* be
toppled onto the people of Makkah – and *Al-Akhshaban* are the two
mountains between which Makkah is situated – but he ﷺ said:

«بَلْ أَسْتَأْنِي بِهِمْ لَعَلَّ اللهَ يُخْرِجُ مِنْ أَصْلَابِهِمْ مَنْ يَعْبُدُهُ لَا يُشْرِكُ بِهِ
شَيْئًا»

"I would rather have someone from their loins who will
worship Allâh, the All-Mighty with no associate."

When he stopped at Nakhlah[2] on his return, he stood up to pray at
night and Allâh sent towards him a number of persons from among
the jinn and they heard his recitation, and he was unaware of them
until it was revealed to him:

﴿وَإِذْ صَرَفْنَآ إِلَيْكَ نَفَرًا مِّنَ ٱلْجِنِّ﴾

"And (remember) when We sent towards you (Muhammad
ﷺ) a group (three to ten persons) of the jinn."[3]

He remained at Nakhlah for a number of days and Zaid ؓ said to
him: "How will you enter among them when they (i.e. Quraish) have

---

[1] Mentioned by Ibn Hisham in his *'Seerah'*, it was narrated by Ibn Ishaq;
however Ibn Ishaq was known to commit *Tadless*.

[2] Nakhlah: The name of a valley.

[3] *Sûrah Al-Ahqâf* 46:29, according to Ibn Katheer in his *'Tafseer'*, this event
took place not after the Prophet's visit to Ta'if, but two years before. Ibn
Al-Qayyim has followed Ibn Ishaq in stating that it took place during the
return from Ta'if.

expelled you?" He (ﷺ) replied:

«يَازَيْدُ إِنَّ اللَّهَ جَاعِلٌ لِمَا تَرَىٰ فَرَجًا وَمَخْرَجًا، وَإِنَّ اللَّهَ نَاصِرٌ دِينَهُ، وَمُظْهِرٌ نَبِيَّهُ»

"Oh, Zaid! Allâh has made what you see as a relief and a way out and verily, Allâh will help His Religion and grant His Prophet victory."

When he reached Makkah, he sent a man from Khuza'h to Mut'im Ibn 'Adi saying:

«أَدْخُلُ فِي جِوَارِكَ»؟

"May I enter your protection?"

He replied: "Yes." And he called his sons and his people and said: "Put on your weapons and stand at the corners of the house, for I have granted asylum to Muhammad." So the Messenger of Allâh ﷺ entered Makkah until he reached the Sacred Mosque and he had with him Zaid bin Harithah ، while Mut'im sat on riding beast and announced: "Oh, people of Quraish! I have given asylum to Muhammad, so let none of you harm him." The Prophet ﷺ reached the (Yemeni) Corner and touched it and then offered a two *Rak'ah* prayer, then left to go to his house, while Mut'im and his sons encircled him bearing their weapons until he had entered his house.

Chapter

Then the Messenger of Allâh ﷺ was taken physically – according to the correct opinion – from the Sacred Mosque to Bait Al-Maqdis (in Jerusalem), riding on Al-Buraq, accompanied by Jibreel 🕊 where he descended and he led the Prophets in prayer,[1] having tied up Al-Buraq to the ring of the door of the mosque. It was said that he descended in Bethlehem, but nothing at all authentic has been reported to that effect.

Then he was taken up on that night from Bait Al-Maqdis to the lowest heaven and Jibreel 🕊 asked for it to be opened for him and it was opened for them. There he saw Adam, the father of mankind and he gave salutations of peace to him and he returned his greeting and welcomed him, affirming his Prophethood. Then Allâh showed him the souls of those of his descendants who are fortunate (i.e. who will enter Paradise) on his right and those who will be wretched (i.e. who will be in the Hell-fire) on his left.

Then he was taken up to the second heaven wherein he saw John (Yunûs 🕊) and Jesus ('Isa 🕊). After that, he was taken up to the third heaven and there he saw Joseph (Yusûf 🕊). Then he was taken up to the fourth heaven, in which he saw Idris 🕊. After that, he was taken up to the fifth heaven, where he met Aaron (Harûn 🕊). Then he went onto the sixth heaven, in which he met Moses (Mûsa 🕊), who, when the Prophet ﷺ passed by him cried; when he was asked why he was crying, he said: "Because the nation of a slave who was sent after me who will enter Paradise are greater in number than

---

[1] Narrated by Muslim, on the authority of Anas 👐 and by Ahmad, on the authority of Ibn 'Abbas 👐. Ibn Hajr considered that this prayer took place before the ascent to the heavens, while Ibn Katheer opined that the correct view was that it took place in Bait Al-Maqdis after the ascent.

those of my nation who will enter it." Then he was taken up to the seventh heaven, where he met Abraham (Ibraheem 🕮), after which he was taken up to *Sidrah Al-Muntaha*[1] and then he was raised up to *Al-Bait Al-Ma'mûr*[2] and then he was taken up to the Compeller, Most Exalted be He and he approached Him until,

$$ ﴿فَكَانَ قَابَ قَوْسَيْنِ أَوْ أَدْنَىٰ ۝ فَأَوْحَىٰ إِلَىٰ عَبْدِهِ مَآ أَوْحَىٰ ۝﴾ $$

"And was at a distance of two bows' length or (even) nearer. So (Allâh) revealed to His slave [Muhammad 🕮 through Jibraıl (Gabriel) whatever He revealed."[3]

It was at this time that the prayer was made incumbent upon him and he returned, passing by Moses (Mûsa 🕮), who asked him: "What were you commanded to do?" He 🕮 said:

$$ «بِخَمْسِينَ صَلَاةً» $$

"I was commanded to observe fifty prayers (a day)."

Moses (Mûsa 🕮) said: "Your people will not be able to do that. Return to your Lord and ask Him to reduce it for your people." So he turned to Jibreel 🕮, as if seeking his counsel and he advised: "Yes, if you wish." Then Jibreel 🕮 ascended with him until they came to the Compeller, Most Blessed, Most High and spoke to Him while he was still in his place." This is the wording of Al-Bukhari in his *'Saheeh'*.

In one of the narrations, it is reported that He decreased it by ten for him, then he descended and passed by Moses (Mûsa 🕮) and informed him of it, but he said: "Return to your Lord and ask Him to

---

[1] *Sidrah Al-Muntaha*: The lote tree at the utmost boundary of the seventh heaven.

[2] *Al-Bait Al-Ma'mûr*: The house of worship which is situated over the heavens and which is continually visited by the angels.

[3] *Sûrah An-Najm* 53:9 Although this is one interpretation of Allâh's Words in *Sûrah An-Najm*, in fact, according to Ibn Katheer, the correct interpretation is that it refers to the Prophet's seeing Jibraıl 🕮 and the latter's approaching him until "he was at a distance of two bows' lengths or nearer." Certainly the context of the *Sûrah* supports this, if one reads the preceding Verses.

decrease it." And he continued to go back and forth between Moses (Mûsa ﷺ) and Allâh, Most Blessed, Most High, until He had made it five. Moses (Mûsa ﷺ) ordered him to return and ask for a further decrease, but he said:

«قَدِ اسْتَحْيَيْتُ مِنْ رَبِّي، وَلَكِنِّي أَرْضَى وَأُسَلِّمُ»

"I am embarrassed before my Lord, but I accept and submit."

Then when he departed a voice called, saying:

«قَدْ أَمْضَيْتُ فَرِيضَتِي وَخَفَّفْتُ عَنْ عِبَادِي»

"I have ordained My Obligation (upon the slaves) and I have reduced (the burden) on My slaves."[1]

The Companions ﷺ disagreed as to whether or not he saw his Lord on this night. It has been authentically reported on the authority of Ibn 'Abbas ﷺ that he saw Him and it has been authentically reported from him that he said: "He saw Him with his heart."[2] And it has been authentically reported on the authority of 'A'ishah and Ibn Mas'ûd ﷺ that they rejected this; they said that the Words of Allâh:

﴿وَلَقَدْ رَءَاهُ نَزْلَةً أُخْرَىٰ ۝﴾

"And indeed he (Muhammad ﷺ) saw him [Jibraıl (Gabriel)] at a second descent (i.e. another time)."[3]

refer only to Jibreel ﷺ.[4] And it has been authentically reported on the authority of Abu Dharr ﷺ that he asked the Prophet ﷺ: "Did you see your Lord?" He ﷺ replied: "(He is) Light, how could I see him?"[5] That is:

«نُورٌ أَنَّى أُرَاهُ»

---

[1] Narrated by Al-Bukhari and Muslim.

[2] Narrated by Muslim At-Tirmzi.

[3] *Sûrah An-Najm* 53:13

[4] Narrated by Al-Bukhari and Muslim.

[5] Narrated by Muslim, At-Tirmidhi and Ahmad, on the authority of Abu Dharr ﷺ.

"A Light screened me from seeing Him."

As in the wording of the other *Hadeeth*:

$$«رَأَيْتُ نُورًا»$$

"I saw a light."[1]

Ad-Darimi reported that the Companions ﷺ were agreed
unanimously that he did not see Him. *Shaikh Al-Islam* (Ibn
Taimiyyah): "The saying of Ibn 'Abbas ﷺ does not contradict this.
Nor does his saying: "He saw Him with his heart." And it has been
authentically reported from him ﷺ that he said:

$$«رَأَيْتُ رَبِّي تَبَارَكَ وَتَعَالَى»$$

"I saw my Lord, the Most Blessed, Most High." But this was in
Al-Madinah in a dream."

Upon this Imam Ahmad based his opinion that he saw Him, because
the visions of the Prophets are real and they must be true; but he did
not say that he saw Him when he was awake. However, on one
occasion, he said: "He saw Him," and on another occasion, he said:
"He saw Him with his heart." And it has been related from him in the
writings of some of his Companions that he said that he saw Him with
his own eyes; but the texts of Imam Ahmad are with us and there is
nothing of that in them. As for the saying of Ibn 'Abbas ﷺ that he saw
Him with his heart twice, if his evidence is the Saying of Allâh:

$$﴿مَا كَذَبَ ٱلْفُؤَادُ مَا رَأَىٰ ۝﴾$$

"The (Prophet's) heart lied not in what he (Muhammad ﷺ)
saw."[2]

Then His Saying:

$$﴿وَلَقَدْ رَءَاهُ نَزْلَةً أُخْرَىٰ ۝﴾$$

"And indeed he (Muhammad ﷺ) saw him [Jibraıl (Gabriel)] at
a second descent (i.e. another time)."[3]

---

[1] Narrated by Muslim.

[2] *Sûrah An-Najm* 53:11

[3] *Sûrah An-Najm* 53:13

And it would appear that this is his evidence – then (it should be known that) it has been authentically reported from him ﷺ that this vision was of Jibreel ﷺ whom he saw in his true form twice. And the evidence for Ahmad's saying that he saw Him with his heart is this saying of Ibn 'Abbas ﷺ.

As for His Words:

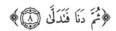

"Then he [Jibrail (Gabriel)] approached and came closer,"[1]

this is not the same as the approach and coming closer mentioned in the story of the Prophet's night journey, for that which is mentioned in the Qur'ân is Jibreel ﷺ as 'A'ishah and Ibn Mas'ûd ﷺ said and as is proven by the context, because He said:

$$ \text{﴿عَلَّمَهُ شَدِيدُ ٱلْقُوَىٰ ۝﴾} $$

"He has been taught (this Qur'an) by one mighty in power [Jibrail (Gabriel)]."[2]

As for the approach and coming closer mentioned in the *Hadeeth*, it is clear that it is the approach and coming closer of the Lord, Most Blessed, Most High.

In the morning, when the Prophet ﷺ told his people, their disbelief in him was greater than ever and they asked him to describe Bait Al-Maqdis to them and so Allâh gave him a vision of it so that he could see it and he began to describe it to them and they were unable to refute what he said.[3] And he informed them about their caravan which he had seen during his night journey and on his return and of the time of its arrival and the camel which was leading it and the matter was as he had said,[4] but this did nothing but increase them in rejection.

And it has been transmitted from Ibn Ishaq, on the authority of

---

[1] *Sûrah An-Najm* 53:8

[2] *Sûrah An-Najm* 53:5

[3] Narrated by Al-Bukhari and Muslim, on the authority of Ibn 'Abbas ﷺ.

[4] Narrated by Ahmad, on the authority of Ibn 'Abbas ﷺ.

'A'ishah and Mu'awiyah 🙏 that they said that the night journey took place with his spirit; but it is necessary to know the difference between saying that the night journey was a dream and saying that it was a spiritual journey, for there is a great difference between them. And they did not say that the night journey was a dream, because that which is seen by the sleeper could be an example of something which is connected to reality in a tangible form[1] and so he sees in a vision as if he was taken up to the heaven, or taken to Makkah, but his spirit does not ascend and it does not leave; it is only that the angel of visions has made an image for him. And those who said that he was taken up by his spirit did not intend to say that it was a dream, but that the spirit was actually taken up and that it left the body in the same manner as it does when a person dies; but because the Messenger of Allâh 🙏 had the status of one who exceeded the norm, so that his chest was split open while he was alive and he felt no pain, he was actually taken up by his spirit without him dying, whereas the souls of others cannot achieve this except after death. This is because the souls of the Prophets remain in *Ar-Rafeeq Al-A'la*[2] after their death, but at the same time they are able to control their bodies, so that they may reply to the salutations of peace delivered to them in *Ar-Rafeeq Al-A'la* – and due to this connection, the Prophet 🙏 was able to see Moses (Mûsa 🙏) praying in his grave and he also saw him in the sixth heaven.

And it is well known that he was not taken up from his grave and then returned, for that is the place of his soul and that is where it remains, while his grave is where his body lies and where it will remain until the return of the souls to their bodies (on the Day of Resurrection). And whoever found difficulty in comprehending this should look at the example of the sun which is high above and its effect on the earth and on the lives of plants and animals. And the importance of the soul is greater than this.

---

[1] Such as a person seeing someone in a dream drowning in a sinking ship and later he hears that that person is terminally ill, or is drowning in debt for example.

[2] *Ar-Rafeeq Al-A'la*: A place on high heavens, where the souls of the Prophets gather.

So say unto the inflamed eyes, – beware of looking at the sun,
And cover yourselves with the darkness of night.

Ibn 'Abdil Barr said: There was a year and two months between the night journey and the *Hijrah* (to Al-Madinah).

The night journey took place once, although it was said that it took place twice: Once while he was awake and once while he was asleep; it would seem as though those who propounded this wished to reconcile the *Hadeeth* of Shuraik and others due to the fact that the Prophet ﷺ said in it:

«ثُمَّ اسْتَيْقَظْتُ وَأَنَا فِي الْمَسْجِدِ»

"Then I awoke and I was in the mosque."

And he said:

«وَذَلِكَ قَبْلَ أَنْ يُوحَىٰ إِلَيْهِ»

"And that was before Revelation came to him."

And there were those who said that it occurred three times, but all of this is conjecture and it is the opinion of the weak scholars of *Hadeeth* transmission among the Zahiris. The correct view is that which is held by the leaders among the scholars of *Hadeeth* transmission, which is that the night journey took place once. How amazing it is that those people should think that the obligation to pray fifty prayers was enjoined upon him each time!

Al-Hafiz Ibn Hajr exposed the mistake of Shuraik regarding some of the wording of the *Hadeeth* of the night journey. Muslim reported it with its complete chain of narrators, then he said: "He advanced and delayed things and added and left out things and he did not present the facts of the *Hadeeth* correctly and in detail." And he (i.e. Muslim) spoke well – may Allâh have mercy on him.

Chapter

Az-Zuhri said: "Muhammad Ibn Salih told me, on the authority of 'Asim Ibn 'Umar Ibn Qatadah and Yazeed Ibn Rooman and others, who said: The Messenger of Allâh ﷺ remained for three years in Makkah, from the beginning of his Prophethood, attending the *Hajj* every year and following the pilgrims in their camps and showing up at the festivals in 'Ukaz, Majannah and Dhul Majaz and calling upon them to protect him so that he could communicate the Messages of his Lord that they might be rewarded with Paradise, but he did not find anyone to support him, nor anyone who responded positively to his call. He even used to ask the whereabouts of the different tribes one after another and he would say:

«يَا أَيُّهَا النَّاسُ قُولُوا: لَا إِلَهَ إِلَّا اللهُ. تُفْلِحُوا وَتَمْلِكُوا بِهَا الْعَرَبَ، وَتُدِينُ لَكُمْ بِهَا الْعَجَمُ فَإِذَا مُتُّمْ كُنْتُمْ مُلُوكًا فِي الْجَنَّةِ»

"Oh, people! Say: *"La Ilaha Illallah"* (None has the right to be worshipped except Allâh) and you will be successful and by it you will rule over the Arabs and the non-Arabs will offer allegiance to you and when you die, you will be kings in Paradise."

And Abu Lahab would follow behind him, saying: "Do not obey him, for he is an innovator and a liar." So they would reply to him with the ugliest of replies and they would hurt him and say: "Your own people know you better, since they did not follow you." And he would call them to Allâh and he would say:

«اللَّهُمَّ لَوْ شِئْتَ لَمْ يَكُونُوا هَكَذَا»

"Oh, Allâh! If You willed, they would not be so."

He (Az-Zuhri) said: "Among the names of the tribes to whom he presented himself which have been mentioned to us are: Banu 'Amir Ibn Sa'sa'ah, Muharib Ibn Khasfah, Fazarah, Ghassan, Murrah, Haneefah, Sulaim, 'Abs, Banu Nadhr, Banul Buka', Kindah, Kalb, Al-Harith Ibn Ka'b, 'Uzrah and Al-Hadharamah, and none of them accepted his call to Islam.[1]

One of the things which Allâh accomplished for His Messenger ﷺ was that the tribes of Al-Aws and Al-Khazraj heard from their allies, the Jews of Al-Madinah that: "A Prophet will appear in our time and we will follow him and kill you with him, in the same manner in which 'Ad and Iram were killed." The Ansar used to perform *Hajj* as did the Arabs, but not the Jews, so when they saw the Messenger of Allâh ﷺ calling the people to Allâh and they observed his circumstances, one of them said to the others: "You know, by Allâh, O, my people, that this is the one of whom you were warned by the Jews; so do not let them precede you in following him. As-Suwaid Ibn As-Samit Ibn Al-Aws had come to Makkah and the Messenger of Allâh ﷺ preached to him and soon after that, Anas Ibn Rafi' arrived with some young men from Banu Abdil Ashhal, seeking a treaty (with Quraish) and the Prophet ﷺ called them to Islam. Iyyas Ibn Mu'adh, who was a youth, said: "O, my people! By Allâh, this is better than that which we came for." At this, Anas struck him and rebuked him, upon which he fell silent and they left and returned to Al-Madinah.

Then during the *Hajj* season, in Al-'Aqabah the Messenger of Allâh ﷺ met six persons from Al-Khazraj: As'ad bin Zurarah, Jabir Ibn 'Abdillah, 'Awf Ibn Al-Harith, Rafi' Ibn Malik, Qutbah Ibn 'Amir and 'Uqbah Ibn 'Amir and he called them to Islam and they accepted Islam,[2] then they returned to Al-Madinah, where they called the

---

[1] Narrated by Ibn Sa'd in *'At-Tabaqat'* by way of Al-Waqidi upon whose weakness there is a consensus of opinion. It was also narrated by Ahmad, by way of 'Abdur-Rahman Ibn Abi Az-Zanad, on the authority of his father and by Ibn Hibban, on the authority of Tariq Ibn 'Abdillah Al-Muharibi.

[2] Narrated by Ibn Hisham, from Ibn Ishaq and all of the narrators are trustworthy, according to scholars of *Hadeeth*, apart from Ibn Ishaq himself, who used to commit *Tadlees*.

people to Islam and it spread until there was not a house which Islam had not entered.

The following year, twelve men from among them came: The original six, apart from Jabir, and they had with them Mu'adh Ibn Al-Harith, the brother of 'Awf, Zakwan Ibn 'Abdi Qais – who remained in Makkah until he migrated to Al-Madinah, so he is both *Ansari* and *Muhajir* – 'Ubadah Ibn As-Samit, Yazeed Ibn Tha'labah, Abul Haitham Ibn At-Teehan and 'Uwaimir Ibn Sa'idah. Abu Az-Zubair reported on the authority of Jabir that the Prophet ﷺ remained for ten years following the people in their camps during the *Hajj* season and in Al-Majannah and 'Ukaz, saying:

«مَنْ يُؤْوِينِي وَمَنْ يَنْصُرُنِي حَتَّى أُبَلِّغَ رِسَالَاتِ رَبِّي وَلَهُ الْجَنَّةُ»

"Who will shelter me and support me so that I may convey the Messages of my Lord and have Paradise (as his reward)."

But he did not find anyone. A man might even travel from Egypt or Yemen to visit his family (in Makkah) and his people would come to him and say: "Beware of the son of Quraish." And he would walk among their men and call them to Allâh and they would point their fingers at him, until Allâh sent us from Yathrib and a man from among us would go to him and he believes in him and he would recite the Qur'ân to him, then he would return to his family and they would embrace Islam through his Islam. Then we gathered together and we said: "How long shall the Messenger of Allâh ﷺ be exiled in the mountains of Makkah?" So we traveled until we came near to him during the *Hajj* season and we took the pledge of allegiance (*Bai'ah*) of Al-'Aqabah and Al-'Abbas ﷺ said to him: "Oh, my nephew! I do not know these people and I know the people of Yathrib." So we gathered around him in ones and twos and when Al-'Abbas ﷺ looked in our faces, he said: "These are a people whom we do not know; these people are new." We said: "Oh, Messenger of Allâh! Upon what should we pledge allegiance to you?" He replied:

«عَلَى السَّمْعِ وَالطَّاعَةِ فِي النَّشَاطِ وَالْكَسَلِ، وَعَلَى النَّفَقَةِ فِي الْعُسْرِ وَالْيُسْرِ، وَعَلَى الأَمْرِ بِالْمَعْرُوفِ وَالنَّهْيِ عَنِ الْمُنْكَرِ، وَعَلَى أَنْ

تَقُومُوا فِي اللهِ لَا تَأْخُذُكُمْ فِيهِ لَوْمَةَ لَائِمٍ، وَعَلَى أَنْ تَنْصُرُونِي إِذَا
قَدِمْتُ عَلَيْكُمْ، وَتَمْنَعُونِي مِمَّا تَمْنَعُونَ مِنْهُ أَنْفُسَكُمْ وَأَزْوَاجَكُمْ
وَأَبْنَاءَكُمْ وَلَكُمُ الْجَنَّةُ»

"That you will hear and obey, whether you feel active or lazy, that you will spend (in Allâh's Cause) whether you are in difficulty or at ease, that you will order *Al-Ma'rûf* (Islamic Monotheism and all that is good) and forbid *Al-Munkar* (polytheism and all that is evil), that you will stand in Allâh's Cause and you will not care for the rebukes of the censurer, that you will support me if I come to you and protect me from all that you would protect yourselves, your wives and your families from and (if you do so) you will have Paradise (as a reward)."

So we stood up to take the oath of allegiance to him and Asa'd Ibn Zurarah 🙰 took him by the hand and said: "Slowly, oh, people of Yathrib! We have not traveled all this way without knowing that he is the Messenger of Allâh and removing him today will cause a split between all of the Arabs and they will take up arms against you; so either you bear this patiently and take him and your reward will be with Allâh, or you fear within yourselves (that you will not be able to support him) and you abandon him and it will be an excuse for you with Allâh." But they said: "Stay your hand from us, oh, As'ad, for by Allâh, we will not abandon this pledge, nor will we accept its annulment." So we stood up to him one by one and he accepted the pledge from us, giving us thereby (the way to) Paradise."[1]

Then they left for Al-Madinah and the Messenger of Allâh 🙰 sent with them Ibn Ummi Maktûm and Mus'ab Ibn 'Umair 🙰 to teach them the Qur'ân and call them to Allâh and they stayed with Asa'd Ibn Zurarah 🙰. Mus'ab Ibn 'Umair 🙰 would lead them in prayer and he performed the Friday prayer for them when their number had reached forty.[2] At their hands many embraced Islam, including

---

[1] Narrated by Ahmad, on the authority of Jabir 🙰.

[2] Narrated by Abu Dawûd, Al-Hakim and Al-Baihaqi. This *Hadeeth* should not be taken as evidence that the minimum number of worshippers required for the Friday prayer to be held is forty, as this is not the case.

Usaid bin Hudhair and Sa'd bin Mu'adh ﷺ; and through their Islam, the whole of the tribe of 'Abdul Ashhal embraced Islam, except Al-Usairim ﷺ, who did not embrace Islam until the day of the Battle of Uhud and after embracing Islam on that day, he fought until he was killed without ever having prostrated once to Allâh; the Messenger of Allâh ﷺ said:

$$ «عَمِلَ قَلِيلًا وَأُجِرَ كَثِيرًا» $$

"His deeds were few, but his reward will be great."[1]

And Islam increased and became the Religion of the majority in Al-Madinah. Then Mus'ab ﷺ returned to Makkah and that year a large number of people from the *Ansar* including Muslims and polytheists attended the *Hajj* and the leader of the people was Al-Bara' Ibn Ma'rûr and on the night of the pledge of allegiance of Al-'Aqabah, the first person to pledge his allegiance to him was Al-Bara' Ibn Ma'rûr and this was a great honour for him, because he confirmed the agreement and hastened to do so. The Messenger of Allâh ﷺ chose from among them that night twelve leaders and when the pledge of allegiance was completed, they sought permission from him to attack the people of Mina with their swords, but he did not permit them to do so. And the devil cried out over Al-'Aqabah in the most piercing of voices ever heard: "O, inhabitants of the houses of Mina! Beware! Muhammad and the Sabians[2] who are with him have agreed to make war upon you!" The Messenger of Allâh ﷺ said:

$$ «هَذَا أَزَبُّ الْعَقَبَةِ، أَمَا وَاللهِ يَا عَدُوَّ اللهِ لأَتَفَرَّغَنَّ لَكَ» $$

"This is Azabb[3] of Al-'Aqabah. By Allâh, oh, enemy of Allâh, I will attend to you."[4]

Then he ordered them to disperse to their riding beasts and in the

---

[1] Narrated by Al-Bukhari, Muslim and Ahmad.

[2] It was the habit of Quraish to refer to those who embraced Islam as Sabians, meaning that they were apostates.

[3] *Azabb*: The name of a devil.

[4] Narrated by Ibn Hisham, Ahmad and At-Tayalisi, on the authority of Ibn Ishaq; and as mentioned previously, Ibn Ishaq was a *Mudallis*.

morning, the notables of Quraish came to them and said: "We have been informed that you met our companion (i.e. Muhammad 鄴) last night and you agreed to pledge allegiance to him to make war against us. By Allâh, there is no one among the Arabs against whom we would hate more to make war than you. Then some men were dispatched from among the polytheists of Al-Khazraj who said: "By Allâh, that did not happen." And Ibn Ubayy said: "This is false; my people would not betray me in this manner. If I were in Yathrib, my people would not do this without consulting me." So Quraish returned and Al-Bara' rode to the centre of Ya'jaj, where he met up with his companions from among the Muslims and Quraish followed them and they came upon Sa'd Ibn 'Ubadah and began to beat him until they brought him to Makkah, then Mut'im bin 'Adi and Al-Harith bin Harb bin Umayyah came and they rescued him from them. When the Ansar realized that they had lost him, they consulted with each other as to whether they should return for him, but then they saw him coming towards them, so they went on together.

The Messenger of Allâh 鄴 permitted the Muslims to migrate to Al-Madinah and the people hastened to do so. The first of them to leave was Abu Salamah and his wife, but she was held back from him for a year and she was kept away from her child; then later she left with her child for Al-Madinah being escorted by 'Uthman Ibn Abi Talhah.[1]

Then the people left in groups until none remained in Makkah except the Messenger of Allâh 鄴, Abu Bakr and 'Ali 鄴 – who remained at his command – and those who were forcibly prevented from leaving by the polytheists. The Messenger of Allâh 鄴 prepared his outfit for departure, awaiting the Command (from Allâh) and Abu Bakr 鄴 did likewise.

When the polytheists saw that the Companions of the Messenger of Allâh 鄴 had left and sent their children and belongings to Al-Madinah and that it was a place of strength and its people were

---

[1] Narrated by Ibn Hisham in his *'Seerah'*, on the authority of Ibn Ishaq; all of the narrators in the sanad are reliable, according to Shu'aib and 'Abdul Qadir Al-Arna'ût, except Ibn Ishaq, who used to commit *Tadlees*.

strong and courageous, they feared that the Messenger of Allâh ﷺ would leave and then dealing with him would be more difficult for them. So they gathered in the meeting hall and Satan attended with them, in the guise of an important *Shaikh* from among the people of Najd, wrapped in a heavy garment. Each of them voiced his opinion, but the *Shaikh* did not accept it, until Abu Jahl said: "I think that we should take a strong young man from each tribe, then give him a sharp sword and let each of them deal him one blow; then Banu 'Abdi Manaf will not know what to do after that, and we shall pay his blood money." The *Shaikh* said: "By Allâh, this is the (best) opinion!" And so they dispersed having agreed upon this; but Jibreel ﷺ came to him and informed him of their plan and ordered him not to sleep in his bed that night.[1]

The Messenger of Allâh ﷺ came to Abu Bakr ؓ in the middle of the day, at a time when he did not normally visit him, with his face covered and he said to him:

«أَخْرِجْ مَنْ عِنْدَكَ»

"Send out those who are with you."

Abu Bakr ؓ said: "There is no one here except your family, oh, Messenger of Allâh!" He ﷺ said:

«إِنَّ اللهَ قَدْ أَذِنَ لِي فِي الْخُرُوجِ»

"Allâh has permitted me to leave."

Abu Bakr ؓ asked: "Shall I accompany you?" He ﷺ answered: "Yes." Abu Bakr ؓ said: "Then take, may my father and mother be ransomed for you, one of my two mounts." The Messenger of Allâh ﷺ said: "(I will pay) its price." And he ordered 'Ali ؓ to sleep in his bed that night. Those people (from Quraish) gathered and peered through a gap in the door, intending to attack him as he slept and they discussed which of them would do the criminal deed and the

---

[1] Narrated by Ibn Hisham, on the authority of Ibn Ishaq, but it is a weak narration, since the person from whom Ibn Ishaq reported is unknown, as Ibn Ishaq says only: "I was informed by one in whom I have trust."

Messenger of Allâh ﷺ came out and took up a handful of dust and threw it on their heads, while he recited:

$$﴿وَجَعَلْنَا مِنْ بَيْنِ أَيْدِيهِمْ سَدًّا وَمِنْ خَلْفِهِمْ سَدًّا فَأَغْشَيْنَاهُمْ فَهُمْ لَا يُبْصِرُونَ ٩﴾$$

"And We have put a barrier before them, and a barrier behind them, and We have covered them up, so that they cannot see."[1]

Then he proceeded to the house of Abu Bakr ؓ and they left by an opening therein at night. A man came and saw the people at his door and asked: "What are you waiting for?" They replied: "Muhammad." He said: "You have failed and lost, for by Allâh, he has passed by you and thrown dust on your heads." So they stood up and shook the dust from their heads. Then in the morning, 'Ali stood up from his bed and they asked him where the Prophet ﷺ was, but he replied: "I have no knowledge concerning him."[2]

Then he and Abu Bakr proceeded to the cave known as *Ghar Thawr* and they entered it, after which, a spider spun a web across the entrance.[3] They had hired Ibn Uraiqit Al-Laithi, who knew the road well, although he followed the religion of his people, for they trusted him to do this and they delivered their riding bests to him and agreed to meet him at the cave three days hence.[4] Quraish exerted all of their efforts to find them, taking with them trackers and they searched until they reached the opening of the cave. 'Amir Ibn Fuhairah had herded sheep belonging to Abu Bakr ؓ cover their tracks. They remained in the cave for three days until the heat of the search for them had died down, then Ibn Uraiqit came to them with

---

[1] *Sûrah Ya Seen* 36:9

[2] Narrated by Ibn Sa'd, by way of Al-Waqidi, who is weak and by Ibn Hisham, on the authority of Ibn Ishaq, who used to commit *Tadlees* and by Ahmad, by way of 'Uthman Ibn 'Amr Ibn Saj, who is weak, according to Ibn Hajr.

[3] The story of the spider has not been narrated from any authentic source, nor has the story of the pigeons laying eggs in front of the cave.

[4] Narrated by Al-Bukhari.

the mounts and they rode off, Abu Bakr ⚬ seating 'Amir Ibn Fuhairah behind him and the guide went ahead of them – and they were under Allâh's observation and Help from Him accompanied them and carried them on their way.

When the polytheists had given up searching for them, they placed a bounty on the head of each of them, which caused the people to exert themselves in searching for them, but Allâh was Master of his affair. When they passed by the tribe of Banu Mudlaj, ascending from Qadeed, they were seen by a man from the tribe, who said to them: "I have recently seen near the coast silhouettes which I believe to be none other than Muhammad and his Companions." And Suraqah Ibn Malik came to hear of the matter and he desired that the prize be for him alone (but in the end, he got something which was far beyond his expectations), so he said: "No, they are so-and-so and so-and-so, who have gone out on some errand of their own.

Then he remained for a short while, then he stood up and entered his tent and said to his servant: Go out with the horse from the back of the tent and meet me behind the hill." Then he took his spear and lowered its point, so that it made a line in the ground, then he mounted his horse. When he came near to them, he heard the recitation of the Prophet 쁖, but he did not look towards him, though Abu Bakr ⚬ was looking around him much and he said: "Oh, Messenger of Allâh! This is Suraqah who has caught up with us." So the Messenger of Allâh 쁖 invoked Allâh against him and the forelegs of his horse sank into the ground and he said: "I know that what has afflicted me is because of your supplication, so please supplicate for me and I will divert the people away from you." So the Messenger of Allâh 쁖 supplicated for him and his horse was freed. Then Suraqah asked him to give him something in writing and so Abu Bakr ⚬ wrote for him at the Prophet's request on a piece of tanned leather.[1] He kept that piece of leather until the day of the Conquest of Makkah and then he came to the Messenger of Allâh 쁖 and he fulfilled the promise made therein, saying:

---

[1] Narrated by Al-Bukhari and Al-Hakim, on the authority of Suraqah ⚬.

«الْيَوْمَ يَوْمُ وَفَاءٍ وَبِرٍّ»

"Today is a day of fulfillment and kindness."

He offered to give them provisions and horses, but they said: "We have no need of them, but distract our pursuers." Suraqah replied: "Well enough." Then he returned and found the people searching for them and he said to them: "I have already checked this way." At the start of the day, he was hunting for them and at the end of the day, he was protecting them.

Then they continued on their way and passed by the tents of Umm Ma'bad of the Banu Khuza'. Ibn Al-Qayyim mentioned the whole story, then he said: A voice called out in Makkah which was heard by the people, but they could not see who was speaking (and it said):

> May Allâh, the Lord of Mankind reward with the best of rewards,
> The two companions who sat in the tents of Umm Ma'bad,
> They stayed with kindness and they departed with it,
> And successful is he who becomes Muhammad's companion,
> Oh, sons of Qusai! Allâh has granted you much glory,
> For which we cannot reward you enough, and leadership (in Makkah),
> Ask your sister about her ewe and her container (of milk),
> For if you were to ask the ewe, it would testify,[1]
> He called for a ewe which was not giving milk,
> And it gave much milk for him, like that of a feeding mother,
> A Prophet sees that which those around him do not see,
> And he recites the Book of Allâh in every place,
> And if he says something one day,
> Belonging to the knowledge of the unseen,
> You will see it fulfilled today or tomorrow,
> He left a people and they lost their minds,
> And he came to a people with the light of renewal,

---

[1] Narrated by Al-Hakim and Al-Haithami, who attributed it to At-Tabarani. The remaining verses are not mentioned in the complete version of 'Zad Al-Ma'ad'

Their Lord guided them thereby after they had been lost,
The most righteous of them is he who follows the truth and is successful,
Let Abu Bakr rejoice at the reward of his efforts, For his accompanying the Prophet (ﷺ),
For whomsoever Allâh ordains happiness, he will be happy,
And let Banu Ka'b rejoice for the place of their daughter,
Who prepared the place of rest for the Believers.

Asma' ﵂ said: "We did not know in which direction the Messenger of Allâh ﷺ was going, then a man from among the jinn came up from lower Makkah chanting these verses and the people were following him, hearing his voice, but not seeing him until he went out from upper Makkah." She said: "When we heard what he said, we knew in which direction the Messenger of Allâh ﷺ was going and that he was going to Al-Madinah."[1]

---------- ❖ ❖ ❖ ----------

---

[1] According to Shaikh Nasir Ad-Deen Al-Albani, this is a weak narration, having a mixed up *Sanad*, however, Ibn Katheer says that there are two other chains which support it. And Allâh knows better.

Chapter

The *Ansar* were informed of the departure of the Messenger of Allâh ﷺ and so they used to go out to the lava plains each day and wait until the heat of the sun became too intense, then they would return to their houses.

Then on Monday, the twelfth of Rabee' Al-Awwal, at the end of the thirteenth year of his Prophethood, they went out as was their custom and when the sun became hot, they returned. Then a man from among the Jews climbed one of the hillocks of Al-Madinah for his own reasons and he saw the Messenger of Allâh ﷺ and his companions in white, standing out clearly from the heat haze and he called out in his loudest voice: "Oh, Banu Qailah! Here is your companion! Here is your grandfather whom you are awaiting! The *Ansar* hastened to fetch their weapons in order to meet him while the roars of the voices and *"Allâhu Akbar"* was heard among Banu 'Amr Ibn 'Awf and the Muslims made *Takbeer* out of joy at his arrival and went out to meet him and they received him and greeted him with the greeting of Prophethood, surrounding him and circling him while tranquillity encompassed him and Revelation came down to him

$$﴿هُوَ مَوْلَىٰهُ وَجِبْرِيلُ وَصَٰلِحُ ٱلْمُؤْمِنِينَ وَٱلْمَلَٰٓئِكَةُ بَعْدَ ذَٰلِكَ ظَهِيرٌ﴾$$

"Allâh is his *Maula* (Lord, or Master, or Protector), and Jibrail (Gabriel), and the righteous among the believers; — and furthermore, the angels are his helpers."[1]

He proceeded until he stopped at Quba' among the tribe of Banu 'Amr Ibn 'Awf and he stayed with Kulthûm Ibn Al-Hidm and it was said with Sa'd Ibn Khaithamah and he stayed with them for fourteen nights and built there Quba' Mosque, which was the first mosque

---

[1] *Sûrah At-Tahreem* 66:4

built after the start of the Prophethood.[1] Then on Friday, he mounted his camel by Allâh's Command and Friday prayer over took him at Banu Salim Ibn 'Awf and so he performed the Friday prayer in the mosque which is in the bottom of the valley, then he mounted his camel and they took it by its halter, (saying): "Come to where there are many men, weapons and protection," but he said:

«خَلُّوا سَبِيلَهَا فَإِنَّهَا مَأْمُورَةٌ»

"Let her go where she will, for she is under (Divine) Command."

The camel continued to go on with him and it did not pass by any house from among the houses of the *Ansar* without them wishing for him to descend, but he said:

«دَعُوهَا فَإِنَّهَا مَأْمُورَةٌ»

"Leave her, for she is under (Divine) Command."

The camel continued until it reached the place where his mosque stands today and there it knelt down and he did not descend from it until it had risen and gone on a little, then it turned and went back to its original place and knelt down again and he descended from it; and that was on the land of Banu An-Najjar, his maternal uncles. It was good fortune from Allâh that made the camel kneel there, for the Prophet ﷺ desired to alight there, in order to honour them thereby. They began to solicit him to enter their abodes, but Abu Ayyûb ﷺ stepped forward to his saddle and took it into his house; the Prophet ﷺ said:

«الْمَرْءُ مَعَ رَحْلِهِ»

"A man goes with his saddle."

Then Abu Zurarah ﷺ came and took his camel and it stayed with him.[2] He became as Qais Ibn Sirmah Al-Ansari said – and Ibn 'Abbas ﷺ used to visit him frequently and memorized these verses

---

[1] Narrated by Ibn Sa'din '*At-Tabaqat*' and Al-Bukhari narrated something similar, on the authority of 'Urwah Ibn Az-Zubair ﷺ.

[2] Narrated by Al-Bukhari and Muslim.

from him - :

> He remained among Quraish for thirteen years,
> Reminding them (of Allâh) and hoping to find someone,
> Who would be a friend to him and support him, presenting
> himself to the people in the festivals,
> But he found none who would give him a home, And he found
> none who would invite him,
> Then when he came to us, having made up his mind,
> And he became happy and pleased with *Taibah* (Al-Madinah),
> And he no longer feared the oppression of a far off tyrant,
> Nor feared a rebel from among mankind,
> We sacrificed our lawful wealth for him,
> And (we sacrificed) ourselves in times of war,
> And we shared with him our worldly goods,
> Opposing all of those people who opposed him,
> Even though they had been beloved to us,
> And we know that there is no lord besides Allâh,
> And the Book of Allâh became our only guide.

Ibn 'Abbas ﷺ said: "The Prophet ﷺ was in Makkah and he was ordered to migrate to Al-Madinah and the following Verse was revealed to him:

$$﴿وَقُل رَّبِّ أَدْخِلْنِي مُدْخَلَ صِدْقٍ وَأَخْرِجْنِي مُخْرَجَ صِدْقٍ وَاجْعَل لِّي مِن لَّدُنكَ سُلْطَانًا نَّصِيرًا﴾(٨٠)$$

"And say (O Muhammad ﷺ): "My Lord! Let my entry (to the city of Al-Madinah) be good, and (likewise) my exit (from the city of Makkah) be good. And grant me from You an authority to help me (or a firm sign or a proof)."[1]

Qatadah said: "Allâh removed him from Makkah to Al-Madinah with a good exit and the Prophet of Allâh (ﷺ) knew that he would be unable to carry out this Command except with authority and so he asked Allâh to grant him authority to help him and then Allâh showed him *Dar Al-Hijrah*[2] while he in Makkah and he said:

---

[1] *Sûrah Al-Isra'* 17:80

[2] *Dar Al-Hijrah*: The Land of Migration (Al-Madinah).

«أُرِيتُ دَارَ هِجْرَتِكُمْ بِسَبْخَةٍ ذَاتِ نَخْلٍ بَيْنَ لَابَتَيْنِ»

"I was shown the land of your migration: (It is) near a salt marsh, where date palms grow and it lies between two lava fields."[1]

Al-Bara' ﷺ said: "The first person to come to us from among the Companions of the Messenger of Allâh ﷺ was Mus'ab Ibn 'Umair and Ibn Ummi Maktûm ﷺ and they began to teach the people the Qur'ân, then 'Ammar Ibn Yasir arrived with Bilal and Sa'd, then 'Umar Ibn Al-Khattab came among twenty riders ﷺ, then the Messenger of Allâh ﷺ arrived and I have never seen the people as happy as they were when he came; I even saw women, children and slave girls saying: "This is the Messenger of Allâh ﷺ who has come." He stayed in the house of Abu Ayyûb ﷺ until his rooms and his mosque were built. While he was in Abu Ayyûb's ﷺ house, he sent Zaid Ibn Harithah and Abu Rafi' ﷺ to Makkah with two camels and five hundred dirhams and they returned to him with Fatimah and Umm Kalthûm, his daughters, Sawdah, his wife, Usamah Ibn Zaid and his mother, Umm Ayman ﷺ.

As for Zainab ﷺ, her husband, Abul 'As, did not allow her to leave. 'Abdullah, the son of Abu Bakr ﷺ left with them, bringing Abu Bakr's family, including 'A'ishah ﷺ and they stayed in the house of Harithah Ibn An-Nu'man ﷺ.

---

[1] Narrated by Al-Bukhari, on the authority of 'A'ishah ﷺ.

Chapter

Regarding the Building of the Mosque

Az-Zuhri said: "His she-camel knelt down at the place where his mosque was to be built and today men from among the Muslims pray therein. It was a place for drying dates owned by two orphans in the care of As'ad Ibn Zurarah ﷺ. The Messenger of Allâh ﷺ bargained with them over the price, but they said: "No, we will give it to you." But he refused and purchased it from them for ten *Deenars*. It consisted of a wall without a roof and its *Qiblah* faced towards Bait Al-Maqdis. As'ad Ibn Zurarah ﷺ used to pray therein and perform the Friday prayers before the arrival of the Messenger of Allâh ﷺ. In it there were date-palms and *Gharqad* trees[1] and graves of the polytheists, so the Messenger of Allâh ﷺ ordered that the graves be disinterred and that the date palms and the trees be cut down and placed in rows, facing towards the *Qiblah* of the mosque. He made its length from the *Qiblah* to the back a hundred cubits, and from side to side, it was a similar distance or less. He made its foundation approximately three cubits, then they built it from adobe bricks and the Messenger of Allâh ﷺ built with them, transporting the bricks and stones and singing:

"O, Allâh, there is no goodness except that of the Hereafter,
So forgive the *Ansar* and the *Muhajirûn*."

And he sang:

---

[1] *Gharqad*: A thorny bush native to the Middle East, which according to the Prophet ﷺ is the friend of the Jews. (See: *'Saheeh Muslim'*, the Book of Trials and Portents of the Hour).

This (carrying) work is not the work of Khaibar, this is more pious, oh, our Lord and purer.

And they began to recite poetry while they were transporting the bricks and one of them said in his poetry:

Were we to sit while the Messenger works, That would be a misguided action on our part.

He made its *Qiblah* to face towards Bait Al-Maqdis and he made three doors for it, one at the back, one which was known as *Bab Ar-Rahmah* (the Door of Mercy) and a door by which the Messenger of Allâh ﷺ entered. He made its pillars from tree trunks and its roof from palm leaves. It was said to him: "Will you not provide it with a (proper) roof?" He said:

«لَا عَرِيشَ كَعَرِيشٍ مُوسَىٰ»

"No, a palm leaf roof, like that of Moses."

To its sides, he built houses for his wives from adobe brick and he made roofs for them from branches and palm leaves.

When he had completed the building, he consummated his marriage with 'A'ishah ﷺ in the house which he had built for her to the east of the mosque and he built another house for Sawdah ﷺ.[1]

Then the Prophet ﷺ declared brotherhood between the *Muhajirûn* and the *Ansar*; and they were ninety men – half of them from the *Muhajirûn* and half of them from the *Ansar* – that they might share their worldly goods and inherit each other after death, until the Battle of Badr took place. Then when the Verse:

﴿وَأُوْلُوا۟ ٱلْأَرْحَامِ بَعْضُهُمْ أَوْلَىٰ بِبَعْضٍ﴾

"And blood relations among each other."[2]

was revealed, the rights of inheritance were returned to the close relatives. It was also said that he declared another brotherhood between members of the *Muhajirûn* and that he took 'Ali ﷺ as a

---

[1] Narrated by Ibn Sa'd in *'At-Tabaqat'*.
[2] *Sûrah Al-Ahzab* 33:6

brother,[1] but the first report is more strongly confirmed. If he had taken anyone as a brother, Abu Bakr As-Siddeeq ﷺ would have been more entitled to it, he of whom he said:

$$\text{«لَوْ كُنْتُ مُتَّخِذًا مِنْ أُمَّتِي خَلِيلًا لَاتَّخَذْتُ أَبَا بَكْرٍ خَلِيلًا، وَلَكِنْ أَخِي وَصَاحِبِي»}$$

"If I were to take anyone of my people as a *Khaleel* (close friend), I would have taken Abu Bakr as a *Khaleel*, but he is my brother and my companion."[2]

And this is (Islamic) brotherhood, albeit of a general kind, as he ﷺ said:

$$\text{«وَدِدْتُ أَنَّا قَدْ رَأَيْنَا إِخْوَانَنَا»}$$

"I wished that we could see our brothers."

The Companions ﷺ said: "Are we not your brothers?" He said:

$$\text{«أَنْتُمْ أَصْحَابِي، وَإِخْوَانِي قَوْمٌ يَأْتُونَ مِنْ بَعْدِي، يُؤْمِنُونَ بِي وَلَمْ يَرَوْنِي»}$$

"You are my Companions; my brothers are a people who will come after me and they will believe in me without having seen me."[3]

And Abu Bakr Siddeeq has the highest level of this brotherhood, just as he has the highest level of companionship.

The Messenger of Allâh ﷺ made a treaty of non-hostility with the Jews of Al-Madinah and wrote a document to that effect. Their Rabbi, 'Abdullah Ibn Salam set out without delay and entered Islam,[4] but the majority refused except to disbelieve. They were three tribes: Banu Qainuqa', Ban An-Nadheer and Banu Quraizah – and all three of them fought him. He pardoned Banu Qainuqa', banished Banu

---

[1] All of the *Ahadeeth* in which it is claimed that the Prophet ﷺ took 'Ali ﷺ as a brother are weak, according to Shu'aib and 'Abdul Qadir Al-Arna'ût.

[2] Narrated by Al-Bukhari and Muslim.

[3] Narrated by Muslim, on the authority of Abu Hurairah ﷺ.

[4] Narrated by Al-Bukhari on the authority of Anas Ibn Malik ﷺ.

An-Nadheer and killed the men of Banu Quraizah and enslaved their women and children. *Sûrah Al-Hashr* was revealed concerning Banu An-Nadeer and *Sûrah Al-Ahzab* regarding Banu Quraizah.

He ﷺ used to pray towards Bait Al-Maqdis and he said to Jibreel ﷺ:

«وَدِدْتُ أَنَّ اللهَ صَرَفَ وَجْهِي عَنْ قِبْلَةِ الْيَهُودِ»

"I wished that Allâh would turn my face away from the *Qiblah* of the Jews."

Jibreel ﷺ replied:

«إِنَّمَا أَنَا عَبْدٌ فَادْعُ رَبَّكَ وَاسْأَلْهُ»

"I am only a slave, so supplicate your Lord and ask Him."

So he began to turn his face towards the heaven, asking for that and then Allâh revealed:

﴿قَدْ نَرَىٰ تَقَلُّبَ وَجْهِكَ فِى ٱلسَّمَآءِ﴾

"Verily, We have seen the turning of your (Muhammad's) face towards the heaven."[1]

This took place sixteen months after his arrival in Al-Madinah and two months before the Battle of Badr occurred.[2] In this there were great wisdoms and a trial for the Muslims, the polytheists, the Jews and the hypocrites. As for the Muslims, they said:

﴿ءَامَنَّا بِهِۦ كُلٌّ مِّنْ عِندِ رَبِّنَا﴾

"We believe in it; the whole of it (clear and unclear Verses) are from our Lord."[3]

It was they whom Allâh guided and it was not hard for them. As for

---

[1] *Sûrah Al-Baqarah* 2:144

[2] This *Hadeeth* was narrated by Ibn Sa'd in '*At-Tabaqat*' by way of Al-Waqidi, on the authority of Ibn 'Abbas ﷺ, however, as mentioned previously, Al-Waqidi is weak (Ash-Shafi'i called him a forger of *Hadeeth*) (See: '*Tahzeeb Al-Kamal*'). Nonetheless, the substance of the *Hadeeth* was narrated by Al-Bukhari, on the authority of Al-Bara'.

[3] *Sûrah Âl 'Imrân* 3:7

the polytheists, they said: "Just as he has returned to our *Qiblah*, he will soon return to our religion." But he did not return to it, except that it was the truth. As for the Jews, they said: "He has gone against the *Qiblah* of the Prophets who were before him." And as for the hypocrites, they said: "He does not know in which direction to pray: If the first was correct then he has abandoned it and if the second was correct, then he was previously doing something invalid." The sayings of the foolish people were many and varied and they were, as Allâh, Most High said:

﴿وَإِن كَانَتْ لَكَبِيرَةً إِلَّا عَلَى الَّذِينَ هَدَى اللَّهُ﴾

"Indeed it was great (heavy) except for those whom Allâh guided."[1]

And it was a trial from Allâh to see who would obey the Messenger and who would turn on their heels. And because the matter of the *Qiblah* was a momentous one, Allâh, Most Glorified prepared before it the matter of abrogation and His Ability to do that and that He brings something better than the thing which was abrogated or something like it, then He added to that a rebuke to those who sought to confuse His Messenger and did not obey him.

Then He mentioned the differing between the Jews and the Christians and their testimony against each other that they follow nothing and He warned His slaves against agreements with them and following their vain desires. Then He mentioned their disbelief in Him and their saying that He, Most Glorified, Most High has a son.

Then He informed us that the east and the west belong to Him and that wherever His slaves turn their faces, His Countenance is there and that He is All-encompassing, All-knowing and because of His Greatness, the All-encompassing nature of Him and His Knowledge of all things, wheresoever the slave turns his face, there is the Countenance of Allâh. Then He informed us that His Messenger ﷺ will not be asked about the inhabitants of the blazing Fire, who did not obey him.

After that, He informed us that the People of the Scripture (the Jews

---
[1] *Sûrah Al-Baqarah* 2:143

and Christians) would not be happy with him until he followed their religion; then He reminded the People of the Scripture of the Blessings which He has given them and He made them fear His Punishment. Then He mentioned His *Khaleel* Abraham (Ibraheem🕮) and how he built His House and lauded Him and He informed us that He made him an *Imam* for the people; then He mentioned His Sacred House and Abraham's building of it, in the course of which, He mentioned that just as its builder was an *Imam* for the people, so the House that he built is an *Imam* (i.e. a place of resort) for them.

Then He informed us that no one rejects the Religion of this *Imam* Abraham (Ibraheem 🕮) except the most foolish of people; then He commanded His slaves to follow his Messenger 🕮 and believe in what was revealed to him and to the (other) Prophets 🕮. Then He responded to those who claim that Abraham (Ibraheem 🕮) and his family were Jews or Christians. And He declared all of this to be a preparation before the changing of the *Qiblah* and He, Most Glorified confirmed the matter time and time again and commanded His Messenger 🕮 to turn his face towards it wheresover he might be and from whencesoever he started out (on a journey, for a military engagement etc.).[1]

And He, Most Glorified informed us that the One Who guides whom He wills to the Straight Path is the One Who guided them to this *Qiblah* and that it is for them and that they are its people, because it is the best of *Qiblahs* and they are the best of peoples and likewise, He chose for them the best of Messengers and the best of Books and that He raised them up from the best of generations and chose for them the best of Laws and gave them the best of characters and made them to dwell in the best of lands and made for them dwellings in Paradise which are the best of dwellings and their position on the Day of Resurrection will be the best of positions, for they will be on a high hill, while the (remainder of) the people will be below them. Glorified be He, Who selects for His Mercy whom He wills. That is the Bounty of Allâh, which He bestows upon whom he wills; and Allâh is the Owner of Great Bounty. And He, Most Glorified informs us that He

---

[1] See *Tafseer Ash-Shawkani*.

did that so that men may have no argument against the Muslims; but the wrongdoers argue against them using these aforementioned arguments. And the apostates do not oppose the Messengers with any arguments besides these or ones similar to them. And all those who give preference to something other than the sayings of the Messenger ﷺ, his argument is of the same type as the arguments of those people. And He, Most Glorified informed us that He did this in order to complete His Blessings upon them and to guide them. Then He mentioned His Blessings upon them in revealing His Book to them to purify them, to teach them the Book and the *Hikmah* (i.e. the *Sunnah*, Islamic Laws and Islamic Jurisprudence) and to teach them what they did not know.

Then He commanded them to remember Him (by prayer and glorifying Him) and be grateful to Him, for through them (i.e. remembrance and gratitude) their supplications will be answered with the most complete Blessings and more and they will win His Remembrance and His Love for them. Then He commanded them to do that without which they could not achieve that – and that is patient perseverance (in the face of hardship and adversity) and prayer and He informed us that He is with those who patiently persevere (i.e. by His Hearing, His Seeing and His Knowledge) and that He Has Completed His Blessing upon them along with the (changing of the *Qiblah*) by prescribing the *Adhan* for them five times during the day and night and He increased the *Zuhr* and *'Asr* prayers by two *Rak'ahs*, they having previously been two *Rak'ah* prayers. And all of this occurred after the arrival of the Prophet ﷺ in Al-Madinah.

Chapter

When the Messenger of Allâh 鷺 had settled in Al-Madinah and Allâh had supported him with His Help and with the Believers and He had united their hearts after their former enmity and the Helpers of Allâh (the *Ansar*) and the Battalions of Islam protected him from all mankind, sacrificed themselves for him, preferred their love for him over their love for their fathers, their sons and their wives and they preferred him over their ownselves and the Arabs and the Jews fired at them from the same bow, rallying the forces of enmity against them and clamoured against them on every side; but Allâh, Most High commanded them to patiently persevere, to pardon them and forgive them until they became strong and their forces were potent, at which point, He permitted them to fight, but He did not enjoin it upon them, for He, Most High said:

$$﴿أُذِنَ لِلَّذِينَ يُقَتَلُونَ بِأَنَّهُمْ ظُلِمُواْ وَإِنَّ اللَّهَ عَلَى نَصْرِهِمْ لَقَدِيرٌ ۝﴾$$

"Permission to fight (against disbelievers) is given to those (believers) who are fought against, because they have been wronged; and surely, Allâh is Able to give them (believers) victory —."[1]

It was said that this referred to Makkah, because the *Sûrah* is a Makkan one, but this is wrong for the following reasons:

The First: That Allâh did not permit fighting in Makkah.

The Second: That the context proves that the permission to fight was given after they were unrightfully expelled from their homes.

The Third: That the Words of Allâh:

$$﴿هَٰذَانِ خَصْمَانِ اخْتَصَمُواْ فِي رَبِّهِمْ﴾$$

"These two opponents (believers and disbelievers) dispute with

---

[1] *Sûrah Al-Hajj* 22:39

each other about their Lord;"[1]

were revealed regarding those who fought on the day of the Battle of Badr.

The Fourth: That He addressed them in the Verse saying:

$$﴿يَـٰٓأَيُّهَا ٱلَّذِينَ ءَامَنُوٓاْ﴾$$

"Oh, you who believe!"

And such an address is Madinan.

The Fifth: That He commanded *Jihad* therein, which includes *Jihad* by the hand and other forms and there is no doubt that the general command to observe *Jihad* was after the *Hijrah*.

The Sixth: That Al-Hakim narrated in '*Al-Mustadrak*' on the authority of Ibn 'Abbas ﷺ, which conforms to the conditions of acceptance laid down by Al-Bukhari and Muslim, in which he said: "When the Messenger of Allâh ﷺ departed from Makkah, Abu Bakr ﷺ said: "They have expelled their Prophet. Truly, we are for Allâh and to Him shall we return; surely, they will be destroyed." Then Allâh revealed:

$$﴿أُذِنَ لِلَّذِينَ يُقَـٰتَلُونَ﴾$$

"Permission to fight (against disbelievers) is given to those (believers) who are fought against."[2]

And this was the first Verse revealed regarding fighting.

And the context of the *Sûrah* proves that there are Makkan and Madinan Verses in it, because the story of the devil's throwing words in the Messenger's recitation is Makkan. And Allâh knows better.

Then Allâh enjoined fighting upon those who are attacked, for He, Most High said:

$$﴿وَقَـٰتِلُواْ فِى سَبِيلِ ٱللَّهِ ٱلَّذِينَ يُقَـٰتِلُونَكُمْ﴾$$

"And fight in the way of Allâh those who fight you,"[3]

---

[1] *Sûrah Al-Hajj* 22:19
[2] *Sûrah Al-Hajj* 22:39
[3] *Sûrah Al-Baqarah* 2:190

Then He enjoined fighting against all of the polytheists upon them. So it was forbidden, then it was permitted, then it was commanded for those who are attacked, then it was commanded against all of the polytheists – either *Fard 'Ain*[1] or *Fard Kifayah*,[2] according to what is generally accepted.

The fact is that *Jihad* is *Fard 'Ain* – either by one's heart, one's tongue one's hand or one's wealth. It is an obligation upon every Muslims to undertake one or another of these forms of *Jihad*. As for *Jihad* with one's self (i.e. fighting), it is *Fard Kifayah*; and as for *Jihad* with one's wealth, there are two opinions regarding its obligation, but the correct view is that it is obligatory because the command to perform *Jihad* with one's wealth and to perform it with one's self in the Qur'ân is the same: Allâh has linked salvation from the Fire, forgiveness and entering Paradise to it, for He, Most High says:

$$﴿يَٰٓأَيُّهَا ٱلَّذِينَ ءَامَنُواْ هَلۡ أَدُلُّكُمۡ عَلَىٰ تِجَٰرَةٖ تُنجِيكُم مِّنۡ عَذَابٍ أَلِيمٍ ۝﴾$$

"O you who believe! Shall I guide you to a trade that will save you from a painful torment?"[3]

And He, Most Glorified informs us that He has: [4] And that He has recompensed them with Paradise and that this covenant and this promise were laid down in the most excellent of His Books (the Torah, the *Injeel* [Gospel] and the Qur'ân), then He confirms it by informing them that no one is truer to his promise than He, Most Blessed, Most High and then He confirms it by commanding them to rejoice at that and that it is the supreme success. So let the person who makes a contract with his Lord consider how splendid is this contract, for it is Allâh, the Almighty, the All-Powerful Who is the Purchaser and the price is Paradise and the one through whose hands this contract has passed is the most honourable of the Messengers from among the angels and mankind and verily, the commodity of this sale has been prepared for a great thing.

---

[1] *Fard 'Ain*: An obligation upon all of the Muslims.

[2] *Fard Kifayah*: An obligation upon the Muslims which is considered to have been fulfilled if a sufficient number of them undertake it.

[3] *Sûrah As-Saff* 61:10

[4] *Sûrah At-Tawbah* 9:111

They have prepared you for something which, if you comprehend it,

Then disdain from keeping company with the foolish folk,

The price of Paradise and love (of Allâh), is to strive with one's own self and one's wealth, for the sake of their Owner (Allâh).

How cowardly is the rejecter, the penniless man who seeks to bargain for this merchandise.

Are they joking with Allâh, those penniless people who bargain (with Allâh)?

The price has not decreased, that those in financial difficulty may sell it on (their own) terms.

It is on display in the market of those who wish to buy, and its Owner will not accept a price for it, less than striving with one's self.

The lazy ones are hesitant, but those who love (Allâh) wait, to see which of them deserves that his soul may be the price.

The goods pass between them and fall into the hands of:

$$ ﴿أَذِلَّةٍ عَلَى ٱلْمُؤْمِنِينَ أَعِزَّةٍ عَلَى ٱلْكَٰفِرِينَ﴾ $$

"Humble towards the believers, stern towards the disbelievers."[1]

And because those who claim to love Him are many, they are required to prove it, for if the people were given (Paradise) solely on the basis of their claims, every unqualified person would claim to be entitled to it and they would bring all kinds of different proofs for their claim, then it would be said: This claim cannot be verified except by clear evidence:

$$ ﴿قُلْ إِن كُنتُمْ تُحِبُّونَ ٱللَّهَ فَٱتَّبِعُونِي يُحْبِبْكُمُ ٱللَّهُ﴾ $$

"Say (O Muhammad ﷺ to mankind): "If you (really) love Allâh, then follow me (i.e. accept Islamic Monotheism, follow the Qur'ân and the *Sunnah*), Allâh will love you."[2]

And all of mankind would hesitate, except the followers of the Messenger ﷺ, who emulated his deeds, his sayings, his guidance and his character and they were requested to show firm evidence and it

---

[1] *Sûrah Al-Ma'idah* 5:54
[2] *Sûrah Âl 'Imrân* 3:31

would be said: The evidence is not accepted without attestation:

$$﴿ يُجَٰهِدُونَ فِى سَبِيلِ ٱللَّهِ وَلَا يَخَافُونَ لَوْمَةَ لَآئِمٍ ﴾$$

"Fighting in the way of Allâh, and never fear of the blame of the blamers."[1]

So most of those who claimed to love Him hesitated, then the *Mujahidûn* did what was required and it was said to them: Truly, the lives and the wealth of those who love Allâh do not (in truth) belong to them, so give what was agreed upon in the contract , for a contract of sale requires that something be given by both parties.

Then when the merchants saw the greatness of the Purchaser and the value of the price and the splendour of him who made the bargain and the measure of the contract in which it was confirmed, they realized that the sale goods had an importance second to none and they realized that selling them for the small price of a sum of *Dirhams* was an act of criminal fraud, for the pleasure of them departs, while the consequence of them remains and so they made a bargain with the Buyer of their own free will and choice, without the option of return. Then when the bargain was complete, they handed over the sold goods and it was said: Your lives and property have become Ours and now We return them to you more abundantly than they were and we have increased your wealth therein.

$$﴿ وَلَا تَحْسَبَنَّ ٱلَّذِينَ قُتِلُوا۟ فِى سَبِيلِ ٱللَّهِ أَمْوَٰتًا ﴾$$

"Think not of those as dead who are killed in the way of Allâh."[2]

We did not buy your lives and your wealth from you except in order to make apparent (Our) Generosity and Kindness in accepting the sale and in giving in return for it the most splendid of prices, then We combined for you the price and the goods (and returned them both to you).

Observe the story of Jabir ﷺ and his camel, how the Messenger of Allâh ﷺ bought his camel from him and then returned the full

---

[1] *Sûrah Al-Ma'idah* 5:57
[2] *Sûrah Âl 'Imrân* 3:169

amount and more to him, then he returned the camel to him.[1] The Prophet ﷺ reminded him of this deed with regard to the situation of his father with Allâh and he informed him that Allâh has given him life and spoken directly to him and He said to him:

«يَا عَبْدِي تَمَنَّ عَلَيَّ أُعْطِكَ»

"Oh, My slave! Ask Me and I will give you."[2]

Glorified be He Whose Generosity and Kindness are so great that He encompasses thereby all of creation. He gave the merchandise and He gave its price and it was He who guided (the slave) to the completion of the bargain and accepted the merchandise, in spite of its imperfection and gave in return for it the most splendid of prices and He purchased His slave from himself by His Wealth (i.e. Paradise) and He combined for him the price and the goods and extolled him and praised him for this contract, while it was He Who granted it to him and willed it from him:

Come and welcome, if you have firm resolve,
For the call of love is urging you, so traverse the distance,

And say to those who call you to love and happiness:
If you call, I will say: "I answer your call" a thousand times,

And do not look at the effects which they left behind, for if you look at their effects, you will only be saddened,
But take from them the supplies for the trip,

And follow the path of guidance and love, and you will reach your destination,

And do not wait for the companion who remains sitting,
But leave him, for the desire to see your loved ones,

Will suffice to carry you, and keep alive by their memory
When your riding beast comes near, for the remembrance will renew your efforts,

---

[1] Narrated by Al-Bukhari, Muslim and the compilers of the '*Sunan*', on the authority of Jabir Ibn 'Abdillah ﷺ.

[2] Narrated by At-Tirmidhi and Ibn Majah, on the authority of Jabir Ibn 'Abdillah ﷺ.

And if you fear weariness, then say to it (i.e. the camel):
Ahead of you is the watering place, so seek the sources of the water,

And take a firebrand from their light and travel by it,
For it is their light which guides you, not their torches,

And hurry to Wadi Al-Arak and say therein:
"I hope that I see them there," if indeed you say anything,

And if not, then in Na'man, I have one who can show,
The way to those whom you love, so seek them, if you should ask,

And if not, then you will meet with them by night,
But if you miss them, then alas for him who is unaware,
Come to the Gardens of *'Adn*, for they are
A more fitting abode if you intend to stay somewhere,

But the enemy have captured you,
Because you tarried over the effects, crying over the houses,

And come to a Day of plenty in an eternal Garden,
And strive with yourself if you are willing to sacrifice,

And leave them as ruined buildings, for there is no place of rest therein,
And pass by them, for they are not houses,
Turn away from them to the path
Which was taken by those you love,

And say: "Be patient, oh, my soul for an hour,"
For when you meet (with them) the weariness will be no more,
For it is no more than an hour,
Then it will pass, then he who was sad will rejoice.

The one who calls to Allâh and to *Dar As-Salam*[1] motivates the reluctant souls and (calls them to) the highest endeavours and the one who calls to *Eeman* makes to hear those with attentive ears; and Allâh makes to hear anyone (whose heart is) alive and his hearing it elevates him to the ranks of *Al-Abrar*[2] and it encourages him on his

---

[1] *Dar As-Salam*: The Abode of Peace, i.e. Paradise.

[2] *Al-Abrar*: Those who were obedient to Allâh and follow strictly His Commands.

journey and he does not stop until he reaches *Dar Al-Qarar*.[1]

The Prophet ﷺ said:

«انْتَدَبَ اللهُ لِمَنْ خَرَجَ فِي سَبِيلِهِ، لَا يُخْرِجُهُ إِلَّا إِيمَانٌ بِي، وَتَصْدِيقٌ بِرُسُلِي أَنْ أَرْجِعَهُ بِمَا نَالَ مِنْ أَجْرٍ أَوْ غَنِيمَةٍ أَوْ أُدْخِلَهُ الْجَنَّةَ، وَلَوْلَا أَنْ أَشُقَّ عَلَى أُمَّتِي، مَا قَعَدْتُ خَلْفَ سَرِيَّةٍ، وَلَوَدِدْتُ أَنِّي أُقْتَلُ فِي سَبِيلِ اللهِ، ثُمَّ أُحْيَا، ثُمَّ أُقْتَلُ، ثُمَّ أُحْيَا، ثُمَّ أُقْتَلُ»

"The person who participates in (*Jihad*) in Allâh's cause and nothing compels him to do so except belief in Allâh and His Messengers, will be recompensed by Allâh either with a reward, or booty (if he survives) or will be admitted to Paradise (if he is killed in the battle as a martyr). Had I not found it difficult for my followers, then I would not remain behind any expedition (going for *Jihad*) and I would have loved to be martyred in Allâh's cause and then made alive, and then martyred and then made alive, and then again martyred in His cause."[2]

And he ﷺ said:

«مَثَلُ الْمُجَاهِدِ فِي سَبِيلِ اللهِ، كَمَثَلِ الصَّائِمِ الْقَائِمِ الْقَانِتِ بِآيَاتِ اللهِ، لَا يَفْتُرُ عَنْ صِيَامٍ وَلَا صَلَاةٍ حَتَّى يَرْجِعَ»

"The example of a *Mujahid* in Allâh's Cause – and Allâh knows better who really strives in His Cause –is like a person who fasts and prays continuously. Allâh guarantees that He will admit the *Mujahid* in His Cause into Paradise if he is killed, otherwise He will return him to his home safely with rewards and war booty."[3]

«وَقَالَ: غَدْوَةٌ فِي سَبِيلِ اللهِ، أَوْ رَوْحَةٌ، خَيْرٌ مِنَ الدُّنْيَا وَمَا فِيهَا»

"A single endeavour (of fighting) in Allâh's Cause in the

---

[1] *Dar Al-Qarar*: The Everlasting Abode, i.e. the life of the Hereafter.

[2] Narrated by Al-Bukhari, An-Nasa'i and Ahmad, on the authority of Abu Hurairah ﷺ.

[3] Narrated by Al-Bukhari, Muslim, Ibn Majah, Ahmad and Malik, on the authority of Abu Hurairah ﷺ, except Ibn Majah, who narrated it on the authority of Abu Sa'eed Al-Khudri ﷺ.

forenoon or in the afternoon, is better than the world and whatever is in it."

And he ﷺ said:

«أَنَا زَعِيمٌ - أَيْ: كَفِيلٌ - لِمَنْ آمَنَ بِي وَأَسْلَمَ، وَجَاهَدَ فِي سَبِيلِ اللهِ بِبَيْتٍ فِي رَبَضِ الْجَنَّةِ، وَبِبَيْتٍ فِي وَسَطِ الْجَنَّةِ، وَبِبَيْتٍ فِي أَعْلَى الْجَنَّةِ، مَنْ فَعَلَ ذَلِكَ لَمْ يَدَعْ لِلْخَيْرِ مَطْلَبًا، وَلَا مِنَ الشَّرِّ مَهْرَبًا، يَمُوتُ حَيْثُ شَاءَ أَنْ يَمُوتَ»

"I am the *Za'eem* – that is responsible for – whoever believes in me and submits (to Allâh) and fights in Allâh's Cause for an abode in the outskirts of Paradise, an abode in the middle of Paradise and an abode in the loftiest heights of Paradise; whoever did that, never leaving his quest for goodness, nor fleeing from evil, he will die where he wished to die."[1]

And he ﷺ said:

«مَنْ قَاتَلَ فِي سَبِيلِ اللهِ - مِنْ رَجُلٍ مُسْلِم - فَوَاقَ نَاقَةٍ، وَجَبَتْ لَهُ الْجَنَّةُ»

"Whoever fought in Allâh's Cause – from among the Muslim men – for the equivalent of the time between two milkings of a she-camel, Paradise is ordained for him."[2]

And he ﷺ said:

«إِنَّ فِي الْجَنَّةِ مَائَةَ دَرَجَةٍ، أَعَدَّهَا اللهُ لِلْمُجَاهِدِينَ فِي سَبِيلِ اللهِ، بَيْنَ كُلِّ دَرَجَتَيْنِ كَمَا بَيْنَ السَّمَاءِ وَالْأَرْضِ، فَإِذَا سَأَلْتُمُ اللهَ، فَاسْأَلُوهُ الْفِرْدَوْسَ، فَإِنَّهُ أَوْسَطُ الْجَنَّةِ، وَفَوْقَهُ عَرْشُ الرَّحْمٰنِ، وَمِنْهُ تَفْجُرُ أَنْهَارُ الْجَنَّةِ»

"Verily, in Paradise, there are a hundred levels which Allâh has prepared for the *Mujahidûn* in Allâh's Cause and the distance between each Paradise is like the distance between the heaven

---

[1] Narrated by An-Nasa'i, on the authority of Fadhalah Ibn 'Ubaid ؓ and declared authentic by Ibn Hibban and Al-Hakim and this was confirmed by Az-Zahabi.

[2] Narrated by the compilers of the '*Sunan*', Ahmad and Ad-Darimi on the authority of, Mu'adh Ibn Jabal ؓ.

and the earth; so if you ask Allâh, ask Him for *Al-Firdaws*, for it is the best Paradise and it is the highest Paradise; above it is the Throne of the Most Beneficent and from it originate the rivers of Paradise."[1]

And he ﷺ said:

«مَنْ أَعَانَ مُجَاهِدًا فِي سَبِيلِ اللهِ، أَوْ غَارِمًا فِي غُرْمِهِ، أَوْ مُكَاتَبًا فِي رَقَبَتِهِ، أَظَلَّهُ اللهُ فِي ظِلِّهِ يَوْمَ لَا ظِلَّ إِلَّا ظِلُّهُ»

"Whoever helped a *Mujahid* in Allâh's Cause, or helped a debtor with his debts, or helped a slave to obtain his freedom, Allâh will shade him with His Shade on the Day when there will but no shade but His."[2]

And he ﷺ said:

«مَنِ اغْبَرَّتْ قَدَمَاهُ فِي سَبِيلِ اللهِ، حَرَّمَهُمَا اللهُ عَلَى النَّارِ»

"Anyone whose feet became covered in dust in Allâh's Cause, Allâh will forbid the Fire to him."[3]

And he ﷺ said:

«لَا يَجْتَمِعُ شُحٌّ وَإِيمَانٌ فِي قَلْبِ رَجُلٍ، وَلَا يَجْتَمِعُ غُبَارٌ فِي سَبِيلِ اللهِ، وَدُخَانُ جَهَنَّمَ فِي وَجْهِ عَبْدٍ»

"Miserliness and *Eeman* cannot be combined in the heart of a man, nor can dust obtained in Allâh's Cause and smoke from the Hell-fire be combined in the face of a slave."[4]

And he ﷺ said:

«رِبَاطُ يَوْمٍ وَلَيْلَةٍ خَيْرٌ مِنْ صِيَامِ شَهْرٍ وَقِيَامِهِ، وَإِنْ مَاتَ جَرَى عَلَيْهِ الَّذِي كَانَ يَعْمَلُهُ، وَأُجْرِيَ عَلَيْهِ رِزْقُهُ، وَأَمِنَ الفَتَّانَ»

"Keeping watch for a day and a night is better (in point of

---

[1] Narrated by Al-Bukhari, on the authority of Abu Hurairah ﷺ.

[2] Narrated by Ahmad, on the authority of Sahl Ibn Hunaif ﷺ.

[3] Narrated by Al-Bukhari, At-Tirmidhi and Ahmad.

[4] Narrated by An-Nasa'i and Ahmad, on the authority of Abu Hurairah ﷺ and this is the wording of Ahmad.

reward) than fasting for a whole month and standing in prayer every night. If a person dies (while, performing this duty), his (meritorious) activity will continue and he will go on receiving his reward for it perpetually and will be saved from the torture of the grave."[1]

And he ﷺ said to a man who had been guarding the Muslims sitting on his horse, from the start of the night until the morning, without getting off except to pray or to answer the call of nature:

«قَدْ أَوْجَبْتَ، فَلَا عَلَيْكَ أَلَّا تَعْمَلَ بَعْدَهَا»

"You have merited Paradise, so there would be no sin upon you if you did nothing else after it."[2]

And Abu Dawûd reported that he (ﷺ) said:

«مَنْ لَمْ يَغْزُ، وَلَمْ يُجَهِّزْ غَازِيًا، أَوْ يَخْلِفْ غَازِيًا فِي أَهْلِهِ بَخَيْرٍ،
أَصَابَهُ اللهِ بِقَارِعَةٍ قَبْلَ يَوْمِ الْقِيَامَةِ»

"Whoever did not fight and did not prepare a warrior or take the place of a warrior in caring for his family, Allâh will afflict him with destruction before the Day of Resurrection."[3]

Abu Ayyûb Al-Ansari explained that throwing oneself into destruction is by abandoning *Jihad*.

And it has been authentically reported from the Prophet ﷺ that he said:

«إِنَّ النَّارَ أَوَّلَ مَا تُسْعَرُ بِالْعَالِمِ وَالْمُنْفِقِ وَالْمَقْتُولِ فِي الْجِهَادِ إِذَا
فَعَلُوا ذَلِكَ لِيُقَالَ. . . . »

"The first people to be consumed by the Fire will be the scholar, the one who spends in charity and the one killed in *Jihad* – if they did so in order to be spoken well of."[4]

---

[1] Narrated by Muslim, on the authority of Salman ⬥.

[2] Narrated by Abu Dawûd, on the authority of Sahl Ibn Al-Hanzaliyyah ⬥.

[3] Narrated by Abu Dawûd, Ibn Majah and Ad-Darimi, on the authority of Abu Umamah ⬥.

[4] Narrated by Muslim and At-Tirmidhi, on the authority of Abu Hurairah ⬥.

Chapter

The Prophet ﷺ used to prefer to fight at the start of the day, just as he preferred to set out on a journey at the start of the day. If he did not fight in the early part of the day, he would delay the fighting until the sun had passed its meridian, the winds blew and (Allâh's) Help came down.[1]

He used to take an oath from his Companions ؓ in war that they would not run away and he might take an oath from them upon (fighting to) death and he would take an oath from them upon *Jihad* as he did upon Islam and he took an oath from them upon the *Hijrah* and upon *Tawheed* and the obligation to obey Allâh and His Messenger ﷺ. He also took an oath from some of his Companions ؓ that they would not ask the people for anything: A whip would fall from the hand of one of them and he would descend and pick it up himself and he would not say: "Pass it to me."[2]

He would consult his Companions ؓ regarding *Jihad*, engaging the enemy and choosing the campsites and he used to keep to the rear when traveling and urge on the weak. He would take someone who had no mount up behind him and he was the kindest of traveling companions to them on the journey.[3] And when he wished to do battle, he would allude to something else and he said:

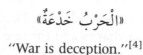

"War is deception."[4]

---

[1] Narrated by At-Tirmidhi, Abu Dawûd and Ahmad.

[2] Narrated by Muslim and Abu Dawûd, on the authority of 'Awf Ibn Malik Al-Ashja'i ؓ.

[3] Narrated by Abu Dawûd, on the authority of Jabir Ibn 'Abdillah ؓ.

[4] Narrated by Al-Bukhari, Muslim, Abu Dawûd and At-Tirmidhi, on the authority of Jabir Ibn 'Abdillah ؓ.

He would send out spies and they would bring him news of the enemy and he would send out advance parties and post guards.[1] And when he encountered the enemy, he would stand and supplicate and seek Allâh's Help and he and his Companions 🙵 would remember Allâh much and they would lower their voices.[2]

He would order the troops and the fighting and would place in charge of each wing a capable leader and fighters would engage in single combat in front of him at his command. He would put on his equipment for battle and sometimes, he might don two coats of chain mail[3] and he had flags and banners.[4] And when he defeated a people, he would stay in their town for three days, then he would return home.[5] And when he wished to raid a town or village, he would wait and if he heard the *Adhan* in the area, he would not attack, but if he did not, he would attack.[6] Sometimes he would attack his enemy by night and sometimes he would surprise them by day. He liked to depart early on a Thursday morning[7] and when the army camped, they would remain close together, so much so, that it was said that if a cloth had been spread over them, it would have covered them all.[8]

He would order the ranks and prepare them for battle with his hand, saying:

«تَقَدَّمْ يَا فُلَانُ، تَأَخَّرْ يَافُلَانُ»

"Stand forward, so-and-so, stand back, so-and-so!"

And he preferred that a man should fight under the banner of his people. Upon engaging the enemy, he would say:

---

[1] Narrated by Muslim, Ahmad and Abu Dawûd.

[2] Narrated by Al-Bukhari, Muslim, Abu Dawûd and Ahmad.

[3] Narrated by Abu Dawûd, At-Tirmidhi, Ibn Majah and Ahmad.

[4] Narrated by Abu Dawûd.

[5] Narrated by Al-Bukhari, At-Tirmidhi, Abu Dawûd and Ibn Majah.

[6] Narrated by Al-Bukhari and Muslim, on the authority of Anas 🙵.

[7] Narrated by Al-Bukhari, on the authority of Ka'b Ibn Malik 🙵.

[8] Narrated by Abu Dawûd and Ahmad, on the authority of Abu Dawûd Al-Khushani 🙵.

«اللَّهُمَّ مُنْزِلَ الْكِتَابِ، وَمُجْرِيَ السَّحَابِ، وَهَازِمَ الْأَحْزَابِ اهْزِمْهُمْ، وَانْصُرْنَا عَلَيْهِمْ»

"Allâhumma, Munzil Al-Kitabi, Wa Mujriyas-Sahabi, Wa Hazimal-Ahzabi, Ihzimhum Wansurna 'Alaihim"

"Oh, Allâh, Who sent down the Book, Who moves the clouds and Who vanquishes the clans (of disbelievers)! Vanquish them and make us victorious against them."[1]

And sometimes he might say:

﴿سَيُهْزَمُ الْجَمْعُ وَيُوَلُّونَ الدُّبُرَ ۝ بَلِ السَّاعَةُ مَوْعِدُهُمْ وَالسَّاعَةُ أَدْهَىٰ وَأَمَرُّ ۝﴾

"Their multitude will be put to flight, and they will show their backs. Nay, but the Hour is their appointed time (for their full recompense), and the Hour will be more grievous and more bitter."[2]

And he used to say:

«اللَّهُمَّ أَنْزِلْ نَصْرَكَ»

"Allâhumma, Anzil Nasrak"

"O, Allâh! Send down your help."

And he used to say:

«اللَّهُمَّ أَنْتَ عَضُدِي وَأَنْتَ نَصِيرِي، بِكَ أُقَاتِلُ»

"Allâhumma, Anta 'Adudee Wa Anta Naseeree Bika Uqatil"

"Oh, Allâh! You are my Strength and You are my Helper and in Your Name I fight."[3]

And when the fighting became fierce and the enemy made straight for him, he announced himself, saying:

«أَنَا النَّبِيُّ لَا كَذِبْ، أَنَا ابْنُ عَبْدِالْمُطَّلِبْ»

---

[1] Narrated by Al-Bukhari, on the authority of Salim Abu An-Nadr ﷺ and by Muslim, on the authority of 'Abdullah Ibn Abi Awfa ﷺ.

[2] *Sûrah Al-Qamar* 54:45-46.

[3] Narrated by Abu Dawûd, on the authority of Anas Ibn Malik ﷺ.

"I am the Prophet and that is no lie, I am the son of 'Abdul Muttalib."[1]

And when the fighting became fierce, they would protect him.[2]

He was always the closest of them to the enemy and he used to make a watchword for the Companions ﷺ in battle by which they would be known if they spoke. One time, their watchword was: *"Amit, Amit"* (Put to death, put to death)[3] and another time, it was: *"Ya Mansûr!"* (Oh, Mansûr [One who is helped by Allâh])[4] and another times, it was: *"Ha Meem, La Yunsarûn"* (*Ha Meem*, They [i.e. the disbelievers] will not be helped).[5]

He used to wear armour and a helmet and he would wear a sword and carry a spear and an Arabian bow and he would protect himself with a shield. He loved pride in battle and he said:

«إِنَّ مِنْهَا مَا يُحِبُّ اللهُ، وَمِنْهَا مَا يُبْغِضُ اللهُ، فَأَمَّا الَّتِي يُحِبُّ اللهُ، فَاخْتِيَالُ الرَّجُلِ بِنَفْسِهِ عِنْدَ اللِّقَاءِ، وَاخْتِيَالُهُ عِنْدَ الصَّدَقَةِ، وَأَمَّا الَّتِي يُبْغِضُ اللهُ عَزَّ وَجَلَّ، فَاخْتِيَالُهُ فِي الْبَغْيِ وَالْفُجُورِ»

"Verily, there is pride which Allâh hates and pride which Allâh loves. That which Allâh loves is a man's pride in himself when fighting and when giving charity and that which Allâh, the Almighty, the All-Powerful hates is pride shown by injustice and oppression."[6]

On one occasion, he fought with a mangonel against the people of Ta'if. He prohibited the killing of women and children. He would examine the (enemy) combatants and those of them who had begun to grow

---

[1] Narrated by Al-Bukhari and Muslim, on the authority of Al-Bara' Ibn 'Azib ﷺ.

[2] Narrated by Muslim, on the authority of Al-Bara' Ibn 'Azib ﷺ.

[3] Narrated by Abu Dawûd, on the authority of Salamah Ibn Al-Akwa' ﷺ, it was declared authentic by Al-Hakim and Az-Zahabi confirmed this.

[4] Narrated by Abu Ash-Shaikh in *'Akhlaq An-Nabi'*, on the authority of Yahya Al-Hamani, its chain of narrators is incomplete.

[5] *Sûrah Fussilat* 41:1, 16.

[6] Narrated by Abu Dawûd, on the authority of Jabir Ibn 'Ateek ﷺ.

pubic hair were killed, while those who had not were spared.[1]

When he sent out a military expedition, he would advise them to fear Allâh and he would say:

«سِيرُوا بِسْمِ اللهِ وَفِي سَبِيلِ اللهِ، قَاتِلُوا مَنْ كَفَرَ بِاللهِ، وَلَا تُمَثِّلُوا وَلَا تَغْدُرُوا وَلَا تَغْلُوا وَلَا تَقْتُلُوا وَلِيدًا»

"Go forth in Allâh's Name and in Allâh's Cause; fight those who disbelieve in Allâh, do not mutilate the enemy dead, do not break treaties, do not embezzle the spoils of war and do not kill children."[2]

He prohibited traveling with the Qur'ân to the lands of the enemy and he ordered the commander of his expedition to call the enemy before engaging in fighting – either to Islam and migration or Islam without migration, in which case, they would be like the Bedouins among the Muslims, who had no share in the spoils of war, or to pay the *Jizyah*.[3] If they acceded to the call, it was accepted from them; if it was not, he would seek help from Allâh and fight them.

If he vanquished an enemy, he would order a caller to gather all of the spoils and he would start by sharing the booty with those who had a right to it, then he would deduct the *Khumus*[4] from the remainder and he would use it in the manner which Allâh deemed appropriate and commanded, for the benefit of the Muslims. Then he would give a small amount from the remainder to those who had no share, such as the women and children and the slaves; and then he would divide what remained into equal-sized shares and give three shares to the cavalryman and one to the infantryman. This is what has been authentically reported from him ﷺ.[5] He would also give extra from the spoils according to what he considered beneficial: He combined

[1] Narrated by Abu Dawûd, on the authority of 'Atiyyah Al-Qurazi ﷺ.

[2] Narrated by Muslim, the compilers of the *'Sunan'*, Ahmad, Malik and Ad-Darimi.

[3] *Jizyah*: A tax paid by Jews and Christians living under Muslim protection.

[4] *Khumus*: One fifth, which is deducted from the spoils of war.

[5] Narrated by Al-Bukhari and Muslim, on the authority of 'Abdullah Ibn 'Umar ﷺ.

for Salamah Ibn Al-Akwa' ﷺ on one campaign the share of a cavalryman and the share of an infantryman, so he gave him four shares, due to the great use he had been in that particular battle.[1]

He used to give the strong and the weak equal shares, aside from the aforementioned extra. When he was fighting in the land of the enemy, he would send an expedition ahead of him and whatever spoils they collected, he would take the *khumus* from it, then from the remainder he would take one quarter and give it to them as extra shares, then he would divide what remained between the members of the expedition and the rest of the troops. And he would do likewise upon returning, giving them one third.[2] In spite of this, he disliked giving extra shares, for he said:

«لِيَرُدَّ قِوِيُّ الْمُؤْمِنِينَ عَلَى ضَعِيفِهِمْ»

"The strong Believer and the weak Believer should receive an equal share."[3]

The Prophet ﷺ had a share in the booty which was known as *As-Safiyy*:[4] If he wished, a slave and if he wished, a horse and he would choose it before the *Khumus* was taken from the spoils.[5]

'A'ishah ﷺ said: "Safiyyah ﷺ was from *As-Safiyy*." (Narrated by Abu Dawûd)[6] And his sword, *Zul Fiqar*, was from *As-Safiyy*. He used to

[1] Narrated by Muslim and Abu Dawûd.

[2] Narrated by Abu Dawûd, on the authority of Habeeb Ibn Maslamah Al-Fihri ﷺ.

[3] Narrated by Ahmad, on the authority of 'Ubadah Ibn As-Samit, but the *Hadeeth* is weak due to the presence in the *Sanad* of Abu Ishaq, of whom Muhammad Ibn Sa'd said: "He makes many mistakes in his *Ahadeeth*." Also in the *Sanad* is Sulaiman Ibn Mûsa, of whom Abu Hatim Ar-Razi said: "There is *Idhtirab* (contradiction) in some of his *Ahadeeth*." Ibn Hajr said of him that he was lax regarding some of his *Ahadeeth* and that towards the end of his life, he mixed things up.

[4] *As-Safiyy*: The Pure.

[5] Narrated by Abu Dawûd, on the authority of Ash-Sha'bi, who was a *Tabi'i*, so it is a *Mursal* narration.

[6] Narrated by Abu Dawûd, on the authority of 'A'ishah ﷺ and declared authentic by Ibn Hibban.

give a share to those who had been absent from the fighting due to some benefit to the Muslims, as he gave to 'Uthman ☙ after the Battle of Badr, when he nursed his (i.e. the Prophet's) daughter and he said:

«إِنَّ عُثْمَانَ انْطَلَقَ فِي حَاجَةِ اللهِ وَحَاجَةِ رَسُولِهِ»

"Verily, 'Uthman has left on business of Allâh and of his Messenger." And he gave him his share and his reward."[1]

They used to buy and sell in his presence when in battle and he did not prohibit them from doing so. They used to hire people to fight and such hiring was of two types: (i) That a man would go off to fight and he would hire someone to serve him on the journey; (ii) that he would hire from his wealth someone who would go out for *Jihad* and this was known as *Al-Ja'a'il*; regarding this practice, the Prophet ﷺ said:

«لِلْغَازِي أَجْرُهُ، وَلِلْجَاعِلِ أَجْرُهُ وَأَجْرُ الْغَازِي»

"The warrior gets his reward, and the one who equips him gets his own reward and that of the warrior."[2]

And they used to share the booty in two ways also: (i) Physical participation (i.e. each one fighting and then combining what they had got and sharing it equally) and (ii) that a man would hand over his camel or his horse to another man so that he could do battle on it, on the understanding that he would give him half of his share; they might even divide up the share so that one of them received an arrow shaft and the other the arrow head and the flight; 'Abdullah Ibn Mas'ûd ☙ said: "'Ammar, Sa'd and I became partners in what we would receive on the Day of Badr and Sa'd brought two captives, while 'Ammar and I brought nothing."[3]

---

[1] Narrated by Abu Dawûd, on the authority of 'Abdullah Ibn 'Umar ☙.

[2] Narrated by Ahmad and Abu Dawûd, on the authority of 'Abdullah Ibn 'Amr ☙.

[3] Narrated by Abu Dawûd, An-Nasa'i and Ibn Majah, on the authority of Abu 'Ubaidah, who reported on the authority of 'Abdullah Ibn Mas'ûd ☙, but it is a *Munqati'* narration, because Abu 'Ubaidah did not hear from his father, 'Abdullah Ibn Mas'ûd ☙.

Sometimes, he would send out an expedition on horseback and sometimes on foot and he did not give a share to anyone who arrived after victory had been achieved.[1] He used to give blood relatives from Banu Hashim and Banu Al-Muttalib, but not their brothers from Banu 'Abdi Shams and Banu Nawfal and he said:

«إِنَّمَا بَنُو الْمُطَّلِبِ، وَبَنُو هَاشِمٍ شَيْءٌ وَاحِدٌ»

"Banu Al-Muttalib and Banu Hashim are one thing."

And he interlocked his fingers and said:

«إِنَّهُمْ لَمْ يُفَارِقُونَا فِي جَاهِلِيَّةٍ وَلَا إِسْلَامٍ»

"They neither left us in the *Jahiliyyah*, nor in Islam."

The Muslims used to acquire with him in their battles honey, grapes and food and they would eat it and they would not include it in the war booty; Ibn Abi Awfa ﷺ was asked: "Did you use to take *Khumus* from the food?" He replied: "We acquired food on the day of the Battle of Khaibar and any man would come along and take from it what sufficed him, then leave."[2] One of the Companions ﷺ said: "We would eat a camel on an expedition without dividing it, even though we were returning to our camp and our saddle-bags would be full with its flesh."[3]

The Prophet ﷺ forbade pillaging and mutilation[4] and he said:

«مَنِ انْتَهَبَ نُهْبَةً فَلَيْسَ مِنَّا»

"Whoever pillaged is not one of us."[5]

---

[1] Narrated by Al-Bukhari, on the authority of Abu Hurairah ﷺ.

[2] Narrated by Abu Dawûd, on the authority of 'Abdullah Ibn Abi Awfa ﷺ.

[3] Narrated by Abu Dawûd, on the authority of Al-Qasim, the freed slave of 'Abdur-Rahman, it has in its chain of narrators one Ibn Harshaf Al-Azadi, who is unknown, according to Az-Zahabi, thus the *Hadeeth* is weak.

[4] It is reported on the authority of Anas Ibn Malik ﷺ that he said: "The Prophet ﷺ encouraged charity and prohibited mutilation." (Narrated by Al-Bukhari).

[5] Narrated by Abu Dawûd and Ahmad, on the authority of Anas Ibn Malik ﷺ.

He also forbade that a man should ride an animal which is part of the war booty and then when he has emaciated it, return it, or to wear a garment from the war booty, then when he has worn it threadbare to put it back.[1] He did not forbid that something should be utilized at the time of battle, but he was extremely strict about embezzling the spoils of war and he said:

«عَارٌ وَنَارٌ وَشَنَارٌ عَلَى أَهْلِهِ يَوْمَ الْقِيَامَةِ»

"(Embezzling the spoils of war is) disgrace, fire and ignominy on the Day of Resurrection for those who do it."[2]

And when his slave, Mid'am was killed, some of the Companions ؆ said: "Congratulations to him (the slave) for gaining Paradise." Allâh's Messenger ؅ said:

«كَلَّا وَالَّذِي نَفْسِي بِيَدِهِ، إِنَّ الشَّمْلَةَ الَّتِي أَخَذَهَا يَوْمَ خَيْبَرَ مِنَ الْغَنَائِمِ لَمْ تُصِبْهَا الْمَقَاسِمُ، لَتَشْتَعِلُ عَلَيْهِ نَارًا»

"No! By Him in Whose Hand is my soul, the sheet which he stole from the war booty before its distribution on the day of Khaibar, is now burning over him."

When the people heard that, a man brought one or two leather shoe straps to the Prophet. The Prophet said:

«شِرَاكٌ أَوْ شِرَاكَانِ مِنْ نَارٍ»

"A strap of fire," (or he said:) "Two straps of fire."[3]

And the Prophet ؅ said regarding the man who looked after his belongings (whose name was Kirkirah) when he died:

«هُوَ فِي النَّارِ»

[1] Narrated by Abu Dawûd and Ahmad, on the authority of Ruwaifi' Ibn Thabit Al-Ansari ؆.

[2] Narrated by Ahmad and Malik, on the authority of 'Abdullah Ibn 'Amr Ibn Al-'As ؆.

[3] Narrated by Al-Bukhari, Muslim, Abu Dawûd, An-Nasa'i and Malik, on the authority of Abu Hurairah ؆.

"He is in the Fire."

The people then went to look and found in his place a cloak which he had stolen from the war booty.[1]

And they used to say in some of their battles: "So-and-so is a martyr and so-and-so is a martyr," until they passed by a man and they said of him: "He is a martyr." But the Prophet ﷺ said:

«كَلَّا إِنِّي رَأَيْتُهُ فِي النَّارِ فِي بُرْدَةٍ غَلَّهَا أَوْ عَبَاءَةٍ»

"No! I saw him in the Fire wearing a *Burdah*[2] or a cloak (the narrator is unsure what it was) that he stole from the war booty."

Then he ﷺ said:

«يَا ابْنَ الْخَطَّابِ اذْهَبْ فَنَادِ فِي النَّاسِ إِنَّهُ لَا يَدْخُلُ الْجَنَّةَ إِلَّا الْمُؤْمِنُونَ»

"Oh, Ibn Al-Khattab! Go and announce to the people that none will enter Paradise except the Believers."[3]

And once, when he acquired war booty, he ordered Bilal ﷺ to announce to the people and they came, bringing their booty and he deducted the *Khumus* from it and distributed it; then a man came after that with a camel rope made of hair. The Prophet ﷺ said to him:

«أَسَمِعْتَ بِلَالًا يُنَادِي؟»

"Did you hear Bilal calling?"

He said: "Yes." The Prophet ﷺ asked him:

«فَمَا مَنَعَكَ أَنْ تَجِيءَ بِهِ؟»

"Then what prevented you from bringing it?"

---

[1] Narrated by Al-Bukhari, Ibn Majah and Ahmad, on the authority of Abu Hurairah ﷺ.

[2] *Burdah*: Outer garment.

[3] Narrated by Muslim and Ahmad, on the authority of 'Abdullah Ibn 'Abbas ﷺ and by Ad-Darimi, on the authority of 'Umar Ibn Al-Khattab ﷺ.

The man made some excuses and the Prophet ﷺ said:

«كُنْ أَنْتَ تَجِيءُ بِهِ يَوْمَ الْقِيَامَةِ فَلَنْ أَقْبَلَهُ عَنْكَ»

"Be (as you are), for you may bring it on the Day of Resurrection and I will not accept it from you."[1]

And he ordered that the property of the embezzler of war booty be burnt and that he be beaten and the two Caliphs who came after him (Abu Bakr and 'Umar ﷺ used to beat the embezzler of war booty and burn his property also.[2] It was said that this is abrogated by all of the *Ahadeeth* which I have referred to, because burning was not mentioned in any of them. It was also said – and this is the correct opinion – that it is a form of financial rebuke and punishment which fall under the *Ijtihad* of the Imams,[3] like executing the drinker of alcoholic beverages after the third or fourth time.[4]

---

[1] Narrated by Abu Dawûd and Ahmad, on the authority of 'Abdullah Ibn 'Amr Ibn Al-'As ﷺ.

[2] Narrated by At-Tirmidhi and Abu Dawûd, on the authority of 'Umar Ibn Al-Khattab ﷺ, it contains in its chain of narrators one Muhammad Ibn Salih Ibn Za'idah, who is weak; Al-Bukhari said: "No one narrated this *Hadeeth* except Muhammad Ibn Salih Ibn Za'idah and he is Abu Waqid Al-Laithi, who narrated *Ahadeeth* which are *Munkarah*. Abu Dawûd also narrated something similar on the authority of 'Abdullah Ibn 'Amr Ibn Al-'As ﷺ, but it contains in its *Sanad* one Zuhair Ibn Muhammad Al-Khurasani, of whom Ad-Darimi said: "He is honest, but he has many mistakes." According to Ibn Hajr, *Ahadeeth* narrated from him by the people of Ash-Sham (such as this one) are weak.

[3] This would only be the case if the evidence was authentically reported from the Prophet ﷺ. However, if it was weak – as in this case – it would not be so.

[4] In fact, executing the drinker of alcoholic beverages after the fourth offence is mentioned in an authentic *Hadeeth*: "Whoever drank alcohol, flog him; and if he repeats the offence, flog him a second time; if he repeats it a third time, flog him again and if he repeats it a fourth time, kill him." (Narrated by At-Tirmidhi, Abu Dawûd, An-Nasa'i, Ahmad, Al-Hakim, At-Tabarani and others.

Regarding His ﷺ Guidance With Respect to Prisoners of War

He would pardon some of them, he would kill some of them, he would ransom some of them for money and some of them for the release of Muslim prisoners. He did all of these things in accordance with what was beneficial (to the Muslims). On one occasion, the *Ansar* ﷺ sought permission from him not to pay the ransom of his uncle, Al-'Abbas ﷺ and he said:

«لَا تَدَعُوا مِنْهُ دِرْهَمًا»

"You will not leave a single *Dirham* of it!"[1]

And he returned the captives from Hawazin to them after the distribution of the war booty and the hearts of those who had gained spoils were positively affected by this (and they gave up their captives) and he compensated those who did not forsake their captives with six shares for each captive.

And Ahmad has reported on the authority of 'Abdullah bin 'Abbas ﷺ that some of them had no money and so the Messenger of Allâh ﷺ declared that their ransom would be that they should teach the children of the *Ansar* to write.[2] This proves the permissibility of accepting work as a ransom. And the correct opinion which is based upon his guidance and that of his Companions ﷺ is that the Arabs

---

[1] Narrated by Al-Bukhari, on the authority of Anas Ibn Malik ﷺ.

[2] Narrated by Ahmad, on the authority of 'Abdullah Ibn 'Abbas ﷺ, it contains in its *Sanad* one 'Ali Ibn 'Asim Ibn Suhaib Al-Wasiti, who was declared weak by Ibn Hajr, while Yahya Ibn Ma'een and Yazeed Ibn Harûn called him a liar.

may be taken as slaves and it is permissible to have sexual intercourse with the slave women from among them without it being conditional upon their embracing Islam. And he prohibited parting a mother slave from her child and he used to give the children who were brought to him to their families, hating that he should split them up.

It has been authentically reported from him that he killed a spy from the polytheists,[1] but he did not kill Hatib ☙ when he spied on them, calling to mind the fact that he had fought in the Battle of Badr. Those who held that a (Muslim) spy should not be killed[2] cited this as evidence and those who held that he should be killed also cited it as evidence, such as Malik, due to his proffering an excuse which prevented him being killed and he reasoned that if Islam prohibited killing a Muslim spy, he would not have proffered an excuse; and when a ruling is affected by something more general, the more specific is devoid of effect.

It was a part of his guidance to free the slaves of the polytheists if they went out to the Muslims and embraced Islam.

It was also a part of his guidance that when a person embraced Islam and he had something in his possession, it belonged to him and he did not return to the Muslims their personal property which had been taken by the disbelievers when they embraced Islam. And it has been confirmed from him ﷺ that he distributed the land of Quraizah and An-Nadeer and half of Khaibar between the recipients of the war booty and he set aside half of Khaibar for those who came there, such as arrivals from afar, unexpected matters and the problems or disasters affecting the Muslims, but he did not divide Makkah; some scholars said that this was because it is the House of Pilgrimage Rites and so it is an endowment from Allâh to His slaves. Others said that the *Imam* has the choice of whether to distribute the land or to endow it, based upon the action of the Prophet ﷺ and they said that the land is not included in the war booty, the distribution of which is commanded, because Allâh has not permitted it for anyone except this nation (i.e. the Muslims), but He has made permissible for them the homes and the lands of the disbelievers,

---

[1] Narrated by Al-Bukahri and Abu Dawûd, on the authority of Salamah Ibn Al-Akwa' ☙.

[2] Ash-Shafi'i, Ahmad and Abu Haneefah.

according to the Words of Him, Most High:

$$﴿ كَذَلِكَ وَأَوْرَثْنَاهَا بَنِي إِسْرَٰٓءِيلَ ۝ ﴾$$

"Thus [We turned them (Pharaoh's people) out] and We caused the Children of Israel to inherit them."[1]

And the Prophet ﷺ sometimes distributed land and sometimes he did not and 'Umar ﷺ did not distribute it, instead he placed a permanent land tax upon it, which he paid to the (Muslim) combatants (who had fought to conquer it). This is the meaning of endowment (*Waqf*), not the kind of endowment whose ownership may not be transferred; indeed, it is permissible to sell it as practised by the (Muslim) people. And the scholars in absolute agreement that it may be inherited; Ahmad declared that it is permissible to make it a dowry, whereas it is not permissible to sell *Waqf* due to the fact that it invalidates the right of those upon whom it is endowed. And the right of the fighters is in the tax on the land, so it is not invalidated by selling the land. Similar to this is the selling of a slave who has entered into a written agreement to purchase his freedom (*Mukatab*), because the means for obtaining his freedom has already been agreed upon in the contract and so he is transferred to the purchaser as a *Mukatab*, just as he was with the seller.

The Prophet ﷺ forbade a Muslim from living among the polytheists, if he has the ability to migrate; he said:

$$«أَنَا بَرِيءٌ مِنْ كُلِّ مُسْلِمٍ يُقِيمُ بَيْنَ أَظْهُرِ الْمُشْرِكِينَ»$$

"I am innocent of blame for any Muslim who lives among the polytheists."

It was said to him: "O, Messenger of Allâh! Why is that?" He said:

$$«لَا تَرَاآى نَارَاهُمَا»$$

"Their fires should not be visible to each other (i.e. they should live far apart)."[2]

---

[1] *Sûrah Ash-Shu'ara'* 26:59
[2] Narrated by Abu Dawûd and At-Tirmidhi, on the authority of Jareer Ibn 'Abdillah ﷺ.

And he ﷺ said:

«مَنْ جَامَعَ الْمُشْرِكَ وَسَكَنَ مَعَهُ فَهُوَ مِثْلُهُ»

"Anyone who associates with a polytheist and lives with him is like him."[1]

And he ﷺ said:

«لَا تَنْقَطِعُ الْهِجْرَةُ حَتَّى تَنْقَطِعَ التَّوْبَةُ، وَلَا تَنْقَطِعُ التَّوْبَةُ، حَتَّى تَطْلُعَ الشَّمْسُ مِنْ مَغْرِبِهَا»

"*Hijrah* (migration for Allâh's sake) will not end until repentance ends and repentance will not end until the sun rises in the west."[2]

And he ﷺ said:

«سَتَكُونُ هِجْرَةٌ بَعْدَ هِجْرَةٍ، فَخِيَارُ أَهْلِ الأَرْضِ أَلْزَمُهُمْ مُهَاجَرَ إِبْرَاهِيمَ عَلَيْهِ السَّلَامُ، وَيَبْقَى فِي الأَرْضِ شَرَارُ أَهْلَهَا تَلْفِظُهُمْ أَرَضُوهُمْ تَقْذَرُهُمْ نَفْسُ اللهِ وَيَحْشُرُهُمُ اللهُ مَعَ الْقِرَدَةِ وَالْخَنَازِيرِ»

"There will be one *Hijrah* after another and the best of people will migrate as did Abraham, while those who remain in the land will be the most evil of people; their lands will reject them and Allâh will despise them and He will gather them on the Day of Resurrection with the apes and swine."[3]

---

[1] Narrated by Abu Dawûd, on the authority of Samurah Ibn Jundub ؓ, it contains in its *Sanad* one Ja'far Ibn Sa'd Ibn Samurah Ibn Jundub, who is weak, according to Ibn 'Abdil Barr, while Ibn Hajr says that his status as a narrator is unknown, as does Ibn Al-Qattan. It also contains one Khubaib Ibn Sulaiman, who is also unknown, according to Ibn Hajr and Az-Zahabi. Likewise the status of Sulaiman Ibn Samurah, from whom Khubaib reports is unknown, according to Ibn Al-Qattan.

[2] Narrated by Abu Dawûd, Ahmad and Ad-Darimi, on the authority of Mu'awiyah ؓ, but it contains in its *Sanad* one Abu Hind Al-Bajli, who is unknown, according to Az-Zahabi and Ibn Al-Qattan.

[3] Narrated by Abu Dawûd and Ahmad, on the authority of 'Abdullah Ibn 'Amr Ibn Al-'As ؓ.

Chapter

Regarding His ﷺ Guidance in Peace and in Treaties, Treatment Accorded to Messengers From the Disbelievers, Taking the *Jizyah*, Treatment of the People of the Scripture and the Hypocrites and His Fulfillment of Agreements

It has been authentically reported from the Prophet ﷺ that he said:

«ذِمَّةُ الْمُسْلِمِينَ وَاحِدَةٌ يَسْعَى بِهَا أَدْنَاهُمْ، فَمَنْ أَخْفَرَ مُسْلِمًا، فَعَلَيْهِ لَعْنَةُ اللهِ وَالْمَلَائِكَةِ وَالنَّاسِ أَجْمَعِينَ، لَا يَقْبَلُ اللهُ مِنْهُ يَوْمَ الْقِيَامَةِ صَرْفًا وَلَا عَدْلًا»

"The protection granted by the Muslims is one and must be respected by the humblest of them. He who violated the covenant with a Muslim, there is upon him the curse of Allâh, the angels and all of mankind. Neither an obligatory act nor a supererogatory act would be accepted from him as recompense on the Day of Resurrection."[1]

And it has been authentically reported from him ﷺ that he said:

«مَنْ كَانَ بَيْنَهُ وَبَيْنَ قَوْمٍ عَهْدٌ، فَلَا يَحُلَّنَّ عُقْدَةً، وَلَا يَشُدَّهَا حَتَّى يَمْضِيَ أَمَدُهُ، أَوْ يَنْبِذَ إِلَيْهِمْ عَلَى سَوَاءٍ»

---

[1] Narrated by Al-Bukhari and Muslim on the authority of Abu Hurairah ﷺ and by Ahmad on the authority of 'Ali Ibn Abi Talib ﷺ.

"When one has a covenant with people he must not loosen or strengthen it till its term comes to an end or he brings it to an end in agreement with them (to make both the parties equal)."[1]

And he ﷺ said:

«مَنْ أَمَّنَ رَجُلًا عَلَى نَفْسِهِ فَقَتَلَهُ، فَأَنَا بَرِيءٌ مِنَ الْقَاتِلِ»

"Whoever guaranteed the safety of a man and then killed him, I disavow the killer."

And it is reported from him ﷺ that he said:

«مَا نَقَضَ قَوْمٌ الْعَهْدَ إِلَّا أُدِيلَ عَلَيْهِمُ الْعَدُوُّ»

"Whenever a people violate an agreement, the enemy will triumph over them."[2]

When he arrived in Al-Madinah, he found the disbelievers to be of three types: (i) Those with whom he made a treaty that they would not make war against him, nor side with others against him; (ii) those who fought against him; (iii) those who did not enter into any treaty with him, neither did they make war against him; instead, they waited to see what would happen to him; then there were among them those who secretly hoped that he would defeat his enemies, while others among them wished for him to be defeated. And among them were those who appeared to join him, while secretly, they were his enemy. And he treated each group in accordance with the Commandments of his Lord, Most High.

He made an agreement with the Jews of Al-Madinah, but Banu Qainiqa' fought against him after the Battle of Badr, going over to the east (i.e. to the polytheists forces of Makkah) after it took place, revealing their injustice and envy. Then Banu Nadheer invalidated their agreement and the Prophet ﷺ fought them and laid siege to them, cutting down their date palms and burning them, after which they descended from their forts, on the understanding that they

---

[1] Narrated by At-Tirmidhi, Abu Dawûd and Ahmad.

[2] Narrated by Al-Hakim, on the authority of Buraidah ؓ, it contains in its chain of narrators one Basheer Ibn Al-Muhajir, who was deemed as lax by scholars of *Hadeeth*.

would leave Al-Madinah, being allowed to take with them what could be carried by camel, but excluding their weapons. Allâh mentioned their story in *Sûrah Al-Hashr*. After that, Banu Quraizah broke their treaty, and they were the worst of the Jews in disbelief, this is why what befell them did not befall their brothers (i.e. their men were put to death and their wives and children enslaved). This was his judgement on the Jews of Al-Madinah. And each battle with the Jews took place following a major battle (with the polytheists): Banu Qainuqa' following the Battle of Badr, Banu An-Nadeer following the Battle of Uhud and Banu Quraizah following the Battle of the Trench; as for Khaibar, we shall mention their story shortly.

It was a part of his guidance ﷺ that when he made a peace treaty with a people, if some of them invalidated it, while others of them abided by it and accepted it, he would make war against all of them, as he did in the cases of Ban An-Nadeer, Banu Quraizah and the people of Makkah; this was his practice regarding those with whom he had made agreements. And accordingly the People of the Scripture should be treated, as correctly stated by the companions of Imam Ahmad and others; however the companions of Imam Ash-Shafi'i differed with them on this, for they said that the invalidation of the agreement applies only to those who broke it; and they distinguished between the two based upon the fact that a treaty of protection is firmer; but the first opinion is more correct. And this was the legal ruling given by us to the Ruler when the Christians burnt the property of the Muslims in Ash-Sham and some of the Christians knew of this and agreed to it and they did not inform the Ruler about it and (we ruled) that the punishment for it was a mandatory sentence of death and that the Imam has no choice in the matter, as with a prisoner of war; indeed killing for him becomes a legal punishment. And Islam does not withhold killing if it is a legal punishment from one who is living under the protection of the Islamic State, as it is a duty to impose the Judgements of Allâh, as opposed to the person who is at war with the Muslims and then he embraces Islam; there is a ruling upon such a person.[1] And as for

---

[1] His life and his property are protected by the Islamic State and he may not be killed for what he did prior to embracing Islam.

the person living under the protection of the Islamic State who invalidates the agreement, there is another ruling upon him and that is what is claimed in the works of Ahmad. And our Shaikh Ibn Taimiyyah has ruled accordingly on more than one occasion.

It was a part of his guidance that if he made a peace treaty with a people, then an enemy of his joined them and made a treaty with them, then another people joined with him, the ruling on those disbelievers who made war against the people who had joined him was the same as that on those who made war against him. It was for this reason that he attacked Makkah and thus ruled Shaikh Al-Islam Ibn Taimiyyah regarding the Christians of Al-Mashriq, when they supported the enemies of the Muslims in their war against them and supplied them with money and weapons; he considered that they had thereby invalidated the agreement. So how would it be if those living under Muslim protection helped the polytheists in their war against the Muslims.

And emissaries from his enemies came to him while they were hostile to him and he did not harm them, but when two messengers came to him from Musailamah and said what they said, he said to them:

«لَوْلَا أَنَّ الرُّسُلَ لَا تُقْتَلُ لَضَرَبْتُ أَعْنَاقَكُمَا»

"If it were not for the fact that emissaries may not be killed, I would have cut off your heads."[1]

So his practice was not to kill emissaries; and it was a part of his guidance also not to retain an emissary if he embraced Islam while in his company; instead, he would return him, as Abu Rafi' ﷺ said: "Quraish sent me to him and Islam entered my heart and I said: "Oh, Messenger of Allâh! I will not return." But he said:

«إِنِّي لَا أَخِيسُ بِالْعَهْدِ، وَلَا أَحْبِسُ الْبُرُدَ، ارْجِعْ إِلَيْهِمْ، فَإِنْ كَانَ فِي قَلْبِكَ الَّذِي فِيهِ الآنَ فَارْجِعْ»

---

[1] Narrated by Abu Dawûd and Ahmad, on the authority of Na'eem Ibn Mas'ûd Al-Ashja'i ﷺ, it contains in its chain of narrators one Salamah Ibn Al-Fadl Al-Ansari, of whom Ibn Hajr said: "He is honest, but he makes many mistakes."

"I will not break an agreement and I will not detain an emissary; go back to them, then if there is still in your heart that which is there now, you may return."[1]

Abu Dawûd said: "This took place during the time when it was a condition (of the treaty between the Muslims and the polytheists) that if any of them came to him, he would return him to them. But as for today, this would not be right." And in the words of the Prophet ﷺ:

$$\text{«لَا أَحْبِسُ الْبُرُدَ»}$$

"I will not detain an emissary."

There is evidence that this applies only to emissaries, but as for his returning a person who came to him as a Muslim, that would only be if the stipulation (of the treaty) were present, while as for messengers, there is a different ruling for them.

It was also a part of his guidance that if his enemies made an agreement with one of his Companions without his consent, which did not harm the Muslims, he would uphold it, as was the case when they made an agreement with Huzaifah ؓ and his father that they would not fight with the Messenger of Allâh ﷺ against them and he said:

$$\text{«انْصَرِفَا نَفِي لَهُمْ بِعَهْدِهِمْ، وَنَسْتَعِينَ اللهَ عَلَيْهِمْ»}$$

"Go. We will fulfill their agreement and seek Allâh's Help against them."[2]

And he made a peace treaty with Quraish in which it was stipulated that if anyone came to him (from them) as a Muslim, he would return him, but that if anyone came to them from him, they would not return him;[3] and the wording was general, including men and women; then Allâh abrogated that for women and He commanded that they be examined and if they found that a woman was a Believer,

[1] Narrated by Abu Dawûd and Ahmad, on the authority of Abu Rafi' ؓ.

[2] Narrated by Muslim and Ahmad, on the authority of Huzaifah Ibn Al-Yaman ؓ.

[3] Narrated by Al-Bukhari and Muslim, on the authority of Anas Ibn Malik ؓ.

she would not be returned, but her dowry would be returned to her husband.

And He commanded the Muslims to pay the dowry of a woman who had left her husband and gone to them if they were penalized by it being incumbent upon them to return the dowry of the female emigrant, that they should return it to the person whose wife had left him and they should not return her to her pagan husband. That is the penalty and it is not in truth a punishment.

In this there is evidence that when a woman leaves the authority of her husband, the amount paid to him is estimated and that it is in accordance with the dowry which he paid to her, not based upon the amount given to a woman in similar circumstances, and that the marriages of the disbelievers are valid and also that it is not permissible to return a Muslim woman who migrates from the disbelievers to the Muslims, even if it was a condition of the peace treaty and that it is not permissible for a disbeliever to marry or be married to a Muslim woman and that a Muslim man may marry her if she has completed her *'Iddah*[1] and he gives her a dowry. Here is the clearest evidence that a (Muslim) wife may leave the authority of her (disbelieving) husband and that the marriage is dissolved by her migration. And in it there is a prohibition of marrying polytheist women. These rulings were derived from the two Verses (in *Sûrah Al-Mumtahanah* 60:10-11); there is consensus on some of them and in some of them there exists a difference of opinion. But those who claim that the Verses has been abrogated have no evidence, because if the condition applied only to men, then women are excluded from it, whereas, if it is general for men and women, Allâh has prohibited their return.

And He commanded that the dowry be returned to the husband from whom she had run away; then He informed us that that is His Judgment with which He judges between His slaves and that it emanates from His Knowledge and His Wisdom. And nothing has

---

[1] *'Iddah*: The waiting period which a Muslim woman must observe following divorce or the death of her spouse, which is three menstrual cycles. After this, she is free to marry.

come from Him which invalidates this Judgement.

When the Prophet ﷺ made a treaty with them in which it was stated that he would return the men, he made it possible for them to take those who came to him, but he would not force them to return, nor would he order them to do so. And if the person had killed any of them or taken their property, and he had departed from his jurisdiction and did not return to them, he would not rebuke him for this, nor would he indemnify them for what he had done, because he was not under his jurisdiction, nor would he order him to return to them. And the treaty document did not require the safeguarding of lives and property, except for those who were under his jurisdiction, as in the case of Banu Jazimah, when Khalid killed them and the Prophet ﷺ rejected what he had done and declared himself innocent of it.[1]

And because Khalid had interpreted the Prophet's words (literally)[2] and he had fought them in accordance with the order of the Prophet ﷺ, they were indemnified with half of their blood money, due to the misinterpretation and doubt. And he treated them in this matter as he would have treated the People of the Scripture, who are protected by covenant of protection, not by Islam. And the peace treaty did not necessitate that he help them against those who made war on them, who were not under his jurisdiction, for it was written therein that if they were attacked by those who were not under the *Imam*'s authority, even if he was a Muslim, then it was not incumbent upon the *Imam* to return him, nor to indemnify for damage.

And taking the rulings regarding war, peace and diplomatic policies from his ﷺ guidance is more appropriate than taking them from the opinions of others. So based upon this, if there was a covenant of protection between a Muslim ruler and some of those who are

---

[1] Narrated by Al-Bukhari, on the authority of Abu Salim ﷺ.

[2] The Prophet ﷺ ordered Khalid ﷺ to fight them if they did not say: *"Aslamna"* (We have embraced Islam) and they did not say this, but instead said: *"Saba'na"* (We have changed our religion) and so Khalid ﷺ acting upon the literal meaning of the words of the Prophet ﷺ, killed some of them and took some of them captive.

entitled to such protection (i.e. the People of the Scripture), it would be permissible for another Muslim ruler who did not have a covenant of protection with them to make war against them, as *Shaikh Al-Islam* (Ibn Taimiyyah) ruled in the case of the Christians of Malta, citing as evidence the story of Abu Baseer.

Likewise, he made a peace treaty with the people of Khaibar, when he had defeated them, that he would expel them from there and that they might take away with them what their riding beasts could carry and that their gold and silver and weapons would be for the Messenger of Allâh ﷺ and he stipulated that they should not hide anything and that if they did, they would have no protection, but they concealed a *Mask*[1] which had belonged to Huyay Ibn Akhtab, which he had taken away with him when *Banu An-Nadeer* were expelled. The Prophet ﷺ asked Huyay's uncle about it and he said: "It was all expended in battles and other expenses." The Prophet ﷺ said:

$$\text{«الْعَهْدُ قَرِيبٌ، وَالْمَالُ أَكْثَرُ مِنْ ذَلِكَ»}$$

"It was only a short time ago and the money was more than that."

So he sent him to Az-Zubair to ascertain the truth and he tortured him until he said: "I saw Huyay going around in the ruins here." So they looked and found it there. So the Messenger of Allâh ﷺ killed the two sons of Abul Huqaiq, one of whom was the husband of Safiyyah Bint Huyay. And he enslaved their women and children and divided up their property due to their having broken the terms of the treaty and he wanted to expel them, but they said: "Allow us to live here and we shall work on the land, for we know it better." And since neither he nor his Companions ﷺ had sufficient labourers to work the land, they gave it to them on the understanding that they would pay them half of all that it produced, including dates and crops and that he would confirm them therein for as long as he wished.[2] And he did not kill all of the men as he did with Banu Quraizah, due to their collaboration with those who violated the covenant.

---

[1] *Mask*: A leather bag.

[2] Taken from the *Hadeeth* of Abu Dawûd and that of Ibn Sa'd, on the authority of 'Abdullah Ibn 'Umar ﷺ.

As for the people of Khaibar, those of them who knew about the *Mask* and hid it and had agreed with him on the stipulation that if it became evident that they had hidden anything, the covenant of protection would be revoked, he killed them, based upon the condition which they had agreed to, but he did make this a general order for all of the people of Khaibar, because it was known that not all of them knew of about the *Mask* and that is similar to the case of the person living under Muslim protection or the one with whom there is an agreement, if he invalidates it and no one else supports him.

And his giving the land to the people of Khaibar on the condition that they paid him half of the produce is a clear proof that it is permissible to make a sharecropping agreement. And the fact that the trees were date palms has no effect whatsoever, because the ruling on a thing is that of the thing which is similar to it, so the ruling on a land in which there are grapes and other things is the same as that of land in which there are date palms.

It is also understood from this that it is not a condition that the seeds be from the owner of the land, for he 鐐 never gave them seeds – and that is a settled matter. Indeed, some of the scholars said: If it were said that it is a condition that the worker supplies the seeds, it would be stronger. And those who claim that it is a condition that the owner supply the seeds have no evidence, except for an analogy with silent partnership; but in fact, it is nearer to the truth to say that this is an evidence against them, because in the case of silent partnership, the capital returns to the owner (and the remainder is shared between the two). And if that had been stipulated in the agreement, it would have been corrupted for them. So they considered the seeds to be like the rest of the plants. Also the seeds are considered to be like the water and other requirements, because crops do not grow by themselves, but require irrigation and work. Seeds (left alone) will die in the earth, but Allâh brings forth crops from other components along with them, such as water, wind, sun, soil and labour – this requires that the farmer be more liable to provide the seeds; and what has been reported in the *Sunnah* is in agreement with the analogy.

And in the story, there is evidence for the permissibility of making a covenant of non-hostility without any set time limit; rather, it is in accordance with the wish of the Imam; and absolutely nothing has been reported after it which would abrogate it. However, he would not make war against them without prior warning being given to both sides at the same time, so that they and he would have equal knowledge of the ending of the treaty.

There is also evidence in the story for the permissibility of chastising the accused by torture, for Allâh was Able to inform His Messenger ﷺ of the whereabouts of the treasure, but it was His Will that it be made a *Sunnah* for the Muslims to torture the accused and to expand for them the means of judgements and make them easier for them, as a Mercy from Him.

There is also evidence in it for the permissibility of using factual evidence, based upon the saying of the Prophet ﷺ:

«الْعَهْدُ قَرِيبٌ، وَالْمَالُ أَكْثَرُ مِنْ ذَلِكَ»

"It was only a short time ago and the money was more than that."

And likewise the Prophet of Allâh, Solomon (Sulaimân ﷺ) dealt with the matter of identifying the child's mother. And the Prophet ﷺ did not relate it to us, i.e. the story of Solomon (Sulaimân ﷺ) in order simply to pass the time; rather, so that we should take account of it when passing judgements; indeed, ruling by *Qasamah*[1] and the priority given to the oaths of the accusers of murder is derived from this, based upon the clear evidences; and in fact, the stoning of a woman accused of committing adultery is taken from this, based upon circumstantial evidence which was obtained as a result of his accusation and her refusal to swear that she was innocent.

Also derived from this is the acceptance of the testimony of the People of the Scripture upon the Muslims, if they make a will while traveling (and do not find any Muslims to witness it) and that if the next of kin of the deceased come to know that the witnesses have committed

---

[1] *Qasamah*: An accusation of homicide made in an oath sworn by fifty of the kinsmen of the deceased against another tribe or group of people of whose guilt they feel certain.

deception, it is permissible for them to swear to that and they will have the right to that which they have sworn. And material evidence in financial matters is like material evidence in matters of murder and has more right to be accepted than it. For this reason, if a person from whom property was stolen finds some of it in the hand of a known cheat and there is no evidence that he bought it from another, it is permissible for him to swear that the rest of his property is in that person's possession and that it was he who stole it, based upon the clear material evidence; and this is like the oath sworn by the next of kin of a murder victim in *Qasamah*; indeed the matter of money or property is a less serious one. This is why it is confirmed by a male witness and an oath, or a male witness and two female witnesses, as opposed to murder; and the Qur'ân and *Sunnah* prove the former and the latter. And those who claim that it is abrogated have no evidence at all, because it is mentioned in *Sûrah Al-Ma'idah* and that was one of the last *Sûrahs* to be revealed and the Companions ﷺ ruled in accordance with it after him ﷺ.

Also from this is the evidence of Yusuf's *Qamees*, (which was torn from behind, thus proving that it was his master's wife who had attempted to seduce him and not vice versa); and Allâh related the story in order to confirm it and as an example to be followed, not simply for the sake of narrating it.

And after the Prophet ﷺ established the people of Kahibar on the land, he would send every year a person to estimate their harvest (by looking at the amount of dates on the trees) and then he would see how much was collected from it and he would fix for them the Muslims' share and they would arrange it. And he would suffice himself with one assessor. And in this there is evidence that it is permissible to estimate the harvest in accordance with what appears to be sound on the date palms and to estimate the distribution based upon the number of date palms, after which the yield of either of the two partners will be known, even if it is not clear later and this is for the benefit of the crop.

And it proves that the distribution is collection, not sale and that it is permissible to suffice oneself with one assessor and one distributor and that the person who has the yield in his possession may dispose of it after the assessment and that he may guarantee the share of his partner (who carried out the assessment).

Then in the time of 'Umar ⚬, his son, 'Abdullah ⚬ went to his property in Khaibar and they met him with enmity and threw him from the top of a house, breaking his hand, after which 'Umar ⚬ expelled them to Ash-Sham and distributed it between those who had taken part in the Battle of Khaibar.

Chapter

As for his ﷺ guidance regarding the covenant of protection and the taking of the *Jizyah*, he did not take the *Jizyah* until after *Sûrah Bara'ah* was revealed in the eighth year; then when the Verse of the *Jizyah* was revealed, he took it from the Magians[1] and the People of the Scripture, but he did not take it from the Jews of Khaibar; and some mistakenly thought that it was specially for the people of Khaibar, but was due to their lack of understanding, because he made the peace treaty with them before the Verse was revealed and then Allâh commanded him to fight the People of the Scripture until they pay the *Jizyah*, so they were not included in that. This was because the covenant between him and them was made before it, so he did not request anything else from them, but he requested from others who had not made a covenant with him that they pay the *Jizyah*. Then when 'Umar ؊ expelled them, that covenant was changed and the ruling for them became the same as that for others among the People of the Scripture. Then in some countries where knowledge of the *Sunnah* was scanty, a group of them (i.e. the Jews) produced a book which they had forged, in which it was said that the Prophet ﷺ had lifted from Khaibar the obligation to pay the *Jizyah*; and in it there was a testimony from 'Ali Ibn Abi Talib, Sa'd Ibn Mu'adh and a number of the Companions ؊, and it spread amongst those who were ignorant of the *Sunnah* and thought that it was authentic and implemented its ruling until it was submitted to *Shaikh Al-Islam* (Ibn Taimiyyah) and he was requested to support its implementation and he spat on it and proved that it was a lie by mentioning ten evidences, including that:

---

[1] Narrated by Al-Bukhari and Ash-Shafi'i, on the authority of 'Amr Ibn Deenar ؊.

(i) Sa'd 🙵 died before Khaibar.

(ii) The (Verse of) *Jizyah* had not yet been revealed at the time of Khaibar.

(iii) He 🙵 removed from them the obligations of *Al-Kulaf*[1] and *As-Sukhar*[2] and these did not exist in the time of the Prophet 🙵, but were imposed by unjust rulers and have continued to be implemented.

(iv) This book was not mentioned by any of the scholars, neither by the compilers of the Prophet's *Seerah*,[3] nor by the scholars of *Hadeeth* nor anyone else and they (the Jews) did not reveal it during the time of the *Salaf*, because they knew that they would have known it to be a lie; but when knowledge of the *Sunnah* had decreased, they forged it and some perfidious traitors to Allâh and His Messenger 🙵 assisted them. But this only continued until Allâh revealed the truth of the matter and the successors of the Messengers made clear its falseness.

He did not take the *Jizyah* from idolaters, and it was said: It is not taken from any disbeliever other than these (the Jews, the Christians and the Magians) and those who followed their religion, following the example of the Prophet 🙵 in taking it or not taking it. And it was said: It is taken from the non-Arab idolaters, but not the Arabs. The first opinion is that of Ash-Shafi'i and Ahmad in one narration attributed to him and the second opinion is that of Abu Haneefah and Ahmad in another narration. They said that the Prophet 🙵 did not take it from the Arabs, because it was made obligatory after they had embraced Islam and no polytheist remained in the land of the Arabs. For this reason, after the conquest of Makkah, he made war on Tabuk (whose inhabitants were Christians); and if there had been any polytheists in the land of the Arabs, they would have been closer to him and it would have been more fitting to make war on them before fighting those who were further away. And whoever contemplates this will know that the matter is so. They said: But he took it from the

---

[1] *Al-Kulaf*: A tribute or tax.

[2] *As-Sukhar*: A tax.

[3] *Seerah*: Biography.

Magians and there is no authentic evidence, or anything attributed to the Prophet ﷺ to prove that they have a Scripture. And there is no difference between an idolater and a fire worshipper; indeed, the idolaters adhered to the Religion of Abraham (Ibraheem ﷺ) to an extent, unlike the fire worshippers. In fact, the fire worshippers were enemies of Abraham (Ibraheem ﷺ). And the *Sunnah* proves this, as in '*Saheeh Muslim*':

«إِذَا لَقِيتَ عَدُوَّكَ مِنَ الْمُشْرِكِينَ، فَادْعُهُمْ إِلَى إِحْدَى ثَلَاثٍ»

"If you encounter your enemies from among the polytheists, then call them to one of three things."[1]

Up to the end of the *Hadeeth*.

And Al-Mugheerah said to Kisra's representative: "Our Prophet has ordered us to fight you until you worship Allâh or pay the *Jizyah*."[2]

And the Prophet ﷺ said:

«هَلْ لَكُمْ فِي كَلِمَةٍ تُدِينُ لَكُمْ بِهَا الْعَرَبُ، وَتُؤَدِّي الْعَجَمُ إِلَيْكُمُ الْجِزْيَةَ»؟

"Do you desire a word which will subdue the Arabs and will cause the non-Arabs to pay the *Jizyah* to you?"

They said: "What is it?" He said:

«لَا إِلَهَ إِلَّا اللهُ»

"*La Ilaha Illallah*"

"None has the right to be worshipped except Allâh".[3]

He made a peace treaty with the people of Najran on the understanding that they would pay two thousand garments – half in the month of Safar, and the rest in Rajab, and they would lend (the Muslims) thirty coats of mail, thirty horses, thirty camels, and thirty

---

[1] Narrated by Muslim, on the authority of Buraidah· ﷺ.

[2] Narrated by Al-Bukhari, on the authority of Jubair Ibn Hayyah, who narrated from An-Nu'man Ibn Muqrin and Al-Mugheerah Ibn Shu'bah ﷺ.

[3] Narrated by Ahmad and At-Tirmidhi, on the authority of 'Abdullah Ibn 'Abbas ﷺ.

weapons of each type used in battle and that the Muslims would stand surety for them until they returned them in case there is any plot or treachery in Yemen, on the understanding that no church of theirs would be demolished and no clergyman of theirs would be turned out and there would be no interference in their religion until they bring something new or take usury.[1]

And when he ﷺ sent Mu'adh to Yemen, he ordered him to take from every person who had reached the age of puberty one *Deenar* or its value in *Ma'afiri*, which are the garments of Yemen.[2] In this there is evidence that the form and quantity of the *Jizyah* are not fixed; rather it is in accordance with the needs of the Muslims and the situation of those from whom it is taken. And neither the Prophet ﷺ nor his Caliphs distinguished between the Arabs and the non-Arabs; he took it from the Magians of Hijr and they were Arabs. This was because every group among the Arabs followed the religion of the peoples who were next to them: The Arabs of Bahrain were Magians and Tanookh, Bahrah and Banu Taghlib were Christians; so the Prophet ﷺ did not consider their forefathers, nor when they embraced the religion of the People of the Scripture. And it has been authentically reported from him ﷺ that there were some among the Ansar whose sons had embraced Judaism after the Law of Moses had been abrogated and their fathers wished to force them to embrace Islam, then Allâh revealed:

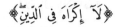

"There is no compulsion in religion."[3]

And the words of the Prophet ﷺ:

---

[1] Narrated by Abu Dawûd, on the authority of 'Abdullah Ibn 'Abbas ﷺ, it contains in its *Sanad* one Isma'eel Ibn 'Abdir-Rahman Al-Qurashi, of whom Yahya Ibn Ma'een said: "There is weakness in his *Hadeeth*." It also contains one Yûnus Ibn Bukair, of whom Ibn Hajr said: "He is honest, but he makes mistakes."

[2] Narrated by the compilers of the *'Sunan'* and by Ahmad, it was declared authentic by Ibn Hibban and Al-Hakim and Az-Zahabi confirmed this.

[3] *Sûrah Al-Baqarah* 2:256

«خُذْ مِنْ كُلِّ حَالِمٍ دِينَارًا»

"Take from every (male) person who has reached puberty one *Deenar*,"

is evidence that it is not taken from children or women. As for the version narrated in which it says:

«مِنْ كُلِّ حَالِمٍ أَوْ حَالِمَةٍ»

"(Take) from every person who has reached the age of puberty, both male and female."

It does not have a complete chain of narrators connected to the Prophet ﷺ; its chain is broken and this addition was not mentioned by the other narrators; possibly it is from the explanatory notes of one of them.

---------- ❖ ❖ ❖ ----------

Chapter

Regarding His ﷺ Guidance in Dealing With the Disbelievers and the Hypocrites – From the Start of His Mission Until He Met Allâh, the Almighty, the All-Powerful

The first thing which his Lord, Most Blessed, Most High revealed to him was to recite in the Name of his Lord, Who created him and that was the start of his Prophethood. Then it was revealed to him:

"O you (Muhammad ﷺ) enveloped in garments! Arise and warn!"[1]

So He announced (his Prophethood) to him by the former Verses and sent him forth as a Messenger by the latter Verses. Then He commanded him to warn his close kin and he warned his people, then he warned those around them from among the Arabs, then he warned all of the Arabs without exception, then he warned all of mankind. He remained for thirteen years warning the people, without fighting and he was commanded to patiently persevere. Then it was permitted for him to migrate to Al-Madinah and then it was permitted for him to fight. After that, he was commanded to fight those who fought him. Then Allâh commanded him to make war on the polytheists until all and every kind of worship was for Allâh Alone.

---

[1] *Sûrah Al-Muddaththir* 74:1-2

After the Command came to undertake *Jihad*, the disbelievers who were with the Prophet ﷺ in Al-Madinah were of three kinds: (i) Those with whom there was a peace treaty, (ii) those with whom they were at war and (iii) those who were living under Muslim protection. As regards to those who had treaties with the Muslims, Allâh commanded his Messenger ﷺ to implement them so long as they abided by them, but that if he feared that they would act falsely, to repudiate the treaty with them and He commanded him to fight against anyone who broke their covenant and *Bara'ah* (*Sûrah At-Tawbah* 9:1) was revealed, making clear the three groups and commanding him to fight the People of the Scripture until they agree to pay the *Jizyah*; and He commanded him to undertake *Jihad* against the disbelievers and the hypocrites. He made *Jihad* against the disbelievers with the sword and against the hypocrites by argument. And He commanded him to declare himself free from the covenants with the disbelievers and He declared them (the disbelievers) to be of three types: (i) Those whom Allâh had commanded him to fight – and they were those who had broken their covenants, (ii) those who had a covenant lasting for a fixed period of time and who had not violated it; Allâh commanded him to complete the covenants with them until they expired and (iii) those who had an unlimited covenant or who had no covenant and did not make war against him ﷺ. Allâh commanded him to give a respite to such people lasting for four months, then once they had passed, to fight them – and they are the months mentioned in the Words of Allâh:

$$﴿فَإِذَا ٱنسَلَخَ ٱلۡأَشۡهُرُ ٱلۡحُرُمُ﴾$$

"Then when the Sacred Months (the 1st, 7th, 11th, and 12th months of the Islamic calendar) have passed."[1]

And the first day of it was the tenth of Dhul Hijjah, *Yawm Al-Adhan*[2] and the last day of it was the tenth of Rabe' Al-Akhar. And they are not the four months mentioned in the Words of Allâh, Most High:

$$﴿مِنۡهَآ أَرۡبَعَةٌ حُرُمٌ﴾$$

---

[1] *Sûrah At-Tawbah* 9:6
[2] *Yawm Al-Adhan*: The day on which the call to *Hajj* is made.

"Of them four are Sacred (i.e. the 1st, the 7th, the 11th and the 12th months of the Islamic calendar)."[1]

And he did not make the polytheists travel during them, because that was not possible, since they are not consecutive months and Allâh only gave them a respite of four months. After the passing of these four months, Allâh commanded him 鐢 to fight them so he fought those who had violated their covenants and gave a respite of four months to those without any covenant and those with an unlimited covenant. And Allâh commanded him 鐢 to complete the duration of the covenant of those who had fulfilled their agreements and all of them embraced Islam and they did not remain disbelievers until the end of the time period. For those living under the protection of the Muslims state (*Dhimmis*), he imposed upon them the *Jizyah*. After *Bara'ah* was revealed, the disbelievers continued as three types: (i) Those who were at war, (ii) those who had covenants and (iii) those who lived under Muslim protection. Then those who had covenants became Muslims and they became two groups: (i) Those who were at war with the Muslims and (ii) those who lived under Muslim protection, which meant that the people living in the land were of three types: (i) Muslims (ii) those granted safety and security by the Prophet 鐢 and (iii) those who were in fear and at war with him 鐢.

As for the Prophet's treatment of the hypocrites, he was commanded to accept their declarations and to make *Jihad* against them with argument and evidence; and he was commanded to avoid them, to speak harshly to them and to speak to them with words which would affect their hearts. And he was prohibited from offering funeral prayers over them or from standing at their gravesides (to supplicate for them) and he was informed (by Allâh) that it was the same whether he sought forgiveness for them or he did not, for Allâh will not forgive them.

---

[1] *Sûrah At-Tawbah* 9:36

Chapter

As for his conduct towards his Companions 🌸, he was commanded to be patient with those who called upon their Lord morning and evening seeking His Countenance and not to let his eyes overlook them[1] and to pardon them, seek forgiveness for them, consult them[2] and pray for them.[3] And He commanded him to cut off relations with those who disobey him and stay away from him, until they repented to Allâh, as he did with the three who were left behind. And He commanded him to implement the legal punishments upon them, regardless of whether they were eminent or humble.

And He commanded him to repel his enemies among the devils from mankind by that which is better and to answer a bad deed with a good deed and to respond to ignorance with gentleness and to injustice with pardon and to cutting off relations by mending them and He informed him that if he did that, his enemy would become as though he was a close friend.[4]

And He commanded him to repel his enemies among the devils from the *Jinn* by seeking protection with Allâh from them; and He combined both of the Commands for him in three places in the Qur'ân: (ii) *Sûrah Al-A'raf*, (ii) *Sûrah Al-Mu'minûn* and (iii) *Sûrah Fussilat*. And He listed for him in the Verse in *Sûrah Al-A'raf* all noble traits of character, for the one placed in authority over the Muslims has three ways with regard to those in his charge: There are rights upon them which they must discharge and there are commands which he orders them to implement and it is inevitable that there will

---

[1] See *Sûrah Al-Kahf* 18:28.
[2] See *Sûrah Âl 'Imrân* 3:159.
[3] See *Sûrah At-Tawbah* 9:103.
[4] See *Sûrah Fussilat* 41:34.

be remiss or neglectful with regard His rights upon them. So he was commanded to take from the obligations which were upon them those things which they did willingly and which were easy for them and which were not a hardship for them and that is the (aforementioned) pardon. And Allâh commanded him to order them to observe *Al-'Urf* (kindness) – and that is what is understood by the rational mind and the sound *Fitrah*[1] – and not *Al-'Unf* (harshness). And he was commanded to respond to their ignorance with avoidance. This was his manner of conduct towards those who live in the earth – both the humans and the jinn among them and the Believers and the disbelievers among them.

---

[1] *Fitrah*: The innate sense of what is true and right.

Chapter

Regarding the Conduct of His ﷺ Battles

The first military expedition sent out by the Prophet ﷺ was undertaken by Hamzah Ibn 'Abdil Muttalib ؓ in the month of Ramadan, at the end of the seventh month after the migration to Al-Madinah. He sent him out with thirty men picked from the *Muhajirûn* to attack a caravan belonging to Quraish which was returning from Ash-Sham in which Abu Jahl was present with three hundred men. When they met, Majdi Ibn 'Amr Al-Juhani interceded between them, for he was friendly towards both sides.

Then the Prophet ﷺ sent 'Ubaidah Ibn Al-Harith ؓ to a place called Batn Rabigh in the month of Shawwal, with sixty of the *Muhajirûn* and they encountered Abu Sufyan who had two hundred men with him. An exchange of arrow shooting took place between them, but swords were not drawn; and the first one to shoot an arrow in Allâh's Cause was Sa'd Ibn Abi Waqqas ؓ. Ibn Ishaq placed this expedition chronologically before that of Hamzah ؓ.

After that, he ﷺ sent out Sa'd bin Abi Waqqas ؓ to Al-Kharrar, in the month of Dhul Qa'dah after nine months with twenty riders to attack a caravan belonging to Quraish, but they found that the caravan had passed by the day before.

Then he himself took part in the expedition of Abwa', which was the first expedition in which he personally took part. He went out with men picked from the *Muhajirûn* to attack a caravan belonging to Quraish, but he did not find it.

Then he ﷺ took part in the expedition of Buwat in the month of Rabee' Al-Awwal with two hundred of his Companions ◈ to attack a caravan belonging to Quraish until they reached Buwat, but they did not find it, so they returned.

Then he went out after thirteen months to find Kurz Ibn Jabir who had raided the pastures of Al-Madinah; he searched for him until they reached a valley known as Safawan, which was in the area of Badr, but he missed Kurz.

Then he ﷺ went out after sixteen months with a hundred and fifty of the *Muhajirûn* intending to attack a caravan belonging to Quraish which was heading towards Ash-Sham. He reached Dhul 'Asheerah, but found that it had already passed him and it was this caravan which he had gone out in search for when it was on its way back and it was the cause of the Battle of Badr.

Then he sent 'Abdullah Ibn Jahsh ◈ to Nakhlah with twelve men from among the *Muhajirûn*, each two of them mounted on one camel; they reached the middle of Nakhlah, where they lay in wait for a caravan belonging to Quraish. Sa'd Ibn Abi Waqqas and 'Utbah Ibn Ghazwan ◈ had lost their camel and fallen behind. The expedition proceeded to the middle of Nakhlah and the caravan of Quraish passed by them. They said: "We are now at the end of the month of Rajab (which was considered a sacred month wherein fighting was forbidden) and if we leave them this night, they will enter the Sacred Precincts (of Makkah)." Then they agreed to attack them and one of them fired at 'Amr Ibn Al-Hadrami and killed him. They took 'Uthman Ibn Al-Mugheerah and Al-Hakam Ibn Keesan prisoner and Nawfal Ibn Al-Mugheerah escaped. They set aside the *Khumus* – and it was the first *Khumus* in Islam. The Messenger of Allâh ﷺ disapproved of what they had done and Quraish strongly criticized it, claiming to have found a basis to censure the Muslims, saying: "Muhammad has declared permissible fighting in the forbidden months." This became very hard upon the Muslims, then Allâh revealed:

$$﴿ يَسْأَلُونَكَ عَنِ ٱلشَّهْرِ ٱلْحَرَامِ قِتَالٍ فِيهِ ﴾$$

"They ask you concerning fighting in the Sacred Months (i.e.

1st, 7th, 11th and 12th months of the Islamic calendar."[1]

Allâh, Most Glorified says: What they have done may be serious, but the sins of which you are guilty, such as disbelief, preventing people from following the Way of Allâh and from making pilgrimage to His House, expelling the Muslims who were residents of Makkah from their homes, the *Shirk* which you practise and the *Fitnah* which has resulted from your actions is a greater sin in Allâh's Sight. And most of the scholars have explained the word *Fitnah* here as meaning *Shirk*; and the truth of it is the *Shirk* which its owner calls to and he punishes those who are not put to trial by it (i.e. those who do not accept it). This is why it will be said to them in the Fire:

$$﴿ذُوقُوا فِتْنَتَكُمْ﴾$$

"Taste you your trial (punishment, i.e. burning)!"[2]

'Abdullah Ibn 'Abbas ﷺ said: "(It means) your denial." And the truth of it is that it means: Taste the end result of your *Fitnah*, such as in His Words:

$$﴿ذُوقُوا مَا كُنتُمْ تَكْسِبُونَ﴾$$

"Taste what you used to earn!"[3]

And similar to it is the Saying of Allâh:

$$﴿إِنَّ ٱلَّذِينَ فَتَنُوا ٱلْمُؤْمِنِينَ وَٱلْمُؤْمِنَٰتِ﴾$$

"Verily, those who put into trial the believing men and believing women,"[4]

which was explained as meaning the burning of the Believers by fire, but the wording is more general and the reality of it is: They tortured the Believers, in order to turn them away from their Religion.

As for the *Fitnah* which is associated with Allâh, as in His Words:

$$﴿فَتَنَّا بَعْضَهُم بِبَعْضٍ﴾$$

---

[1] *Sûrah Al-Baqarah* 2:217
[2] *Sûrah Ad-Dhariyât* 51:14
[3] *Sûrah Az-Zumar* 39:24
[4] *Sûrah Al-Burûj* 85:10

"We have tried some of them with others."[1]

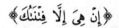

"It is only Your trial."[2]

And it is the trial by blessings and calamities; this is one type of *Fitnah* and the *Fitnah* of the polytheists is of another type altogether, as is the *Fitnah* of a Believer by his children, his wealth and his neighbour. And the *Fitnah* between the followers of Islam, such as the people involved in the incident of the camel and *Saffain* is still another type. And it is in this kind of *Fitnah* that the Messenger of Allâh ﷺ commanded us to avoid both parties.

And sometimes what might be meant by *Fitnah* is disobedience or sin, such as in the Words of Allâh:

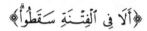

"Surely, they have fallen into trial."[3]

That is, they fell into the *Fitnah* of hypocrisy and they ran to it from the *Fitnah* of the daughters of Banu Al-Asfar[4] And what is meant is that Allâh, Most Glorified has judged between His followers and His enemies with justice and He has not deprived His followers of hope if they err due to misinterpretation or are deficient in any way that He will forgive them for what they have done because of their affirmation of Allâh's Oneness, their acts of obedience to Him and their migration to Al-Madinah.

---------- ❖ ❖ ❖ ----------

---

[1] *Sûrah Al-An'am* 6:53
[2] *Sûrah Al-A'raf* 7:155
[3] *Sûrah At-Tawbah* 9:50
[4] Banu Al-Asfar: The Sons of Rome, i.e. the Christians. This refers to those hypocrites who excused themselves from fighting in the Battle of Tabuk, by saying that they feared to do so because of the *Fitnah* of the women of Tabuk.

Chapter

Then in Ramadan of that year, news reached the Prophet ﷺ that a caravan was approaching from Ash-Sham and so he prepared a force to intercept it, but he did not equip it well because he left in haste with a little over three hundred men, including two horsemen and seventy camels, each of which carried two or three riders on it. A call for help (from the caravan) reached Makkah and they went out, as Allâh, Most High says:

$$﴿بَطَرًا وَرِئَآءَ ٱلنَّاسِ﴾$$

"Boastfully and to be seen of men."[1]

and Allâh joined them (in battle) without a mutual appointment, as He, Most High says:

$$﴿وَلَوْ تَوَاعَدتُّمْ لَٱخْتَلَفْتُمْ فِى ٱلْمِيعَٰدِ﴾$$

"Even if you had made a mutual appointment to meet, you would certainly have failed in the appointment."[2]

When the Messenger of Allâh ﷺ was informed of the departure of the troops from Makkah, he consulted his Companions ﷺ. The *Muhajirûn* spoke and they spoke well, then he consulted them again and they spoke, then he consulted them a third time and the *Ansar* realized that he meant them, so Sa'd Ibn Mu'adh ﷺ hastened forth and gave his famous speech and Al-Miqdad ﷺ gave his well known speech. The Messenger of Allâh ﷺ was pleased by what he heard from his Companions ﷺ and he said:

«سِيرُوا وَأَبْشِرُوا، فَإِنَّ اللهَ وَعَدَنِي إِحْدَى الطَّائِفَتَيْنِ، وَإِنِّي قَدْ رَأَيْتُ

---

[1] *Sûrah Al-Anfal* 8:47
[2] *Sûrah Al-Anfal* 8:42

مَصَارِعَ الْقَوْمِ»

"Go forth and rejoice, for Allâh has promised me one of two courses (either war booty or *Jihad* in His Cause) and I have seen the enemy lying prostrate."[1]

So he went forth to Badr and when the two sides came into each others' view, he stood up and raised his hands and sought victory from his Lord and the Muslims sought victory from Allâh and help from Him, then Allâh revealed to him:

﴿أَنِّي مُمِدُّكُم بِأَلۡفٖ مِّنَ ٱلۡمَلَٰٓئِكَةِ مُرۡدِفِينَ﴾

"I will help you with a thousand of the angels each behind the other (following one another) in succession."[2]

The Word (*Murdifeen*) was recited with *Kasrah* and also with *Fathah* and it was said that the meaning is that they (i.e. the angels) are behind you and it was also said that it means that they are one behind another, that they did not come all at one time. And if it was said: Here it is mentioned that they were a thousand and in *Sûrah Al-'Imrân* it says three thousand and five thousand, there are two opinions regarding this:

The First: That it (the Verse in *Sûrah Âl 'Imrân*) refers to the day of the Battle of Uhud and that it is dependent up a condition which was not met, and so the Help was not forthcoming.

The Second: That it refers to the day of the Battle of Badr and the evidence is that the context proves it, as in His Words:

﴿وَلَقَدۡ نَصَرَكُمُ ٱللَّهُ بِبَدۡرٖ وَأَنتُمۡ أَذِلَّةٞ فَٱتَّقُواْ ٱللَّهَ لَعَلَّكُمۡ تَشۡكُرُونَ ۝ إِذۡ تَقُولُ لِلۡمُؤۡمِنِينَ أَلَن يَكۡفِيَكُمۡ﴾

"And Allâh has already made you victorious at Badr, when you were a weak little force. So fear Allâh much that you may be grateful. (Remember) when you (Muhammad ﷺ) said to the believers, "Is it not enough for you.""

---

[1] Narrated by Ibn Hisham without any *Sanad*.
[2] *Sûrah Al-Anfal* 8:9

Up to His Words:

$$\text{﴿وَمَا جَعَلَهُ ٱللَّهُ إِلَّا بُشْرَىٰ لَكُمْ وَلِتَطْمَئِنَّ قُلُوبُكُم بِهِۦۚ﴾}$$

"Allâh made it not but as a message of good news for you and as an assurance to your hearts."[1]

So when they sought His Help, He supported them with a thousand angels, then three, then five and this succession of Help had a better effect on them and strengthened them more and was more pleasing to them.

Those who supported the first opinion said: The context of the story is that of Uhud and mention of Badr was only included in it as a remonstrance, for He reminded them of His Blessing upon them in Badr, then He returned to the story of Uhud and He informed them of the words of His Messenger to them:

"Is it not enough for you".[2]

Then He promised them that if they patiently persevered and were pious and God-fearing, He would help them with five thousand and this is from the speech of His Messenger ﷺ, while the Speech concerning the Help extended to them in Badr is that of Him, Most High and it is general, while the other was dependent upon a condition being fulfilled. And the story told in *Sûrah Âl 'Imran* concerns the Battle of Uhud and is told in great detail and at great length and it is explained by His Words:

$$\text{﴿وَيَأْتُوكُم مِّن فَوْرِهِمْ هَٰذَا﴾}$$

"And the enemy comes rushing at you."[3]

Mujahid said: "It is the day of the Battle of Uhud." And this necessitates that the Help was on that day, so it is not correct to say that the Help was on the day of the Battle of Badr and that the enemy

---

[1] *Sûrah Âl 'Imrân* 3:132-135

[2] *Sûrah Al 'Imrân* 3:124

[3] *Sûrah Âl 'Imrân* 3:125

came rushing down on them on the day of the Battle of Uhud.

When they (i.e. Quraish) had decided to go out, they remembered the war between them and Banu Kinanah and *Iblees* appeared to them in the form of Suraqah Ibn Malik and said:

$$﴿لَا غَالِبَ لَكُمُ ٱلْيَوْمَ مِنَ ٱلنَّاسِ وَإِنِّ جَارٌ لَّكُمْ﴾$$

"No one of mankind can overcome you this day (of the battle of Badr) and verily, I am your neighbour (for every help)."[1]

Against the possibility that Kinanah should bring you something which you detest (i.e. defeat)." Then when they had prepared to fight and he saw that the Army of Allâh had come down from the heaven, he turned upon his heels and fled. They said: "Where are you going, O, Suraqah? Did you not say that you are our neighbour?" He said: "I see what you do not see; I fear Allâh and Allâh is Severe in punishment." And in his saying: "I see what you do not see" he spoke the truth, but in his saying: "I fear Allâh" he lied. It was said that he feared that he would be killed with them and that is more obvious. And when the hypocrites and those in whose hearts was a disease saw the small number of the Party of Allâh and the large number of His enemies, they thought that victory would be achieved through weight of numbers and they said: {These people are deceived by their Religion},[2] Allâh, Most Glorified informed the Muslims that victory is achieved by *Tawakkul* and not by strength of numbers and that He is Almighty and cannot be defeated and that He is Most Wise and He helps those who deserve, even though they are weak.

The Messenger of Allâh concluded the matter of Badr and the captives in Shawwal, then he ﷺ set off seven days after that to make war on Banu Sulaim and he reached a well known as Al-Kudr and stayed there for three days and then he departed.

When the fleeing polytheists reached Makkah, Abu Sufyan vowed that water should not touch his head until he did battle with the Messenger of Allâh ﷺ and so he journeyed with two hundred riders until he reached the outskirts of Al-Madinah and he stayed for a

---

[1] *Sûrah Al-Anfal* 8:48
[2] *Sûrah Al-Anfal* 8:49

night with Salam Ibn Al-Mishkam (a Jew) and he gave him secret information about the people, then in the morning, he cut the small date palms and killed a man from among the Ansar and an ally of his, then the Messenger of Allâh ﷺ set out in search of him, but he missed him. The disbelievers had discarded a great deal of *Saweeq*[1] in order to lighten their load in a place called Qarqarah Al-Kudr and because of this, the expedition was known as the Expedition of *Saweeq*.

After that, the Prophet ﷺ made war against Najd, making for Ghatafan; he stayed there for the whole of the month of Safar in the third year of the *Hijrah* and he did not encounter any fighting. Then he returned, intending to attack Quraish and he reached Buharan, a mine in the Hijaz, but he did not encounter any fighting. There he remained for the month of Rabee' Al-Akhar and Jumad Al-Awwal, after which he departed.

After that, he made war against Banu Qainuqa', then he killed Ka'b Ibn Al-Ashraf and he was given permission to kill any of the Jews found there due to their breaking of the covenant and their waging war against Allâh and His Messenger ﷺ.

When Allâh killed the most eminent personages of Quraish in Badr and Abu Sufyan became their leader, he gathered the hosts and set out with them towards Al-Madinah and he stopped near Mount Uhud and this is where the well known Battle of Uhud took place. On that day, the Prophet ﷺ inspected the young men and he sent back those who were too young to fight, and they included 'Abdullah Ibn 'Umar, Usamah, Zaid Ibn Thabit and 'Arabah ﷺ but he permitted those of them whom he considered able to fight, including Samurah Ibn Jundub and Rafi' Ibn Khadeej ﷺ and they were both fifteen years of age. It was said: He permitted those whom he permitted due to their having reached adulthood and they declared the minimum age for adulthood to be fifteen years. Another group said that he permitted them to fight due to their ability to do so and that there is not effect from adulthood or its absence in this matter. And they said that in one narration of the *Hadeeth* of 'Abdullah Ibn 'Umar ﷺ, he

---

[1] *Saweeq*: A kind of porridge made from wheat or barley.

said: "When he saw that I was able, he permitted me (to fight)."[1]

Then the story of Al-Usairim was mentioned and the words of Abu Sufyan on the mountain, which were narrated by Al-Bukhari in his *'Saheeh'*, on the authority of Al-Bara' Ibn 'Azib 🙏, who said: "Abu Sufyan looked down and said: "Is Muhammad among you?" The Prophet 🕌 said to his Companions 🙏: "Do not answer him." Then he said: "Is Ibn Abi Qahafah (i.e. Abu Bakr) among you?" The Prophet 🕌 said:

$$«لَا تُجِيبُوهُ»$$

"Do not answer him."

Then he asked: "Is 'Umar Ibn Al-Khattab among you?" The Messenger of Allâh 🕌 said: "Do not answer him." Then he said: "These people have been killed, for if they were alive, they would have answered." At this, 'Umar 🙏 unable to control himself said: "You have lied, oh, enemy of Allâh! Allâh has maintained what you hate." Abu Sufyan answered: *"Hail Hubal! Hail Hubail!"* The Prophet 🕌 said: "Answer him." They said: "What shall we say?" He 🕌 said: "Say: "Allâh is Most High and Most Powerful." He said: "We have Al-'Uzza, but you do not have any 'Uzza." The Prophet 🕌 said: "Answer him." They said: "What shall we say?" He 🕌 said:

$$«قُولُوا: اللهُ مَوْلَانَا وَلَا مَوْلَى لَكُمْ»$$

"Say: Allâh is our Protector and you have no protector."

Abu Sufyan said: "Today is vengeance for the Day of Badr; and war is a matter of alternate success." 'Umar 🙏 answered him, saying: "They are not the same; our dead are in Paradise and your dead are in the Fire." Then Abu Sufyan said: "You will find that your dead have been

---

[1] What has been narrated by Al-Bukhari and Muslim, the compilers of the *'Sunan'* and Ahmad, on the authority of 'Abdullah Ibn 'Umar 🙏 contradicts this, for they reported that he said: "The Messenger of Allâh 🕌 inspected me on the Day of Uhud, when I was fourteen years of age, but he did not permit me (to fight), and he inspected me on the Day of Al-Khandaq (the Battle of the Trench) and at that time, I was fifteen years of age and he permitted me (to fight).

mutilated. I did not order it, but I am not sorry."[1] Here we see that the Prophet ﷺ ordered his Companions ﷺ to answer Abu Sufyan when he spoke proudly of his deity and his *Shirk*, in order to extol the Oneness of Allâh and to declare the Might of the God of the Muslims; but he did not order them to answer him, or he prohibited them from doing so when Abu Sufyan asked: "Is Muhammad among you?" etc. This was because, the injury they had suffered in the Battle of Badr had not yet healed and the fire of their anger still burned. But when he said (to his soldiers): "You have killed them," 'Umar ﷺ was unable to restrain his anger and he said: "You have lied, oh, enemy of Allâh!" In this reply there was courage and the desire to show the enemy at that time something which would acquaint them with the Muslims' bravery and that he and his people were worthy foes, who were not afraid. And his answer caused anger to the enemy and sapped their resolve which it would not have done had they answered him when he asked about them. So ignoring the first question ("Is Muhammad among you" etc.) was better and answering his next statement ("You have killed them") was best. Also not answering him was an affront to him; then when he had convinced himself that they were dead and he was filled with pride and satisfaction, 'Umar's reply caused insult and humiliation to him. And in answering him, 'Umar ﷺ had not disobeyed the Prophet's injunction: "Do not answer him."[2]

---

[1] Narrated by Al-Bukhari, on the authority of Al-Bara' Ibn 'Azib ﷺ and by Ahmad, on the authority of 'Abdullah Ibn 'Abbas ﷺ.

[2] This is because the Prophet ﷺ only forbade the Companions ﷺ from answering his questions: "Is Muhammad among you" etc. not from answering Abu Sufyan's boasting and taunts.

Regarding the Rulings Derived From This Battle

These include the fact that *Jihad* is obligatory upon one who sets out to do it; therefore whoever donned his coat of mail may not return (without fighting the enemy).

Also, it is not incumbent upon the Muslims to leave their homes and go out to meet the enemy, if they strike at them in their homes. Another benefit derived from this story is that it is not permissible for those youths who do not possess the ability to fight to do so. Likewise, it is permissible for women to fight and it is permissible to seek their help in *Jihad* and that it is permissible to go into the midst of the enemy, as Anas Ibn An-Nadr and others did. Also, if the *Imam* is injured, he may lead them in prayer while sitting and they should sit behind him. Another benefit is that asking Allâh to be martyred and hoping for it – as Ibn Jahsh ﷺ did – is not prohibited. Also, if a Muslim kills himself, he will be one of the inhabitants of the Fire, like Quzman. Another benefit derived is that the martyr should not be washed, nor should he be prayed over, nor should he be shrouded except in the garments he is wearing, unless they have been looted from him, in which case, he may be shrouded in something else. Also, if he was in a state of ritual impurity (*Janabah*) when he died, he must be washed, as in the case of Hanzalah ﷺ. It is also derived from this story that the martyrs are buried in the place where they died, in accordance with his order to return the dead to them.[1] And it is

---

[1] Narrated by Ahmad, on the authority of Jabir Ibn 'Abdillah ﷺ.

permissible to bury two or three in one grave.[1] Scholars have differed regarding the order of the Prophet ﷺ to bury the martyrs of Uhud in their clothes – is it something recommended, or is it an obligation? The latter would appear to be more correct. Another benefit derived from the story is that one who is excused from fighting, such as a lame person may perform *Jihad*. And if the Muslims kill a Muslim, thinking him to be a disbeliever, his blood money (*Diyah*) is paid from the Muslim Treasury (*Bait Al-Mal*), because the Prophet ﷺ wanted to pay the blood money for Abu Huzaifah Ibn Al-Yaman ؤ.

As for the wisdoms derived from this battle, Allâh, Most Glorified has indicated the major ones in *Sûrah Âl 'Imrân* in His Words:

﴿وَإِذْ غَدَوْتَ مِنْ أَهْلِكَ﴾

"And (remember) when you (Muhammad ﷺ) left your household in the morning,"[2]

up to the completion of sixty Verses.

Another wisdom is that it informed them of the consequences of disobedience, faintheartedness and disputing with one another, in order that they might be vigilant and watchful against the causes of humiliation and that the Wisdom of Allâh dictates that the Messengers and their followers are sometimes granted victory and at other times, victory is granted against them, but the end result is for them. This is because, if they were always victorious, the Believer and others would join with them and they would be indistinguishable from each other and if other than they were always to achieve victory, the aim of sending the Messenger ﷺ would not be accomplished.

Allâh, Most High says:

﴿مَّا كَانَ ٱللَّهُ لِيَذَرَ ٱلْمُؤْمِنِينَ عَلَىٰ مَآ أَنتُمْ عَلَيْهِ حَتَّىٰ يَمِيزَ ٱلْخَبِيثَ مِنَ ٱلطَّيِّبِ﴾

---

[1] Narrated by Al-Bukhari and the compilers of the '*Sunan*', on the authority of Jabir Ibn 'Abdillah ؤ.

[2] *Sûrah Âl 'Imrân* 3:121

"Allâh will not leave the believers in the state in which you are now, until He distinguishes the wicked from the good."[1]

That is, Allâh will not leave you in this state of the Believers being indistinguishable from the hypocrites until he distinguishes between them.

$$﴿وَمَا كَانَ اللَّهُ لِيُطْلِعَكُمْ عَلَى الْغَيْبِ﴾$$

"Nor will Allâh disclose to you the secrets of the *Ghaib* (Unseen),"

by which He distinguishes between them; rather, it is the Will of Him, Most Glorified that He distinguish between you in a manner that is witnessed by many. And His Words:

$$﴿وَلَكِنَّ اللَّهَ يَجْتَبِي مِن رُّسُلِهِ مَن يَشَاءُ﴾$$

"But Allâh chooses of His Messengers whom He wills,"

are an exception to His negation of having granted knowledge of the unseen to anyone, i.e. except the Messengers ﷺ, for He informs them of what He wills from the Unseen, as mentioned in *Sûrah Al-Jinn*, so your success will come through belief in the Unseen of which He has informed His Messengers ﷺ, for if you believe in it and fear Allâh, you will have the greatest of rewards.

And among them is the deduction that worship of Allâh by His *Awliya'* should be both in prosperity and in adversity, for if they are firm in practising obedience to Allâh by doing both the things which they like and the things which they dislike, then they are not like those who worship Him only when circumstances are good.

Also, if He granted them victory at all times, they would be as they would if He granted them (unlimited) sustenance,[2] for He disposes of their affairs in accordance with His Wisdom and He is All-knowing and All-seeing. Also, If they acknowledge that they have no power and no strength except in Him, they will be entitled to victory, for victory cannot be achieved without humility, as Allâh, Most High says:

---

[1] *Sûrah Âl 'Imrân* 3:179

[2] See *Sûrah Ash-Shûra* 42:27.

$$\left\{ وَلَقَدْ نَصَرَكُمُ ٱللَّهُ بِبَدْرٍ وَأَنتُمْ أَذِلَّةٌ \right\}$$

"And Allâh has already made you victorious at Badr, when you were a weak little force."[1]

And:

$$\left\{ وَيَوْمَ حُنَيْنٍ إِذْ أَعْجَبَتْكُمْ كَثْرَتُكُمْ \right\}$$

"And on the day of Hunain (battle) when you rejoiced at your great number,".[2]

And also that He has prepared for His slaves abodes in the Hereafter which cannot be attained by (righteous) deeds alone, nor will they attain them except by being subjected to trials and He has ordained for them the means (trials) to achieve Paradise, just as He granted them success in performing righteous deeds.

Also, perpetual protection, victory and wealth give rise to dependence on the life of this world and hinder the souls and hold them back from the Path of Allâh. So if Allâh wants to honour a slave, He ordains trials for him, which is a cure for this sickness.

Likewise, in Allâh's Sight, martyrdom is one of the highest ranks and He, Most Glorified loves to take martyrs from among His *Awliya'*.

Also, when He, Most Glorified wants to destroy His enemies, He ordains for them the means due to which they deserve to be destroyed, such as their transgression, and the extreme harm which they visited upon His *Awliya'* and thereby He purifies His *Awliya'* of their sins and it becomes one of the causes of the destruction of Allâh's enemies. And He, Most Glorified mentioned that in His Words:

$$\left\{ وَلَا تَهِنُوا وَلَا تَحْزَنُوا \right\}$$

"So do not become weak (against your enemy), nor be sad,"[3]

$$\left\{ وَيَمْحَقَ ٱلْكَٰفِرِينَ \right\}$$

"And destroy the disbelievers."

[1] *Sûrah Âl 'Imrân* 3:123
[2] *Sûrah At-Tawbah*: 9:25
[3] *Sûrah Âl 'Imrân* 3:139-142

So Allâh has combined encouragement for them and the best words of consolation with mention of the great wisdoms which necessitated the victory of the disbelievers, saying:

$$﴿إِن يَمْسَسْكُمْ قَرْحٌ فَقَدْ مَسَّ ٱلْقَوْمَ قَرْحٌ مِّثْلُهُۥ﴾$$

"If a wound (or killing) has touched you, be assured a similar wound (and killing) has touched the others (disbelievers)."[1]

That is: Why are you sad and disheartened at this, when they have been visited by the same thing in the path of Satan? Then He informed them that He gives these days to men by turn, because they are material things which He divides between His *Awliya'* and His enemies in the life of this world, as opposed to the life of the Hereafter, then He mentioned another wisdom, which is that He distinguishes thereby between Believer and the hypocrite and He gives them knowledge of martyrdom, because mere knowledge of the unseen does not result in reward or punishment. Then He mentioned another wisdom, which is that He takes the martyrs from them. And His Words:

$$﴿وَٱللَّهُ لَا يُحِبُّ ٱلظَّـٰلِمِينَ﴾$$

"And Allâh loves not the *Zalimûn* (polytheists and wrong-doers)."

Are a gentle reminder that He did not take martyrs from those who deserted His Prophet ﷺ on the Day of Uhud, because He does not love them. Then He mentioned another wisdom, which is the purification of the Believers from their sins and also from the hypocrites (since they became known thereby). Then He mentioned another wisdom and that is the destruction of the disbelievers. Then He rejected their (the Muslims') belief that they might enter Paradise without *Jihad* and patient perseverance. And His Words:

$$﴿وَلَمَّا يَعْلَمِ ٱللَّهُ ٱلَّذِينَ جَـٰهَدُواْ مِنكُمْ﴾$$

"Before Allâh tests those of you who fought (in His Cause)."[2]

---

[1] *Sûrah Âl 'Imrân* 3:140
[2] *Sûrah Âl 'Imrân* 3:142

That is: When you have not performed *Jihad*, for the Reward of Allâh is given for what we do. Then He censured them for their flight from something which they had desired (i.e. martyrdom). Another wisdom is that the Battle of Uhud was a forewarning of the death of the Messenger of Allâh ﷺ. And the thankful ones are those who realized the value of the Blessing (bestowed upon them) and remained firm upon it when the Messenger of Allâh ﷺ died and He made the end result in their favour. Then He informed them that He Has appointed a term for every soul and then He informed them that many of the Prophets were killed and many of those who followed them were killed along with them, but those who remained of them did not become disheartened, or (it was said that it means:) those who were killed did not become disheartened at the time of their death. And the truth is that it carries both meanings. Then He, Most Glorified informed them of the words used by the Prophets and their peoples when they sought help from Allâh, including their acknowledgement (of their weakness), their repentance and seeking of forgiveness and their request to Him to make their feet firm and grant them victory over their enemies; He said:

$$﴿وَمَا كَانَ قَوْلَهُمْ إِلَّآ أَن قَالُوا۟ رَبَّنَا ٱغْفِرْ لَنَا ذُنُوبَنَا وَإِسْرَافَنَا فِىٓ أَمْرِنَا وَثَبِّتْ أَقْدَامَنَا وَٱنصُرْنَا عَلَى ٱلْقَوْمِ ٱلْكَٰفِرِينَ﴾$$

"And they said nothing but: "Our Lord! Forgive us our sins and our transgressions (in keeping our duties to You), establish our feet firmly, and give us victory over the disbelieving folk."[1]

They asked Him for forgiveness for their sins and to make their feet firm and grant them victory when they came to know that their enemies were only victorious over them due to their sins and that Satan seeks to cause them to backslide them and thus to defeat them and that they are of two types: Dereliction of obligations or exceeding the limits – and that victory is conditional upon obedience to Allâh:

$$﴿قَالُوا۟ رَبَّنَا ٱغْفِرْ لَنَا ذُنُوبَنَا وَإِسْرَافَنَا فِىٓ أَمْرِنَا﴾$$

"Our Lord! Forgive us our sins and our transgressions (in

---

[1] *Sûrah Âl 'Imrân* 3:147

keeping our duties to You)."

Then they knew that if He, Most Glorified, Most High did not make their feet firm and help them, they would not be able to do that. They asked Him for that Which is in His Hand and they fulfilled both of the conditions necessary for their supplications to be answered: (i) Affirming Allâh's Oneness and having recourse to Him and (ii) removing that which prevents the achievement of His Help, which is the commission of sins and acts of extravagance. Then Allâh, Most Glorified warned them against obedience to the enemy and that if they did so, they would be losers in this world and in the Hereafter. And in it there is a reference to the hypocrites who obeyed the polytheists when they were victorious over the Muslims on the Day of Uhud. Then He, Most Glorified informed them that He is the Protector of the Believers and the Best of helpers and whoever takes Him as a Protector, he will be helped. Then He informed them that He will cast terror into the hearts of their enemies which will prevent them from overcoming them and that is because of their *Shirk* and the level of fear is commensurate with the degree of *Shirk*, while the Believer who does not mix his faith with *Shirk* will have security and guidance.

Then He informed them of the truth of His Promise of Help and that if they had remained steadfast in obedience, His Help would have continued, but that they lost the protection given them due to their obedience and so they lost His Support and that He caused them to flee from their enemies as a trial for them and to let them know the punishment for disobedience. Then He informed them that He had pardoned them after that. Al-Hasan was asked: "How could they be pardoned after the disbelievers had overcome them?" He said: "If it had not been for His Pardon, they would have been annihilated, but because of His Pardon, the enemy were repelled from them after they had gathered to exterminate them. Then He mentioned their condition at the time they fled, how they fled wildly, intent upon (naught but) flight, or climbing the mountain, without even sparing a glance for their Prophet ﷺ and his Companions ﷺ and the Messenger ﷺ was in their rear calling them back: "To me, O, slaves of Allâh! I am the Messenger of Allâh!" And so He recompensed them for this flight with one affliction after another: The affliction of flight and the affliction of Satan's shout that Muhammad ﷺ had been killed. It was also said that it means: Allâh recompensed you with an affliction due to the affliction you imposed upon His Messenger ﷺ by your flight. But the first opinion is more apparent for a number of reasons:

The First: That His Words:

$$﴿ لِكَيْلَا تَحْزَنُوا عَلَى مَا فَاتَكُمْ ﴾$$

"To teach you not to grieve for that which had escaped you,"[1]

up to the end of the Verse – to point out to them the wisdom behind this affliction, which was that He made them forget the sadness caused to them by the victory which had been lost and the defeat inflicted upon them. And this only occurs when one affliction is followed by another.

The Second: That it agrees with the facts, because the affliction of losing the war booty occurred and then the affliction of the rout, then the affliction of injury and death, then hearing that the Prophet ﷺ had been killed, then the enemy's ascent of the mountain. And it does not mean that they suffered only two afflictions, but that they suffered one affliction after another, until their trial was complete.

The Third: That His Saying:

$$﴿ غَمًّا ﴾$$

Means that it was the result of the recompense, not that it was the cause of it. And that means: He recompensed you with an affliction connected to (another) affliction as a requital for their flight, their abandonment of their Prophet ﷺ, their failure to respond to his call, their disobedience to his command to remain at their posts, their disputing and their faintheartedness – and each one of these things was the cause of an affliction specific to it. And it was from His Kindness towards them that these things they did were a result of their natures which they cannot control which are an obstacle to them attaining constant support, so He decreed for them the means

---

[1] *Sûrah Âl 'Imrân* 3:153

which He brought out from power to action and (evil) consequences were the outcome of that, so that they realized repentance was one of them, as was being on their guard against such things and repelling them with their opposites is an obligation: And it may be that a body is made healthy by diseases.

Then Allâh, Most Glorified showed Mercy to them and removed from them the affliction by the drowsiness which He sent down to them; and in war, that is a sign of victory, as it was sent down in the Battle of Badr. And He informed them that anyone who was not affected by it was concerned only with himself and not his Religion, or his Prophet or his companions and that they:

﴿يَظُنُّونَ بِاللَّهِ غَيْرَ الْحَقِّ ظَنَّ الْجَاهِلِيَّةِ﴾

"And thought wrongly of Allâh — the thought of ignorance."[1]

And this belief was explained as their belief that Allâh, Most Glorified does not help His Messenger and that his Religion will disappear. And it was explained as meaning that they thought that what had befallen them was not from Allâh's *Qadar*, nor was there any wisdom behind it. It was also explained as being a denial of wisdom, a denial of *Qadar* and a denial that Allâh's Religion will succeed. And this bad belief was the belief of the disbelievers and the hypocrites mentioned in *Sûrah Al-Fath* (48:6) And this belief was only described as a bad and ignorant belief because it entails thinking of Allâh that which is not befitting to Him, His Attributes and Names, His Wisdom, His praise, His Oneness in matters of Lordship and worship and His Truthfulness in fulfilling His Promises. And whoever believed that He would not make the Religion of his Messenger successful (over all others) and that He would cause falsehood to triumph permanently over truth, causing the truth thereby to disappear completely and not to reappear thereafter has believed evil of Allâh and attributed to Him things unbefitting His Perfection and His Divine Attributes. And whoever denied that this was from His *Qadar* does not know Him, nor does he know His Dominion. And likewise, whoever denied the wisdom of it

---

[1] *Sûrah Âl 'Imrân* 3:154

which demands praise and thanks to Allâh, but rather, claimed that it was *Mashee'ah Mujarradah*,[1] then that is the belief of those who reject (Allâh's Religion) – and woe to those who disbelieve from the Fire!

And most people think badly of Allâh in matters relating to themselves and to others; and none is saved from that except those who know Allâh, know His Names and Attributes and what is entailed by praising and thanking Him and know His Wisdom. And those who despaired of His Mercy thought badly of Him and whoever claimed that He would punish the righteous man and that He would place him on the same level as His enemy has thought badly of Him. And whoever thought that He would abandon His creation without guidance to distinguish between what is commanded and what is prohibited has thought badly of Him. Likewise, whoever thought that He would neither reward them nor punish them and that He would not make the truth clear to them in those matters in which they differed (has thought badly of Allâh), as has one who thought that He would cause righteous deeds to be lost without cause from the slave and that He would punish him for deeds over which he had no control or in which he had no choice, or claims that He would support His enemies with the same miracles with which He supports the Messengers ﷺ and that everything is good in His Sight (i.e. bad deeds and good deeds), even that He would cause one who spent his life in obedience to Him to dwell forever in the Hell-fire and that He would bless one who frittered away his life in disobedience to Him and that the two are of equal goodness in His Sight and that which prevents either of them from reaching his rightful abode cannot be known without strong evidence (from the Qur'ân and *Sunnah*); and if there is none, then logic cannot judge which of them is good and which of them is evil.

Likewise, one who thought that He has informed us about Himself, His Attributes and His Actions that which is manifestly false and that He has failed to speak the truth and has not informed us of it, but

---

[1] *Mashee'ah Mujarradah*: Something which Allâh allows to happen without reason or purpose, as opposed to something which He loves and approves of.

only referred to it in some obscure way, or indicated it in some mysterious manner and always explained things by that which is false and that He wants them to tire their minds in elucidating His Words and that He wants them to depend for their understanding His Names and Attributes on their own understanding, and not on His Book and that rather, He wanted them not to understand His Words in accordance with what they understood from their language, in spite of His Ability to make the truth clear and to remove the expressions which cause them to have false beliefs and believed that he and those of like mind have interpreted the truth without Allâh and His Messenger 鑾 and that guidance was in their sayings and that nothing but misguidance will be obtained by understanding the Speech of Allâh according to its apparent meaning, such a person has thought badly of Allâh. And all of those people are guilty of thinking badly of Allâh and they believe other than the truth of Allâh, the belief of the former times of ignorance (*Jahiliyyah*). And whoever believes that something can occur in His Dominion which He does not will to be, and that He is unable to bring it into being has thought ill of Him. And whoever thought that He was without ability to do a thing from throughout eternity and that at that time He could not be thus described and then He became able to do it, such a person has thought ill of Allâh. And whoever believed that He does not hear and that He does not see and that He does not know about the things which exist has thought badly of Allâh. And whoever thinks that He does not will and that He does not speak and that He has not spoken to anyone and that He never speaks and that He neither commands nor forbids, has thought badly of Him. And whoever believed that He is not Above His heavens, over His Throne and that with regard to Him, all places are equal and that whoever said: "Glorified be my Lord, Most Low" is the same as one who said: "Glorified be my Lord Most High" has believed the most wicked thing of Allâh. And whoever believed that He loves disbelief, iniquity and disobedience just as He loves obedience has thought evil of Allâh. And whoever denies for Him the Attributes of Pleasure and Anger and denies that He takes friends and enemies and that He does not draw near to anyone and that no one draws near to Him, has thought ill of Him. Likewise, whoever believes that He considers opposites equal and that He distinguishes between things which are equal in every way and that He invalidates the good deeds of a lifetime due to the commission of a major sin, causing him to dwell eternally in the Fire of Hell – and in short, believed of Him other than that by which He has described Himself or that by which His Messengers ﷺ have described Him, or negated the Attributes by which He has described Himself, has indeed thought ill of Allâh, as has one who believes that He has a son or a partner or one who can intercede with Him without His Permission, or that there are intermediaries between Him and mankind who submit their requests to Him and that the Reward which is with Him may be attained through acts of disobedience (i.e. sins) just as it is attained through obedience (i.e. good deeds), or he thought that when he leaves something for His sake, He will not give him something better than it in its place, or believed that He punishes simply in accordance with His Will and without cause from the slave, or believed that if he was sincere in his desire (for Allâh's Reward) and his fear (of Allâh's Punishment), that He will frustrate his hopes and desires, believed that He would make His enemies ever victorious over His Messenger, Muhammad ﷺ during his life and after his death – he has thought ill of Him.

And they believed that when he died, they (the Companions ﷺ voiced opinions in the Religion without authority and wronged the members of the Prophet's family and that the power was in the hands of His enemies and their enemies without any sin on the part of His *Awliya'* while He was able to help them (but did not do so), then that He made those who changed the Religion to lie with him ﷺ in his grave, where his nation send greetings of peace upon him and upon them. And every liar, disbeliever and subjugated and oppressed person believes this of his Lord. Indeed, most of mankind, or rather, all of them – except those whom Allâh wills – believe of Allâh that which is untrue, believe ill of Him. And whoever searched within himself will find in it hidden there like the fire which is hidden within the flint: Strike the flint of anyone you will, and its sparks will inform you of what is in it – whether it be little or much. So examine yourself – are you free of it?

If you are saved from it, you are saved from a great misfortune, and if not, then I am not sure of your salvation.

So let the intelligent person who wishes good for himself pay regard in this matter and let him repent to Allâh and seek His Forgiveness whenever he thinks ill of his Lord.

And what is meant by this is what is said regarding the Words of Allâh, Most High:

$$﴿يَظُنُّونَ بِٱللَّهِ غَيْرَ ٱلْحَقِّ ظَنَّ ٱلْجَٰهِلِيَّةِ﴾$$

"And thought wrongly of Allâh — the thought of ignorance."[1]

Then He informed them that the words proceeding from their thoughts i.e.

$$﴿هَل لَّنَا مِنَ ٱلْأَمْرِ مِن شَيْءٍ﴾$$

"Have we any part in the affair?"

And their saying:

$$﴿لَوْ كَانَ لَنَا مِنَ ٱلْأَمْرِ شَيْءٌ مَّا قُتِلْنَا هَٰهُنَا﴾$$

"If we had anything to do with the affair, none of us would have been killed here."

And they did not mean by this to affirm their belief in Allâh's *Qadar*, for if it were so, they would not have been critical and it would not have been fitting that Allâh should reply to them:

$$﴿قُلْ إِنَّ ٱلْأَمْرَ كُلَّهُ لِلَّهِ﴾$$

"Say you (O, Muhammad): "Indeed, the affair belongs wholly to Allâh."

This is why more than one scholar said: This is a denial of Allâh's *Qadar*. And as for their belief that if the matter had been left to them, they would not have been afflicted by killing, Allâh has belied them in His Words:

$$﴿إِنَّ ٱلْأَمْرَ كُلَّهُ لِلَّهِ﴾$$

_____
[1] *Sûrah Âl 'Imrân* 3:154

"Indeed, the affair belongs wholly to Allâh."

So nothing happens except that which has been preceded by Allâh's Ordainment, therefore, if Allâh wrote that he who remained in his house would be killed, he would still have gone forth to his place of death and he would have had no alternative. This is the clearest evidence of the falseness of the saying of the *Qadariyyah*.

Then Allâh, Most High informed them of another wisdom, which is the test of that which is in their hearts and that is the test of the *Eeman* or hypocrisy which is in them; for the Believer increases thereby in naught but *Eeman*, while the hypocrite and he in whose heart there is a disease shows the hypocrisy which is within him by his actions. Then Allâh mentions another wisdom, which is the *Tamhees* of that which is in the hearts of the Believers and that means their purification, for the things which contaminate hearts include being overcome by one's natural disposition, love for oneself, decisions based upon custom and things being made to seem attractive by Satan being overcome by indifference which opposes the *Eeman* therein. And if they were left in continuous well-being, they would not be rid of this, therefore, it was His blessing upon them that they suffered this defeat and it was equivalent to His blessing them with victory. Then He, Most High informed them about those who turn away from among the Believers, that it was because of their sins that the devil caused them to backslide, for deeds can be an army for the slave or an army against him, so a person's fleeing from an enemy when he is able to fight him is only due to an army from his own deeds.

Then He informed them that He has pardoned them, because their flight was not caused by doubt, but by some accident. Then He, Most High repeated that this was due to their deeds, for He said:

$$﴿أَوَ لَمَّا أَصَٰبَتْكُم مُّصِيبَةٌ قَدْ أَصَبْتُم مِّثْلَيْهَا﴾$$

"(What is the matter with you?) When a single disaster smites you, although you smote (your enemies) with one twice as great."[1]

And He mentioned the same thing in a more general manner in the Makkan *Sûrahs*, saying:

---

[1] *Sûrah Âl 'Imrân* 3:165

﴿وَمَا أَصَـٰبَكُم مِّن مُّصِيبَةٍ فَبِمَا كَسَبَتْ أَيْدِيكُمْ وَيَعْفُوا۟ عَن كَثِيرٍ﴾

"And whatever of misfortune befalls you, it is because of what your hands have earned. And He pardons much."[1]

And He said:

﴿مَّآ أَصَابَكَ مِنْ حَسَنَةٍ فَمِنَ اللَّهِ وَمَآ أَصَابَكَ مِن سَيِّئَةٍ فَمِن نَّفْسِكَ﴾

"Whatever of good reaches you, is from Allâh, but whatever of evil befalls you, is from yourself."[2]

And the good and the bad here refer to blessings and disasters; and He closed the Verse (in *Sûrah Âl 'Imrân*) with His Words:

﴿إِنَّ اللَّهَ عَلَىٰ كُلِّ شَىْءٍ قَدِيرٌ﴾

"Verily, Allâh has power over all things."

After His Words:

﴿هُوَ مِنْ عِندِ أَنفُسِكُمْ﴾

"It is from yourselves (because of your evil deeds)."

In order to acquaint them with the prevalence of His Ability along with His Justness and in that there is an affirmation of His *Qadar* and the cause and He has attributed the cause to themselves and the prevalence of His Ability to do all things to Himself. So the former negates the predicate (in the Verse: "From where does this come to us?") and the latter negates their invalidation of Allâh's *Qadar*; and it is similar to His Words:

﴿لِمَن شَآءَ مِنكُمْ أَن يَسْتَقِيمَ ۝ وَمَا تَشَآءُونَ إِلَّآ أَن يَشَآءَ اللَّهُ رَبُّ الْعَـٰلَمِينَ ۝﴾

"To whomsoever among you who wills to walk straight. And you cannot will unless (it be) that Allâh wills — the Lord of the *'Alamın* (mankind, jinn and all that exists)."[3]

---

[1] *Sûrah Ash-Shûra* 42:30

[2] *Sûrah An-Nisa'* 4:78

[3] *Sûrah At-Takweer* 81:28-29

And in the mention of His Ability to do all things there is a very good point, which is that the affair is in His Hand, so do not seek explanation of the like of it from other than Him. And the explanation of this and clarification of it is in the Words of Allâh:

$$﴿وَمَآ أَصَٰبَكُمۡ يَوۡمَ ٱلۡتَقَى ٱلۡجَمۡعَانِ فَبِإِذۡنِ ٱللَّهِ﴾$$

"And what you suffered (of the disaster) on the day (of the Battle of Uhud when) the two armies met, was by the Leave of Allâh."[1]

And this Permission is from *Al-Qadar*; then He informed them about the wisdom behind this Determination, which is that He may distinguish clearly thereby between the Believers and the hypocrites, for the hypocrites spoke of what was within themselves and the Believers heard it and they heard Allâh's reply to them and they realized the result of hypocrisy and what it leads to. So see how many wisdoms and benefits Allâh has in this story and how many warnings and guidances there are therein. Then He consoles them for those among them who were killed with the best consolation, saying:

$$﴿وَلَا تَحۡسَبَنَّ ٱلَّذِينَ قُتِلُوا۟ فِي سَبِيلِ ٱللَّهِ أَمۡوَٰتَۢا بَلۡ أَحۡيَآءٌ عِندَ رَبِّهِمۡ يُرۡزَقُونَ ۝$$
$$فَرِحِينَ بِمَآ ءَاتَىٰهُمُ ٱللَّهُ مِن فَضۡلِهِۦ﴾$$

"Think not of those as dead who are killed in the way of Allâh. Nay, they are alive, with their Lord, and they have provision. They rejoice in what Allâh has bestowed upon them of His bounty."[2]

So He has combined for them the everlasting life (of the Hereafter) and near to Him and that they are with Him and that they have continuous provision and that they rejoice at the Bounty which He bestows upon them and that rejoicing is greater than pleasure and they rejoice (also) at being with their brothers, by whose company their happiness and their bliss and are made complete and they rejoice at the constant renewal of His blessings upon them. And He, Most Glorified reminded them during this time of trial of what is the

---

[1] *Sûrah Âl 'Imrân* 3:166
[2] *Sûrah Âl 'Imrân* 3:169-170

greatest blessing upon them, which if they compared it to every trial, they would dwindle away – and that is the sending of a Messenger from among themselves, for every trial after this great goodness is a very simple thing. So He informed them that the disaster was from themselves in order that they take care and that by His *Qadar*, it occurred that they might affirm His Oneness and depend upon Him. And He informed them of the Wisdoms which are His, that they may not doubt Him regarding His *Qadar* and in order to acquaint them with many of His Names and Attributes and to remind them of that which is greater than victory and spoils and to console them for their dead, that they might compete with them and be not sad for them. For all praise and thanks are due to Him, in the manner which He deserves and which befits His Generosity of Countenance and the Greatness of His Majesty.

Chapter

When the battle was over, the polytheists retreated and the Muslims thought that they intended to attack Al-Madinah, which was unbearable to them, then Abu Sufyan called: "We will meet you again at Badr next year." The Messenger of Allâh (ﷺ) said:

«قُولُوا : نَعَمْ»

"Say: "Yes."

Then they left.

When they had traversed a part of the road, they began mutual recriminations and they said: "You gained power over them, then you left them to gather against you, so return and let us annihilate them. This reached the Messenger of Allâh ﷺ and so he called the people and appointed a detachment to go in pursuit of the Makkan army, saying:

«لَا يَخْرُجْ مَعَنَا إِلَّا مَنْ شَهِدَ الْقِتَالَ»

"Nobody will go out with us except those who took part in the fighting."

The Muslims responded to his call due to the injuries which had befallen them; Jabir asked permission to stay behind, as his father had entrusted him to stay and care for his family and so he ﷺ gave him permission. So they went out until they reached Hamra' Al-Asad and Abu Sufyan said to one of the polytheists who desired to attack Al-Madinah: "Can you convey a message to Muhammad, and I will load your camel with raisins when you arrive in Makkah?" He said: "Yes." He said: "Inform him that we have gathered to attack and annihilate him and his Companions." When he informed them of what Abu Sufyan had said, they said:

﴿حَسْبُنَا ٱللَّهُ وَنِعْمَ ٱلْوَكِيلُ ۝ فَٱنقَلَبُواْ بِنِعْمَةٍ مِّنَ ٱللَّهِ وَفَضْلٍ لَّمْ يَمْسَسْهُمْ سُوٓءٌ وَٱتَّبَعُواْ رِضْوَٰنَ ٱللَّهِ وَٱللَّهُ ذُو فَضْلٍ عَظِيمٍ ۝﴾

"Allâh (Alone) is Sufficient for us, and He is the Best Disposer of affairs (for us)." So they returned with grace and bounty from Allâh. No harm touched them; and they followed the good Pleasure of Allâh. And Allâh is the Owner of great bounty."[1]

The Battle of Uhud took place in the month of Shawwal, in the third year after the *Hijrah* and he remained in Al-Madinah for the rest of the year. Then when the month of Muharram began, he was informed that Talhah and Salamah, the sons of Khuwailid had set out with their followers, calling for war with him and so he sent Abu Salamah ❀ with a hundred and fifty men. They captured some camels and sheep but did not see any fighting.

On the fifth of Muharram, he ﷺ was informed Khalid Ibn Sufyan Al-Huzali had gathered forces and so he sent out 'Abdullah Ibn Unais ❀, who killed him.

Then in the month of Safar, some people from 'Udal and Qarah came to him and they told him that there were some among them who had embraced Islam and they asked him to send someone to teach them the Religion, so he sent six persons,[2] including Khubaib and he appointed as their leader Marthad[3] and that which had been ordained occurred. And it was in this month that the Battle of Ma'ûnah Well took place.

Then in the month of Rabee' Al-Awwal, the conflict with Banu An-Nadeer took place. Az-Zuhri claimed that it took place six months after Badr, but this is pure conjecture on his part, or else, it has been wrongly attributed to him. In fact there is no doubt that it took place

---

[1] *Sûrah Âl 'Imrân* 3: 173-174

[2] This is according to Ibn Ishaq; according to Al-Bukhari, they were ten.

[3] This again is according to Ibn Ishaq, however in *'Saheeh Al-Bukhari'*, it is narrated on the authority of Abu Hurairah ❀ that the Prophet ﷺ appointed 'Asim Ibn Thabit ❀ as their leader.

after Uhud and that the battle which took place after Badr was that against Banu Qainuqa' and that which took place after the Battle of the Trench was that against Banu Quraizah, while the battle against Khaibar took place after the Battle of Hudaibiyyah – so he had four battles with the Jews.

Then the Messenger of Allâh ﷺ personally took part in the Battle of Zat Ar-Riqa' in the month of Jumad Al-Awwal, and that was the Battle of Najd, in which he was in search of some people from among the tribe of Banu Ghatafan. On that day, he led them in the fear prayer.[1] This is how it was reported by Ibn Ishaq and a number of scholars regarding the history of this battle, but this is problematic; what is apparent is that the first fear prayer which he performed was at 'Usfan, as mentioned in a *Hadeeth* declared authentic by At-Tirmidhi. And it has been authentically reported that he ﷺ prayed it in Zat Ar-Riqa', so it is known that this was after 'Usfan and there is no dispute regarding the fact that 'Usfan took place after the Battle of the Trench; and this is supported by the fact that Abu Hurairah and Abu Mûsa ﷺ took part in the Battle of Zat Ar-Riqa'.

Then in the month of Sha'ban or Dhul Qa'dah, the Messenger of Allâh ﷺ went out to keep the appointment with Abu Sufyan and he reached Badr and he remained there waiting for the polytheists; the pagans had set out, but when they were only a day's journey from Makkah, they turned back, saying: "The year is one of drought."

Then they set out in the month of Rabee' Al-Awwal of the year 5 A.H. for Dûmah Al-Jandal and they captured their cattle, but news had come to them from the Jews of the Prophet's expedition and they had fled.

Then in the month of Sha'ban, in 5 A.H.,[2] he sent Buraidah Al-Aslami to Banu Al-Mustaliq, which was known as the Battle of Al-Muraisee' – and Al-Muraisee' was a well. They chose to fight and the

---

[1] Narrated by Al-Bukhari, on the authority of Abu Mûsa Al-Ash'ari ﷺ.

[2] This was the date given by Al-Baihaqi, based upon the narrations of Qatadah, 'Urwah and others and it was declared to be the most authoritative by Al-Hakim, but Al-Bukhari narrated on the authority of 'Abdullah Ibn 'Umar that it was in the year 4 A.H.

exchange of arrows went on for an hour, then the Prophet ﷺ gave the command to his Companions ﷺ and they advanced as one man and annihilated the polytheists and the Messenger of Allâh ﷺ captured their women and children and their property.

It was during this battle that a necklace belonging to 'A'ishah ﷺ was lost and they were held up searching for it and then the Qur'ânic Verse regarding *Tayammum* was revealed. In the *Hadeeth* narrated by At-Tabarani, it was reported that 'A'ishah ﷺ said: "When the events surrounding the loss of my necklace occurred, the people of *Al-Ifk*[1] said what they said. Then I went out with the Prophet ﷺ on another occasion and my necklace was also lost, causing the people to be held up searching for it and I met with the treatment from Abu Bakr that Allâh willed and he said to me: "Oh, my daughter! On every journey you are a trouble and a trial to us when the people have no water." Then Allâh revealed the license to perform *Tayammum*."[2] This proves that *Tayammum* was after this battle (i.e. the Battle of Al-Muraisee'. But the story of *Al-Ifk* was because of the loss of a necklace and so the two stories became mixed up in the minds of some people.

As for the story of *Al-Ifk*, it was in this battle, up to where he (Ibn Al-Qayyim) said: 'Ali suggested that he separate from her via some indirect indication, not an open declaration, when he saw that what had been said had caused him to doubt, advising the Messenger of Allâh ﷺ to leave the doubt so that he would be freed from the worry which he had been caused due to the people's gossip.

Usamah ﷺ advised that he keep her with him, since it was known that he ﷺ loved her and her father and because her chastity and her religiousness were well known and that Allâh would not make the

---

[1] *Al-Ifk*: Falsehood, untruth. What is referred to here is the disgraceful calumny spread by the hypocrites regarding 'A'ishah's chastity after she was lost on the journey and rescued by Safwan Ibn Mu'attal ﷺ.

[2] Narrated by At-Tabarani, on the authority of 'A'ishah ﷺ, it contains in its *Sanad* one Muhammad Ibn Humaid Ar-Razi who is weak, according to Ibn Hajr in '*Fath Al-Bari*', but the story – including the Revelation of *Tayammum* – is narrated by Al-Bukhari and Muslim, on the authority of 'A'ishah ﷺ.

Prophet's loved one and the daughter of his friend to be of the character claimed by the people of *Al-Ifk*.

As Abu Ayyûb and other notables among the Companions ﷺ said:

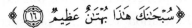

"Glorified are You (O Allâh)! This is a great lie."[1]

Observe from their glorification of Allâh how they knew Him and their declaration that Allâh would never give to His Messenger a woman who was evil.

And if it was said: Why did he ﷺ hesitate and ask? It would be said in reply: This was part of the completion of the great wisdoms of which Allâh made this story a cause and by which He tested His Messenger ﷺ and all of the Muslim nation until the Day of Resurrection – that some people be raised up thereby, while others be degraded. The completion of the test necessitated that the Revelation to His Prophet ﷺ cease for a month, in order that His Wisdom be made clear in the most perfect manner and that the faithful might increase in *Eeman* and become firmer in justice and *Husn Az-zan*[2] and that the hypocrites might increase in their lying, and hypocrisy and that their secret thoughts be revealed, and that the worship required of her and her parents be completed, and that Allâh's Favour upon them be completed and that their need for Allâh and their humility to Him be increased; and their hope of His Mercy and that her hopes from mankind be cut off. And in this, she gave the situation its full due, whereas if Allâh had apprised His Messenger immediately of the truth, these wisdoms and many, many more would have been lost.

Also, it was Allâh's Will that the high status of His Messenger ﷺ and the members of his household in His Sight be made clear and that He undertake the defence Himself and reply to the enemies and humiliate them in a manner in which His Messenger (ﷺ) had no hand.

Also, he was the object of this harm, therefore, it was not fitting that

---

[1] *Sûrah An-Nûr* 24:16

[2] *Husn Az-Zann*: To think the best of someone, rather than the worst.

he should testify to her innocence, even though he had more evidences of her innocence than did the Believers; but due to the perfection of his constancy, his fortitude and his kindness, he displayed the patient perseverance which was expected of him.

Then when the Revelation came, he punished those who had declared her guilt, except 'Abdullah Ibn Ubayy, even though he was the architect of this lie. It was said: This was because the punishment was an expiation for them, whereas Ibn Ubayy had no right to that, because he had been promised a painful punishment and that was sufficient for him, without any other punishment. It was also said that the punishment could not be confirmed upon him because he had only spoken of the matter among his companions (i.e. without expressing an opinion as to her guilt or innocence). It was also said that the punishment for slander is a human right which cannot be carried out unless it is sought. And if it was said that it is a right of Allâh, then it must be sought by the slandered person. It was also said that he did not punish him for a greater benefit than would have been attained by punishing him, just as he did not kill him, even though his hypocrisy was apparent. This was to unite his people and avoid causing them to flee from Islam; for these reasons, it is likely that he did not punish him. And on their return from this battle, Ibn Ubayy said:

$$ ﴿وَلَئِن رَّجَعْنَآ إِلَى ٱلْمَدِينَةِ لَيُخْرِجَنَّ ٱلْأَعَزُّ مِنْهَا ٱلْأَذَلَّ﴾ $$

"If we return to Al-Madinah, indeed the more honourable ('Abdullah bin Ubai bin Salûl, the chief of hyprocrites at Al-Madinah) will expel therefrom the meaner (i.e. Allâh's Messenger ﷺ)."[1]

---

[1] *Sûrah Al-Munafiqûn* 63:8

Chapter

Regarding the Battle of the Trench (Ghazwah Al-Khandaq)

This took place in the year 5 A.H., in the month of Shawwal and the reason for it was that the Jews, when they saw the victory of the polytheists on the Day of Uhud and they came to know of Abu Sufyan's appointment with the Muslims (in the following year) and that he had set out and then returned, the notables among them went out to Quraish to incite them to make war against the Messenger of Allâh ﷺ and Quraish responded to their call; then they went out to Ghatafan and called upon them to join in and they responded to their call. Then they went round the Arab tribes. Then he (Ibn Al-Qayyim) mentioned the story up to where he related the tale of the people from the 'Uranah tribe and he said: In it, as regards Islamic Jurisprudence, there is the permission to drink camel's urine and the purity of the urine of animals whose meat it is permissible to eat and combining the cutting of the hand and foot of the *Muharib*[1] and of killing him if he stole property and that the murderer should be killed according to the manner in which he killed his victim, for they gouged out the eyes of the camel herder, so their eyes were gouged out. It would appear that the story is *Muhkam*,[2] even though the events referred to, occurred before the legal punishments were revealed, for the punishments were revealed to confirm them.

---

[1] *Muharib*: One who makes war on Islam and the Muslims.
[2] *Muhkam*: Legally valid, as opposed to *Mansûkh* (abrogated).

Regarding the Story of Al-Hudaibiyyah

He (Ibn Al-Qayyim) narrated the story up to his words: The treaty stipulated that hostilities should cease ten years, that the Muslims would return to Al-Madinah that year and come back to Makkah the following year, when they would be allowed to remain for three days, that they would not be allowed to enter it with weapons except those of a rider and sheathed swords, that those who came to the Makkans from Al-Madinah would not be returned to them, but that any Muslims who came to Al-Madinah from Makkah would be returned to them.

And in the story of Al-Hudaibiyyah, Allâh revealed the compensation to be paid by Ka'b Ibn 'Ujrah (who had shaved his head due to illness).[1] Also in it, the Prophet ﷺ supplicated Allâh three times for those who shaved their heads and once for those who shortened their hair. And in it, he slaughtered a camel and also a cow on behalf of seven persons. Also in it, he sacrificed a camel which had belonged to Abu Jahl, in order to anger thereby the polytheists. And in it, *Sûrah Al-Fath* was revealed.

After he had returned to Al-Madinah, some believing women came to him and Allâh forbade him from returning them; it was said that this was an abrogation of the condition in the treaty with regard to women. It was also said that this was a restriction imposed by the Qur'ân on the generality of the *Sunnah* – and this is very rare. It was also said that the condition had not been imposed except upon men,

---

[1] See *Sûrah Al-Baqarah* 2:196

but that the pagans wished to make it general, so Allâh revealed.[1]

Regarding matters of Islamic Jurisprudence, there is the fact that the *'Umrah* of the Prophet ﷺ was in the months of *Hajj* and that one assumes *Ihram* for *'Umrah* from the starting point (*Meeqat*). As for the *Hadeeth* in which it is stated: "Whoever assumed *Ihram* from Bait Al-Maqdis, all of his previous and future sins will be forgiven."[2] it is not authentic. Also, it is understood from it that it is sanctioned by the *Sunnah* for one who is performing *Hajj Al-Ifrad* to drive the sacrificial animal, and that marking the animal (with a garland etc.) is a *Sunnah*, but not mutilating it (with a knife etc.). Also, the desirability of causing anger to the enemies of Allâh and that the leader should send out spies ahead of him in the direction of the enemy. Also, it is permissible to seek help from a polytheist who is trustworthy when the need arises, because 'Uyainah Al-Khaza'i was a disbeliever. Likewise, it is desirable to hold consultations. Also, that it is permissible to capture family members separated from the men before fighting starts. And that replying to false statements made by the enemy is permissible even if they are spoken by one who is not Islamically responsible, such as their saying: "Al-Qaswa' (the Prophet's camel) has become stubborn." Also, that it is desirable to swear to Religious information when one wishes to emphasize it. It has been recorded from him ﷺ that he swore on more than eighty occasions and Allâh, Most High commanded him to swear to the truth of what he had said on three occasions, in *Sûrah Yûnus*, *Sûrah Saba'* and *Sûrah At-Taghabun*. Likewise, that if the polytheists and the profligate ones request something thereby venerating the sacred things of Allâh, it should be granted to them, even of they deny it to others, for whoever sought something based upon that which Allâh, Most High loves, his request should be acceded to, so long as it does not entail something which is hated by Allâh and is greater than it. This is a very critical matter and a very difficult one, which is why it

---

[1] *Sûrah Al-Mumtahanah* 60:10

[2] Narrated by Abu Dawûd, Ibn Majah and Ibn Hibban, it has in its *Sanad* has two narrators who are unknown. And among those who disliked that *Ihram* should be assumed before reaching the starting place are Al-Hasan Al-Basri, 'Ata' Ibn Abi Rabah and Imam Malik.

was so burdensome for some of the Companions ﷺ. And (Abu Bakr) *As-Siddeeq* responded as did the Prophet ﷺ, which proves that he was the best of the Companions ﷺ, the most perfect of them and the most knowledgeable of them regarding Allâh, His Messenger ﷺ and His Religion and the strictest of them in conforming to it. Likewise, 'Umar ﷺ did not ask anyone except the Prophet ﷺ and As-Siddeeq ﷺ.

And it is narrated by Ahmad regarding this story that the Messenger ﷺ was praying in *Al-Haram*[1] and he was staying in *Al-Hill*[2] In this there is evidence that the multiplied reward for prayers performed in Makkah applies to all of *Al-Haram* and not only to the Mosque and that the words of the Prophet ﷺ: "A prayer in the Sacred Mosque,"[3] is like the Words of Allâh, Most High:

$$﴿فَلَا يَقْرَبُواْ ٱلْمَسْجِدَ ٱلْحَرَامَ﴾$$

"So let them not come near *Al-Masjid Al-Haram* (at Makkah),"[4] and His Words:

$$﴿سُبْحَٰنَ ٱلَّذِىٓ أَسْرَىٰ بِعَبْدِهِۦ لَيْلًا مِّنَ ٱلْمَسْجِدِ ٱلْحَرَامِ﴾$$

"Glorified (and Exalted) is He (Allâh) [above all that (evil) they associate with Him] Who took His slave (Muhammad ﷺ) for a journey by night from *Al-Masjid Al-Haram* (at Makkah)."[5]

We also derive from it that whoever stopped near to Makkah should stop in *Al-Hill* and pray in *Al-Haram*. This is what 'Abdullah Ibn 'Umar ﷺ used to do.

Another benefit derived from this is the permissibility of the *Imam* initiating moves to seek a peace treaty, if he considers that it is in the interests of the Muslims. And the standing of Al-Mugheerah at the head of the Prophet ﷺ – when it was not his normal custom to have

---

[1] *Al-Haram*: The Sacred Precincts of Makkah.

[2] *Al-Hill*: The area outside the sacred Precincts of Makkah.

[3] Narrated by Al-Bukhari and Muslim, on the authority of Abu Hurairah ﷺ.

[4] *Sûrah At-Tawbah* 9:28

[5] *Sûrah Al-Isra'* 17:1

anyone do so when he was sitting. – is a *Sunnah* when the disbelievers approach, in order to make a show of strength and to venerate the *Imam*; it is not the kind of standing which is censured, just as haughtiness and pride in war are not censured.

And in the sending of the camels in front of the other messenger there is evidence of the desirability of showing the Symbols of Islam to the messengers of the disbelievers. And as for the saying of the Prophet ﷺ) to Al-Mugheerah:

«أَمَّا الإِسْلَامُ فَأَقْبَلُ، وَأَمَّا الْمَالُ فَلَسْتُ مِنْهُ فِي شَيْءٍ»

"As for your embracing Islam, I accept it, but as for their property, I will not take anything of it."[1]

There is evidence that the property of the polytheist who has an agreement with the Muslims is inviolate and that it may not be appropriated; rather, it should be returned to him, because Al-Mugheerah ؓ accompanied them on the understanding that they were protected, then he betrayed them, but the Messenger of Allâh ﷺ did not intervene in the matter of their property, nor did he defend it, nor did he indemnify them for it, because it occurred before Al-Mugheerah embraced Islam.

And in the words of Abu Bakr As-Siddeeq ؓ to 'Urwah: " Suck Al-Lat's clitoris!"[2] – there is a permissibility of speaking plainly the name of the private parts if there is some benefit to be gained thereby, just as he (ﷺ) permitted a plain response to the one who made the claims of the *Jahiliyyah* (i.e. claims of tribal superiority), by saying: "Bite your father's penis!"[3] And for every situation there is a (fitting) saying.

Also, there is the permissibility of enduring the rudeness displayed by the messenger of the disbelievers in order to attain some benefit, because he ﷺ did not retaliate against 'Urwah when he seized him by his beard.

---

[1] Narrated by Al-Bukhari and Ahmad, on the authority of Al-Miswar Ibn Makhramah ؓ and Marwan Ibn Al-Hakam.

[2] This is in Ahmad's version.

[3] Narrated by Ahmad, on the authority of Ubayy Ibn Ka'b ؓ.

We also derive from it the fact that sputum and used water are not impure and the desirability of optimism, based upon the words of the Prophet:

«سَهُلَ أَمْرُكُمْ»

"Now the matter has become easy for you,"[1]

when Suhail came. And we also understand from it that making a peace treaty with a polytheist in which there is harm is permissible if there is some benefit in it. Also, that if anyone swore an oath, made a vow or made a promise and he did not fix a time for its fulfillment, he is not obliged to do so immediately. Likewise, we derive from it that shaving the head is a rite of *Hajj* and that it is preferable to shortening the hair and also that it is a rite of *'Umrah*, like *Hajj* and that it is a rite for one who is prevented from performing *Hajj* or *'Umrah*.

Also that the one who is prevented from performing *Hajj* or *'Umrah* must slaughter his sacrificial animal at the place at which he is prevented – whether it is in *Al-Hill* or in *Al-Haram* and that he is not required to arrange with someone to slaughter the animals in *Al-Haram*, if he does not reach his destination, according to the Words of Allâh:

﴿وَٱلْهَدْىَ مَعْكُوفًا أَن يَبْلُغَ مَحِلَّهُ﴾

"And detained the sacrificial animals, from reaching their place of sacrifice."[2]

Also, we understand from the Verse that the place in which they slaughtered their sacrificial animals was a part of *Al-Hill*, because all of *Al-Haram* is a place of slaughter for sacrificial animals. Also, that the one who is prevented from performing *'Umrah* is not required to make up for it and the *'Umrah* which is made after it is known as *'Umrah Al-Qadiyyah*, because it was that with which He compensated them. Likewise, we derive from it that an absolute command must be obeyed immediately, for if it were not so, he ﷺ would not have been

[1] Narrated by Al-Bukhari, on the authority of Al-Miswar Ibn Makhramah ﷺ and Marwan Ibn Al-Hakam.

[2] *Sûrah Al-Fath* 48:25

angry with them for delaying its implementation. And their delay was merely an action for which they were forgiven, not a praiseworthy action and Allâh has forgiven them for it and granted them Paradise.

Also, we understand from it that the fundamental principle is that he is included in the commands given to his nation, unless there is some evidence to indicate that it is particular, based upon the words of Umm Salamah 鑾.

Also, we derive the permissibility of making a peace treaty which stipulates that Muslim men must be returned, but not women, for it is not permissible to return women, for that is something which has been particularly abrogated by the text of the Qur'ân; so there is no way to claim that this abrogation applies to anyone else.

Likewise, there is the fact that when a woman leaves her husband's authority, the amount paid to him is estimated and that it is in accordance with the dowry which he paid to her, not based upon the amount given to a woman in similar circumstances.

Also, the condition does not cover one who departed to a country other than that of the Muslim leader and that if he then arrived in the land of the leader, he is not obliged to return him unless he is requested to do so.

Another benefit derived from this is that if he should kill the people who were delivering him, he does not have to pay compensation for them nor has the *Imam* any responsibility.

Another benefit is that if there is an agreement between a Muslim ruler and the Christians, it is permissible for another Muslim ruler to fight against them, as ruled by Shaikh Al-Islam Ibn Taimiyyah and he cited as evidence the story of Abu Baseer. And the wisdoms which may be derived from this story are greater than may be encompassed by any besides Allâh.

Another wisdom is that it was a prelude before the greater conquest (of Makkah) and that is Allâh, Most Glorified's custom in the most important matters, both in legal affairs and in matters relating to His Ordainments, that He places before them preludes.

Also, it was one of the greatest conquests, because the people began to mix freely and exchange opinions and (as a result of that,) as those whom Allâh willed entered the fold of Islam during this period. And by these conditions Allâh strengthened His Messenger ﷺ and his army and as a result of which, the polytheists were humbled due to a condition from which they had sought strength and the Muslims were strengthened by humbling themselves to Allâh and so strength based upon falsehood became humbleness and true humility became strength.

Another wisdom was the increase in *Eeman* and obedience to a command which they disliked which Allâh brought about in the Muslims and their acceptance of His Decree and their anticipation of His Promise and their experience of the tranquility which He granted them in this situation which shook the mountains.

Also, He, Most Glorified made it a cause of forgiveness for His Messenger ﷺ and for the completion of His Favour upon him, His Guidance, His Help, the opening of his heart thereby and the removal from it of any sense of wrongdoing or injustice. This is why Allâh has mentioned it as a recompense and an objective. And this is only as a result of something which happened to the Messenger ﷺ and his Companions ﴾.

And observe His description of the hearts of the Believers in this situation in which they (the hearts) were agitated and then through the calmness and tranquility which descended on them, they increased in *Eeman*. Then He confirmed that the oath of loyalty which they made to His Messenger ﷺ was an oath to Him and that whoever breaks it only breaks it to the detriment of Himself and that every Believer has taken the pledge of allegiance to Allâh from the lips of His Messenger ﷺ based upon *Eeman* and the things which it entails. Then He mentioned the belief of the Bedouins and that it was due to their ignorance of Him, Most Glorified, then He informed them of His Pleasure with the Believers and their pledge of allegiance and that then He knew the sincere obedience which was in their hearts and so He sent down the *Sakeenah* (calmness and tranquility) upon them and He rewarded them with the conquest (of Makkah) and abundant spoils, the first of which were in Khaibar and then they continued without ceasing; and He has restrained the hands from them. It was said that this referred to the hands of the Makkans and it was also said that it referred to the hands of the Jews, when they intended to fight those in Al-Madinah after the Companions ﷺ and it was said that it referred to the people of Khaibar and their allies from Banu Ghatafan and Banu Asad, but the correct opinion is that it includes all of them. And Allâh says:

$$ ﴿وَلِتَكُونَ ءَايَةً لِّلْمُؤْمِنِينَ﴾ $$

"That it may be a sign for the believers."[1]

It was said that "it" refers to Allâh's restraining their hands and it was said that it refers to the conquest of Khaibar. Then He added Guidance to all of this.

Then He promised them many spoils and many other victories which were not in their power at that time. It was said that this referred to Makkah and it was also said that it referred to Persia and Rome and it was said that it referred to all that came after Khaibar from the east and the west.

Then He said that if the disbelievers fought against them, they would certainly turn their backs and that is the Way of Allâh. If it was said: Then what of the Battle of Uhud? – the reply would be that it is a promise with a condition attached to it and that condition is that the Muslims are equipped with patient perseverance and fear of Allâh and the Battle of Uhud was lost due to the faintheartedness which negates patient perseverance and the disobedience which negates fear of Allâh. Then He mentioned that He has stayed their hands in Makkh due to the presence of (believing) men and women mentioned and that the punishment had been withheld from them due to their presence, just as He withheld it from them due to His Messenger ﷺ when he was in their midst.

Then he informed them of the pride and haughtiness which was in their hearts whose origin was ignorance and injustice. And He informed them of the calm and tranquility which He sent down to the hearts of His *Awliya'* to counter the pride and haughtiness of the

---

[1] *Sûrah Al-Fath* 48:20

disbelievers and how He made them (the Believers) stick to the word of piety and that is a word which encompasses every word by which fear of Allâh is expressed and the highest of them is the word if sincerity: "*La Ilaha Illallah*" (None has the right to be worshipped except Allâh).

Then He informed them that He,

"sent His Messenger (Muhammad ﷺ) with guidance and the religion of truth (Islam), that He may make it (Islam) superior to all religions."[1]

So Allâh has undertaken the responsibility to perfect this Religion (i.e. Islam) and to make it victorious over all other religions, so do not think that what happened on the Day of Al-Hudaibiyyah indicates otherwise. Then Allâh mentions His Messenger ﷺ and his party with the best of praises, while the *Rafidah*[2] describe them with the opposite of that.

---------- ❖ ❖ ❖ ----------

---

[1] *Sûrah Al-Fath* 48:28
[2] *Rafidah*: Rejectors, i.e. the Shiites.

Chapter

Regarding the Battle of Khaibar

Mûsa Ibn 'Uqbah said: "When the Messenger of Allâh ﷺ returned to Al-Madinah from Al-Hudaibiyyah, he remained for twenty days or thereabouts, then he set out for Khaibar, leaving Siba' Ibn 'Urfutah ؓ in charge of Al-Madinah. At that time, Abu Hurairah ؓ arrived and he found Siba' Ibn 'Urfutah ؓ reciting *Sûrah Maryam* and *Sûrah Al-Mutaffifeen* in the *Fajr* prayer and he said to himself during his prayer: "Woe to the father of so-and-so, for he has two measures; when he measures out (for others) he is deficient and when he measures for himself, he measures generously. After Siba' ؓ had finished the prayer, he supplied him with food, then he went to the Messenger of Allâh ﷺ and he spoke to the Muslims and they made him and his companions partners in their shares.

When the Messenger of Allâh ﷺ reached Khaibar, he performed the morning prayer there, then he mounted his riding beast and the people of Khaibar came out carrying their shovels and baskets in order to work in their fields, being unaware of any danger. The Prophet ﷺ called out:

«اللهُ أَكْبَرُ، خَرِبَتْ خَيْبَرُ، إِنَّا إِذَا نَزَلْنَا بِسَاحَةِ قَوْمٍ، فَسَاءَ صَبَاحُ الْمُنْذَرِينَ»

"*Allâhu Akbar*! Khaibar is destroyed! When we arrive in a people's quarters, the day turns bad for those who have been warned."[1]

---
[1] Narrated by Al-Bukhari, on the authority of Anas ؓ.

Then he (Ibn Al-Qayyim) mentioned the *Hadeeth* in which it is reported that the Prophet ﷺ gave the standard to 'Ali ؓ and his single combat with Marhab. And then he mentioned the story of 'Amir Ibn Al-Akwa' ؓ.[1] Then he besieged them and the Muslims became exhausted and hungry and they slaughtered their donkeys, but the Prophet ﷺ forbade them from eating them. Then he ﷺ made a peace treaty with the Jews in which it was stipulated that they could take away with them all that their riding beasts could carry, but that the gold and silver were his. He also stipulated that anyone who hid anything or carried anything away would have no protection, but they hid a leather bag belonging to Huyai. Then he mentioned the *Hadeeth*. But when the Prophet ﷺ wanted to expel them, they said: "Leave us in the land," so he gave it to them, on condition that they would pay a half of its produce, if he would confirm them in the land. He did not kill anyone except Ibn Abil Huqaiq, who was killed due to his violation of the treaty.

The Messenger of Allâh ﷺ took Safiyyah as a captive and she had been under the guardianship of Ibn Abil Huqaiq and he invited her to embrace Islam and she did so, so he freed her and married her, making her dowry her manumission.[2] He divided Khaibar into thirty-six shares, each share being subdivided into a hundred shares. He and the Muslims took half and the other half was designated for catastrophes and to cover any exigencies afflicting the Muslims.[3] Al-Baihaqi said: "This was because half of Khaibar was conquered by treaty and half of it by force." One of the fundamentals of jurisprudence laid down by Ash-Shafi'i is based upon this: That the land which was conquered by force must be shared out (as the remainder of the spoils of war are shared out).

And whoever studied the matter, it will be clear to him that all of the land of Khaibar was conquered by force and this is the truth of which there is no doubt. And the Imam is free to choose regarding the land whether to divide it or to donate it, or whether to divide some of it and donate the other part. The Prophet ﷺ did all of these things: He

---

[1] Narrated by Al-Bukhari, on the authority of Salamah Ibn Al-Akwa' ؓ.

[2] Narrated by Al-Bukhari and Muslim, on the authority of Anas ؓ.

[3] Narrated by Abu Dawûd, on the authority of 'Umar Ibn Al-Khattab ؓ.

divided Quraizah and An-Nadeer, but he did not divide Makkah; and he divided half of Khaibar and left half of it. No one was absnet from those who had been present at Hudaibiyyah, except Jabir 🕮 and he gave him a share. Ja'far and his companions came to him, along with the Abu Mûsa Al-Ash'ari and his companions 🕮. A woman from among the Jews poisoned him with a leg of mutton which she had given to him, but he did not punish her,[1] although it was said that he killed her after Bishr Ibn Al-Bara' died.[2]

Quraish had wagers as to who would win in the battle between the Muslims and the Jews of Khaibar; some of them contended that Muhammad and his Companions would win, while others said that the two confederates (i.e. among the Arab tribes) and the Jews of Khaibar would triumph. When the Prophet 🕮 emerged victorious, Al-Hajjaj Ibn 'Ilat embraced Islam and took part in the Battle of Khaibar, then he (Ibn Al-Qayyim) related his story.

Among the matters relating to Islamic Jurisprudence which may be derived from this story are: The fighting took place in the forbidden months, because he 🕮 had set out for Khaibar in the month of Muharram. Also, the division of the spoils, three shares for the cavalryman and one for the infantryman. Also that it is permissible for individuals in the army to eat food if they find it and there is no need to deduct the *Khumus* from it, based upon the fact that 'Abdullah Ibn Al-Mughaffal took a bag of fat.[3] Also that if reinforcements arrive after the fighting, there is no share for them in the spoils unless the army permit it and are agreeable to it, because the Prophet 🕮 spoke to his Companions 🕮 regarding the people of the ship (i.e. the returning migrants from Abyssinia). Also, we derive from it the prohibition of eating the meat of the donkey; it was said that the reason for this is that it is unclean and this reason is more acceptable than any other reason suggested such as those who said that it is because it had not been included in the *Khumus*, or that it is because it eats excrement. We also derive from it the permissibility of

---

[1] Narrated by Al-Bukhari and Muslim.

[2] Narrated by Abu Dawûd.

[3] Narrated by Al-Bukhari and Muslim, on the authority of 'Abdullah Ibn Al-Mughaffal 🕮.

making a peace treaty and the fact that the leader may abrogate it whenever he wishes and that there may be a condition attached to the guarantee of safety and that it is permissible to order torture for those who are under suspicion. Also, that one may act upon evidences, according to his words: "It was only a short time ago and the money was more than that." Also, if someone says something and then evidence is established that he is lying, no heed is paid to his words. Also, if those living under Muslim protection break any of the conditions imposed upon them, they will no longer have any protection. Likewise, if anyone takes anything from the spoils before they are distributed, it does not belong to him even if it less than his right, according to the words of the Prophet ﷺ:

$$ «شِرَاكٌ مِنْ نَارٍ» $$

"It is a shoelace of fire."[1]

Also that it is permissible to regard something as a good omen, indeed, it is highly recommended, as the Prophet ﷺ regarded the sight of the spades, axes etc. as omens of Khaibar's destruction. Also that the invalidation of the treaty applies also to the women and children, if those who violated it were numerous and strong. However, if it was only one of a group who did not support him, then it does not apply to his wife and his children, like those whose blood the Prophet ﷺ ordered shed who maligned him and he did not take their women or their children captive. This was his guidance in this matter and in that. Also, we derive from it that it is permissible to make the dowry of a slave woman her manumission – without her permission, without witnesses and without a legal guardian and without pronouncing the words of marriage. Also, it is permissible for a person to lie about himself and about others, so long as it does not entail harm to others, if thereby he able to attain his rights, as Al-Hajjaj did. We also derive from this the permissibility of accepting a gift from a disbeliever.

After leaving Khaibar, the Prophet ﷺ set out for Wadi Al-Qura where

---

[1] Narrated by Al-Bukhari, Muslim, An-Nasa'i, Abu Dawûd and Malik, on the authority of Abu Hurairah ﷺ.

the Jews resided. When they reached it, the Jews met them with arrows and Mid'am was killed. The Companions ☸ said: "Congratulations to him on attaining Paradise." Bu the Prophet ﷺ said:

$$«كَلَّا وَالَّذِي نَفْسِي بِيَدِهِ إِنَّ الشَّمْلَةَ الَّتِي أَخَذَهَا يَوْمَ خَيْبَرَ مِنَ الْمَغَانِمِ لَمْ تُصِبْهَا المَقَاسِمُ، لَتَشْتَعِلُ عَلَيْهِ نَارًا»$$

"No, by Him in Whose Hand is my soul, the sheet (of cloth) which he took (illegally) on the Day of Khaibar from the booty before the distribution of the booty, has become a flame of fire burning him."

Then the Messenger of Allâh ﷺ prepared his Companions ☸ for battle and he called the people of the valley to Islam, then a man from among them came out to fight and he was met by Az-Zubair ☸ who killed him. Then another came out and he was met by 'Ali ☸ who killed him, until eleven of them had been killed in single combat. And every time one of them was killed, the Prophet ﷺ would call upon the rest of them to embrace Islam. They continued to fight them until the evening, then the morning came upon them and the sun had risen no more than was sufficient to cast a shadow of a spear's length when it was conquered by force. The Prophet ﷺ left the land and the date palms in the hands of the Jews. When news of the fate of Khaibar, Fadak and Wadi Al-Qura reached the people of Taima', they made a treaty with the Prophet ﷺ and they remained on their property. It was considered that from Wadi Al-Qura to Al-Madinah is Hijaz, while what lies beyond it is a part of Ash-Sham.

Then the Prophet ﷺ left for Al-Madinah. They came out of the road to take rest and he said to Bilal ☸:

$$«اكْلَأْ لَنَا الْفَجْرَ»$$

"Keep looking for the *Fajr* time for us."

And he (Ibn Al-Qayyim) mentioned the *Hadeeth*.[1] It was also reported that the incident took place on the return from Al-Hudaibiyyah and it was also said that it took place on the return

---

[1] Narrated by Muslim, At-Tirmidhi, Abu Dawûd, Ibn Majah and Malik.

from Tabûk.[1]

It is derived from this *Hadeeth* that when a person sleeps through a prayer or forgets it, its time is when he wakes up or remembers it. It is also derived from it that the regular *Sunnah* prayers should be made up and that the *Adhan* and *Iqamah* are called for prayers which were missed and that they are made up in congregation and that they should be made up immediately, in accordance with the words of the Prophet ﷺ:

$$ «فَلْيُصَلِّهَا إِذَا ذَكَرَهَا» $$

"He should make it up as soon as he remembers it."[2]

And he only delayed it a little, in order to leave the place where they took rest, as this is the place where Satan abides. There is also a warning against praying in areas frequented by devils, such as bathrooms and toilets in particular.

When they returned, the *Muhajirûn* returned to the *Ansar* the gifts of kindness they had given them (when they first arrived in Al-Madinah).

The Prophet ﷺ remained in Al-Madinah until the month of Shawwal, sending out military expeditions, including that of Ibn Huzafah, who commanded his companions to enter the fire. The Messenger of Allâh ﷺ said:

$$ «لَوْ دَخَلُوهَا مَا خَرَجُوا مِنْهَا، إِنَّمَا الطَّاعَةُ فِي الْمَعْرُوفِ» $$

"If they had entered it (i.e. the fire), they would not have come out of it till the Day of Resurrection. Obedience (to somebody) is required when he enjoins what is good."[3]

If it was asked: How can this be, when (if they had entered it) they would have been acting in obedience to Allâh and His Messenger ﷺ

---

[1] However, the *Hadeeth* narrated by Muslim, on the authority of Abu Hurairah ؓ mentions specifically that it took place on the return from Khaibar.

[2] Narrated by Muslim, the compilers of the '*Sunan*', Ahmad and Ad-Darimi.

[3] Narrated by Al-Bukhari, on the authority of 'Ali Ibn Abi Talib ؓ.

(according to their understanding)? We should answer: Because they intended to enter the fire, even though they knew that Allâh has forbidden them from killing themselves, they are not excused. And if this is the case regarding one who tortures himself in obedience to those in authority whose commands he is supposed to obey, then what of one who tortures a Muslim, whom it is forbidden to torture in obedience to those in authority? And if after entering it, they would not leave it, in spite of their intention being to obey Allâh, then what may be said of those among the brothers of Satan who entered it and they instilled the delusion in the minds of the ignorant that it was a part of the inheritance of Ibraheem, Allâh's *Khaleel* ?!

Regarding the Great Victory

By which Allâh strengthened His Religion, His Messenger ﷺ and His protected sanctuary and by which the people entered into the Religion of Allâh in crowds. The Prophet ﷺ set out for it in 8 A.H., when ten days of Ramadan had passed. Then he (Ibn Al-Qayyim) mentioned the story.

Included in the matters relating to Islamic Jurisprudence which may be derived from this story are: That if those who have a covenant with the Muslims make war on those who are under the protection of the Muslim leader, they will be in a state of war with him and he may attack them in their homes at night and he may do so without informing them. This is only if he fears betrayal on their part. If betrayal is ascertained on their part, then (they have breached the covenant with him) and there is no need to inform them.

It is also derived from this that the agreements of all parties are invalidated thereby if they accepted it, just as they enter the agreement as a consequence of their allies' entry into it.

Also, in it is the permissibility of making a peace treaty for a period of ten years; and the correct opinion is that it is permissible to do so for longer than that if necessary and there is some benefit for the Muslims in doing so. Also, if the *Imam* is asked something and he remains silent, it is not considered to be an offer, because Abu Sufyan asked him to renew the treaty and he remained silent. Also derived from it is that the enemy messenger may not be killed because Abu Sufyan was one of those who invalidated the treaty. It is also understood from it that the Muslim spy should be killed and that a woman may be stripped in case of need. Also, if a man accuses a

Muslim of hypocrisy or disbelief based on his own interpretation and due to anger for Allâh's sake – not based upon his own whim – he is not guilty of sin. It is also derived from it that a serious major sin may be atoned for by a great good deed, as Allâh, Most High says:

$$ ﴿إِنَّ ٱلْحَسَنَٰتِ يُذْهِبْنَ ٱلسَّيِّئَاتِ﴾ $$

"Verily, the good deeds remove the evil deeds (i.e. small sins)."[1]

And vice versa, according to the Words of Allâh, Most High:

$$ ﴿لَا تُبْطِلُواْ صَدَقَٰتِكُم بِٱلْمَنِّ وَٱلْأَذَىٰ﴾ $$

"Do not render in vain your *Sadaqah* (charity) by reminders of your generosity or by injury."[2]

And His Words:

$$ ﴿أَن تَحْبَطَ أَعْمَٰلُكُمْ وَأَنتُمْ لَا تَشْعُرُونَ﴾ $$

"lest your deeds should be rendered fruitless while you perceive not."[3]

Then he (Ibn Al-Qayyim) related the story of Hatib and the story of Dhul Khuwaisarah and its like. Then he said: And anyone possessing a rational mind understands the importance of this matter. Also, we derived from it the permissibility of entering Makkah in order to wage a permitted fight without entering into the state of *Ihram*. And there is no disagreement regarding the fact that anyone who wishes to perform the pilgrimage rites may only do so in a state of *Ihram*. As for matters other than these two, there is no obligation except that which Allâh and His Messenger ﷺ have imposed. In it, we also find the clear statement that Makkah was conquered by force and that those who maligned the Prophet ﷺ were killed.

As for the statement of the Prophet ﷺ:

$$ «إِنَّ اللهَ حَرَّمَ مَكَّةَ، وَلَمْ يُحَرِّمْهَا النَّاسُ» $$

---

[1] *Sûrah Hûd* 11:115

[2] *Sûrah Al-Baqarah* 2:64

[3] *Sûrah Al-Hujurat* 49:3

"Verily, Allâh has made Makkah a sanctuary, not the people."[1]

And his words:

«إِنَّ إِبْرَاهِيمَ حَرَّمَ مَكَّةَ»

"Verily, Abraham has declared Makkah a sanctuary,"[2]

This declaration is one of Divine Decree and is from the Islamic Law. It had already been decreed on the day when Allâh created the world and then it was put into words by Abraham (Ibraheem ﷺ). As for the saying of the Prophet ﷺ:

«لَا يُسْفَكُ بِهَا دَمٌ»

"Blood may not be spilled therein."[3]

It refers to the blood which may be legally spilled elsewhere, like the prohibition of cutting trees. In one version, the *Hadeeth* states:

«لَا يُعْضَدُ شَوْكُهَا»

"Its thorn trees may not be cut down."[4]

And it is very clear from this that it is unlawful to cut down thorn trees and boxthorn trees, but they (the scholars) permitted that a dry tree may be cut, because it is like the dead tree. And in the version in which it was stated:

«لَا يُخْبَطُ شَوْكُهَا»

"The leaves of its thorn trees may not be removed,"[5]

is clear evidence that it is unlawful to cut the leaves. As for the words of the Prophet ﷺ:

«لَا يُخْتَلَى خَلَاهَا»

---

[1] Narrated by Al-Bukhari, on the authority of Abu Shuraih ﷺ.

[2] Narrated by Muslim, on the authority of Rafi' Ibn Khadeej ﷺ.

[3] Narrated by Al-Bukhari, on the authority of Abu Shuraih ﷺ.

[4] Narrated by Al-Bukhari, on the authority of Mujahid.

[5] Narrated by Muslim, on the authority of Abu Hurairah ﷺ.

"Nor should its vegetation or grass be uprooted."

There is no dispute that what is intended is that which grows by itself; and *Al-Khala* refers to moist grass; and the exception of *Al-Izkhir* from this prohibition is evidence that the *Hadeeth* is general for all other grasses. But truffles and things hidden in the earth are not included in this prohibition, because they are like fruits.

As for his saying ﷺ:

«وَلَا يُنَفَّرُ صَيْدُهَا»

"Its game should not be chased."

It is a clear forbiddance of all of the causes due to which game is killed and hunted, even including a prohibition of chasing them from their place, because an animal is protected in this place, as it was there first and so it has more right to it. And from this, it is clear that if a protected animal was already in its place, it should not be disturbed from it. As for his saying ﷺ: '

«لَا تُلْتَقَطُ سَاقِطَتُهَا ، إِلَّا لِمُنْشِدٍ»

"'Nor should its lost things be picked up, except by one who makes a public announcement about it."

It is clear from this that lost property in the Sacred Precincts may not be taken possession of, nor may they be picked up, unless it is in order to inform people about them. This is one of two narrations reported from Ahmad. So he must announce it continuously until its owner come forward. This is the correct opinion and the *Hadeeth* is clear regarding it. The *'Munshid'* (mentioned in the *Hadeeth*) is one who announces it and the *'Nashid'* is the one who is seeking it, such as in the saying:

«إِصَاخَةُ النَّاشِدِ لِلْمُنْشِدِ»

"The listening of the seeker to the anouncer."

As for his not entering the House until the pictures were eliminated from it, it is inferred from this that it is hated to pray in a place in which there are pictures and the dislike of praying there is greater than that of praying in the bathroom, because while the former is the place of Satan, the latter is a place where one is likely to find *Shirk* and the majority of *Shirk* committed by people has its origins in pictures and graves.

Also in the story there is the permissibility of one or two men accompanying and protecting a woman, such as Umm Hani' 🌸 and also the killing of those whose apostasy was compounded (by other sins) and who did not repent, based upon the story of Ibn Abi Sarh.[1]

---

[1] Ibn Abi Sarh had embraced Islam in Al-Madinah and then apostatized and fled to Makkah. He was brought to the Prophet 🍃 on the day of the conquest of Makkah by 'Uthman Ibn 'Affan 🌸, who had taken him under his protection; and because he had repented and returned to the fold of Islam, his life was spared.

Chapter

Regarding the Battle of Hunain

Ibn Ishaq said: When Hawazin heard of the conquest, Malik Ibn 'Awf gathered Hawazin and Thaqeef and Jusham gathered and came to him and among them was Duraid Ibn As-Simmah, who was of no use except for his advice; then he (Ibn Al-Qayyim) mentioned the story.

Then he (Ibn Al-Qayyim) said: Allâh promised His Messenger ﷺ that once Makkah was conquered, the people would enter His Religion in great numbers, so when Makkah was defeated, Allâh's Wisdom dictated that He seize the hearts of Hawazin and those allied with them and those who followed them in order that Allâh's Religion and the Help given to His Messenger ﷺ should be manifest and so that their spoils might be a reward for those who took part in the conquest of Makkah and that Allâh make apparent His Might to those the like of whom the Muslims had not previously encountered and so that none from among the Arabs could resist them after that.

At first, He gave them a taste of the bitterness of defeat, in spite of their strength, in order to lower heads which had been raised by the conquest of Makkah and which had not entered Allâh's Sacred Precincts as the Messenger of Allâh ﷺ entered it, with bowed head, riding on horseback, so much so that his beard was almost touching his saddle and (they were given a taste of defeat) in order to show those who said: "We shall not be beaten this day by a smaller force." – that victory comes from Allâh. Then when their hearts had become remorseful, He sent to them support along with news (of victory):

﴿ثُمَّ أَنزَلَ ٱللَّهُ سَكِينَتَهُۥ عَلَىٰ رَسُولِهِۦ وَعَلَى ٱلۡمُؤۡمِنِينَ﴾

"Then Allâh did send down His *Sakeenah* (calmness, tranquillity and reassurance) on the Messenger (Muhammad ﷺ), and on the believers."[1]

And His Wisdom dictated that the bestowal of His Help only comes to those who are remorseful:

﴿وَنُرِيدُ أَن نَّمُنَّ عَلَى ٱلَّذِينَ ٱسْتُضْعِفُوا۟ فِى ٱلْأَرْضِ وَنَجْعَلَهُمْ أَئِمَّةً وَنَجْعَلَهُمُ ٱلْوَٰرِثِينَ ۝ وَنُمَكِّنَ لَهُمْ فِى ٱلْأَرْضِ وَنُرِيَ فِرْعَوْنَ وَهَٰمَٰنَ وَجُنُودَهُمَا مِنْهُم مَّا كَانُوا۟ يَحْذَرُونَ ۝﴾

"And We wished to do a favour to those who were weak (and oppressed) in the land, and to make them rulers and to make them the inheritors. And to establish them in the land, and We let Fir'aun (Pharaoh) and Haman and their hosts receive from them that which they feared."[2]

Allâh opened the wars with the Arabs with the Battle of Badr and He closed them with the Battle of Hunain and the angels fought in both of them and the Prophet ﷺ hurled gravel in both of them; and through them both the fire of the Arabs was extinguished, for Badr caused them to fear and disunited them, while Hunain exhausted their strength.

It is also derived from it the permissibility of borrowing weapons from a polytheist and that complete trust in and dependence on Allâh requires that one undertake the necessary measures to achieve one's objective and that Allâh's guarantee of protection to him ﷺ does not negate undertaking the causes, just as His informing us that He would manifest His Religion over all others does not negate all forms of *Jihad*.

And he ﷺ stipulated to Safwan that he would guarantee the loan, which raises the question: Is this a guarantee to return them, or a guarantee against damage? Scholars have differed regarding this matter. It is also derived from this story that it is permissible to kill the enemy's riding beast, if that helps to kill him and that is not

---

[1] *Sûrah At-Tawbah* 9:26
[2] *Sûrah Al-Qasas* 28:5-6

considered torture of animals, which is prohibited. Also we derive from it that he ﷺ pardoned the one who had intended to kill him[1] and stroked his chest and supplicated for him. Also derived from it is the permissibility of the Imam delaying the distribution of the spoils until after some of the disbelievers have embraced Islam and then returning to them what was taken from them. And in this there is evidence that spoils may only be rightfully possessed through division of them. So if a person died before they were distributed or stored in the Muslim land, his share would be returned to the remaining recipients of the spoils. This is the *Mazhab* of Abu Haneefah. Ahmad declared that the *Anfal* are from four- fifths of the booty and that this gift is from the *Nafl* (which the Messenger of Allâh granted to the chiefs of the tribes in order to strengthen their faith) and this is more fitting than giving a third after the *Khumus* and then a quarter after it. And (had they understood this,) Dhul Khuwaisarah and his like would not have been blind to the wisdom behind it. Their spokesman said to the Prophet ﷺ: "Be fair."

The *Imam* is the representative of the Muslims and he acts in accordance with what is best for them and with what helps to establish the Religion so if that was set aside in order to attract the enemies of Islam to it, to protect against their evil, it is permissible to do so – indeed it is obligatory to do so, for it is a basic principle of Islamic Law that one permit the lesser of two evils in order to repel the greater of them and in order to attain the greater of two benefits by letting pass the lesser of them; indeed the benefits of the life of this world and the Religion are based upon these two things.

We also derive from it that it is permissible to sell slaves, indeed even animals, exchanging some of them for others by *Nasee'ah*[2] or by *Tafadul*[3] and that if the two participants in the sale make a deferment for an unspecified period of time, it is permissible,

---

[1] This refers to the story of Fudalah Ibn 'Umair; however, according to Al-Albani, it is a weak *Hadeeth* reported by Ibn Hisham with a mixed up chain of narrators.

[2] *Nasee'ah*: Deferred payment.

[3] *Tafadul*: Immediate payment.

according to the most authoritative opinion, since there is nothing to beware of and no risk.

As for the words of the Prophet ﷺ:

«مَنْ قَتَلَ قَتِيلًا لَهُ عَلَيْهِ بَيِّنَةٌ فَلَهُ سَلْبُهُ»

"Anyone who has killed an enemy and has a proof of that, will posses his spoils."[1]

Scholars have differed regarding whether that is according to the Islamic Law, or whether it is a stipulation (of the *Imam*). And the source of the dispute is whether he said this based upon his position as the Messenger of Allâh ﷺ, such as his words:

«مَنْ زَرَعَ بِأَرْضِ قَوْمٍ بِغَيْرِ إِذْنِهِمْ، فَلَيْسَ لَهُ مِنَ الزَّرْعِ شَيْءٌ، وَلَهُ نَفَقَتُهُ»

"Whoever farmed in the land of a people without their permission, he has no share of the crop, but he is entitled to his costs."[2]

Or whether it was based upon his position as *Mufti*,[3] as in his words:

«خُذِي مَا يَكْفِيكِ وَوَلَدَكِ بِالْمَعْرُوفِ»

"Take what is sufficient and reasonable for you and your sons."[4]

Or whether it was based upon his position as *Imam*, in which case it would be because there was some benefit in it at that time and it would be incumbent upon those who came after him to bear it in mind, according to what was beneficial. Due to this, the scholars have

---

[1] Narrated by Al-Bukhari, on the authority of Abu Qatadah.

[2] Narrated by At-Tirmidhi, Abu Dawûd, Ibn Majah and Ahmad, on the authority of Rafi' Ibn Khadeej ؓ, it contains in its chain of narrators one Shareek Ibn 'Abdillah An-Nakha'i, who was described by Yahya Ibn Ma'een, Abu Dawûd, Abu Hatim Ar-Razi and others as being guilty of mistakes.

[3] *Mufti*: One who delivers legal verdicts (*Fatawa*).

[4] Narrated by Al-Bukhari, Ibn Majah, An-Nasa'i, Ahmad and Ad-Darimi.

differed regarding a great number of matters in which there is a statement reported from him, such as his saying:

«مَنْ أَحْيَا أَرْضًا مَيْتَةً فَهِيَ لَهُ»

"Whoever gave life to dead ground, it belongs to him."[1]

It is also derived from this story that in such matters, one witness is sufficient and he does not need to swear an oath, nor is it a condition that he says: "I testify".

Also, that the arms stripped from an enemy warrior are not subject to the *Khumus*, that they are a part of the spoils, that one who has no share of women or children has a right to them and that he has the right to the arms of all those whom he killed, even if they are numerous.

---

[1] Narrated by Al-Bukhari, Abu Dawûd, Ahmad, Malik and Ad-Darimi.

Regarding the Battle of At-Ta'if

When Thaqeef had been defeated, they entered their fort and prepared to fight. The Messenger of Allâh ﷺ went forth and halted near to their fort and they rained arrows heavily on the Muslims, so that it was as if they were a swarm of locusts, until twelve of them were killed. Because of this, the Prophet ﷺ moved to higher ground, to a place where now stands At-Ta'if Mosque. From there he besieged them for eighteen days or for twenty-something days.[1] He fired upon them with a mangonel – and he was the first to do so in Islam – and he ordered that their grape vines be cut down and the people began to do so. Ibn Sa'd said: "They asked him to leave them for Allâh's sake and for the sake of kinship and he ﷺ said:

$$\text{«فَإِنِّي أَدَعُهَا لله وَلِلرَّحِم»}$$

"Then I will leave them for Allâh's sake and for the sake of kinship."

Then his caller announced: "Any slave who comes down to us, he will be free," upon which, a number of men came out,[2] including Abu Bakrah ﷺ. The Prophet ﷺ entrusted each man to the care of one of the Muslims, which was a great hardship to the people of At-Ta'if. It was not possible to conquer it, so the Prophet ﷺ ordered the return to Al-Madinah. At this, the people set up a hue and cry, saying: "Shall

---

[1] It is reported by Muslim, on the authority of Anas Ibn Malik ﷺ that he said: "then we left for At-Ta'if and we besieged it for forty nights."

[2] According to Al-Bukhari, they were twenty-three in number.

we depart without having conquered At-Ta'if?" He said:

$$\text{«اغْدُوا عَلَى الْقِتَالِ»}$$

"Then start fighting in the morning."

In the morning, they fought and were wounded and the Prophet ﷺ said:

$$\text{«إِنَّا قَافِلُونَ غَدًا إِنْ شَاءَ اللهُ»}$$

"If Allâh wills, we shall depart."

Upon hearing this, they were pleased and they began to leave and the Messenger of Allâh ﷺ laughed. Once they were mounted and had started moving, the Messenger of Allâh said: "Say:

$$\text{«آيِبُونَ تَائِبُونَ عَابِدُونَ لِرَبِّنَا حَامِدُونَ»}$$

"Here we are returning, repenting and worshipping (Allâh) and to our Lord we offer praise."

It was said to him: "Oh, Messenger of Allâh! Supplicate Allâh against Thaqeef." He said:

$$\text{«اللَّهُمَّ اهْدِ ثَقِيفًا وَائْتِ بِهِمْ»}$$

"Oh, Allâh! Guide Thaqeef and bring them to us (as Muslims)."[1]

Then he ﷺ left for Al-Ji'ranah and from there, he donned the garments of *Ihram* and performed *'Umrah*, then returned to Al-Madinah. When he arrived in Al-Madinah from Tabûk in the month of Ramadan a delegation from Thaqeef came to him and when he left them, he was followed by 'Urwah Ibn Mas'ûd, who overtook him before he entered Al-Madinah and he embraced Islam and sought permission from him to return to his people with Al-Islam. The Messenger of Allâh ﷺ knew the pride of opposition which was in them. 'Urwah said: "I am dearer to them than their first born children." And in truth, he was beloved by them and they were obedient to him. So he left and went to call his people to Islam,

---

[1] Narrated by Al-Bukhari.

hoping that they would not oppose him due to his position among them. When he looked down upon them and preached to them, they fired arrows at him from every direction and he was killed. It was said to him before he died: "What do you think about your blood (i.e. your imminent death)?" He said: "It is martyrdom with which Allâh has honoured me and there is naught within me save that which is within the martyrs who were killed with the Messenger of Allâh ﷺ before he went away from you, so bury me with them." So he was buried with them. It is claimed that the Messenger of Allâh ﷺ said regarding him:

«إِنَّ مِثْلَهُ فِي قَوْمِهِ كَمَثَلِ صَاحِبِ يْس فِي قَوْمِهِ»

"Urwah among his people is like the man of *Ya Seen* among his people."

Thaqeef remained for some months after killing 'Urwah ﷺ, then they decided that they could not fight all those Arabs around them and so they decided to send a man to the Messenger of Allâh ﷺ as they had sent 'Urwah ﷺ before. They spoke to 'Abdu Yalail, but he refused, fearing that they would do to him what they had done to 'Urwah ﷺ and so they sent with him two men from Al-Ahlaf and three men from Banu Malik, including 'Uthman Ibn Abil 'As; when they were near to Al-Madinah, and they stopped at a place called Qanah, they met Al-Mugheerah bin Shu'bah ﷺ and he rushed to give the glad tidings to the Messenger of Allâh ﷺ. Abu Bakr ﷺ met him and said: "I implore you by Allâh not to precede me (in going to the Prophet ﷺ, so he agreed and Abu Bakr ﷺ entered the presence of the Messenger of Allâh ﷺ and informed him, then Al-Mugheerah ﷺ went out to them and brought back the camels with them. The Messenger of Allâh ﷺ erected a tent for them near his mosque. Khalid bin Sa'eed acted as intermediary between them and the Messenger of Allâh ﷺ. One of the things which they asked of the Messenger of Allâh ﷺ was that he leave for them Al-Lat (their idol) and not destroy it for three years, so that they might be saved thereby from the wrath of the ignorant among them, but he refused. They continued to ask him, but he refused; they even asked him for a month's respite, but he refused to allow them any respite.

Another thing that they asked him was that he excuse them from praying and that they should not have to destroy their idols themselves. He said:

$$«أَمَّا كَسْرُ أَوْثَانِكُمْ بِأَيْدِيكُمْ، فَسَنُعْفِيكُمْ عَنْهُ، وَأَمَّا الصَّلَاةُ فَلَا خَيْرَ$$
$$فِي دِينٍ لَا صَلَاةَ فِيهِ»$$

"As for the destruction of your idols by your own hands, we shall excuse you that, but as for the prayer, there is no goodness in a religion which has no prayer."

When they had embraced Islam, he appointed 'Uthman bin Abil 'As in charge of them, although he was the youngest of them, because he was the keenest of them on studying and understanding the Religion.

When they set out for their land, the Messenger of Allâh ﷺ sent Abu Sufyan and Al-Mugheerah ﷺ with them to destroy Al-Lat. When they entered, Al-Mugheerah ﷺ, attacked it with a pickaxe, while Banu Mu'attib, fearful that would be fired upon like 'Urwah ﷺ. The women of Thaqeef came out with their heads uncovered, crying over it. After he had destroyed it, he took its wealth. The son of 'Urwah and Qarib bin Al-Aswad had approached the Messenger of Allâh ﷺ before the delegation, when 'Urwah ﷺ had been killed, desiring to leave Thaqeef and they embraced Islam and the Messenger of Allâh ﷺ said to them:

$$«تَوَلَّيَا مِنْ شِئْتُمَا»$$

"Choose whomsoever you will as your *Wali*."[1]

They said: "We will not take anyone as a *Wali* except Allâh and His Messenger." The Prophet ﷺ said:

$$«وَخَالَكُمَا أَبَا سُفْيَانَ بْنَ حَرْبٍ»$$

"And your maternal uncle, Abu Sufyan Ibn Harb?"

They said: "And our uncle, Abu Sufyan." Then when the people of At-Ta'if embraced Islam, Ibn 'Urwah ﷺ asked the Messenger of Allâh to pay the debt of his father from the wealth of Al-Lat and he said:

---

[1] *Wali*: Friend, supporter.

"Yes." Qarib 🌸 said: "And for Al-Aswad, oh, Messenger of Allâh?" So he paid it and 'Urwah 🌸 and Al-Aswad were brothers from the same mother and father, so the Messenger of Allâh ﷺ said:

$$«إِنَّ الأَسْوَدَ مَاتَ مُشْرِكًا»$$

"Al-Aswad died as a polytheist."

But Qarib 🌸 said: "Oh, Messenger of Allâh! But it comes to a Muslim who is related," meaning himself "and the debt is only upon me." So he paid "Urwah's debt and Al-Aswad's from Al-Lat's wealth.

Regarding matters of Islamic Jurisprudence, it is derived from this story that it is permissible to fight in the forbidden months, because the Messenger of Allâh ﷺ set out for Makkah at the end of Ramadan and he stayed in Makkah for nineteen nights. Then he left for Hawazin and he fought them and then left them and set out for At-Ta'if and he besieged them for twenty-odd nights, or eighteen nights, according to Ibn Sa'd. If you consider this, you will realize that a part of the siege was in Dhul Qa'dah and there is no escaping this conclusion; but the fighting did not begin until Shawwal and there is a difference between the beginning and the continuation of it.

Also, we derive from it the permissibility of a man taking his family with him, because in this story, Umm Salamah and Zainab 🌸 were with him ﷺ.

Also, it is permissible to fire a mangonel on the disbelievers, even if it leads to the death of women and children.

Likewise, it is permissible to cut down their trees, if that weakens them and angers them.

We also derive from it that if a slave runs away and joins up with the Muslims, he becomes free. Ibn Al-Munzir reported that there is a consensus of opinion among the scholars on this.

Also, if the *Imam* besieges a fort and he considers that it is to their benefit to withdraw, he may do so.

We also derive from it that he assumed his *Ihram* for 'Umrah from Al-Ji'ranah – and it is the *Sunnah* for whoever entered it from the direction of At-Ta'if. As for leaving Makkah for Al-Ji'ranah in order to assume *Ihram* from there, none of the scholars has declared it to be desirable.

We also derive from it the perfect kindness and mercy which the Prophet 鷺 displayed in his supplication for Thaqeef for guidance, even though they had fought against him and killed a number of his Companions ﷺ and they killed the messenger he sent to them.

We also see the perfect love which Abu Bakr As-Siddeeq ﷺ had for him and his desire to get nearer to him in any way possible and this proves the permissibility of a man asking his brother to give preference to him by doing something in order to seek another's favour and that it is permissible for him to do so. And the opinion of those who said that it is not permissible is not correct, because 'A'ishah ﷺ gave preference to 'Umar ﷺ in being buried in her house and he asked that of her and she did not display any dislike of that request nor did she dislike to accede to it.

We also derive from it that it is not permissible to allow the objects of *Shirk* to remain for even a day once one has achieved the ability to remove them, for they are the signs of disbelief and they are the greatest evil. And that is the ruling on the shrines which are built over graves and which are taken as idols worshipped besides Allâh and the stones which are intended for veneration and the seeking of blessings and which share the status of Al-Lat, Al-'Uzza and Manat, the other third (idol) – or even worse acts of *Shirk* – we seek Allâh's Help (against falling into) that. And none of those who worshipped these *Tawagheet*[1] believed that they created, provided sustenance, gave life or caused death. They only used to do before them what their brothers among the polytheists do before their *Tawagheet* today. These people followed the ways of those who came before them in an identical manner, adopting their practices inch-by-inch and yard-by-yard until *Shirk* overcame most of them due to the appearance of ignorance and the lack of knowledge, so that *Al-Ma'rûf* (right-eousness) came to be considered *Al-Munkar* (evil) and *Al-Munkar* came to be considered *Al-Ma'rûf* and *Sunnah* came to be considered *Bid'ah* and *Bid'ah* came to be considered *Sunnah* and the small child

---

[1] *Tawagheet*: Objects of worship besides Allâh.

would be reared upon that and the adult grew old upon it; the signposts (of knowledge) were erased. Separation from Islam increased greatly. The scholars became few in number, the foolish people gained ascendancy and the situation became very serious and hardship increased both on land and at sea due to that which the people's hands earned. However, there will remain a group from the Muhammadan group who continue to call to the truth and who oppose the people of *Shirk* and innovation, until such time as Allâh inherits the earth and those upon it – and He is the Best of inheritors.

We also derive from this story the permissibility of the *Imam* utilizing the wealth from shrines in the cause of *Jihad* and other beneficial deeds and to give it to the warriors and to make use of its value in benefitting the Muslims. This is also the ruling on making an endowment of it – and this is something which is disputed by no one among the scholars of Islam.

Chapter

When the Messenger of Allâh ﷺ arrived in Al-Madinah and the ninth year began, he sent out the collectors to take the *Zakah* from the desert Arabs; he sent 'Uyainah to Banu Tameem and he sent 'Adi Ibn Hatim to Tai' and Banu Al-Asad and he sent Malik Ibn Nuwairah to collect the *Zakah* of Banu Hanzalah. The *Zakah* of Banu Sa'd he divided between two men, sending Az-Zibraqan to one area and Qais Ibn 'Asim to another and he sent Al-'Ala' to Bahrain and 'Ali to Najran.

And in that year the Battle of Tabuk took place; it was in the month of Rajab at a time when the people were suffering hardship and there was drought in the land and fruit was ripe.

It was the usual custom of the Messenger of Allâh ﷺ when he went out on a military expedition to name a different destination from which he intended to raid except when the destination was remote and the weather was severe. So one day, he said to Al-Judd Ibn Qais (a hypocrite): "Would you like to fight the Byzantines this year?" He replied: "Permit me to stay behind and do not tempt me, for there is no man fonder of women than I and I fear that if I saw their women, I would not be able to bear it." The Messenger of Allâh ﷺ turned away from him and said:

«قَدْ أَذِنْتُ لَكَ»

"I permit you."[1]

It was regarding him that the following Verse was revealed:

﴿وَمِنْهُم مَّن يَقُولُ ٱئْذَن لِّي وَلَا تَفْتِنِّيٓ﴾

---

[1] According to Al-Albani, this *Hadeeth* was transmitted by Ibn Hisham and Ibn Jareer from Ibn Ishaq and its chain of narrators is weak.

"And among them is he who says: "Grant me leave (to be exempted from *Jihad*) and put me not into trial."[1]

Some of the hypocrites said to each other: "March not forth in the heat." So Allâh revealed:

$$﴿وَقَالُوا لَا تَنفِرُوا فِي ٱلْحَرِّ﴾$$

"And they said: "March not forth in the heat."[2]

The Messenger of Allâh ﷺ ordered *Jihad* and he urged the wealthy to finance the expedition. 'Uthman ؓ provided three hundred camels and all their equipment and a thousand *Deenars*[3] and those known as the weepers came and they were seven in number and they asked the Messenger of Allâh ﷺ to provide mounts for them, but he said:

$$﴿لَا أَجِدُ مَا أَحْمِلُكُمْ عَلَيْهِ تَوَلَّوْا وَّأَعْيُنُهُمْ تَفِيضُ مِنَ ٱلدَّمْعِ حَزَنًا أَلَّا يَجِدُوا مَا يُنفِقُونَ﴾$$

"I can find no mounts for you," they turned back, while their eyes overflowing with tears of grief that they could not find anything to spend (for *Jihad*)."[4]

His Companions ؓ sent Abu Mûsa ؓ to him to ask him to provide mounts for them, but he found him angry and he said:

$$«وَاللهِ لَا أَحْمِلُكُمْ وَلَا أَجِدُ مَا أَحْمِلُكُمْ عَلَيْهِ»$$

"By Allâh, I cannot provide mounts for you, nor do I have anything which I can give you as a ride."

Then some camels were brought to him and he sent for them, saying:

$$«مَا أَنَا حَمَلْتُكُمْ، وَلَكِنَّ اللهَ حَمَلَكُمْ، وَإِنِّي وَاللهِ لَا أَحْلِفُ عَلَى يَمِينٍ، فَأَرَى غَيْرَهَا خَيْرًا مِنْهَا إِلَّا كَفَّرْتُ عَنْ يَمِينِي، وَأَتَيْتُ الَّذِي هُوَ خَيْرٌ»$$

---

[1] *Sûrah At-Tawbah* 9:49

[2] *Sûrah At-Tawbah* 9:81

[3] Narrated by Ahmad, on the authority of 'Abdur-Rahman Ibn Samrah ؓ.

[4] *Sûrah At-Tawbah* 9:92

"It was not I who gave you mounts, but Allâh gave you mounts. By Allâh, If I swear an oath and then see something better than it, I perform expiation for it and then do that which is better than it."[1]

A man stood up and offered the night prayer and he cried, then he said: "Oh, Allâh! You have commanded *Jihad*, but You have not placed in the hand of Your Messenger the means to carry me. Therefore, I give away in charity all the wrongs that have been committed against me, whether against my property, my body or my honour." Then he awoke in the morning and the Prophet ﷺ said:

«أَيْنَ الْمُتَصَدِّقُ هَذِهِ اللَّيْلَةَ؟»

"Where is the person who gave charity last night?"

Nobody stood up, so he repeated the question, then a man stood up and informed him of what he had done and the Prophet ﷺ said:

«أَبْشِرْ وَالَّذِي نَفْسُ مُحَمَّدٍ بِيَدِهِ، لَقَدْ كُتِبَتْ فِي الزَّكَاةِ الْمُتَقَبَّلَةِ»

"Rejoice, for by Him in Whose Hand is my soul, it has been recorded among the accepted charities."

Some Bedouins came to him offering excuses for not going, but he did not permit them. Ibn Ubayy had camped in Thaniyyah Al-Wada', among his allies from the Jews and the hypocrites and it was said that his camp was not the lesser of the two camps.

The Messenger of Allâh ﷺ left Muhammad Ibn Maslamah ؓ in charge of Al-Madinah. When he ﷺ went on, Ibn Ubayy fell behind. The Prophet ﷺ left 'Ali ؓ behind to take care of his family, but 'Ali ؓ said: "Would you leave me behind with the women and children?" The Prophet (ﷺ) replied:

«أَمَا تَرْضَى أَنْ تَكُونَ مِنِّي بِمَنْزِلَةِ هَارُونَ مِنْ مُوسَى غَيْرَ أَنَّهُ لَا نَبِيَّ بَعْدِي»

"Are you not content to be to me as Aaron was to Moses, (he

---

[1] Narrated by Al-Bukhari and Muslim, on the authority of Abu Mûsa Al-Ash'ari ؓ.

added:) except that there will be no Prophet after me)?"[1]

Some persons whose faith was not in doubt stayed behind, including: Ka'b bin Malik, Hilal bin Umayyah, Murarah bin Ar-Rabee', Abu Khaithamah and Abu Dharr ﷺ, then Abu Khaithamah and Abu Dharr ﷺ caught up with him. The Messenger of Allâh ﷺ arrived there with thirty thousand men, including ten thousand horsemen and he remained there for twenty nights, shortening the prayers. At that time, Heraclius was in Hims. Abu Khaithamah ﷺ returned to his family a few days after the Prophet's departure and he found two of his wives in their huts in his garden. Each of them had sprinkled her hut with water and cooled water for him and prepared food for him. When he entered, he stood at the door of the hut and looked at his two wives and what they had prepared for him and said: "The Messenger of Allâh ﷺ is out in the sun, the wind and the heat and Abu Khaithamah is in the cool shade with food prepared and a beautiful woman. This is not fair." By Allâh, I will not enter the hut of either of you until I meet up with the Messenger of Allâh ﷺ." Then he went to his camel and saddled it and set off in pursuit of the Messenger of Allâh ﷺ and caught up with him as he arrived in Tabuk.

He met up with 'Umair Ibn Wahb ﷺ on the road and they kept company until, when they were near to Tabuk, Abu Khaithamah ﷺ said to him: "I have committed a sin, so you should stay behind me until I come to the Messenger of Allâh ﷺ." So he did so. Then when he approached, the people said: "There is a rider on the road." The Messenger of Allâh ﷺ said:

«كُنْ أَبَا خَيْثَمَةَ»

"Be Abu Khaithamah."

They said: "Oh, Messenger of Allâh! By Allâh, it is Abu Khaithamah." When he had dismounted, he approached the Messenger of Allâh ﷺ greeted him with salutations of peace and then told him what had happened. The Prophet ﷺ spoke kindly to him and supplicated for him.

---

[1] Narrated by Al-Bukhari and Muslim, on the authority of Sa'd Ibn Abi Waqqas ﷺ.

When the Messenger of Allâh passed by the abodes of Thamûd, he said:

«لَا تَشْرَبُوا مِنْ مَائِهَا، وَلَا تَتَوَضَّؤُوا مِنْهُ لِلصَّلَاةِ، وَمَا كَانَ مِنْ عَجِينٍ فَأَعْلِفُوهُ الإِبِلَ، وَلَا يَخْرُجَنَّ أَحَدٌ مِنْكُمْ إِلَّا وَمَعَهُ صَاحِبٌ لَهُ»

"Neither drink from their water nor make ablution with it for prayer and whatever dough you have made from it, give it to the camels and none of you should leave without having a companion with him."

The people did as he ordered, except for two men, one of them to answer call of nature and the other to find his camel. As for the former, he had an epileptic fit in the place where he had gone to answer the call of nature, while as for the latter, the wind carried him and threw him in the mountains of Tai'. The Messenger of Allâh ﷺ said:

«أَلَمْ أَنْهَكُمْ؟»

"Did I not forbid you?"

Then he supplicated for the one who had suffered the seizure and he was cured and Tai' gave him to the Messenger of Allâh ﷺ when he returned to Al-Madinah.[1]

Az-Zuhri said that when the Prophet ﷺ passed by Al-Hijr, he wrapped his garment around his face and he urged on his mount, then he said:

«لَا تَدْخُلُوا بُيُوتَ الَّذِينَ ظَلَمُوا أَنْفُسَهُمْ إِلَّا وَأَنْتُمْ بَاكُونَ، خَوْفًا أَنْ يُصِيبَكُمْ مَا أَصَابَهُمْ»

"Do not enter the houses of those who wronged themselves unless you do so weeping and in fear that that which afflicted them may afflict you."[2]

And it is authentically reported that he ordered them to throw away

---

[1] Narrated by Ibn Hisham.
[2] Narrated by Ahmad, on the authority of 'Abdullah Ibn 'Umar ﷺ.

the water and to water from the well from which the she-camel (of Salih ﷺ used to drink.

Ibn Ishaq said that the people were without water and so the Messenger of Allâh ﷺ supplicated Allâh and so He sent to him a cloud and it rained until they had quenched their thirst. Then he continued his journey and men began to fall behind. When the Messenger of Allâh ﷺ was told that so-and-so had fallen behind, he would say:

«دَعُوهُ فَإِنْ يَكُ فِيهِ خَيْرًا فَسَيَلْحَقُهُ اللهُ بِكُمْ، وَإِنْ يَكُ غَيْرَ ذَلِكَ، فَقَدْ أَرَاحَكُمُ اللهُ مِنْهُ»

"Leave him, for if there is any good in him, Allâh will make him join you and if there is no good in him, Allâh has relieved you of him."

Abu Dharr's camel caused him to tarry and so he placed his baggage on his back and when the Messenger of Allâh ﷺ halted at one of his stopping places, a man said: "Oh, Messenger of Allâh! It is Abu Dharr." He ﷺ said:

«رَحِمَ اللهُ أَبَا ذَرٍّ، يَمْشِي وَحْدَهُ، وَيَمُوتُ وَحْدَهُ، وَيُبْعَثُ وَحْدَهُ»

"May Allâh have mercy on Abu Dharr. He walks alone, he will die alone and he will be raised alone."[1]

And in '*Saheeh Ibn Hibban*', it is reported that when Abu Dharr ﷺ was close to death, his wife cried and he said: "What makes you cry?" She said: "You die in this wilderness and I have not a garment sufficient with which to shroud you and I have no hands with which to wash you." He said: "Do not cry, for I heard the Messenger of Allâh ﷺ say to a group of people of whom I was one:

«لَيَمُوتَنَّ رَجُلٌ مِنْكُمْ بِفَلَاةٍ مِنَ الأَرْضِ، يَشْهَدُهُ عِصَابَةٌ مِنَ الْمُسْلِمِينَ»

---

[1] Narrated by Ibn Katheer, on the authority of 'Abdullah Ibn Mas'ûd ﷺ, it contains in its *Sanad* one Buraidah Ibn Sufyan Al-Aslami, who is described as weak by scholars of *Hadeeth*. In spite of this, Ibn Katheer declared it to be *Hasan*. Al-Hakim also narrated it and Az-Zahabi declared it to be authentic, but he added: "It is *Mursal*."

"A man from among you shall die in the desert of the earth and a group of the Believers will attend his burial."

And all of those people died in a town, so I am the man. By Allâh, I have not lied, nor have I been lied about, so look out at the road." So I was racing to the top of a sandhill in order to see, then I would return and nurse him. While I was engaged thus, I observed some men on camels, as if they were a flock of vultures moving forward on their mounts, so I waved to them and they hurried forward until they stopped by me and said: "Oh, bondwoman of Allâh! What is wrong with you?" I said: "A Muslim man is dying, so enshroud him." They said: "Who is he?" I said: "Abu Dharr." They asked: "The Companion of the Messenger of Allâh 襲?" I replied: "Yes." They said: "May our fathers and mothers be ransomed for him," and they hastened to him and entered and he said: "Rejoice, for I heard the Messenger of Allâh 襲 saying" and he related the *Hadeeth* to them. Then he said: "If I had a garment which would suffice me as a shroud belonging to me or my wife, I would not be wrapped except in that shroud, so I implore you by Allâh that a man from among you who is a leader, or in-charge, or a messenger, or a headman may enshroud me." But there was none among them who responded to his words except a young boy from the *Ansar*, who said: "Oh, uncle! I will enshroud you in my *Rida'* or in my bag, I have a piece of cloth woven by my mother." He said: "You enshroud me." So he did so and they stood and prayed over him, then they buried him and they were all men from Yemen.

And in *'Saheeh Muslim'*, it is reported that the Messenger of Allâh 襲 said before he arrived in Tabûk:

«إِنَّكُمْ سَتَأْتُونَ غَدًا إِنْ شَاءَ اللهُ عَيْنَ تَبُوكَ، وَإِنَّكُمْ لَنْ تَأْتُوهَا حَتَّى يُضَحِّيَ النَّهَارُ، فَمَنْ جَاءَهَا مِنْكُمْ فَلَا يَمَسَّ مِنْ مَائِهَا شَيْئًا حَتَّى آتِيَ»

"Tomorrow, if Allâh wills, you will arrive at Tabuk spring and you will not get there before daytime and he who amongst you happens to go there should not touch its water until I come."

(Mu'adh Ibn Jabal ﷺ said:) "We came to it and two persons (amongst) us reached that fountain ahead of us. It was a thin flow of water like a shoelace. Allâh's Messenger 襲 asked them whether they had touched the water. They said: "Yes." The Messenger of Allâh ﷺ scolded them and he said to them what he had to say by the Will of Allâh. The people then took the water of the spring in the palms of their hands, little by little and Allâh's Messenger (may peace be upon him) washed his hands and his face in it, and then he put it back again and there gushed forth abundant water from that spring, until all the people had drunk their fill. He then said:

«يُوشِكُ يَا مُعَاذُ إِنْ طَالَتْ بِكَ حَيَاةٌ أَنْ تَرَى مَا هَاهُنَا قَدْ مُلِىءَ جِنَانًا»

"Mu'adh, it is hoped that if you live long you will see here fields full of vegetation."[1]

When he reached Tabûk, the Head of Ailah came to him and made a peace treaty with him and paid him the *Jizyah*. And the people of Jarba and Adhruh came to him and paid the *Jizyah* to him. To the Head of Ailah, he wrote:

«بِسْمِ اللهِ الرَّحْمٰنِ الرَّحِيمِ: هٰذِهِ أَمَنَةٌ مِنَ اللهِ وَمِنْ مُحَمَّدٍ رَسُولِ اللهِ ﷺ لِيُحَنَّةَ بْنِ رُؤْبَةَ وَأَهْلِ أَيْلَةَ، لِسُفُنِهِمْ وَسَيَّارِتِهِمْ فِي الْبَرِّ وَالْبَحْرِ لَهُمْ ذِمَّةُ اللهِ، وَذِمَّةُ النَّبِيِّ، وَمَنْ كَانَ مَعَهُمْ مِنْ أَهْلِ الشَّامِ، وَأَهْلِ الْيَمَنِ، وَأَهْلِ الْبَحْرِ، فَمَنْ أَحْدَثَ مِنْهُمْ حَدَثًا فَإِنَّهُ لَا يَحُولُ مَالُهُ دُونَ نَفْسِهِ، وَإِنَّهُ لِمَنْ أَخَذَهُ مِنَ النَّاسِ، وَإِنَّهُ لَا يَحِلُّ أَنْ يُمْنَعُوا مَاءً يَرِدُونَهُ، وَلَا طَرِيقًا يُرِيدُونَهُ مِنْ بَرٍّ أَوْ بَحْرٍ»

"In the Name of Allâh, the Most Beneficent, the Most Merciful, this is a guarantee of protection from Allâh and from the Prophet Muhammad, the Messenger of Allâh to Yuhannah Ibn Ru'bah and the people of Ailah; their ships, their caravans on land and at sea shall have the Protection of Allâh and the protection of the Prophet, he and whosoever is with him from among the people of Ash-Sham, the people of Yemen and the people at sea. Whosoever contravenes this treaty, his wealth shall not save him and it will be for anyone among the people who takes it. It is not lawful for them to prevent access to water

---

[1] Narrated by Muslim, on the authority of Mu'adh Ibn Jabal ﷺ.

for anyone who wants it nor from any journeys they want to make by land or by sea."[1]

Then he ﷺ sent Khalid Ibn Al-Waleed ؓ to Ukaidir Ibn 'Abdil Malik Al-Kindi, the ruler of Dûmah Al-Jandal and he said to him:

«إِنَّكَ سَتَجِدُهُ يَصِيدُ الْبَقَرَ»

"You will find him hunting oryx."

So Khalid ؓ went on until he was within eyesight of the fort on a moonlit night and there was Ukaidir on a rooftop and with him was his wife. The wild oryx remained rubbing their horns against the door of the fort and his wife said: "Have you ever seen the like of this?" He said: "No, by Allâh." So he mounted his horse and with him were members of his household, including his brother, whose name was Hassan. When they went out, the Messenger of Allâh's riders met them and they took him and killed his brother. He was wearing a garment of brocade embroidered with gold. Khalid ؓ stripped him of it and sent it to the Messenger of Allâh ﷺ and then he came to him with Ukaidir, and the Prophet ﷺ spared his life and made a peace treaty with him that he would pay the *Jizyah*, for he was a Christian. Ibn Sa'd said: "Khalid ؓ spared his life and he had with him four hundred and twenty riders for the purpose of conquering Dûmah Al-Jandal, which he did and he made a peace treaty with him in which it was stipulated that he would pay two thousand camels, eight hundred head of cattle, four hundred pieces of armour and four hundred spears. He set aside Safiyyah for the Messenger of Allâh ﷺ, then he divided up what remained of the spoils (after deducting the *Khumus*) among his Companions ؓ and every one of them received five shares.

The Messenger of Allâh ﷺ remained in Tabûk for between thirteen and nineteen days, then he left.

And it is reported on the authority of 'Abdullah Ibn Mas'ûd ؓ that he said: "I got up in the middle of the night when I was with the Messenger of Allâh ﷺ during the Tabûk campaign and I saw a torch burning in a corner of the camp, so I went to it and I saw the

---

[1] Narrated by Ibn Hisham.

Messenger of Allâh ﷺ with Abu Bakr and 'Umar ﷺ and I saw that 'Abdullah Dhul Bijadain ﷺ had died and they had dug a hole for him and the Messenger of Allâh ﷺ was in the hole and Abu Bakr and 'Umar ﷺ were passing him down to him and he ﷺ was saying:

«اللَّهُمَّ إِنِّي قَدْ أَمْسَيْتُ رَاضِيًا عَنْهُ، فَارْضَ عَنْهُ»

"Oh, Allâh! I have been well pleased with him, so be You (also) Well Pleased with him."

'Abdullah Ibn Mas'ûd ﷺ said: "Would that I were the inhabitant of that hole."[1]

And it is reported on the authority of Abu Umamah Al-Bahili ﷺ that he said: "Jibreel ﷺ came to the Messenger of Allâh ﷺ when he was in Tabuk and said to him: "Oh, Muhammad! Perform the funeral prayer for Mu'awiyah Ibn Mu'awiyah Al-Mizani." So the Messenger of Allâh ﷺ went out and Jibreel ﷺ came down with seventy thousand angels and he placed his right wing on the mountains and they were humbled and he placed his left wing on the lands and they were humbled, then he looked towards Makkah and Al-Madinah and the Messenger of Allâh ﷺ prayed over him (Mu'awiyah) along with Jibreel and the angels. After he had finished praying, he said:

«يَا جِبْرِيلُ بِمَ بَلَغَ مُعَاوِيَةُ هَذِهِ الْمَنْزِلَةَ»

"Oh, Jibreel! Due to what has Mu'awiyah attained this high rank?"

He replied: "Due to his recitation of

﴿قُلْ هُوَ اللَّهُ أَحَدٌ﴾

"Say: "He is Allâh, One."[2]

When sitting and when standing, while riding and while walking."[3]

---

[1] Narrated by Ibn Hisham from Ibn Ishaq, according to Al-Hafiz, in '*Al-Isabah*', it's chain of narrators is broken.

[2] *Sûrah Al-Fatihah*.

[3] Narrated by Ibn As-Sunni and Al-Baihaqi.

And the Messenger of Allâh ﷺ said:

«إِنَّ بِالْمَدِينَةِ أَقْوَامًا مَا سِرْتُمْ مَسِيرًا وَلَا قَطَعْتُمْ وَادِيًا إِلَّا كَانُوا مَعَكُمْ»

"Verily, in Al-Madinah there are those who were with you when you marched and whenever you crossed a valley."

They said: "And they were in Al-Madinah?" He ﷺ said:

«نَعَمْ حَبَسَهُمُ الْعُذْرُ»

"Yes, they were held back by some lawful excuse."[1]

The Messenger of Allâh ﷺ set out on the return journey from Tabûk to Al-Madinah until, on the way, some of the hypocrites plotted against him; they conspired to toss him from the top of a mountain pass on the road. When they reached the pass, they tried to traverse it with him, but Allâh informed him of their plan. He said to the people: "Whoever wishes to go by the bottom of the valley, (he should do so) for it is wider for him." And he took the mountain pass while the people went via the bottom of the valley, except those conspirators, who covered their faces. The Messenger of Allâh ﷺ ordered Huzaifah Ibn Al-Yaman and 'Ammar Ibn Yasir ﷺ to go with him and they walked with him; he ordered 'Ammar ﷺ to take hold of the camel's reins and he ordered Huzaifah ﷺ to drive it. While they were proceeding, they heard the sound of the people behind them, so he ordered Huzaifah ﷺ to turn them back; he did so and he had a staff in his hand with which he touched the faces of their mounts with it and they became fearful when they saw Huzaifah ﷺ, believing that their plot had become known, so they hurried on until they mixed with the people. Then the Messenger of Allâh ﷺ said to Huzaifah ﷺ:

«هَلْ عَرَفْتَ مِنْهُمْ أَحَدًا»

"Did you recognize any of them?"

He said: "I recognized the mount of so-and-so and of so-and-so." And it was dark. The Prophet ﷺ said:

---

[1] Narrated by Al-Bukhari, on the authority of Anas Ibn Malik ﷺ and by Muslim, on the authority of Jabir Ibn 'Abdillah ﷺ.

«هَلْ عَلِمْتَ شَأْنَهُمْ»؟

"Do you know what their plan was?"

He replied: "No." The Prophet ﷺ said:

«فَإِنَّهُمْ مَكَرُوا لِيَسِيرُوا مَعِيَ، حَتَّى إِذَا طَلَعَتْ فِي الْعَقَبَةِ طَرَحُونِي»

"They plotted to go with me, so that when I ascended the mountain path, they would throw me over."

Huzaifah ؓ said to him: "Will you not cut off their heads?" He ﷺ said:

«أَكْرَهُ أَنْ يَتَحَدَّثَ النَّاسُ أَنَّ مُحَمَّدًا قَدْ وَضَعَ يَدَهُ فِي أَصْحَابِهِ»

"I dislike that the people should say that Muhammad has laid his hands on his Companions."

Then he ordered him to keep it a secret.

The Messenger of Allâh ﷺ traveled from Tabûk until he was only an hour away from Al-Madinah – and the people of Adh-Dhirar Mosque had come to him when he was preparing to leave for Tabûk and said to him: "We have built a mosque for the sick and needy and for the rainy nights and we would like you to pray in it." He ﷺ said:

«إِنِّي عَلَى جَنَاحِ سَفَرٍ، وَلَوْ قَدِمْنَا إِنْ شَاءَ اللهُ أَتَيْنَاكُمْ»

"I am on the point of traveling, but when we return, if Allâh wills, I will come to you."

Then he was informed about this mosque by Allâh and so he summoned Malik Ibn Ad-Dukhsum and Ma'n Ibn Adi ؓ and he said:

«انْطَلِقَا إِلَى هَذَا الْمَسْجِدِ الظَّالِمِ أَهْلُهُ، فَاهْدِمَاهُ وَحَرِّقَاهُ بِالنَّارِ»

"Go to go to that mosque of evil and demolish it and burn it."

So they rushed out until they reached Banu Salim and Malik ؓ said to Ma'n ؓ: "Wait for me until I bring fire from my people." So he went inside and took a palm leaf and set fire to it, then they dashed out and entered the mosque with it and the people were inside it; they burnt it and destroyed it and the people dispersed from it and Allâh, Most Glorified revealed:

﴾ وَٱلَّذِينَ ٱتَّخَذُوا۟ مَسْجِدًا ضِرَارًا وَكُفْرًا وَتَفْرِيقًۢا بَيْنَ ٱلْمُؤْمِنِينَ ﴿

"And as for those who put up a mosque by way of harm and disbelief and to disunite the Believers."[1]

When the Prophet ﷺ was close to Al-Madinah, the people came out to meet him, including the women and the children and they were chanting:

The full moon has risen upon us
From *Thaniyyat Al-Wada'*,
We must give thanks
As long as a caller calls to Allâh.

Some narrators have said that this was when he arrived as an emigrant to Al-Madinah, but this is pure fancy, because Thaniyyat Al-Wada' lies in the direction of Ash-Sham. And when he looked down on Al-Madinah, he said: "This is Tabah," and he said:

«هَذَا أُحُدٌ جَبَلٌ يُحِبُّنَا وَنُحِبُّهُ»

"This is Uhud, a mountain which loves us and we love it."[2]

When he entered the city, he went to the mosque first and offered a two *Rak'ah* prayer, then he sat in it to greet the people and those who had stayed behind came to him to make their excuses; and they were over eighty in number.[3] He accepted their excuses and prayed for their forgiveness, leaving their secrets to their Creator. It was regarding them that the Words of Allâh were revealed:

﴾ يَعْتَذِرُونَ إِلَيْكُمْ إِذَا رَجَعْتُمْ إِلَيْهِمْ ﴿

"They (the hypocrites) will present their excuses to you (Muslims), when you return to them."[4]

----------  ----------

---

[1] *Sûrah At-Tawbah* 9:107
[2] Narrated by Al-Bukhari and Muslim, on the authority of Anas ﷺ.
[3] '*Fath Al-Bari*'.
[4] *Sûrah At-Tawbah* 9:94

Chapter

An Indication of Some of the Benefits Which May be Derived From This Story

These include the permissibility of fighting in a forbidden month, if it is confirmed that he set out in Rajab.

Also, the permissibility for the *Imam* to announce a matter to the people which would harm them were it kept secret and for him to keep hidden from matters other than it, if there is some benefit in doing so.

Likewise, if the *Imam* calls upon the army to go to war, they must go and it is not permissible for anyone to stay behind without his permission. And it is not a condition of the obligation that every person be individually called upon. And this is one of the three situations in which *Jihad* is *Fard 'Ain*. The second is when the enemy is surrounding the city and the third is when he (i.e. the Muslim) is between the Muslim and the enemy lines.

Also, it is obligatory to perform *Jihad* with one's wealth, just as it is obligatory to perform it with one's body. This is the correct opinion of which there is no doubt. And it takes precedence over the obligation to wage *Jihad* with one's body in all circumstances except one, which proves that it is more imperative than *Jihad* with one's body, for if it is incumbent upon one who is unable to perform *Hajj* himself to pay someone to perform it on his behalf, then the obligation to perform *Jihad* with one's wealth is more worthy.

It is also mentioned in it the great financial contribution made by 'Uthman ﷺ.

And we also understand from it that one who is unable to wage *Jihad* with his wealth is not excused unless he has exerted himself to the utmost, because Allâh, Most Glorified only negated the sin upon those who were unable after they had come to His Messenger ﷺ to ask him to provide mounts for them, then they returned, weeping.

We also derive from this that the *Imam* may leave behind a man from among the citizens (to take charge of affairs) and that he will be one of the *Mujahidûn*, because he is of the greatest help to them.

Also, we derive from it that it is not permissible to drink the water in the wells of Thamûd, nor is it permissible to make ablution with it, nor to cook with it, nor to make dough using it, but it is permissible to give it to the animals to drink. However it is permissible to drink and utilize the water from the well of the she-camel (of Salih ﷺ. And it was well known and still in existence up to the time of the Messenger of Allâh ﷺ and the knowledge has continued to be with the people century after century up to our time, so the riding beasts should not be watered from any other well.

Also, if anyone passes by the dwellings of those upon whom is Allâh's Wrath and those who were punished, he should not enter them, nor should he stay in them; instead he should hasten his steps and he should cover his face with his garment until he has passed them and he should not enter them without weeping and taking warning from their fate.

We also derive from it that he ﷺ used to combine the prayers when he was traveling and in this story, it is reported in the *Hadeeth* of Mu'adh ﷺ that he combined them by offering the second of them at the time of the first (*Jam'at-Taqdeem*). But we have mentioned the reason for this and it has not been reported from him ﷺ that he practised *Jam'at-Taqdeem* on a journey other than this, although it has been authentically reported from him that he did so before entering 'Arafah.

Also we derive from it the permissibility of performing *Tayammum* with sand, because the Prophet ﷺ and his Companions ﷺ were crossing the sands and they were not carrying dust with them; and these deserts cause great thirst and so they complained to the

Messenger of Allâh ﷺ.

And we derive from it that he ﷺ remained in Tabuk for twenty days shortening his prayers the whole time. And he did not say: No man should shorten his prayers if he remains longer than that." Ibn Al-Munzir said: "The scholars are in agreement that the traveller may shorten his prayers, so long as he has not decided to take up residence, even if a number of years passed.

We also derive from it the permissibility, indeed the desirability of breaking one's oath if he considered that doing something else would be better. And if he wishes, he may atone for it at once, or if he wishes, he may delay it.

Also, an oath made in anger is valid, if the anger is not so intense that it causes the person to be unaware of what he was saying. Likewise his judgement is binding and any contracts he makes are valid. But if his anger causes him to be unaware of what he was saying, then his oath is not valid, nor is his pronouncement of divorce.

Also the saying of the Prophet ﷺ:

$$\text{«مَا أَنَا حَمَلْتُكُمْ»}$$

"It was not I who provided mounts for you" etc.,

The Jabari[1] might cite it as evidence for his belief, but there is no evidence in it for him, for it is only like his saying:

$$\text{«وَاللهِ لَا أُعْطِي أَحَدًا شَيْئًا، وَلَا أَمْنَعُ، وَإِنَّمَا أَنَا قَاسِمٌ»}$$

"By Allâh, I do not give anyone anything, nor do I prevent anyone; I am only a distributor, I place it as I am commanded."

So he only acts upon what he is commanded to do.

We may also derive from it that if a person belonging to a community which has an agreement with the Muslims violates it by doing something harmful to Islam and the Muslims, he invalidates the agreement with regard to his life and his wealth and if the Imam is

---

[1] Jabari: One who belongs to *Al-Jabariyyah*, an heretical school of philosophy which held that man has no free will at all and is forced to do everything.

unable to seize him, then his life and his property are open and may be taken by anyone who is able to do so, as in the peace treaty of the people of Ailah.

Also, a dead person may be buried at night if it is due to necessity or some particular benefit as the Messenger of Allâh ﷺ buried Dhul Bijadain at night.

Also, if the *Imam* sends out an expedition and they gain some spoils, whatever they get is for them after the deduction of the *Khumus*, because the Prophet ﷺ divided up the spoils of Dûmah Al-Jandal among the members of the expedition. However, if the expedition went out from the army during a battle and attained it due to the strength of the army, then this is not the case, because what they have attained is war booty for all involved, after the deduction of the *Khumus* and the *Nafal*. And this was the guidance of the Prophet ﷺ.

And in it is the saying of the Prophet ﷺ: "Verily, in Al-Madinah there are those who were with you when you marched and whenever you crossed a valley." This is *Jihad* by one's heart and it is one of the four levels of *Jihad*.

We also derive from this story the permissibility of burning places of sin and disobedience, as the Prophet ﷺ burnt *Masjid Ad-Dirar* (the Mosque of Harm); and it is incumbent upon the *Imam* to destroy it, either by demolishing it or by burning it, or by altering its shape and changing its function. And if that was the case regarding *Masjid Ad-Dirar*, then the shrines where *Shirk* is practised should with all the more reason be destroyed and likewise the houses of the wine merchants and those who do evil deeds; 'Umar ﷺ burnt down a whole village in which wine was sold. And he burnt down the palace of Sa'd when he secluded himself in it from the people. And the Prophet ﷺ intended to burn the houses of those who did not attend the Friday prayer or the congregational prayers; and the only thing which prevented him from doing so was the presence therein of persons upon whom it was not obligatory (i.e. women and small children).

We also understand from it that an endowment is not valid unless it is done as an act of righteousness, so a mosque which was built over a grave should be demolished, just as a dead body should be exhumed from a mosque if it was buried therein, for the mosque and the grave do not go together in Islam. This is the religion of Islam with which Allâh sent His Messenger and it has become something strange among the people, as you see.[1]

---

[1] This is a reference to the *Hadeeth* of the Prophet ﷺ in which he said: "Islam started as something strange and it will again return to being something strange, just as it started." (Narrated by Muslim, At-Tirmidhi, Ibn Majah, Ahmad and Ad-Darimi)

Chapter

Regarding the Three Who Stayed Behind and They Were Ka'b Ibn Malik, Hilal Ibn Umayyah and Murarah Ibn Ar-Rabee'

Some commentators have said that the first of their names is Makkah and the last of them is 'Akkah. And it has been narrated to us in the *'Saheehayn'* in the wording of Al-Bukhari – may Allâh, Most High have mercy on him – on the authority of Ka'b Ibn Malik ⚔, who said: "I did not remain behind Allâh's Messenger ﷺ in any battle that he fought except the Battle of Tabuk, and I failed to take part in the Battle of Badr, but he did not admonish anyone who had not participated in it, for in fact, Allâh's Messenger ﷺ had gone out in search of the caravan of Quraish till Allâh made them (i.e. the Muslims) and their enemy meet without any appointment. I witnessed the night of Al-'Aqabah (pledge) with Allâh's Apostle when we pledged for Islam, and I would not exchange it for the Battle of Badr although the Battle of Badr is more popular amongst the people than it (i.e. the pledge of Al-'Aqabah). As for my news (in this battle of Tabûk), I had never been stronger or wealthier than I was when I remained behind the Prophet ﷺ in that battle.

By Allâh, never had I two she-camels before, but I had them at the time of this battle.

Whenever the Messenger of Allâh ﷺ intended to do battle, he would conceal his intention by declaring that he was going somewhere else, until this campaign, for he fought it in severe heat and he faced a long journey through the desert and an enemy who was great in numbers and so he disclosed his intention to the Muslims, so that they might prepare to do battle with their enemy. So he informed them of his true objective, and the Muslims who accompanied the Messenger of Allâh ﷺ were many in number and there was no register of their names and numbers. Ka'b ◈ said: "Any man who intended to be absent would think that the matter would remain hidden unless Allâh revealed it through Divine Revelation. So Allâh's Messenger ﷺ fought that battle at the time when the fruits had ripened and the shade looked pleasant. Allâh's Messenger ﷺ and his Companions ◈ prepared for the battle and I started to go out in order to get myself ready along with them, but I returned without doing anything. I would say to myself: "I can do that." So I kept on delaying it every now and then till the people got ready and the Messenger of Allâh ﷺ and the Muslims along with him departed, and I had not prepared anything for my departure, and I said: "I will prepare myself (for departure) one or two days after him, and then join them." In the morning following their departure, I went out to get myself ready but returned having done nothing. Then again in the next morning, I went out to get ready but returned without doing anything.

Such was the case with me till they hurried away and the battle was missed (by me). Even then I intended to depart to catch them. I wish I had done so! But it was not ordained for me. So, after the departure of Allâh's Messenger ﷺ, whenever I went out and walked amongst the people (i.e. the remaining persons), it grieved me that I could see none around me, but one accused of hypocrisy or one of those weak men whom Allâh had excused. The Messenger of Allâh ﷺ did not remember me till he reached Tabuk. So while he was sitting amongst the people in Tabûk, he said: "What did Ka'b do?" A man from Banu Salamah said: "Oh, Messenger of Allâh! He has been stopped by his two *Burdas* (i.e. garments) and his looking at his own flanks with pride." Then Mu'adh Ibn Jabal said: "What a bad thing you have said! By Allâh, Messenger of Allâh, we know nothing about him but good." Allâh's Messenger ﷺ kept silent." Ka'b Ibn Malik added: "When I heard that he (i.e. the Prophet ﷺ) was on his way back to Al-Madinah, I became engrossed with my concern, and began to think of false excuses, saying to myself: "How can I avoid his anger tomorrow?" And I took the advice of a wise member of my family in this matter. When it was said that the Messenger of Allâh ﷺ had come near, my mind abandoned all the evil, false excuses and I knew well that I could never come out of this problem by forging a false statement. Then I decided firmly to speak the truth. So the Messenger of Allâh ﷺ arrived in the morning; and whenever he returned from a journey, he would visit the Mosque first of all and offer a two *Rak'ah* prayer therein and then sit for the people. So when he had done all that (this time), those who had failed to join the battle (of Tabuk) came and started offering (false) excuses and taking oaths before him. They were something over eighty men; the Messenger of Allâh ﷺ accepted the excuses they had expressed, took their pledge of allegiance asked Allâh's Forgiveness for them, and left the secrets of their hearts for Allâh to judge. Then I came to him, and when I greeted him, he smiled the smile of an angry person and then said: "Come!" So I came walking till I sat before him. He said to me: "What prevented you from joining us? Had you not purchased an animal to carry you?" I answered: "Yes, Oh Messenger of Allâh! But by Allâh, if I were sitting before any person from among the people of the world other than you, I would have avoided his anger with an excuse. By Allâh, I have been bestowed with the power of speaking fluently and eloquently, but by Allâh, I knew well that if today I tell you a lie to seek your favor, Allâh would surely make you angry with me in the near future, but if I tell you the truth, though you will get angry because of it, I hope for Allâh's Forgiveness. Really, by Allâh, there was no excuse for me. By Allâh, I had never been stronger or wealthier than I was when I remained behind you." Then the Messenger of Allâh ﷺ said:

«أَمَّا هَذَا فَقَدْ صَدَقَ، فَقُمْ حَتَّى يَقْضِيَ اللهُ فِيكَ»

"As regards this man, he has surely told the truth. So get up till Allâh decides your case."

I got up, and many men of Banu Salamah followed me and said to me: "By Allâh, we never witnessed you doing any sin before this. Surely, you failed to offer an excuse to the Messenger of Allâh ﷺ as did the others who did not join him. The prayer of Allâh's Messenger

🌸 to Allâh to forgive you would have been sufficient for you." By Allâh, they continued blaming me so much that I intended to return (to the Prophet 🌸) and accuse myself of having told a lie, but I said to them: "Is there anybody else who has met the same fate as I have?" They replied, "Yes, there are two men who have said the same thing as you have, and both of them were given the same order that was given to you." I said: "Who are they?" They replied: "Murarah Ibn Ar-Rabi' Al-'Amri and Hilal bin Umayyah Al-Waqifi." They mentioned to me two pious men who had attended the Battle of Badr, and in whom there was an example for me. So I did not change my mind when they mentioned them to me. The Messenger of Allâh 🌸 forbade all of the Muslims from speaking to us, the three aforesaid persons out of all those who had remained behind in that battle. So we kept away from the people and they changed their attitude towards us till the very land (where I lived) appeared strange to me as if I did not know it.

We remained in that condition for fifty nights. As regards my two fellows, they remained in their houses and kept on weeping, but I was the youngest of them and the firmest of them, so I used to go out and witness the prayers along with the Muslims and roam about in the markets, but none would talk to me, and I would come to the Messenger of Allâh 🌸 and greet him while he was sitting in his gathering after the prayer, and I would wonder whether the Prophet 🌸 had moved his lips in return to my greetings or not. Then I would offer my prayer near to him and look at him stealthily. When I was busy with my prayer, he would turn his face towards me, but when I turned my face to him, he would turn his face away from me. When this harsh attitude of the people lasted long, I walked till I scaled the wall of the garden of Abu Qatadah who was my cousin and the dearest person to me, and I offered my greetings to him. By Allâh, he did not return my greetings. I said: "Oh, Abu Qatadah! I beseech you by Allâh! Do you know that I love Allâh and His Messenger 🌸?" He kept quiet. I asked him again, beseeching him by Allâh, but he remained silent. Then I asked him again in the Name of Allâh. He said: "Allâh and His Prophet know better." Thereupon my eyes flowed with tears and I returned and jumped over the wall." Ka'b added:

"While I was walking in the market of Al-Madinah, suddenly I saw a Nabatean from the Nabateans of Ash-Sham who came to sell his grains in Al-Madinah, saying: "Who will lead me to Ka'b Ibn Malik?" The people began to point (me) out to him till he came to me and handed me a letter from the King of Ghassan in which the following was written:

"To proceed, I have been informed that your companion (i.e. the Prophet ﷺ has treated you harshly and Allâh does not desire for you to live in a place where you feel inferior and your right is lost. So join us, and we will console you." When I read it, I said to myself: "This is also a kind of test." Then I took the letter to the oven and made a fire therein by burning it. When forty out of the fifty nights had elapsed, behold! There came to me a messenger from Allâh's Messenger ﷺ and said: "Allâh's Messenger ﷺ orders you to keep away from your wife." I said: "Should I divorce her, or else what should I do?" He said: "No, only keep away from her and do not have intimate relations with her." The Prophet sent the same message to my two fellows. Then I said to my wife: "Go to your parents and remain with them till Allâh gives His Verdict in this matter." Ka'b added: "The wife of Hilal Ibn Umayyah ﷺ came to the Messenger of Allâh ﷺ and said: "Oh, Messenger of Allâh! Hilal Ibn Umayyah is a helpless old man who has no servant to attend him. Do you dislike that I should serve him?" He said:

«لَا وَلَكِنْ لَا يَقْرَبُكِ»

"No, (you can serve him) but he should not come near (i.e. have sexual relations with) you."

She said: "By Allâh, he has no desire for anything. By Allâh, he has never ceased weeping since this matter began till this day."

On that, some of my family members said to me: "Will you also ask the Messenger of Allâh ﷺ to permit your wife (to serve you) as he has permitted the wife of Hilal Ibn Umayyah to serve him?" I said: "By Allâh, I will not ask permission from Allâh's Messenger ﷺ regarding her, for I do not know What Allâh's Messenger ﷺ would say if I asked him to permit her (to serve me) while I am a young man." Then I remained in that state for ten more nights after that till the period of fifty nights was completed starting from the time when the Messenger of Allâh ﷺ prohibited the people from talking to us. When I had offered the *Fajr* prayer on the fiftieth morning on the roof of one of our houses and while I was sitting in the condition which Allâh described (in the Qur'ân) i.e. my very soul seemed straitened to me and even the earth seemed narrow to me for all its spaciousness, there I heard the voice of one who had ascended the mountain of Sala' calling with his loudest voice: "Oh, Ka'b Ibn Malik! Rejoice (at the good tidings)." I fell down in prostration before Allâh, realizing that relief had come. The Messenger of Allâh ﷺ had announced the acceptance of our repentance by Allâh when he had offered the *Fajr* prayer. The people then went out to congratulate us. Some bringers of good tidings went out to my two fellows, and a horseman came to me in haste, and a man of Banu Aslam came running and ascended the mountain and his voice was swifter than the horse. When he (i.e. the man) whose voice I had heard, came to me conveying the good tidings, I took off my garments and dressed him with them; and by Allâh, I owned no other garments than them on that day. Then I borrowed two garments and wore them and went to the Messenger of Allâh ﷺ. The people started receiving me in groups, congratulating me on Allâh's Acceptance of my repentance, saying: "We congratulate you on Allâh's Acceptance of your repentance." Ka'b further said: "When I entered the Mosque, I saw the Messenger of Allâh ﷺ sitting with the people around him. Talhah Ibn Ubaidillah ؓ swiftly came to me, shook hands with me and congratulated me. By Allâh, none of the *Muhajirûn* got up for me except he and I will never forget this action of Talhah's." Ka'b continued: "When I greeted the Messenger of Allâh ﷺ, his face was bright with joy and he said:

«أَبْشِرْ بِخَيْرِ يَوْم مَرَّ عَلَيْكَ مُذْ وَلَدَتْكَ أُمُّكَ»

"Be happy with the best day that you have had ever since your mother delivered you."

Ka'b said: "I said to the Prophet ﷺ: "Is this forgiveness from you or from Allâh?" He said:

«لَا بَلْ مِنْ عِنْدِ اللهِ»

"No, it is from Allâh."

Whenever Allâh's Prophet became happy, his face would shine like a piece of the moon, and we all knew that characteristic of him. When I sat before him, I said: "Oh, Allâh's Prophet! As a part of my repentance I will give up all my wealth as charity in the Cause of Allâh and that of His Messenger. Allâh's Messenger ﷺ said:

«أَمْسِكْ عَلَيْكَ بَعْضَ مَالِكَ، فَهُوَ خَيْرٌ لَكَ»

"Keep some of your wealth, as it will be better for you."

I said: "Then I will keep my share from Khaibar with me," and added: "Oh, Messenger of Allâh! Allâh has saved me for telling the truth; so as a part of my repentance will be to speak naught but the truth as long as I live. By Allâh, I do not know anyone of the Muslims whom Allâh has helped in telling the truth more than me. From the time I mentioned that to Allâh's Messenger ﷺ until today, I have never intentionally told a lie. I hope that Allâh, Most High will also save me (from telling lies) for the rest of my life." And Allâh, Most High revealed to His Messenger ﷺ the Verse:

﴿لَّقَد تَّابَ ٱللَّهُ عَلَى ٱلنَّبِيِّ وَٱلْمُهَٰجِرِينَ وَٱلْأَنصَارِ ٱلَّذِينَ ٱتَّبَعُوهُ فِي سَاعَةِ ٱلْعُسْرَةِ مِنۢ بَعْدِ مَا كَادَ يَزِيغُ قُلُوبُ فَرِيقٍ مِّنْهُمْ ثُمَّ تَابَ عَلَيْهِمْ إِنَّهُ بِهِمْ رَءُوفٌ رَّحِيمٌ ۝ وَعَلَى ٱلثَّلَٰثَةِ ٱلَّذِينَ خُلِّفُوا حَتَّىٰ إِذَا ضَاقَتْ عَلَيْهِمُ ٱلْأَرْضُ بِمَا رَحُبَتْ وَضَاقَتْ عَلَيْهِمْ أَنفُسُهُمْ وَظَنُّوٓا۟ أَن لَّا مَلْجَأَ مِنَ ٱللَّهِ إِلَّآ إِلَيْهِ ثُمَّ تَابَ عَلَيْهِمْ لِيَتُوبُوٓا۟ إِنَّ ٱللَّهَ هُوَ ٱلتَّوَّابُ ٱلرَّحِيمُ ۝ يَٰٓأَيُّهَا ٱلَّذِينَ ءَامَنُوا۟ ٱتَّقُوا۟ ٱللَّهَ وَكُونُوا۟ مَعَ ٱلصَّٰدِقِينَ ۝﴾

"Allâh has forgiven the Prophet ﷺ, the *Muhâjirûn* (Muslim emigrants who left their homes and came to Al-Madinah) and the *Ansâr* (Muslims of Al-Madinah) who followed him (Muhammad ﷺ) in the time of distress (Tabûk expedition), after the hearts of a party of them had nearly deviated (from the Right Path), but He accepted their repentance. Certainly, He is unto them full of kindness, Most Merciful. And (He did forgive also) the three who did not join [the Tabûk expedition and whose case was deferred (by the Prophet ﷺ) for Allâh's Decision] till for them the earth, vast as it is, was straitened and their own selves were straitened to them, and they perceived that there is no fleeing from Allâh, and no refuge but with Him. Then, He forgave them (accepted their repentance), that they might beg for His Pardon [repent (unto Him)]. Verily, Allâh is the One Who forgives and accepts repentance, Most Merciful. O you who believe! Be afraid of Allâh, and be with those who are true (in words and deeds)."[1]

By Allâh, Allâh has never bestowed upon me, apart from His guiding me to Islam, a greater blessing than the fact that I did not tell a lie to the Messenger of Allâh ﷺ which would have caused me to perish as those who have told a lie perished, for Allâh described those who told lies with the worst description He ever attributed to anybody; Allâh said:

$$﴿سَيَحْلِفُونَ بِٱللَّهِ لَكُمْ إِذَا ٱنقَلَبْتُمْ إِلَيْهِمْ لِتُعْرِضُوا۟ عَنْهُمْ فَأَعْرِضُوا۟ عَنْهُمْ إِنَّهُمْ رِجْسٌ وَمَأْوَىٰهُمْ جَهَنَّمُ جَزَآءَۢ بِمَا كَانُوا۟ يَكْسِبُونَ ۝ يَحْلِفُونَ لَكُمْ لِتَرْضَوْا۟ عَنْهُمْ فَإِن تَرْضَوْا۟ عَنْهُمْ فَإِنَّ ٱللَّهَ لَا يَرْضَىٰ عَنِ ٱلْقَوْمِ ٱلْفَٰسِقِينَ ۝﴾$$

"They will swear by Allâh to you (Muslims) when you return to them, that you may turn away from them. So turn away from them. Surely, they are *Rijsun* [i.e. *Najasun* (impure) because of their evil deeds], and Hell is their dwelling place — a recompense for that which they used to earn. They (the hypocrites) swear to you (Muslims) that you may be pleased with them, but if you are pleased with them, certainly Allâh is not pleased with the people who are *Al-Fâsiqûn* (rebellious, disobedient to Allâh)."[2]

You should know – may Allâh grant us and you success in attaining the deeds which are pleasing to Him – that in this *Hadeeth* of Ka'b ﷺ there are (many) benefits:

---

[1] *Sûrah At-Tawbah* 9:117-119

[2] *Sûrah At-Tawbah* 9:95-96

They include the permissibility of informing a man of his abandonment of acts of obedience and the result of his action and that is giving advice which is one of the most important things.

We also derive from it the desirability of responding to one who backbites a Muslim, as Mu'adh 🙵 did.

Also, there is the obligation to tell the truth, even if it is a hardship, for the result of it will be goodness.

Likewise, there is the desirability of offering a two *Rak'ah* prayer in the mosque upon returning from a journey before doing anything else.

Also, it is desirable for one who arrives from a journey if people desire to see him, to sit for those who wish to see him in an open place, such as the mosque or the like.

Likewise, a person should be judged in accordance with what is apparent, and the secrets (which he may conceal in his heart) are for Allâh to determine.

Also, we derive from it the obligation to avoid the innovators and the open sinners and to avoid greeting them with salutations of peace in order to show disdain for them and a punishment for them.

Likewise, it is desirable for a person to weep for himself if he commits a sin and it is his right to do so.

Also, it is permissible to burn a paper in which the Name of Allâh, Most High is mentioned, if there is some benefit in doing so, as Ka'b 🙵 did.

We also derive from it that indirect expressions for divorce, such as the saying: "Go to your parents" do not constitute divorce without an intention.

Also, it is permissible for a wife to serve her husband without being forced or compelled to do so.

Likewise, it is desirable to perform *Sujûd Ash-Shûkr*[1] when one receives some blessing or some clear misfortune is removed and to give charity at that time.

---

[1] *Sujûd Ash-Shukr*: Prostration of thanks.

It is also desirable to give glad tidings and to congratulate someone and to honour the bearer of glad tidings by giving him a garment or the like.

Also, it is desirable to stand up to greet a person who has just arrived in order to honour him, if he is respected and honoured and also the permissibility of the people displaying pleasure at that, as Ka'b ﷺ did when Talhah ﷺ stood up and it does not contradict the *Hadeeth*:

«مَنْ سَرَّهُ أَنْ يَتَمَثَّلَ لَهُ الرِّجَالُ قِيَامًا فَلْيَتَبَوَّأْ مَقْعَدَهُ مِنَ النَّارِ»

"Whoever liked that men should stand up for him, let him take his place in the Fire."[1]

This is because this warning is for the arrogant and those who get angry if one does not stand for them; and the Prophet ﷺ used to stand up for Fatimah ﷺ out of pleasure at seeing her and she would stand out of respect for him. Likewise every standing which causes love for Allâh's sake, which is to exhibit happiness for one's brother when he receives some blessing from Allâh, to show kindness towards one who deserves kindness – and deeds are purely according to intentions. And Allâh knows better.

Also, it is permissible for a person to praise himself by the attributes he possesses, if it is not due to pride.

Also we derive from it that there was no military administration or directorate during the life of the Prophet ﷺ and the first person to establish these departments was 'Umar ﷺ.

Likewise, when an opportunity to do some good deed comes one should energetically seize the opportunity, because resolve quickly breaks down and Allâh punishes those to whom He grants the opportunity to do goodness and they do not act upon it by coming between his heart and his intention; Allâh, Most High says:

﴿يَٰٓأَيُّهَا ٱلَّذِينَ ءَامَنُواْ ٱسۡتَجِيبُواْ لِلَّهِ وَلِلرَّسُولِ إِذَا دَعَاكُمۡ لِمَا يُحۡيِيكُمۡ وَٱعۡلَمُوٓاْ أَنَّ ٱللَّهَ يَحُولُ بَيۡنَ ٱلۡمَرۡءِ وَقَلۡبِهِۦ﴾

---

[1] Narrated by At-Tirmidhi and Abu Dawûd, on the authority of Mu'awiyah Ibn Abi Sufyan ﷺ.

"O you who believe! Answer Allâh (by obeying Him) and (His) Messenger when he (ﷺ) calls you to that which will give you life, and know that Allâh comes in between a person and his heart (i.e. He prevents an evil person to decide anything)."[1]

And He explained this in His Words:

$$ ﴿وَنُقَلِّبُ أَفْئِدَتَهُمْ﴾ $$

"And We shall turn their hearts."[2]

And He says:

$$ ﴿فَلَمَّا زَاغُوٓا۟ أَزَاغَ ٱللَّهُ قُلُوبَهُمْ﴾ $$

"So, when they turned away (from the path of Allâh), Allâh turned their hearts away (from the Right Path)."[3]

And He says:

$$ ﴿وَمَا كَانَ ٱللَّهُ لِيُضِلَّ قَوْمًۢا بَعْدَ إِذْ هَدَىٰهُمْ حَتَّىٰ يُبَيِّنَ لَهُم مَّا يَتَّقُونَ﴾ $$

"And Allâh will never lead a people astray after He has guided them until He makes clear to them as to what they should avoid."[4]

And examples of this are numerous in the Qur'ân.

Likewise, we derive from it that none stayed behind except one who was held in contempt due to his hypocrisy, or a man who was among those who were excused, or one whom the Messenger of Allâh ﷺ had left in charge.

Also, we derive from it that the *Imam* should not be careless regarding one who lags behind him in certain matters; rather, he should remember him so that he may return to obedience, for the Prophet ﷺ said:

---

[1] *Sûrah Al-Anfâl* 8:24
[2] *Sûrah Al-An'am* 6:110
[3] *Sûrah As-Saff* 61:5
[4] *Sûrah At-Tawbah* 9:115

«مَا فَعَلَ كَعْبٌ؟»

"What did Ka'b do?"

And he did not mention anyone else in order to show his acceptance of him and his disregard of the hypocrites.

We also understand from it the permissibility of maligning a man according to what seems most probable to the one who maligns him, in defence of Allâh and His Messenger ﷺ

It is also permissible to reply to the maligner, if it appears probable to the one replying that what he says is pure fancy, as Mu'adh ﷺ did; and the Prophet ﷺ did not rebuke either of them.

We also derive from it that the *Sunnah* for one who arrives from a journey is to enter the city in a state of ritual ablution (*Wudhû'*) and to begin by going to the House of Allâh before going to his house and pray two *Rak'ahs* there.

Also, the *Imam* may avoid answering the greeting of one who has committed some such sin.

We also derive from it that the one placed in authority may rebuke one whom he loves, for the Prophet ﷺ censured those three and no others and people constantly rebuke loved ones.

We also derive from it that Allâh granted Ka'b and his two companions ﷺ success due to their telling the truth and He did not leave them so that they lied in which case, they would have saved themselves in the life of this world at the expense of the Hereafter, while those who are truthful may suffer somewhat in this world, but they achieve a good end (in the Hereafter). And upon this the life of this world and the life of the Hereafter are based.

And in the Prophet's singling them out for prohibition against speaking to them, there is evidence of their truthfulness and the untruthfulness of the others, for he wished to teach the truthful ones a lesson. But as for the hypocrites, this medicine would not treat their disease. And this is how the Lord, Most Glorified punishes the crimes of His slaves.

And in Ka'b's saying: "Till I scaled the wall of the garden of Abu

Qatadah" there is evidence for the permissibility of entering the house of one's companion or neighbour if it is known that he accepts it without giving permission.

And in the *Hadeeth* is the command of the Prophet ﷺ to them to separate from their wives, which is like good tidings of relief from suffering, in two respects: (i) that he was now speaking to them and (ii) that he ordered them to separate from their wives.[1]

And in his saying: "Go to your parents," there is evidence that divorce does not take place as a result of this expression or similar ones, as long as he did not intend it.

And in his prostration when he heard the voice of the bearer of glad tidings, there is evidence that this was the habit of the Companions. – and that is *Sujûd Ash-Shukr* when blessings are renewed or adversities are repelled; and the Prophet ﷺ prostrated when Jibreel ﷺ gave him the glad tidings that whoever sent prayers on him once, Allâh would send prayers on him ten times because of it. And he prostrated when he interceded for his nation and Allâh granted him intercession for them three times. And Abu Bakr ﷺ prostrated when news came to him of the killing of Musailamah.[2] And 'Ali ﷺ prostrated when he found that Dhu Ath-Thudayyah had been killed among the Khawarij.

And in the competing of the owner of the horse and the one who ascend Sala' with each other there is evidence of the people's desire to do good deeds and of how they used to compete with each other in making others happy.

We also derive from it that giving something to a bearer of glad tidings is a part of having noble manners and that it is permissible for the one who receives the good news to give him all of his clothes.

And we derive from it that it is desirable to congratulate one for whom religious blessings have been renewed and that to stand up for

---

[1] This is because it meant that they were being punished for their sin and that therefore, there was an end in sight to their plight, as opposed to the hypocrites, whose punishment was deferred until the Hereafter, but would be everlasting.

[2] Narrated by Al-Baihaqi.

him and shaking his hand, for this is a highly recommended *Sunnah* and it is also permissible in the case of one for whom some earthly blessings have been renewed.

And we derive from it that it is preferred to say: May that which Allâh has given you be pleasing to you," or the like, for therein is acknowledgement that these blessings are from Allâh and supplication for the one who receives them that he will enjoy them.

And we derive from it that the very best day of a slave's life is the day on which he repents to Allâh and on which is repentance is accepted and in the Prophet's pleasure at it, there is his perfect love and compassion for his nation.

We also derive from it the desirability of giving charity at the time of repentance and that whoever vowed to give of his wealth in charity is not obliged to give all of it.

And we derive from it the great value of truthfulness and how much happiness in the life of this world and the life of the Hereafter depend upon it. And Allâh has divided mankind into two groups: (i) Those who are happy – and they are the truthful, believing ones and (ii) the wretched – and they are the untruthful and the deniers and it is a division which is all-encompassing, widespread and reflected (in deeds).

And the Saying of Allâh:

$$﴿لَّقَد تَّابَ ٱللَّهُ عَلَى ٱلنَّبِيِّ وَٱلْمُهَٰجِرِينَ وَٱلْأَنصَارِ ٱلَّذِينَ ٱتَّبَعُوهُ فِي سَاعَةِ ٱلْعُسْرَةِ مِنۢ بَعْدِ مَا كَادَ يَزِيغُ قُلُوبُ فَرِيقٍ مِّنْهُمْ ثُمَّ تَابَ عَلَيْهِمْ إِنَّهُۥ بِهِمْ رَءُوفٌ رَّحِيمٌ ﴿١١٧﴾ ﴾$$

"Allâh has forgiven the Prophet ﷺ, the *Muhâjirûn* (Muslim emigrants who left their homes and came to Al-Madinah) and the *Ansâr* (Muslims of Al-Madinah) who followed him (Muhammad ﷺ) in the time of distress (Tabûk expedition), after the hearts of a party of them had nearly deviated (from the Right Path), but He accepted their repentance. Certainly, He is unto them full of kindness, Most Merciful."[1]

___
[1] *Sûrah At-Tawbah* 9:117

This is the greatest description of the value of repentance and it is the utmost perfection of the Believer, for Allâh, Most Glorified, Most High has given them this perfection after the last of the battles.

This is only known by those who really know Allâh and know His rights. So Glorified be He, besides Whose Pardon and Forgiveness none encompasses the slaves. And He repeated His Forgiveness of their sins twice: He turned to them with Forgiveness firstly by guiding them to repent and secondly by accepting their repentance. And all goodness comes from Him and through Him and all of it belongs to Him.

Regarding the Pilgrimage of Abu Bakr 🙵

In the year 9 A.H., after his return from Tabûk, he set out with three hundred men from among the Muslims and the Verses of *Bara'ah* (in *Sûrah At-Tawbah*) were revealed regarding the invalidation of the agreements between the Messenger of Allâh 🙵 and the polytheists. So 'Ali 🙵 went out (to proclaim these Verses to the people) on the she-camel of Allâh's Messenger 🙵 and he met Abu Bakr 🙵; when Abu Bakr 🙵 saw him, he asked: "Did you come to lead or to be led?" He replied: "To be led; Allâh's Messenger 🙵 has sent me to proclaim *Bara'ah* to the people and to renounce the agreements of all those who have made covenants (with the Messenger of Allâh 🙵, so their agreements will remain in effect until they expire."

'Ali 🙵 said: "I have been sent with four things (to tell them): (i) None will enter Paradise except a believing soul, (ii) no naked persons will be allowed to circumambulate the Ka'bah, (iii) the Believer and the disbeliever will not worship side-by-side in the Sacred Mosque after this year and (iv) whosoever has a covenant with the Prophet 🙵, it will be valid only until it expires (i.e. it will not be renewed or extended)."

Ibn Ishaq said: "After the Messenger of Allâh 🙵 had conquered Makkah and returned from Tabuk and Thaqeef had embraced Islam, delegations from the Arabs came to him from every quarter." And he (i.e. Ibn Al-Qayyim) mentioned among them the delegations of: Banu Tameem, Tai', Banu 'Amir, 'Abdul Qais, Banu Haneefah, Kindah, Al-Ash'ariyyûn, Al-Azad, the people of Najran, Hamdan, the Christians of Najran and others. Then he mentioned the guidance of the Prophet ﷺ in writing to the kings, then he mentioned his guidance in medicine and then he mentioned his guidance in treatment by spiritual medicines, both singular and compound. And he mentioned the natural medicines, saying: Muslim narrated on the authority of 'Abdullah Ibn 'Abbas ﷺ in a *Marfû'* form:

«الْعَيْنُ حَقٌّ وَلَوْ كَانَ شَيْءٌ سَابَقَ الْقَدَرَ لَسَبَقَتْهُ الْعَيْنُ»

"(The influence of) *Al-'Ain*[1] is a fact; if anything had preceded *Al-Qadar*, it would have been (the influence of) the evil eye."

And when you are asked to take bath (as a cure) from the influence of the evil eye, you should take a bath."[2] It is also reported in his *'Saheeh'*, on the authority of Anas ﷺ that the Messenger of Allâh ﷺ permitted incantations against *Al-'Ain*, ulcers and poison (by snakebite, scorpion sting etc.)[3]

And Malik Ibn Shihab narrated on the authority of Abu Umamah Ibn Sahl bin Haneef that he said: "'Amir bin Rabee' ﷺ saw Sahl ﷺ bathing and he said: "I have not seen the like of what I see today, not even the skin of a maiden who has never been out of doors." Sahl ﷺ fell to the ground. The Messenger of Allâh ﷺ came to 'Amir ﷺ and was furious with him and said:

«عَلَامَ يَقْتُلُ أَحَدُكُمْ أَخَاهُ أَلَا بَرَّكْتَ؟ اغْتَسِلْ لَهُ»

"Why does one of you kill his brother? Why did you not say: 'May Allâh bless you? Make *Ghusl* for it.'"

'Amir ﷺ washed his face, hands, elbows, knees, the ends of his feet, and inside his lower garment in a vessel. Then he poured it over him, and Sahl ﷺ went off with the people, and there was nothing wrong with him."[4] And 'Abdur-Razzaq reported on the authority of Ma'mar, who reported on the authority of Ibn Tawûs, who reported from his father in a *Marfû'* form:

---

[1] *Al-'Ain*: The evil eye of envy.
[2] Narrated by Muslim, on the authority of 'Abdullah Ibn 'Abbas ﷺ
[3] Narrated by Muslim, on the authority of Anas Ibn Malik ﷺ.
[4] Narrated by Imam Malik, on the authority of Abu Umamah Ibn Sahl ﷺ.

«الْعَيْنُ حَقٌّ، وَإِذَا اسْتُغْسِلَ أَحَدُكُمْ، فَلْيَغْتَسِلْ»

"Al-'Ain is a fact, so if one of you is asked to bathe, he should make major ritual ablution."[1]

And its connection (to the Prophet ﷺ) is correct. Az-Zuhri said: "The one who casts the evil eye is commanded to take a drinking vessel full of water and put the palm of his hand in it and rinse his mouth with it, then spit into the vessel and wash his face in the vessel, then to put his left hand in the vessel and pour it over his right knee into the vessel, then to put his right hand into it and pour it over his left knee, then wash what is inside his *Izar* and the vessel should not be placed on the ground; then it should be poured over the head of the man who has been afflicted by the evil eye from behind and in a single pouring."[2]

And *Al-'Ain* is of two types: (i) That of humans and (ii) that of the jinn, for it has been authentically reported from Umm Salamah ﷺ that the Prophet ﷺ saw a slave girl in her house and in her face was a *Saf'ah* (a dark spot) and he said:

«اسْتَرْقُوا لَهَا، فَإِنَّ بِهَا النَّظْرَةَ»

"Make incantation for her, for she has been afflicted by *An-Nazrah* (i.e. the evil eye)."[3]

Al-Baghawi said: "*Saf'ah* means *An-Nazrah* from the jinn. He ﷺ was saying that she has been afflicted by the evil eye from the jinn, which was more piercing than the points of spears."

The Prophet ﷺ used to seek protection with Allâh from the jinn and from the evil eye of human beings. A group from among those with deficient hearing and intelligence have denied the matter of *Al-'Ain*, whereas the intelligent people in all nations do not reject it, although they may differ regarding its causes.

---

[1] Narrated by 'Abdur-Razzaq in *'Musannaf'*. It is a *Mursal* narration, but Muslim has reported it in a connected form in his *'Saheeh'*, by way of Ibn Tawûs from his father, on the authority of 'Abdullah Ibn 'Abbas ﷺ.

[2] Narrated by Al-Baihaqi in his *'Sunan'*.

[3] Narrated by Al-Bukhari and Muslim.

And there is no doubt that Allâh, Most Glorified has created in human bodies and spirits different powers and characteristics and He has created in many of them attributes and qualities which can affect others, so it is not possible for any rational person to reject the effect of some souls on bodies, because that is something which is apparent (to all).

And it is not actually the eye which affects a person, but rather the spirit, but because of its strong connection to the eye, the deed has been attributed to it. And the spirit of the envious person is harmful to the person of whom he is envious in a manner which is most clear. For this reason, Allâh commanded His Messenger ﷺ to seek refuge from the evil of it. And the most similar thing to it is the poisonous, because the power of its poison is concealed within it, for when it encounters its enemy, the strength of anger is emitted from it.

Some of them cause miscarriage, while others cause blindness, as the Prophet ﷺ said regarding *Al-Abtar*[1] and *Dhu At-Tufyatain*:[2]

$$ \text{«إِنَّهُمَا يَلْتَمِسَانِ الْبَصَرَ، وَيُسْقِطَانِ الْحَبْلَ»} $$

"They cause blindness and they cause miscarriage."[3]

And the effect is not dependent upon physical contact. And the one who emits the evil eye is not dependent upon seeing the object of his envy; indeed, he might even be blind and the thing (which incites his envy) might be described to him. And many of them have their effect through a description, without having seen the object of their envy. So every person from whom *Al-'Ain* is emitted is envious (*Hasid*), but not every envious person causes *Al-'Ain*, but because envy is more general than it, seeking protection from it means seeking protection from *Al-'Ain*. And it is an arrow which emanates from the soul of the envious one and the one who emits *Al-'Ain*; if it strikes him when is unprotected, it will affect him, but if he is on his guard and he is armed, it will not affect him and it might even be returned to the one who cast it in like manner. A person might even afflict himself with

---

[1] *Al-Abtar*: A kind of venomous snake with a short tail.
[2] *Dhu At-Tufyatain*: A poisonous snake with two white stripes on its back.
[3] Narrated by Muslim, At-Tirmidhi, Abu Dawûd, Ibn Majah and Ahmad, on the authority of 'Abdullah Ibn 'Umar ﷺ

the evil eye, or he might afflict someone unintentionally, but rather by his (evil) nature and this is the worst kind of evil eye.

Abu Dawûd has reported in his *'Sunan'*, on the authority of Sahl Ibn Hunaif ﷺ, that he said: "passed by a river and I entered it and took a bath in it. When I came out, I had fever. The Messenger of Allâh ﷺ was informed about it. He said:

$$\text{«مُرُوا أَبَا ثَابِتٍ فَلْيَتَعَوَّذْ»}$$

"Ask Abu Thabit to seek refuge in Allâh from that."

I asked: Oh, my master! will an incantation be useful?" He replied:

$$\text{«لَا رُقْيَةَ إِلَّا فِي نَفْسٍ، أَوْ حُمَةٍ، أَوْ لَدْغَةٍ»}$$

"No, an incantation is not to be used except in the case of *Nafs*, or *Humah* (fever) or *Ladghah* (a snake bite)."[1]

And *Nafs* means *Al-'Ain*, while *Al-Ladghah* means the sting of a scorpion or the like. And among the forms of seeking refuge and incantations is to recite *Al-Mu'awwidhatan*,[2] *Sûrah Al-Fatihah* and *Ayah Al-Kursi* frequently. Among the Prophetic ways of seeking refuge with Allâh is to say:

$$\text{«أَعُوذُ بِكَلِمَاتِ اللهِ التَّامَّاتِ مِنْ كُلِّ شَيْطَانٍ وَهَامَّةٍ؛ وَمِنْ كُلِّ عَيْنٍ لَامَّةٍ»}$$

"*A'ûdhu Bikalimatillahit-Tammati Min Kulli Shaitanin Wa Hammatin Wa Min Kulli 'Ainin Lammah*"

"I seek refuge with the Perfect Words of Allâh from every devil, from every poisonous creature and from the affliction of every envious eye)"[3]

And the like of:

---

[1] Narrated by Abu Dawûd and Ahmad on the authority of Sahl Ibn Hunaif ﷺ.

[2] *Al-Mu'awwidhatan*: The two Seekers of Refuge (with Allâh) – *Sûrah Al-Falaq* and *Sûrah An-Nas*.

[3] Narrated by Al-Bukhari, At-Tirmidhi, Abu Dawûd, Ibn Majah and Ahmad, on the authority of 'Abdullah Ibn 'Abbas ﷺ.

«أَعُوذُ بِكَلِمَاتِ اللهِ التَّامَّاتِ الَّتِي لَا يُجَاوِزُهُنَّ بَرٌّ وَلَا فَاجِرٌ مِنْ شَرِّ
مَا خَلَقَ، وَذَرَأَ وَبَرَأَ، وَمِنْ شَرِّ مَا يَنْزِلُ مِنَ السَّمَاءِ، وَمِنْ شَرِّ مَا
يَعْرُجُ فِيهَا، وَمِنْ شَرِّ مَا ذَرَأَ فِي الأَرْضِ، وَمِنْ شَرِّ مَا يَخْرُجُ مِنْهَا،
وَمِنْ شَرِّ فِتَنِ اللَّيْلِ وَالنَّهَارِ، وَمِنْ شَرِّ طَوَارِقِ اللَّيْلِ، إِلَّا طَارِقًا
يَطْرُقُ بَخَيْرٍ يَا رَحْمٰنُ»

*"A'ûdhu Bikalimait-Tammatil-Latee La Yujawizuhunna Barrun Wa
La Fajirun Min Sharri Ma Khalaqa Wa Dhara'a Wa Bara'a Wa Min
Sharri Ma Yanzilu Minas-Sama'i Wa Min Sharri Ma Ya'ruju Feeha Wa
Min Sharri Ma Dhara'a Fil-Ard Wa Min Sharri Ma Yakhruju Minha
Wa Min Sharri Fitanil-Laili Wan-Nahari Wa Min Sharri Tawariqil-
Laili Illa Tariqan Yatruqu Bikhairin Ya Rahman"*

"I seek refuge with the Perfect Words of Allâh Which neither a
righteous man nor a profligate man may surpass from the evil
of what He has created, wrought and brought forth from
naught and from the evil of what descends from the heaven
and what ascends to it and from the evil of what He has
wrought in the earth and from the evil of what emanates from
it and from the evil of the trials of the night and the day and
from the night visitors, except a visitor who brings good, oh,
Most Beneficent!."[1]

Another supplication is:

«أَعُوذُ بِكَلِمَاتِ اللهِ التَّامَّاتِ مِنْ غَضَبِهِ وَعِقَابِهِ وَشَرِّ عِبَادِهِ، وَمِنْ
هَمَزَاتِ الشَّيَاطِينِ وَأَنْ يَحْضُرُونَ»

*"A'udhu Bikalimatillahit-Tammati Min Ghadabihi Wa 'Iqabihi Wa
Sharri 'Ibadihi Wa Min Hamazatish-Shayateeni Wa An Yahdurûni"*

"I seek refuge with the Perfect Words of Allâh from His Anger
and His Punishment and from the evil of His slaves and from the
evil suggestions of the devils and from their coming to me."[2]

---

[1] Narrated Ahmad, on the authority of 'Abdur-Rahman Ibn Khanbash ☙.

[2] Narrated by Abu Dawûd, on the authority of 'Abdullah Ibn 'Amr Ibn Al-
'As ☙.

Another is:

«اللَّهُمَّ إِنِّي أَعُوذُ بِوَجْهِكَ الْكَرِيمِ، وَكَلِمَاتِكَ التَّامَّةِ مِنْ شَرِّ مَا أَنْتَ آخِذٌ بِنَاصِيَتِهِ، اللَّهُمَّ أَنْتَ تَكْشِفُ الْمَأْثَمَ وَالْمَغْرَمَ، اللَّهُمَّ لَا يُهْزَمُ جُنْدُكَ، وَلَا يُخْلَفُ وَعْدُكَ سُبْحَانَكَ وَبِحَمْدِكَ»

"Allâhumma, Innee A'ûdhu Bika Biwajhikal-Kareemi Wa Kalima-tikat-Tammati Min Sharri Ma Anta Akhidhun Binasiyatihi; Allâhumma, Anta Takshiful-Ma'thama Wal-Maghrama; Allâhumma La Yuhzamu Junduka Wa La Yukhlafu Wa'duka Subhanaka Wa Bihamdik"

"Oh, Allâh, I seek refuge in Your Noble Countenance and in Your Perfect Words from the evil of what You seize by its forelock; O, Allâh! You remove sin and dept; oh, Allâh! Your troops are not routed, nor is Your Promise broken. Glory and praise be unto You."[1]

And another is:

«أَعُوذُ بِوَجْهِ اللهِ الْعَظِيمِ الَّذِي لَا شَيْءَ أَعْظَمُ مِنْهُ، وَبِكَلِمَاتِهِ التَّامَّاتِ الَّتِي لَا يُجَاوِزُهُنَّ بَرٌّ وَلَا فَاجِرٌ وَأَسْمَاءِ اللهِ الْحُسْنَى، مَا عَلِمْتُ مِنْهَا وَمَا لَمْ أَعْلَمْ مِنْ شَرِّ مَا خَلَقَ وَذَرَأَ وَبَرَأَ، وَمِنْ شَرِّ كُلِّ ذِي شَرٍّ لَا أُطِيقُ شَرَّهُ، وَمِنْ شَرِّ كُلِّ ذِي شَرٍّ أَنْتَ آخِذٌ بِنَاصِيَتِهِ، إِنَّ رَبِّي عَلَى صِرَاطٍ مُسْتَقِيمٍ»

"A'ûdhu Biwajhillahil-'Azeemil-Ladhee La Shay'un A'zama Minhu Wa Bikalimatihit-Tammati-Al-Latee La Yujawizuhunna Barrun Wa La Fajirun Wa Bi-Asma'illahil-Husna Ma 'Alimtu Minha Wa Ma Lam A'lam Min Sharri Ma Khalaqa Wa Dhara'a Wa Bara'a Wa Min Kulli Dhee Sharrin La Uteequ Sharrahu Wa Min Sharri Kulli Dhee Sharrin Anta Akhidhun Binasiyatihi; Inna Rabbee 'Ala Siratin Mustaqeem"

"I seek refuge with Allâh's Mighty Countenance, that which there is nothing greater and by His Words which neither a righteous man nor a profligate man may surpass and with His

---

[1] Narrated by Abu Dawûd, on the authority of 'Ali Ibn Abi Talib ﷺ.

Beautiful Names – those which I know and those which I do not know – from the evil of that which He has created, wrought and brought forth from naught and from the evil of every wicked person against whose evil I cannot prevail and from the evil of every wicked person whom You will seize by the forelock. Verily, my Lord is on a Straight Path."[1]

And if he wishes, he may add:

«تَحَصَّنْتُ بِاللهِ الَّذِي لَا إِلَهَ إِلَّا هُوَ إِلَهِي وَإِلَهُ كُلِّ شَيْءٍ، وَاعْتَصَمْتُ بِرَبِّي وَرَبِّ كُلِّ شَيْءٍ، وَتَوَكَّلْتُ عَلَى الْحَيِّ الَّذِي لَا يَمُوتُ وَاسْتَدْفَعْتُ الشَّرَّ بِلَا حَوْلَ وَلَا قُوَّةَ إِلَّا بِاللهِ، حَسْبِيَ اللهُ وَنِعْمَ الْوَكِيلُ، حَسْبِيَ الرَّبُّ مِنَ الْعِبَادِ، حَسْبِيَ الْخَالِقُ مِنَ الْمَخْلُوقِ، حَسْبِيَ الرَّازِقُ مِنَ الْمَرْزُوقِينَ لَا إِلَهَ إِلَّا هُوَ عَلَيْهِ تَوَكَّلْتُ وَهُوَ رَبُّ الْعَرْشِ الْعَظِيمِ»

"Tahassantu Billahil-Ladhee La Ilaha Illa Huwa, Ilahee Wa Ilahu Kulli Shay'in, Wa'tasamtu Birabbee Wa Rabbi Kulli Shay'in Wa Tawakkaltu 'Alal-Hayyil-Ladhee La Yamûtu Wastadfa'tush-Sharra Bila Hawla Wa La Quwwata Illa Billahi, Hasbiyallahu Wa Ni'mal-Wakeelu, Hasbiyar-Rabbu Minal-'Ibadi, Hasbiyal-Khaliqu Minal-Makhlûqi, Hasbiyar-Raziqu Minal-Marzûqi, Hasbiyallahu Wa Kafa, Sami'allahu Liman Da'a, Laisa Wara'allahi Marma, Hasbiyallahu La Ilaha Illa Huwa 'Alaihi Tawakkaltu Wa Huwa Rabbul-'Arshil-'Azeem"

"I am fortified by Allâh, besides Whom there is none who has the right to be worshipped, My *Ilah* and the *Ilah* of everything, and I have sought refuge with my Lord and the Lord of all things and I have placed my trust in the Ever-living, Who does not die and I have warded off evil with (the words): *"La Hawla Wa La Quwwata Illa Billah"* "There is no power and no strength

---

[1] Narrated by Malik, up to the words: "from the evil of that which He has created, wrought and brought forth from naught." It was reported on the authority of Al-Qa'qa' Ibn Hakeem, a *Tabi'i*, from Ka'b Al-Ahbar, who is also a *Tabi'i*, therefore it is *Mu'an'an*.

save in Allâh) Allâh is Sufficient for me and He is the best Disposer of affairs. Sufficient for me is the Lord against the slaves, Sufficient for me is the Creator against the created, Sufficient for me is the Sustainer against the sustained, Sufficient for me is Allâh and Enough. Allâh hears the one who supplicates; there is no object besides Him, Allâh is Sufficient for me, none has the right to be worshipped but He. In Him I trust and He is the Lord of the Mighty Throne."

Whoever tried these ways of seeking refuge with Allâh knows their benefit and they prevent one being afflicted by Al-*'Ain* and the alleviate it once it has struck, according to the strength of the person's *Eeman* and the strength of his soul, for it is a weapon and a weapon is as strong as the person who wields it.

And if the person from whom the evil eye emanates fears the harm of his eye, he should say:

«اللَّهُمَّ بَارِكْ عَلَيْهِ»

"Allâhumma, Barik 'Alaihi"

"Oh, Allâh! Bless him," as the Messenger of Allâh commanded 'Amir to say to Sahl ﷺ. And among the things which alleviates it is the saying:

«مَا شَاءَ اللهُ لَا قُوَّةَ إِلَّا بِاللهِ»

"Ma Sha'allahu La Quwwata Illa Billah"

"That which Allâh wills (will come to pass)."

(There is no strength except with Allâh). Whenever 'Urwah ﷺ saw something he admired, or he entered any of his gardens, he would say this.[1]

Among them is also the incantation of Jibreel ﷺ for the Prophet ﷺ, which is in *'Saheeh Muslim'*:

---

[1] Allâh, Most High says: {It was better for you to say when you entered your garden: "That which Allâh wills (will come to pass)! There is no power but with Allâh } (*Sûrah Al-Kahf* 18:39).

«بِسْمِ اللهِ أَرْقِيكَ مِنْ كُلِّ شَيءٍ يُؤْذِيكَ، مِنْ شَرِّ كُلِّ نَفْسٍ أَوْ عَيْنٍ حَاسِدٍ، اللهُ يَشْفِيكَ بِسْمِ اللهِ أَرْقِيكَ»

"In Allâh's Name I make this incantation for you against everything which might harm you, from the evil of every soul or envious eye. May Allâh cure you, in Allâh's Name I make this incantation for you."[1]

Then he (i.e. Ibn Al-Qayyim) mentioned the guidance of the Prophet ﷺ regarding the treatment of every complaint with the Divine Incantation, and he mentioned in this regard the *Hadeeth* of Abu Dawûd, narrated on the authority of Abu Ad-Darda', who attributed it to the Prophet ﷺ:

«مَنِ اشْتَكَىٰ مِنْكُمْ شَيْئًا فَلْيَقُلْ: رَبُّنَا اللهُ الَّذِي فِي السَّمَاءِ»

"If any of you complained of something, he should say: (*Rabbunallahul-Ladhee Fis-Sama'*) etc. (Our Lord, Allâh, Who is in *As-Sama'*."[2]

Then he mentioned the aforementioned incantation of Jibreel ﷺ. Then he (Ibn Al-Qayyim) mentioned the guidance of the Prophet ﷺ regarding incantations for ulcers and wounds and he mentioned the narration which is in the '*Saheehayn*', in which it is stated that the Prophet ﷺ said:

«إِذَا اشْتَكَى الإِنْسَانُ، أَوْ كَانَ بِهِ قُرْحَةٌ، أَوْ جُرْحٌ قَالَ بِإِصْبُعِهِ هٰكَذَا»

"If a person is complaining of something, or he has an ulcer or a sore, he should recite, with his finger thus."

And Sufyan ﷺ placed his finger on the ground, then he raised it and said:

«بِسْمِ اللهِ تُرْبَةُ أَرْضِنَا بِرِيقَةِ بَعْضِنَا، يُشْفَى سَقِيمُنَا بِإِذْنِ رَبِّنَا»

"*Bismillahi, Turbatu Ardina Bireeqati Ba'dina, Yushfa Saqeemuna Bi'idhni Rabbina*"

---

[1] Narrated by Muslim, on the authority of Abu Sa'eed Al-Khudri ﷺ.
[2] *As-Sama'*: Literally, the highest place.

"In the Name of Allâh, the soil of our land and the saliva of some of us cure our patient with the permission of our Lord."[1]

As to whether the earth of the land refers to all land or it refers to the land of Al-Madinah, the scholars hold two opinions regarding it.

---

[1] Narrated by Al-Bukhari, Muslim, Abu Dawûd, Ibn Majah and Ahmad, on the authority of 'A'ishah ﷺ.

Chapter

Regarding His ﷺ Guidance in Treating Afflictions

Allâh, Most High says:

﴿وَلَنَبْلُوَنَّكُم بِشَيْءٍ مِّنَ ٱلْخَوْفِ وَٱلْجُوعِ وَنَقْصٍ مِّنَ ٱلْأَمْوَٰلِ وَٱلْأَنفُسِ وَٱلثَّمَرَٰتِ ۗ وَبَشِّرِ ٱلصَّٰبِرِينَ ۝ ٱلَّذِينَ إِذَآ أَصَٰبَتْهُم مُّصِيبَةٌ قَالُوٓاْ إِنَّا لِلَّهِ وَإِنَّآ إِلَيْهِ رَٰجِعُونَ ۝ أُوْلَٰٓئِكَ عَلَيْهِمْ صَلَوَٰتٌ مِّن رَّبِّهِمْ وَرَحْمَةٌ ۖ وَأُوْلَٰٓئِكَ هُمُ ٱلْمُهْتَدُونَ ۝﴾

"And certainly, We shall test you with something of fear, hunger, loss of wealth, lives and fruits, but give glad tidings to *As-Sâbirûn* (the patient). Who, when afflicted with calamity, say: "Truly, to Allâh we belong and truly, to Him we shall return." They are those on whom are the *Salawât* (i.e. who are blessed and will be forgiven) from their Lord, and (they are those who) receive His Mercy, and it is they who are the guided ones."[1]

Then he (i.e. Ibn Al-Qayyim) mentioned the *Hadeeth* of *Al-Istirja'*[2] and then he said: This expression is one of the most effective and most beneficial treatments for one who is afflicted by calamities, because it contains two fundamental principles, which if they are realized, the slave will be consoled thereby from his calamity.

---

[1] *Sûrah Al-Baqarah* 2:155-157

[2] *Al-Istirja'*: Saying the words: *"Inna Lillahi Wa Inna Ilaihi Raji'ûn"* (Verily, we are for Allâh and to Him we shall return). This *Hadeeth* was narrated by Muslim and Ahmad, on the authority of Umm Salamah ﷺ.

The first of them is that the slave and his wealth belong to Allâh and He has given it to him as a loan.

The second of them is that the return is to Allâh and it is inevitable that he will leave the life of this world behind; so if this is his beginning and his end, then his thinking about them is one of the greatest treatments for this illness and a part of his treatment is that he knows that what was ordained to afflict him cannot miss him and what was ordained to miss him cannot afflict him.

And a part of it is that his Lord has set aside for him the like of that which he missed or better and He has stored up for him that which is many times better than the calamity and that if He had willed, He could have made the calamity greater than it was.

Another part of it is His extinguishing the fire of his misfortune by the coolness of comfort and consolation, so he should look to his right and to his left (i.e. at the world around him) and he should know that the pleasures of this life are an illusion, though they may cause him to laugh a little, they will cause him to weep much.

 Also a part of it is the knowledge that discontent does not alleviate the misfortune; indeed, it increases it.

 And another part of it is the knowledge that losing the reward which Allâh has guaranteed for patience and *Istirja'* is greater than it.

And another part of the treatment is the knowledge that discontent causes his enemy to take pleasure and grieves his friend and makes his Lord Angry.

Still another part of it is the knowledge that the pleasure which follows patient perseverance and the expectation of Allâh's Reward is many times greater than that which he would have experienced from the thing which he lost, if it had remained with him.

Another part of it is that he should soothe his heart by seeking recompense for it from Allâh.

And a part of it is the knowledge that his reaction to the calamity will determine what happens to him, for whoever accepts (Allâh's *Qadar*), Allâh will be pleased with him and whoever is angry at it, Allâh will be Angry with him.

Also a part of the treatment is the knowledge that even if he was patient sometime after the calamity struck, that being the patience of one who is resigned, that is not praiseworthy and it is not rewarded.

And another part of it is the knowledge that one of the most effective medicines is the success granted by Allâh in attaining that which He loves and which is pleasing to Him and that it is the essence of love.

Another part of it is for him to compare between the greater and the lesser of the two pleasures: between the pleasure which he enjoys due to (his acceptance of) the calamity which befell him and the pleasure which he enjoys due to the reward of Allâh (which he receives due to his acceptance and patient perseverance).

And a part of it is the knowledge that the One Who puts him to trial is the Best of judges and the Most Merciful of those who show mercy and that He has not subjected him to misfortune in order to destroy him, but in order to test him and to hear entreaties and see him prostrating at His door.

Another part of it is the knowledge that misfortunes are a means of preventing sickness which will cause his destruction, such as pride, arrogance, and hardness of heart.

Still another part of it is the knowledge that the bitterness of this life is the sweetness of the afterlife and vice versa. And if this is not apparent to you, examine the words of the truthful one, whose words are believed:

$$\text{«حُفَّتِ الْجَنَّةُ بِالْمَكَارِهِ، وَحُفَّتِ النَّارُ بِالشَّهَوَاتِ»}$$

"Paradise is surrounded by hardships and the Hell-Fire is surrounded by temptations."[1]

And in this matter, the minds of mankind are at fault and the reality of men is made clear (i.e. that they prefer the temporary pleasures of this world to the everlasting pleasures of the Hereafter).

---

[1] Narrated Muslim, At-Tirmidhi, Ahmad and Ad-Darimi, on the authority of Anas Ibn Malik.

Regarding His Guidance in the Treatment of Worry, Anxiety and Sadness

It is reported in the '*Saheehayn*' that the Messenger of Allâh ﷺ used to say whenever he was worried:

«لَا إِلَهَ إِلَّا اللهُ الْعَظِيمُ الْحَلِيمُ، لَا إِلَهَ إِلَّا اللهُ رَبُّ الْعَرْشِ الْعَظِيمِ، لَا إِلَهَ إِلَّا اللهُ رَبُّ السَّمَوَاتِ وَرَبُّ الأَرْضِ رَبُّ الْعَرْشِ الْكَرِيمِ»

"*La Ilaha Illallahul-'Azeemul-Haleemu, La Ilaha Illallahu Rabbul-'Arshil-'Azeemi, La Ilaha Illallahu Rabbus-Samawati Wa Rabbul-Ardi, Rabbul-'Arshil-Kareem.*"

"None has the right to be worshipped except Allâh, the Most Great, the Most Forbearing, none has the right to be worshipped except Allâh, the Lord of the Mighty, Throne, none has the right to be worshipped except Allâh, the Lord of the Heavens, the Lord of the earth and the Lord of the Supreme Throne."

And it is narrated by At-Tirmidhi, on the authority of Anas ﷺ that the Messenger of Allâh ﷺ used to say:

«يَا حَيُّ يَا قَيُّومُ بِرَحْمَتِكَ أَسْتَغِيثُ»

"*Ya Hayyu Ya Qayyûmu, Birahmatika Astagheeth.*"

"O, You, the Ever-living, the Sustainer and Protector of all that exists, By Your Mercy, I seek aid."

And At-Tirmidhi also narrated on the authority of Abu Hurairah ﷺ

that whenever the Messenger of Allâh ﷺ was anxious about something, he would raise his eyes to the heaven and say:

«سُبْحَانَ اللهِ الْعَظِيمِ»

"Subhanallahil-'Azeem."

"Glorified be Allâh, the Most Great."

And if he applied himself in supplication, he would add:

«يَا حَيُّ يَا قَيُّومُ»

"Ya Hayyu Ya Qayyûm"

"O, You, the Ever-living, the Sustainer and Protector of all that exists."

And Abu Dawûd has narrated on the authority of Abu Bakr As-Siddeeq ﷺ in a *Marfû'* form that he said:

«دَعْوَةُ الْمَكْرُوبِ: اللَّهُمَّ رَحْمَتَكَ أَرْجُو، فَلَا تَكِلْنِي إِلَى نَفْسِي طَرْفَةَ عَيْنٍ، وَأَصْلِحْ لِي شَأْنِي كُلَّهُ لَا إِلَهَ إِلَّا أَنْتَ»

"The supplication for one seized by calamity is: *"Allâhumma, Rahmataka Arju, Fala Takilnee Ila Nafsee Tarfata 'Ainin Wa Aslih Lee Sha'nee Kullahu La Ilaha Illa Anta"*

"O, Allâh! I seek Your Mercy, so do not entrust me to myself (even) for the blink of an eye; remedy all of my affairs, for there is none worthy of worship except You."[1]

Abu Dawûd also narrated on the authority of Asma' Bint 'Umais that she said: "The Messenger of Allâh ﷺ said to me:

«أَلَا أُعَلِّمُكَ كَلِمَاتٍ تَقُولِينَهُنَّ عِنْدَ الْكَرْبِ: اللهُ رَبِّي لَا أُشْرِكُ بِهِ شَيْئًا»

"Shall I not teach you words which you may say in times of distress? (They are): *"Allâhu Rabbee, La Ushriku Bihi Shay'an"* (Allâh is my Lord, I will not associate anything with Him."

---

[1] Narrated by Abu Dawûd and Ahmad, on the authority of Abu Bakr As-Siddeeq ﷺ.

And Ahmad has narrated on the authority of Ibn Mas'ûd 🌸 in a *Marfû'* form that he said: "Whenever a slave is afflicted by anxiety or sadness and he says:

«اللَّهُمَّ إِنِّي عَبْدُكَ، وَابْنُ عَبْدِكَ، وَابْنُ أَمَتِكَ نَاصِيَتِي بِيَدِكَ، مَاضٍ
فِيَّ حُكْمُكَ، عَدْلٌ فِيَّ قَضَاؤُكَ، أَسْأَلُكَ بِكُلِّ اسْمٍ هُوَ لَكَ سَمَّيْتَ بِهِ
نَفْسَكَ، أَوْ أَنْزَلْتَهُ فِي كِتَابِكَ، أَوْ عَلَّمْتَهُ أَحَدًا مِنْ خَلْقِكَ، أَوِ
اسْتَأْثَرْتَ بِهِ فِي عِلْمِ الْغَيْبِ عِنْدَكَ أَنْ تَجْعَلَ الْقُرْآنَ الْعَظِيمَ رَبِيعَ
قَلْبِي، وَنُورَ صَدْرِي، وَجِلَاءَ حُزْنِي وَذَهَابَ هَمِّي»

*"Allâhumma, Innee 'Abduka Wabnu 'Abdika Wabnu Amatika;
Nasiyatee Biyadika Madhin Fiyya Hukmuka 'Adlun Fiyya Qada'uka;
As'aluka Bikullismin Huwa Laka, Sammaita Bihi Nafsaka Aw
Anzaltahu Fee Kitabika Aw 'Allamtahu Ahadan Min Khalqika
Awista'tharta Bihi Fee 'Ilmil-Ghaibi 'Indaka An Taj'alal-Qur'anal-
'Azeema Rabee'a Qalbee Wa Nûra Sadree Wa Jala'a Huznee Wa
Dhahaba Hammee"*

"O, Allâh! I am Your slave and the son of your male slave and your female slave; I am in Your Power. Your Command concerning me prevails and Your Decision concerning me is just. I call upon You by every one of the beautiful Names by which You have described Yourself, or which You have revealed in Your Book, or have taught anyone of Your creatures, or which You have chosen to keep in the Knowledge of the unseen with You, to make the Mighty Qur'ân the delight of my heart, the light of my breast and the remover of my anxieties and sorrows), Allâh will remove his anxiety and sadness and substitute in place of it happiness."[1]

At-Tirmidhi narrated on the authority of Sa'd 🌸 in a *Marfû'* form:

«دَعْوَةُ ذِي النُّونِ لَمْ يَدْعُ بِهَا رَجُلٌ مُسْلِمٌ فِي شَيْءٍ قَطُّ إِلَّا اسْتُجِيبَ
لَهُ»

"A Muslim man never supplicates using the words of Dhun-

---

[1] Narrated by Ahmad, Ibn Hibban and Ibn As-Sunni.

Nûn[1] except that it is answered."[2]

And in another version:

«إِنِّي لَأَعْلَمُ كَلِمَةً لَا يَقُولُهَا مَكْرُوبٌ إِلَّا فَرَّجَ اللهُ عَنْهُ، كَلِمَةُ أَخِي يُونُسَ»

"Verily, I will teach you words which, whenever a person afflicted by grief says them, Allâh will relieve him of it: They are the words of my brother, Jonah."[3]

And Abu Dawûd has narrated that the Prophet ﷺ said to Abu Umamah ؓ:

«أَلَا أُعَلِّمُكَ كَلَامًا إِذَا أَنْتَ قُلْتَهُ أَذْهَبَ اللهُ عَزَّ وَجَلَّ هَمَّكَ، وَقَضَى دَيْنَكَ؟ قُلْ إِذَا أَصْبَحْتَ وَإِذَا أَمْسَيْتَ:

"Shall I not teach you words which, if you said them, Allâh, the Almighty, the All-Powerful will remove your anxiety and discharge your debt? Say in the morning and at night:

اللَّهُمَّ إِنِّي أَعُوذُ بِكَ مِنَ الْهَمِّ وَالْحُزْنِ، وَأَعُوذُ بِكَ مِنَ الْعَجْزِ وَالْكَسَلِ، وَأَعُوذُ بِكَ مِنَ الْجُبْنِ وَالْبُخْلِ، وَأَعُوذُ بِكَ مِنْ غَلَبَةِ الدَّيْنِ وَقَهْرِ الرِّجَالِ»

"Allâhumma Innee A'ûdhu Bika Minal-Hammi Wal-Hazni Wa A'ûdhu Bika Minal-'Ajzi Wal-Kasali Wa A'ûdhu Bika Minal-Jubni Wal-Bukhli Wa A'ûdhu Bika Min Ghalabatid-Daini Wa Qahrir-Rijal"

"Oh, Allâh! I seek refuge with You from anxiety and sadness and I seek refuge with You from inability and laziness and I seek refuge with You from cowardice and miserliness and I seek refuge with You from being overcome by debt and from the oppression of men). (Abu Umamah ؓ said:)

"So I did that and Allâh, the Almighty, the All-Powerful removed my anxieties and discharged my debts."[4]

---

[1] *Dhun-Nûn*: Jonah (Yûnus) ﷺ.

[2] Narrated by At-Tirmidhi and Ahmad on the authority of Sa'd Ibn Abi Waqqas ؓ.

[3] See *Sûrah Al-Anbiya'* 21:87.

[4] Narrated by Abu Dawûd, on the authority of Abu Umamah ؓ, it contains

And Abu Dawûd narrated on the authority of Ibn 'Abbas 🙵 in a *Marfû'* form:

«مَنْ لَزِمَ الاسْتِغْفَارَ جَعَلَ اللهُ لَهُ مِنْ كُلِّ هَمٍّ فَرَجًا، وَمِنْ كُلِّ ضِيقٍ مَخْرَجًا، وَرَزَقَهُ مِنْ حَيْثُ لَا يَحْتَسِبُ»

"Whoever was constant in seeking forgiveness from Allâh, Allâh will make a release for him from every trouble and a way out for him from every oppression and He will sustain him from whence he does not expect."[1]

And in the *'Sunan'*:

«عَلَيْكُمْ بِالْجِهَادِ، فَإِنَّهُ بَابٌ مِنْ أَبْوَابِ الْجَنَّةِ، يَدْفَعُ اللهُ بِهِ عَنِ النُّفُوسِ الْهَمَّ وَالْغَمَّ»

"*Jihad* is an obligation upon you, for it is a gate from among the gates of Paradise, by which Allâh removes anxiety and affliction."[2]

And in *'Al-Musnad'* (by Imam Ahmad), it is reported that when something serious happened to the Messenger of Allâh ﷺ would seek refuge in prayer.[3]

And it is reported from Ibn 'Abbas 🙵 in a *Marfû'* form:

«مَنْ كَثُرَتْ هُمُومُهُ وَغُمُومُهُ، فَلْيُكْثِرْ مِنْ قَوْلٍ:

"Whoever was seized by many anxieties and afflictions should repeat frequently the words:

لَا حَوْلَ وَلَا قُوَّةَ إِلَّا بِاللهِ»

---

in its chain of narrators one Ghassan Ibn 'Awf Al-Basri, who is considered weak by As-Saji and Al-Azadi. Ibn Hajr described him as lax in *Hadeeth*.

[1] Narrated by Abu Dawûd and Ibn Majah, on the authority of Ibn 'Abbas 🙵. It contains in its *Sanad* Al-Hakam Ibn Mus'ab, who is unknown, according to Abu Hatim Ar-Razi.

[2] Narrated by Ahmad, on the authority of 'Ubadah Ibn As-Samit 🙵. It was declared authentic by Al-Hakim and Az-Zahabi confirmed this.

[3] Narrated by Ahmad, on the authority of Suhaib 🙵.

"*La Hawla Wa La Quwwata Illa Billah*"

"There is nor power and no strength except in Allâh."

And it has been confirmed in the '*Saheehayn*' that it (i.e. the saying: "*La Hawla Wa La Quwwata Illa Billah*")

«إِنَّهَا كَنْزٌ مِنْ كُنُوزِ الْجَنَّةِ»

"Is a treasure from among the treasures of Paradise."[1]

These medicines consist of fifteen effective ingredients, but if they are unable to remove the anxiety and sadness, then it has spread beyond control.

The first: The affirmation of Allâh's Oneness in matters of Lordship (*Tawheed Ar-Rubûbiyyah*).

The second: The affirmation of Allâh's sole right to be worshipped (*Tawheed Al-Ulûhiyyah*).

The third: Tawheed of knowledge.

The Fourth: The declaration that the Lord, Most High is far above committing injustice against His slave or seizing him without any cause on the part of the slave which would necessitate that.

The fifth: The slave's acknowledgement that it is he who is the wrongdoer.

The sixth: Seeking mediation with Allâh (*Tawassul*) by the most beloved thing to Allâh which is by His Names and Attributes and the most comprehensive of them for the meanings of the Names of Attributes is: *Al-Hayyu* and *Al-Qayyûmu*.

The seventh: Seeking help from Him Alone.

The eighth: The slave's affirmation of belief in Him by placing his hopes in Him.

The ninth: The affirmation of trust in Allâh and dependence on Him (*Tawakkul*) and the acknowledgement of the slave that he is in Allâh's Power and that His Command concerning him prevails and His Decision concerning him is just.

---
[1] Narrated by Al-Bukhari and Muslim, on the authority of Abu Mûsa ﷺ.

The tenth: That his heart takes pleasure in the garden of the Qur'ân, like spring for animals and that he is enlightened by it in the darkness of doubts and uncertainties and that he is consoled by it against every calamity and he seeks a cure in it from the diseases of his heart and so it removes his sadness and cures his anxiety and grief.

The eleventh: Seeking forgiveness from Allâh.

The twelfth: Repenting to Allâh (*Tawbah*).

The thirteenth: Jihad.

The fourteenth: Prayer.

The fifteenth: The acceptance that man is without power or strength and the acknowledgement that they belong only to Allâh.

Chapter

Regarding His ﷺ Guidance in the Treatment of Fear and Sleeplessness

At-Tirmidhi narrated on the authority of Buraidah ﷺ that he said: "Khalid complained to the Messenger of Allâh ﷺ, saying: "Oh, Messenger of Allâh! I cannot sleep at night, due to insomnia." He ﷺ said:

«إِذَا أَوَيْتَ إِلَى فِرَاشِكَ، فَقُلْ:

"When you repair to your bed, say:

اللَّهُمَّ رَبَّ السَّمٰوَاتِ السَّبْعِ، وَمَا أَظَلَّتْ، وَرَبَّ الأَرَضِينَ السَّبْعِ وَمَا أَقَلَّتْ، وَرَبَّ الشَّيَاطِينِ وَمَا أَضَلَّتْ، كُنْ لِي جَارًا مِنْ شَرِّ خَلْقِكَ كُلِّهِمْ جَمِيعًا أَنْ يُفْرِطَ عَلَيَّ أَحَدٌ مِنْهُمْ، أَوْ يَبْغِي عَلَيَّ، عَزَّ جَارُكَ، وَجَلَّ ثَنَاؤُكَ، وَلَا إِلَهَ غَيْرُكَ»

"Allâhumma, Rabbas-Samawatis-Sab'i Wa Ma Azallat Wa Rabbal-Ardeena-Sab'i Wa Ma Aqallat Wa Rabbash-Shayateeni Wa Ma Adallat, Kun Lee Jaran Min Sharri Khalqika Kullihim Jamee'an An Yafruta 'Alayya Ahadun Minhum Aw Yabghiya 'Alayya 'Azza Jaruka Wa Jalla Thana'uka Wa La Ilaha Ghairuka."

"O, Allâh! Lord of the seven heavens and all that they contain, Lord of the earths and all that they carry, Lord of the devils and all those whom they send astray, be a Protector for me against the evil of all of Your created beings, that they may not transgress against me and that they may not commit injustice against me. Mighty is Your Protection and Exalted is Your

Praise and there is no *ilah* besides You."[1]

Also in At-Tirmidhi's *'Sunan'* is the *Hadeeth* of 'Amr Ibn Shu'aib, in which it is stated that the Messenger of Allâh ﷺ used to teach them the following supplication as a protection against fear:

$$\text{«أَعُوذُ بِكَلِمَاتِ اللهِ التَّامَّاتِ مِنْ غَضَبِهِ، وَشَرِّ عِبَادِهِ، وَمِنْ هَمَزَاتِ}$$
$$\text{الشَّيَاطِينِ، وَأَعُوذُ بِكَ رَبِّ أَنْ يَحْضُرُونَ»}$$

"A'ûdhu Bikalimatillahit-Tammati Min Ghadabihi Wa Sharri 'Ibadihi Wa Min Hamazatish-Shayateeni Wa A'ûdhu Bika Rabbi An Yahdurûn"

"I seek refuge with the Perfect Words of Allâh from His Anger and from the evil of His slaves and from the whisperings of the devils and I seek refuge with You, Lord, from their coming to me."[2]

And 'Abdullah Ibn 'Umar ؓ used to teach it to those of his children who were of sufficient age to memorize it and he used to write it and hang it around the necks of those who were not.[3]

And it is mentioned in the *Hadeeth* of 'Amr Ibn Shu'aib in a *Marfû'* form:

$$\text{«إِذَا رَأَيْتُمُ الْحَرِيقَ فَكَبِّرُوا، فَإِنَّ التَّكْبِيرَ يُطْفِئُهُ»}$$

"If you see burning, say: "*Allâhu Akbar*", because *Takbeer* extinguishes it."[4]

---

[1] Narrated by At-Tirmidhi, on the authority of Buraidah Ibn Al-Haseeb ؓ, it contains in its chain of narrators Al-Hakam Ibn Zuhair, of whom Yahya Ibn Ma'een said: "He is a liar," while Al-Bukhari said: "His *Ahadeeth* are abandoned."

[2] Narrated by Abu Dawûd, At-Tirmidhi and Ahmad, Shaikh Nasir Ad-Deen Al-Albani declared it to be "*Hasan Lighairihi*" (i.e. it is raised to the level of *Hasan* by another supporting narration).

[3] According to Shaikh Nasir Ad-Deen Al-Albani, this addition is *Munkar*, since it is prohibited in Islam to wear amulets, whether they be Qur'ânic Verses or supplications.

[4] Narrated by Ibn As-Sunni in *"Amal Al-Yawmi Wal-Lailah"*, it contains in its *Sanad* Al-Qasim Ibn 'Abdillah, who was described as a liar by Imam Ahmad. Shaikh Al-Albani says that a number of its narrators are weak.

Burning is caused by fire, from which Satan was created and in it there is destruction which is beloved by Satan; and fire naturally seeks to rise high and to destroy and these two attributes are the guidance of Satan, to which he calls and by which he destroys mankind, while remembrance of the Lord, the Almighty, the All-Powerful restrains Satan. So when the Muslims extols his Lord by saying: *"Allâhu Akbar"*, it extinguishes the burning and we and others have tried this and have found that it is so.

---------- ❖ ❖ ❖ ----------

Chapter

Regarding His ﷺ Guidance
in Preserving Health

Allâh, Most High says:

﴿وَكُلُوا۟ وَٱشْرَبُوا۟ وَلَا تُسْرِفُوٓا۟﴾

"And eat and drink but waste not by extravagance."[1]

So He instructed them to put in their bodies the food and drink which would sustain them, rather than eating and drinking excessively which is just excreted, and that the amount and the quality of it be should sufficient to benefit the body, so preservation of health is enshrined within these two words (i.e. quantity and quality). And because health and wellbeing are among the greatest of blessings – indeed general wellbeing is without exception the greatest of blessings – it is only fitting that you should preserve it.

This is why the Prophet ﷺ said:

«نِعْمَتَانِ مَغْبُونٌ فِيهِمَا كَثِيرٌ مِنَ النَّاسِ: الصِّحَّةُ وَالْفَرَاغُ»

"There are two blessings which many people lose: Health and free time (for doing good deeds)."[2]

And it is reported by At-Tirmidhi and others in a *Marfû'* form:

---

[1] *Sûrah Al-A'raf* 7:31

[2] Narrated by Al-Bukhari, At-Tirmidhi, Ibn Majah and Ahmad.

«مَنْ أَصْبَحَ مُعَافًى فِي جَسَدِهِ، آمِنًا فِي سِرْبِهِ، عِنْدَهُ قُوتُ يَوْمِهِ، فَكَأَنَّمَا حِيزَتْ لَهُ الدُّنْيَا»

"Whoever enjoyed good health in his body and safety among his people and had enough food for the day, it is as if he had gained possession of the whole world."[1]

Also narrated by At-Tirmidhi in a *Marfû'* form is the *Hadeeth*:

«أَوَّلُ مَا يُسْأَلُ عَنْهُ الْعَبْدُ يَوْمَ الْقِيَامَةِ مِنَ النَّعِيمِ أَنْ يُقَالَ: أَلَمْ نُصَحِّ لَكَ جِسْمَكَ؟ وَنَرْوِكَ مِنَ الْمَاءِ الْبَارِدِ»

"The first blessing about which the slave will be asked on the Day of Resurrection is that it will be said to him: "Did We not give you a healthy body? And did We not give you cold water to drink?"[2]

Due to this, some of the *Salaf* said regarding the Words of Allâh:

﴿ثُمَّ لَتُسْـَٔلُنَّ يَوْمَئِذٍ عَنِ ٱلنَّعِيمِ﴾

"Then on that Day you shall be asked about the delights (you indulged in, in this world)!"[3]

That it (the delight) refers to health.

And Ahmad has narrated in a *Marfû'* form:

«سَلُوا اللهَ الْيَقِينَ وَالْمُعَافَاةَ، فَمَا أُوتِيَ أَحَدٌ بَعْدَ الْيَقِينِ خَيْرًا مِنَ الْعَافِيَةِ»

"Ask Allâh for certainty and well-being, for no one is given anything better after certainty than well-being."[4]

---

[1] Narrated by At-Tirmidhi, on the authority of 'Abdullah Ibn Mihsan Al-Ansari, it contains in its *Sanad* 'Amr Ibn Malik, who is declared weak by a number of scholars, including Abu Hatim Ar-Razi, Ibn 'Adi and others. It also contains one Salamah Ibn 'Ubaidillah, who is unknown, according to Imam Ahmad.

[2] Narrated by At-Tirmidhi, on the authority of Abu Hurairah ﷺ.

[3] *Sûrah At-Takathur* 102:8

[4] Narrated by Imam Ahmad, on the authority of Abu Bakr ﷺ.

So he has combined well-being in the Religion with wellbeing in worldly matters.

And in *'Sunan An-Nasa'i'*, it is reported in a *Marfû'* form: "Ask Allâh for forgiveness, health and well-being, for no one is given anything after certainty better than well-being."[1] These three things include removal of past evils by forgiveness, present evils by health and future evils by maintaining well-being.

It was not the custom of the Prophet ﷺ to restrict himself to one type of food, because that is harmful, even if it is the best of food. Instead, he used to eat what was customary among the people of his land.

Anas ؓ said: "The Messenger of Allâh ﷺ never disparaged any food. If it appealed to him, he would eat it and if it did not, he would leave it."[2] Whenever a person eats a food which he does not like, it is more harmful than beneficial to him.

He ﷺ used to love meat (i.e. mutton) and his favourite part was the leg and the front portion of the sheep, because that is lighter and more quickly digested.

He also used to like sweets and honey; and meat, sweets and honey are among the most beneficial foods.

He would eat all of the fruits available in his land whenever they arrived and that is one of the ways of maintaining good health, because Allâh, Most Glorified, in His Wisdom has placed fruits in every land which are a means of preserving the health of its people. And in most cases, when a person avoids eating fruit due to fear of illness, one finds that he is the sickest of people in body. And it has been authentically reported from him ﷺ that he said:

$$\text{«لَا آكُلُ مُتَّكِئًا»}$$

"I do not eat while leaning."[3]

---

[1] Narrated by An-Nasa'i, in *''Amal Al-Yawmi Wal-Lailah'*.

[2] Narrated by Al-Bukhari, Abu Dawûd and Ahmad, on the authority of Abu Hurairah ؓ – not Anas ؓ, as the author says.

[3] Narrated by Al-Bukhari, At-Tirmidhi, Ibn Majah, Abu Dawûd, Ahmad and Ad-Darimi, on the authority of Abu Juhaifah ؓ.

And he ﷺ said:

«إِنَّمَا أَجْلِسُ كَمَا يَجْلِسُ الْعَبْدُ، وَآكُلُ كَمَا يَأْكُلُ الْعَبْدُ»

"I sit only as the slave sits, and I eat as the slave eats."[1]

Leaning or supporting one's weight (*Ittika'*) has been explained as meaning to sit cross-legged and it has been explained as meaning to lean on something and it has been explained as meaning to lean on one side. All three of these are considered *Ittika'*.

He used to eat with three fingers and that is the most beneficial way to eat. He used to drink honey mixed with cold water.

And it has been authentically reported from him that he prohibited drinking in a standing position and it has been authentically reported from him that he commanded one who did so to vomit it out.[2] And it has been authentically reported from him that he drank while standing[3] and so it was said that the prohibition was abrogated and it was said that this made it clear that the prohibition was not one of *Tahreem*[4] and it was said that he drank standing out of necessity.

He used to take three breaths when drinking and he said:

«إِنَّهُ أَرْوَى وَأَمْرَأُ، وَأَبْرَأُ»

"It is more thirst-quenching, healthier and more wholesome."

That is, it is better to quench the thirst, healthier in that it frees one from thirst and more nourishing for the body when it enters it, and it mixes with it easily and is tastier and more beneficial, as in Allâh's Words:

﴿فَكُلُوهُ هَنِيئًا مَّرِيئًا﴾

"Take it, and enjoy it without fear of any harm (as Allâh has made it lawful)."[5]

---

[1] Narrated by Abu Ash-Shaikh, on the authority of 'A'ishah ☙, it contains in its *Sanad* one 'Ubaidullah Ibn Al-Waleed Al-Wassafi, who is weak, according to Imam Ahmad, Yahya Ibn Ma'een and others.

[2] Narrated by Muslim and Ad-Darimi.

[3] Narrated by Al-Bukhari, Muslim, An-Nasa'i, Ibn Majah and Ahmad.

[4] *Tahreem*: Strict forbiddance.

[5] *Sûrah An-Nisa'* 4:4

That is, delight in the result of it and enjoy the taste of it.

And At-Tirmidhi has narrated from the Prophet ﷺ that he said:

«لَا تَشْرَبُوا نَفْسًا وَاحِدًا كَشُرْبِ الْبَعِيرِ، وَلَكِنِ اشْرَبُوا مَثْنَى، وَسَمُّوا اللَّهَ إِذَا شَرِبْتُمْ، وَاحْمَدُوا إِذَا أَنْتُمْ فَرَغْتُمْ»

"Do not drink in one breath as the camel does, but drink in two or three breaths and mention Allâh's Name when you drink and praise and thank Him when you finish."[1]

And it is authentically reported from the Prophet ﷺ that he said:

«غَطُّوا الْإِنَاءَ، وَأَوْكُوا السِّقَاءَ، فَإِنَّ فِي السَّنَةِ لَيْلَةً يَنْزِلُ فِيهَا وَبَاءٌ، لَا يَمُرُّ بِإِنَاءٍ لَيْسَ عَلَيْهِ غِطَاءٌ وَلَا سِقَاءٍ لَيْسَ عَلَيْهِ وِكَاءٌ، إِلَّا وَقَعَ فِيهِ مِنْ ذَلِكَ الدَّاءِ»

"Cover the drinking vessels and tie the waterskins, for there is a night in the year when a pestilence descends and it does not pass over any vessel without a cover or any waterskin which is not tied except that some of that disease goes into it."[2]

Al-Laith Ibn Sa'd, one of the narrators said: "The non-Arabs in our community protect themselves against that night in Kanûn Al-Awwal."[3]

And it has been authentically reported from him ﷺ that he ordered vessels to be covered even if it be only with a stick.[4]

And it has been authentically reported from him ﷺ that he ordered his Companions ؓ to mention Allâh's Name when covering vessels and tying waterskins and he prohibited them from drinking from the

---

[1] Narrated by At-Tirmidhi, on the authority of Ibn 'Abbas ؓ, it contains in its Sanad one Yazeed Ibn Sinan Al-Jazari, who is described as weak by Ahmad Ibn Hanbal and Yahya Ibn Ma'een.

[2] Narrated by Muslim and Ibn Majah, on the authority of Jabir Ibn 'Abdillah ؓ.

[3] Kanûn Al-Awwal: December.

[4] Narrated by Al-Bukhari and Muslim on the authority of Jabir Ibn 'Abdillah ؓ.

mouth of the waterskin[1] and from breathing and blowing into the water vessel and from drinking from cracked or chipped cups.[2]

He would not refuse perfume[3] and he said:

«مَنْ عُرِضَ عَلَيْهِ رَيْحَانٌ، فَلَا يَرُدَّهُ، فَإِنَّهُ طَيِّبُ الرِّيحِ، خَفِيفُ الْمَحْمَلِ»

"Whoever is offered *Raihan*, he should not refuse it, because it is light to carry and it has a pleasant odour."[4]

And in Abu Dawûd and An-Nasa'i's version: "Whoever is offered perfume."

In Al-Bazzar's '*Musnad*', it is reported from him ﷺ that he said:

«إِنَّ اللهَ طَيِّبٌ يُحَبُّ الطَّيِّبَ، نَظِيفٌ يَحِبُّ النَّظَافَةَ، كَرِيمٌ يُحِبُّ الْكَرَمَ، جَوَادٌ يُحِبُّ الْجُودَ، فَنَظِّفُوا أَفْنَاءَكُمْ وَسَاحَتَكُمْ، وَلَا تَشَبَّهُوا بِالْيَهُودِ يَجْمَعُونَ الأَكِبَّاءَ فِي دُورِهِمْ»

"Verily, Allâh is Good and He loves that which is good and He is Clean and He loves cleanliness and He is Kind and He loves kindness and He is Generous and He loves Generosity, so clean your doorways and your courtyards and do not imitate the Jews whoever collect their rubbish in their houses."[5]

And regarding perfume, one special characteristic of it is that the angels like it and the devils flee from it and good souls love good souls and evil souls love evil souls, so:

---

[1] Narrated by Al-Bukhari, on the authority of Abu Hurairah ﷺ.

[2] Narrated by Abu Dawûd, on the authority of Abu Sa'eed Al-Khudri ﷺ, it contains in its chain of narrators one Qurrah Ibn 'Abdir-Rahman, who is described as weak by Yahya Ibn Ma'een, Ibn Hibban, Ahmad Ibn Hanbal and others.

[3] Narrated by Al-Bukhari, on the authority of Anas Ibn Malik ﷺ.

[4] Narrated by Muslim, Abu Dawûd, An-Nasa'i and Ahmad, on the authority of Abu Hurairah ﷺ.

[5] Also narrated by At-Tirmidhi, on the authority of Sa'd Ibn Abi Waqqas, it contains in its *Sanad* one Khalid Ibn Ilyas, who is abandoned in *Hadeeth*, according to scholars.

﴾ٱلۡخَبِيثَٰتُ لِلۡخَبِيثِينَ وَٱلۡخَبِيثُونَ لِلۡخَبِيثَٰتِ وَٱلطَّيِّبَٰتُ لِلطَّيِّبِينَ وَٱلطَّيِّبُونَ لِلطَّيِّبَٰتِ ﴿

"Bad statements are for bad people (or bad women for bad men) and bad people for bad statements (or bad men for bad women). Good statements are for good people (or good women for good men) and good people for good statements (or good men for good women)."[1]

And although this may refer to men and women, it also includes deeds and words, foods and drinks, clothing and odours, either based upon the generality of its wording or by the generality of its meaning.

---

[1] *Sûrah An-Nûr* 24:26

Regarding His Guidance ﷺ in His Judgements

The aim is not to mention the general legislation, even though his particular judgements are general, but to mention his guidance in the courts of summary jurisdiction in which he ruled between the opposing parties and to mention along with it the cases from his general rulings. It has been confirmed from him that he imprisoned a man on suspicion.[1]

And in the *Hadeeth* of 'Amr Ibn Shu'aib, on the authority of his father, on the authority of his grandfather, it is reported that a man intentionally killed his slave and the Prophet ﷺ flogged him with a hundred stripes and he banished him for a year and ordered him to free a slave and he did not make the punishment fit the crime.

And Ahmad has reported on the authority of Anas ؓ in a *Marfû'* form:

«مَنْ قَتَلَ عَبْدَهُ قَتَلْنَاهُ»

"Whoever killed his slave, we shall kill him."[2]

But even if this is authentic, it is for the *Imam* to reprimand, according to what he considers beneficial.

---

[1] Narrated by At-Tirmidhi, Abu Dawûd and An-Nasa'i.

[2] Narrated by An-Nasa'i, Abu Dawûd, Ibn Majah, Ahmad and Ad-Darimi, on the authority of Samurah Ibn Jundub ؓ, not Anas ؓ, as mentioned by the author.

And he ﷺ ordered a man to pursue a person who was in debt to him.[1] This was reported by Abu Dawûd.

Abu 'Ubaid narrated that he ﷺ ordered that the murderer be killed and that the *Sabir* (one who locked up another without food or water until he died) be (likewise) imprisoned until death."[2] Abu 'Ubaid said: "That is, he should be locked up until he dies." And 'Abdur-Razzaq mentioned in his *'Musannaf'* on the authority of 'Ali ؓ that he said: "The kidnapper should be imprisoned until he dies."

Regarding *Al-'Uraniyyûn*, he ordered that their hands and feet be cut off and their eyes gouged out as they had done to the camel-herder, and he left them until they died of hunger and thirst, as they had done to the camel-herder.[3]

And in *'Saheeh Muslim'* it is reported that a man claimed that another man had killed his brother and so he sent him to his brother and when he turned back, he said: "If he kills him, he will be like him." When he returned, the man said: "I only took him away by your command." The Prophet ﷺ said:

«أَمَا تُرِيدُ أَنْ يَبُوءَ بِإِثْمِكَ وَإِثْمِ صَاحِبِكَ؟»

"Do you not prefer that he should bear the burden of your sin and that of your brother?"

The man said: "Yes." So he set him free.[4] It was said that the meaning of this is that if the killer is led with a strap around his neck, he is absolved of the crime of which he is accused and so he becomes like the one who leads him; and in it (the saying of the Prophet ﷺ) there is indemnity by pardon. It was also said that it means: If the man did not intend to kill his brother and he killed him because of it, then he is a murderer like him. And this is proven by the *Hadeeth* narrated by Imam Ahmad, on the authority of Abu Hurairah ؓ in a *Marfû'* form, in which it was said: "Oh, Messenger of Allâh! I did not

---

[1] Narrated by Abu Dawûd, on the authority of Abu Habeeb ؓ.

[2] Narrated by 'Abdur-Razzaq in *'Al-Musannaf'*.

[3] Narrated by Al-Bukhari, Muslim, the compilers of the *'Sunan'* and Ahmad, on the authority of Anas ؓ.

[4] Narrated by Muslim, on the authority of 'Alqamah Ibn Wa'il ؓ.

intend to kill him." The Messenger of Allâh ﷺ said to the deceased's next of kin:

$$«أَمَا إِنَّهُ إِنْ كَانَ صَادِقًا، ثُمَّ قَتَلْتَهُ دَخَلْتَ النَّارَ»$$

"If he has spoken the truth and you then kill him, you will enter the Fire."

And so he let him go.[1] And he ruled against a Jew who had crushed the skull of his slave girl between two rocks that his head be crushed between two rocks.[2] In this there is evidence that a man should be killed for killing a woman and that the murderer is killed in the same manner in which he killed his victim and that the murderer is executed without asking the permission of the next of kin of the victim. This is the *Mazhab* of Imam Malik and it was the opinion of Shaikh Al-Islam Ibn Taimiyyah. And whoever claimed that he did so due to the Jew's invalidation of the covenant is incorrect, because one who violates a covenant of protection does not have his head crushed. And regarding a woman who threw a stone at another woman, killing her and the child in her belly, he ruled that the payment of one tenth of the blood money for a male slave or a female slave (*Ghurrah*) for the fetus and the blood money for the murdered woman upon the kin of the murderess.[3]

And in '*Saheeh Al-Bukhari*', it is reported that he ruled on the fetus of a woman the payment of one tenth of the blood money for a male or female slave, then the woman upon whom he had pronounced judgement died, so he ruled that her estate was for her children and her husband and that the blood money was to be paid by her heirs.[4] From this it is proven that a semi-intentional act does not necessitate retaliation and that the relatives of the accused bear the responsibility

---

[1] It is not in Imam Ahmad's '*Musnad*'; it was narrated by At-Tirmidhi, Abu Dawûd and Ibn Majah. The former said that it is *Hasan Saheeh*.

[2] Narrated by Al-Bukhari and Muslim, on the authority of Anas Ibn Malik ﷺ.

[3] Narrated by Al-Bukhari and Muslim, on the authority of Abu Hurairah ﷺ.

[4] Narrated by Al-Bukhari, Muslim, An-Nasa'i, Abu Dawûd and Ahmad, on the authority of Abu Hurairah ﷺ.

of paying the *Ghurrah*, in the same manner as the *Diyah* and that the husband is not included among them, nor are her children.

And he ﷺ ruled upon a man who married his father's wife that he be killed and that his property be taken;[1] and that is the *Mazhab* of Imam Ahmad and it is the correct opinion. The three[2] said that his punishment is that of the adulterer, but the judgement of the Messenger of Allâh ﷺ is more appropriate and more correct.

And he ruled that if a man looked into someone's house without his permission and he threw a stone at him or poked him with a stick and put out his eye, then there is no sin upon him.[3]

And it has been authentically reported from him ﷺ that he invalidated the payment of blood money for the mother of the children of the blind man (who was her master) when he killed her for maligning the Prophet ﷺ.

And he killed a number of Jews for slandering him and hurting him. Abu Bakr said to Abu Barzah ؓ when he wished to kill someone who had slandered him: "It is not allowed for anyone to do that after the Messenger of Allâh ﷺ."[4] And regarding this there are more than ten *Ahadeeth* some of which are *Saheeh*, some of which are *Hasan* and some of which are *Mashhûr*.[5] Mujahid reported on the authority of Ibn 'Abbas ؓ that he said: "Any man who curses Allâh or curses any of His Prophets ﷺ has belied the Messenger of Allâh ﷺ and it is an act of apostasy, for which the one who does it must be compelled to repent to Allâh; if he goes back on what he said (all well and good), but if not, he must be killed."

And it is reported in the '*Saheehayn*' that he ﷺ pardoned the woman who poisoned him.[6]

---

[1] Narrated by Ahmad, An-Nasa'i and Abu Dawûd.

[2] Abu Haneefah, Malik and Ash-Shafi'i.

[3] Narrated by Al-Bukhari and Muslim, on the authority of Abu Hurairah ؓ.

[4] Narrated by An-Nasa'i, on the authority of Abu Barzah ؓ, all of its narrators are described as reliable by scholars of *Hadeeth*.

[5] *Mashhûr*: This term is defined by the scholars of *Hadeeth* as follows:

[6] "A *Hadeeth* which is not *Mutawatir* (reported by such a large group of

He did not kill the one who bewitched him, but it is authentically reported on the authority of 'Umar, Hafsah and Jundub 🙏 that he killed one who practised magic. And it has been authentically reported from him 🙻 regarding the captives of war that he killed some of them, that he ransomed other, freed some of them and enslaved some of them. But it is not known that he enslaved any male adults. And these judgements have not been abrogated; rather the *Imam* is free to choose between them, according to what is most beneficial.

And he 🙻 made a number of judgements regarding the Jews: He made a covenant with them when he first arrived in Al-Madinah, then Banu Qainuqa' made war on him and so he conquered them, then he freed them. Then he fought Banu An-Nadeer and he banished them, then Banu Quraizah and he killed them. Then he made war on the people of Khaibar and he conquered them.

Regarding His ﷺ Rulings on the Spoils of War

He ﷺ ruled that the cavalryman is entitled to three shares and the infantryman to one share and he ruled that the loot from the dead enemy soldier belongs to the one who killed him. And Talhah and Sa'eed Ibn Zaid ﷺ did not attend the Battle of Badr, but he allotted a share for them and they said: "And our recompense?" He replied: "And your recompense." And no one disagrees that 'Uthman ﷺ stayed behind to take care of his wife, Ruqayyah ﷺ and the Prophet ﷺ allotted a share for him and he said: "Andy my recompense?" And he ﷺ replied: "And your recompense." Ibn Habeeb said: "This was the exclusive right of the Prophet ﷺ. And the scholars are in agreement that one who stays away from the battle has no share of the spoils.

I say: Ahmad, Malik a number of the *Salaf* and the scholars from the later generations have said that if the *Imam* sends someone on a mission which is for the benefit of the army, he may allot a share to him.

The Prophet ﷺ did not deduct the *Khumus* from spoils of the fallen enemy (i.e. his armour, weapons etc.), but that he deducted it from the war booty. And he ruled that a person was entitled to his share based upon the testimony of one witness.

Kings and rulers would send him gifts and he would accept them and divide them among his Companions ﷺ. And Abu Sufyan gave him a gift and he accepted it.

Abu 'Ubaid has reported from him ﷺ that he rejected the gift of 'Amir

Ibn Malik, saying: "We do not accept gifts from a polytheist." And he said: "He only accepted the gift of Abu Sufyan because it was in peacetime. Likewise, he accepted the gift of Al-Muqawqas because he had dealt kindly with Hatib  and he had not despaired of his embracing Islam. But he never accepted a gift from a polytheist who was at war with him. Sahnûn said: "If the Leader of the Christians gives a gift to the *Imam*, there is no objection and it belongs solely to him." Al-Awza'i said: "It should be shared between the Muslims and he may be compensated for it from the Muslims' treasury. Ahmad said: "The ruling on it is that of spoils of war."

---------- ❖ ❖ ❖ ----------

Regarding His ﷺ Ruling on the Sharing of Property

They are of three types: *Zakah*, spoils of war and war booty gained without fighting.

As for *Zakah* and war booty, we have mentioned previously the ruling on them and made clear that he did not give it to all of the eight categories[1] and that he might sometimes give it to one category.

As for spoils obtained without fighting (*Al-Fai'*), he distributed them on the Day of Hunain between the new converts to Islam, in order to attract their hearts.[2] And 'Ali ﷺ sent him a piece of gold from Yemen and he divided it among four persons.[3]

And in the '*Sunan*', it is reported that he designated a share for his kin among Banu Hashim and Banu Al-Muttalib, but he did not give to Banu Nawfal and 'Abdu Shams, and he said: "We and Banu Al-Muttalib did not disunited in the *Jahiliyyah*, nor in Islam; we and they

---

[1] Narrated by Al-Bukhari and Muslim. However, Abu Dawûd narrated on the authority of 'Abdur-Rahman Ibn Ka'b Ibn Malik, on the authority of his mother, that the Prophet ﷺ had her killed. And it was said that he forgave her for trying to kill him, but that he ordered her to be killed when Bishr Ibn Al-Bara' ﷺ, who also ate the poisoned meat died.

[2] See *Sûrah At-Tawbah* 9:60.

[3] Narrated by Al-Bukhari and Muslim, on the authority of Anas Ibn Malik ﷺ.

are one." And he interlocked his fingers.[1] And he did not divide them equally like an inheritance, but instead distributed them between them according to what was beneficial; so he would marry those of them who were unmarried from these spoils and he would pay the debts of the debtor from them and he would give to the poor from them. And what is proven by his guidance is that he made the disbursement of the *Khumus* like that of *Zakah*, not giving it to any except the aforementioned eight categories, not that he distributed it between them like an inheritance. And whoever studied his biography cannot doubt that.

Scholars disagreed regarding whether *Al-Fai'* was his property which he disposed of as he saw fit, or not.

What is proven by his *Sunnah* is that he disposed of it as he was commanded, not as an owner does, for Allâh, Most Glorified gave him the choice whether to be slave and Messenger or a king and Messenger and he chose to be a slave. And the difference is that a slave does not dispose except as he is commanded while the king and Messenger may give to whomsoever he wills and deny whomsoever he wills, as Allâh, Most High said to Solomon (Sulaiman ﷺ):

$$﴿هَٰذَا عَطَآؤُنَا فَٱمْنُنْ أَوْ أَمْسِكْ بِغَيْرِ حِسَابٍ﴾$$

"[Allâh said to Sulaimân (Solomon):] "This is Our Gift, so spend you or withhold, no account will be asked of you."[2]

That is, give whomsoever you wish and deny whomsoever you wish. This was the status which was offered to our Prophet ﷺ and which he disliked, and he said:

$$«وَٱللهِ إِنِّي لَا أُعْطِي أَحَدًا، وَلَا أَمْنَعُ أَحَدًا إِنَّمَا أَنَا قَاسِمٌ أَضَعُ حَيْثُ أُمِرْتُ»$$

"By Allâh, I do not give anyone nor do I deny anyone; I am only a distributor and I give as I am commanded."[3]

---

[1] Narrated by Al-Bukhari and Muslim, on the authority of Abu Sa'eed Al-Khudri ﷺ.

[2] *Sûrah Sad* 38:39

[3] Narrated by Abu Dawûd and An-Nasa'i.

For this reason, he would spend on himself and his family from what was sufficient for a year and he would designate the remainder for fighting and weapons in Allâh, the Almighty, the All-Powerful's Cause. And it is regarding this matter that disagreement has occurred up to this day.

As for *Zakah* and inheritance, they have not caused difficulties or doubts for those in authority who came after him ﷺ, as the matter of *Al-Fai'* has done. Were there no doubts or difficulties in it, Fatimah ؓ would not have requested her inheritance; and Allâh, Most High has said:

﴿مَّآ أَفَآءَ ٱللَّهُ عَلَىٰ رَسُولِهِۦ مِنْ أَهْلِ ٱلْقُرَىٰ فَلِلَّهِ وَلِلرَّسُولِ وَلِذِى ٱلْقُرْبَىٰ وَٱلْيَتَٰمَىٰ وَٱلْمَسَٰكِينِ وَٱبْنِ ٱلسَّبِيلِ كَىْ لَا يَكُونَ دُولَةَۢ بَيْنَ ٱلْأَغْنِيَآءِ مِنكُمْ﴾

"What Allâh gave as booty (*Fai'*) to His Messenger (Muhammad ﷺ) from the people of the townships — it is for Allâh, His Messenger (Muhammad ﷺ), the kindred (of Messenger Muhammad ﷺ), the orphans, *Al-Masâkin* (the poor), and the wayfarer, in order that it may not become a fortune used by the rich among you."

Up to His Words:

﴿فَأُو۟لَٰٓئِكَ هُمُ ٱلْمُفْلِحُونَ﴾

"... such are they who will be the successful."[1]

So Allâh, Most Glorified has informed us that what Allâh has given as spoils (*Al-Fai'*) to His Messenger is all for those who were mentioned in these Verses and he did not bestow the *Khumus* of it only upon those mentioned; instead, he distributed it generally, freely and to all. So he would distribute it among those with a specific right to it, i.e. those who were permitted to receive *Al-Khumus*, then those with a general right and they were the *Muhajirûn*, the *Ansar* and those who followed them until the Day of Resurrection.

So what he and his Caliphs did is what was intended by the Verses, which is why 'Umar ؓ said: "There is none who has a greater right to this money than another and I do not have a greater right to it than

---

[1] *Sûrah Al-Hashr* 59:7-9

another; and by Allâh, there is no one among the Muslims who does not have a share of it except a bonded slave, but we are obliged to distribute it in accordance with the Book of Allâh and the shares fixed for us by the Messenger of Allâh, so a man is given in accordance with his striving in Islam and according to how early was his acceptance of Islam and how wealthy he is and how great is his need. By Allâh, if I remained for them, the shepherd would be brought a share as great as the mountain of San'a' while he is still in his place."[1] So those people named in the Verse of *Al-Fai'* are the ones named in the Verse of *Al-Khumus*; and the *Muhajirûn* and the *Ansar* and those who follow them are not included in the Verse of *Al-Khumus*, because they are entitled to the whole of *Al-Fai'* and those who are entitled to *Al-Khumus* have two special rights: A special right to *Al-Khumus* and a general right to *Al-Fai'*, because they are included in both shares. And just as the division of *Al-Fai'* between those to whom he gave it is not the division of complete ownership, but rather according to what is needed and beneficial, likewise, *Al-Khumus* is shared between those who have a right to it and we derive from the stipulation of its being confined to the five categories[2] that they are included in it. and that they are not excluded from those who have a right to *Al-Fai'* and that *Al-Khumus* does not bypass them and go to others. This is why the Imams of Islam, such as Malik, Ahmad and others ruled that *Ar-Rafidah*[3] do not have any right to *Al-Fai'*. And Allâh, Most Glorified has determined that those who are entitled to receive *Al-Khumus* are entitled to receive *Al-Fai'* and He has specified them out of concern for their situation and in order to show preference to them and because the spoils are only for those who have a right to them, He has stipulated that the *Khumus* from them is only for those who have a right to it and because *Al-Fai'* is not especially designated for anyone, He has made it for them, for the *Muhajirûn*, the *Ansar* and those who follow them.

---

[1] Narrated by Ahmad, on the authority of Aws Ibn Al-Hadathan, it contains in its *Sanad* one Muhammad Ibn Muyassar and he is weak, according to Yahya Ibn Ma'een, An-Nasa'i, Ibn 'Adi and others.

[2] See *Sûrah Al-Anfal* 8:41.

[3] *Ar-Rafidah*: The Rejecters, i.e. the Shiites.

Regarding the Wisdom Behind not Killing or Imprisoning the Enemies' Messengers and in Repudiating the Treaties of Those With Whom He Had Made Them in Equality, if He Feared That They Would Invalidate Them

It has been authentically reported that he said to the two messengers from Musailamah, when they said: "We say that he is the Messenger of Allâh," –

«لَوْلَا أَنَّ الرُّسُلَ لَا تُقْتَلُ لَقَتَلْتُكُمَا»

"Were it not that messengers may not be killed, I would have killed you both."[1]

And it has been authentically reported from him that he said to Abu Rafi' ؓ when Quraish had sent him to the Prophet and he desired not to return:

«إِنِّي لَا أَخِيسُ بِالْعَهْدِ، وَلَا أَحْبِسُ الْبُرُدَ، وَلَكِنِ ارْجِعْ، فَإِنْ كَانَ فِي نَفْسِكَ الَّذِي فِيهَا الآنَ فَارْجِعْ»

"I do not break agreements, nor do I detain messengers, but if you return and still find within yourself that which you feel now, you may return."[2]

---

[1] Narrated by Abu Dawûd and Ahmad, on the authority of Na'eem Ibn Mas'ûd ؓ.

[2] Narrated by Abu Dawûd, on the authority of Abu Rafi' ؓ.

And it has been authentically reported from him that he returned Abu Jandal ﷺ to them (i.e. Quraish) and Subai'ah Al-Aslamiyyah ﷺ came to Al-Madinah and her husband set out in search of her, then Allâh, Most High revealed:

$$﴿يَٰٓأَيُّهَا ٱلَّذِينَ ءَامَنُوٓاْ إِذَا جَآءَكُمُ ٱلْمُؤْمِنَٰتُ مُهَٰجِرَٰتٍ فَٱمْتَحِنُوهُنَّ ٱللَّهُ أَعْلَمُ بِإِيمَٰنِهِنَّ فَإِنْ عَلِمْتُمُوهُنَّ مُؤْمِنَٰتٍ فَلَا تَرْجِعُوهُنَّ إِلَى ٱلْكُفَّارِ...﴾$$

"O you who believe! When believing women come to you as emigrants, examine them; Allâh knows best as to their Faith, then if you ascertain that they are true believers send them not back to the disbelievers..."[1]

So he made her swear an oath that nothing had caused her to leave except her desire for Islam and that she had not left because of something which she had done among her people, nor because she was angry with her husband and she swore to that, and so he gave her husband his dowry and he did not return her to him.

And Allâh, Most High says:

$$﴿وَإِمَّا تَخَافَنَّ مِن قَوْمٍ خِيَانَةً فَٱنۢبِذْ إِلَيْهِمْ عَلَىٰ سَوَآءٍ إِنَّ ٱللَّهَ لَا يُحِبُّ ٱلْخَآئِنِينَ﴾$$

"If you (O Muhammad ﷺ) fear treachery from any people throw back (their covenant) to them (so as to be) on equal terms (that there will be no more covenant between you and them). Certainly Allâh likes not the treacherous."[2]

And the Prophet said:

$$«مِنْ كَانَ بَيْنَهُ وَبَيْنَ قَوْمٍ عَهْدٌ، فَلَا يَحُلَّنَّ عَقْدًا، وَلَا يَشُدَّنَّهُ، حَتَّى يَمْضِيَ أَمَدُهُ، أَوْ يَنْبِذْ إِلَيْهِمْ عَلَى سَوَاءٍ»$$

"Whoever has an agreement between him and a people, he should not dissolve it, nor should he change it until it expires."[3]

---

[1] *Sûrah Al-Mumtahanah* 60:10

[2] *Sûrah Al-Anfal* 8:59

[3] Narrated by At-Tirmidhi, Abu Dawûd and Ahmad, on the authority of 'Amr Ibn 'Abasah.

And it has been authentically reported from him that he said:

«الْمُسْلِمُونَ تَتَكَافَأُ دِمَاؤُهُمْ وَيَسْعَى بِذِمَّتِهِمْ أَدْنَاهُمْ»

"Muslims are equal in respect of blood. The humblest and weakest of them is entitled to give protection on behalf of them."[1]

And in another *Hadeeth*, he said:

«يُجْبَرُ عَلَى الْمُسْلِمِينَ أَدْنَاهُمْ، وَيُرَدُّ عَلَيْهِمْ أَقْصَاهُمْ»

"The humblest of the Muslims may give protection on their behalf and the farthest of them must return to them (i.e. if an expedition goes out from the main force and obtains booty in a far off place, it is to be shared by them and the main force)."[2]

These are four cases, in which it is mentioned that they are a united hand (of authority) over others, which means that it is not permitted to appoint the disbelievers to positions of authority. And his words: "The farthest of them must return to them" necessitates that if a military expedition acquires booty through force of arms, the booty is distributed among them and whatever comes to the treasury from *Al-Fai'* is for the farthest of them and the humblest of them, even if the cause of its being taken was the humblest of them.

He took the *Jizyah* from the Christian Arabs of Najran and Ailah and from the people of Dûmah, most of whom were Arabs and he took it from the People of the Scripture in Yemen, they being Jews and he took it from the Magians, but he did not take it from pagan Arabs. Ahmad and Ash-Shafi'i said that it may not be taken except from the People of the Scripture and the Magians.

A number of scholars said that it may be taken from all people: The People of the Scripture, according to the Qur'ân, the Magians according to the *Sunnah* and from others following on from that, because the Magians are polytheists who do not have a Scripture and that the only reason he did not take it from the pagan Arabs was that

---

[1] Narrated by Abu Dawûd, on the authority of 'Abdullah Ibn 'Amr Ibn Al-'As ﷺ.

[2] This explanation was given by Ibn 'Abdil Barr in *'Al-Istizkar'*.

they had all embraced Islam before the Qur'ânic injunction was revealed and they did not accept that the disbelief of the idol worshippers was any worse than that of the Magians; rather, they said, the disbelief of the Magians was worse, because the idol worshippers acknowledged the Oneness of Allâh in matters of Lordship (*Tawheed Ar-Rubûbiyyah*) and they only worshipped their idols (according to their claim) in order to bring them closer to Allâh and they did not claim that they were creators, nor did they make lawful the marrying of mothers, daughters or sisters, for they were upon the remnants of the Religion of Abraham (Ibraheem 鐌) and he had Scriptures and a Divine Law, whereas regarding the Magians, it is not known that they adhere to anything of the Laws of the Prophets 鐌. And he wrote to the people of Hajar and the kings, calling upon them to embrace Islam or pay the *Jizyah* and he did not distinguish between Arabs and non-Arabs. And he ordered Mu'adh 鐌 to take from every adult male one *Deenar* or its equivalent in *Ma'afiri*, which is the clothing of Yemen and 'Umar 鐌 made it four *Deenars*; this was because during the time of the Messenger of Allâh 鐌, he knew the weakness of the people of Yemen, whereas during the time of 'Umar 鐌, he knew of the wealth of the people of Ash-Sham.

And it has been confirmed from him 鐌 that he deemed it lawful to make war on Quraish without repudiating the treaty, when their allies committed aggression against his allies, thus betraying them, which Quraish accepted and he considered their compliance with this deed to be tantamount to them having done it themselves.

Regarding His ﷺ Rulings on Marriage and Matters Relating to it

It has been authentically reported from him ﷺ that he rejected the marriage of a matron who had been given in marriage by her father against her will.

And in the *'Sunan'*, it is reported from him ﷺ that he allowed a virgin whose father had given her in marriage against her will to choose (whether or not she accepted the marriage).

And it has been authentically reported from him ﷺ that he said:

«لَا تُنْكَحُ الْبِكْرُ حَتَّى تُسْتَأْذَنَ وَإِذْنُهَا أَنْ تَسْكُتَ»

"A virgin should not be married until her permission is sought and her permission is her silence."[1]

And he ruled that the orphan girl may be consulted and he said:

«وَلَا يُتْمَ بَعْدَ احْتِلَامٍ»

"There is no orphanhood after puberty."[2]

This proves the permissibility of marrying an orphan and it is proven by the Qur'ân.[3]

---

[1] Narrated by Ahmad, on the authority of 'Abdullah Ibn 'Amr ﷺ.

[2] Narrated by Abu Dawûd, on the authority of Abu Hurairah ﷺ.

[3] Narrated by Al-Bukhari, Muslim, At-Tirmidhi, An-Nasa'i, Ahmad and Ad-Darimi, on the authority of Abu Hurairah ﷺ.

And also in the '*Sunan*', it is reported from him ﷺ that he said:

«لَا نِكَاحَ إِلَّا بِوَلِيٍّ»

"There is no marriage without (the consent of) a legal guardian."[1]

Also in the '*Sunan*', it is reported that he said:

«لَا تُزَوِّجُ الْمَرْأَةُ نَفْسَهَا ، فَإِنَّ الزَّانِيَةَ هِيَ الَّتِي تُزَوِّجُ نَفْسَهَا»

"A woman may not give herself in marriage, for it is the adulteress who gives herself in marriage."[2]

And he ruled that if a woman is given in marriage by two guardians, she is for the first (suitor).[3]

And he ﷺ ruled regarding a man who had married a woman without fixing a dowry for her and who did not have sexual intercourse with her before he died, that she should have the same dowry as other women of her status, no less and no more, that she should have a share of his inheritance and that she must observe a waiting period ('*Iddah*) of four months and ten days.[4]

In '*Sunan At-Tirmidhi*', it is reported that he said to a man:

«إِذَا أُزَوِّجُكَ فُلَانَةَ»

"Do you accept that I should marry you to so-and-so?"

He said: "Yes." Then he said to the woman:

«أَتَرْضَيْنَ أَنْ أُزَوِّجَكِ فُلَانًا»؟

"Do you accept that I should marry you to so-and-so?"

She replied: "Yes." So he married them and the man consummated the marriage, but he had not fixed a dowry for her and he had not

---

[1] Narrated by Al-Bukhari, At-Tirmidhi, Abu Dawûd, Ibn Majah, Ahmad and Ad-Darimi.

[2] Narrated by Ibn Majah, on the authority of Abu Hurairah ﷺ

[3] Narrated by At-Tirmidhi, An-Nasa'i, Abu Dawûd, Ahmad and Ad-Darimi, on the authority of Samurah Ibn Jundub ﷺ

[4] Narrated by Muslim, At-Tirmidhi, An-Nasa'i, Abu Dawûd and Ahmad.

given her anything, so when death approached him, he compensated her with his share of the booty from Khaibar.[1]

These rulings imply the permissibility of marrying without naming a dowry, the permissibility of consummating the marriage before naming the dowry, the fixing of a dowry equal to that which other women of similar status receive, if the husband should die, even if he has not consummated the marriage, that she is obliged to observe the waiting period of death, even though he had not consummated the marriage; this was the view taken by Ibn Mas'ûd ﷺ and the scholars of 'Iraq.

These rulings also imply the permissibility of taking the responsibility of giving both parties in marriage and that it is sufficient to say: "I have married so-and-so to so-and-so," restricting oneself to this.

And he ﷺ commanded those who embraced Islam and had more than four wives to choose four of them. And he ﷺ ordered those who embraced Islam and had as wives two sisters to choose one of them. This implies the validity of the marriage of the disbelievers and that he should choose whom he wishes from the among those whom he married before embracing Islam and (if he retained less than four) from others after embracing Islam and that is the opinion of the majority of scholars. At-Tirmidhi has reported in a *Hadeeth* which he declared to be *Hasan*, that the Prophet ﷺ said:

«إِذَا تَزَوَّجَ الْعَبْدُ بِغَيْرِ إِذْنِ مَوَالِيهِ فَهُوَ عَاهِرٌ»

"If a slave marries without the permission of his masters, he is an adulterer."[2]

THE END

And Allâh knows better and is Wiser, and all praise and thanks be to Allâh, the Lord of the worlds.

---

[1] Narrated by Abu Dawûd, on the authority of 'Uqbah Ibn 'Amir ﷺ.
[2] Narrated by At-Tirmidhi, Abu Dawûd, Ahmad and Ad-Darimi, on the authority of Jabir Ibn 'Abdillah ﷺ.